FROM MILTON TO McLUHAN

THE IDEAS BEHIND AMERICAN JOURNALISM

FROM

THE IDEAS

MILTON

BEHIND AMERICAN

TO

JOURNALISM

McLUHAN

J. HERBERT ALTSCHULL
Johns Hopkins University

New York & London

FROM MILTON TO MCLUHAN
The Ideas Behind American Journalism

Longman, 95 Church Street, White Plains, N.Y. 10601

Associated companies:
Longman Group Ltd., London
Longman Cheshire Pty., Melbourne
Longman Paul Pty., Auckland
Copp Clark Pitman, Toronto

Executive editor: Gordon T.R. Anderson
Production editor: Dee Josephson
Production supervisor: Joanne Jay

Library of Congress Cataloging-in-Publication Data

Altschull, J. Herbert.
From Milton to McLuhan: ideas and American journalism/
J. Herbert Altschull.
p. cm.
Includes bibliographical references.
ISBN 0-582-28562-3
1. Journalism–Philosophy. 2. Freedom of the press–History.
3. Journalism–United States–Philosophy. I. Title.
PN4731.A389 1990 90-30932
070.4′01–dc20 CIP

3 4 5 6 7 8 9 10-AL-9594939291

This book is lovingly dedicated to my faithful children: Jo Ellen (Gessford), Susan (Saigger), Elizabeth (Gaudu), Nicole, and John.

For their help and encouragement in the long preparation of this book, I would like to give special thanks to the following persons: Walter Jaehnig, George Test, Andy Naden, Joy Naden, Kristina Rascher, Dave Nord, John Merrill, and Judy Norwood. I would also like to express my thanks to my editor, Elaine Luthy Brennan, and to my indexer, Dawn Lewellan.

Contents

FROM MILTON TO McLUHAN

THE IDEAS BEHIND AMERICAN JOURNALISM

Introduction: Journalism as Fire and Light

Deep in the first act of Tom Stoppard's *Night and Day*—a play of the late 1970s about reporters and revolution in a troubled African nation—the practice of modern journalism comes under examination. Stoppard's antihero, veteran Australian reporter Dick Wagner, has a very simple vision of his work. He disdains the title of "foreign correspondent" because correspondents merely file essays from foreign places. Rather, he sees himself as "a fireman. I go to fires. Swindon or Kambawe—they're both out-of-town stories and I cover them the same way. I don't file prose. I file facts."[1]

The image of the rumpled reporter, relentless in his or her pursuit of speeding fire trucks or erring politicians, has become a familiar figure in the contemporary world. So has the reporter's love of *facts*, or what media scholars criticize as the "facticity" of journalists—their tendency to provide graphic descriptions of a single tree when what readers need is a wider view of the forest. The pursuit of facts is part of a time-honored tradition in journalism. Two centuries ago Voltaire spoke to journalists from the French Enlightenment with advice that is deeply respected today: stand firm, as the quintessential enlightened skeptic; never trust the statements of others in the absence of clear and unshakable evidence.[2] In the early years of the twentieth century, German sociologist Max Weber observed that American newspapers are repositories of facts because readers want it that way:

> *For the American . . . wants nothing but facts from his paper. Whatever opinions are published in the press about these facts he regards as not worth reading; as a democrat he is convinced that, in principle, he can interpret as well as the newspaper writer, perhaps even better.*[3]

In our own time, Jack Webb's *Dragnet* character, Sergeant Friday, repeatedly stated what may well be the essence of the American journalist's operating philosophy: "Just the facts, ma'am, just give us the facts."

But this view of journalists as fire fighters or fact-chasers tells only part of the story, as reflected in the suggestion that journalists do, in fact, have an *operating philosophy*. Of course, journalists are reluctant to confess to holding a philosophy. They are, after all, dedicated empiricists; it is *facts* that they are after, not philosophy. Still, we all hold ideas, whether we call them that or not, and when we claim to reject a particular body of ideas we are in fact proclaiming a philosophy, the simplest, most clear-cut philosophy of all. For a philosophy, as William James has observed, is no mere technical matter, but rather "our more or less dumb sense of what life honestly and deeply means."[4]

One of the chief purposes of this book is to demonstrate that American journalists, in their pursuit of facts, do indeed have a philosophy, a professional philosophy of life composed of a complex of ideas, and that this belief system has been arrived at through the assimilation, usually unnoticed, of intellectual concepts that form the basis of Western civilization. This book aims to explore these ideas, especially the major turns in the stream of ideas that flows from the libertarian polemics of John Milton in seventeenth-century England to the controversial essays of media prophet Marshall McLuhan in the second half of the twentieth century, and to show how the practice of journalism has been indelibly influenced by the evolution of the American intellectual tradition.

The journalist—or journalism student—or ordinary citizen—might well raise this legitimate question: why is it important to study philosophy? If we understand how to write, how to edit, how to recognize what constitutes news, what will be read and what will not, why then is it necessary to interest ourselves in philosophy? After all, journalism is a *practical* pursuit. So American journalists have some kind of world view, some kind of belief system. So what? Let's get on with our job of reporting the news.

Although this line of reasoning appears to be a rejection of philosophy, it could well be seen as a faulty expression of the philosophical concept, pragmatism, which is associated with William James. It will be pointed out later in this book that of all the philosophies that have been introduced in the Western world, this is the one system with which journalists have been most comfortable. Since the journalist who asks why it makes sense to study philosophy might be seen as a follower of James, he or she needs to be knowledgeable about James's ideas. Perhaps from this example alone it can be seen how important it is for journalists to understand where the ideas they hold originated, and then to check out the original sources to see whether they make sense. If, for example, what James himself wrote doesn't make sense, then ideas derived from his writings may turn out to be equally nonsensical. (Most readers, however, will likely find James convincing.)

One of the sources of James's ideas was the iconoclastic English novelist and essayist, G. K. Chesterton, who addressed the issue of philosophy in the preface to his *Heretics*, a collection of essays:

> *There are some people—and I am one of them—who think that the most practical and important thing about a man is still his view of the universe. We think that for a landlady considering a lodger it is important to know his income, but still more important to know his philosophy. We think that for a general about to fight an enemy it is important to know the enemy's numbers, but still more important to know the enemy's philosophy. We think the question is not whether the theory of the cosmos affects matters, but whether in the long run anything else affects them.*[5]

I mean to endorse entirely the wisdom here given expression by Chesterton. It is *practical* to search for one's views about the universe. It is not an idle exercise in academic game-playing but rather something that directly affects the behavior of the journalist. It is as important to the journalist as knowing how to write a good lead or a dramatic headline. A clear picture of the ideas that have influenced American life in general and journalists in particular will inevitably assist the reporter and editor to a better understanding of the mind and motives of his or her sources. A faulty picture will just as inevitably lead to inaccurate, even erroneous, news reports. It is very important, therefore, for every journalist and every student of journalism to examine his or her own philosophy and the ideas that fit into that philosophy, as well as to understand the philosophy of those persons with whom they come into professional contact: their sources, their colleagues in the newsroom, and the readers of what they write.

In light of this, it may be worthwhile for the readers of this book to know something about its author, the reader's lodger for the pages that follow. I am a former professional journalist and remain an avid student of the news media. I was a reporter and editor (and "foreign correspondent") for the Associated Press, the *New York Times*, NBC, King Broadcasting Company in Seattle, and *Newsweek* before earning a doctorate in history at the University of Washington. In much of my work in completing this book, I was assisted by my colleague, Walter B. Jaehnig, the son of a newspaper editor, who was a reporter and editor for the *Louisville* (Ky.) *Courier-Journal* before studying for a doctorate in sociology at the University of Essex in England. Jaehnig and I each lived outside the United States for an extended period, operating in another culture while observing the dance of American politics and culture from afar. We shared similar teaching assignments in the School of Journalism at Indiana University in the 1970s, including a course titled "The Media as Social Institutions," which dealt with journalism in the political, economic, and social environment and its philosophy, including the study of ethics. Out of many back-corridor conversations in Ernie Pyle Hall emerged the idea for this book, which is drawn from social theory and intellectual history and their traces in the practice of everyday journalism.

I see this book as practical, not as distant and dry theory. I have been struck by how quickly aspiring journalists acquire the rhetoric and behaviors of professional journalists but still seem confused as to what they are supposed to believe, and why. I am convinced that the ideas expressed and clarified in the pages to come offer information and analysis that journalists can and should be using in their daily lives, both as individuals and as professionals. C. Wright Mills noted in 1959 that in his "Age of Fact," people need more than the information that dominates their attention and overwhelms their ability to assimilate it:

> *What they need, and what they feel they need, is a quality of mind that will help them to use information and to develop reason in order to achieve lucid summations of what is going on in the world and of what may be happening within themselves. It is this quality . . . that journalists and scholars, artists and publics, scientists and editors are coming to expect of what may be called the sociological imagination.*[6]

It is, of course, always to be kept in mind that journalism does not exist in a vacuum, apart from the world of human experience and the society in which the journalist lives. Reporters and editors are part, often a significant part, of their political, economic, aesthetic, and cultural environment. The practice of journalism never has been and cannot ever be separated from the values present in the cultural tradition of America.

Whatever philosophy is held by an American, it is derivative; that is, it came to the United States from abroad. Western philosophy had its origins in Greece some 3,000 years ago. The many twistings and turnings of Western philosophy have been analyzed, refined, and propagandized for three millennia by the Romans, the churchmen of the Middle Ages, the thinkers of the Renaissance and the Enlightenment, romantic philosophers of England, France, Germany, and other European countries, and, in more recent times, by Americans themselves. Although the ideas that emerged among Native Americans and in the countries of the Middle East, Asia and Africa have made some inroads into the traditional beliefs of Americans, they have had up to now much less influence.

The historical development of the Western philosophical tradition has been uneven, marked by frequent ebbs and flows. But consistently present have been pendulumlike swings between seemingly opposing ideas or dualisms. Optimism reigns, then is at least temporarily replaced by a greater sense of pessimism. Humankind is perceived as naturally and fundamentally good, created by a higher power, then seen to possess an irredeemable dark side. The best government is that which governs least, until problems of so vast a scale are encountered that only collective solutions seem possible. The press is granted liberty but is then confronted by the logic of license. People swear that they should be guided by the reason of their minds, but find that they remain pulled by the emotions in their hearts. They swell with unquestioning patriotism in defending their national interests—and then are drawn to a yearning for international brotherhood. The dualisms of big and small, of urban and rural, of belief in freedom and trust in authority, all play their parts. The dualistic debates that characterize the American experience continue and may never be resolved, unless perhaps we learn to master a philosophy of paradox. Some of the theories that we now see as eternal may well be turned upside down one day. Such was the vision of this country of Thomas Jefferson, who held that "no society can make a perpetual constitution," since the dead cannot—and ought not—direct the fate of those alive today. "The earth," Jefferson wrote, "always belongs to the living generation."[7]

Still, despite the magnetic pull of the extremes of the many dualisms in the mainstream of the American intellectual tradition, certain ideas have dominated—and continue to dominate—the belief system of the citizens of this country, journalists foremost among them. It is among the tasks undertaken in the writing of this book to bring these mainstream concepts into sharper focus by illuminating their historical roots. For the ideas described and examined in this study are products of other times, born in response to specific sets of problems and conditions and tested in the cauldron of the Great Debates of their eras before being handed down to us. As we study the origins of these ideas, we begin to hear in our own discussions of journalism and public affairs the voices of those who have gone before us. As the authors of a recent book on the values held by middle-class Americans recognized:

> *In talking to our contemporaries, we were listening not only to voices present but to voices past. In the words of those we talked to, we heard John Calvin, Thomas Hobbes, and John Locke, as well as Winthrop, Franklin, Jefferson, Emerson, and Whitman.*[8]

The journalist who is able to identify these voices can play a role more useful to society than that of scribbler about events and recorder of gossip because he or she is able not only to report and interpret events but also to demonstrate the *ideas* that lie behind them. By recognizing the historical and intellectual roots of those ideas, the journalist can locate them in the only perspective we all have, the perspective of time and space, and thereby bring the underlying reality of the story into focus. No benefit of a liberal education is greater than acquiring the ability to bring objects and ideas into focus. If something is new, then it is proper for the journalist to report it as new, but before the journalist does this, he or she had better know enough about the past to recognize whether or not it is in fact new.

Not every idea or concept examined in this book relates directly to the practice of journalism, but it is critically important for the journalist to be aware of the intellectual traditions that have shaped his society. Whether he recognizes it or not, those traditions determine the way he prepares and writes his stories.

To say that a journalist needs a sound sense of history is to state the obvious. Still, American journalists are often with reason criticized for lacking that sense of history, for lacking the long-term perspective required to explain and analyze the complex web of political, economic, social, and psychological events that are the stuff of news reports. As the Twentieth century was drawing to a close, the National Endowment for the Humanities issued a report lamenting the "cultural illiteracy" of Americans, announcing that surveys demonstrated that more than half the college students of America did not know the "basic landmarks of history and thought." No job or profession requires a higher order of cultural literacy than does journalism. The student of this book will never be guilty of the charge of cultural illiteracy.

In presenting this history of ideas, I would have preferred to accompany the text with extensive excerpts from the writings of the past, but found it necessary in the interests of time and space to limit the extent of these excerpts. Still, important contributions are included, dating from the English thinkers of the seventeenth century, whose ideas had a powerful impact on those of American journalists, writers, and political leaders. Since it is difficult to argue that one is truly educated if one has studied nothing but secondary sources, readers are encouraged to supplement this reading by seeking out the original works cited in the endnotes. Only when we have read the original words of an author can we avoid someone else's misunderstanding or misinterpretation.

The pages that follow attempt to clarify the writings of the philosophers whose ideas have helped shape the American experience, and to relate the ideas expressed in those writings to the beliefs of contemporary American journalists. An effort has been made at every point to place these philosophers in their own time frames and not to put into their heads ideas they could not have held during their lifetimes. From time to time, illustrations are presented of how journalists gave direct expression to the ideas of philosophers in articles published in their newspapers, but my interest lies more in the ideas circulated in the press and appropriated by reporters and editors than in reproducing newspaper articles. Reprints of articles from the American press are plentiful and are to be found in any library.

This volume is divided into ten parts, subdivided for purposes of clarity into a number of shorter chapters, each of which covers a specific theme. Part 1 explores the subject of philosophy and its impact upon the worldview of journalists and the practice of journalism. Part 2 and 3 examine the ideas developed and circulated by the English and French theorists whose influence on the thinking of the American revolutionaries was decisive. It was the beliefs of the men of the English and French Enlightenment of the seventeenth and eighteenth centuries that fired the imagination of the American settlers and of the men (and some women) who pioneered an American press. We encounter the ideas of Milton, Hobbes, Locke, and Hume, whose empiricism was the bedrock of what we now speak of as the "American Way of Life." We meet also the ideas of the French *philosophes*, Montesquieu, Voltaire, and Rousseau, whose views were equally influential in the development of the American experience, but which all too often are ignored because they come down to us in a foreign language. The Founding Fathers were all quite at home in the French language; in fact, the writings of Franklin, Jefferson, and Paine were as familiar to the French revolutionaries as they were to the American rebels. These two parts move us a bit closer to the present in an examination of the impact on American thinking of the young French nobleman, Alexis de Tocqueville, who found much to applaud and much to condemn in the American democratic experience.

Part 4 turns to the ideas of the Founding Fathers. Here we see how the ideas of the European Enlightenment thinkers were applied to the American setting and how they influenced the thinking of early editors from the young Franklin to the more radical Jeffersonians at the turn of the nineteenth century. We explore the ways in which the thinking of Jefferson, Madison, Hamilton, and other revolutionary leaders provided a pattern for the belief system of later American journalists. In this part, we call attention to the division between optimists such as Thomas Paine and pessimists in the spirit of Edmund Burke and how that division influenced journalists. In addition, we examine the romantic counterrevolution that was born in Germany and then imported from across the seas by Ralph Waldo Emerson and other Americans who traveled and studied abroad.

In Part 5, we introduce another set of ideas whose roots lay in that romantic movement, ideas associated chiefly with Karl Marx. Over the years, Marx's writings have exerted a strong influence on American journalism, even when journalists were not aware of the origin of their thoughts. We contrast the ideas of Marx the collectivist with those of the foremost prophet of individualism, John Stuart Mill. These men were contemporaries as America moved from an agrarian to an industrial society. The still unresolved struggle between the ideas of Marx and Mill, between collectivism and individualism, has resounded through the decades in the thoughts of American journalists. Here we also examine the radical economics of Malthus, Ricardo and Adam Smith as well as the pivotal work of Jeremy Bentham, Mills's colleague and mentor in the utilitarian movement that has exerted such a profound impact on American thought.

In the second half of this volume, we move away from the European roots of American ideas and examine the fallout of journalists' ideas and beliefs, of shifts in philosophy and growth in science and technology. In Part 6, we concentrate on the power of optimism, which might well be described as the Gospel of America: pride of country, confidence in the future, pride and confidence manifest in the poetry of Walt Whitman and the great nineteenth-century editors. In this context, we explore the impact on frontier America of perhaps the greatest contribution of nineteenth-century scientific thought, the biological explanations of Charles Darwin.

The unifying principle of Part 7 is the most significant American contribution to the world of ideas: the philosophical construct we call pragmatism, a system of beliefs that arrived with the twentieth century, growing out of increasing devotion to the methods of science, to the empiricism that had its roots in the English and French Enlightenment. Here, we explore the ideas of the great American pragmatists, William James and John Dewey, and see their impact on some of the most fundamental beliefs of journalists, concepts such as "the public's right to know."

In Part 8, we trace the ideas behind another basic ingredient in the belief system of journalists: the conviction that the reporter and editor are properly investigators, watchdogs checking up on abuse of power by persons in high places. This is a belief that predated the days of the yellow journalists and muckrakers, whose views are explored in this part; in fact, we can easily trace this idea to roots both in the Enlightenment and in the romantic movement. Still, as with the other ingredients in the belief system of American journalists, conflicting ideas can be found in the pattern of the dualisms that have arisen throughout our intellectual history: conflicts, for instance, between a yearning for freedom and a need for security; between optimism, faith in the future, and pessimism, dark forebodings about the future; between overweening pride in our own country and a passion for universal brotherhood; between devotion to the wishes of the individual, the One, and belief in society, in Many. Here, we examine ideas that incline both to praise and condemnation of investigative journalism and to the impact of new codes of journalistic conduct envisaged by commissions of independent scholars and by newspersons themselves.

Part 9 explores yet another controversial element in the philosophical constructs of journalism: power. We trace a number of twentieth-century philosophical threads: shifts in viewpoints of thinkers identified as New Conservatives and New Radicals, and especially the contributions of the theologian Reinhold Niebuhr and the journalist Walter Lippmann. We direct our attention to the thought processes set in motion by the phenomenon known today as McCarthyism. Next, we explore the question of the power of journalists themselves, questions dramatically raised in 1969 by the then vice president of the United States, Spiro Agnew.

In Part 10, the ideas explored throughout this volume are placed in contemporary perspective. Of all the models journalists prescribe for themselves, none is more far-reaching than the ideal of skepticism, a concept that goes all the way back to the Greeks, from whom the Enlightenment thinkers borrowed so extensively. Some commentators have argued that the ideal of skepticism, combined with the thirst for investigative work, has resulted in the establishment by modern journalism of a kind of "adversary culture" among journalists, one that is no longer in the mainstream of American ideas but, somehow opposed now to the traditional American Way of Life. Here, two Canadian scholars have played a key role, Harold Innis and Marshall McLuhan. The study concludes with an examination of the contemporary fascination with ethical issues, bringing us to the conclusion of a study of what we like to identify as the professional ideology of American journalists. Or perhaps the professional ideolog*ies* of American journalists.

The scope of this volume is admittedly ambitious. But no more so than the craft of journalism itself. The names of many newspapers symbolize some of the roles journalism has knit for itself in the fabric of American society: the *Times*, the *Sentinel*, the *Tribune*, the *Examiner*, the *Intelligencer*. In fulfilling these roles, journalists and journalism often displease and offend the very people and institutions they mean to serve. Few Americans would, however, be likely to argue that we would be better off without the unpleasant things that journalism calls to our attention. Perhaps the final words in this introduction properly belong to playwright Tom Stoppard, himself a former reporter. Near the end of *Night and Day*, after a young, idealistic reporter has been killed while covering a military firefight and his scoop blocked by a strike in the London newsroom, the crucial question is asked. Did he die for the cause of democracy, for some romantic notion of his own importance, or perhaps for the more prosaic profits of the newspaper's owners? Stoppard gives us several interpretations, including one bitter comment that he died in the cause of "junk journalism," that is to say, the cause of glitzy sensationalism. The answer provided by the laconic photographer, George Guthrie, is the one that echoes through the centuries as the major philosophical justification for free journalism in an open society, a sentiment to which I and no doubt many of the readers of this book subscribe:

> *"I've been around a lot of places. People do awful things to each other. But it's worse in places where everybody is kept in the dark. It really is. Information is light. Information, in itself, about anything, is light. That's all you can say, really."*[9]

PART I

Journalism and the Study of Philosophy

CHAPTER 1

Introduction: To Keep "Us Always Alive with Excitement"

From our twentieth-century perspective, it is easy to think of the Civil War as a tragic episode that fractured the American nation, leaving behind a legacy of bitterness and regional distrust. It is surprising, therefore, to read the words of a contemporary observer who, in September 1861, could look at the brighter side and see the war as providing a new experience with evident benefits for all his countrymen. Oliver Wendell Holmes, physician and poet, commented that the coming of the telegraph and the railroad gave the nation "iron nerves" and "iron muscles" that linked Americans as they had never been connected before—through a complex communications network bringing them news reports of the progress of the war.

"This perpetual intercommunication, joined to the power of instantaneous action, keeps us always alive with excitement," he wrote in a magazine column.[1] Holmes may have had other thoughts about the war later. His son with the same name, one day to become the renowned U.S. Supreme Court justice, was wounded three times while serving in the Union army, and on one occasion, after Holmes received a message that his son had been wounded, perhaps fatally, at the Battle of Antietam, he searched for him for six days from the back of a horse.[2] But the elder Holmes, like many Americans of his day, was a staunch believer in social progress. Noting that the journalism of the day of "almost hourly paragraphs, laden with truth or falsehood as the case may be, mak[es] us restless always for the last fact or rumor they are telling," Holmes was confident that the new communications would have important long-term benefits for Americans and the concept of democracy:

> *And this instant diffusion of every fact and feeling produces another singular effect in the equalizing and steadying of public*

opinion. We may not be able to see a month ahead of us; but as to what has passed, a week afterwards it is as thoroughly talked out and judged as it would have been in a whole season before our national nervous system was organized.[3]

No doubt the good doctor was right. There can be little argument that the railroads and the telegraph—and later the high-speed printing press, the telephone, radio, television, the communication satellite—provided the means by which Americans can be among the best-informed people in the world. But technology itself does not inform anyone. Someone or something must produce the "almost hourly paragraphs" in a form that provides an accurate representation of what is happening, in a form that the audience can comprehend.

And this information must be what its audience *needs* to know, it must be added. Seven years before Holmes's elegy to the newspaper, a distinguished contemporary, Henry David Thoreau, presented an entirely different perspective on those "almost hourly paragraphs." From his retreat at Walden Pond, Thoreau complained that the "news" that was being circulated was mainly gossip that no one in the United States needed to know: "We are in great haste to construct a magnetic telegraph from Maine to Texas; but Maine and Texas, it may be, have nothing important to communicate."[4] Indeed, Thoreau predicted wryly, a cable under the Atlantic would mean that "perchance the first news that will leak through . . . will be that Princess Adelaide has the whooping cough." Thoreau's harsh complaints about a sensational, celebrity-oriented press represents a theme that has echoed through American history:

I am sure that I have never read any memorable news in a newspaper. If we read of one man robbed, or murdered, or killed by accident, or one house burned, or one vessel wrecked, or one steamboat blown up, or one cow run over on the Western Railroad, or one mad dog killed, or one lot of grasshoppers in the winter,—we never need read of another. One is enough.[5]

Has the "communications revolution" that began with the telegraph had the effect of equalizing and steadying public opinion, as Holmes predicted? Or has it simply excited us about things not worth reading about, as Thoreau feared? Most observers would likely take a position somewhere in the middle, viewing Holmes as too optimistic and Thoreau as too caustic and remote. In any case, while Americans have an abundance of information at their disposal, there is little to suggest that they uniformly welcome and understand this information, or that public opinion has become a stable factor in American life through the efforts of the news media. To many, failure of the media to rise above the level of gossipmonger and to insure a consistent, steadfast public opinion serves as an indictment of journalism.

Throughout the American experience, the perceived need for an informed citizenry—Thoreau notwithstanding—has been intertwined with the idea of a free and open access to information that people "need to know." Critics of the press have repeatedly seen a connection between flaws in the functioning of the democratic order and the practice of journalism. In Part 1 we will consider some of these criticisms. Before we do so, however, we must clarify two important concepts: philosophy and ideology. Everything that follows will in one way or another be influenced by these concepts, and by the meanings that we assign to them.

First, let us consider how philosophy differs from ideology or a system of beliefs. Sadly, it must be acknowledged that the words *philosophy* and *ideology* may in everyday usage have been robbed of precise meaning. We sometimes say such and such a person has a "philosophy" of life when what we really mean is that this person believes in government control or a free press or saving the environment. Those are not really philosophies; they are beliefs; they represent the person's ideology, or at least a part of it.

The word *philosophy* derives from the Greek and means, literally, "love of wisdom." In the beginning, then, philosophy was simply the search for wisdom by people whose object in life was to become as wise as possible. That took thought and a great deal of study. Later, philosophy came to mean not only the search for wisdom but also the wisdom itself that was being sought. From the beginning there have been two main branches of philosophy, one known as *epistemology*, which is the study of knowledge, the other as *ontology*, which is the study of the nature of existence. From these branches have come many other aspects of philosophy for, since the goal is wisdom, the area in which one may become wise may consist of anything on earth—or beyond earth, for that matter. Metaphysics deals with things that cannot be explained by our senses: God, for example, or life in outer space, or the occult.

Because philosophy deals with anything, it is the father of all other studies. Sometimes the term has been used as synonymous with *science*, which is a word of Latin rather than Greek origin whose literal meaning is "knowledge." *Science* and *epistemology* have equivalent meanings, so that one may justifiably use the terms *science* and *philosophy* interchangeably. But, even as the nature of philosophy has been blurred by usage, so has that of science. We speak not only of such things as the biological sciences but also the science of swimming. We often refer to science more in terms of its *methods* than of its content. To employ the scientific method is to apply the knowledge that we have acquired through the study of philosophy to a search for further knowledge. The *ends* of philosophy and science are virtuous: to achieve justice and to arrive at what philosophers ever since Plato have identified as the "summum bonum" or Supreme Good.

Once we introduce the concept of the Good, we find that we have reached another important aspect of philosophy and science: ethics. The meaning that the Greeks assigned to ethics was "moral philosophy," a term that often is applied also to other special concerns of philosophy, such as aesthetics (the study of beauty) and logic (mathematical analysis).

Every one of these concerns, of course, has some bearing on the lives and practices of journalists.

Ideology is quite a different matter. The term itself is of more recent origin. If was first used in France at the end of the eighteenth century, when DeStutt de Tracy established what he called "the science of ideas."[6] This "science," which was clearly a product of the same liberal passion that had fired the French Revolution, was committed to an entirely rational political and social order from which all emotional biases were to be removed and all problems were to be solved on the basis of logic. In other words, the only way you could solve a problem was by freeing yourself of emotion and tackling it with pure logic. Before he came to power, Napoleon allied himself with the *idéologues*, but as soon as he became the emperor, he wrote them off as idle dreamers peddling "visionary moonshine" and "idealistic trash."[7] Many persons over the years have defended the concept of a science of ideas, but ever since Napoleon derided the movement, the term *ideology* has tended to be used in a pejorative sense. In the United States, for instance, we often hear derisive references to "Marxist ideology," with the criticism equally divided between Marxism and ideology as its primary target. Interestingly enough, Marx himself condemned the concept of ideology, but what he meant by the term was totally different from the meaning assigned it by DeStutt de Tracy.[8] Marx's own ideology—although he never called it that—was rooted in the belief that social events are caused by *material* factors and not by ideas. He specifically rejected ideas, which he said were nothing but devices that capitalists thought up in order to preserve their own power base. On the other hand, Napoleon and those who followed in his footsteps maintained that ideas were devices thought up by revolutionaries and liberals in order to uproot the status quo and overcome their leaders, the "legitimate" holders of power. It is easy to see the muddle and to recognize why, in many places, ideology is seen as a dirty word. In any case, we will return to this theme in Part 5, when we examine the ideas of Marx and their role in the belief system of American journalists.

Modern thinking about ideology was influenced substantially in 1960 by sociologist Daniel Bell's *The End of Ideology*.[9] Bell's position, widespread at the time, was that Marxist, or leftist, "ideology" had lost its force in the United States. Bell and his fellow thinkers saw contemporary America as made up of practical men and women who inhabit a world in which people are no longer motivated by ideas. In this view, technology has replaced ideas, and the world is being run not by people dedicated to particular ideas but by bureaucrats carrying out the dictates of politically neutral technology—by, for instance, programmers feeding data into computers without any regard to the nature of that data.

Time has shown that Bell's thinking was premature, if not wholly off the mark. In fact, in the generation that has passed since Bell's book appeared, ideology has come to dominate American life as perhaps never before. The 1960s was an era marked by ideological turmoil over war and peace, over racial and sexual divisions. The so-called "Reagan Revolution" of the 1980s was fueled by the election to office of a man committed to a specific set of ideas on things such as prayer and abortion. Patriotism and political symbols, all related to ideas, emerged as major issues in the election of George Bush in 1988.

Increasingly, the role of journalists in the dissemination of information on such ideological questions has become a topic of public and private discussion. Now that it is universally held that American journalists are by nature neither saints nor sinners, neither heroes nor villains, what can we say of the ideologies they hold not only as individuals but as a group with a *professional* ideology?

Here, we are seeing ideology in terms of a certain, specialized view of the world, in terms of ideas held by members of a particular group, professional journalists. In a recent study of the news media, W. Lance Bennett defined ideology as a formal "system of beliefs about the nature, origins, and means of promoting values that people regard as important."[10] What do journalists see as important? Bennett maintained that ideologies, both individual and professional, provide us not only with a clear sense of the purpose of life, but also with a logic for interpreting the world. It is only a short step, then, to the notion that journalists—like members of all occupational groups—use their professional ideology to address questions about the purpose of their job and how that job is supposed to operate. This is the sense in which the term *ideology* is used in this book, as we examine together the origins of the practices, codes, ethics, and operating rules of journalistic work.

Mark Fishman found in his examination of a California newspaper that a set of professional practices and routines gives news organizations a uniform view of the world that is, in our sense, ideological.[11] The professional ideology of journalists takes its shape from how reporters and editors understand the philosophical ideas that are fundamental in the American culture. These understood ideas then burrow down so deep inside the journalist's personality that he or she clings to them passionately, although often unconsciously. The less conscious one's ideology is, the more intensely one tends to protect it. It is important, therefore, to recognize the emotional context of ideology.

In this sense, the journalist's ideology is roughly equivalent to his "belief system." Robert Lane found an unexpressed but powerful belief system buried in the subjects of his fascinating study of the thinking and attitudes of a blue-collar society.[12] This kind of buried belief system is obviously even more clearly demonstrated among persons working in identical occupations. One's professional ideology is drawn from four primary sources: the codes of conduct and practices that have developed throughout the history of the occupation, the opinions that have been arrived at on the basis of conscious thought, the attitudes that are rooted in feelings or emotions, and the public statements by admired practitioners and leaders. The journalist's professional ideology then is a complex of practices, opinions, attitudes, and public statements—of conscious thought and powerful feelings. Like all ideologies, it serves as a guide to thought and to political and social action. When William James spoke of a philosophy as "our more or less dumb sense of what life honestly and deeply means," he was suggesting that our ideology was *part* of our philosophy. We get this philosophy, he went on, "only partly from books; it is our individual way of just seeing and feeling the total push and pressure of the cosmos."[13]

CHAPTER 2

Ideology and the Missing Theory of News

Walter Lippmann noted as far back as 1915 that it is easy for editors to take a strong editorial position in their newspapers when there is little or no opposition to that stance in the community.[1] It is then that a stance is the least dangerous, flatters everyone who holds it, and risks no offense to any significant segment of the readership. No one is angered by endorsement of mom, the flag, and apple pie. To avoid offense is good business for newspapers operated, as nearly all are, as commercial enterprises. But is such a position necessarily *right*? Does it provide the best solution to the problems that face the community, or the nation? Is it reasonable to expect the press—which depends upon community acceptance for its daily bread—to present an argument that is likely to offend the majority of its readers and financial supporters, even if it believes it to be the best argument? Lippmann raised this question in the context of the debate over American entry into the war in Europe and pointed out that it is always easy for the press to be patriotic because few will question a position in favor of American interests in international disputes. But for this very reason, Lippmann argued, the practices of the American press do not meet the informational needs of the public. While such "easy" editorial positions are understandable, this did not make them sufficient to Lippmann:

> *In following the easiest way . . . [the editor] is not guilty of any malevolent plan. He does it with a good conscience, for the human conscience is never so much at ease as when it follows the line of least resistance. Only saints, heroes, and specialists in virtue feel remorse because they have done what everybody was doing and agreed with what everybody was thinking.*[2]

Edward Jay Epstein, a contemporary student of the press, goes even further than Lippmann. Not only does Epstein consider journalists far removed from sainthood, but he questions whether they can be considered seekers after truth:

> *The problem of journalism in America proceeds from a simple but inescapable bind: journalists are rarely, if ever, in a position to establish the truth about an issue for themselves, and they are therefore almost entirely dependent on self-interested "sources" for the version of reality that they report.*[3]

Despite the fact that today's journalists are better educated and perhaps more highly motivated than those of Lippmann's time, Epstein argues that it is unlikely that anything better than a "truncated version of reality" can be provided to the public. This is so, he says, because of the constraints of time and space imposed by the news production system, including such things as deadlines and limited budgets, and by the journalist's relationship with sources. What journalism can do, according to Epstein, is serve "as an important institution for conveying and circulating information, and signaling changes in the direction of public policy."[4] But to do even this, he argues, journalists must reconsider how they represent themselves, and be more explicit in identifying the sources of their information.

Journalists are, according to John C. Merrill, paradoxical creatures in terms of the way they view themselves and their work: they consider themselves individualists, but seek a "sense of unity" with other journalists. While they perceive themselves as social critics,

> *[they] accept criticism badly; they talk of objectivity while reflecting the world through a prism; they talk of news without really knowing what it is, they see themselves as adversaries of government without knowing just why they should be.*[5]

These and other contradictions in the practice of journalism, according to Merrill, result from a lack of serious philosophical awareness or interest among American journalists. Journalists avoid reflection about fundamental ideas important to their craft, even though these ideas might force them to look at their work in a "deeper, more profound way."

On this, Merrill finds agreement in fellow critic Dennis Chase, who argues that American journalism lacks philosophical introspection because, to reporters and editors, the practical always dominates the theoretical:

> *The problems of journalism are, at base, philosophical problems. They involve questions of definition and function: What is news? What is truth? How can one know Truth? These are the recurring and unstated issues behind most journalism disputes. Yet, when*

it comes to this matter of philosophy, publishers, editors, broadcasters and journalism educators are virtually unanimous in their conviction that any theories about journalism should take second place to the hard reality of practice.[6]

Chase proposes that journalists are *aphilosophical*, that is, they tend to passively accept whatever philosophy is culturally dominant at any given period. This tendency, he argues, is "strangling the chance for a science of journalism." Although the present book is not meant as an attempt to promote a "science of journalism," it may—by directing the reader's attention to the ideas that have dominated the American landscape and the practice of journalism—enable the reader to judge for himself or herself whether such a science of journalism is possible of achievement and whether, indeed, such a universally accepted "science" would be desirable.

A number of modern critics, primarily nonjournalists, have observed in the professional ideology of journalists the absence of a theory of news, an epistemology, that might raise the practice of journalism to the level of a genuine profession, to the status of a science or even an art. All sciences, Daniel Patrick Moynihan has pointed out, have "a professional tradition of self-correction," that is, a clearly defined sense of what is right and what is wrong so that through research errors might be found, discussed, and ultimately corrected. "This practice is of course the great invention of western science," Moynihan says. Every true profession has such a tradition and, ideally, an epistemology

which is shared by all respected members of the profession, so that when a mistake is discovered it can be established as a mistake to the satisfaction of the entire professional community . . . Ideally, also, no discredit is involved: to the contrary, honest mistakes are integral to the process of advancing in the field. Journalism will never attain to any such condition. Nevertheless, there is a range of subject matter about which reasonable men can and will agree, and within this range American journalism even of the highest order, is often seriously wide of the mark.[7]

Moynihan's point is that because journalists have no generally accepted guidelines about what is right and what is wrong, research to identify, discuss, and correct errors makes no sense. The criterion each journalist uses to evaluate right and wrong, good and bad, is simply his or her professional news judgment, a quality that can never be defined with precision. Mistakes by journalists are inevitable, according to Moynihan, since they have no alternative but to interpret what they see and hear on the basis of their own subjective evaluation. In the world of journalism, he says, "the *Rashomon* effect is universal."[9] The reference is to the well-known Japanese novel and film in which different eyewitnesses to the same event offer widely different interpretations of that event on the basis of what works best for them. Thus, without definable guidelines, criticism of the press becomes simply personal opinion, to be accepted or rejected by others based on *their* personal opinions or their news judgment.

Since journalists do not articulate a professional ideology, it must be found in a set of *conventional* usages and practices.[9] Lacking an epistemology shared by all members of the profession, journalists arrive at their philosophy through an ideology of faith, one that is not based on scientific inquiry. The standards and value system of journalists derive from their news judgment and a series of conventional definitions of news developed over time, conventions that come more or less from what is "in the air," what "everybody knows."[10]

In fact, one of the beliefs held by American reporters and editors is that journalism should *not* have a shared epistemology. It ought to be irreverent. It ought to be unpredictable and just a little bit disreputable. Moynihan recognizes this romantic value system and even endorses it. So do most libertarians. Nowhere has this value system been stated more cogently and movingly than in the opinion of Judge Gurfein in the *Pentagon Papers* case:

> *The security of our Nation is not at the ramparts alone. Security also lies in the value of our free institutions. A cantankerous press, an obstinate press, a ubiquitous press must be suffered by those in authority in order to preserve the even greater values of freedom of expression and the right of the people to know.*[11]

We will return later to the intriguing issue of the people's right to know raised by Gurfein. Meanwhile we should note that Moynihan has plenty of company in his concern that journalists have no consciously shared epistemology and no tradition of professional self-correction. James Carey, for instance, argues that journalists must develop a critical tradition so that they can clarify just what it is they do believe.[12] In the course of a month, he points out, more people read the work of one *New York Times* reporter than have read the poetry of Wordsworth or Keats over nearly two centuries. But whereas literary critics regularly debate the merits of the work of the romantic poets, there is next to no serious analysis of the output of the reporter aside from widespread general grumbling about the news media. Carey, who does not consider this genuine criticism, observes that not only do experts provide too little criticism of the quality of journalistic work but so do fellow reporters and editors: "At journalistic gatherings, professionals do not critique one another's work; they give one another awards."[13]

Carey has a prescription. He wants the news media to help set up a genuine system of "cultural criticism," whereby in the pages of their newspapers the work of journalists could be judged by other journalists as well as by those among their readers who are "most qualified by reason of motive and capacity to enter the critical arena."[14] If such a practice were adopted, newspapers and presumably broadcasting stations would devote at least a portion of their space to the kind of debate that is expected to take place in the pages of scholarly journals. In this way, perhaps, the belief system of American journalists would become manifest and a shared epistemology might emerge.

According to another student of the modern press, sociologist Gaye Tuchman, the daily pressures of putting out a newspaper or preparing a broadcast make it simply impossible for the journalist to engage in this kind of critical activity. "Processing news leaves no time for reflexive epistemological examination," she says.[15] Moreover, journalists are not "thinkers" in the sense that social scientists are thinkers; rather, says Tuchman, the reporter is a "man of action" who has time only to make instantaneous decisions about the validity, the reliability, or the "truth" in his daily diet of news.

Of course the argument of the present book is that journalists do indeed have time to reflect about what they are dealing with or, rather, that they must make the time to think. Developing a conscious philosophy is one way to promote the habit of reflection and thus to avoid slanting one's writing in unconscious, unexamined ways. For example, one pitfall into which journalists regularly stumble as a result of their emphasis on the practical and their contempt for the mere theoretical is the tendency to ignore just what it means to rely on figurative language when reporting reality. Journalists who identify the "front-runner" in an election campaign or speak of a football team "roaring" down the field are falling prey to what students of logic identify as the aesthetic fallacy. They are taking a metaphor and substituting it for the facts—the empirical reality—that they pride themselves on presenting. If they *intend* to substitute a metaphor for reality, all well and good. But if not, they are deceiving both their readers and themselves, for they are confusing two different kinds of knowledge and truth: the aesthetic, symbolic, beautiful and the empirical or observable.

David Hackett Fischer, in a delightfully witty study of fallacies in historical writing, calls attention to scholars from Aristotle to the present who have found more truth in poetry than in a recitation of bare facts.[16] Journalists rarely if ever present bare facts, almost never in the exact order in which they took place. What purports to be reality in the newspapers and on radio and television is inevitably a *reconstruction* of reality, to fit the needs and requirements of journalism. A story rarely starts with a "lead" that begins at the beginning of an event. Events are reorganized so that the most important (that is, the most important in the judgment of the writer) comes first. Journalists who seek to make their stories interesting by pulling out for the lead the most dramatic aspect of an event are inevitably distorting reality, for reality is always neutral. Reconstruction and reorganization of events into the forms of journalism are aesthetic pursuits, retellings of happenings in the style of literature. Novelist Virginia Woolf made the point clearly: "Truth of fact and truth of fiction are incompatible."[17] The journalistic "story" is inevitably a mixture of fact and fiction and hence unreal.

The head of the news department of the National Broadcasting Company at one point openly urged his staffers to present their news reports "in fictive form," relying on the stuff of drama, tales with rising and falling action, with clearly defined beginnings, middles and ends.[18] Yet, the reality we experience consists almost entirely of middles. The professional ideology of American journalists holds that what appears in the news media represents the truth or is at least "accurate" in the sense of being real.

Yet, figurative speech is not real. It substitutes stylistic structure for reality. Fischer calls attention to the fallacy of figures, defining it as "a form of ambiguity which consists in the abuse of figurative language, so that a reader cannot tell whether or not a literal meaning is intended."[19] The reader cannot know whether a candidate is or is not a front-runner or whether the football team actually did roar down the field. Images arise in the mind in both cases. Exactly how far in front of the field must a horse be running before he is a front-runner? Are all horses that are ahead front-runners? Or is the horse in first place there only because those who are running behind actually want him there and do not wish to challenge him too quickly? Finally, of course, political candidates are not in fact racehorses. But the journalist without a philosophical orientation can easily mistake such reconstructions for reality, such fictions for fact. And his or her public, in turn, receives a mistaken picture of reality.

CHAPTER 3

Philosophy and Some Fundamental Questions

The criticisms of journalism reported in the previous section are harsh, perhaps overstated. But recent years have seen an increasing number of journalists, educators, humanists, and social scientists turning to questions of philosophy, especially of ethics, as they wrestle with the processes of mass communications and the role of the news media in contemporary life. Often these inquiries result from controversies over journalistic handling of specific issues, such as privacy matters involving AIDS patients or political candidates, terrorism and other forms of political violence, or the portrayal of certain groups, such as rape victims or members of racial minorities or elderly people, in newsprint or on television screens. Increasingly, discussions of journalistic ethics have found their way onto the agendas of gatherings of newspeople and political groups or into the pages of magazines, scholarly journals, and trade publications of the media industries. Yet, there can be little doubt that journalists, like workers in other crafts and professions, are more concerned with their daily work, with turning out their daily products, than with philosophy, theories, or ideology.

When journalists are asked to discuss their philosophy, the concept that is mentioned most frequently is pragmatism. John Chancellor of NBC has said that newspeople have "a bias toward pragmatism and common sense." Harry Reasoner of CBS has identified himself as an empiricist and said that philosophically this means he believes in "finding out areas where people can agree on good things—wide areas of agreement."[1] Observations of a similar nature dot the literature on the mass media in the United States. There appears to be a tendency among journalists as well as among Americans generally to equate "pragmatism" with "practicality." This is an error, for pragmatism is, as we will see later, not a philosophy of common sense, but one that roots itself in rigorous scientific inquiry.

This is not to say that journalists are unethical or never address themselves to the subject of philosophy. However, the thrust of their lives is practical, and their awareness or understanding of the complexities of philosophy is severely limited. This is largely due to the fact that, as sociologist Warren Breed observed in his classic study of 1955, the ultimate rewards that come to journalists are for producing more and more news:

> *Newsmen do talk about ethics, objectivity, and the relative worth of various papers, but not when there is news to get. News comes first, and there is always news to get. They are not rewarded for analyzing the social structure, but for getting news. It would seem that this instrumental orientation diminishes their moral potential.*[2]

Breed concluded that journalists' emphasis on the practical not only influences the nature of the news they report, but also comes to bear on the ethics of journalism, or at least on the capacity of journalists to make moral decisions. Editors are indeed committed to pursuing moral ends. They are especially concerned lest their articles lower public taste or subject individuals to danger. Yet these concerns inevitably take second place to the overriding journalistic value of printing the story. At the end of a study of the moral values of American editors, this author concluded that "the clear moral philosophy" of American editors was "to publish rather than to conceal."[3]

Ethics, it is to be remembered, is a branch of philosophy often referred to as "moral philosophy"; it is concerned with "right action" or proper conduct, what one "ought" to do, what are defensible motives for one's action, all in pursuit of the Good. There is obviously some confusion as to what we mean by ethics—especially whether it is something we *have*, as in the contention that reporters who rummage through someone's garbage in search of material for a story "have no ethics", or something we *do*, as in learning how to develop considered responses to the moral problems that confront reporters and editors.[4]

A careful distinction needs to be made also between one's individual ethical values and those that one holds and carries out as part of the professional code of one's occupation. There is inevitably a difference between the two, as Joseph Leighton pointed out more than half a century ago:

> *Since the key question of ethics is the relation between the individual's own preferences or interests or valuations and his obligations as a member of various groups or communities, it is impossible to solve ethical problems without a social philosophy. The heart of ethics is the heart of social philosophy. The central*

question is: How may the individual's life be ordered so that he can be a moral self as a member of the community of moral selves?[5]

As a sociologist, Leighton's concern was essentially with a person's moral philosophy in terms of his position in society, especially in terms of the special standards of his occupation. Here, it is important to examine the "social role" of the journalist. What expectations do journalists have for themselves? What do others expect of journalists? What kinds of professional relationships do journalists have with others, such as media owners, colleagues, news sources, and the reading and viewing public? Journalism is a collective practice; the great majority of American journalists practice their craft within institutional settings. The values and standard of these organizations exert a powerful influence upon the ethical practices of the journalists who work within them.

There are, nevertheless, times when the standards of behavior a journalist adopts as part of his or her career conflicts with the standards he or she holds as an individual. A reporter may, for instance, consider it morally repugnant to rummage through a trash can in search of personal documents. That journalist then faces a difficult choice: to carry out a directive from his boss that he considers immoral, or to maintain his personal morality by refusing to carry out the directive. In the latter case, he is placing himself and his family at risk, for he may be fired for insubordination or suffer other painful consequences.

An ethical choice cannot be other than a free one; otherwise, one cannot be held responsible for one's actions. A choice to carry out a directive at gunpoint, for example, is obviously not an ethical one since the question of ethics arises only when it is possible to make a judgment or take action freely. Nor is a person who refrains from killing another necessarily behaving ethically; since society has established a law against murder, to obey it is to be law-abiding, not ethical.

The social nature of ethics is entangled in the American tradition of individualism. A recent study of American values led researchers to conclude that the worth placed on individual autonomy in the American tradition of rugged individualism makes it difficult to perceive any "objectifiable criteria of right and wrong, good or evil" that apply to all of us.[6]

Also to be kept in mind are the undeniable cultural influences that color the ethical judgments of individuals. American journalists share the Western intellectual tradition with other members of their society, and have been educated in its values and premises. While their understanding of this tradition may not be perfect or complete, nonetheless it provides the foundation for this worldview. The point is made in a report by 31 newspaper editors describing their toughest ethical dilemmas:

As citizens in a democratic society we are all properly leery of anyone who claims to have a patent on moral truth. But, as the cases [in this booklet] plainly reveal, our society expects all its citizens to adhere to a core set of ethical rules and values that constitute a democracy.[7]

Moreover, questions surrounding the various institutions that make up our democratic order are ultimately ethical questions, as Leighton has pointed out:

In the final analysis, the problems of the authority and functions of the state, of the production and distribution of economic goods, of the values of democracy, and the place of education and religion in the community are ethical problems, that is, problems of human values.

Awareness of this truth might be the best reason of all for persons in all occupations, journalists prominent among them, to undertake a study of philosophy in preparing for their life's work. For without such study, practical journalists rarely find themselves comfortable with abstractions. One writer has suggested that abstract ideas or philosophical principles are not quite real to the journalist: "his mind is filled with concrete-bound rules and slogans. . . . Consciously, he is not bound to any principles, and his opinions come and go with the slogans."[9] According to this analysis, slogans and rules of the moment become incontestable truths to journalists who find them obviously true.

Most of what follows in this book is based upon the abstract ideas, many of which found their initial expression in other eras, other cultures, that journalists need to be familiar with. Philosophical ideas are timeless, relevant to every generation that takes the time to consider them. Walter Lippmann put it this way:

We must remember that the least perishable part of the literature and thought of the past is that which deals with human nature. Scientific method and historical scholarship have enormously increased our competence in the whole field of physics and history. But for an understanding of human nature we are still very largely dependent . . . upon introspection, general observation, and intuition. There has been no revolutionary advance here since the hellenic philosophers. That is why Aristotle's ethics is as fresh for anyone who accustoms himself to the idiom as Nietzsche, or Freud, or Bertrand Russell, whereas Aristotle's physics, his biology, or his zoology is of interest only to antiquarians.[10]

While some of these ideas, especially on first reading, may seem bewildering or impenetrable, at their core resides the most important questions ever asked by humankind. Among these are the basic questions listed below, which can serve as useful organizing principles and help the reader place a specific set of ideas in a meaningful context or compare them with the work of other philosophers.

- *What is the nature of humankind?* All philosophy is rooted in a world view or perspective on the nature of human beings. Are people fundamentally good, or do they possess inherent flaws or weaknesses that an operating philosophy must address? Where did people originate? Is there some transcendent authority that created them and, if so, what is their relationship to it?
- *What is the relationship between the individual and society?* What linkages, if any, connect the individual to the wider society? Which is preferable, a world in which the individual is the centerpiece, or one that revolves around the collective society? Are people basically free and independent, or can they be located only by reference to the social order? What is the nature of authority in the society, and where does it reside? What are the limits, if any, on this authority? Where does its power originate?
- *What is a just society?* Philosophy is a means by which humankind has attempted to adjudicate competing claims for resources—for wealth, power, or simply the means of maintaining a desirable life-style. How ought these claims to be decided? By whom? How is justice—or fairness—defined in the society, and who is empowered to write the definition? What is "freedom" or "liberty"? What duties or obligations does a person have to his or her neighbor, and what can that person expect in return?
- *What is truth?* What is truth to the individual and to the society? How important is it to the overall functioning of the social order? Who decides what is true? On what basis? What role does reason play in human relationships? Who or what possesses the authority to locate truth and give expression to it?
- *What is the proper role of the journalist?* How important is it for journalists to pursue truth and report information to the public? Of what value are information and knowledge in the functioning of society? Who uses that information? For what purposes? What is the difference between information and knowledge? Whose responsibility is it, anyway, to disseminate information?

The list is by no means exhaustive, nor is it meant to be. Readers will no doubt add questions of their own. But these sets of questions raise issues that are as contentious and perplexing in American society as it approaches the twenty-first century as they were in sixteenth-century England at the dawn of the period historians refer to as the Enlightenment, and this is where our story begins.

PART II

The English Libertarians and the Theory of Liberty

John Milton (1608–1674): "And though all the winds of doctrine were let loose to play upon the earth, so Truth be in the field, we do injuriously, by licensing and prohibiting, to misdoubt her strength. Let her and Falsehood grapple; whoever knew Truth put to the worse, in a free and open encounter?"

John Locke (1632–1704): "Men being . . . by nature all free, equal, and independent, no one can be put out of his estate and subjected to the political power of another without his own consent . . . Every man, by consenting with others to make one body politic under one government, puts himself under an obligation to every one of that society to submit to the determination of the majority."

CHAPTER 4

Introduction: The Dawn of the Modern World

The discovery and settlement of America coincided with the dawn of the modern world. Anyone who is making an effort to understand the growth of the United States and its institutions must continually bear in mind that vast changes were already underway in the Western world when Columbus set sail in 1492, and that the pace of these changes accelerated throughout the colonial period. Four critical, and related, developments hastened these decisive changes. First, Gutenberg's use of movable metal type to print documents opened up a new world of information for all people. Second, the Roman Catholic church, which for a thousand years had been the center of all political, economic, social and cultural activity, was declining in power, and Protestant sects, both Lutherans and Calvinists, were challenging the very underpinnings of Roman power over thought. Third, science was emerging as a direct threat to the church's monopoly as the primary source of knowledge. And, finally, the secular state was rising to fill the power vacuum created by the political decline of the church. No men were more conscious of these developments than the settlers and developers of the American colonies. They were tuned in carefully to the turmoil that was rocking the countries of western Europe, from where the settlers had come. They were fascinated by ideas and wanted to apply them to New World institutions. George Washington made the point with faultless clarity:

> *The treasures of knowledge, acquired by the labours of Philosophers, Sages, and Legislators, through a long succession of years, are laid open for our use, and their collected wisdom may be happily applied in the Establishment of our forms of Government.*[1]

In 1455, a generation before the first voyage of Columbus, the German inventor Johannes Gutenberg of Mainz produced the first large book printed from movable metal type, a Bible, the first ever printed and thus the first available for reading outside the control of the church. Gutenberg's Bible was on sale to the public a year later. Suddenly, there came a public demand for literacy; the church, which previously had directed all education, including reading and writing, could no longer exercise its monopoly over literacy and biblical interpretations. Protestant challenges to those interpretations came swiftly. Calvin's rebellious doctrine spread quickly to Scotland and launched a century of warfare. By 1560, Presbyterianism, an offshoot of the Calvinist doctrine that had produced direct church government, or "theocracy," in Geneva, had become the state religion of Scotland. In quick order, it moved south into England, where it played a decisive role in civil warfare and the triumph of the Puritan Revolution, which ultimately conquered England and was exported to the colonies on the *Mayflower*. Actually, Puritanism and its democratic impulses had established a beachhead in New England even earlier, under the leadership of Roger Williams.

The challenges of Luther, Calvin, and other Protestants were made possible by the introduction and spread of printing. Before Gutenberg, all Bibles had been hand-produced in beautiful editions by church scribes, whose biblical interpretations reflected the official doctrines promulgated by the church. The new technology gave the public access not only to different interpretations of the Bible and religious dogma but also to the outpouring of new scientific information, including the revolutionary discoveries of Copernicus, Galileo, and Newton, and to the political reflections of Machiavelli, More, and Hobbes. The revolutionary spirit that swept Europe was made possible by the expansion of knowledge and information. Now, for the first time in Western history, ordinary people could be exposed to the ideas and thoughts of philosophers, scholars, and writers. Before Gutenberg, the church and its royalist allies were able to restrict the broadcasting of ideas and hence to control the thinking of the multitudes. No longer could authority exercise a monopoly over access to books. A mighty blow was struck for literacy. And when ordinary people may read and write, what control can their rulers retain over their thoughts—or indeed their actions?

By the time of Milton's birth in 1606, the success of the Protestant Reformation was already assured. Expansion of the Protestant movement required the spread of discussions and arguments begun in the assaults on Rome by Luther, Calvin, and the other great Protestant leaders of the sixteenth century. What better medium than the public print? Milton's friend Samuel Hartlib predicted in 1641, a year after the triumph of Cromwell: "The art of Printing will so spread knowledge that the common people, knowing their own rights and liberties, will not be governed by way of oppression. . . ."[2]

For the first time in history, public opinion became an important element in political controversy. Appeals came from tracts written by pamphleteers on all sides of the issues raised by the Puritan Revolution, sometimes couched in the language of polite discourse, sometimes in direct assertions, as in James Harrington's remarkable antimonarchical argument, later widely quoted in the United States, that a proper government was "an empire of laws and not of men."[3]

The Old Guard did not accept its fall passively. In England, the Tudor and Stuart monarchs fabricated a patchwork of schemes designed to keep the flames of revolution under control by censoring all expressions of opposition to official dogma. Henry VIII ordered the execution of dozens of challengers, including Sir Thomas More, the distinguished writer-statesman, for fear that their ideas would stir the people to revolt. The infamous Star Chamber came, during the reigns of Henry VIII and his daughters, Mary and Elizabeth, to stand for all time as the symbol of oppressive censorship. The proceedings in the Star Chamber, so named because it was conducted in a hall whose ceiling was decorated with stars, were held in secret. Torture, which was not permitted under the English common law, was recognized as a prerogative of the king in Council. The Court of the Star Chamber, established under Elizabeth I in 1586, made books subject to licensing by the archbishop of Canterbury or the bishop of London. Under the 1586 decree, any "unlawful" writing, meaning writing unacceptable to the church, was to be dealt with in the harshest of ways. All printing equipment used in publishing unlawful material was to be taken away by a kind of Star Chamber police force charged with "defacing, burning, breaking, and destroying" the presses.[4]

The Star Chamber rules were modified in 1637, but the damage had been done, and five years later England was torn by civil war, a war that brought the only execution of royalty in modern England and 11 years of army rule under the Protectorate of the commoner Oliver Cromwell. Although Cromwell was no democrat, it was during his regime that there was written what has come down to us as perhaps the most stirring of all challenges to censorship written in the English language, the *Areopagitica* of John Milton.

That essay appeared in 1644, a generation after the *Mayflower* arrived at Plymouth Rock. Seven years later, the English Enlightenment, that great philosophical challenge to the orthodoxy of the past, was set in motion by the remarkable treatise, *The Leviathan*, by Thomas Hobbes. In this part, we will examine the thought and the writings of Milton and Hobbes and their successors, John Locke and David Hume, whose influence is incalculable on the thinking patterns that grew up in the United States and profoundly affected the beliefs and attitudes of American journalists.

CHAPTER 5

John Milton and the Self-Righting Principle

John Milton's preeminence as a poet is unchallenged. His epic in blank verse, *Paradise Lost*, is one of the greatest achievements in English literature. In the lexicon of journalism, however, Milton's fame rests less on his genius as a wordsmith than on the electric content of one great pamphlet written in defiance of censorship. This paean to free expression was published on November 24, 1644, under the title, *Areopagitica; A Speech of Mr. John Milton/For the Liberty of Unlicensed Printing/to the Parliament of England.* It was sent to Parliament as an appeal from official complaints lodged against Milton for two tracts on divorce that he had written within the past year. In those pamphlets, he had spoken out in support of divorce, in part perhaps because he was displeased with his 16-year-old bride but, more importantly, as a declaration on freedom of expression.[1] In a passage that was clearly anathema to the Anglican church authorities, Milton envisioned "three species of liberty which are essential to the happiness of social life—religious, domestic, and civil."[2] In his remarkable comparison of domestic life to public life, Milton argued:

> *He in vain makes vaunt of liberty in the senate or the forum, who languishes under the vilest of servitude, to an inferior at home.*[3]

Latter-day feminists arguing for equality for women would endorse Milton's sentiments, but certainly not his intention, for he was extolling *male* rights, drawing from the fact that he was a well-educated student of the classics while his bride, Mary Powell, was no intellectual match for him. In any case, the response of the clergy was one of horror. In a sermon before Parliament, an Anglican minister named Herbert Palmer summed up the reaction of the church by blasting Milton's defense of divorce as "a wicked book" that had escaped English censorship laws and deserved nothing better than burning.[4] Incidentally, despite Mary's departure from Milton's home a month after their wedding, she soon returned, to live with him and bear four children before her death seven years later.[5]

It was indeed the era of the pamphleteer. In England, political tracts were pouring without pause from the pens of men swept away by what Bertrand Russell calls "the fire and passion appropriate to a new revolutionary movement."[6] Censorship provisions had been a fixture in English law during the Tudor and Stuart eras, enforced often enough by punishment before the Star Chamber, but Milton's tracts on divorce led clerics to push Charles I into a new, tougher law that provided that no pamphlet could be published without a specific church license. Milton's writings were already anathema to Anglican prelates. He had, with proper Puritan self-righteousness, condemned the worldliness of the clergy in an earlier pamphlet in which he had even raised questions about the potential tyranny of monarchs. In retrospect, one is led to wonder how Milton survived this period unscathed, while some of his fellow pamphleteers were imprisoned and others were ordered to the scafford to have their ears cut off.[7] Later, with the end of the Protectorate and the restoration of the Stuarts to the throne in 1660, Milton was indeed arrested. Other followers of Cromwell were murdered but Milton survived to write his greatest poetry.[8]

Interestingly, Milton's *Areopagitica*, with its fierce assault on censorship, caused scarcely a ripple in the flow of English rhetoric at the time of its publication; it was not until 1728, when nearly a century had passed, and just after the most dramatic confrontation on censorship in the American colonies, the trial of John Peter Zenger, that a new edition of the *Areopagitica* was published, setting off a serious clamor for an end to censorship and for freedom of expression.

When Milton published the *Areopagitica*, the Puritan Revolution was a scant two years old. To understand the environment in which this passionate argument for a free press was published, a word or two about historical developments is necessary. As Calvinism was gaining a foothold in Scotland and threatening to expand into England, Mary Tudor waged a rear-guard action by reestablishing Catholicism as the state religion of England, a doctrine that Milton, however democratic he may have been in other areas, hated with an undying and unreasonable passion. We will return to this uncomfortable aspect of Milton's personality. When Elizabeth assumed the throne in 1558 at the start of her 44-year reign, she announced a compromise—in an attempt to reconcile the libertarian residents of the towns and cities, who had tended to support Presbyterianism, and the conservative people of the rural areas, who were still leaning towards Catholicism. Her compromise was to establish the Anglican church, which was nominally Protestant but which retained many of the forms of Catholicism. It was under the banner of this Anglican church that the Star Chamber and other authoritarian forces grew increasingly repressive, thus sowing the seeds of the Puritan Revolution.[9]

Milton was, like Cromwell, a Protestant, chafing under the rule of the Stuarts, who had succeeded to the throne of England on the death of Elizabeth and who were, if anything, more repressive than the Tudors in enforcing political and religious orthodoxy inside and outside the Star Chamber. In the end, the Roundheads who rallied behind Captain Oliver Cromwell rebelled and swept the Stuart king, Charles I, from power. At first, the goals of the dissenting middle classes were modest, mainly to limit the power of the monarchy, to increase the role of Parliament, and to substitute a Calvinist state for the Anglican church. But as the repression heightened, Cromwell's men, spearheaded by his army troops known as the Ironsides, turned increasingly radical. The civil war that began in 1642 brought an outpouring of fervent democratic agitation.[10]

Nevertheless, it would be an error to cast Cromwell's regime as democratic, or as opposed to monarchical rule. In 1648, Cromwell's officers were even prepared to return Charles to the throne in return for safeguards guaranteeing the political and religious changes that they had already put into force. Yet a few months later, on January 30, 1649, these same officers were driven to execute Charles, not so much on republican principles but rather on the conviction that they could not make a permanent settlement with him.[11] It was not until 11 years later, in 1660, that the Protectorate was ended and Charles's son was returned to England to assume the throne as constitutional monarch, Charles II.

Milton was a remarkable man who lived in remarkable days. Like the Italian and French writers, artists, scientists, and political theorists of the Renaissance, he was deeply grounded in the Greek and Roman classics. But he also had a foot in the door of the commercial explosion that dominated the Puritan world and which was exported full-blown to the American colonies. He was the son of a self-made man of good but not aristocratic background; the elder Milton rose to wealth and prominence as a scrivener, a career that combined the roles of legal stationer, notary, and writer of law journals. His son grew up in the company of middle-class scholars and merchants who were early adherents of Puritanism and in whose ranks rebellion seethed. Milton was an avid student of the Bible, and his great poetic epic, *Paradise Lost*, published in 1667 when he was 59 years old and already blind, was a blending together of beliefs, feelings, and political wisdom generated from the ancient classics, Christian tradition, and the new winds of freedom blowing across Europe.

Milton was an optimist par excellence, like his friend Roger Williams, who brought religious freedom to the American colony of Rhode Island. To Milton, man was inherently good (in this view, Milton differed strikingly from Hobbes), and sin was identified with political ignorance. Here, Milton was kin to Thomas Jefferson, James Madison, and the other optimistic Founding Fathers, who believed that education and knowledge would inspire virtuous humankind to work to build a kind of paradise on earth. Milton's Satan was the tragic hero of *Paradise Lost*,[12] far removed from the traditional horned monster with claws and a tail, but rather a proud, daring, commanding, even beautiful figure of gigantic size who rejected servitude, whatever the cost.[12]

> . . . Here at least
> We shall be free; th' Almighty hath not built
> Here for his envy, will not drive us hence:
> Here we way reign secure, but in my choice
> To reign is worth ambition though in Hell:
> Better to reign in Hell than serve in Heaven.[13]

This is not to say, of course, that Satan is an altogether admirable figure in Milton's imagination; he is after all the Demon, the Tempter of humankind. But he operates in a thoroughly modern manner, gaining his ends and driving humankind away from God by appealing to the pride and envy in the spirit of men and women. Milton's Satan was a figure of matchless mental skills, coldly and calculatedly finding his pleasure in the destruction of the human spirit through appeals to man's rationality. "The mind," Milton has Satan say, "is its own place, and in itself/Can make a heaven of hell, a hell of heaven."[14] Indeed, while Milton admired Satan's independence of spirit, he also condemned him for rebelling against a just aristocracy of virtue under God.[15] However brilliant and powerful in thought and poetry Milton may have been, he was nonetheless a man of the seventeenth century and subject to the confusions of his times, confusions that continue to afflict us today.

American journalists, schooled in the fire of Milton's ideas, have not yet resolved the inconsistencies that surged through *Paradise Lost* and Milton's prose works. Of all those inconsistencies, the most enduring among the ideas of journalists revolves around censorship: what are in fact the virtues or evils inherent in the concept of freedom of the press?

We must return now to 1644, after Milton had published his two pamphlets on divorce and had experienced the enactment of a tough new censorship law which, though not directed specifically at himself, elevated his poetic wrath to heights of eloquence rarely if ever equalled in the literature of a free press. The title of the *Areopagitica* is drawn from a hill in Athens called Areopagus, where the Athenians placed their highest judicial court. A speech before the court was called an areopagitic; the most famous speech, by the lawyer Isocrates, was an appeal for a system of government in which all the people possessed equal political power.[16] Milton's essay is many things. It is at once a scholarly history of the practice of censorship; cautious propaganda against church efforts to legislate conformity to its own teachings; a graceful hymn to reason, logic, rationality, and the wonder of books; and above all a passionate affirmation of the open mind.

How absurd and self-destructive, Milton wrote, for the church to impose the threat of licensing in order to instruct its adherents away from evil, for how can one know evil if he has not encountered it? How can he then tell evil from good? "He that can apprehend and consider vice with all her baits and seeming pleasures, and yet abstain, and yet distinguish, and yet prefer that which is truly better, he is the true wayfaring Christian."[17]

Milton went on to assert what has come down to us as one of the most enduring elements in the belief system of journalists: that only by reading all sides of issues can the human being approach not only understanding but also decency and goodness—or, to use Milton's phrasing, "human virtue."[19]

> *Since therefore the knowledge and survey of vice is in this world so necessary to the constituting of human virtue, and the scanning of error to the confirmation of truth, how can we more safely, and with less danger, scout into the regions of sin and falsity than by reading all manner of tractates and hearing all manner of reason? And this is the benefit which may be had of books promiscuously read.*[18]

Of equal fervor was Milton's paean to diversity, another value paramount among the values of today's journalists. It is incumbent upon all freedom-loving people to unite in "one general and brotherly search" for truth. "Where there is much desire to learn," Milton wrote, "there of necessity will be much arguing, much writing, many opinions; for opinions in good men is but knowledge in the making."[19] To avoid opening the mind to contrary opinion, however heretical, Milton wrote, is to reject truth, to allow its streaming fountain to "sicken into a muddy pool of conformity and tradition."[20]

A special phrase has been created as a symbolic expression of Milton's well-known argument that whenever truth and falsehood come to grips with each other—in what today we often describe as "the marketplace of ideas"—it will always be truth that emerges triumphant. This idea is known today as "the self-righting principle," the idea that truth needs no champion in the arena of that marketplace, that truth wins even without the authority of someone in power. So strong is truth, Milton said, that "she needs no policies, nor stratagems, nor licensings to make her victorious."[21]

Of course, Milton was being wildly utopian, and perhaps he knew so himself but, swept away by the surge of republicanism in the air in Puritan England, and perhaps also by the electricity in his own prose, Milton provided for American journalists a kind of codex that stands above all other ingredients in the philosophy of journalists: the unflinching search for the truth in the cause of all that is virtuous. "For who knows not," Milton asked, "that Truth is strong, next to the Almighty?"[22]

The essence of the self-righting principle is expressed in this passage:

> *And though all the winds of doctrine were let loose to play upon the earth, so Truth be in the field, we do injuriously, by licensing*

> *and prohibiting, to misdoubt her strength. Let her and Falsehood grapple; whoever knew Truth put to the worse, in a free and open encounter?*[23]

Praise for Milton's arguments in the *Areopagitica* is universal. It is, biographer Don Wolfe writes, "the unique and unanswerable classic of intellectual freedom."[24] George Sabine, who is repelled by Milton's failure to accord Catholics the same freedom from censorship that he demanded for others, nonetheless acknowledges that the *Areopagitica* "is the finest argument ever written against the stupidities and futilities of censorship."[25] Similar mountains of praise come not only from Milton's biographers, but from just about everyone who has examined the philosophical questions involved in freedom of expression.

At the same time an especially interesting challenge to Milton's self-righting principle is raised by Isaiah Berlin, who suggests that, while it is presented as a "brave and optimistic" judgment, there is a cost to society of permitting all sides of every issue to compete freely in Milton's arena:

> *Are demagogues and liars, scoundrels and blind fanatics, always, in liberal societies, stopped in time, or refuted in the end? How high a price is it to pay for the great boon of freedom of discussion?*[26]

The thoughtful questions raised by Berlin will remain central throughout this study of the ideas of American journalists. Again and again philosophers have returned to the question of the power of truth. Two centuries after the appearance of the *Areopagitica*, the great libertarian philosopher, John Stuart Mill, pursued Milton's ideas to their logical end by holding that the suppression of any point of view, however vile and hateful, works to the detriment of humankind. To Mill, liberty is an *end* to which humankind aspires; to Milton, liberty is a *means* to the end of truth.[27] Berlin of course questions the arguments of both Mill and Milton.

History is full of peculiarities and paradoxes. Chief among those is the fact that Milton the poet, the lover of liberty, could also be Milton the bureaucrat, the enemy of free expression. At the start of Cromwell's rule in 1649, Milton was appointed Latin secretary to the Council of State, a position he held until the fall of the Cromwell Protectorate 21 years later. It was in that bureaucratic role that Milton muzzled Catholic writings and condemned Catholics, especially the Irish, as "rabble . . . papists . . . savages" who, he wrote, were the "grand enemy and persecutor of the true church."[28] Not only was Milton false to the uncompromising stance on censorship that he had taken in the *Areopagitica*, but he was also sufficiently bloodthirsty in his hatred of Catholic opposition to the "true church" that he, the believer in reason and deliberation, could provide philosophical justification for the beheading of Charles I. His work, he wrote in justifying regicide, was "an abstract consideration of . . . what might lawfully be done against tyrants."[29]

Like so many thinkers before and after, Milton was unable to bridge the gap between abstract principle and concrete behavior, a dilemma that has vexed journalists as well as philosophers. Despite Milton's behavior as Cromwell's censor, his self-righting principle endures today as the pinnacle of the doctrine that truth is strong next to the Almighty. Milton's abstract defense of free expression spread across the Western world to give succor not only to the Founding Fathers in the colonies and to American journalists then and now, but also to thinkers as disparate as Voltaire in France and Marx in Germany. Voltaire was, like Milton, to uphold the cause of free expression not only in order to evoke great ideas but also to give us all recreation and joy through music and dance, and in fact in just having fun. Censors, he wrote, would be tempted to ban all songs that were not properly "grave and Doric."[30] And Marx was, like Milton, to argue that even the most perfect form of licensing demanded judges of superhuman quality. Marx would later agree with Milton's declaration that censors were bound to be "either ignorant, imperious, and remiss, or basely pecuniary."[31] Whatever Milton's flaws, it remains true, as his biographer William Parker concludes, that what mattered most to Milton "was political liberty earned and then preserved by unswerving national morality."[32]

CHAPTER 6

Thomas Hobbes and Society by Contract

Two opposing threads run through the history of ideas in the United States to make their conflicting claims on the outlook of American journalists. Our perception of the world depends very much on whether we are optimistic or pessimistic about the nature of humankind. Are men and women good by nature? Are they wicked? If they are good, after all, they may pretty much be left to their own resources. We can be sure that they will behave honorably; so they need little if any authority or coercive agency such as police to control them. If they are wicked, then they may not be left to carry out their own will. They need authority; they need police; they need to be controlled. All governments, all systems of thought, are woven from one or the other of these threads.

The American system of government is an unmistakably optimistic one. The Founding Fathers, for the most part, believed in the goodness of humankind. But not altogether. They believed that there was a need for government, for police forces, for checks on excessive power in the hands of a majority, and for social control. But they believed in a *minimum* of those kinds of control.

Milton, as we have seen, was convinced of the goodness of humankind. People, he thought, would always search for the truth; they would never be satisfied with falsehood. No matter how clever Milton's Satan may have been, he was in the end overcome by the forces of good. Truth would always come out on top.

But while Milton was the incorrigible optimist, to his contemporary, Thomas Hobbes, men were naturally savage and unprincipled, in need of authority and control if they were ever to survive in a social setting. No one in the state of nature, Hobbes wrote, would ever seek decency and goodness; rather, he would murder his fellow creatures to gain his own selfish ends.

The solution to this natural human depravity, Hobbes argued, was the political state—or, to use his terminology, the commonwealth. And this commonwealth could be ruled by only an absolute, all-powerful force. In Hobbes's vision, that force ought to be a monarch.

While Milton's early life was sunny, Hobbes's was not. He was always a worrier, a characteristic that is sometimes illustrated by the almost certainly apocryphal story that he was born prematurely when his mother heard of the approach of the Spanish Armada.[1] That was in 1588, 20 years before Milton's birth. Hobbes liked to say that his mother had given birth to twins: himself and fear. Hobbes's father was an irascible vicar who beat up a fellow parson and ran away from home, leaving young Thomas to be raised by a wealthy uncle who sent him to Oxford to study the classics. Hobbes's life was marked by civil war and the threat of further warfare, so that to him, the dominant, driving force of human life was fear—fear of war, fear of anarchy, fear of death. Twice, Hobbes fled a country, once from England, once from France, believing that his life was at stake. Recovering from poor health in his early years, he nevertheless lived to the great age of 91. The record shows that, despite his gloomy assessment of people, he was a man of integrity, honest and kindly in all his dealings.[2]

Hobbes's great achievement, an historical landmark in political philosophy, was the *Leviathan*, published in 1651, two years after the execution of Charles I and seven years after Milton's *Areopagitica*. It sets forth the doctrine of the social contract, which stands today as the philosophical underpinning of the American experiment.

Before we turn our attention to the *Leviathan*, let us take a closer look at the passage of Hobbes's life through the dramatic years of the seventeenth century. Where Milton was an enemy of the Stuarts, and even argued in favor of the execution of Charles I, Hobbes was a thoroughgoing royalist who fled to France at the start of the Civil War. Indeed, while in exile in France, Hobbes tutored the future Charles II in mathematics. His bad luck held firm, however, when he found, on the publication of the *Leviathan*, that the French monarch was responding with hostility to his attacks on the Catholic church. So he escaped back to England again, this time swearing allegiance to Cromwell. He remained quiet politically until the monarchy was restored in 1660, at that time receiving a small pension from Charles II. Even then, the superstitious, whom Hobbes detested, forced an investigation of his alleged atheism after the Plague and the Great London Fire of 1666.[3]

Hobbes gained his central position in the revolution in philosophy that swept Europe during the seventeenth century by being the first thinker to apply the model of the physical sciences to social studies. Indeed, he is often said to be the inventor of social *science*.[4] Hobbes was acquainted with many of the philosophers of science, including Galileo, to whom Milton also had made a pilgrimage.[5]

Whether or not Hobbes actually was an atheist is unclear, but there is little doubt that he was suspicious of all religions.[6] In any case, he was a materialist; that is, he believed that there is at bottom no difference between matter, life, and the mind, and that the world consists simply of matter in motion. It is not our purpose here to attempt to examine in depth Hobbes's metaphysics; it is sufficient to say that to Hobbes the vital biological motions of the human animal pass through the central nervous system to emerge in the heart, as feelings. Thus, what starts out in the mind as a feeling of hunger is replaced after a meal by a feeling in the heart of satisfaction. From this idea, Hobbes developed his concept of "desire" and "aversion," desire being what leads to the good of our total being, body and mind, and aversion being what leads to our death.[7] There is thus a kind of self-correcting device in our biological nature, the sort of "invisible hand" that Adam Smith, a century later, would see as operating in the arena of economics if one let people do as they wish, that is, under "laissez-faire." We will return to this concept later.

It is equally important to recognize that Hobbes was also a nominalist; that is to say, he refused to take anything for granted and rejected belief in an objective world. This aspect of Hobbes's thinking, later to be expanded by David Hume, is of special interest to journalists, since to Hobbes the only universal was names. Without names, without words, without language, there can be no truth or falsehood, for the words *true* and *false* have no intrinsic meaning; they are not attributes of *things* but rather of *speech*. Thus, if there is no language, there can be no untruth. In reasoning, "a man must take heed of words," for what one person calls wisdom, Hobbes said, another might call fear or cruelty.[8] He had contempt for metaphors, arguing for plain, simple speech. He spoke out angrily against "names that signify nothing; but are taken up, and learned by rote from the schools."[9]

Hobbes is of special interest to journalists, whose trade is in precisely those words which Hobbes cautioned us to "take heed of." Indeed, it is also interesting to note that Hobbes was a brilliant writer, with a style of limpid clarity. Modern American science writers would do well to study Hobbes for inspiration.

In any case, Hobbes the materialist, the nominalist, was driven by his studies of the natural sciences to try to develop a science of society. He located it in his doctrine of self-preservation—which he saw as the most basic of all human drives. It is this fundamental egoism that has given Hobbes such a bad press, especially among American progressives. The historian Vernon Parrington, for example, attacked Hobbes as a "state absolutist" who "violently condemned democracy."[10]

Indeed, Hobbes did condemn democracy. In his belief system, there is no room for the idea that men would work together voluntarily and cooperatively towards a mutually desired goal. Men are simply not naturally cooperative, Hobbes held. In nature, before there is any kind of state, or government, or commonwealth, "every man is enemy to every man." Moreover, there is "continual fear, and danger of violent death; and the life of man, solitary, poor, nasty, brutish, and short."[11] The only time when men can be led to work together is under the control of the state. And it was to the state that Hobbes was referring in his conception of the leviathan.

The word *leviathan* is drawn from the Book of Job; it is the word used in the King James translation to describe the fierce, uncompromising, implacable sea monster that God showed to Job to illustrate God's own power, and to demonstrate how vain it is for mortal man to stand against that power. When Job submitted to God, God forgave him his past sins of pride and arrogance, and bestowed blessings on him.[12] Such a powerful creature, Hobbes wrote, is the leviathan of the state. At one point, he calls the state the "mortal God."[13] The original edition of the *Leviathan* makes the point graphically. The top of its famous pictorial title page portrays the state as a king, implacable and mighty, rising high above the buildings, cities, and people over which he held sway.[14] Above the head of the king is written a motto from Job: "Upon earth there is not his like, who is made without fear."[15] The next line in Job is equally relevant: "He is a king over all the children of pride."

Anarchy, Hobbes said, marks humanity living in the state of nature. Life is short and brutish; it is also competitive. Each man is selfishly seeking to preserve his own life, but the result is the opposite, because in the fierce competition he is likely to lose his life. Since men are also reasonable, Hobbes said, they are also looking for a solution to the problem caused by the murderous anarchy of the state of nature. Peace is the answer to war; security is the answer to anarchy. The only force powerful enough to insure peace and to abolish anarchy is, in Hobbes's imagery, the leviathan of the state, the sovereign ruler over naturally warring mankind. When men are prepared to yield their own sovereignty to the leviathan, they can live in peace and order and seek higher ends than mere self-preservation. Nobody loves a leviathan, Hobbes said, but it is a rational action to invoke such a monster in the form of a commonwealth, and then to draw up a contract, or a covenant, under which the obligation of the commonwealth, the sovereign state, is to guarantee peace and order, and the obligation of the citizens is to yield up the rights they enjoyed in the state of nature, and to swear obedience to the sovereign state.[16]

This in essence is the contract theory under which the United States was established. Later philosophers, in England, France, and the United States, were to amend and soften Hobbes's leviathan, but all contract theories are based on his idea that when men enter society, they give up their individual freedoms in return for the security provided by the state. Rules are set forth for both the individual and society. Where in this scheme of things lies that most fundamental of all elements in the ideology of journalists, freedom of the press?

Hobbes is clear enough on this question. There is simply no freedom of the press when such freedom is not acceptable to the sovereign state. In fact, under Hobbes's covenant, there can be no political parties or labor unions. All teachers must be ministers of the sovereign, and may teach only what they consider useful.[17] Of course, there was no such thing as the modern press in the seventeenth century, but by extension it is clear there can be no independent press in Hobbes's commonwealth. Like teachers, journalists are obliged to present only information that the sovereign considers useful. The power of the sovereign being unlimited, he may impose censorship whenever he considers the expression of opinions detrimental to the interests of the state. Thus, Milton's move to censor the Catholic press would have been entirely acceptable under Hobbes's covenant.

If one accepts the underlying premise of Hobbes's theory, that man is naturally selfish and seeks only his own security, it follows that he is gaining more than he loses in yielding to the leviathan his private freedom, for only then is he safe from war and anarchy. To Hobbes, despotism is always preferable to anarchy. If a man refuses to obey the sovereign, he is in a sense cutting his own throat, for the system could not work without the universal obedience of all those who are protected by the covenant. Hobbes is telling men that not only are *they* surrendering their individual rights, but so are all other persons subject to the covenant. You, then, Hobbes says, are protected by the sovereign from whatever harm your neighbor may want to do unto you.

Not only must a man give his consent to the covenant, Hobbes tells us, but he must also submit his will to the sovereign state, whether that sovereignty resides in the hands of a single monarch or an assembly such as Parliament or Congress. It is thus that the sovereign state becomes the "mortal God," standing in the place of the immortal God:

> *For, by this authority, given him by every particular man in the commonwealth, he hath the use of so much power and strength conferred on him, that by terror thereof he is enabled to perform the wills of them all, to peace at home and mutual aid against their enemies abroad. And in him, consisteth the essence of the commonwealth. . . .*[18]

Coercion and terror, Hobbes writes, are justifiable weapons of the leviathan, the state, and of its sovereign ruler. The covenant to which all members of the commonwealth agree empowers the sovereign to "use the strength and means of them all, as he shall think expedient, for their peace and common defense." The all-powerful sovereign will practice justice, because it is part of the law of nature. To behave unjustly would be self-contradictory, a logical absurdity in Hobbes's scheme of things.[19] Without the authority of an unlimited sovereign, there would be no way to move from the natural state to the civil state.[20] Everyone, sovereign and subjects, would be acting in his own enlightened self-interest, a phrase that has won universal approval among today's journalists.

The members of the commonwealth surrender to this harsh authority, therefore, because they are operating in their own self-interest; after all, they have a natural "aversion" to war and anarchy. Here is the origin of the modern theory of utilitarianism, which we will encounter in greater detail later. Utilitarianism and its daughter, pragmatism, provide the framework not only for the professional ideology of American journalists, but for the essence of the American polity as well.

In Hobbes's imagery, human beings are motivated to seek what they desire and to avoid anything for which they have an aversion. They desire peace; they have an aversion to war. They desire security; they have an aversion for anarchy. What was to Hobbes the bipolar principle of desire versus adversity became to Helvétius, Hume, Bentham, Mill, and others whose thoughts we will encounter later, the principle of pleasure versus pain. "Pleasure" is whatever we desire, and "pain" is whatever we have an aversion to. If we cast this concept in terms of morality, we find that love is the same as desire and hate is the same as aversion. Thus, we call "good" whatever it is that we desire and we call "bad" whatever it is we have an aversion to.[21] The utilitarian interpretation was by no means original with Hobbes; it was the centerpiece of the world view of the Stoics in ancient Greece and of Cicero in Rome. Hobbes's contribution was to convert the utilitarian doctrine into a justification of the modern state, and to provide the philosophical foundation for the widely held belief of journalists that publishing "the news" is good for the people. This doctrine is justified on the ground that the people desire—and derive pleasure from—the publication of news and that they are averse to—and thus suffer pain from—the suppression of news. It is important to bear in mind that Hobbes did not envisage the covenant as one that people actually sign. The covenant was a figure of speech, a metaphor to describe the terms under which the modern state exists. Indeed, to Hobbes the state itself is artificial, just as the leviathan was an artificial animal. It is in fact only through something that is artificial that society can be made to survive, to preserve itself against what is natural—hatred, selfishness, and war.[22] And self-preservation is the absolute goal.

Hobbes imagined the ideal sovereign to be a monarch rather than an assembly. Locke was to differ sharply with Hobbes on this point, but then by the time Locke wrote his principal works on government the period of civil wars had ended and the British social order seemed far more stable than it had appeared during Hobbes's lifetime. Indeed, it was civil warfare that Hobbes feared most of all. He seemed in fact to pay little attention to the king as human being. It is an abstract, just, and honorable monarch that Hobbes envisioned. Locke, a century later, saw it as the worst evil "to be subject to the inconstant, uncertain, arbitrary will of another man."[23] Across the Channel in France, Rousseau would reject *all* individual wills and substitute the General Will of the citizens of the state.

CHAPTER 7

John Locke and the Paradox of Democracy

Of all the philosophers we will encounter in this volume, none has had a greater impact on the ideas and the behavior of Americans than John Locke, a younger contemporary of Hobbes. To consider some of the personal and intellectual qualities of Locke tells us something very important about ourselves as Americans. For it is Locke who for more than two centuries Americans have admired above all other thinkers. Locke was a gentle man, fiercely optimistic about the nature of human beings, a man of great erudition but one who rarely paraded his erudition and instead preached the cause of common sense. He was a revolutionary, but a conservative revolutionary, a man whose ideas were used to ignite the rebellion of the American colonies but who distanced himself from all kinds of bloodshed. He is the father of American democracy, but he was himself no democrat. His guiding light was the precise opposite of revolutionary fire. It was prudence.

Some of the ideological confusion that has marked the American experience from the very beginning grows from the fact that the gentle Locke refrained from joining the battle and looked always for ways to avoid conflict, holding that what we must do is steer clear of the ardor and the fury of our passions and search, quietly and calmly, with our reason for the answers to the complex questions that face us all. He elevated the head above the heart, but he preached with dogmatic intensity the overriding importance of private property, which he took to be the most important ingredient of a just society.

Although Locke himself detested paradoxes, his philosophy is rooted in the greatest of all paradoxes in a democratic society: how can the individual be supreme when the political and economic order are created to serve the interests of society, not of people as individuals but as a *collective* of individuals?

Locke was the very embodiment of the moderate. He challenged the idea that there are absolute answers to our questions, and he insisted that our obligation as individuals and as members of society is to search for those answers one by one, through direct experimentation.

American history books and examinations of American citizenship, naturally enough, emphasize Locke's influence on government. Certainly, it was Locke's treatises on government that most influenced the Founding Fathers, but Locke's importance goes well beyond his political theories. We can, without much hesitation, identify him as the father of empiricism. And it is empiricism on which the American social order is constructed. There are two ways in which we can gain knowledge. On the one hand, we can acquire knowledge because *it comes to us from outside ourselves, handed down to us*, by God, by his priests, by kings and emperors, by teachers, in short by those in authority, or because it is given to us without the intercession of someone in authority, through our own capacity for thought and our intuition, which are gifts from God. There are inevitably religious overtones whenever knowledge comes from outside. On the other hand, empirical knowledge *comes to us from inside, as a result of our own efforts*, through piecemeal and tentative acquisition of data, through trial and error, through the conduct of experiments. The empirical approach is, of course, at the center of the scientific method, and Locke, like Hobbes, was committed to the new science. Indeed, he was a friend of Isaac Newton, the greatest English scientist and the discoverer of the principle of gravity. Knowledge, then, can be gained by deduction (in which we make use of our God-given capacity for thought) or by induction (by the piecemeal acquisition of information through experience and experimentation).

To argue that our knowledge is arrived at empirically is to raise the most profound challenge to the authority of churches. The gentle, prudent John Locke was the serpent in the church's Garden of Eden, for not only did he reject the idea of revealed wisdom handed down by organized religions, but he also rejected the notion that ideas come to us from God. We are not born with ideas in our head, Locke said in his famous doctrine of the "tabula rasa." Instead, we are born with a mind that is blank, like a clean slate, and the knowledge that we gain comes not from God, but from our own experiences. No greater blow has ever been struck to the idea of revealed knowledge. And yet, characteristically, Locke was no atheist. Indeed, he pictured God as the ultimate judge, able and prepared to overthrow not only the authority of organized churches but of kings and emperors as well. Whenever people are oppressed by unjust and tyrannical rulers, Locke wrote, they have the right to "appeal to heaven" and then rise up in rebellion. On this foundation, the revolutionary journalists of the American colonies preached rebellion against the British—less than a hundred years after Locke had given them their philosophical justification.

Locke was, like Hobbes, a nominalist in that he dismissed the idea of taking things for granted. Here, too, he was a bit inconsistent, since he also believed that some things were self-evident, a belief that found its way into the American Declaration of Independence. In any case, as we shall see, there were substantial differences between Hobbes and Locke, especially in their view of human nature. In fact, despite having read Hobbes with care, Locke did not acknowledge any debt to him.

One thing that was self-evident to Locke was the existence of God. This was so despite the fact that Locke's belief that it was experience, not God, that put ideas into the human head was absolutely destructive of the teachings of the church. Empiricism and intuition are simply ideas in opposition. Locke was in fact the first significant political thinker of modern times to look at theological disputes with complete indifference. The poet, Percy Bysshe Shelley, used Locke as his chief source a century and a half later in his *Necessity of Atheism*, an essay for which he was expelled from Oxford.[1] Locke's restless mind was always attracted to what was new and modern; he raised challenge after challenge to everything that was traditional, and as a result drew the wrath of learned divines and philosophers, as well as medical doctors, monarchs, and political thinkers.[2] Indeed, like Hobbes, he found himself compelled to flee to Holland to escape political retribution, later to return in triumph upon the success of the great English revolution of 1688.

It is not Locke's writings about the nature of knowledge that have made him famous and beloved among Americans; rather, it has been his love of freedom and the resulting prescription he laid out for the political and social institutions that arose in America. Still, it is important to understand the underpinning of Locke's general philosophy. It is also important to recognize his contribution to the study of language, which he saw as functional, that is, useful to convey thought. One should never argue about words, Locke maintained, on the ground that they are all inventions of man, created to ease communications with one another and to stimulate the transmission of knowledge. Disputes, Locke held, should be about "essences," not words, a position pursued, with considerable wit, by Lewis Carroll in *Alice Through the Looking Glass*.[3]

Locke's name is forever associated with two elements of what we can safely identify as the American belief system and indeed the professional ideology of American journalists: the contract theory, which holds that our government thrives under the consent of the governed, and the doctrine of the right of revolution, which holds that we have the absolute right, indeed the duty, to rise up against tyrannical leaders and throw the rascals out, by force and violence if that is necessary. These two doctrines undergird our most basic and fundamental civil liberties, the freedom to say what we want and the freedom to print and publish our opinions and beliefs.

Locke's political philosophy was set forth in his *Two Treatises of Government*, published in 1690, which is generally held to have been aimed at defending the Glorious Revolution that took place two years earlier.[4] Of course, the *Treatise* did much more than that. It served as a blueprint for the American and the French revolutions, providing conceptual and moral justification for republican governments everywhere.

Locke was well qualified to play such an important role in history.[5] Born in 1632 to a country lawyer who served in Cromwell's revolutionary army, Locke attended Christ Church, Oxford, and came under the influence both of the antimonarchical movement sweeping the country and also of the scientific advances that had excited Hobbes before him. He was, as Hobbes had been, especially impressed by René Descartes (1596–1650), the French mathematician whom Bertrand Russell considers the "founder of modern philosophy," a man who contributed substantially to the development of the scientific method, and whose famous assertion, *Cogito, ergo sum* [I think; therefore, I am], set the British empiricists to questioning the revealed wisdom of the church.[6]

Like Milton and Hobbes, Locke was a man of action. He served at a diplomatic mission in Germany and drafted the constitution for the Carolinas in the American colonies, working under one of the chief proprietors of Carolina, Anthony Ashley Cooper, later Lord Shaftesbury, who was accused of treasonable acts while serving as chancellor under Charles II and fled to Holland. Locke, aware that government spies were keeping watch over him, went to Holland also. When at last the Stuarts were dethroned in 1688, William of Orange, a grandson of Charles I, was invited to London to succeed to the throne, after accepting a Bill of Rights that guaranteed British citizens a passel of civil liberties. This was the bloodless Glorious Revolution that, among other things, pronounced the death in England of the long-enduring concept of the divine rights of kings, and introduced that celebrated English contribution to the political world, the constitutional monarch. Locke sailed for England with William, and two years later published his *Two Treatises*.

The first treatise was written as a direct response to the doctrine of hereditary power laid out by Sir Robert Filmer in his *Patriarcha: or the Natural Power of Kings*, which was published posthumously in 1680 and on which the Stuart monarchs were relying in order to maintain their right to the throne. Filmer, ignoring Hobbes's contract theory as well as any consideration of the public good, wrote that the authority under which monarchs hold political power over their subjects is the same authority that enables fathers to exercise power over their children. Filmer argued that God had given to Adam the authority to transfer his power to his oldest son, and that this had been the source of political power ever since.[7]

Nonsense, Locke replied. The power that the father has over his sons, the younger ones as well as the oldest, derives from the consent that they have given him. Otherwise, said Locke, the father, the monarch, whoever is in authority, has no right to expel a son or a citizen from his property. This is so, Locke declared, enunciating a theme that has inflamed the imagination of free men ever since, because men are "by nature, all free, equal, and independent," and no one may ever be "put out of his estate, and subjected to the power of another, without his own consent."[8] The consent does not have to be carved in granite; it is enough, Locke wrote, for the citizen to give his "tacit consent," and in fact that is what he does when he joins a community.[9]

Unlike Hobbes and the other great contract theorist, Jean-Jacques Rousseau, whom we will meet later, Locke distinguished between the contract that creates a civil society and the contract that establishes a government. In fact, he saw two separate contracts, a device that made it relatively easy for him to conceive a theory of revolution that was written into the Declaration of Independence. The complexities involved in the two contracts need not detain us here. It suffices to point out that in the end, Locke's contract was not irrevocable.[10] It could be altered, violently if necessary, when it led to tyranny and substantial abuse of power.

We must now turn to Locke's perception of a state of nature. It will be recalled that Hobbes's natural world was a cruel, competitive place, where each man warred against every other man. Locke, on the other hand, pictured a kind of happy, primitive, communal Garden of Eden. Locke's optimistic vision of a state of nature was traditional; it was Hobbes's pessimistic vision that was original. Locke's state of nature was very similar to the Judeo-Christian portrait of the happy world of the biblical patriarchs.

Bertrand Russell, otherwise an admirer of Locke, remarked that, in his lack of originality here, Locke is similar to all people who gain fame for their ideas. "As a rule," Russell wrote, "the man who first thinks of a new idea is so much ahead of his time that every one thinks him silly, so that he remains obscure and is soon forgotten. Then, gradually, the world becomes ready for the idea, and the man who proclaims it at the fortunate moment gets all the credit."[11] Locke certainly did.

As happy as he thought nature to be, Locke nevertheless detected a serious flaw in his state of nature. It provides no mechanism for judging disputes. In short, there are no written laws, only the natural law, which is subject to reasonable disagreement. Since every man, in Locke's view, is a reasonable person, he is capable of judging disputes with his neighbor. But the neighbor, through his own reason, may come to a different judgment. There has to be some way out, and this Locke discovered in his concept of civil society, which is based on written—or positive—laws. Here, he was following the Leveler, James Harrington, whose ideal society was "an empire of law, not men." For Locke, reasonable men (feminism was still far in the future) had consented to join a civil society that provides equal protection under its laws. To gain this protection, men had agreed to yield to the civil society the authority to abridge their absolute liberty in the interest of the greater good. They had consented to give up their ideal state of nature to become subjects of a government that limited their freedoms. It was a way to make sure that they retained a thoroughgoing defense of their individual liberty, in a union strong enough and powerful enough to resist oppression by mighty rulers. The resolution was majority rule:

> *Thus every man, by consenting with others to make one body politic under one government, puts himself under an obligation to every one of that society to submit to the determination of the majority, and to be concluded by it.*[12]

It can be seen how Locke struggled to resolve the paradox of a democratic society: how to insure *individual* liberty and at the same time how to protect the rights of *society*. His resolution, majority rule, was manifest in a legislative body chosen by the individual members of the society. Not all members, however; Locke was not that far ahead of his time. The vote for the legislature was restricted to men and, although Locke never said so in so many words, to men who owned property. The decisive factor was majority rule, in which Locke, and indeed America's Founding Fathers, placed great trust. It remained for the Frenchman, de Tocqueville, to point out that majorities are quite as capable of tyranny and oppression as monarchs. But that is another story. In any case, Thomas Cook takes the position that Locke did not believe in majorities absolutely, that he argued that the majority may legislate only to interpret and not to limit rights.[13]

The government that Locke envisaged as being established by the community is, above all, balanced. It does not have a monarch at its head, although Locke was careful not to reject the idea of monarchy. As an empire of laws, Locke's government was to be run by the lawmakers, the legislature. The gentle, moderate revolutionary made it clear that he was not recommending a democracy.[14] Instead, he gave the name *commonwealth* to his "society of men." And the goal, above all others, of his commonwealth was the defense of property.

CHAPTER 8

A Blueprint for Revolutionary Thought

To the eye of the late-twentieth-century reader, Locke's emphasis on property seems curious, certainly overstated. The fact is, however, that 300 years ago, property played quite a different role in human affairs than it does today in our world of heavy mortgages and apartment and condominium living. To own property, in Locke's day, was to be a free man, capable of defending oneself against the might of kings and emperors. When Locke wrote that a father could not claim eternal power over his sons, his reference point was "estate," and he said, quite simply, that a father did not have the right to transfer his estate to his oldest son without the consent of all his sons and indeed without what today we would refer to as "due process of law." In drawing up their contract, men consented to yield the freedom that they enjoyed in the state of nature in return for the protection of their property:

> *[Fear over his ability to protect his property in the state of nature] makes him willing to quit this condition, which, however free, is full of fears and continual dangers; and it is not without reason that he seeks out and is willing to join in society with others, who are already united, or have a mind to unite, for the mutual preservation of their lives, liberties, and estates, which I call by the general name property.*[1]

Locke went on to identify as "the great and chief end" of men in putting themselves under governments "the preservation of their property."[2] Indeed, Locke perceived property as an extension of man's personality into his land through his work and his energy. "Every man has a property in his own person; this nobody has any right to but himself," he said, adding, with a touch of mischievous wit, "the labor of his body and the work of his hands we may say are properly his."[3] This concept, one of Locke's most far-reaching, plays a major role in both capitalistic and socialistic economics. Capitalism argues, with Locke, that one of the highest duties of the state is to protect private property. Socialism argues, also with Locke, that each man is entitled to the benefits of his own labor, a doctrine that excludes profit for anyone else over and above the fruit of that labor. The conflict is obvious. Locke was no economist, and thus his lack of clarity made it possible for later generations to claim him as both conservative and liberal. The fact is that Locke did not bother with these distinctions. His main purpose in his *Treatise* was to defend the particulars of the Glorious Revolution.

Certainly, Locke was no capitalist. His reference point, long before the Industrial Revolution, was land, not capital. He was a spokesman for the landed gentry, and his vision of the world was similar to that of Thomas Jefferson, who was never happy with industrial development and perceived America as a land of agrarian plenty, a land of self-motivated and self-reliant yeoman farmers. This perception has never ceased to be an element of the American journalist's professional ideology. Rural values, including the image of the self-made man, rising through his own hard work and his reliance on himself, have been a staple in the "human interest" story as long as there have been American newspapers.

In his own lifetime, Locke was considered a liberal. This has become a very troublesome word, and Locke, who was always suspicious about arguments over words, would no doubt find himself amused if he were to return to earth today to learn how the definition of the word has changed and how so many quarrels have risen over who is or is not a liberal. The liberal of Locke's day would be a conservative today. His devotion to the cause of property made Locke a liberal in seventeenth-century England, for he was rejecting the idea that all land belonged to the monarch. He offered no plan for turning land over to poor people. The right to private property, he believed, is a natural right like life and liberty, and no reasonable man would give his consent to joining a government unless that government guaranteed to protect his property. Locke's middle-class ideology defended individual liberty in terms of the right to possess property as a defense against oppression from government. The question of whether oppression might come from society rather than government is apparently something that did not trouble Locke. Property rights were Locke's concern, not human rights. In fact, economic *power* was not Locke's primary concern; it was, rather, economic *possessions*. Locke's commitment to moderation and to balancing all the great interest groups—the crown, the church, the nobility, and the common people—made him a forerunner also of the great English conservative, Edmund Burke, whom we will meet later. Burke, like Locke, did not desire to overturn a monarchy; they both wanted a supreme king, but not a king that was *too* supreme. The inevitable solution was the elevation of the legislature, the Parliament, to equal, if not greater, power than the king.

Rousseau, as we will see, held an opposite view of property. He maintained that property was the root of all political and social inequality, and his contract raised the power of the people over that of the government. In this connection, Thomas Paine and, to a lesser extent, Thomas Jefferson were followers of Rousseau rather than Locke. In any case, it is interesting to note that in adapting Locke's ideas for the American colonies, Jefferson revised Locke's triad, and substituted "the pursuit of happiness" for "property."

It was from his recognition of property as the foremost value of the community that Locke drew his right of rebellion, a right that has been adopted, in one form or another, by American journalists from the very beginning. Although mainstream journalists almost never pursue this right to its natural ending, the legalizing of force and violence, it certainly undergirds the idea of reporters as watchdogs over lawmakers and executives who, as Locke wrote, violate the trust of the people "either by ambition, fear, folly, or corruption."[4]

In the end, Locke argued, the people must be the earthly judge of the behavior of those they have sent to the legislature and of the executive acceptable to that body—in his days, this meant the constitutional monarch—and since they did not have the power to appeal to anyone on earth against an unjust government, their appeal had to be to heaven.[5] And God, being just, would inevitably empower the people, acting not as individuals but as a community, to remove the government "by force."[6]

True to his moderate self, Locke made it clear that there were severe limits to the right of rebellion. It could not be invoked for any minor transgressions, but only when the legislators "endeavor to take away and destroy the property of the people, or to reduce them to slavery under arbitrary power."[7] Locke rejected a potential challenge that his theory would lead to "a ferment for frequent rebellion" and asserted:

> *. . . such revolutions happen not upon every little mismanagement in public affairs. Great mistakes in the ruling part, many wrong and inconvenient laws, and all the slips of human frailty will be borne by the people without mutiny or murmur. But if a long train of abuses, prevarications and artifices, all tending the same way, make the design visible to the people . . . it is not to be wondered that they should then rouse themselves. . . .*[8]

The Declaration of Independence, with its ringing phrases that have been written into the bloodstream of American journalists, was the handiwork of John Locke as much as of Thomas Jefferson. Interestingly, Locke had no fondness for political parties, another strain that found friendly acceptance in the United States and in the belief system of American journalists, devoted as they have always been to independent thought. Himself a Whig, Locke rejected political parties on the ground that they were so subject to prejudice and passion that they interfered with rational judgment.[9] It was a small step from this Lockean stance to the Founding Fathers' contempt for "factions," as evidenced by an influential essay by James Madison.

Locke demonstrated his political skill in working for an end to the licensing system that had so offended Milton 50 years earlier. He argued that to continue the licensing rules would have serious economic impact. It would, he said, damage the English printing trade and make it difficult for English printers to compete with foreigners. In 1694, Locke prepared for the House of Commons a statement listing 18 reasons for ending government censorship. He was careful to avoid making a forceful statement in defense of a free press, but he gained his ends by attacking the licensing machinery as cumbersome and by arguing that licensing wasn't necessary since the common law already gave adequate protection against licentiousness.[10] The linkage of a free press to property rights has long been a salient element in the professional ideology of American journalists.

Although Locke was much more robust in his defense of religious liberty than of a free press, his stress on property rights served as a powerful stimulus for freedom of the press. Anyone who could acquire a printing press would be in possession of property that could not be taken away by the government, and the owner could not be denied the right to use that property as he saw fit unless that use were to break the law. Locke was not altogether clear on this point, but he stressed that "the safeguard of men's lives, and of the things that belong unto this life, is the business of the commonwealth; and the preserving of those things unto their owner is the duty of the magistrate."[11] Leonard Levy points out, however, that although a convinced seventeenth-century liberal, Locke required his magistrate to refuse to tolerate opinions "contrary to human society, or to those moral rules which are necessary to the preservation of civil society."[12]

Locke's ideas provided a blueprint for revolutionary thought in the American colonies and in eighteenth-century France, where Rousseau accepted Locke's thinking on social contracts but dismissed his cool moderation and intellectualism in favor of exactly the kind of crimson passion that Locke feared so much. Where Locke was optimistic about the nature of human beings, Rousseau was skeptical. Where Locke built his republican model on the rock of property, Rousseau dismissed property as the chain that enslaved men. We will turn to Rousseau and the other French philosophers who influenced the course of American life and ideas in Part 3.

CHAPTER 9

David Hume: The Roots of a Skeptical Press

The success of the Glorious Revolution brought an end to the experimental liberalism of the seventeenth century, and while the fervor for change was bubbling away beneath the surface in France, Britain was experiencing a remarkable return to conservatism, a blind resistance to change, that led the country on the one hand to expand its trade and commerce, including the settling of the United States, while on the other hand indulging in the political and economic stupidity that led the American colonies to rebel.[1]

The central figure in British philosophy in the eighteenth century was unquestionably the Scot, David Hume, a man who unlike Locke looked more backward to an historical past than forward to a brave new world. His biographer, A. J. Ayer, calls him "the greatest of all British philosophers."[2] In any case, Hume's philosophy is of special importance in the professional ideology of today's American journalists, for it is he who is accorded above all other philosophers the position of chief skeptic. So skeptical was Hume that he could take the position that we can never prove that anything causes anything else.

In a very real sense, Hume was the relativist supreme. Like most contemporary journalists, he rejected absolutes of any kind. He had no use for metaphysics and argued that it was custom rather than thinking on which our reasoning was based. Our values, he wrote, anticipating what in the late twentieth century would be called "whim ethics," are determined not by general principles but by individual cases, each of them growing out of customs and conventional behavior. Interestingly enough, it was Hume whose writings inspired those of the German philosopher Immanuel Kant, who asserted that Hume had awakened him from his "dogmatic slumbers," but who, ironically, would thereupon erect absolute standards of morality that were the exact opposite of what Hume was proposing.[3]

Paradoxically, it was Hume's rejection of the idea that metaphysics and indeed religion are no more valid than customs and circumstances that led Kant and the German idealist, Hegel, to produce an elaborate metaphysics that inspired a religious revival and restored belief in absolute ethical values.[4]

Hume was born in 1711, seven years after Locke's death, and died in August 1776, one month after the signing of the Declaration of Independence. It was in that same year that Adam Smith, another Scot and a student of Hume, wrote his famous book, *The Wealth of Nations*, that was to serve as the philosophical underpinning of modern capitalism. Smith idolized Hume and wrote, upon his death, that he approached "as nearly to the idea of a perfectly wise and virtuous man, as perhaps the nature of human frailty will permit."[5]

Hume's masterpiece, *A Treatise of Human Nature*, was published in 1739 and 1740, when he was still in his 20s. It was a depressing failure for him. His skepticism led critics for more than a century to revile him. It was not until the twentieth century that Hume's reputation was solidified in England, although in America he exerted a strong influence on the Founding Fathers, particularly James Madison.[6] Hume's contemporary fame in philosophy came after he published an abbreviated version of the *Treatise* in 1748 under the title, *Inquiries Concerning Human Understanding*. It was this latter study that appealed to Kant and indeed to the new breed of French philosophers, who lionized Hume when he set up residence in France several years later.[7]

Hume's skepticism grew out of his conviction that we can never know anything for certain, even what we see and hear. In this, Hume was following the teaching of the Stoics of ancient Greece and their spokesman in Rome, Cicero.[8] All that we can know, Hume said, are *probabilities*. We cannot even be certain that what we perceive is true. This line of reasoning was of course a total dismissal of any kind of natural law based on the idea of a state of nature. Hume called the state of nature "a mere fiction, not unlike the golden age, which poets have invented."[9] Hume's epistemology—his philosophy of knowledge—is not easy to follow. It divides perceptions into two general categories, which he called "impressions" and "ideas."[10] Impressions are more powerful than ideas—they are, Hume said, "strong and vivid" perceptions.[11] Although Hume lived long before Freud and modern psychology, it can be said that in general his "impressions" come close to what we would today speak of as drives.

All ideas are derived from impressions, Hume wrote, and are rooted in imagination. Impressions are immediate, "strong and vivid," drawn from our natural passions and the images of external objects that we see and experience.[12] Although ideas are not inborn, emotions are part of human nature. In this, Hume disagrees with Locke who, he said, "perverted" the concept of ideas by failing to distinguish them from impressions.[13]

As the complete empiricist, Hume takes the position that we cannot know whether there is such a thing as a self, a personal identity. Since everything is based on perceptions, the self is "nothing but a bundle or collection of different perceptions."[14] Thus, we can never prove the existence of a soul or an afterlife. Nor can we perceive the future. In fact, Hume, the complete nominalist, dismissed abstract ideas altogether, except as inferences, verbal or symbolic, existing only through habit and general acceptance. When we speak of government or negotiations, for instance, we rarely think of "all the simple ideas, of which the complex ones are compos'd," but we "avoid talking nonsense" about them because we tend to agree on a mutually acceptable definition.[15]

The best we can do, according to Hume, is draw probable conclusions based on what we can in fact perceive, a line of reasoning that is wholly compatible with the professional ideology of most journalists. Since "both sides" of any issue may be valid, each must be presented to those who would make judgments about them. This argument can, of course, be made on moral grounds, but Hume bases it on a thoroughly skeptical view of human knowledge:

> *When I am convinced of any principle, 'tis only an idea, which strikes more strongly upon me. When I give the preference to one set of arguments above another, I do nothing but decide from my feeling concerning the superiority of their influence.*[16]

The affable Hume said he saw no reason to study philosophy unless that study appealed to one's temperament and unless it squared with one's skepticism:

> *In all the incidents of life we ought still to preserve our scepticism. If we believe, that fire warms, or water refreshes, 'tis only because it costs too much pain to think otherwise. Nay if we are philosophers, it ought only to be upon sceptical principles, and from an inclination, which we feel to be employing ourselves after that manner.*[17]

Even if it is true, as some commentators argue, that Hume was nowhere near so skeptical as he portrayed himself, Hume's reputation, then and now, is of the quintessential modern skeptic, the true son of the philosophical skeptics of Greece and Rome.[19] In any case, Hume, who was often given to a wry and amusing irony, said at one point that he considered skeptical doubt to be "a malady, which can never be radically cured." As we will see, American journalists certainly suffer from—or revel in—this malady.

From his theory of knowledge and his commitment to skepticism, Hume went on to his greatest contribution to philosophy, his theory of cause and effect. Experience shows us that performing a certain thing, say A, seems to cause something else, say B, to behave in a certain way, so that we assume that A caused B. But this, Hume said, is merely an assumption; it is not proof. He used the example of a billiard ball being propelled into another one, "causing" it to move. This "necessary conjunction," he said, is made by inference and habit, not by scientific proof.[19] There is a correlation between A and B, Hume acknowledged, but there is no proof of cause and effect. We may think, he said, that we are basing our cause-and-effect conclusions on our reasoning, but not so; instead, we are acting on the basis of *customs* or *conventions*. In fact, all our beliefs about cause and effect are drawn from "nothing but custom"; indeed, those beliefs are rooted more in our feelings than in our reasoning.[20] For Hume, conventions are simply factors that seem rational but cannot be proved.[21] They are useful too, he said, because it is only by means of these conventions that more or less stable rules of behavior can be made. It was this insight of Hume's that impressed Kant and led him to establish a rigid set of rules of behavior.

Two centuries later, examination of the practices of journalism would lead a number of analysts, including Walter Lippmann, to conclude that reporters identify news on the basis of conventions, such as topicality, proximity, authoritative sources, and the presence of celebrities. We will hear more of journalistic conventions later. Suffice it, for the moment, to recognize that the father of this concept is David Hume. It makes sense; it brings order and psychological comfort to our lives to base our behavior and thoughts on customs and conventions, Hume wrote.

Journalists might ponder Hume's argument that we are acting more on the basis of our feelings (impressions) than rational thought when we expect certain kinds of behavior to follow others, when we expect something to cause something else. "The mind," he says, "is carried by habit, upon the appearance of one event, to expect its usual attendant." It is something that "we *feel* in the mind, this customary transition of the imagination from one object to its usual attendant."[22]

It was a natural step from Hume's epistemology, his theory of knowledge, to his theory of ethics. Since there are no absolutes, there are no rational principles of right and wrong. Reason cannot tell us what is virtuous, but customs and conventions can. In fact, Hume said, since people are addicted to mixed emotions, "'tis impossible to separate the good from the ill."[23] Foes of Hume would accuse him of being a relativist without any standards of morality. Not so, said Hume. What was important for him was to recognize that morality is a matter of our feelings, not of our thinking. Morality is like aesthetics, he said, a matter of taste. "'Tis not solely in poetry and music, we must follow our taste and sentiment, but likewise in philosophy," Hume asserted.[24] Beauty, or goodness, is in the eye of the beholder. As one biographer commented: "It is the democratic view of morals; what most people feel to be right is right."[25]

Curiously and despite his skepticism, Hume was, unlike Hobbes, generally optimistic about the nature of man. He tried to dodge the question by arguing that it didn't really make any difference whether men were naturally wicked or good, wise or foolish, but he nevertheless agreed with Hobbes that man is motivated by his own self-interests and loves no one more than himself. In this view, Hume was in complete agreement with Hobbes that human beings are driven by a desire to avoid pain, or indeed anything to which they have an aversion. In fact, it was through Hume that Hobbes's utilitarianism made its way to France and also to Jeremy Bentham, who is recognized today as the chief exponent of the pleasure–pain philosophy that we will encounter later. But Hume distanced himself from Hobbes in claiming that man's natural quality of "sympathy," the capacity for pity and compassion that "takes us . . . out of ourselves," helps us to work for the good of humankind however otherwise selfish we may be.[26] It is man's imagination, Hume said, that makes possible the "sympathy" that counters self-interest and is absolutely required to establish a successful society.

That imagination helps human beings to be aware *both* of their selfish self-interests and of their altruistic sympathy, and thus to recognize that a government is necessary to curb those selfish impulses and to enable those sympathetic qualities to work for the benefit of all. The social contract, which Locke envisaged as based on the consent of the governed, was for Hume of a somewhat different quality. He dismissed the idea of tacit consent as absurd, since no one can be bound by a promise he has not consciously made. Promises are based entirely on "human conventions," that is, on the moral values that human beings have developed through acting in their own interests. These interests, Hume said, "consist in the security and protection, which we enjoy in political society, and which we can never attain, when perfectly free and independent."[27] Hume followed Locke in endorsing revolution, but found it "pernicious and criminal" to resist the power of the government except in cases of "grievous tyranny and oppression."[28]

Hume pictured governments as rising from the "passions of lust and natural affection." He turned to the family for his "original principle of human society." It is under a combination of their selfishness and sympathy that parents govern their children, both harshly and affectionately. After a while, the children come to recognize the advantages of parental rule. So it is with governments, in which the selfishness and sympathy of their citizens combine for the good of society as a whole.[29]

Hume's fame is based not only on his major philosophical works, but also on a large number of essays and his *History of England*, which was published in 1755 and which, according to the irascible Bertrand Russell, "devoted itself to proving the superiority of Tories to Whigs and of Scotchmen to Englishmen."[30] In one essay that was circulated in the American colonies, Hume offered glowing tributes to civil liberties and press freedom.[31] Following Milton, Hume saw liberty of the press as offering no threat to rulers, however that liberty might be abused. Press freedom, he said, "can scarce ever excite popular tumults or rebellions."

> *We need not dread from this liberty any such ill consequence as followed from the harangues of the popular demagogues of Athens and tribunes of Rome. A man reads a book or pamphlet*

> *alone and coolly. There is none present from whom he can catch the passion by contagion. He is not hurried away by the force and energy of action. And should he be wrought up to never so seditious a humor, there is no violent resolution presented to him by which he can immediately vent his passion.*[32]

Moreover, since people are likely to believe bad things about their governors one way or another, it is safer for the ruler to have those bad things put down in writing, because then they can come to his attention more easily.

Hume wrote extensively about the passions and was even critical of Milton for being "stiff and pedantic." However much he might have criticized Locke and other English philosophers for being inelegant writers, Hume was every bit in the mainstream of English rationality and intellectualism. He applauded English philosophy, but admired French art and theatre and especially the French skill at conversation.[33] His dispute with Rousseau, however irrational, resulted at least in part from basic differences between them.[34] Hume was cool and self-controlled while Rousseau was feverishly, perhaps pathologically, animated. To some degree, the divergent legacies bequeathed by English and French philosophy can be summed up in the differences in temperament of Hume and Rousseau. But then there were important differences between Rousseau and his fellow French philosophers, to whom we now turn.

PART III

The French, Society, and the Power of Feelings

François-Marie Arouet de Voltaire (1694–1778): "History has scarcely yet been more than chronological accounts written neither as a citizen nor as a philosopher . . . How miserable to make a study out of what can neither instruct, nor please, nor improve anyone. [We need] the story of people's morals and manners, sciences, laws, customs, superstitions. Practically all I see are the stories of kings. I want the stories of men."

Jean-Jacques Rousseau (1712–1778): "Of itself the people wills always the good, but of itself it by no means always sees it. The General Will is always in the right, but the judgment which guides it is not always enlightened . . . It is therefore necessary to make the people see things as they are . . . to guide them from the seducing voice of private wills."

CHAPTER 10

Introduction: Les Philosophes

In contemporary America the journalist easily justifies his work on the ground that he is serving the public, providing the information the individual needs to perform the duties of democratic citizenship. It is a matter of education—and no idea is more widely accepted by Americans than the idea that the more information you have the better off you are. Education is a positive good; no one speaks ill of learning, even those who have no interest in it.

In the doctrine of individualism, however, as preached by Hobbes and Locke and the English thinkers of the seventeenth century, there is no place for public service. Each man is free to follow his own path, to acquire whatever property he can, and to use that property however he chooses so long as he does not break the law or harm his fellow man. How he uses his property is his own business.

Thus, a man might acquire a printing press, compose his thoughts on paper, and circulate that paper as he wishes so long as he does not preach sedition. Only then might government interfere to abridge his freedom. Whether or not he informs or educates the public is irrelevant. It is the freedom itself that counts. This is a laissez-faire doctrine, one with which the later capitalist philosophers were quite comfortable. Most likely, Locke would have said, the printer in his activities seeks to earn income as profit, since it is through profit that he can acquire additional property—and the measure of his freedom is determined by the extent of his property.

The image of man, in the Hobbesian and Lockean world, is rational. Human beings are motivated by self-interest; it was in their self-interest that they formed the social contract, and it is self-interest that induces them to cooperate with one another since, if they do not, there would likely be a return to the Hobbesian jungle. There is little room for emotion in the community, since indulgence of feelings would likewise bring a return to the jungle. These ideas are fundamentally conservative. Government and the institutions of government are valuable as correctives. They are not good in themselves. Ideally, the individual ought to be left alone, but one could not go quite that far, because in the state of nature men would take the law into their own hands and no doubt bring harm to one another. In the Hobbesian view, man is by nature a savage and government is needed to protect a person from his fellows. Locke and Hume saw man as neither good nor evil, but they considered government necessary to make sure that each person is allowed the freedom to carve out his future in his own way; only thus can he have a sense of security. Isaiah Berlin interprets this kind of freedom as "negative" freedom.[1]

In the view of the English libertarians, keeping yourself informed is your own responsibility; a rational man would *want* information so that he might use it for his own purposes. Government plays a primarily negative role. So indeed do the other institutions of the social order. They are designed to protect, not to nurture.

The genius of the English thinkers who influenced the course of the United States and its institutions lay in their *political* philosophy. The politics of the press in the United States draws extensively on the concepts generated by these thinkers, especially Locke. To the English thinkers, the essence of government and its laws lies in the very nature of things, a notion derived from the Greek Stoics and their chief Roman spokesman, Cicero, who saw law as essentially "natural."[2] Laws exist simply because they are part of the natural order of things, part of God's plan; they are reasonable.

The journalist who defies a court order that he reveal his sources publicly is following natural law; he is rejecting positive law, those that are written by governments and men. The natural law, in this view, is the law of reason. On the other hand, men in their role as legislators might very well write positive laws that were irrational and unreasonable. The laws of men might forbid rebellion, but natural—or higher—law might require it. To Locke, natural law is not religious. It is the law of reason. Locke was cautious enough, in an age when absolute monarchy was still practiced, to suggest that rebellion is permissible only under repeated and extreme violations of the natural law, but the underlying idea was clear enough to those who read him, including the American colonists and the editors of the colonial newspapers.

Expression of such political ideas, including justification for revolution, was severely limited on the European continent in the sixteenth and seventeenth centuries, for the monarchs there were far more absolute than those in England. Thus the outpouring of political ideas on the European continent was delayed until the eighteenth century. It was not until the death of Louis XIV in 1715 that a flowering of thought similar to what had already taken place in England occurred in France. And when it did, it moved in a somewhat different direction. Rather than being essentially political, the French thrust was chiefly *social.*[3] Rather than political liberty, the primary emphasis in France was on civil liberty. The French philosophers chose for the development of these ideas a rubric, devised by the physicist Jean le Rond d'Alembert, that has become a household phrase: the Age of Enlightenment. There was nothing humble about these French thinkers; Denis Diderot, who created the world's first encyclopedia (1747–1772), identified himself and his fellow thinkers as *les philosophes*, or "the philosophers."

The ideas of John Locke were well known to the *philosophes*. Some among them, including Voltaire, Helvétius, and Montesquieu, lived and studied for long periods in England. Indeed, it was often as amended by the French that Lockean ideas reached the American colonists. Benjamin Franklin and Thomas Jefferson served as diplomats in France and lived in Paris for extended periods in the eighteenth century. Through them there was an extensive cross-fertilization of ideas. In the years prior to the revolution, much of this cross-fertilization derived from Franklin, who was an intimate of the *philosophes* during his years of residence in Paris. Franklin was lionized at his home in the Parisian suburb of Passy, where he published his writings on his own printing press. So closely were the American and French philosophers in contact with one another that the solitary Franklin proposed marriage to the widow of the philosopher Claude-Adrien Helvétius, a beautiful and lively woman who maintained a salon for liberals in the latter years of the century.[4] Upon being turned down, Franklin composed two of his most amusing little essays.[5] An essay addressed to Madame Helvétius, titled "The Elysian Fields," began:

> *Vexed by your barbarous resolution, announced so positively last evening, to remain single all your life in respect to your dear husband, I went home, fell on my bed, and believing myself dead, found myself in the Elysian Fields.*[6]

Franklin survived that rejection, though, and was later to play an important role in the establishment of the U.S. Constitution, in which he and his colleagues concocted an intriguing amalgam of the ideas of the English and French enlightenments. The French emphasis was primarily social—and social concerns direct themselves, as the phrase specifies, more to the activities and interests of society than to those of individuals, that is to say, to groups of people, to collectives. The chief spokesman for these social ideas was Jean-Jacques Rousseau, whose impact on American ideas, particularly as they relate to the ideas behind American journalism, is extensive. In fact, few persons in the history of ideas have had a greater impact on the world at large. Rousseau was to some extent the intellectual father of Karl Marx. Not only that. His commentaries shifted the direction of schooling; he can justifiably be credited as the originator of the idea of progressive education. *Alice in Wonderland* is based on the teachings of Rousseau; so are the schools of education in the

United States. Indeed, Rousseau's ideas had a powerful impact on the concepts of free expression as they appeared in the Declaration of Independence and the Constitution.

Rousseau was by no means the only *philosophe* to influence American thinking. Montesquieu's *The Spirit of Laws* was well known to the Founding Fathers who gathered in Philadelphia to draft the Constitution in 1787. James Madison, the leader of the drafters, often went to Montesquieu for support when he argued the idea, familiar to all American schoolchildren today, of a system of checks and balances guaranteeing that no branch of the American government could grow too powerful and thus lead to tyranny and the abuse of liberty.[7] Voltaire was also widely read, and his eloquent defense of a free press had an extensive readership among the founders. So did the writings of Diderot and d'Alembert. Lesser-known *philosophes* such as Helvétius and Pierre Bayle were also known to the colonists and influenced the patterns of their thought.

No one can, of course, say that this or that idea ever transferred itself into direct action. Ideas germinate and flower. They do not move in a direct line from thought to action. And since time passes between ideas and action, there is inevitably space for examination, interpretation, and modification. These changes are often not recognized, for they are subtle and filter into a person's brain without conscious effort. Thus it is impossible to prove that Locke directly influenced the American Revolution. His influence, substantial as it was, came through the actual perpetrators of the revolution, men who had read Locke, assimilated his thought, and interpreted it as suited their objectives. Their interpretations also took into account the judgments and opinions of others who had read Locke and had drawn somewhat different interpretations. It can be seen that the ideas of Locke, like those of Milton or Cicero, or Aristotle or Plato, were leavened in American thought by the views and attitudes of the *philosophes* and the experiences of the colonists themselves. As the political concepts of the English were adapted to the American scene, they were inevitably altered by the social environment.

While the English rationalists were comfortable with direct intellectual statements, the French, for whatever reason, were given to lofty flights of speculation, to broad and often unfathomable abstractions. In the colonies this bent of the Frenchmen found fertile soil, for many of the Founders were themselves abstract thinkers, devoted to speculation on grand subjects. Moreover, there was in the French reading of the Enlightenment a kind of passionate involvement, a removal from the more disinterested, scientific mien of the English.

The *philosophes* were not democrats, any more than was Hobbes or Locke. Perhaps Rousseau alone among the French philosophers can be called an avid democrat. In fact Rousseau has sometimes been called the first democrat or, in the words of Lytton Strachey, the first modern.[8] Certainly, the libertarian Voltaire was not prepared to turn society over to "the people," whom he despised. Rousseau was remarkable even among this remarkable assemblage. It is to be remembered that the *philosophes* were men of the eighteenth century who lived in a social order under the control of a monarch and an aristocracy that was only grudgingly beginning to surrender its prerogatives. The *philosophes* inhabited a world in which literacy was limited primarily to those who enjoyed positions of economic and social prestige, the nobility, the clergy, the merchants, the artisans, the property holders.

When they urged freedom of expression, they were speaking of such freedom for representatives of their own class. They did not expect leadership to emerge from the workers or peasants. The revolution did not begin until 1789, and (although it probably would have surprised them) the radical ideas let loose by the *philosophes* had by that time established a firm grasp on the minds of the literate in America as well as in France. With surprising speed, the ideas then circulated to the underprivileged social orders. The ground was prepared for the Jacobins and the spread of democratic principles, giving rise of course to the belief that the press ought properly to be free of all external controls. Among the chief architects of these ideas were Montesquieu, Helvétius, Voltaire, and especially Rousseau.

CHAPTER 11

Montesquieu: The Spirit of Laws

Of all commentaries, Montesquieu's *The Spirit of Laws* (1748) played the largest part in the Founding Fathers' creation of American institutions. Montesquieu's ideas slipped quietly into "the American system," beloved of journalists as well as teachers and scholars in high school civics classes. Madison summarized large parts of Montesquieu's book; Jefferson who in later years became critical of him, filled 20 pages of his *Commonplace Book* with passages from *Spirit*. Hamilton and Madison relied on Montesquieu in their defense of the Constitution in the *Federalist Papers*. The Bill of Rights was based in large part on Montesquieu's conception of civil liberties. In much the same way, Montesquieu's views were enshrined in the celebrated preamble to the French constitution of 1791, the Declaration of the Rights of Man and the Citizen.

Some commentators consider *Spirit* to be in fact an "American classic"; it was well known in the colonies as early as 1750.[1] In the last half of the eighteenth century, New York and Philadelphia booksellers found a ready market for the works of Montesquieu as well as those of the more renowned *philosophes*, Voltaire and Rousseau.[2]

Montesquieu has long been celebrated in the United States as the father of the concept of a mixed government where separate branches of government keep their eyes on one another in a system of checks and balances, although the idea was by no means original with him. Aristotle and Polybius had endorsed the idea of mixed government in the days of antiquity; Plato had envisaged a separation of government powers in his *Laws*. Yet it was Montesquieu who infused these concepts with the liberating ideas and especially the passions of the French Enlightenment—and disseminated them far and wide. To Aristotle, there were three possible forms of government—monarchy, aristocracy, and democracy—all potentially good for the society. But each of these, he said, would inevitably decay into something that was harmful, monarchy into dictatorship, aristocracy into oligarchy, democracy into mob rule. A mixture of all three was preferable. Montesquieu agreed and in the eighteenth century became the leading exponent of the form of government that was put into force under the American Constitution. Montesquieu was especially persuasive to the rational, antidogmatic Founding Fathers, for he was of like mind; moreover, he was one of the first thinkers to recognize clearly the importance of social conditioning on the growth of ideas and ideals.

While his writings have become a cornerstone of democratic ideology, Montesquieu himself was a member of the nobility, born Charles-Louis de Secondat in 1689, heir to the title of baron de Montesquieu. A lawyer by training, he studied in England for two years (1729–1731) and having fallen in love with the spirit of the unwritten English constitution, passed along his somewhat idealized view of that document to the American colonists and to the rising radical movement in France. The distinguished historian of political ideas, George H. Sabine, an unabashed anglophile suspicious of the lack of precision in French thought, wrote that Montesquieu was saved "from the charge of being an elegant amateur (horrors) by his unquestioned enthusiasm for liberty and his devotion to moral values."[3]

To Montesquieu, justice is the chief virtue and the only justification for laws. That is, laws should be adopted by governments only in order to insure the triumph of justice. Montesquieu fiercely attacked the atrocities of the legal system of his time and the cruelty of the laws. Indeed, it should be noted that the Italian marquess of Beccaria, Cesare Bonesana (1738–1794), converted Montesquieu's ideas into an influential vehicle for the reform of penal laws. Beccaria was also well known in colonial America, revered especially for his passionate sympathy for victims of injustice and the oppressed. His goal, Beccaria wrote, was to uphold "the rights of man and the rights of invincible truth."[4] Beccaria anticipated the ethical system of Immanuel Kant, which has played a major role in the contemporary resurgence of interest in journalism ethics, by asserting: "Liberty vanishes whenever the law . . . allows a man to cease to be a *person* and to become a thing."[5] For Montesquieu, laws ought to be aimed entirely at insuring justice, at securing the liberty of the citizen and the prosperity of the nation.[6] Voltaire was to say later that for him freedom meant nothing more than the right to depend on the law to be rational and to apply equally to all, an early statement of what we recognize today as the principle of due process.[7]

The best form of government, Montesquieu said, was one that, as he imagined England to have, enabled each citizen to pursue wealth and power with a minimum of restraint. This pursuit could take place only if neither the monarch nor the law-writing parliament held a monopoly over power. Critical in the carrying out of this pursuit was freedom of expression.

In endorsing freedom of expression, Montesquieu was giving utterance to an idea celebrated by all the *philosophes* even as it had been applauded by Milton, Locke, and Hume. It needs to be kept in mind, of course, that it could not have occurred to Montesquieu in the middle of the eighteenth century that the yeoman farmer or the carpenter or the hairdresser would ever have entertained much interest in free expression, especially in print, since it was unlikely that such persons could read or write, but the seeds were sown nevertheless.

Montesquieu contributed to the long-standing confusion over the terms *republic* and *democracy* by occasionally using them interchangeably in his attempt to classify different forms of government. It remained for Madison to clarify the difference in his brilliant *Federalist* No. 10 but, unfortunately, not everyone who discusses the subject of democracy pays close attention to Madison.[8]

In the *Spirit*, the republican (or democratic) form was favorably compared with the monarchical and the despotic. While Montesquieu, a son of his times, actually preferred the constitutional monarchy, it was, he said, the republican (or democratic) state that the common people could be expected to love. In fact, he saw as the very principle of democracy—its "virtue," as he put it—that the people could be passionately devoted to it. That passion for democracy, he said, was "a sensation that may be felt by the meanest as well as the highest person in the state."[9]

The republican form of government was to Montesquieu a moral system of government. Good laws would simply guarantee the triumph of justice and liberty. But still, it was possible for a republic to degenerate into the rule of the mob. Liberty and justice could be as readily undone by mobs as by dictators. Divided power was part of the answer; so was education.

In the American colonies, it was Madison, that great admirer of Montesquieu, who extended the thoughts of his French mentor. It was all very well, Madison said during the debates on the establishment of a constitution for Virginia, to speak of the virtue of democracy, but virtue could never exist as an abstract quality in a government. It was necessary, in concrete terms, that people themselves be virtuous. "No theoretical checks, no form of government, can render us secure," said Madison, rejecting the idea of paper checks and balances without the force of law. "To suppose that any form of government will secure liberty or happiness without any virtue in the people is a chimerical idea."[10]

In Montesquieu's analysis, education was always a critical factor in the prevention of abuses by the powerful. Madison was entirely at home with this view and was to expand the concept of education to include the writings of pamphleteers and other journalists. This stress on education in the very foundation of the state is of immense significance in the development of the belief system of American journalists. Journalism as an institution providing "news" to a general public was, of course, as unfamiliar a concept to Montesquieu as it was to Locke before him, but although he does not refer to the press, Montesquieu's words can be seen as implicitly carving out an educational role for the press, as they do explicitly for parents and teachers. The expressed goal of education was to insure love of a free, democratic government. "Everything," he wrote, "depends on establishing this love in a republic":

> *To inspire it ought to be the principal of education: but the surest way of instilling it into children is for parents to set them an example. People have it generally in their power to communicate their ideas to their children; but they are still better able to transfuse their passions.*[11]

While education could promote patriotism and love of liberty, wicked governments might still abuse their power. Such abuses, Montesquieu asserted, could not be checked by anything but counterpower.[12] The concept of the press as a "fourth estate," as a form of counterpower, fits comfortably into Montesquieu's scheme of good government. While he himself was no revolutionary, the logic of his ideas was radical indeed. For since liberty and justice were absolute virtues to him, it was but a small step to maintain that when governments grow unjust and deprive their citizens of their freedom, they must be overthrown. On this score, there was little difference between the ideas of Montesquieu and Locke.

On another, however, Montesquieu's views were fiercely radical and remarkably contemporary, serving as a philosophical springboard not only for the "big government" advocates of the twentieth century but also the "social responsibility" doctrine of the press. The state had not only the right but the duty to intervene in the private lives of its citizens when it was necessary to work, in effect, for the redistribution of the wealth of the nation. "The obligations of the state are not discharged by a few alms given to the naked in the street," Montesquieu wrote. "It owes to all its citizens assured subsistence, adequate clothing and a livelihood compatible with their health."[13] The concept of the press as a spokesman for the downtrodden, as an instrument of reform, is in complete harmony with the ideas of Montesquieu about education and the duties of the state, for how might the state better be informed of the ills of the common folk than by a press playing its role as educator?

Montesquieu spread across Europe and to the colonies a concept that was quintessentially French as opposed to English rationalism, a concept that has been adopted by American journalists as one of their most deeply cherished beliefs: that not only is a system of checks and balances demanded in the calculating political arena but also in the *passionate* world of conscience and feelings. The idea of a conflict of ideas was not a new one, for in the *Areopagitica*, Milton had envisioned a battle between truth and falsehood, but Montesquieu added a different slant. It was to him less a matter of the intellectual content of ideas than was it a collision of passions. To the English the idea of passion checking passion was ignoble; to the *philosophes* it was central to the human condition.

Who knows the truth? Montesquieu asked. Who can say that mere words can harm the political world? Writings, even those sharply critical of governments, are rarely damaging. To punish someone for what he writes without the closest prior definition of what is unacceptable is the hallmark of despotism. Here, Montesquieu was publicizing and popularizing an idea that was emerging in England as well, that prior restraint, the censoring of something in advance of publication, was unlawful, not maintaining the spirit of the law. "Words," he wrote, "do not constitute an overt act; they remain only in idea." The overt-acts test later became a judicial rule in the United States. The Supreme Court was to agree with Montesquieu's argument that only action may be punished, not thought. Even satirical commentaries, he said, are unlikely to bring harm: "They may amuse the general malevolence, please the malcontents, diminish the envy against public employments, give the people patience to suffer, and make them laugh at their sufferings."[14]

How these ideas were adapted to the American scene will be shown in Part 4. In any case, part of Montesquieu's message was that free and open commentary must be tolerated, even words that are themselves politically unacceptable or not in accord with popular taste. And there was no requirement that they make sense.

CHAPTER 12

Voltaire: "I Will Defend to the Death . . ."

While the English Libertarians—Hobbes, Locke, Hume—furnished much of the light in the Enlightenment, it was the French writers and thinkers who provided the fire, two in particular, allies in spirit but often enemies in the social and political world of their times: Jean-Jacques Rousseau, to whom we turn in the next chapter, and François-Marie Arouet de Voltaire. So overwhelming was the fame and influence of the latter that historians have often spoken of the eighteenth century as the Age of Voltaire.

The professional ideology of American journalists owes much to Voltaire, for however many plays and novels, political and social pamphlets, letters and essays he may have written, he was first and foremost a journalist. To him, the password to progress and to the triumph of good on earth was enlightened understanding. And no journalist has cheerfully shouldered the burden of providing this kind of enlightened understanding more than Voltaire. An outspoken foe of organized religion, Voltaire found instead a secular trinity: toleration, the rule of law, and freedom of opinion, which for him set forth the conditions under which human beings could live on earth in dignity and happiness.[1] This trinity underlay Voltaire's program of social reform, about which he wrote passionately. Indeed, one could without too great exaggeration speak of Voltaire as the first great advocacy journalist.

Students of Voltaire have long disagreed among themselves about his stature and significance. Some have depicted him as flighty and superficial; others have seen him as vigorous and profound. Some have seen him as a dedicated activist; others, as a remote figure who talked a good game but refused to take to the barricades.[2] Still, few persons today would deny Voltaire's overwhelming influence over the course of history and over the way we view the world, in short over the ideas we carry about in our heads. And indeed over the professional ideology of American journalists.

To begin with, it is important to note that Voltaire was the skeptic par excellence, and that he did as much as anyone to spread the methods of science among historians, humanists, and writers, journalists foremost among them. Believe nothing that has not been proved, Voltaire wrote in the introduction to his famous *Essay on the Customs and Spirit of Nations*. Accept only what can be established with "the greatest and most recognized probability," he affirmed.[3]

Voltaire's collected works cover no fewer than 52 volumes. Counted among them are novels and short stories, essays on politics and society, full-scale histories, and a massive assortment of letters addressed to the great and near-great of the eighteenth century. An indefatigable writer, certainly the most journalistically inclined of the *philosophes*, Voltaire was never reluctant to offer advice, not only to kings and popes but to journalists as well. His 1737 *Lettre à un journaliste* is one of the earliest lectures ever written on how to be a good reporter.[4] Voltaire would have made a great professor of journalism had he been so inclined.

Today, Voltaire is best known for his eloquent style, his biting and sarcastic wit, and his unswerving devotion to the basic principles of human liberty, especially freedom to communicate the written word. Voltaire was a patrician by birth and taste, and it was not until the last two decades of his long life—he died at 83—that one could speak of him in any way as a radical, but few persons have defended human liberty with greater enthusiasm. One prominent scholar has credited Voltaire's condemnation of Christian persecutions with being "probably the greatest contribution to freedom of speech ever made."[5]

For most of his life, Voltaire does not appear to have been concerned about *political* liberty. The work of governments did not attract his interest, nor did the activities of the masses. In fact, from his lofty position Voltaire regarded the general public as cruel and stupid. It did not apparently occur to him that there could be no civil liberty without political liberty. To Voltaire, the people were "a rabble" who "will always be stupid and barbarous. They are oxen who need a yoke, a goad and hay."[6] Faced with the repression of the authorities in his adopted residence just outside Geneva, however, Voltaire decided that maybe even the "unthinking masses" would rally to the cause of reason and logic if only they were told the truth, an ideological stance with which American journalists, no matter how they may deride the reading public, are entirely comfortable.[7]

In Geneva and indeed elsewhere in France, Voltaire's ideas so offended the religious authorities that some of his famous writings were publicly burned, along with Rousseau's *Social Contract* and other works that were thought in those years prior to the French Revolution to be incitements to rebellion.[8] It was at this time that Voltaire flirted with the idea of democracy, but never too seriously. He continued to assail Rousseau not only for what he saw as his lack of a sense of humor but also for his radicalism, this despite the fact that many of his views were quite close to those of his revolutionary colleague. The checkered relationship between Voltaire and Rousseau makes up the stuff of fiction.

On the whole, Voltaire's ideas differed little from those of Locke, and it was his well-known and fiercely seditious essay on Locke that had much to do with the spread of Locke's thought through France.[9] Still, it is important to keep in mind that it is French, not English, that is the language of radicalism—and Voltaire's sarcastic wit managed to convert the carefully structured words of Locke into something that sounded far more radical than the paler language of the original. Jefferson was a great admirer of Voltaire and it may well have been through Voltaire's essay that Locke became for him a revolutionary. In any case, Jefferson was to wax as eloquent as Voltaire in his defense of free expression. "I have," the Virginian wrote in words hallowed in stone on the Jefferson Memorial in Washington, "sworn upon the altar of God, eternal hostility against every form of tyranny over the mind of man."[10] In this context, Jefferson and Voltaire were brothers; their impassioned words have through the years coursed through the blood of the American journalist.

The admiration for Voltaire by Jefferson and his American contemporaries was apparently derived only from certain passages. Jefferson would certainly not have approved Voltaire's expressed contempt for the public, but he much admired not only Voltaire's defense of free expression but also his conviction that reason was the guiding principle of human endeavor. Moreover, Voltaire's image of history as cultural, not based merely on wars and great men, was fascinating to the builders of a New World.

Certainly, one of Voltaire's greatest contributions to the ideas of American journalists lay in his insistence that human understanding was not to be advanced by simply piling fact upon fact—he expressed only contempt for "mere compilers"—but rather through painstaking attention to detail, especially about the customs and behavior of the people:

> *It seems to me that one cannot consider history as nothing more than a compilation of chronological material. This tells us nothing about what has been written, nothing about ordinary people, nothing about philosophy.*[11]

How shameful it is, Voltaire went on, to write history about "what can neither instruct, nor please, nor improve anyone!" What more attractive advice could a contemporary journalist receive. "Practically all I see are histories of kings. I want histories of men." And, he said, those histories ought to include what today is the daily bread of newspapers and broadcasting outlets, stories about "people's morals and manners, sciences, laws, customs, superstitions." Voltaire invited not only the historian but the journalist as well to devote his efforts to writing what today would be identified as "human interest" stories. Before Voltaire, the idea of the chronicler spending time over the activities of the common man was unknown. In Voltaire's conception of universal or cultural history, this idea was central. For the journalist, Voltaire wrote, the most fascinating events of all are "the tidbits of history," because they tell the most that can be told about human beings and their tastes.[12]

Not only is it important for the reporter to search for the "tidbits of history," Voltaire told journalists, but also to express what he has to say in language that can be easily understood. Avoid the pedantic, Voltaire said, foreshadowing the advice that journalist George Orwell would offer two centuries later. Use familiar words rather than making up new ones, and tell it straight, said Voltaire.[13] Indeed, Voltaire saw the journalist as educator as much as writer. "Above all," Voltaire told journalists, "inspire in our youth a taste for the history of recent times, for that is far more important for us than accounts of ancient times, which do nothing but tease our curiosity."[14]

Voltaire's advice to journalists has a remarkably modern ring to it. Be skeptical about the information that is given you. Do not trust anything that you have been told unless it can be confirmed by independent examination. Adopt the methods of science. Voltaire, who was more committed an empiricist than Locke or Hume, embodied qualities that today would be celebrated as professional. His specific advice to journalists was not circulated extensively in the American colonies at the time, but Voltaire's works were so widely read in colonial America that the basic thrust of his ideas was manifest to the colonists, including the numerous journalists among them. In France, even today it is no exaggeration to speak of Voltaire as the patron saint of the Gallic journalist.

To reporters and editors everywhere, the most attractive side of Voltaire was perhaps the far-ranging nature of his interests. He was, for instance, the supreme example of the generalist, the Renaissance man whose interests were so wide and varied that there was almost nothing about which he did not demonstrate a lively curiosity. The practice of journalism in today's increasingly specialized world is almost the last refuge of the generalist.

Voltaire was also an adamant spokesman for religious tolerance, another element that endeared him to Jefferson, to the American colonists, and to the American journalists who circulated their ideas. On religion, Locke had been exceedingly cautious, seeking to avoid offending the church establishment. Voltaire on the other hand had no such inhibitions. In his essay on Locke, he observed that some devout Englishmen were alarmed by Locke's argument that ideas came from the brain, not from God, and had complained that Locke was trying to turn religion upside down. Not so, said Voltaire at his ironic best: "But it is common with theologians to begin by pronouncing that God is offended whenever we happen not to think as they do."[15]

Voltaire's essay on Locke provided an equally ironic and quite unique defense against the allegation that printed matter might circulate subversive ideas. Ever the skeptic, Voltaire found the no-nonsense essence of British empiricism much to his liking, and he propaganized enthusiastically on its behalf. In any case, he wrote, no philosophical belief such as Locke's could ever harm the religion of a nation. "Never," he said, "will philosophers create a religion sect . . . because they do not write for the whole people, and they are without enthusiasm." His pen dipped in sarcasm, he continued in this vein:

> *Divide the human race into twenty parts; nineteen will be composed of those who work with their hands and who will never know if there is Locke in the world. In the twentieth part which remains, how few men will be found who read! And among those who read, there are twenty who read the Roman authors for every one who studies philosophy. The number of those who think is excessively small, and these do not care to disturb the world.*[16]

Voltaire turned again and again to his love of books. His defense of press freedom, one of the shortest and most eloquent ever penned, testifies to his endorsement of free thought and to his determination to express those free thoughts in print. Voltaire's paean to the press was included in his masterful *Philosophical Dictionary*, a remarkable collection of the liberal thought of the ages, which Peter Gay characterizes, appropriately enough, as "a bomb thrown at the Old Regime."[17] Rome, Voltaire wrote in rejecting the idea of censorship, was not conquered by books but because she had revolted Europe through her rapacity and wickedness. A devotee of luxurious, epicurean living, Voltaire used the occasion of that essay to condemn the clergy for its rejection of the pleasures of living, including singing and dancing: "You fear books as certain small towns have feared violins. Let people read and let them dance; these two amusements will never do the world any harm."[18]

Voltaire's acerbic style has caused him to appear to some readers as gloomy and pessimistic about life, which would certainly put him outside the mainstream of American journalism. But, although Voltaire specifically dismissed an "optimistic" outlook on life, he was not at all given to gloom and despair. He saw himself as a realist, and above all an activist, a stance that would be echoed a century and a half later by the great American pragmatist, William James. "Dare to think for yourself," Voltaire admonished. It was in *action*, he argued, that mankind fulfils itself. "Man is born for action," he wrote. "Not to be occupied and not to exist are the same thing."[19] This was the same Voltaire who at times found peace and happiness in living the quiet, bookish, thoughtful life. At the same time, he gave expression to an enduring element in the professional ideology of inquiring American journalists. Don't wait for someone to come to you, Voltaire was saying. Find out for yourself. Much of his quarrel with Rousseau lay in his (erroneous) assessment that Rousseau was a mere dabbler while he was an activist. "Jean-Jacques," he wrote in a razor-sharp Voltairean riposte, "writes just for the sake of writing, but I write to stir things up."[20]

The work of Beccaria and Montesquieu on justice stimulated Voltaire to a series of ferocious assaults on the French criminal justice system, especially after a young man named Jean Chevalier de La Barre, alleged without clear proof to have defaced a crucifix, was found to have Voltaire's *Philosophical Dictionary* in his possession and then condemned to a horrible death. Following the execution, La Barre was buried along with a copy of Voltaire's book.

Joining other *philosophes* in outraged assault on the French system of criminal justice, Voltaire campaigned for a change in the law that would insure that punishment was never exacted for moral or religious reasons, only to insure the social order. The professional ideology of journalists would follow Voltaire and his colleagues in promoting the American doctrine that it is better to let a guilty man go free than condemn an innocent man. Endorsing the Roman maxim, Voltaire argued that "offenses against the gods concern only the gods."[21] Rousseau was to go even further: "There is not a single evil-doer whom one cannot render good for something. One has the right to put to death, even as an example, only the man one cannot preserve without danger." Voltaire's comment, on reading this passage from the *Social Contract*, was simply "*Bon.*"[22]

Voltaire's life was intimately associated with that of another *philosophe*, Claude-Adrien Helvétius, renowned for developing the fundamentals of the movement that we know today as utilitarianism, a philosophy that freed science from the chains that had bound it throughout all the centuries when ideas and morality were thought to be altogether religious in origin, coming only from God. It is in utilitarianism that the cross-fertilization of English and French thought in developing the great ideas of the Enlightenment can best be seen.

Helvétius, the son of a well-to-do physician, was introduced to the writings of Hume when he visited England with his father. It was, as we have seen, Hume's *Treatise of Human Nature* that had attacked the foundations of natural law, arguing that inasmuch as no one could establish scientifically the existence of laws of human morality, one must ultimately conclude that morality is determined not by deity but by customs, habits, and popular conventions.

Men act on the basis of what they can use, of what has *utility* for them, Hume argued, and since it is human nature to seek pleasure and to avoid pain, conventional vitue and happiness lie largely in escaping pain. Helvétius brought the ideas of Hume and other English utilitarians back to France with him and incorporated them into his masterpiece, *Essays on the Mind*, which appeared in Paris in 1758, shocking not only the clerics but his fellow *philosophes* as well.[23] Denis Diderot, who had worked with Helvétius on the celebrated Encyclopedia of knowledge, condemned *Mind* for ignoring hereditary factors in human development. Voltaire, certainly no friend of the church, was at first shocked by its frank materialism, but it was to Helvétius that he delivered his famous maxim, "I disapprove of what you say but I will defend to the death your right to say it."[24]

Mind achieved some kind of a record for burnings. It was condemned by the Sorbonne shortly after it was published and burned on the order of the French parliament a year later; it was condemned once again by the national Assembly of the Clergy in 1765.[25]

Curiously, it was the work of the Frenchman Helvétius, more radical than Voltaire or the Scot Hume whom he admired, that was later to exert the greatest influence over the development of English utilitarianism, so called by its chief spokesman, Jeremy Bentham, to whom we turn later. It was largely from his reading of utilitarianism that Bentham was able to construct what has become the unspoken but fundamental ideology of the "socially responsible" contemporary American journalist. In language that Bentham was later to borrow, Helvétius maintained that pleasure and pain are "safeguards" inborn in human beings. These safeguards then help people as they travel the path to progress and happiness.[26] This line of reasoning rejects the individualism of Locke. The special interests of individuals must yield to those of the collective, to the "greatest number." Morality rests, then, in enlightening the people as to what precisely constitutes the greatest good. For people to be enlightened, they must be educated, an assignment Helvétius gave to the legislature, but which of course could also be given to the journalist. In any case, the contemporary journalist, like his fellows of the eighteenth and nineteenth centuries, has taken that task upon himself.

Anyone who holds the people in ignorance, Helvétius wrote, brings upon himself universal contempt:

> *If audacious and powerful wickedness so often puts justice and virtue in chains and oppresses the nations, this is brought about only with the assistance of ignorance, which conceals from every nation its true interest, hinders the action and union of its strength, and by that means shields the guilty from the sword of justice.*[27]

The tone that Helvétius brought to utilitarianism was secular, not ecclesiastical, as had been the case with the pleasure-pain principle as it developed in England before Bentham. In England, theologians had stressed the pleasures and pains of the afterlife. No friend of organized religion, Helvétius turned utilitarianism into a mechanism for social reform, wherein legislators educated individuals and then enacted laws to bring about their private happiness as well as public reforms. It was a radical idea that was adopted by Bentham when he campaigned for social reform in England, and which was later to unfurl as the banner of *responsibility* under which a free press was justified because it served the interests of its readers.

In comparison with Voltaire's style, Helvétius's was heavy-handed, and Voltaire certainly considered him a lightweight. Indeed, at the same time that he was defending Helvétius's right to say whatever he wished, Voltaire let it be known that he considered *Mind* nothing but an "omelet . . . an airy trifle."[28] But behind Voltaire's light-hearted manner and his deprecating wit lay the powerful message that progress and virtue are secure only when those with something to say may say it undisturbed. The rule applied to hated ideas as well as admired ideas, a basic concept in the ideology of American journalists, who traditionally report "both sides" of issues, those they agree with and those they despise, in order to be "objective" communicators. Reporters and editors do not hesitate to endorse Voltaire's message to Helvétius.

CHAPTER 13

Rousseau: The General Will and Social Responsibility

Few persons have had greater impact on the ideas of modern men and women than Rousseau. Isaiah Berlin has written: "If Voltaire created the religion of man, Rousseau was the greatest of its prophets." To Tolstoy, Rousseau was one of the two men (Stendhal was the other) to whom he owed the most.[1] Rousseau was a hero and an inspiration both to the Jacobins who remade the world by igniting the French Revolution and to a number of the rebels who launched the American Revolution. The English philosopher-statesman, Edmund Burke, saw Rousseau as "the mad Socrates" of the French revolutionaries.[2] Even those who found Rousseau's radical views distasteful, as Burke did, recognized how great was his influence—on individuals as widely different in view as Jefferson and Hegel, John Stuart Mill and Karl Marx, Thoreau and Kant. Rousseau was no doubt correct in remarking that there had never been anyone like himself.[3] To George Sabine, the fact that Rousseau could appeal to persons with such opposing philosophies is testimonial to the imprecision of his own thought.[4]

It is indeed true that Rousseau was fascinated by paradox; if he were alive today, this fascination might very well have led him to pursue the modern career of journalist. The paradox of the man who bites the dog is always more interesting to the journalist than the straightforward case of the carnivorous canine.

A careful reading of Rousseau shows that in his analysis of history, politics, the arts, philosophy, and morality, he gave intellectual support to such widely held elements in the dogma of the press as the doctrines of social responsibility and the people's right to know. And, like Voltaire and today's American journalist, Rousseau was thoroughly skeptical about the "theories" of intellectuals; as far as Rousseau was concerned, people behaved on the basis of their gut reactions rather than cognitive thought. The first question the inquiring reporter asks of a news source is "How do you *feel* about . . . ?" not "What do you *think* about . . . ?"

Naturally, these and other basic beliefs of the contemporary American journalist were never consciously adopted from Rousseau's writings. More likely, the typical American newsperson is only peripherally familiar with Rousseau. But ideas, as we have had occasion to note before, infiltrate our behavior unbidden and unrecognized. Since journalists rarely concern themselves with philosophy, their ideas, indeed the dogmas and conventions under which they operate, come from outside the craft (or profession) they pursue.[5] And in the arrival of these dogmas, conventions, and practices, Rousseau is a towering figure.

The most complete account we have of Rousseau's life comes from his own posthumously published *Confessions*, a remarkable work in itself. From the pages of that autobiography there emerges a portrait of a very complex man, one who could be—and has been—characterized as a revolutionary, a totalitarian, a romantic, a progressive, a neurotic, indeed as the world's first anthropologist.[6] One can certainly doubt that complete accuracy was uppermost in Rousseau's intentions in the *Confessions*, but the account is gripping and quite revealing. It has been suggested that the Rousseau described in the *Confessions* was largely a fictional self created to compensate for his own personal inadequacies.[7] In any case, even in his own account, Rousseau was anything but a lovable figure. Born at some distance from Paris, the intellectual capital of the French world, Rousseau was the product of a family of genteel poverty. His mother died in childbirth; his father deserted him soon after. The victim of a humiliating disease (inflammation of the bladder, stricture of the urethra), he was shy but passionate, ever argumentative, particularly with authority.[8] In the Age of Reason, when his fellow *philosophes* were unswervingly committed to the idea that rational thought could solve anything, Rousseau was a rebel, a man who found greater joy in nature and quiet solitude than in the intellectual ferment of the city, a man who revered innocence and despised the rich and the powerful. His colleagues came to return his loathing. The encyclopedist, Diderot, once Rousseau's closest friend and ally, was to declare that between himself and Rousseau lay the "vast chasm between heaven and hell."[9]

In an almost throwaway line in his *Confessions*, Rousseau gives expression to what we might well identify as the guiding principle of his life. In a reference to his experiences with his first love, an older woman, the baroness of Warens, Rousseau wrote: "Instead of listening to her heart, which gave her good counsel, she listened to her reason, which gave her bad."[10] The reversal, the about-face, that Rousseau gave to the Enlightenment, came from his challenge to the ascendancy of reason and his claim of primacy for passion. For Rousseau, the heart was above the head.

The impact of this reversal on American journalism is apparent. Wisdom in all things, statecraft as well as love, resides not in the intellectual elite, not in the holders of power, but rather in the people. Modern American journalists, well-paid and university-trained, can no longer be included among "the people," Voltaire's rabble, but the dogma of democracy, enshrined in the concept of "the people's right to know," remains nevertheless a firm linchpin in the journalist's professional ideology. In Rousseau's powerful imagery, intellect might go astray, but the voice of the people, directed by their feelings, will always take the path of decency. Of course, for intelligent choices to be made, those feelings have to be fed with sound information; thus, education is a dominant force in Rousseau's thinking. Informed people, acting on their feelings, provided the only kind of government worth having. The concept of the people's right to know is clearly at hand.

In his admiration for information, Rousseau was a man of his time. Belief in the virtues of education was crucial to all the *philosophes*. But to Rousseau, education was more than merely intellectual. It was a *moral* necessity, and it was necessary, furthermore, that the passions be educated as well as the mind. Indeed Rousseau was, like the American journalists who have followed in the spirit of Rousseauism, more the moralist than the philosopher or the recorder of events. He was, according to one scholar, preaching a "civil religion"; he was envisaging a New Jerusalem.[11]

The centerpiece of Rousseau's political philosophy is the concept of the General Will, a somewhat mystical concept to which the Genevan gave birth in 1762 in his most famous political pronouncement, the *Social Contract*. Seven years earlier, Rousseau's *A Discourse on the Origin of Equality* had stirred the interest of intellectuals and had even reached down to the eighteenth-century version of the "general public." The earlier book bitterly condemned the capitalist state and associated all the evils of the world with private property. Despite the severe criticism of many of the *philosophes*, who were strong supporters of Locke's attachment to private property and capitalism, Rousseau made no effort to backtrack. The *Social Contract* begins with the ringing words: "Man was born free but is everywhere in chains."[12] To Rousseau, these chains were created as a defense of private property or—to use a contemporary restatement of a Rousseauean idea—as a means whereby the haves keep out the have-nots. It was to insure equal rights for all citizens, Rousseau wrote, that men organized themselves under social contracts:

> *Instead of destroying the natural equality of mankind, the fundamental compact substitutes . . . a moral and legal equality for that physical inequality which nature placed among men, and that, let men be ever so unequal in strength or in genius, they are all equalized by convention and legal rights.*[13]

Such, Rousseau wrote, is the essence of *good* governments. "Under bad governments," he said, 'this equality is only apparent and illusory; it serves only to keep the pauper in his poverty and the rich man in the position he has usurped." The social state, he concluded, is of value to all persons only "when all have something and none too much."[14]

The chief reason perhaps for the uncertainty of analysts about Rousseau's General Will lies in the fact that he did not define the term precisely, for the very good reason no doubt that the concept is itself neither precise nor objective. It is in fact dogmatic, doctrinal, and religious, this idea that somehow there is in "the people" an underlying awareness of what is moral, virtuous, valuable, and good. The people understand these things in a way that cannot be analyzed empirically. Americans ought to have little difficulty in recognizing this mystical idea, for it is similar to belief in the virtue of the American Way of Life, as understood in the *hearts* of the American people. In similar vein, freedom of the press is recognized as good because it too is willed by the people. It is the expression of the General Will.

Rousseau was careful to distinguish between the General Will (*volonté générale*) and the Will of All (*volonté de tous*). The Will of All, representing the sum total of individual wills and desires, is a quite different thing from the General Will. The Will of All need not be good, for it represents a hodgepodge of individual selfish wishes. It destroys all social ties, placing the individual first and ignoring the legitimate wants and needs of the group. It is on the basis of this concept that Rousseau is sometimes considered to be the father of modern sociology. The General Will, in this view, cannot possibly be wicked or selfish. The Will of All may be selfish, ignorant, and full of prejudice, but never the General Will. Or, as Rousseau himself saw the difference, the Will of All is simply the sum of all *private* interests while the General Will constitutes the *public* interest. In Rousseau's moralistic vision of the New Jerusalem, the General Will replaces the self-love of individuals with the self-esteem of community consciousness.[15]

Not only did Rousseau reject the Will of All, but he also condemned the culture of the *philosophes* themselves. In so doing, he incurred their undying hatred. Rousseau, a product of the "lower orders" of prerevolutionary France, rejected salon society—what Voltaire identified as his "church"—or *le monde*, as it was known then, and embraced the disenfranchised, the poor, the peasantry. In so doing he became the intellectual hero of those who were to storm the Bastille 11 years after his death. To Voltaire and the others, including even his close friend, Diderot, another product of the "lower orders," Rousseau became an outcast, a traitor to the cause of the *philosophes*.[16]

The General Will "is always right and tends to the public advantage," Rousseau wrote, "but it does not follow that the deliberations of the people are always correct. Our will is always for our own good, but we do not always see what it is; the people are never corrupted, but are often deceived."[17]

And who is it who will *undeceive* the people, who will work to avoid corruption? Rousseau suggests this is the task of those who enact the laws, the legislators, but it is apparent that he means to include also the teachers and the writers, journalists significant among them:

> *Of itself the people wills always the good, but of itself it by no means always sees it. The General Will is always in the right, but the judgment which guides it is not always enlightened. . . . Public enlightenment leads to the union of understanding and will in the social body. It is therefore necessary to make the people see things as they are . . . to guide them from the seducing voice of private wills.*[18]

No clearer philosophical support for the concept of the "people's right to know" has ever been provided. Moreover, Rousseau wrote, it is the task of the legislator (and, one is compelled to add, of the teacher and the journalist) to feel himself "capable, so to speak, of changing human nature, of transforming each individual." What a powerful calling! "The legislator occupies in every sense an extraordinary position in the state."[19] He is not to exercise power like a king but he ought to possess such skill with words that he can persuade the people to follow the dictates of the General Will. Even more than Voltaire, Rousseau insisted on the rejection of lofty and obscure language above the intellectual level of the people: "Wise men, if they try to speak their own language to the common people instead of its own cannot possibly make themselves understood. There are a thousand kinds of ideas which it is impossible to translate into popular language."[20] Not all of us are skillful writers, nor are we all well-educated, but we all can understand plain speech—this was Rousseau's message.

These sentiments, too, are an integral part of the way American journalists view the world and their jobs as well. It is important that everyone understand what they write, including, as it used to be said, the Kansas City milkman.[21]

Rousseau's philosophical output was concerned in almost equal degrees with culture, politics, and education. To him, education was the key not only to a civilized society or to culture, not only to good government, but also to the good life for the individual. The educational system that he saw in France was, Rousseau believed, something to be despised, to be revolutionized from top to bottom. His ideas on education, expressed in a number of books, the most remarkable of which was *Émile: A Treatise on Education*, influenced the development of education everywhere, especially in the United States where, a century or more later, John Dewey was to apply them to American teaching methods. This was so although Dewey was a firm believer in human progress while Rousseau tended to view human history as a step backward from its innocent youth.

In fact, Rousseau leveled his considerable verbal artillery at those who force children to grow up too quickly, who do not allow them the pleasures of their innocent, somewhat idealized pastoral childhood, who insist on compelling them into a world of reason where they are not permitted to give expression to their feelings. "What does wisdom avail you," he asked, "except as it concerns humanity?"

> *By trying to make a learned man out of a child, fathers and tutors begin all too soon tormenting, correcting, reprimanding, flattering, threatening, bribing, instructing, and reasoning. Rather than that, be reasonable and never reason with your pupil, especially when you want him to change his dislikes; for by dragging reason into unpleasant matters you make it distasteful to him and discredit it early in a mind that is not ready to understand it.*[22]

"For us to exist is to feel," Rousseau asserted. "We have feelings before we have ideas."[23] Rousseau, the moralist extraordinary, perceived education as far more than book learning. Not only is it necessary that education be universal and compulsory, but it must be in a real sense designed for character building, to include physical education as well as academic learning.[24] Rousseau was in fact suspicious of the "sophisticated Parisian culture" of the decadent French ruling circles that had won over his fellow *philosophes*, especially Voltaire.[25] The verbal education that they sought to impose on society, Rousseau thought, was a way to prevent a return to innocence and integrity. Lewis Carroll's Alice was a child of *Émile*, learning with Humpty Dumpty the importance of words: " 'When I use a word,' Humpty Dumpty said, in a rather scornful tone, 'it means what I choose it to mean—neither more nor less.' "[26] America's muckraking journalists were Rousseau's disciples as well, insofar as they sought to enlighten the people in order that they could exercise the General Will and bring down the corrupt barons of the marketplace.

There were muckrakers aplenty in prerevolutionary France. The "antisocial smut" raked up by these writers was, however, a good deal more salacious than anything imagined by Lincoln Steffens or even Upton Sinclair.[27] These authors of what was then known as *libelles* (libels) and *chroniques scandaleuses* (scandal sheets), took Rousseau as their hero-example, and produced a kind of underground journalism that sneered at the high and mighty, reported about the exotic sex lives of kings and courtiers—their chief target was Madame DuBarry, the mistress of Louis XV—and predicted the fall of the Old Regime. One scholar speaks of their writings as "gutter Rousseauism."[28] It is not likely that any of their accounts was true to the facts, but their outpourings must have played a part in the general sense of decadence that pervaded French society and helped prepare the public for the turmoil of the revolution. Rigid censorship was imposed by the Bourbon rulers, not only on the writings of the *libellistes* but on much of the works of Rousseau as well. The split between Voltaire and Rousseau was complete, enduring until 1778, the year that both men died. It was 11 years later that the

Jacobins stormed the Bastille. Voltaire had railed at the *libellistes*, condemning them as "satanic works [that] spread a terrible poison on everything one respects and loves."[29]

In discussing the political journalism of the *libellistes*, historian Robert Darnton has written:

> *In such crude media, politics was reported crudely—as a game for kings, their courtiers, ministers, and mistresses. Beyond the court and below the summit of salon society, the "general public" lived on rumors; and the "general reader" saw politics as a kind of nonparticipant sport, involving villains and heroes but no issues—except perhaps a crude struggle between good and evil or France and Austria.*[30]

The public in Darnton's portrait of the eighteenth century bears a painful similarity to the readers of today's gossip columns and televised accounts of the alleged private lives of celebrities. Darnton does, however, draw a sharp distinction between the "investigative journalism" of the *libellistes* and that of the contemporary American reporter, but certainly modern journalists have come under attack on similar grounds. We will return to this topic later.

In any case, Rousseau was not a genuine revolutionary, nor indeed could he be counted as a libertarian since in his view the people are not free to disobey the General Will. Freedom lies in carrying out the General Will, since it is always good. Those who oppose it are subject to punishment. It is the collective will that counts, not the total will of individuals. Isaiah Berlin, in his fascinating contrast between Locke and Rousseau, "Two Concepts of Liberty," argues that the kind of liberty Locke proposed is a negative one, Rousseau's a positive one.[31] In Locke's concept, liberty consists of preventing those in power from interfering with the behavior of the individual so that each person can become what he wants to be. For Rousseau, liberty brings with it a positive duty to carry out the commandments of the General Will. It did not matter to Locke whether an individual participates in government; to Rousseau it did.

Governments formed under Locke's social contract are instruments to open up opportunities for the individual. In Rousseau's social compact, however, liberty means not only accepting those opportunities but also doing something about them, participating in government rather than accepting it passively. To Rousseau, liberty and morality are the same thing.[32] One is "free" only when one is behaving morally, that is, following the spirit of the General Will. Locke was an optimist about the nature of man. At bottom, Rousseau was a pessimist about the nature of man, not at all convinced that men *would* work individually to safeguard their freedom. Only in the group, only in the collective, can the General Will find expression—then only when the people have been educated and enlightened about the deceptions of those who would seduce them into slavery. This is a concept with which Marx was thoroughly at home. Men are naturally good, Rousseau argued in extolling the virtuous peasant, the noble savage, but society, with its misdirected worship of the crass and the ugly, has bound him in chains. Only a new kind of society can release those chains, a new kind of society created by intelligent partisans, wise and altruistic lawmakers, dedicated journalists, and clear-minded teachers. Marx thought so, too.

On the other hand, Rousseau was never impressed by dogma, and the rigidity of Marxism-Leninism, especially with its glorification of urban, industrial life, would have appalled him. He might have found happier intellectual companionship in Immanuel Kant, the German philosopher, and Leo Tolstoy, the Russian historian-novelist. Kant and Tolstoy acknowledged their intellectual debt to Rousseau. Kant, for whom good was an absolute—live your life as though each of your actions could serve as a universal rule for behavior, he advised—hung a picture of Rousseau on the wall of his study and pronounced him the Newton of the moral world.[33] Reason is not enough to guarantee morality, Kant wrote.[34] One needs above all one's moral sense, and that comes from feelings, not from reason. Tolstoy linked himself indelibly with Rousseau's analysis of education and his profound moralistic suspicion of the rich and the powerful. Devotion to an innate sense of morality and suspicion of the powerful are integral elements in the attitudes of American journalists, ideas that were communicated to the world by Rousseau.

In part, the spread of Rousseau's ideas to the United States grew out of the remarkable cross-fertilization of thought between France and the American colonies in the final years of the eighteenth century. The French seized with approval the practical wisdom of Benjamin Franklin and Thomas Jefferson and the fiery pronouncements of Thomas Paine. And the Americans took into their rationale for rebellion against the British the intellectual excitement generated by Montesquieu and Voltaire, by Diderot and d'Alembert, by Helvétius and Rousseau. On both sides of the Atlantic there was profound support for the idea of free expression, especially in opposition to the powerful and the corrupt.

CHAPTER 14

Revolution: The Rights of Majorities and Minorities

Looked at from the comfortable vantage point of hindsight, the French Revolution seems an inevitable result of the unfolding of the ideas of the *philosophes*. Perhaps it was not inevitable, though, that the circulation of those militant ideas bring on the violence and bloodshed of the Reign of Terror. Still, when a social system is destroyed, its demise is never an easy one. Louis XVI tried to head off the violence by announcing his acceptance of the basic document put together by the Jacobin revolutionaries. It was called the Declaration of the Rights of Man and the Citizen, created by a committee of five, who in drawing it up consulted the then American ambassador, Thomas Jefferson.[1] The Declaration was presented to the National Assembly in August 1789. In concise form it summarized, often in ringing language, the social and political philosophies of Montesquieu, Helvétius, Voltaire, and Rousseau. Article 11 proclaimed in essence an ideology that has entered the belief system of American journalists and indeed of journalists everywhere:

> *The free communication of thoughts and opinions is one of man's most precious rights. Every citizen may therefore speak, write, and publish freely, except that he shall be responsible for the abuse of that freedom in cases determined by law.*[2]

Not all journalists, however, would accept the final clause on possible abuse. In any case, when the First Amendment to the U.S. Constitution went into force two years later, no mention was made of abuse. We will return to this topic.

The Declaration was presented to the Estates General by the marquis de Mirabeau, an eloquent and liberal representative of the

French nobility. Mirabeau's death shortly after the Declaration was completed prevented him from seeking, as he wished, to set up a constitutional monarchy similar to that of Britain. Whatever the depth of his devotion to republican ideas, Mirabeau was a passionate supporter of a free press. "Let the first of your laws consecrate forever the freedom of the press," Mirabeau told the Estates. "This is the most untouchable, the most unconditional, freedom—without which the other freedoms can never be secured."[3] He might have been speaking for any association of American journalists.

The Declaration with its guarantee of press freedom was adopted by the Constituent Assembly without difficulty, but it was in force no longer than two years, for in August 1791 the Assembly adopted its first limitation on press freedom, declaring unlawful "voluntary slander against the integrity of civil servants." New rules and regulations, often unwritten, followed rapidly. In fact, no sooner had a political leader lost his power than the newspapers supporting him were banned, their plants confiscated, and their editors thrown into prison. Under Napoleon, all traces of a free press vanished and Voltaire's call for freedom from censorship was ignored. Only the newspapers that supported Napoleon were tolerated. Recognizing the impact of this captive press outside the French borders, Metternich was said to have observed that "the French newspapers were worth 300,000 men for Napoleon."[4]

Still, the words of the Declaration had been written on the hearts of French journalists as well as those of other countries, including the United States. Thomas Paine, the journalist and pamphleteer, achieved just renown for his two-volume defense of the French Revolution which he appropriately titled *the Rights of Man*.[5] Thanks to Paine and those who came after him, the revolutionary goals of the French Declaration became somehow associated with the civil liberties guaranteed under the American Bill of Rights and with the lofty position it reserved for the press.

The battle over freedom of the press in France continued unrelentingly for yet a generation, and was still raging when the monarchy was restored after the fall of Napoleon. Under the Restoration kings, Louis XVIII and Charles X, a series of controls was imposed on the French newspapers, seeking to force them to speak only good of the monarchs and their ministers. Among those who rallied to the support of the embattled press was the marquis de Lafayette, hero of the American Revolution, who was then living in retirement in France.[6] Despite the imposition of heavy fines and prison sentences, the Parisian newspapers continued to ridicule the Bourbon rulers and their ministers. The press won few friends at the palace for naming Charles "the bigot king" or "Charles the Simple."[7]

So punitive was the censorship that the deputies in the Assembly rallied to the defense of the press in a debate that provided what is very likely the most extensive display of public polemics over press freedom in human history. The occasion was the introduction by Charles's ministers of a draft law that would have turned the clock back to the days of rigorous censorship prior to the revolution. Under the measure, named by the sardonic opposition "the law of justice and love," all but a handful of the French newspapers would have been abolished and those that remained would have been barred from virtually all criticism of the government.

For a solid month in the winter of 1827 the Chamber of Deputies wrestled with the draft law.[8] No fewer than 78 members rose to speak while large crowds gathered outside the building to await word on the tenor of the debate and to cheer wildly for the defenders of a free press. Even though Charles's forces commanded a majority in the chamber, the number of speakers was divided nearly evenly in support and opposition. To deny the press the right to speak its mind was to shatter all hopes for achievement of the Rights of Man, said the leader of the opposition, Pierre-Paul Royer-Collard, in a speech reprinted in an edition that was said to have achieved a circulation of a million.

In the end, Charles's ministers managed to carry the day in the Chamber, but the public outcry was so great that the government ultimately withdrew the draft measure from the Assembly and found no alternative but to impose censorship by decree. The irate public, led by angry opponents of censorship, took to the streets and three years later felled the government. Some historians claim it was the assault on the press that brought down the Bourbon monarchy, a claim that seems a bit exaggerated, although there can be little doubt that yearning for an avenue for free expression was a factor in the Revolution of 1830.[9]

In the very next year, a 25-year-old French nobleman journeyed to the United States to examine for himself the visible fruit of the political ideas of the *philosophes* in the struggling nation across the Atlantic. This was Alexis-Charles-Henri Clérel de Tocqueville, who a year later was to publish one of the most enduring accounts of the ideas and behavior of that nation in a two-volume book titled *Democracy in America*.[10] In it, he explored among other things the early behavior of the American press.

Although his heritage was in no way democratic (his grandfather had been guillotined in the Reign of Terror), de Tocqueville was fascinated by the American attempt to carry out the vision of "liberty, fraternity, and equality" that had inspired the French Revolution. His comments on and analysis of the American scene gathered in nine months of on-the-scene examination have been justly celebrated; in fact few commentators on the United States before or since have been more perceptive.

What fascinated de Tocqueville most about the Americans he encountered was their utter devotion to the "equality" element in the famous French triumvirate. On the whole, Americans seemed less interested in brotherhood than did Frenchmen. Moreover, they were prepared to surrender their liberty if it was necessary to do so to maintain their sense of equality with their fellow men. The demand for equality in America, de Tocqueville wrote, had swollen "to the height of fury."[11] For men to be *free* required sacrifices that were easily recognizable. Not so for *equality*, whose charms are "instantly felt and are within the reach of all." No one needs to work hard for "the pleasures of equality [because] each of the petty incidents of life seem to occasion them, and in order to taste them, nothing is required but to live."[12]

De Tocqueville generally admired the American experiment, but even so he was alarmed at the possibility that holding equality above liberty might lead to the trampling of the rights of minorities. He feared the "tyranny of the majority," which might be tempted to use its power without considering the just claims to freedom of those who were not part of the majority.

It was a lonely life, this life of equality, de Tocqueville wrote, for it rejected the conservative benefits that came from a recognition of ancestry and family. Democracy, he said, "throws him [the individual] back forever upon himself alone, and threatens in the end to confine him entirely within the solitude of his own heart."[13]

As for press freedom, de Tocqueville confessed himself no flaming advocate. He approved it more because of the evils it prevented than because of the advantages it might insure. His turn of mind was more intellectual and far less emotional than that of Rousseau. Indeed, many persons both in and out of the field of journalism are in accord with de Tocqueville's fears and concerns about the behavior of the American press.

To de Tocqueville, American journalists were men of the people inspired by their native intelligence and inquiring minds, not by their advanced learning or university educations. Because they spoke the language of the people, they exercised a great impact on what the people thought and how they perceived the world.[14] Novels and motion pictures of the early and middle years of the twentieth century testify to the image of the "common man" journalist that persisted for more than a century, at least until the period after World War II when higher education became acceptable for journalists and other "democrats."[15] Even so, for many persons, there is something rather un-American about journalists who are university educated and members of some kind of elite, especially an "eastern elite." Spiro Agnew, the former vice president, hit a responsive chord when he referred to the leading American journalists as "effete snobs" who inhabited the wealthy domains of the "Eastern Establishment" and did not speak the language of "middle America."[16] We will return to Agnew and his doctrine in Chapter 53.

The language of the uneducated was, in de Tocqueville's estimate, precisely the language spoken by the American journalists of 1831. Again identifying an important strain in the ideology of the American journalist, de Tocqueville commented that it was possible for almost any journalist who wanted to do so to start his own newspaper and begin exerting his personal influence immediately. This was possible, de Tocqueville wrote, because of the great expanse of territory on the American continent. Almost every little hamlet had its own paper and in his own paper the journalist was free to write as he pleased.[17] No dream has been more powerful for the American journalist than that of starting his own newspaper and running it his own way, without the influence of hard-to-please editors.

Because there were so many newspapers, de Tocqueville said, there was considerable diversity of opinion in the American press. Journalists tended to be investigative, but since they were spread out across the country, their opinions on political issues tended to cancel each other out. Besides, he said, American journalists are not much interested in political opinion. "In America," he wrote, "three quarters of the enormous sheet are filled with advertisements, and the remainder is frequently occupied by political intelligence or trivial anecdotes."[18] Only occasionally did one find "a corner devoted to passionate discussions, like those which the journalists of France every day give to their readers."[19]

The majority ruled in America, he said, and the General Will decreed the contents of the newspapers, which the journalists cheerfully produced. Journalists were in fact the voice of the people. What greater praise could an American journalist desire?

Still, it was a case of damning with faint praise. And contemporary American journalists are uncomfortable when identified as being "of a vulgar turn of mind" although they probably would not take offense at being told they were different from those French journalists who engaged in "an eloquent and lofty manner of discussing great interests of the state." To de Tocqueville:

> *The characteristics of the American journalist consist in an open and coarse appeal to the passions of his readers; he abandons principles to assail the characters of individuals, to track them into private life, and disclose all their weaknesses and vices. . . .*[20]

Each journal in America, according to de Tocqueville, exercised only a limited influence but together the American press had an "immense" power. Public opinion would inevitably yield to the *combined* impact of a press that was everywhere, that was always bringing to light the hidden weaknesses and vices of the nation's leaders.[21] The saving grace was the size of the country. Of course, de Tocqueville could not have imagined the narrowing of the size through modern transportation and communications. Those who condemn today's newspaper and broadcasting journalists do so in the spirit of de Tocqueville, whose greatest fear for democracy was that it would degenerate into a tyranny of the majority that would run contemptuously over minority individuals, groups, and institutions.

The debt owed by American journalists to the ideas of de Tocqueville is substantial. At the very dawn of the American newspaper, de Tocqueville recognized the impact of community life and of *localism* on the American continent. The traditional demand of the busy city editor has always been to "localize" the story, to find the "local angle" and concentrate on it. When a plane crashes in a distant state, the reporter is compelled to check whether any local passengers were on board. The localizing impulse would, de Tocqueville believed, encourage a strong sense of involvement by Americans in their local communities and produce an active, socially conscious citizenry. For the utilitarians Helvétius, Bentham, and John Stuart Mill, it was the greatest good of the greatest number that counted. For de Tocqueville, it was the protection of minorities that counted. Who better than the journalist in his small communities could seek to protect the interests of the minorities against the vested power of the majorities?[22]

The ideas that grew and flourished in France in the eighteenth and early nineteenth centuries powerfully influenced the development of the growing ideology of American journalists, although this influence has been little recognized. That of Milton and Locke has long been noted, especially in admiration for the blessings of liberty and for belief that scientific inquiry and rationality will influence one's way of thinking. Hosannas have long been sung to the power of the mind to affect human behavior. To a certain degree, of course, the *philosophes* placed their trust in this dogma, but they were Frenchmen and had no doubts about the power of passion. Rousseau above all recognized the primacy of feelings in the creation of attitudes. The *philosophes* understood the power of the idea of the Rights of Man and preached this gospel far and wide, especially across the Atlantic, where Paine, Jefferson, Madison, and their allies added the *experiences* of the colonies to the development of the *idea* of the Rights of Man. Half a century later, de Tocqueville recognized the power of the idea in America and saw where it had led and where it would lead in the future.

PART IV

The American Belief System Arises

James Madison (1751–1836): "Some degree of abuse is inseparable from the proper use of everything; and in no instance is this more true, than that of the press. It is better to leave a few of its noxious branches to their luxuriant growth, than by pruning them away, to injure the vigour of those yielding the proper fruits, [for] to the press alone, chequered as it is with abuses, the world is indebted for all the triumphs which have been gained by reason and humanity, over error and oppression."

Thomas Paine (1739–1809): "The revolutions of America and France have . . . provoked people to think by making them feel; and when once the veil begins to rend, it admits not of repair. Ignorance is of a peculiar nature; once dispelled, it is impossible to re-establish it. It is not originally a thing of itself, but is only the absence of knowledge; and though man may be kept *ignorant, he may not be* made *ignorant . . . Such is the irresistible nature of truth, that all it asks, and all it wants, is the liberty of appearing. The sun needs no inscription to distinguish him from darkness."*

CHAPTER 15

Introduction: Call for Rebellion

British and French ideas about liberty and equality emerged against the backdrop of a class structure so rigid that it was next to impossible for a commoner to rise to a position of power, be it political or economic or intellectual. Even the so-called "Great Commoner," William Pitt of England, was an aristocrat who took the title of earl of Chatham. In France it required a revolution to overthrow the aristocracy, in Britain the humiliation of the American rebellion to weaken the power of the landed gentry. It was in the colonies across the Atlantic that the liberating ideas of the Enlightenment philosophers of Britain and France found the fertile ground they needed to flower.

Press ideology in the United States did not of course develop as pure theory, the spinnings of the brains of Locke and Rousseau, of Hume and Montesquieu, but as the product of actual experience. It arose in the crucible of conflict, in outright rebellion against authority, stimulated by one of the most remarkable collection of creative minds ever to appear in a single environment. Journalism, American style, thus began in an atmosphere of experimentation and conflict. The earliest mission of journalists in the new colonies was to fight, in print, against censorship, against restraints on their saying what they wanted to say in their writings. This mission existed even before the rebellion of 1776, but it did not win universal praise until it was enlisted in the cause of secession from the British Empire.

It is for these reasons above all that American journalists from the very beginning have campaigned passionately for the freedom to report as they pleased, to assail, as it suited their fancy, the high and the mighty—in short to publish what clearly had been considered to be seditious libel. That much of this freedom was illusion was not recognized then any more than it is apparent to journalists today. It does not matter. The legends of the past, however far into antiquity they may extend, are not significantly weakened by inaccuracy. In fact, the very unlikelihood of the legend may itself strengthen it.

One of the cardinal principles given utterance during the Enlightenment was belief in free expression—in both the spoken and written word. Only through communication might knowledge be expanded and the emergence of wisdom assured. Yet few people in the eighteenth century were prepared to allow an equal right of free expression to those who thought differently. Milton considered Catholic thought simply wrong and hence saw no contradiction in denying Catholics freedom of expression. The same mind set was found among the free-expression Founding Fathers in the American colonies: the Tory viewpoint was seen as simply wrong-headed and not deserving of the right to be expressed freely. Apparently unaware of the contradiction, the Founding Fathers remained utterly convinced that free expression was an absolute necessity for free men. Perhaps they thought the supporters of King George were not really free and hence did not deserve the right to express their views freely. Driven by their powerful emotional commitment to the *ideal* of a new nation free from the orthodoxy they saw as imposed by the British Crown, the Founding Fathers failed to see that they were not living up to the scientific method of inquiry they admired so passionately. To analyze, to experiment, to derive answers from one's inquiry, however those answers may contradict one's beliefs, and ultimately to publish those answers—these they saw as the methods of science, and these were the techniques they were convinced they were following in the search for understanding and wisdom. To *publish* was central to their way of thinking. And, thus, the press was of consummate importance to them.

The celebrated comment by John Milton a century earlier was a commonplace in their belief system: that truth must be given a chance to compete with falsehood and that in such an encounter, truth must always win out. The expression was not original with Milton. A Baptist minister little known to history, Leonard Busher, had written 30 years earlier that "Even as the chaff before the wind cannot stand, so error before truth cannot abide."[1] This comment, often cited as Milton's self-righting principle, was to be modified substantially over the years, but in its essence it has remained remarkably intact. Today's American journalist, however sophisticated, clings to the romantic illusion that truth is somehow more powerful than falsehood and that when faced with a choice, the reader will always select the truth. Oddly enough, this belief system seems to survive even a certain contempt for the wisdom of the reader.

In the eighteenth century, Milton's self-righting principle was ratified by no less a personage than Benjamin Franklin, the most universally honored of the Founders. In the colonies, his personal endorsement added a mighty stimulus to that principle. So did the support of Thomas Jefferson, although true to his fundamentally skeptical nature, Jefferson was never entirely sure that truth would always triumph, not in any case if it were to be suppressed by political authority.[2]

Free expression in print was revered as essential to personal liberty. And it was to maintain personal liberty that the rebellion against Britain took place. Americans saw themselves as in every way equal to the British, quite competent to raise their own taxes and run their own affairs. British persistence in forcing Americans to obey Britain's rules and regulations, no matter how punitive they might be, ultimately drove the Americans to rebellion.[3]

The instrument of communication among the colonies was the printed word, as contained in personal letters and messages and, more importantly, in newspapers. There was no other way to communicate over distances. These were far too great to permit much word-of-mouth discourse. The 13 colonies had only limited communication among themselves prior to the time of rebellion, for each had been settled under its own charter and each had occupied itself primarily with its own growth. Naturally, hostilities had developed between and among the colonies, but in the face of the threat to their liberties from across the seas these were largely ignored.

The first clear call for a unified rebellion came in 1772. The Virginia House of Burgesses proposed the creation of an intercolonial network of Committees of Correspondence to enable the colonies to seek a joint response to sanctions the British had imposed on Rhode Island for an attack on a British customs schooner. To its Committee of Correspondence the Virginians appointed Jefferson and Patrick Henry, whose writings helped stir the fire of rebellion among all the colonies.[4] A dominant role for the early press was apparent: it was to serve as an arm of persuasion, as propagandist in the cause of liberty; it was in short the "Voice of the People," summoned to righteous wrath by the transgressions of Authority. One revolutionary writer argued that "in establishing American independence, the pen and the press had a merit equal to the sword."[5] Here was Rousseau's General Will speaking out through the press against tyranny. Not only was the press enlisted in the cause of the people in general, however. It was speaking no less in the name of the American individual, in the spirit of Locke, who already had authorized rebellion when the monarch and his minions had engaged in a long train of intolerable abuses. Leading the Americans to rebellion were the writers, the essayists and the journalists of the late eighteenth century. Thus were joined the Philosophers of the Individual and the Philosophers of the Collective, in mutual quest for the blessings of liberty and equality.

It was not recognized then that there was an unbridgeable gap between those belief systems that glorified the individual and those that extolled the collective. American press philosophy has been struggling to reconcile these differences ever since and, no doubt, will continue to do so as long as there remains an American press.

The gap is most apparent when one examines the gulf that separates the markedly different perceptions of the nature of humankind and the nature of governments. The extent of that gap came to be recognized in the philosophical dispute that arose between the ideas of Edmund Burke and those of Thomas Paine. To the individualists, to the followers of

Locke, the motives and behavior of men must always be suspect. Institutions are required to keep man's baser nature in check. Hobbes, of course, went much further, holding that in the absence of the social contract men were fundamentally brutish. To the collectivists, to the followers of Rousseau and Paine, it was the institutions themselves that were evil. Thus, institutions had to be made subject to the wisdom of the collective people, through the General Will. In the state of nature, men might very well be good but in society, they became wicked. The result of this unresolved conflict is that the press in the United States has itself grown up in a state of unresolved conflict.

Even Jefferson was unable to make up his mind. There were times when he applauded a press utterly free to write as it pleased, on the ground that the doctrine of individual liberty properly guarantees anyone the right of unlimited self-expression. At other times, Jefferson rejected mercilessly a press that flouted the will of the people. For help in understanding the growth of press ideology on the American continent, let us take a closer look at the ideas of the early heroes of American journalism.

CHAPTER 16

Benjamin Franklin and the "Price of Truth"

The very first periodicals in the United States—it would be presumptuous to identify the seventeenth- and eighteenth-century press as "newspapers" in the modern sense—were prepared to challenge their governors. This challenge might be political or religious or both. In early colonial days, civil authority and religious authority were virtually synonymous. In New England, home of the Puritan religious rebels, the association between church and state was strongest of all. To attack the church and its ministers was to attack both God and Caesar. Inevitably, the first major collision on American soil between entrenched power and the heady new concept of unrestrained free expression took place in the capital of the colonial theocracy, Boston. There, the *New-England Courant* appeared in 1721, with James Franklin, the older brother of Ben, as its printer. That paper promptly launched an attack on the powerful Mather family, the leaders of the Boston theocracy. When the clergy threatened to close down the paper, James Franklin claimed in his defense the right to publish freely opinions that themselves might not be acceptable to those in authority. The validity of opinions was not up to journalists to decide, Franklin maintained; that was a matter for leaders of the community. "To anathemize a printer for publishing the different opinions of men, is as injudicious as it is wicked," Franklin wrote in the pages of the *Courant*.[1] This early declaration of journalistic objectivity was not enough to save his paper. James Franklin found himself in jail and later sent into exile in Rhode Island. At first he tried to head off the authorities, who were furious with him for attacking Cotton Mather in print, by placing the name of his 16-year-old brother Ben on the masthead, but the ruse was in the long run unsuccessful. It did, however, provide Ben an opportunity to learn the ins and outs of the newspaper trade under unusual circumstances.

The time, it was clear, was not yet ripe for the establishment in law of Milton's self-righting principle. Ben, already the consummate politician, was less forthright than his brother. A believer himself in free expression, Ben was prepared to seek the same ends but in a more roundabout way. His effort came in Philadelphia where, after his brother was imprisoned, he journeyed to seek his own fortune. In the *Pennsylvania Gazette*, which Ben began publishing in 1729, he made his mark on history and on the establishment of the ideology of American journalism.

Ben Franklin was a Renaissance man, a man of enormous breadth, the most celebrated American of his time, both at home and abroad. He was a printer, a wit, a writer, an editor, a diplomat, a politician, a revolutionary, an inventor, a ladies' man, and ultimately an elder statesman who helped draft the American Constitution. The journalism historian, Edwin Emery, is inclined to wax lyrical over Franklin, identifying him as the greatest writer of his time, distinguished both as diplomat and citizen, the man who made journalism respectable.[2] Emery's adulation is a bit extreme, but it is clear that Franklin was of heroic stature; and no one can doubt that the image of this distinguished citizen as a writer and editor helped establish the self-image of journalists as men of stature.

Yet Franklin was no fire-eating, rabble-rousing muckraker, either as journalist or as diplomat. Rarely did he lose his equanimity, and he was careful not to copy his brother by issuing direct challenges to the political powers. His approach was indirect. Appealing to principles that today are presented under the banner of "objectivity," Franklin endorsed Milton's doctrine of combat between truth and falsehood.[3] Leonard Levy has held that Franklin contributed nothing to libertarian theory, that his essays on press freedom were mere platitudes, "unanalytical, almost anti-intellectual."[4] Yet, there is no reason for journalists' ideas to be thought of as intellectual concepts. They take root in an emotional atmosphere largely free of reflection. Franklin's homilies constituted the precise mold in which to contain the ideas of American journalism. Clinton Rossiter has pointed out that Franklin's views accurately reflected "popular thinking in eighteenth-century America."[5]

In the first issue of the *Pennsylvania Gazette*, which appeared October 2, 1729, Franklin identified his ideal editor. There are remarkable similarities between Franklin's ideal and that of Voltaire, which was recorded seven years later.[6] There is no reason to imagine that Voltaire was familiar with Franklin's writings at the time, however. Journalistic ideals were, apparently, simply in the air at that time.

This is how Franklin defined his ideal editor:

> *He ought to be qualified with an extensive Acquaintance with Languages, a great Easiness and Command of Writing and Relating Things clearly and intelligibly, and in a few Words; he should be able to speak of War both by Land and Sea; be well*

> *acquainted with Geography, with the History of the Time, with the several interests of Princes and States, the Secrets of Courts, and the Manners and Customs of all Nations. Men thus accomplish'd are very rare in this remote Part of the World. . . .*[7]

Such men (or women) are rare anywhere, but the model is a powerful one and has continued to attract men and women to the field of journalism from Franklin's day to this.

Milton's self-righting principle found an echo in Franklin's "An Apology for Printers," which appeared in the June 10, 1731, issue of the *Gazette*. Printers, wrote printer Franklin in "a standing Apology for my self," are educated in the belief that "when men differ in Opinion, both Sides ought equally to have the Advantage of being heard by the Publick." For then, "when Truth and Error have fair Play, the former is always an overmatch for the latter." In the case of Franklin the merchant, the printer whose columns were open for sale to other writers, the Miltonian doctrine had, however, a different slant, quite in tune with the principles of capitalism. The newspaper was to Franklin always a profit-making instrument. For, he wrote, printers "chearfully serve all contending Writers that pay them well, without regarding on which side they are of the Question in Dispute."[8]

It was in Franklin's essays that the commercial realities of a free press were for the first time clearly stated. In short, he raised questions about "the price of truth." As no other writer of his generation, Franklin embodied both of the main threads in the fabric of the American press system, as he gave expression to what can be described as the central tension in American press ideology.[9] On the one hand there is the drive to operate in the interest of the public, to provide information for the good of mankind and a free society; on the other there is the drive for private profit in the commercial world of the free marketplace. In much of the writings about the American press, the second half of this tension is lightly dismissed.

In his "Apology," Franklin observed that he would be able to realize higher profits if the reports of his newspaper were more sensational, but he would not, he said, stoop to the lowest common denominator. His picture of the heavy demands placed on the editor is also in keeping with the dogma that asserts the weighty burdens of the conscientious journalist. Yet Franklin never lost sight of the fact that he was a businessman in a competitive field. His newspaper, he informed his readers in the introductory issue of the *Gazette*, would not be ponderous and dull but in fact "as agreeable and useful Entertainment as the Nature of the Thing will allow."[10]

Moreover, Franklin commented, not only would his publication serve all sides to a dispute; it would also pay well those who used its pages to express their views. Even though truth may be the highest calling, he wrote, his paper avoided "printing such Things as usually give Offence either to Church or State."[11] Since Ben certainly had no intention of going to prison as his brother had done, he made it clear he would not undertake a direct assault on the authorities of Pennsylvania. Indeed, 27 years after he had published his "Apology," Franklin, by then a prominent Pennsylvania politician, managed the state's case against a clergyman who had attacked state authorities in print, condemning what he wrote as the work of "a common Scribbler of Libels against Publick Bodies."[12]

What interested Franklin most, in any case, was not "news" as we know it today but opinions. The business of printing, he wrote, "has chiefly to do with Mens Opinions."[13] It was too early, in 1730, to consider the newspaper a source of general "news." Its contents were largely opinion, commercial information, and reports of criminal or unusual activities.

Eight years later, Franklin presented to the readers of the *Gazette* his own interpretation of the historical development of the idea of a free press in the English-speaking world. The purpose of the press, Franklin wrote, was to promote the truth.[14] Those who publish lies are reprehensible and deserve to be punished. "But to whom," he asked, "dare we commit the care of doing it?"

> *An evil magistrate intrusted with power to* punish for words, *would be armed with a weapon the most destructive and terrible. Under pretence of pruning off the exuberant branches he would be apt to destroy the tree.*[15]

Therefore under no circumstances should anyone be punished for publishing what is true. And anyone who tries to use the powers of government to bring legal action against a publication that tells the truth, Franklin said, placing the key words in italics, "*ought to be repudiated as an enemy to liberty*."[16] Half a century later, in 1789, Franklin sought to distinguish between liberty and licentiousness. If press freedom was supposed to mean the liberty for editors to slander one another maliciously, the elderly Franklin wrote, then the legislature ought to limit that liberty, but if it meant the freedom to discuss the propriety of public measures and political opinion, then "let us have as much of it as you please."[17] But he went beyond that statement to remark that if such slander were indeed to appear in the public print, "we should, in moderation, content ourselves with tarring and feathering [the slanderers] and tossing them in a blanket."[18] One historian says that remark has ugly overtones, but another considers it mere horseplay.[19]

The question of malice has not yet been entirely resolved, but certainly in the two centuries following the death of Franklin, American journalists have never failed to rally under the banner of truth that Franklin proclaimed as a young man. Nor have they permitted those who would seek to impose restraints on them to escape being labeled enemies of liberty; it is as if the tar and feather is now in their own hands. To close ranks in the face of any action they see as a restraint on their search for truth has become an automatic response by American journalists.

CHAPTER 17

James Madison and Free Expression

The thorny question of how to identify what limitations, if any, are appropriate limitations on press freedom has dogged practitioners and students of journalism throughout the centuries that followed Franklin. In the eighteenth century, the question was usually associated with the concepts of liberty and license. The distinction was made perhaps most graphically in an article in Andrew Bradford's *American Weekly Mercury* of Philadelphia. Bradford, a rival of Franklin, was the son of William Bradford, the first Philadelphia printer. The elder Bradford had been run out of town by the Quaker leadership for printing an article written by a rival Quaker faction. In colonial days, few printers stayed around to fight for untrammeled press freedom, especially when it interfered with their livelihood.

Andrew Bradford's paper was founded in 1721, the same year the *New-England Courant* began publication. A decade later, in 1734, Bradford ardently defended press liberty as the right of a man to express his views on religion and government "within the bounds of law," and to ferret out the truth about the villainous and wicked in high places.[1] But, Bradford asserted, press *liberty* does not permit "that unwarranted *license* . . . of endeavoring to subvert the fundamental points of religion or morality" nor the "treasonable license" that to him was manifest whenever one challenged the authority of the king.[2] Press freedom was to Bradford "the great palladium of all other liberties." Still, he was opposed to Andrew Hamilton, the Philadelphia lawyer who achieved journalistic immortality with his powerful pleas on behalf of John Peter Zenger, the immigrant printer accused of seditious libel in New York a year after Bradford published the disputed article.[3] In fact, Hamilton also condemned Bradford on similar charges of seditious libel.[4]

Liberty in those days rarely referred to a right, absolute and inviolate, to say or write anything one wanted to say, including comments critical, even seditious, about church or state or about individuals in high places. Few persons in fact defended such far-ranging liberty, especially if it was seen as giving an editor "license" to slander or even attack the basic belief system of the social order. Francis Hutchinson, who served as both chief justice and royal governor of Massachusetts, gave expression in 1767 to the commonly held view of that period that liberty of the press (which he defended) could simply not be construed to mean freedom to revile and slander "all ranks of men with impunity." Such an idea, he said, was "absurd."[5] The legal issue at stake in the Zenger case was not whether a journalist had a right to attack a legislature or a public official, but whether he could be punished for such an attack if what he wrote happened to be true.

It was in that case that the Philadelphia lawyer Andrew Hamilton (no relation to the more famous Alexander Hamilton) argued, with memorable persuasiveness, that for American printers to write freely about tyrannical acts of the mighty was not only an important goal for colonial society, but indeed "the best cause . . . the cause of liberty."[6] Hamilton told the members of the jury that by freeing Zenger they would be blessed and honored by every free person not only for frustrating tyranny but for laying "a noble foundation" for securing for all Americans the right to expose and condemn all arbitrary power. That "noble foundation" has become one of the cornerstones of American press ideology—the very essence of the watchdog principle. Belief in the press as a restraint on tyranny and the abuse of power runs very deep in the ideology of the American press; it predates the muckrakers by more than a century.

Hamilton's appeal to the jury was successful. Zenger was acquitted of the charge of seditious libel. It was the first case in recorded history in which the truth of comments written in a journal was accepted as a proper defense against libel. Yet, the Zenger case was an isolated event; others were to be jailed for seeking to write what they perceived to be truth for half a century still to come. The seed had been planted, however, and agitation for free expression in print was to become part of the American Way of Life.

It is Zenger, an immigrant German printer, whose name is celebrated in the history of press freedom and in the ideology of American journalists, but in fact he was merely recording the ideas of his boss, James Alexander, an attorney, just as James Franklin before him was the printer of his employers' opinions. Alexander is justly renowned as the author of a standard commentary on Zenger's trial;[7] he was also less well known as a press theorist in his own right. In late 1737, two years after Zenger's trial, at the same time Franklin was expressing his own opinions about press liberty, Franklin published in his *Pennsylvania Gazette* an extended essay by Alexander (it appeared in four installments) on freedom of expression. Alexander was, in Leonard Levy's view the first person to develop a full-blown philosophy of press freedom.[8] Madison was of course familiar with Alexander and the Zenger case and may well have based his own theory of a free press on Alexander's observation that, "An evil Magistrate entrusted with a power to punish words is armed with a weapon the most destructive and terrible."[9]

A decade earlier, two English essayists, John Trenchard and Thomas Gordon, writing in Zenger's *New-York Weekly Journal* under the pseudonym Cato, made a major contribution to the ideology of American journalists. Zenger published their 138 essays under the title of *Cato's Letters*. In the development of American political ideas, *Cato's Letters* were quoted far more extensively than the writings of Locke, especially in extolling press freedom in a republican society. In their turn, Franklin, Alexander, Jefferson, and Madison all drew on Cato's assertion that free speech is "the right of every man, as far as by it he does not hurt and control the right of another."[10]

That remarkable American invention, the Constitution of 1787, was the most ambitious effort to codify the theories of the Enlightenment. Despite the fact that press theorists inevitably hark back to the Constitution as the source of the special position accorded the press in the American governmental structure, the Constitution of 1787 was silent on the subject. Not once is the press mentioned in the Constitution; in fact, the issue of press freedom went almost unmentioned at the Constitutional Convention. When the delegates were asked to write a guarantee of press freedom into the document, they voted unanimously in opposition.[11] The question of press freedom did, however, surface when the Constitution came up for ratification. In fact, it was only after the Framers agreed to attach to the Constitution by amendment a Bill of Rights guaranteeing several forms of free expression that ratification was achieved.[12]

During the dispute over ratification, there appeared the greatest of all American contributions to political philosophy, the 87 essays that have come to be known as *The Federalist Papers*. The majority of the essays were written by Alexander Hamilton, although several of the most significant were the work of James Madison and a few others were written by John Jay. *The Federalist Papers* were instruments of political propaganda, designed to win support among the states for ratification of the Constitution. In *Federalist* No. 84, Hamilton argued that no Bill of Rights had been attached to the original document because none was needed. In none of the other 86 essays was the issue of press freedom more than barely mentioned; in No. 84, Hamilton argued there was no need to pronounce the press free since the Constitution had given the federal government no power to control it anyway.[13] Hamilton maintained that the federal government could not exercise any power that was not specifically granted to it under the precise language of the Constitution. Moreover, Hamilton argued, since it is just about impossible to define press freedom to the satisfaction of everyone, this means that in the end a free press can be secure only so long as it is backed by the weight of public opinion. If the public doesn't want a free press, Hamilton was saying, there will not be one. If it does, the press will be free. The idea, then as now, was that the final arbiter was the public—and the public was thought to be as passionately devoted to free expression as the journalist. That this is not clearly so has in no way altered the belief.

In *Federalist* No. 10, the most profound of the 87, Madison addressed himself to the subject of public opinion. It was clear to Madison that whenever the majority of Americans stood behind a principle, that principle was in no danger at all.[14] Madison did not in *Federalist* No. 10 relate his argument to the press, but unquestionably a free press was among the principles in his mind. Danger to free institutions, he argued, lay in the presence of "factions" that might, for whatever selfish reason, seek to restrict freedom.

Madison was the principal author of both the Constitution and the Bill of Rights; no other person has exerted a greater influence on the American belief system. And although Madison was more the democrat than most of the Founders, even he was opposed to establishing a democracy in the 13 colonies. In *Federalist* No. 10, he explained why. It was a republic that was being created in America, he said, not a democracy, for in a democracy where majority ruled, it was entirely possible that a faction made up of that majority would run roughshod over minorities and destroy free institutions.[15] As protection against the majority, *many* factions were required so that they might balance each other out; no single faction could then become strong enough to repress minorities. Madison was skeptical about minorities having to rely on the written law, or "parchment barriers," to protect themselves from cruel majorities.[16] An ironclad system incorporating the checks and balances advanced by Montesquieu would guard against excessive power; to Madison in the eighteenth century, as to journalists today, an unfettered press is a powerful protection against the influence of oppressive and tyrannical factions. This self-image of the press was observed by de Tocqueville half a century later.

Throughout his writings, Madison argued that republican government was rooted in the sovereignty of the people. Historian Edmund Morgan maintains that this idea was simply a "fiction," and that Madison "was inventing a sovereign American people to overcome the sovereign states," just as Milton and his friends had invented sovereign power for Parliament in its fight with the Stuart kings. Morgan assigns enormous credit to Madison for, he says, Madison's "invention" became *fact* under the stewardship of the Founding Fathers, aided of course by a popular press.[17]

It is likely that the Constitution would not have been ratified, even with the philosophical pressure supplied by *The Federalist Papers*, if the Framers had not agreed to append a Bill of Rights embodying the civil liberties that were not expressly guaranteed in the Constitution. Jefferson, at that time ambassador to France and consequently absent from the United States, provided plenty of ammunition for Madison to use in his ultimately successful efforts to win approval of a Bill of Rights. Such a series of civil liberties, Jefferson wrote Madison, was demanded in order to protect the people against the potential for tyranny that was raised under the powers granted by the Constitution to both Congress and the president.[18]

In 1791, after the adoption of the Bill of Rights, Madison joined Hamilton in arguing that public opinion was the true sovereign in the United States. As Rousseau had maintained, it was public opinion that gave expression to the General Will. What clearer spokesman for public opinion could be found than the circulating newspaper, which protected the individual citizen against bigness and against the loss of his significance as an individual! It was through the press that the voice of the private citizen could be heard. In a republic, Madison wrote, every good citizen is "a sentinel over the rights of the people." That citizen has a duty to express his opinion publicly in support of his "political scriptures"—in a kind of "holy zeal."[19]

We can see that by 1791 the chief architect of the American constitutional system was using religious imagery to assert the importance of a free press in the United States. Yet in the same document, Madison expressed concern that a free press might seriously abuse its power by engaging in licentious behavior. The dilemma apparent in a free press troubled even Thomas Jefferson, the most stalwart defender of press liberty among the Founding Fathers. He was to resolve it, for himself at least, some years later.

CHAPTER 18

The "Best Friend" of the Press: Thomas Jefferson

What of Thomas Jefferson? Was it not Jefferson rather than Madison who should be identified as the press's best friend among the Founders? After all, it was Jefferson in his celebrated letter of 1787 who said he would prefer newspapers without government to government without newspapers.[1] Jefferson's ringing words, by now indelibly written into the hearts of American journalists, are displayed in placards on the walls of editors across the country. These words, it should be noted, were written before Jefferson took office as president; it was the same Jefferson who two years into office would urge the states to conduct a "few prosecutions" to curb the opposition press of licentious abuse.[2] Jefferson's writings illustrate that it is not only later presidents who are inconsistent on the subject of a free press but that Jefferson as well held different opinions at different times in his career. In his early years and in the public print after he became president, he extolled the press as a powerful agent of freedom which, even when its artillery was aimed at his own administration, was not to be censored except at the bar of public opinion. Yet in the private pages of his correspondence in his mature years, Jefferson regularly assailed the excesses, the licentiousness, of the American press. Well aware of his impact on public opinion, however, he exercised extreme caution in requesting his correspondents not to make public his letters critical of the press.

Jefferson was an inveterate letter writer; the extent of his correspondence was so overwhelming that a century and a half after his death, scholars and librarians were still attempting to assemble it all. It is not surprising that Jefferson did not want his letters published, nor is it unlikely that many of the things he wrote on paper were mere reflections, observations, and comments that were not carefully thought through. Perhaps his pen was his instrument for thinking out loud.

Like all the Founders, Jefferson was influenced by the compact theory of government espoused by the men of the Enlightenment, Hobbes and Locke, Montesquieu and Rousseau. In the Declaration of Independence, Jefferson asserted that the United States was now dissolving the political bands that had linked the colonies to England and instituting a new government that derived its just powers "from the consent of the governed."[3] Moreover, the new nation drew its justification from *natural law*: certain truths were held to be self-evident. No man-made law was necessary to proclaim the rights of life, liberty, and the pursuit of happiness. In retirement, Jefferson went even beyond the Declaration when he wrote—and to a newspaper editor at that—that to adhere strictly to the written laws was "one of the high duties of a good citizen, but it is not the highest." Still higher were the "laws of necessity, of self-preservation, of saving our country when in danger."[4]

Those stirring words provide comfort to all partisans, journalists definitely included, who in the name of some cause, often to protect the principles of democracy, swim against the tide of majority sentiment. That the same words might be used in the service of some other, less worthy, cause is a troublesome concept usually honored by being ignored.

One finds many Jefferson debunkers among American scholars, a refreshing departure from the army of uncritical Jefferson admirers who outnumber the detractors by a substantial majority.[5] Both groups understandably tend to exaggerate their positions. Critics call attention to Jefferson's apparent support in 1777 for a loyalty oath in Virginia, at which time he commented: "A Tory has been properly defined to be a traitor in thought, but not in deed."[6] They also point out that a year later, in supporting a constitutional amendment to guarantee freedom of the press, Jefferson made it clear that he believed printers should be held accountable when they printed "false facts." In 1788, he wrote Madison:

> *A declaration that the federal government will never restrain the presses from printing anything they please, will not take away the liability of the printers for false facts printed. The declaration that religious faith shall be unpunished does not give impunity to criminal acts dictated by religious error.*[7]

On the other hand, in the document of which he himself was most proud, the act establishing religious freedom in Virginia, Jefferson stood solidly behind the overt-act principle enunciated by Hume and Montesquieu, that no one ought to be punished only for the words he speaks or writes: "To suffer the civil magistrate to intrude his own power into the field of opinion and to restrain the profession or propagation of principles, on the supposition of their ill tendency, is a dangerous fallacy."[8] Some commentators hold that Jefferson never applied the overt-acts test to *political* as well as religious statements,[9] although the record seems a bit muddy on this score.

Certainly, one would do well to view the observations in Jefferson's letters with caution; he very likely did not mean everything he wrote. His Second Inaugural Address may in fact summarize Jefferson's views best of all. In it, he spoke, somewhat sadly, of what he considered the abusiveness, the undue licentiousness, of some elements of the press during his first term in office.[10] Yet Jefferson was not ready to punish the press by official acts; better, he said, to leave the decision to public opinion. In the end Jefferson appears to have placed greater trust in the public than in the press. In this, Jefferson was in the mainstream of American thought, of the twentieth as well as the eighteenth century. Journalists were surprised when Vice President Spiro Agnew won the applause of the public in 1969 for his speech condemning the press but saluting the views of the public, which he characterized as "middle America."[11]

Over the years Jefferson has been quoted more often perhaps than any other political figure in the country's history.[12] What he believed (or, more precisely, what he is said to have believed) has been endorsed by Americans for 200 years, as much by journalists as by anyone else. If Jefferson believed in it, then, so the dogma has it, so should we. What exactly *did* Jefferson believe? Three elements in his belief system, each described below, seem particularly relevant in a discussion of the ideas of American journalists.

First, Jefferson believed that in certain instances man has the right, indeed the duty, to base his actions on "natural" laws rather than on "positive"—or man-made—laws. The appeal here is to the journalist's conscience, to standards higher than any that can be written down on paper. Those journalists who announce their intention to go to prison rather than reveal the names of persons who gave them information in confidence are following to the letter Jefferson's view of the natural law. The laws of mere men, those written laws that decree that a reporter must speak out in court when ordered to do so—those laws, in this system of values, must yield to the natural law under which the journalist does what is naturally good, that is to say, he keeps his promises, whatever the cost.[13]

Second, Jefferson believed in the merit system, that is, in a world in which success is determined by talent and skill, not by birth or connections.[14] The muckraking or investigating journalist who seeks to track down and expose those who achieve prominence simply because they are born wealthy or to prominent families is following Jefferson. To gain a position of power through nepotism is in this view quite as wicked as it is to rise through dishonesty or trickery.

Jefferson's belief in the triumph of virtue over wealth, of talent over birth, is best stated in his remarkable letter to John Adams when both men were in retirement. Any artificial aristocracy, Jefferson wrote, is but a "mischievous ingredient in government," and should never be permitted.[15] Here is an early affirmation of the virtues that would be embodied in Andrew Jackson's so-called Age of the Common Man. For the journalist, however lowly born, however uncertain of his economic or social status, no political figure is so powerful as to be beyond the reach of his pen, his typewriter, or his camera.

Interestingly, Adams in his reply to Jefferson, said he saw no difference between the two former presidents on the subject of aristocracy. Adams also endorsed the triumph of the talented over the untalented, no matter which was well born and which was lowly born, but the more pessimistic Adams observed that he would no more trust the talented common man with unlimited power than he would the well-born aristocrat. All men, Adams said, are corruptible. With consummate irony he wrote:

> *Both artificial Aristocracy, and Monarchy, and civil, military, political and hierarchical Despotism, have all grown out of the Natural Aristocracy of "Virtues and Talents." We, to be sure, are far remote from this. Many hundred years must roll away before We shall be corrupted. Our pure, virtuous, public spirited federative Republic will last for ever, govern the Globe and introduce the perfection of Man, his perfectability already being proved by Price, Priestley, Condorcet, Rousseau, Diderot and Godwin. . . .*[16]

American journalists do not for the most part scoff at idealism or at a utopian belief in the goodness of humankind, nor do they poke fun at the idea that the United States ought to be governed by virtuous and public-spirited leaders. Not for them, at least in the public print, the apparent cynicism of John Adams. (Not for Jefferson, either. For this complex man was also a follower of Rousseau, who saw in education the way to a virtuous and public-spirited leadership.) It was not until two centuries had passed that some prominent American journalists began to give expression to the profound pessimism of John Adams, largely out of opposition to the war in Vietnam and to the abuse of power symbolized by the word *Watergate*. Even in opposition to government power, however, American journalists as a whole have remained Jeffersonian optimists. The psychologist William James was later to identify Jefferson as tender-minded, Adams as tough-minded.[17]

Third, Jefferson believed in the Miltonian self-righting principle—that truth will emerge triumphant in a contest with lies or error. "Let us freely hear both sides," Jefferson wrote in 1814 from his retirement home in Monticello to a French bookseller.[18] In saying this, Jefferson was embracing a long tradition, reaching from the seventeenth century to today's newsrooms: respect for the wisdom of the American citizen who is permitted to decide for himself or herself which statements that appear in print are true and which are false. Still, Jefferson believed the Miltonian view needed to be qualified:

> *. . . the truth is great and will prevail if left to herself . . . she is the proper and sufficient antagonist to error, and has nothing to fear from the conflict, unless by human interposition disarmed of her natural weapons, free argument and debate, errors ceasing to be dangerous when it is permitted freely to contradict them.*[19]

In other words, one must at all cost avoid censoring the reports of those who present various points of view, even in conflicts between truth and error, for if truth is to have a fair chance of combatting error, "free argument and debate" must be assured. This is an important modification of the Miltonian principle, and it has been adopted as a fundamental article of faith by the American journalistic community.

CHAPTER 19

That "Great Bulwark of Liberty"

We cannot be certain what was in the minds of the Founding Fathers when they reached a compromise on the language of the First Amendment. The distinguished historian, Zechariah Chafee, arrived at the conclusion that the Framers "had no very clear idea of what they meant" by freedom of speech or of the press.[1] On the other hand, the equally distinguished legal scholar, Alexander Meiklejohn, held that the Founding Fathers intended to place over those in political power "an absolute, unqualified prohibition" against interfering with the press.[2] In the years preceding the approval of the First Amendment, both Benjamin Franklin and Alexander Hamilton confessed they were unable to define freedom of the press.[3] Today's political philosophers, scholars, judges, and journalists, like those of earlier generations, continue to debate the issue and to arrive at different interpretations. What we do know is that Madison's original draft followed closely the language of the constitution of his own state of Virginia with reference to the press. The third article of the original draft of a federal Bill of Rights guaranteed religious freedom. The fourth declared:

> *The people shall not be deprived or abridged of their right to speak, to write, or to publish their sentiments; and the freedom of the press, as one of the great bulwarks of liberty, shall be inviolable.*[4]

The reference to the press as a bulwark of liberty appears to have been an eighteenth-century cliché. The Virginia Declaration of Rights adopted in 1776 had identified the press as "one of the greatest bulwarks of liberty" and declared that the press "could never be restrained but by despotic Governments." It needs to be noted, however, that Virginia's free press clause provided freedom only for the views of Patriots. The Tory newspapers, those loyal to Britain, were clearly excluded from the right to publish what they desired. Patriots were encouraged to tar and feather anyone who dared to oppose the rebels, and by 1778 every state had declared it illegal to write or speak out against acts of Congress or of the state legislatures.[5]

In introducing the planned Bill of Rights to Congress, Madison turned to the Virginia constitution and those of other states for his sources. After a protracted fight, Madison won approval in the House of Representatives for 17 amendments to be submitted to the states for ratification. He had a more difficult time gaining the favor of the Senate. That body rejected a proposal of Madison that he had judged "the most valuable," one that would have protected the civil liberties of free speech, press, and religion, and of trial by jury not only from abridgement by the Congress but by the states as well. Ultimately the two Houses agreed on 12 amendments to be submitted to the states. The free press clause, now including also freedom of speech, religion, and assembly, was listed as the third amendment. It became the First Amendment only after the first two submitted to the states, establishing a numerical formula for proportional representation in the House and denying congressmen the right to raise their own salaries without an intervening election, failed to win ratification by the states.[6]

Explanations of what Madison and his colleagues meant by the phrase, "Congress shall make no law . . . abridging the freedom of speech, or of the press," have tended to fall into four general classifications.[7]

First, to deny *Congress* the power to legislate in areas of free expression, but to leave to the *states* the power to restrain speech—whether orally or in print—when they saw fit to do so. In this view, it was recognized that speech could be abused, but that the national legislature could not punish the citizen for making public utterances against those in power, whether those criticisms were political or religious. That there were members of Congress who insisted on preserving such a right for the states can be seen by the fact that the Senate, whose delegates were at that time chosen by the state legislatures, refused to make the important civil liberties guaranteed in the Bill of Rights binding on the states. (It was not until the adoption of the Fourteenth Amendment following the Civil War that the federal civil liberties were made binding on the states.) Most states had already adopted codes of civil liberties by the time the Constitutional Convention met in 1787, although those codes differed in wording and indeed in interpretation.

Second, to codify into American law the "prior restraint" provision of the British common law, as defined by Sir William Blackstone in his widely endorsed *Commentaries on the Laws of England* (1765–1769). In Book 4 of his *Commentaries*, Blackstone had written: "The liberty of the press is indeed essential to the nature of a free state; but this consists in laying no previous restraints upon publications, and not in freedom from censure for criminal matter when published."[8] In other words, a citizen might freely publish what he chose, but once his words were in print he was subject to any punishment the law might provide for sedition, libel, or other offenses. Blackstone, who was at the time regarded as an advanced libertarian, opposed any restrictions whatever on freedom of thought or inquiry, holding that the only crime that society sought to correct was that of "bad sentiments destructive of the ends of society."[9]

Third, to repudiate the common law as set forth by Blackstone, to go beyond the "prior restraint" provision and to expand the area of press freedom, although not to the extent that such freedom becomes absolute. This view was similar to that enunciated in 1919 by Justice Oliver Wendell Holmes, when he set forth the doctrine that free speech or free press was protected so long as what one said or wrote did not constitute "a clear and present danger" to society.[10] Holmes was, as a matter of fact, about as inconsistent as the Founding Fathers on the question of free speech. In 1907, he held that the main purpose of the First Amendment was to protect against prior restraint while 12 years later he maintained that the First Amendment had not merely reaffirmed Blackstone on prior restraint but that it had in fact abandoned the common law crime of seditious libel, which Blackstone had specifically retained in force.[11]

Fourth, to declare a guarantee for the press of absolute freedom from any and all governmental restraints. Madison and the American followers of Rousseau were to take this stand a decade after the adoption of the First Amendment, but there is no evidence Madison or anyone else of prominence in the new country held such views in 1789.

Each of these four explanations has attracted supporters, but it is safe to say that it is the third explanation that has by now gained the widest acceptance although it is likely that at the time the amendment was approved, it was seen primarily as incorporating Blackstone into the American code of justice. At the time of the adoption of the amendment, all signs point to a general interest among the Founding Fathers in some form of free expression about issues of public importance and in the right to engage in public criticism, whether about political, civic, or religious questions. In general, the view was widespread that mere words, unaccompanied by action, ought not to be punished.

Supreme Court Justice Potter Stewart maintained in 1974 that the primary purpose of the First Amendment guarantee was "to create a fourth institution outside the government as an additional check on the three official branches."[12] Stewart's views on the First Amendment represented a minority view on the Court; apparently he was providing the Founding Fathers with some twentieth-century hindsight. It is doubtful that Madison or the other Framers had developed a theory of such sophistication as early as 1791. In the twentieth century, it has become fashionable to describe the press as a "fourth branch of government."[13] Leonard Levy maintains that although the Founders may not have clearly understood what they were doing, they were nevertheless implying a Fourth Estate role for the press as part of a semiofficial system of checks and balances.[14] This imagery clearly expresses a status for the press that editors and reporters have for so long claimed that it has become a commonplace in the world of journalism. It is doubtful that the Framers had any institutional status in mind for the press, but the legend persists.

From a historical perspective, it needs to be remembered that the Framers were united in a common goal: the establishment of a new government on American shores free of interference from abroad. Soon, however, serious divisions began to occur, divisions that turned friends into enemies and gave birth to bitter political wrangling. From the constitutional crisis that followed passage of the Sedition Act of 1798 there evolved a widespread acceptance of the third explanation: Blackstone modified. In the second year of the administration of John Adams, the newly created United States found itself facing the threat of a potentially dangerous foreign war against the victorious French republicans who had overthrown the Bourbon monarchy. Jefferson and his more radical allies, led by Thomas Paine, welcomed the triumph of the French Revolution, but Adams, Alexander Hamilton, and the ruling Federalist party feared not only the might of France but also the possibility of subversion from within by native Americans and by French immigrants. In what they thought of as a defense of national security interests, they gained passage of the Alien and Sedition Laws of 1798. The Alien Law permitted the president to deport French citizens, especially writers, whom he considered dangerous to the peace and safety of the United States. The Sedition Law punished false writings designed to stir up contempt for the American government or encouragement for any foreign nation against the interests of the United States. To many of its backers, including President Adams, the Sedition Act represented also a victory for the backers of a free press, since for the first time it incorporated into law the principles of the Zenger case: that truth is a proper defense against charges of seditious libel and that juries, not judges, have the final say as to whether a statement is libelous or not.[15]

Both laws came under vigorous attack from Jefferson, Madison, and their followers. When Jefferson became president in 1801, he pardoned all prisoners jailed under the Alien and Sedition Acts. Even before he ascended to the presidency, he had joined Madison in publishing a series of resolutions and articles sharply critical of what was seen as a challenge to the just-won guarantees of freedom of the press. In the Virginia Resolutions,[16] Madison argued that the Alien and Sedition Laws were unconstitutional, in fact subversive, because they sought to deprive the people of a free press, which he called "the only effectual guardian of every other right"—another grain of wheat in the porridge of press glorification that is part of contemporary journalistic ideology.

Madison and his fellow Virginians went on in a remarkable commentary on the Virginia Resolutions to a declaration that was brand new in the history of Western political thought: an absolute restriction on the authority of the national government to issue any restraints at all on the press. It was ludicrous, Madison held, to imagine that the Founding Fathers meant nothing more in the First Amendment than a restatement of the common law definition of a free press as one free of prior restraint. The guarantee of a free press would be nothing but "a mockery," Madison maintained, if a printer could later be punished for what he had published. Such an extensive guarantee for a free press was quite dangerous, Madison acknowledged, since the press was capable of being licentious and abusive. "Some degree of abuse is inseparable from the proper use of anything," Madison said, and then went on to argue that the citizen had to put up with the abuse because restraints on newspapers would sap their courage so much they would lose their capacity to serve the public.[17] This view is similar to the position taken by Marx half a century later. Laws designed to punish a writer or editor for expressing his own convictions were, Marx wrote, "the most horrible terrorism."[18] The arguments of Madison and Marx have become familiar in the twentieth century: efforts to place restraints on the press are seen as attacking their independence and threatening to have "a chilling effect" on their ability to operate in the public interest. With a remarkable rhetorical flourish, Madison went on to declaim:

> *To the press alone, chequered as it is with abuses, the world is indebted for all the triumphs which have been gained by reason and humanity, over error and oppression.*[19]

Rarely has any public figure praised the press so extravagantly. No pronouncement by an association of editors, publishers, or journalists is likely to be any more laudatory. The ideological importance of Madison's remark cannot be overstated. It sums up in a single sentence the substance of the American journalist's belief system about the significance of the work he or she does.

There is, however, no reason to believe that the position taken by Madison was an accurate reflection of the attitudes of his fellow Framers. After all, his commentary on the Virginia Resolutions was a political document, directed against the Adams administration and designed to win popular support in opposition to the Alien and Sedition Acts. Probably, he allowed his passions to alter his memory a bit here and there. But he nonetheless gave powerful impetus to the ideology of the press. Not only had he proclaimed for the press a kind of absolute freedom from governmental restraint but he also had asserted the watchdog principle, had given in rather embryonic form what later came to be identified as "the public's right to know," and indeed had offered an eloquent statement of the educational role of the press.

Madison's letter on education, written in the spirit of Montesquieu and Rousseau, contained his well-known assertion that "knowledge will ever govern ignorance,"[20] and although his concern was with education in the schoolroom, editors and journalists have adopted the declaration as their own. In the world of journalism, the general conviction is that newspapers (and radio and television) are forms of education, indeed speaking both *for* the underprivileged members of society and *to* them as their primary source of knowledge and empowerment.

By the latter part of the 1820s, then, in a series of pronouncements covering more than a generation, Madison appears to have formulated a clear exposition of a philosophical foundation for the American press, borrowing from both British and French thinkers and adding what he and his colleagues had learned from the experiences of revolutionary America. Man is far from perfect, subject to the limitations of human frailty, but he enjoys the capacity for reason and is likely to make wise choices if permitted unrestricted access to information and to ideas from sources both friendly and inimical. The risks are great, both to individuals and to human society, but the risks would be far greater if man were to be cut off from information, if the power of society, as expressed by government, were used to censor rather that illuminate. Community can exist only if information is freely exchanged and men are allowed to make free choices.[21] Not only individual men but society at large gains much from such free interchange of information and ideas. Truth can be found only if access to it is unlimited. In the twentieth century, many troubling questions would be raised about the issue of access.

The world of the Founding Fathers, it needs to be remembered, was circumscribed. To them newspapers were small enterprises in which individual printers or a handful of partners published and distributed information over a small geographical area and to limited audiences. In short, Madison was not looking at the press as a commercial institution. Profits were of course being made, but they were small. No publishing empires had been begun or even contemplated. The power of the government seemed vast in comparison with that of the printers, and Madison was not dismayed by any fear that, however abusive or untrustworthy the press might be or become, it could pose a threat to the survival of free institutions.

Madison's partner in the writing of *The Federalist Papers*, Alexander Hamilton, was not, however, equally disposed to accord the press unlimited freedom. It was Hamilton, not Madison, who in *Federalist* No. 84 upheld the Constitution for not providing any specific guarantees of press freedom. To Hamilton, only the public could insure a free press. No matter how many constitutional guarantees might have been written, Hamilton said, they were indeed useless if the public thought the press ought not to be free. In this, Hamilton the capitalist par excellence was expressing a view that would later be endorsed by Marx, who wrote in 1849 that an atmosphere in which the public has lost its desire for a free and open press is so "hopelessly sick" that a free press is doomed.[22]

Whom indeed does the press serve? The individual reader? The public at large? The government it lives under? The men and women who finance it? Or does it perhaps serve itself? The core question of whom the press serves is at the center of nearly all philosophical disputes about the press. The answer depends on whether or not the disputant believes that humankind is good or evil. Those who, like Rousseau, distrust institutions and place their trust and confidence in the people, in the ultimate wisdom of the General Will, see the mission of the press as nothing more than to serve the public. Those who, like Hobbes or Locke, fear reliance on human nature or the public at large, see the press essentially as an instrument available to the wise and the virtuous to influence the people to behave in a wise and virtuous manner. The collision between these two visions of humankind can be seen clearly in the quarrel between Thomas Paine and Edmund Burke, to which we will turn shortly.

By the turn of the century, Hamilton had become a bitter enemy of Madison and Jefferson. He had been a key figure in helping President Adams secure passage of the Alien and Sedition Laws; in fact, he and Jefferson had become rival figures in the first major political battle between American editors, that between Philip Freneau of the *National Gazette* and John Fenno of the *Gazette of the United States* in the early 1790s.[23] In 1804, after one Harry Croswell had been convicted on charges of seditious libel for attacking Jefferson in the pages of his New York *Wasp*, he turned to Hamilton for help in appealing the verdict. The Croswell case rivals that of the Zenger case for a position of prominence in the history of courtroom drama in the field of journalism. Now, however, it was the Jeffersonian libertarians who were on the defensive, arguing that abuse in print should be punished by fines and prison terms. Hamilton, however, drew a sharp distinction between merely publishing abusive material about political leaders (which was subject to punishment) and writing articles for good motives and justifiable ends no matter how the material in those articles reflected on persons in power.[24] A democratic society, Hamilton argued, would be foolish to restrict the press to writing only about issues and never about individuals. If there were such restrictions, he asked, how might a citizen raise his voice against tyranny? The truth of what was written should, Hamilton held, echoing the words of the earlier Hamilton in the Zenger case, be the decisive factor.

It is to be noted that Hamilton never agreed with Madison in endorsing unbridled freedom for the press. He insisted on a need for limitations on the power of the press. Juries, he said, should be authorized to punish abuse and calumny when they determined that an article had been written for bad motives or unjust ends. Foreshadowing the bad-tendency test, which later was to be proclaimed a guide for judicial decisions, Hamilton told the court: "The intent is the very essence of the crime." Hamilton, drawing his philosophical strength from Locke, consistently professed his reliance on individual citizens, the members of juries, rather than on the courts, which he suspected were dominated by Jeffersonians. Whether Hamilton was cynical in proclaiming his faith in public opinion is a question that cannot be answered with certainty, but it does need to be remembered that, like Madison in his commentary on the Virginia Resolutions, Hamilton had political as well as philosophical ends in mind when he addressed the court in the Croswell case.

The Croswell case ended indecisively. Hamilton had been seeking a new trial on the charges of seditious libel, but the appeals court split 2–2 on the question of a new trial. Technically, the result permitted the public prosecutor to move for judgment against Croswell, but the prosecutor for whatever reason failed to make the move, and Croswell escaped being punished. The Supreme Court of New York ordered a new trial the following year, but no trial was held. In the intervening period New York had enacted a law permitting truth as a defense in libel actions and Hamilton had been killed in a duel with Aaron Burr.

Of all Hamilton's utterances, none is more remarkable than his forthright assertion before the court of a watchdog function for the press—"to give us early alarm and put us on our guard against the encroachments of power."[25] Rather than acquiesce in suppression of press freedom, Hamilton said in reaffirming the holy dedication others had sworn on the altar of a free press, "Americans ought rather to spill our blood." No doubt he was following in the footsteps of John Milton: no censorship for the truth or those ideas we believe in, but restrictions on error, since it could damage the very institutions we revere.

One of the four judges who heard the Croswell case, James Kent, a distinguished exponent of conservative judicial philosophy, recognized the point. So stirred was Kent by Hamilton's words that he jotted down a note about the attorney's "pathetic, impassioned and most eloquent address" on the threat to liberty whenever the press is stifled. "We ought," Kent wrote, "to *resist—resist—resist* till we hurl the Demagogues and Tyrants from their imagined thrones."[26] The careful observer will note that Kent accepted without question Hamilton's view that the press ought not to go unchecked in the exercise of its "terrible liberty":

> *The novel, the visionary, the pestilential doctrine of an* unchecked *press, [Hamilton] reprobates and this will be an ill-fated country, if the doctrine prevails—it is the pestilence of our country. The best man on earth who is never removed from the reach of calumny felt it—single drops of water will wear out adamant. He does not maintain or contend for this terrible liberty of the press. But he contends for the right of publishing truth with good motive, though the censure light on government or individuals.*[27]

CHAPTER 20

Paine, Burke, and the "Rights of Man"

Among the vast outpourings of writings produced in the revolutionary years that ended the eighteenth century, none is more challenging than the polemics of Thomas Paine and Edmund Burke. Indeed, the public argument between Paine and Burke has been characterized as "perhaps the most crucial ideological dispute ever carried on in English."[1] Both were courageous Englishmen who supported the American Revolution, Burke from a minor position inside the English government, Paine as a fiery radical who was exiled from Britain on account of his revolutionary fervor. Burke, who wrote in effusive, carefully constructed phrases, was a staunch defender of traditional values and historical processes, so much so that he came to despise the philosophical position of Paine, whose *Common Sense* had not only called upon the colonies to rise up in rebellion against Britain but went much further in glorifying the rebellion as a defense of the rights of man against those of entrenched aristocracy.

If Madison was the father of the Constitution, Paine was the prophet of democracy, representative government, and the power of a free press.[2] Perhaps no other journalist has ever had as striking an impact on political action as Paine. His *The Rights of Man* influenced the course of revolution not only in the colonies but in Jacobin France as well; it shook the Old Guard in Britain so fiercely that more than 150 years had to pass after Paine's death in 1809 before his hometown, Thetford, could bring itself to erect a monument to him. At the time of Paine's death, a member of the Thetford Council said that to put up a monument to him "would be an insult to the town."[3]

In the final years of the eighteenth century, the writings of political pamphleteers were themselves dramatic events. It was a time, as Paine himself had written in 1776, that tried men's souls.[4] By 1790, the former

American colonies had launched their experiment in self-government. The Jacobins had stormed the Bastille in Paris and were heading toward the Reign of Terror. It was a world of uncertainty, and those who had been directing its fate were trembling for fear of the future. At this time Burke, then perhaps the most respected of England's political philosophers, was known to be preparing a treatise on the French Revolution. It was certain that, despite his approval of the American rebellion, he would condemn with all the verbal artillery at his command the direction of the French Revolution. In fact, Burke had already spoken out in speeches in Parliament against the fundamental ideas of the rights of man that had inspired the French revolutionaries as well as Paine, whose writings were familiar to the Jacobins. These men, Burke told the House of Commons, were followers of Rousseau and hence dangerous people, because they saw *liberty* as among the rights of man. There is no such thing as abstract liberty, Burke told Commons. As far as he was concerned, the Americans had already subverted the principles in which their rebellion had been rooted. Burke in fact had little sympathy with "rights" of any kind, and to speak of some abstract "rights of man" was nonsense. What to Paine and Jefferson were central to the American experiment, Burke rejected as an alien intrusion of "metaphysics."[5]

Burke's *Reflections on the Revolution in France* appeared in 1790. Since it was already well known that he was preparing the essay, Paine, who at one time had thought well of Burke but now considered him an important political enemy, was already in London, waiting for it to appear so that he might respond. This experienced journalist wasted no time. He was out with his reply by the following February, with a dedication inscribed to the hero of the American rebellion, George Washington. In May, the new Paine pamphlet, its title now employing the phrase detested by Burke, *The Rights of Man*, was in print in the *New York Advertiser*.

The bound version of the book included a highly saleable commodity, a recommendation from Jefferson himself, who wrote: "Something is at length to be publicly said against the political heresies which have sprung up among us."[6] In his private correspondence, Jefferson acknowledged that in speaking of "political heresies," he had been thinking of the published condemnation of the French Revolution by John Adams (not Burke), and said that he regretted his endorsement had ever been published. In any case, with such figures as Burke, Paine, Jefferson, and Adams involved in a print war over the greatest political event of the period, public attention was assured.

What was at the heart of this "crucial ideological dispute"? Nothing short of an open debate on the nature of man and his social and political institutions. The two sides were not always fair with one another. Both Burke and Paine misquoted the other and engaged in some gross distortions and misrepresentations of the other's point of view. Paine in particular was not free of character assassination. But even allowing for political and emotional exaggerations, the critical collision of philosophical viewpoints is clear enough. To Burke, revolution, the destruction of ancient institutions, was wrong. When institutions have lost their purpose and vitality, Burke said, they are in need of reform, not overthrow. There is virtue in tradition and in the leaders that the old institutions have brought to power. To turn power over to hairdressers or candlemakers is ludicrous; since man is inherently weak, to entrust power to a majority of working class individuals is to open the door to political excesses and uncontrolled passions.[7] Following Hobbes and Locke, Burke saw government as a surrender of certain individual rights in favor of a just and orderly civil society.

Paine was utterly disgusted with Burke. "Government is for the living, not the dead," he exclaimed.[8] Moreover, he asserted, Burke despised mankind and considered people contemptible: "He considers them as a herd of beings that must be governed by fraud, effigy and show." Relying not on Hobbes and Locke for spiritual guidance, Paine turned to Rousseau: "Man has no authority over posterity in matters of personal right; and, therefore, no man or body of men, had, or can have, a right to set up hereditary government."[9] Only representative government, which would give equal power to hairdressers, candlestick makers, and the landed gentry, could assure the triumph of nature, reason, and experience, Paine argued, envisioning an American future that would dwarf the glory of Athens: "What Athens was in miniature, America will be in magnitude."[10]

Burke and Paine both appealed to reason, as in fact did Adams and Jefferson, but the conclusions they drew and the future world they foresaw were 180 degrees apart. Although Paine, like the French revolutionaries, referred repeatedly to reason, the reason he revered was one that was stoked with the fire of passion. He was a thoroughgoing Rousseauean, a firm believer in the wisdom of the General Will. The futures perceived by Burke and by Paine were, respectively, those of Locke and Rousseau. Both visions survive in the United States, so that many of the disputes that arise in today's political, economic, social, and cultural environments are philosophical repetitions of the clash between Burke and Paine.

Burke's guiding light was stability. Use traditions to your advantage. Conserve the best of the past. Place your trust in an informed, educated elite, Plato's philosopher-kings. Paine's guiding light was passion. Reject tradition and the past. Strive for a better world in the future. Place your trust in "the people."

Paine has been subjected to one of the most remarkable campaigns of vilification in the American experience. Not only was he disowned by the town fathers of his birthplace, but during his lifetime he was denounced from the pulpit as a wanton blasphemer and condemned in biographies for filthiness, drunkenness, and lechery. Theodore Roosevelt cast him aside as "a filthy little atheist,"[11] and even today he continues to be passed over in the cast of heroes of the American Revolution. In truth, however, he ought more properly to be be revered as the patron saint of the activist journalist, of the fearless seeker after truth in the public print. In fact, Paine endorsed an early version of what is now spoken of as the public's right to know. Mankind must never be told what to think or what to read: "Ignorance . . . once dispelled . . . is impossible to re-establish. It is . . . only the absence of knowledge; and though man may be *kept* ignorant, he cannot be *made* ignorant."[12]

Where Burke was the reformer, Paine was the revolutionary. Where Burke was a pessimist about human nature, Paine was an optimist. Where Burke saw the world as inordinately complex, to Paine the fundamentals were simple and straightforward. To Burke, government was a good and a necessary instrument for the nation's leaders. In fact, leaders could hold power either because of their high birth or their outstanding talent; in whichever case, they needed the institutions of government to keep the people under control. Paine on the other hand saw government as an instrument to be used sparingly, on the ground that it was so easily subject to abuse. Burke believed in the virtue of tradition and religion; Paine dismissed tradition because it served to halt necessary change, and rejected organized religion because it served as a device to enslave the people. Burke denied the idea of abstract liberty; he argued that the only true rights of men were the rights to equality under the law, to enjoy the fruits of their own work and of their inheritance.[13] Freedom, to Burke, must always be limited; moreover, he hated the concept of equality that had appeared in the American colonies and about which de Tocqueville would later write so tellingly. In an outburst of passion (to which he was in fact addicted), Burke once condemned the doctrine of equality as the work of "knavery, and so greedily adopted by malice, envy, and cunning."[14]

Freedom and equality, on the other hand, were decisive in Paine's thinking. Michael Foot, a leader of the modern British Labor party, wrote this glowing defense of Paine:

> *He knew he possessed the implement which could work the miracle—the power of free speech, free writing and free thought. Nothing could induce in him a hairsbreadth of doubt; the bigger the bonfires they made of his books, the bigger would be his sales. No other figure in history can ever have believed in the power of freedom—and not merely its virtue—with Paine's single-minded intensity.*[15]

In 1792, Paine was convicted of seditious libel by a court in Massachusetts for publishing *The Rights of Man*. The jury was in no mood at the height of the French Revolution to endorse freedom of expression for a book that not only supported the Jacobins and downgraded traditional religious practices but also spoke of the people, not their rulers, as the true sovereigns. Paine's lawyer, Thomas Erskine, won few friends at the time but gave expression to an enduring strain in the ideology of American journalists in an impassioned plea to the jury:

> *No legal argument can shake the freedom of the press in my sense of it, if I am supported in my doctrines concerning the great*

> *unalienable right of the people to reform or change their governments. It is because the liberty of the press resolves itself into this great issue that it has been in every country, the last liberty which subjects have been able to wrest from power. Other liberties are held* under *government, but the liberty of opinion keeps governments themselves in due subjection to their duties.*[16]

Classical journalistic ideology, as it has evolved in the United States, derives from that passionate adoration of free expression held by the most revolutionary of the Founding Fathers, the journalist Thomas Paine, who saw the new country as the new Athens; in his crystal ball it was an open society with "no place for mystery."[17] Without restrictions, knowledge must be disseminated throughout the society, he said, by the press and by others, to cast aside ignorance and official dogma. Government and information should exist for the benefit of the governed, not for the benefit of the government and its leaders. Yet even Paine did not believe that a journalist ought to be free of the possibility of being prosecuted for what he had written. True to his belief in the absolute sovereignty of the people, Paine held that if a man says—or writes—"atrocious things," the ultimate judge of whether he is to be prosecuted for his utterances is a jury of the people.[18]

The distinguished American legal scholar, Alexander Bickel, notes that Burke spoke for the side that in the revolutionary period was the losing side. Nevertheless, he points out, Burke's views have continued to play a crucial role in the development of American thought. According to Bickel, Burke recognized that proclamation of the "rights of man" was in fact "an invitation to another round of religious wars and persecutions, not likely to be less fanatical or bloody for the irreligiousness of the new dogma."[19]

In Burke's vision, as in Bickel's, it is wrong for the fraternity of writers and journalists to be made up of true believers in abstract causes, for instance serving as mouthpiece for a mystical General Will. The journalist, rather, like the representative of all institutions, has a positive duty to serve as a realist, not an ideologue, to seek out the true facts so that they might be used to help organize and preserve, as Bickel wrote, "decent, wise, just, responsive, stable government in the circumstances of a given time and place."[20] To Burke, "the restraints on men, as well as their liberties, are to be reckoned among their rights."[21]

Burke in fact attacked Paine's "literary men" who were, like Paine himself, true believers, holding, as Burke wrote, contemptuous disrespect "for the wisdom of others." Rather than practicing true free expression, Burke said, they were denying access to print of any ideas of which they did not approve.[22] In a speech in Parliament at the height of a bitter controversy over the writings of the true believer printer John Wilkes, a hero to the American rebels for his outspoken attacks on King George III in his *North Britain*, Burke wrote that something had to be done about the licentiousness of the press: "Libels have conquered the law. The liberty of the press has run into licentiousness ... too strong for the government."[23] The visions of the press held by Paine and Burke have a curiously modern quality. Each man was in his own way a moralist, and in their differences we can find the conflicting views on liberty and license that not only dominated the growth of press ideology in the eighteenth century but are still very much apparent in the images of the press held in contemporary America.

CHAPTER 21

Revolution: A Mystique for Journalists

Paine referred again and again to Rousseau in his writings; indeed, Paine's reliance on Rousseau's ideas was well known even during his own lifetime.[1] Throughout the former colonies in the 1790s, a series of societies appeared whose aim was to extend the democratic ideas of Rousseau and Paine around the world. These clubs served as the nucleus of the country's first political party, Jefferson's Democratic-Republicans.[2] The party's very name was drawn from the designation the turn-of-the-century radicals gave to their organizations, the "Democratic-Republican Societies." Their concept of democracy was openly based on Rousseau's General Will. To them, government was the organ of the people, whose elected representatives were simply deputies of the people. The centerpiece of their extraordinarily optimistic value system was free and open discussion, including open forums and public debate in the pages of the newspapers. Among the top leadership of these societies were some of the best-known editors of the day, to a man opponents of Federalists Alexander Hamilton and John Adams, whom they held in contempt as, in the words of editor William Duane of Philadelphia, spokesmen for a doctrine of "the inner depravity of man."[3]

Duane was editor of the *Aurora* of Philadelphia, successor in that position to Benjamin Franklin Bache, Franklin's son-in-law and another society member. Following Rousseau and Paine, Duane argued for democratic education, maintaining that it could become a way of life for all Americans; all that was needed then was free speech and the open dissemination of information in the newspapers. Duane was indicted under the Sedition Act, but the charge was dismissed by Jefferson after he succeeded to the presidency in 1801, on the ground that only the states had the authority to interfere with the freedom of the press.[4]

The members of the societies were condemned by Hamilton, Adams, and their Federalist colleagues as "Jacobins," supporters of the French revolutionaries. Under constant attack during their heyday, the societies had by the turn of the nineteenth century vanished from the scene as independent political forces, but not before they had made their mark on the American belief system; for a while they enjoyed considerable popularity. In fact, they were among the staunchest of supporters of Jefferson, including among their leadership journalist-editors such as Duane, Bache, Joel Barlow, Philip Freneau, and Tunis Wortman. Like Rousseau, Paine and to a lesser degree, Jefferson, they were optimistic about the nature of man and about his democratic potential. The poet Barlow made this clear: "It is the *person*, not the property, that exercises the will, and is capable of enjoying happiness; it is therefore the person, for whom government is instituted, and by whom its functions are performed."[5]

A leading student of these societies has written that their major goal was "to translate the classic doctrine of Rousseau's popular sovereignty into actual political life." He adds:

> *New media of communication were imperative, to gain wider public participation. Through interrelated town meetings and associated committees of correspondence, the clubs hoped to make the general will realistic and active. This they accomplished to a large degree.*[6]

Their importance in the development of an American press ideology has not been given adequate recognition. The key member in the furtherance of this ideology was Tunis Wortman, a New York politician-journalist who was at that time the leading American press theorist. Few persons have argued the cause of a free press more powerfully than Wortman, and his influence at the time was extensive. When Wortman launched a paper, *The State of the Union*, in New York in 1813, Jefferson was an enthusiastic subscriber. Wortman's *A Treatise Concerning Political Enquiry, and the Liberty of the Press*, which appeared in 1800, follows Rousseau in arguing that public opinion gives expression to the voice of the General Will. And public opinion, he says, is shaped by the press. Journalists might well abuse the trust placed in them, but their "natural direction will be towards Truth and Virtue."[7] And should the press engage in licentiousness, according to Wortman, "we may securely trust to the wisdom of Public Opinion" to correct it.[8]

The enthusiasm for a free press expressed by New York's Wortman was part of the belief system of the members of the Democratic-Republican clubs. In this, they followed in the spirit of the radical pronouncements made earlier by George Hay, a Virginian and close ally of Jefferson, who served as prosecutor at the treason trial of Aaron Burr in 1807. To Hay, an early absolutist, any restraint at all on the liberty of the press was abhorrent: "If the words freedom of the press have any meaning at all they mean a total exemption from any law making any publication whatever criminal."[9] Otherwise, he said, those words meant nothing. Hay insisted that the Founding Fathers saw "the spirit of inquiry and discussion" as critically important not only in the new nation but "in every free country, and could be preserved only by giving it absolute protection, even in its excesses."[10] The nature of those excesses was not important, Hay said. The comments in the press might be malicious or false, scandalous or absurd, even immoral. They still had a right to be printed for "one was safe within the sanctuary of the press."[11]

Hay's comments provide an early endorsement of the ideas spread by the "new journalists" of the 1960s and 1970s. He argued that it made no sense to try to defend the press by claiming that its attacks on those in power were based on truth because this would give protection only to the "morally right" and would ignore the reality that it is difficult if not impossible to separate fact from opinion. One can find, he wrote, "many truths, important to society, which are not susceptible of that full, direct, and positive evidence, which alone can be exhibited before a court or a jury."[12]

No doubt only a handful of today's journalists have even heard the names of Tunis Wortman or George Hay, and it is not likely that they are more than casually acquainted with the words of Tom Paine. Even so, the ideas that reporters and editors express every day in newsrooms across the country are ideas that were popularized by these men at the turn of the nineteenth century. Entering unrecognized the air breathed by Americans, they have profoundly influenced the way reporters and editors have faced the choices they make in their jobs daily.

To Paine, and to Hay, Wortman, Barlow, and their fellows in the Democratic-Republican societies, a free press was indispensable for the growth of democratic institutions and a better world. The journalists who came after them in the nineteenth century, the Bennetts and the Greeleys, the Danas and the Pulitzers, cheerfully endorsed this theory. To a man, the Jacobin editors saw the press as an instrument of education. Their approach was empirical. As one club statement held: "On information we will speak; and upon deliberation, we will write and publish our statements."[13]

In a sense the American experiment represented an empirical test of Paine's faith in the rights of man. The fear of democracy held by most of the Founding Fathers began to evaporate in the nineteenth century. The revolutionary experiment had begun in earnest.

CHAPTER 22

Kant, Hegel, and the Counterrevolution

The Enlightenment did not lead only in the direction of popular democracy. In fact, the nineteenth century was to produce, not only an experiment in democratic government and free expression, but also a counterrevolution, in which, curiously, the ideas of Rousseau were put to an entirely different use from those of Paine and his followers. As the Democratic-Republican societies were urging expansion of democratic ideas in the new America, across the Atlantic in Prussia, the historian-philosopher Georg Wilhelm Friedrich Hegel was developing quite a different interpretation of history, rejecting democracy altogether. Hegel borrowed Rousseau's General Will, but he gave it a religious twist, something that would have been anathema to the Frenchman. Indeed, Hegel's General Will embodied a metaphysical quality that he identified at various times as the Idea, as God, as Reason, or as the World-Spirit, indeed as "the end of history."[1]

An early enthusiast for the *philosophes* and the French Revolution, Hegel later came to attack Rousseau as being too abstract and Voltaire for his dismissal of traditional religion.[2] It is curious in retrospect to find Hegel condemning others for being abstract while seeing himself as a concrete thinker. This becomes more understandable, however, when one recognizes that Hegel invented his own language, an approach that makes him perhaps the most difficult of all philosophers to follow, but for which he has become a hero to thinkers on both the philosophical Right and the Left. To Hegel something was concrete if it was expressed in the world rather than as something internal or potential, as with Rousseau's conception of the General Will.

In fact, Hegel saw only the mystical, romantic element in Rousseau. He was not at all concerned with popular education, which was so crucial to the Frenchman. Nor was he concerned with Rousseau's revolutionary fervor or with the rights of man.[3]

Hegel's importance in the history of ideas can never be underestimated, but of even greater significance was the research method that he adopted, the concept of *dialectical analysis*. Following Socrates but in a vein unmistakably poetic, Hegel argued that all thought is dynamic, with each concept *becoming* something else. The idea of becoming was crucial. The electric light is used as the classical example. The light being turned on implies it can also be turned off, the Being and the Naught. To understand the phenomenon, it must be seen as a whole, as the conscious unity of opposites.[4] In an important sense Hegel was trying to reconcile the empirical techniques of scientific research, which he criticized sharply, with the rational, intuitive techniques of pure thinkers. He argued that every idea is filled with internal contradictions and that out of a struggle between an idea (thesis) and its contradiction (antithesis) arises a new idea, a synthesis, which contains *its* own contradictions. History is then a struggle between ideas and contradictions, between pure thought and the passions.

Marx would later commit himself whole-heartedly to Hegel's dialectical method of analysis, but would dismiss Hegel's abstract Idea and assert that by turning to *dialectical materialism* rather than Hegelian idealism, he was "standing Hegel on his feet."

The influence of Hegel's ideas on American thought was substantial, although it was not felt until later in the nineteenth century when it was brought back across the Atlantic by the multitude of Americans who had traveled to Germany or had gone there for advanced study at the distinguished universities in Berlin, Heidelberg, and Jena.[5] The German "romantic awakening" of the nineteenth century can be viewed as a counterrevolution, rejecting the concern with individual freedom that had dominated the rational world of the Enlightenment, and reaffirming, in Hegel's metaphysical construction, the mystical concept of society that had been given expression by Rousseau and furthered by Paine and the Democratic-Republican societies.

Hegel was born in 1770. He was 19 years old at the time of the French Revolution and like Burke and Paine was profoundly influenced by it. The greater share of his writings appeared between 1807 and 1821, in the counterrevolutionary post-Napoleonic Era in which powerful rulers imposed new restraints on constitutionalism and civil liberties. At the same time, the United States was being governed under the presidencies of Jefferson and his Virginia colleagues Madison and Monroe. One of Hegel's most important contributions was to make known the philosophy of Immanuel Kant (1724–1804), for it was largely through Hegel's somewhat distorted interpretations that Kant's ideas were disseminated in the nineteenth century. A rebirth of interest in Kant in the twentieth century has gained him his proper place in the history of ideas and given him a major role in, among other things, today's discussions of journalistic ethics.[6]

Both England and France achieved political and social unity long before Germany, which had no tradition of political coherence and which did not emerge as a national entity until late in the nineteenth century, even after the American Civil War. Efforts at social change in the German-speaking world had been frustrated by powerful rulers. Indeed, there was no real tradition of empirical or scientific inquiry in the Germany of Kant and Hegel. In fact, Hegel specifically rejected the empirical methods of science because, he said, they were not dialectical, had no purpose (such as the "actualization" of reason or the Idea) and were abstract, that is to say, outside human experience.

Kant, who influenced Hegel and whose views were somewhat distorted by Hegel, was a gentler spirit. Although he was a contemporary of the great French *philosophes* and although he was familiar with the writings of English and French scholars, he made a point of remaining isolated in his beloved Koenigsberg in East Prussia all his life.[7] Kant considered himself an empiricist dedicated to the scientific method, but even so his tradition was German and therefore more idealistic or, as it was filtered through Hegel, more *romantic* than was that of his French or English contemporaries. Still, Kant stands today as the most influential philosopher of the eighteenth-century Enlightenment.

It is not surprising that in a country made up of numerous contending principalities and dukedoms, the struggle for unity was preeminent in the belief system of the German philosophers. Like Voltaire, Kant saw history, morality, and social customs as universal. What was good in one place was good in another. Yet, at the same time he was profoundly influenced by Hume, whose stance of skeptical empiricism, Kant said, had awakened him from his "dogmatic slumbers."[8] Hume had rejected all absolutes and found that human behavior and moral standards were dictated by conventions and customary uses. Kant moved off in a different direction.

At the center of Kant's philosophy was his concern with "things-in-themselves." The raw material of life, the "objective reality" that exists in time and space, is not an objective characteristic of things-in-themselves. We cannot comprehend the world around us except through what Kant called a transcendental process, that is to say, by our reason, by thinking. The influence of this line of thought on Ralph Waldo Emerson is unmistakable. Things do not exist for us in themselves but only through our *understanding* of them, Kant wrote.[9] It is our *perception* of things that is all-important. Time and space are forms that the mind imposes on what we experience through our senses. Our minds simply transcend reality. By the same token, freedom exists for us because we *will* it to exist. We have the power, by using our rational minds, to create rational laws. In other words, we can be free only to the extent that we will ourselves to be free.

Kant saw this as the practical answer to a metaphysical problem: how to achieve freedom in a world in which the ultimate reality was unavailable to us. Kant's resolution was moral, a kind of philosophical variation on the Golden Rule: do not treat people as means—through whom we can achieve our ends. As rational creatures, Kant said, we have the capacity to exercise our rational wills and to impose on ourselves a law under which we "treat humanity in every case as an end, never as a means only."[10]

Hegel the optimist maintained that human beings would necessarily construct rational laws and behave morally, but Kant saw things differently. Whether we did so, Kant judged, depended on whether we were able to transcend the world of experience. To do this and to achieve freedom was in Kant's view murderously difficult. It required the most rigorous dedication to one's duty, to treat other people as ends, for example.[11] Our moral duty as human beings consisted in never behaving in any way that could not be considered an absolute law. He identified this grim doctrine as "a categorical imperative." Under that doctrine, one must never transgress morality. One must, for instance, never lie, not even to save oneself or one's friend from death. The law of the categorical imperative required absolute commitment to truth.[12]

The crucial problem for Kant, as indeed it had been for Rousseau and the American Founders, was what to do when one's individual freedom collided with the freedom of other people. The social compact was the answer supplied by the Enlightenment. Locke and Rousseau had agreed that he who gives up the freedom that he enjoys in the state of nature to join a community, receives in return the freedom and security that can be enjoyed under the laws of the compact.[13] Kant's solution was specific: create laws that are themselves so rational that they are acceptable to all reasonable persons. True freedom is brought about when the individual "has entirely abandoned his wild, lawless freedom, to find it again, unimpaired, in a state of dependence according to law."[14]

Kant was very cautious about the implications of this statement; he was by no means convinced that human beings could be so rational as all that. The German romantics who borrowed from Kant—Hegel and the poets Schiller and Hoelderlin and to a lesser extent Goethe—had no doubts.[15] Where Kant was a gentle, unobtrusive philosopher, Hegel was arrogant and overbearing. He *knew* the answers; doubt was unknown to him. The followers of Hegel, forgetting Kant's doubts, went on to discover their own version of rationality in the wisdom of Germany or, in Hegel's imagination, of the rising Prussian state. In his wildly enthusiastic way, the poet Schiller envisioned the possibility of the transcendental unity of all knowledge in the German experience. "Each people has its day in history," he wrote, "but the day of the German is the harvest of time as a whole."[16] Kant was so horrified by such declarations that he was moved to issue a denial of the many statements being made in his name. "May God preserve us from our friends," he wrote in a widely circulated comment.[17] It is lamentable that Kant went to his grave before he had a chance to dispute the edifice Hegel had built upon his philosophy.

Hegel was a man with the best of intentions; his vision was of a world of rational morality. Like many German romantics, he longed for a return to ancient Greece, which he called the "paradise of the human spirit." To him, Greece was the land of *Sittlichkeit*, where customs and morals were blended into a harmonious whole. The end of history, the end of the dialectic conflict between ideas and counterideas, was to emerge in what Hegel identified as the World-Spirit, or the Idea, which was a sort of shorthand for a new Greece, a society in which *Sittlichkeit* would once again prevail. The dialectical method presupposed a world of progress, one in which each succeeding step along the way to the Idea was superior to the last.[18]

Freedom in Hegel's complex metaphysical imagery came when one adapted one's individual will to the dictates of history, to the ultimate victory of the Idea (Marx would revise this to the ultimate victory of socialism). To Hegel this was also the essence of morality. Freedom arrived through obedience to the German state, which was the living expression of the triumph of reason, the political incarnation of Hegel's Idea.[19] "The State," Hegel wrote, "is the divine Idea as it exists on earth."[20] Obviously this doctrine provided a philosophical impetus for Hitler and the other pan-Germans of the twentieth century.

Here the doctrine of the General Will was being carried to ends entirely different from those imagined by Madison, Hay, and Wortman, or by Kant for that matter.

Progress to Hegel could be seen in the overthrow of a past dominated by the Catholic church. Protestantism, enshrined in Prussia, was a visible symbol of progress.[21] Hegel's doctrine of freedom was completely rational inside his scheme of rationality:

> *Obedience to the laws of the state, the reason in will and action, was made the principle of human conduct. In this obedience man is free, for the particular obeys the general. Man himself has a conscience; therefore he is free to obey. This involves the possibility of a development of reason and freedom, and of their introduction into human relations.*[22]

Hegel the supreme counterrevolutionary was saying that freedom consists not in a choice that the individual can make but in obeying the choices that have been made for him by the state (or perhaps by the General Will inside the state). Absent is any freedom to refuse to obey. Hegel argued, as do those with a similarly holistic view of the world, that "there is no truth except the whole truth."[23] The press is free, in this imagery, to serve the state, for since the state is moral and embodies the truth, to refuse to obey it is to be irrational and to deny the truth. Well meaning and analytical as he was, Hegel erred murderously in his reliance on an abstract conceptualization and even more so in his refusal to face the hard world of reality. He blindly ignored in his assumption of the virtue of the state the inevitable conflicts between rulers and the ruled.

Whereas the crucial dispute at the turn of the century had pitted the ideas of Burke against those of Paine, in the nineteenth century the battle of ideas tended to focus around those of Hegel on the one hand and those of John Stuart Mill on the other. For if Hegel was the archenemy of popular democracy, Mill was its arch-supporter. In the United States, it was the ideas of Mill that held sway. But not entirely.

PART V

Weighing the Individual Against Society: The Paradox of Democracy

John Stuart Mill (1806–1873): "If all mankind minus one were of one opinion, and only one person were of the contrary opinion, mankind would be no more justified in silencing that one person than he, if he had the power, would be justified in silencing mankind."

Karl Marx (1818–1883): "The purposes of journalistic activity are subsumed under the one general concept of 'truth' . . . Not only the result but also the route belongs to the truth. The pursuit of truth must be true; the true inquiry is the developed truth, whose scattered parts are assembled in the result."

CHAPTER 23

Introduction: Jeremy Bentham and the Pleasure-Pain Principle

We have met up with the paradox of democracy before, but nowhere can this paradox be seen with greater clarity than in the opposing viewpoints of two Europeans who grew to maturity in the middle years of the nineteenth century, Karl Marx and John Stuart Mill. In some ways, these men shared a common vision. Each was a child of Milton, for each glorified, with powerful conviction, the right of free expression. They argued that only when a man has the right to contend for his own beliefs can there be change, and that only change can improve the lot of human beings on this earth. Their greatest point of difference lay in one of the most fundamental of all philosophical issues: is the end of human life to exalt the *individual* or is it instead to achieve the good of *society*? Mill was the greatest of all spokesmen for the individual while Marx was the greatest of all spokesmen for society.

In the United States especially, Marx has been the victim of a bad press, for he and his ideas have often, incorrectly, been associated with the dogmas and doctrines of the Soviet Union. Marx died in 1883, a generation before the Bolshevik Revolution in Russia, and his essentially humanistic value system has never been altogether at home in that country, despite the lip service paid to it by a succession of Soviet leaders and ideologues. In many ways, Marx was, like Mill, a classical nineteenth-century humanist, and his collectivist philosophy has, like the individualism of Mill, exercised a profound influence on American ideas.

Mill was born in 1806, 12 years before Marx, and died a decade before Marx, in 1873. The Old Order perished during their lifetimes, although it has not to this day lost its diehard enthusiasts. At Mill's birth, the fledgling United States of America, under President Thomas Jefferson, had already expanded its territory westward to the Rocky Mountains.

Napoleon, rising to power on the impetus of the French Revolution, strode like a colossus across the face of Europe, inflaming the imagination of all those who dreamed of freeing themselves from the control of royalty and nobility. The vast upheaval set in motion by the Industrial Revolution was just beginning. Burke and the conservatives may have abhorred the rise of the Jacobins in France, but English liberals, basking in the egalitarian breezes that blew across the channel from France and fanned by the ideas of Hobbes, Locke, and Hume, set about establishing a philosophical system with reformist values that they believed fit the times, and that came to exert a profound influence on the belief system of American journalists.

The key figure in the development of this philosophy was Jeremy Bentham, a remarkable figure in a remarkable age. He looked the part, like a benevolent grandfather, a cross between Santa Claus and Benjamin Franklin; dressed in Quakerish simplicity and ill at ease in society, he called himself "a comical old fellow."[1] Around him, he gathered a class of disciples who venerated him as the pupils of Plato and Aristotle had revered their masters. For six decades, Bentham was a dominant figure in philosophical developments in the British Isles. And in practical developments too, for Bentham and his associates were largely responsible for the passage of social legislation that confined the heretofore absolute might of the owners of land and factories in England. It was in 1832, the year that the ancient British election laws were finally reformed, that Bentham died, passing his mantle to his younger associate, the journalist, James Mill, and later to the latter's more famous son, John Stuart Mill.

Bentham is usually identified as "the founder of utilitarianism,"[2] although, as we have seen, the concept that people behave according to what is useful for them is a very old idea indeed, originating with the Greeks and surfacing significantly in the philosophies of Hobbes, Hume, and Helvétius. There can be no doubt that Bentham was the most celebrated of the utilitarians; he was certainly the one most concerned with erecting a formal philosophy based on the concept of utility. Bentham, the son of a wealthy London lawyer, began his career as a conservative, but wound up a liberal reformer. His disciples identified themselves as the "School of Philosophical Radicalism."[3]

Of all the hundreds of thousands of pages he wrote in 64 years of philosophizing, nothing is better known than his unequivocal affirmation of the pleasure-pain principle, which he set down most clearly in the opening paragraphs of his *An Introduction to the Principles of Morals and Legislation*. This work was published in 1789, the year of the French Revolution and a decade after the death of Hume, when Bentham had just turned 40. "Nature," Bentham wrote, "has placed mankind under the governance of two sovereign masters, *pain* and *pleasure*." It is pleasure and pain that tell us what we ought to do, he said, adding:

> *They govern us in all we do, in all we say, in all we think. . . . In words a man may pretend to abjure their empire: but in reality he*

> *will remain subject to it all the while. The* principle of utility *recognises this subjection. . . . Systems which attempt to question it, deal in sounds instead of sense, in caprice instead of reason, in darkness instead of light.*[4]

In Bentham's imagery, men act on the basis of what they can use, of what has *utility* for them. And since it is human nature to seek pleasure and to avoid pain, conventional virtue and happiness lie largely in escaping pain.[5] By pleasure, Bentham and the utilitarians did not mean having a good time or enjoying bodily comfort; to them pleasure was essentially the opposite of pain. Health was pleasure. So was the "good" of humankind. At bottom, all human behavior is motivated by a desire for pleasure. It brings a legislator pleasure, for instance, to make good laws. It reduces the pain of a bad conscience to perform one's moral duty, like paying back debts. Why are justice and moderation virtues? he asks, and then answers: because they promote human happiness.

Bentham credited Hume with causing "the scales [to fall] from my eyes," but it was the work of the Frenchman Helvétius that Bentham considered most influential in his development of English utilitarianism.[6] It was largely from his reading of Helvétius that Bentham was able to construct what has become the unspoken but fundamental ideology of the "socially responsible" contemporary American journalist: the moral principle that it is ethical to publish information that provides the greatest amount of pleasure and the least amount of pain to the greatest number of people.[7]

It is clear that to print a photograph of a victim of a highway accident may well bring pain to the victim's relatives but then it might also contribute to the *greater good* by giving readers a better idea of what might happen if they do not practice highway safety. Whether or not the photograph *would* have this effect is not to be considered under Bentham's doctrine. It *might*, and that is the important factor. The further development and modification of Bentham's ideas by his disciple, John Stuart Mill, contributed much to the American belief system and the ideology of journalism.

Bentham did not claim authorship of the pleasure-pain principle; he said he found it first in the writings of the chemist Joseph Priestley, discoverer of oxygen, and in those of Beccaria, whose work was influential over the *philosophes*. A renowned Bentham scholar said he probably came across the idea in his reading of the Stoic, Cicero, who preached "the citizenship of the world."[8] In any case, Bentham was clearly influenced by Hobbes's distinction between "desires" and "aversions," but his portrait of human motivation was more charitable. Both Hobbes and Bentham saw mankind as selfish, but Bentham hedged a bit, maintaining that experience had taught men that they have one great interest in common: belief in the greatest good of the greatest number.[9]

Consistency was not among Bentham's strong points; over his long life, he made major modifications in his position, sometimes returning to an opinion of his early years that he had himself rejected. As a result of this inconsistency and also of his recurring tendency to eliminate emotional considerations from his world view, Bentham has come under heavy attack over the years, sometimes in highly abusive language.[10] Indeed, in retrospect it seems astonishing that a philosopher could attract such widespread attention, let alone so much criticism. Ralph Waldo Emerson, the New England transcendentalist, condemned Bentham's utilitarianism as "a stinking philosophy." Goethe, the great German liberal poet, condemned Bentham as "that frightfully radical ass." Marx, who read Bentham slavishly, labeled him "the arch philistine . . . the insipid leather-tongued oracle of the commonplace bourgeois intelligence . . . a genius in the way of bourgeois stupidity."[11] His own disciple, John Stuart Mill, was in his later years to condemn Bentham's ethics as "cold, mechanical, and ungenial."[12] It remained for Mill to convert that "cold" ethical system into the warm and benevolent humanism associated with his name.

Bentham was indeed overly cerebral; he saw the world in exclusively intellectual and rational terms, so much so that he failed to see, or in any case to acknowledge, the existence of social classes, a characteristic that troubled the young Mill. There is something fascinating about Bentham: he was personally wholly admirable and generous to the poor and needy, yet, as Mill said, his philosophy was quite mechanical and psychologically disturbing. While he himself retained a sunny, cheerful disposition, many among his followers preached a harsh doctrine, none more than John Stuart's father, James Mill. In any case, Bentham's interpretation of humankind as egoistic and concerned overwhelmingly with avoiding pain led him to hold that men could be discouraged from committing antisocial acts only under the threat of punishment that would bring the evildoer sufficient pain to overbalance the pleasure he might otherwise gain from his action. Bentham's resolution was a kind of "moral arithmetic." Although he was preoccupied with numbers, he was never able to offer a specific plan for how one could decide what was the *greatest* good or how one could determine the *greatest* number. He found himself returning always to his expressed hope that egoistic humankind would find it in their own self-interest to work for the common good.[13] Bentham was, in Mary Peter Mack's words, "a self-styled Romantic frankly chasing an admitted mirage."[14]

It can be seen that Bentham was the very epitome of the individualist. All human behavior was egoistic, with each person seeking his own pleasure and avoiding his own pain. In terms of economics, which we will discuss later, Bentham was a complete devotee of the doctrine of laissez-faire, the egoistic system in which each person is authorized to seek his own fortune without the intervention of government or instruments of society. It was a curious position for a social reformer, and it was the rock on which Benthamite utilitarianism would ultimately founder.

Much given to analogy, Bentham found in medicine the perfect metaphor to characterize the English society he saw around him. The body politic, he wrote, was "afflicted" with "ruinous injury . . . running sores . . . rottenness . . . inflammation, swelling, gout, and cholera . . . deformity and foul nakedness." The nation was sick, choked with the poisons of lies and corruption, he said, and needed reform.[15] In a phrase that may have influenced Marx's famed reference to religion as "the opiate of the masses," Bentham wrote that by means of "a perpetual fever," religion called for "a perpetual demand for opiates."[16]

An individual's devotion to his society and its institutions depended, in Bentham's doctrine, on their *utility*, that is to say, on what they did that was good for him. Hume had used utility as a substitute for natural rights, self-evident truths, eternal morality, and the harmony of nature. Utility measured self-interest. It was under the banner of utility that men worked to reform their environments. Each individual seeking to avoid the pain his institutions might cause him would automatically feel a sense of responsibility to change and modify them for the betterment of the greatest number.

A careful examination of utilitarianism offers some insights into the doctrine of social responsibility, a complex and often contradictory doctrine that has come to play such a major role in the professional ideology of American journalism. Social responsibility, of course, deals with what *ought* to be, but as Bentham pointed out (appropriately in his first major work in the eventful year of 1776), there is inevitably a radical distinction between what *is* and what *ought* to be.[17] Bentham maintained that he had found a way to tie the is and the ought together; he called it a *Novum Organum*, a "Natural System."

Looking, as he usually did, from the point of view of a judge in court, Bentham concluded that the law as then practiced took only one motive for human behavior into account: money. It was as if anybody could be bought, as if there were no psychological motives, such as the love of power or reputation or the passion of sex. In Bentham's Natural System, there were four subordinate motivations for human behavior, rising from equality to abundance to security to subsistence. And above them all was his own Golden Rule, the greatest-happiness principle.[18] A good, socially responsible government would aim at all times for the greatest good of the greatest number of its citizens. At the same time, it would work for the elimination of evil. In fact, that was the only justification Bentham saw for government interference in the lives of individuals: to protect them from a greater evil that might otherwise befall them. Bentham had been a law student of the great Blackstone, and wrote his *Fragment* in part to reply to Blackstone's legal codes. Along the way, the youthful Bentham demolished not only Blackstone's codes but also the popular ideas of the social contract and natural law.[19] True to his devotion to numbers, Bentham found the greatest evil to be one that caused the maximum of suffering.[20] Evil was thus measured in terms of its consequences, a yardstick that was to be adopted by the pragmatists of the twentieth century and was to become a centerpiece of the professional ideology of American journalists.

CHAPTER 24

Radical Economics and the Rise of Capitalism

One of the doleful products of the Industrial Revolution, especially in Britain, was the sharp increase in the numbers of the urban poor, a kind of semipermanent underclass dwelling in the teeming, unhealthy streets of the country's cities. Concern about the condition of the poor and their potential as a revolutionary force was a dominant factor in the Western world throughout the nineteenth century. Novelist Charles Dickens, who never forgot that his first job was in a wretched factory on the slime-ridden banks of the Thames in East London, wrote with power about the plight of the poor, especially in his 1854 novel, *Hard Times*. Both Mill and Marx had an opportunity to read Dickens and indeed to observe for themselves the poor of London; like Dickens, their thinking was profoundly affected by the ubiquitous presence of this underclass. Their solutions to the problem were, of course, sharply different. Mill preached reform; Marx preached revolution. Among other things, Bentham and the philosophical radicals were determined to try to ease the wretched living conditions of the urban poor.

In economics, Bentham was a follower of Adam Smith, who was a student of Hume and is properly revered as the intellectual father of capitalism. In the very year that the Declaration of Independence was announced (and that the youthful Bentham's *Fragment on Government* appeared), Smith was publishing his classic analysis of the basic doctrine of capitalism, *An Inquiry into the Nature and Causes of the Wealth of Nations*. Smith, a moralist and student of human nature as well as a philosopher of economics, exerted an enormous influence on the American Founders, especially John Adams, but also Jefferson and Madison.[1] In the spirit of Hume, Smith pronounced the primary motivation of human beings to be self-interest. It is, he said, in the interests of all of us, the great and the small, to add to our *wealth* and to increase the extent of our *power*. In earlier times, wealth and power might have been thought of as evil, but Smith saw them differently, as "something grand, and beautiful, and noble, of which the attainment is well worth all the toil and anxiety which we are so apt to bestow upon [them]."[2]

By ourselves acquiring wealth and power, by operating in our own self-interest, Smith was saying, we are working for the benefit of all human beings. When we operate in our own interests, he maintained, we are bringing good not only to ourselves but also to other individuals. Thus, the quest for profit is ethically sound. For a man to work for gain is valuable for all society, Smith wrote in a classic statement of the moral foundation of the doctrine of capitalism:

> *He [the individual] intends only his own gain . . . he is in this, as in many other cases, led by an invisible hand to promote an end which is no part of his intention. . . . By pursuing his own interest he frequently promotes that of the society more effectually than when he really intends to promote it. I have never known much good done by those who affected to trade for the public good.*[3]

One's own interest above the public good—that was Smith's message. His "invisible hand" came to symbolize the virtue of capitalism. The hand of nature will see to it that all are provided for, that justice and peace will triumph on earth. Man needs but to leave the market alone under the doctrine of laissez-faire and the invisible hand will do its job. Enlightened self-interest is of more value to humankind than the work of reformers or utopians. Altruism is in fact nothing more than a myth, a seductive narcotic for the simple folk. It is interesting to note that Marx, too, saw a seductive narcotic in capitalist society, but to him the drug was religion, not altruism. Mill, in revising the doctrine of self-interest preached by Smith and Bentham, saw the capacity for altruism and self-sacrifice as a perfectly natural human quality.[4]

Critics of capitalism revile its selfishness, arguing that unrestricted pursuit of wealth and power divides society into two opposing groups: the rich and powerful (in Marxist terminology the exploiters) versus the weak and helpless, the downtrodden, the exploited. Smith, like his modern American follower, Ayn Rand, saw this pursuit of wealth and power as beneficial, as promoting virtue, as fighting vice and corruption.[5] Such a view is the epitome of optimism. It is to take the basest of human motivations, greed, and to make of it a virtue for the social order.

For Adam Smith, nothing in human behavior was more futile than mere talk. "Man," he wrote, foreshadowing the modern doctrine of pragmatism, "was made for action."[6] Only through action, Smith said, can human beings change their environment and work for their own happiness as well as that of other people. To a person who merely reflects and speaks or writes, even though what he expresses may be the most lofty and generous of sentiments, we owe nothing: "We still can ask him.

What have you done? What actual service can you produce, to entitle you to so great a recompence? We esteem you and love you; but we owe you nothing."[7]

As Smith wrote, the Industrial Revolution was just getting underway and enterprise on the part of the rising commercial class, the capitalists, was blocked by the rules laid down by medieval guilds, which were themselves protected by intricate government regulations. Smith's doctrine of laissez-faire was aimed at getting rid of those government regulations and opening up new markets under the banner of free trade. His image of a happy new social order, made possible by the Industrial Revolution, was rooted in his sunny, optimistic attitude about the nature of humankind. Self-interested human beings would naturally work for the benefit of each other, since it is rational to do so.

Not everyone was so optimistic. No commentator stirred a wider reaction than Thomas Malthus, whose words struck terror into an untold number of minds when he wrote, in 1798, that the population of the world was increasing so rapidly that it had to be controlled or disaster would overtake humankind.[8] Malthus, a clergyman, was himself no utilitarian, but he became the leading prophet of the philosophical radicals. His most enduring observation—so powerful that we still today speak of it as "Malthusian"—was that while subsistence advances arithmetically, population increases geometrically.[9] By the year 2003, he wrote, 256 persons would have to live on land that then supported 9 individuals. Starvation, Malthus declared, was the only check to this geometrical population growth. In the spirit of Hobbes, Malthus spoke of a "struggle for existence," a notion that influenced the researches of Charles Darwin, and concluded that it was only the existence of evil—"misery and vice"—that might enable humankind to escape the horrors of limitless population growth.[10]

Poet Laureate Robert Southey condemned Malthus for writing "twopenny trash."[11] Others attacked him for denouncing charity and indeed the benevolence of God's plan. Malthus, on the other hand, considered himself a scientist and maintained that God had imposed moral and physical evils on us as "instruments employed by the Deity" to stimulate us into thinking up ways to solve our problems. Disease, he said, is a sign that we have broken a law of nature; the plague of London was a hint that the city had better improve its system of sanitation. Moral restraint was the ultimate answer, not government intervention, Malthus said. Social inequality, he wrote, was also part of God's plan, since it taught people to, among other things, curb their sexual passions so as to avoid having too many children who could not escape from poverty. In the spirit of laissez-faire, he proposed a kind of do-it-yourself program for rising from poverty. It was simply prudent to *work* to avoid becoming poor.[12]

Malthus's analysis was expanded by David Ricardo, a wealthy banker, in an 1817 book he called *Principles of Political Economy and Taxation*, which has been labeled "the economic Bible of the Utilitarians."[13] In that book, written under the encouragement of his good friend, James Mill, Ricardo drew not only on Smith and Malthus, but also on Locke. His major contribution was his theory of value, which was later to be adapted by Marx into his theory of socialism. Ricardo divided the economic world into three classes: landowners, capitalists, and workers, "the proprietor of the land, the owner of the stock or capital necessary for its cultivation, and the labourers by whose industry it is cultivated."[14] True to the forward-looking utilitarian faith, he dismissed landowners as parasites, vestiges of a dead past, selfishly protecting their own power base as successors to the feudal aristocracy. He denounced landowners for protecting their vested interests, for maintaining tough poor laws that condemned debtors to prison, and for resisting the introduction of machinery that would raise a new class of consumers. Like his friend, James Mill, and like Bentham and Malthus, Ricardo was a kind man, charitable to the poor, and a supporter of education. Again and again, he urged the poor to raise their standards, but, like the other utilitarians, he had a rosy view of human behavior. He too rejected government help for the poor and demanded of them that they rise by their own bootstraps. Leslie Stephen suggests that Ricardo's motto might have been expressed in these words: "Let a man starve if he will not work, and he will work."[15]

Under Ricardo's theory of value, with landowners dismissed from the equation, the profits of capitalists and the wages of laborers were inextricably connected. When wages went up, profits went down. And vice versa. Ricardo wrestled with the question of how to resolve this antagonism which, he said, lay in part in "the niggardliness of nature and the greed of man."[16] To Ricardo, as to many economists who followed him, economics was indeed the dismal science. He turned to Bentham and the greatest-happiness principle for his resolution. Ricardo hedged and found refuge in obscure language when the resolution seemed too difficult for him, but in the end, he took the position that by each seeking his own happiness, capitalists and workers would naturally join forces for the betterment of the political economy. Relying on Adam Smith's analysis of supply and demand and on the invisible hand he saw as directing the market, Ricardo wrote: "The pursuit of individual advantage is admirably connected with the universal good of the whole."[17]

Ricardo's theory of value was an ideal instrument for the philosophical radicals who wanted free trade and an end to "artificial" government regulations. Since the greatest-happiness principle authorized legislators to take action when they wanted to alleviate intolerable pain, the radicals launched a relentless campaign, primarily in the press, to pressure Parliament into action. They founded a new journal, the *Westminster Review*, under the direction of James Mill, who added mightily to the "watchdog" doctrine in the professional ideology of journalists with a ringing declaration that a free press is and properly ought to be a means of "removing the defects of vicious governments."[18]

James Mill plays an important role in the development of a professional ideology for journalists and indeed in the expansion of the utilitarian philosophy. Mill was still a young man when he met Bentham.

A Scot who had failed to earn a post after studying for the Presbyterian ministry, he came to London to take up a career as a journalist and was elected to Parliament in 1802 at the age of 29, one of the first men to make it there strictly on his talents and not through aristocratic birth.[19] The elderly Bentham found Mill's youthful enthusiasm and dedication to utilitarian ideas not only attractive but of enormous value. Bentham set Mill up in a residence formerly occupied by Milton in Queen Square, where he also lived, and supported him financially.[20] Mill, handsome and articulate, served for three decades as Bentham's spokesman in public. Emery Neff tells us that the charm of his conversation was notable, even in an age of great talkers.[21] With unmasked distaste, Bertrand Russell remarks that James Mill's outlook was limited by "the poverty of his emotional nature," but adds that he "had the merits of industry, disinterestedness, and rationality."[22] As we will see later, his influence on his son, John Stuart, was extraordinary.

Before turning to Mill's ideas on journalism, it is useful to examine the political and social environment in which the radicals found themselves. It was a period of great upheaval. Few events in history have stirred the imagination of the civilized world as did the French Revolution. Libertarians like Paine and James Mill were enthusiastic about the promise it offered of a new life under the banner of the Rights of Man. Others, like Burke, were horrified by the bloody excesses that followed the triumph of the Jacobins. In any case, one of the direct results of the revolution was a widespread agitation in the British Isles for sweeping changes in the fabric of society that would lift the poor out of poverty and offer the working classes an opportunity to partake of the good life promised by the Industrial Revolution. Popular support for the writings of Smith, Malthus, and Ricardo, especially from the adherents of the liberal political party, the Whigs, must be seen in this light. On the other hand, the conservatives, the Tories, became increasingly fearful, as the nineteenth century advanced into its third decade, that revolution would come to England.

British and Prussian forces, representing the interests of the conservative governments of those countries, defeated Napoleon at Waterloo and sent him into exile. The peace of 1815 brought a serious depression in the market for English manufactured goods at home and abroad and gave momentum to the radicals' drive for reform.

Fearfully concerned about protecting their privileged position, the Tories in Parliament ratified a series of laws that drew the ire of the radicals. The radicals countered with a program that ultimately brought to an end the chaotic pattern of laws and the obstinate resistance of the church and the universities to modernization.[23] Chief among the hated laws were the notorious Corn Laws, which taxed the bread of the poor. Many of these laws were not to be overturned until 1846, but that action was inevitable following the reform of Parliament a dozen years earlier. It was the precedent-setting Reform Bill of 1832 that prepared the stage for the social legislation of the nineteenth century, as it brought to an end the centuries-old system that had guaranteed seats in Parliament to large landowners and a veto power over all modernizing legislation. Edmund Burke, that staunch defender of tradition and the beneficence of the past, struggled mightily and unsuccessfully against the reform plan, arguing that the Benthamites had failed to see that "the tyranny of the multitude is a multiplied tyranny."[24] James Mill was the chief propagandist for that reform bill and, more importantly, for a doctrine of journalistic activism that has rarely been spelled out more clearly.

CHAPTER 25

James Mill: The Press as Agitators

The question of the power of the press is central in the ideology of journalism. How powerful are newspapers? Or, in modern language, the media? (Philosophically, there is no difference.) Seldom is there a gathering of journalists or journalism educators without that question emerging as a major topic of conversation. Indeed, the question has become central in all conversations whenever power comes under discussion. The contribution of James Mill to this theme is towering, although often overlooked by American historians. For it was Mill who developed a theory that "news" could be a political weapon. Not opinion, not commentary, but news, the reporting of actual events, the dissemination of facts. The heart of Mill's doctrine is contained in an essay he wrote for a supplement to the fifth edition of the *Encyclopedia Britannica* that appeared in 1825.

Mill grew to manhood in troubled times. The world was changing rapidly under the stimulation of new industry. Factory towns sprang up, especially in the northern counties of England and in Mill's Scotland. There emerged, for the first time in history, a mass of urban laborers, a "working class," a proletariat. These workers were without political power; under existing English law, they were disenfranchised. They were not permitted to vote. And when they lost their jobs, they had no claim on public welfare. Although they had no power, to many in England the representatives of this new class were a frightening lot. Memories of the terror that followed the French Revolution were long. Rebellion could, the political leadership feared, come to England as well.

Revolutions have almost always been organized and carried out by intellectuals, but in England, intellectuals like Bentham and his radical followers, were themselves sobered by memories of the French Revolution. They gave their whole-hearted support to the workers, but their hope for reform rested in the benevolence of the ruling classes or, to use the term that originated with Bentham, "the Establishment." They saw the principle of utility as leading inevitably to social reform that would work to the benefit of the greatest number of British citizens.

Mill came up with a better idea: why not use the press as the instrument of reform? He had been writing about press freedom for a dozen years before he got his article, "Liberty of the Press," into the *Encyclopedia*, at a time when fearful government agencies were cracking down on reformist articles by radical journalists. Even Bentham was sufficiently concerned about the threat of censorship that he suppressed one of his own works for a dozen years. Mill's expressed purpose was a revision in the libel law. He concluded that it was proper for the government to ban only one kind of statement in the press: a call to use force and violence against a specific government action, for example, to print a handbill that might "excite a mob" to disturb a particular trial or obstruct police from carrying out their duties.[1] As far as Mill's theory was concerned, anything else was acceptable; even an article that urged resistance in general, since this would be aimed at "some great change in the government at large," not a specific action. Since it was rare for a publication to urge direct, explicit action, Mill's proposal meant almost complete freedom for the press to attack the government, with the clear aim of "removing the effects of vicious governments."[2]

Fundamental change was Mill's goal, and his mechanism for bringing about fundamental change was the press. In fact, it became clear later, Mill perceived the press as the *main* instrument to force the government into making social change. It is important to keep in mind the basic belief of the utilitarians: that human beings always behave in their own interest. Reform would take place only, Mill was convinced, when the government could be made to see that it was in its own self-interest to bring about reforms. Thus, the job of the press was to make the government so afraid of revolution that it would order the reforms itself as being a greater good than rebellion in the streets.

The crucial element in Mill's doctrine was that it was necessary for activist journalists to play the role of public relations specialists, to become in fact "agitators and agents" in behalf of whatever it was that they were striving to accomplish. Their power lay in creating *images of reality* and circulating those images far and wide. One backer of the Reform Bill made the point clearly during debate in Parliament; he said that such press agitators were an inevitable part of any "concerted democratic movement."[3]

Few of the radical journalists who adopted Mill's theory and carried it into practice can be characterized as revolutionaries. The great majority of them, Mill included, were not prepared to take to the barricades. But they were determined to make it appear that the people, especially the new urban working classes, were ready to rebel. Under prodding by Mill's "threat theory," they perfected "the language of menace." To Albany Fonblanque, a journalist for the London *Chronicle* and *Examiner*, Mill wrote:

> *The people, to be in the best state, should appear to be ready and impatient to break out into action, without actually breaking out. The Press, which is our only instrument, has at this moment the most delicate and the most exalted functions to discharge that any power has yet had to perform in this country.*[4]

Dutifully, Fonblanque wrote that if the Reform Bill then before Parliament were defeated, the north of England "would be in insurrection instantly."[5] Mill's friend, John Black, was equally threatening in the *Chronicle*. "Let it never be forgotten," Black wrote, in language readily recognizable today, "that power is with the people, and that the people have merely to resolve, and their purpose is effected." Paraphrasing a comment by Mill, he added: "Nothing but fear will act upon these infatuated persons."[6] Joseph Parkes, one of the ablest of the journalists of that day, remarked cautiously that he himself was a moderate fellow but that he could never discount the irrational impulses of the people, and thus could not "blind himself to the perils of the crisis. If anarchy occurred, its horror in this country would far exceed any ever recorded."[7]

Mill and Parkes were determined to remake the rhetoric of radicalism. Their strategy, rooted in a common perception of the power of the press, was designed to reshape the beliefs of the governing classes about what the people felt and believed, and thus to invent rather than report public opinion. Parkes was anything but modest about the power of the press: it was the steam engine of the political arena. "What James Watt was in science in the application of the power of steam," he said, "we now want in the political science."[8] To Mill and his colleagues, we are indebted for that part of the professional ideology of journalists that portrays the press as the mirror of public opinion. The history of ideas is filled with irony, and rarely is the irony more remarkable than here, where it can be seen that the press, in serving as an agent of change in nineteenth-century Britain, did so to a large extent by consciously creating an image of revolution in a society where revolution was very unlikely indeed.

It is beyond the scope of this study to examine in detail the interesting history of political and social reform in Britain, but it is to be noted that it was in the spring of 1832, under the prodding of the radical journalists, that the so-called Reform Bill was at last enacted. This measure overturned the old system of "pocket boroughs," where English aristocrats could be elected to Parliament to represent districts populated by more cows than people. That bill also extended the franchise to small property owners, but it did not go anywhere near so far as the radicals wanted. And it was not until 1846 that the infamous Corn Laws were repealed. Mill's son, John Stuart Mill, played a part in the agitation for repeal of the Corn Laws.

In retrospect, it seems doubtful that Britain was ripe for revolution in those days, but there were a number of incidents of violence, and there were occasional public riots, notably in 1831 in Bristol and Nottingham, resulting in the execution of seven persons. Leaders in Parliament often expressed opinions in their private correspondence that insurrection was likely, and there can be little doubt that these opinions were fanned by the dramatic, menacing articles in the press. When Marx arrived in Britain, nearly 20 years later, he found historical confirmation of the beliefs he had already developed on the Continent, that the press had great potential as an agitator and agent to raise the level of consciousness of the working classes to the awareness that they were being exploited by capitalists. He saw how the English press, under the guidance of James Mill and his students, had raised the awareness—not only of the workers but also of the politically powerful—that change in the relations between social and economic classes was at hand. He could read it, for instance, in the writings of de Tocqueville, who had hurried to England in 1833 to see for himself.[9]

English journalists watched with interest the events taking place across the Channel in France, where efforts at censorship by a rightist government had led to rioting in the streets and ultimately to the fall of the regime. In the United States, an intensely democratic public was turning to what some writers have called "a coonskin democracy," replacing the patrician presidents of Virginia and Massachusetts with populist leaders, chief among them Andrew Jackson. The American newspapers were extolling the "age of the common man." The impulses in England were similar, but here, the ruling aristocracy was being frightened by newspapers shouting the language of revolution.

Sociologists have pointed out in recent years that one of the functions of the news media is the restructuring of events.[10] Since news stories are not presented in chronological form, the journalist is obviously taking events apart, imposing his own news values—or judgment—on those events, and then giving them a new form, with the most important element going into the lead rather than in the position where it in fact took place. Some facts are included, some are left out. Some facts are emphasized, some are ignored. Reality is lost and replaced by the journalist's construction of that reality. This reconstruction is accomplished for the most part in order to impart drama and order to the news accounts, not for political goals. Mill's reconstruction was, however, for purely political ends. The way in which he and his journalistic friends reconstructed reality was designed to shape the image of reality of readers, the ordinary garden variety type, and the lawmakers, who were being pressed to enact reform legislation. What Mill was after was, in effect, a kind of brainwashing, so that the picture of the world that rose in the heads of readers was the picture the reformers wanted there. Advertisers, of course, follow the same plan of attack in marketing their products.

The mechanism was fear and intimidation. The reform movement in Parliament encouraged Mill's journalists to pour it on. Edward Ellice, a Whig leader, told Parkes to keep it up: "The apprehension of the coming thunder is often greater than the fear of the actual storm, and I suppose you will take all reasonable means to announce it."[11] The goal was to convince the Conservatives that the only "way to avert revolution was to abandon opposition to inevitable causes."[12] Parkes himself was a zealot for what he called "the law of public opinion," and promised to agitate to the death in the cause of reform. The demonstrators, "the out-door men," as he called them, were the hero-fanatics of the journalistic reformers, and "fanaticism is as essential in politics as it is in religion."[13]

It was assuredly a time when rambunctious journalism was the order of the day. One of those who joined in the campaign for reform, although no friend of Mill, was a journalist named William Cobbett, who escaped his native land to go to America and proceeded to heap verbal abuse on the rebels, incurring the wrath of Thomas Jefferson.[14] Writing under the name of "Peter Porcupine," Cobbett became the most prolific defender of the cause of the British during the revolutionary years in the United States. Jefferson acknowledged to a correspondent that in his "implacable hatred," Cobbett had subjected him to such vilification that Jefferson had determined to write letters to associates and not to newspapers, indeed, "never to put a sentence into any newspaper."[15]

Cobbett was driven out of the United States and returned to England to join in the reform movement. He held Mill in contempt, sneering at him as one of the Scottish "feelosophers."[16] Cobbett also had no use for Mill's journalistic tactics and was a sharp critic of the corruption of English journalists, who accepted money and gifts from officials in return for favorable articles. There is no evidence that the upright James Mill was guilty of any misconduct. On the other hand, he would find it difficult today to justify the way he raised his famous son, John Stuart.

CHAPTER 26

John Stuart Mill: Utilitarianism Revisited

No philosopher has commanded a greater following in the United States and among American journalists than John Stuart Mill. Max Lerner, a prominent political scientist and newspaper columnist, wrote in 1961 that Mill was "a towering intellectual who is as fresh as tomorrow morning's newspaper and as relevant as the latest publicized crisis of our time." Of all the figures in Western liberal thought, Lerner wrote, summarizing a widely held view, Mill stands alone in originality of thought, so much so that his ideas have "become part of the intellectual air we breathe."[1] An admiring Isaiah Berlin speaks of Mill as the founder of modern liberalism and "the most passionate and best-known champion in England of the insulted and the oppressed."[2]

Mill is indeed the quintessential liberal, author of the strongest affirmation of the doctrine of free expression since Milton. His *Essay on Liberty*, numbering only 60 pages, appeared in 1859 and has been quoted by supporters of free speech and a free press ever since.[3] As George Sabine has noted, Mill's *Liberty* stands with Milton's *Areopagitica* as "the most classical defenses of freedom in the English language."[4] It was also 1859 that Charles Darwin published *On the Origin of Species*, his report on evolution, and a then little-known German economist named Karl Marx issued his *Critique of Political Economy*.

The eldest son of James Mill, John is renowned not only for his contributions to the literature of freedom and his radical revision of the philosophy of utilitarianism, but also for his personal victory over the stresses of one of the strangest childhoods in history. From his earliest years, Mill was taught the virtues of Benthamism; indeed, he claimed to have coined the word *utilitarianism* for the doctrine preached by Bentham and his father. But, although he continued to consider himself a utilitarian, he redefined the philosophy of utilitarianism, moving it into a new direction, away from the cold, analytical and dispassionate thinking that characterized it under Bentham and indeed under his father.

Mill was the complete synthesizer. He set the tone for all his writings in his first major effort, *A System of Logic*, in which he pronounced his intention "to harmonize the true portions of discordant theories."[5] Mill was 22 years old when he began this effort to overturn the theories of logic that had dominated Western thinking for centuries; he worked at the book off and on for 13 years.

To bring into harmony what was true about all the theories of the past, to discard the false and the disproved, and to demonstrate how the good society could be built on the framework of many contradictory ideas—this was the remarkable goal that Mill had in mind as he set about his task. It was, simply, to build a philosophy that incorporated the best of the eighteenth and nineteenth centuries, the best of the rational thinkers of the Enlightenment and the passionate activists of the romantic movement, the best of the liberal utilitarian Bentham and the conservative romantic poet Samuel Taylor Coleridge. It was, of course, a massive, ultimately unsuccessful, undertaking, but few individuals—perhaps none before him—had been as peculiarly trained to undertake the assignment.

The idea was James Mill's. Seven weeks after John's birth in 1806 and two years before meeting Bentham, Mill challenged a friend (whose wife had also recently delivered an infant son) to a trial that would determine which of them 20 years later could "exhibit the most accomplished & virtuous young man," an excellently informed and perfectly rational being.[6] History does not tell us whether the wager was accepted and, if so, who was declared the winner, but it is difficult to doubt that it would have been James Mill. Believing as he did in the power of education, Mill set about training his son in every field he could imagine, knowledge of which would make John an accomplished and virtuous young man. The education of John Mill is carefully reported, with noteworthy sensitivity, in his *Autobiography*, which he wrote many years later and which has served as the major resource material for the many psychohistorians who have found him a fascinating subject.[7]

In keeping with his plan, James Mill cut his son off from his mother and playmates and undertook to be his sole instructor. By the age of three, the boy was learning Greek and tackling literature, languages, mathematics, logic, political science, economics, geography, history, psychology, and rhetoric. He read extensively the work of Hobbes, Locke, Hume, and Bentham. He spent all his time—when not alone—with his father, discussing his studies, answering questions, and taking long walks. He had no other exercise. His education was almost entirely cerebral. In his training, there was no place for religion or metaphysics and little room for poetry, all of these stigmatized by Bentham as "the accumulation of human idiocy and error."[8] Glassman minces no words in his characterization of James Mill who, he says, emerges from the *Autobiography* "a monster . . . heartless and even psychopathic."[9] The criticism of James Mill seems a bit overdrawn, but one cannot doubt that John grew up emotionally stunted; indeed, he reports in his *Autobiography* that he grew to adulthood without any understanding of the power of human passions, since his father had taught him that all problems could be resolved by thought and careful analysis.[10] Lerner describes the home of James Mill as a "house of intellect."[11]

It is remarkable in retrospect that John was able to recover from the misshaping of his personality. Curiously enough, it was literature—and a trip to France—that enabled the young man to rid himself of a deadly depression that descended on him as he approached the age of 20 and that threatened to destroy him altogether. It was the work of the romantic poets, particularly William Wordsworth, that served as Mill's "medicine." As Mill described it, "What made Wordsworth's poems a medicine for my state of mind was that . . . they seemed to me the very culture of the feelings, that I was in quest of."[12] In France, Mill encountered an intellectual world enriched by the writings of the *philosophes:* Helvétius, whom his father and Bentham admired so thoroughly; Voltaire, whose encyclopedic mind fascinated him; and Rousseau, whose *Confessions* has much the ring of Mill's *Autobiography*. In France, Mill came under the influence of two important nineteenth-century Frenchmen, Henri de Saint-Simon and Auguste Comte, whose writings were important in moving Mill away from classical Benthamism.

Two years after his return from France, at the age of 23, Mill was introduced to Harriet Hardy Taylor, who was destined to succeed his father as his primary influence. Mrs. Taylor was the wife of a prosperous London merchant, and a woman of great charm and powerful intellect. For 19 years, until the death of Taylor, Mill and Mrs. Taylor carried on an intimate but platonic relationship that shocked members of the Victorian world in which they traveled and which Mill described in detail in his *Autobiography*, in glowing words that rival the expression of fictional lovers. They married in 1851, upon the death of Taylor, and worked together until Harriet's death eight years later. Mill dedicated *On Liberty* to her, convinced that it was her ideas more than his that had been expressed in it.[13]

Reformist impulses had seized Mill long before he met Harriet. At the age of 15, he had seen himself as "a reformer of the world."[14] But Harriet added a new dimension to those impulses: social and political radicalism. Together, they envisaged a brave new world, one of nearly total freedom, one of morality without religion. At times, Mill's push for reform led him to the edge of socialism.

Mill was a compulsive writer. Throughout his life, he wrote a continual string of essays and journal articles, none more interesting than his companion essay-critiques of Bentham and Coleridge, studies which, not surprisingly, did not appear until after the death of James Mill. In his teens, he helped his father write his *Elements of Political Economy*, relying extensively on the works of Adam Smith, Malthus, and Ricardo. His own *System of Logic* appeared in 1843 and his *Principles of Political Economy* five years later. The two philosophical works that are most widely read today are *On Liberty* and *Utilitarianism*, the latter a collection of three essays written in 1861 and published as a book two years later. Mill's *Autobiography* appeared shortly after his death in 1873, and has won widespread applause as one of the most fascinating self-examinations of all time.

The essays on Bentham and Coleridge and the book on utilitarianism are of a piece. They represent an attempt on Mill's part to humanize Bentham's doctrine, to rid it of what Mill considered its narrow and heartless qualities, its "cold, mechanical and ungenial air,"[15] and to reinterpret it as a doctrine of reform. Mill wrote as a polemicist, seeking, as he always did, to reconcile opposing points of view. Here, he wanted to convince the disciples of Bentham and the followers of Coleridge that the doctrine of utility could be reinterpreted as a guide to the good life.[16] Mill held the bald egoism of Benthamism in contempt; he rejected the idea that pleasure—or happiness, or utility—could be made to equal goodness. It was more complex than that, Mill said, arguing that Bentham, while correct on many things, was too one-sided, too rigidly legal, on this point. For example, he said, it might have been *right* for Brutus to sentence his son to death, since he was carrying out the law of the land, but that there was certainly nothing *lovable* about that action. The greatest-pleasure principle treated human behavior as if it had only one aspect, rightness, that is to say, a moral aspect. In fact, Mill wrote, there are three aspects to human behavior:

> *Every human action has three aspects: its* moral *aspect, or that of its* right *and* wrong*; its* aesthetic *aspect, or that of its* beauty*; its* sympathetic *aspect, or that of its* lovableness*. The first addresses itself to our reason and conscience; the second to our imagination; the third to our human fellow-feeling.*[17]

In truth, what Mill was doing was destroying the core of Benthamism. He was saying that it rested on a false view of human nature, because it did not comprehend what actually holds society together. It recognized, as Mill said, only the "business" aspects of life and not its ideals, loyalties, love of beauty, love of order, power, even action. In short, the utilitarianism of Bentham and James Mill had no place for what touches the human spirit, or what Coleridge called the "inward man." It had no place, either, for different tastes. Bentham's most often, usually unfavorably, quoted remark, was that "quantity of pleasure being equal, push-pin is as good as poetry." Mill said that Bentham's rigid adherence to his pleasure-pain principle led him into such absurdities.[18] He could make such statements, Mill wrote, because his "knowledge of human nature is bounded," always rational, never recognizing the emotions. Unlike Bentham, Mill accepted altruism, goodness for its own sake, as a human characteristic. Mill spoke of "the social feelings of mankind; the desire to be in unity with our fellows." These feelings, he said, lead one "to identify his *feelings* more and more with their good. . . . He comes, as though instinctively, to be conscious of himself as a being who *of course* pays regard to others."[19] What had caused his own fierce depression at the age of 20 was precisely what was wrong about Bentham's utilitarianism.[20]

Yet, Mill was not prepared to discard Bentham. He continued, despite his efforts at redefinition, to hold that each man inevitably pursues his own pleasure, a moral stance which, as Bertrand Russell points out, tends to reduce ethics to prudence.[21] No doubt Mill was psychologically incapable of repudiating his father in the public print. In a particularly moving passage, he honored his mentor (and incidentally his father):

> *To reject his half of the truth because he overlooked the other half, would be to fall into his error without having his excuse. For our own part, we have a large tolerance for one-eyed men, provided their one eye is a penetrating one: if they saw more, they probably would not see so keenly, nor so eagerly pursue one course of inquiry.*[22]

Bentham and James Mill were eternally to be praised, Mill wrote, because they stood firmly against any form of dogmatism, any transcendental or intuitive understanding of life, or muddiness of thought. To these principles of utilitarianism Mill remained true all his life, and he continued to describe happiness as the sole end of human existence, but his definition of happiness, while never entirely clear, certainly differed sharply from that of Bentham. It was here that he turned to the arguments of Coleridge. The time had come, Mill wrote, for philosophers to sweep away reliance on the purely cerebral doctrines of Locke and his successor, Bentham, and to turn to "the age of real psychology."[23] It was time to unite the rational doctrine of the English philosophers with the more romantic doctrines of Coleridge, which had been taken from the Germans, the philosopher Kant and the poet Goethe, who "saw so much farther into the complexities of the human intellect and feelings."[24]

True to his lifelong quest for synthesis, Mill gave added impetus to the code of objectivity, so dominant a factor in the professional ideology of journalists. There are two sides to all philosophies, Mill wrote in his *Essay on Coleridge*:

> *Thus it is in regard to every important partial truth; there are always two conflicting modes of thought, one tending to give to that truth too large, the other to give it too small, a place: and the history of opinion is generally an oscillation between these extremes. . . . Every excess in either direction determines a corresponding reaction; improvement consisting only in this, that the oscillation, each time, depart rather less widely from the centre, and an ever-increasing tendency is manifested to settle finally in it.*[25]

There may be no more clearly expressed stance on the ethics of journalistic objectivity than this. By presenting "both sides," by demonstrating in print that there is more than one sound opinion, the objective, balanced reporter brings the reader closer to truth, to the moderate center, to the place found only by demonstrating the "oscillation between these extremes." Interestingly, Mill was no admirer of the philosophical doctrines of Coleridge and the Germans, which he found "erroneous"—sound enough psychologically, but far off in their arrogant assumption of truth and in their failure to reject dogmatic certainty. But there was partial truth in Coleridge's romantic doctrine, with its emphasis on culture and history, and especially on the imagination. Coleridge was another "one-eyed man," but to him "the age of psychology" had made it clear that social ties were stronger and more subtle than the legal bonds on which Bentham had relied so heavily.

CHAPTER 27

The Gospel of Liberty

Mill was 53 years old when his *Essay On Liberty* was published. Harriet was only recently dead and Mill himself was ailing, living the life of a recluse in France. In isolation, he was unchanged: tall and spare, bald, bleak, bookish, humorless, a caricature of the Victorian schoolmaster. Mill was a living illustration of that traditional journalistic hero, the lonely fighter for freedom and justice. Few contemporaries recognized the intellectual fire that seethed beneath his austere exterior. Indeed, few philosophers have been as passionate about *ideas* as Mill, a characteristic, as we will see, that divided him sharply from the equally passionate Karl Marx. Mill dreamed large dreams of what a human being might do with his or her intellect, especially to move people to recognize the blessings of freedom. Certainly, this essay is in the nature of a religious poem, a lofty tribute to many of the ideas that infuse American journalism with their vitality. That the essay is flawed in its logic and its consistency is largely irrelevant; its power lies in its central theme.

James Mill had taught his son to refuse to fall into what he thought of as the pitfalls of religion, and John was indeed an agnostic. His religion was freedom, and he stated it with simple clarity: "The only freedom which deserves the name, is that of pursuing our own good in our own way, so long as we do not attempt to deprive others of theirs."[1] Mill's humanism was rooted in freedom of choice: to think as you choose; to express your opinions as you wish, in speech, in writing, in behavior; to frame your own tastes; to join with whomever you wish. Just so long, Mill said, as you do not interfere with someone else's freedom. In fact, the only justification for a government to restrict a person's freedom is when he is trying to harm another, "to produce evil to someone else." Otherwise, Mill said, a man's "independence is, of right, absolute. Over himself, over his own body and mind, the individual is sovereign."[2]

It was in drawing a distinction between the threat to freedom from *society* and the threat from *government* that Mill made his greatest contribution to the idea of liberty. It was not from government, from official sources, that a man's freedom faces the greatest challenge, Mill said, but rather from society, from other human beings—especially when they constitute a majority. Mill met de Tocqueville on several occasions and was in thorough agreement with his French colleague about the damage that might be caused to the fabric of society by a tyranny of the majority. It was public opinion that Mill saw as the gravest threat to individual freedom. Nowhere is this doctrine expressed more powerfully than in Mill's most famous dictum:

> *If all mankind minus one were of one opinion, and only one person were of the contrary opinion, mankind would be no more justified in silencing that one person than he, if he had the power, would be justified in silencing mankind.*[3]

Behind this statement, one can see, lay Mill's serious doubts about democracy, wherein the pressures of public opinion could well result in a society of conformists—and conformity would limit the arrival of fresh ideas, stultify society, and prevent the kind of growth that could come about only with the introduction of new ideas. Mill hated conformity of opinion; social persecution might well tip a democratic society in that direction. "We can never be sure," Mill wrote, "that the opinion we are endeavoring to stifle is a false opinion; and if we were sure, stifling it would be an evil still."[4]

To be a nonconformist was a positive virtue. "The mere example of non-conformity, the mere refusal to bend the knee to custom," he wrote, "is a service."[5] It was "the pressure of public opinion" that concerned Mill, who took the position, in a passage with a very contemporary ring, that the education practices in England had already seen to it that people "now read the same things, listen to the same things, see the same things, go to the same places, have their hopes and fears directed to the same objects."[6] Moved, as was de Tocqueville, to defend dissent and heretics, Mill expressed "his hatred of the human pack in full cry against a victim."[7] Mill was especially fearful of "moral police," who sought to urge conformity even in private affairs, such as one's sexual relations. In this context, Mill was especially distressed when people, including some he thought were his friends, like the essayist-historian, Thomas Carlyle, seemed horrified by his unconventional relationship with Harriet. Mill maintained that men and women ought not be held accountable to society or to public opinion for their actions.

One of the central benefits that comes with liberty, Mill said, is the right to be wrong, the right to make mistakes. It is because the truth cannot be found, Mill believed, that dissent is necessary, that the "many sides" of truth need to be given free expression.[8] There is no way that truth could be self-evident. In *On Liberty* as well as in *Utilitarianism*, Mill spoke out in opposition to so-called philosophers who *knew* what was true on the basis of their own intuition.[9] Thus, there could never be any fixed ethical rules, such as Kant's categorical imperative. Some of Mill's critics believe that he went too far in his opposition to intuitionism, so much so that he did not write into his ethical theory the critical element of Kant's doctrine that it is wrong for one to treat someone else as a means for his attaining his own ends.[10] This criticism is probably unfair, since at the center of all Mill's thought, as well as Kant's, was the idea that we must always bear responsibility for whatever consequences are caused by our behavior.

In holding that human knowledge is never complete, always fallible, Mill gave voice to an idea that has found a home in the professional ideology of American journalists. Mill made his point in an examination of what was known then as the human sciences and today as the social sciences. Since conclusions in these fields are so confused and uncertain, he said, they cannot be legitimately referred to as "sciences." Moreover, he took the position, as do most contemporary journalists, that it is simply impossible to draw valid generalizations or laws about human behavior. Mill was resisting the teachings of the Social Darwinist, Herbert Spencer (whose work we will examine later), and the French positivist, Auguste Comte, both of whom proudly proclaimed "a science of society." Here, too, Mill was in sharp disagreement with Marx. In the spirit of the great skeptic, David Hume, he argued that the best answers we could ever find were *probable* answers, not only in what he called the "ideological" fields—ethics, politics, religion, history—but in the natural sciences as well.[11]

Among other things, Mill sought in *On Liberty* to modify the self-righting principle enunciated by John Milton. Milton, it will be remembered, had written that the Truth must always prevail in a free fight with Falsehood. Mill disagreed. Milton's dictum, he wrote, "is one of those pleasant falsehoods which men repeat one after another till they pass into commonplace, but which all experience refutes." Instead, Mill said, it is "a piece of idle sentimentality that truth, merely as truth, has any inherent power denied to error of prevailing against the dungeon and the stake." There are too many times, he said, when history shows truth suppressed by persecution. But, in a more positive vein, Mill said, such suppression would last only for a while, not forever:

> *The real advantage which truth has, consists in this, that when an opinion is true, it may be extinguished once, twice, or many times, but in the course of ages there will generally be found persons to rediscover it, until some one of its reappearances fall on a time when from favorable circumstances it escapes persecution until it has made such head as to withstand all subsequent attempts to suppress it.*[12]

Despite his unswerving devotion to the cause of liberty, Mill was no democrat. Like de Tocqueville, he remained suspicious about the very workings of democracy. Majorities frightened Mill; he could never be sure that majorities would not invoke their moral police to try to stifle the dissent and nonconformity he believed were essential to the good life. In keeping with a man who believed his life's calling was to synthesize human knowledge, Mill's view of human nature was inconsistent—at times the embodiment of optimism, but at other times exhibiting all the qualities of a pessimist. What more optimistic view of the nature of humankind could there be than in Mill's fundamental assumption that we are rational people, who, when presented with the evidence of good and evil, will choose the good. Certainly, in his lonely isolation, Mill was cut off from awareness of the dark and irrational forces gathering strength in nineteenth-century Europe. Marx understood those forces far better; as would Sigmund Freud in the next century. On the other hand, Mill's pessimism emerges in his distrust of people in groups, in majorities and public opinion. Like his mentor, Jeremy Bentham, he often referred to the social order in medical terms, as sick and diseased. And, while he feared the collapse of democracy into mob rule, he continued to believe that it was only in a democratic society that human beings could experience the liberty he so passionately wished for them. Mill's man was a complex combination of opposites, unpredictable, creative, fallible, incomplete, always restlessly seeking happiness, truth, and freedom, but never able altogether to achieve them.[13]

It is important to keep in mind that although Mill was indeed the complete individualist, he did not, by any means, ignore the interests of the society at large. He was not, in the sense of Adam Smith, a devotee of laissez-faire economics. In fact, Mill was drawn not only to some of the socialist ideas then sweeping Europe, but indeed to the new concept of communism, although neither he nor Marx conceived communism as the system that was later put into practice in the Soviet Union.

Mill was, like his father and like Marx, a staunch defender of a free press. To Mill, the right to express oneself freely on the printed page was one of the most sacred of all rights. An effort to censure the press, Mill wrote, would revive

> *ignorance and imbecility, against which it is the only safeguard. Conceive the horrors of an oriental despotism—from this and worse we are protected only by the press. Carry next the imagination, not to any living example of prosperity and good government, but to the furthest limit of happiness which is compatible with human nature; and behold that which may in time be attained, if the restrictions under which the press still groans, merely for the security of the holders of mischievous power, be removed. Such are the blessings of a free press.*[14]

The causes that Mill endorsed, in his writings and in his brief tenure as a member of Parliament, were politically left causes. He was the leading exponent in the entire nineteenth century of women's suffrage and birth control. He endorsed proportional representation and an end to the corrupt British electoral system. He publicly supported the North in the American Civil War and was an outspoken critic of the practice of slavery. In fact, it was over the issue of minority rights that he broke with Thomas Carlyle, in one of the most sensational public clashes over political issues of that era. Carlyle, who enjoyed a powerful reputation as the leading conservative thinker in Britain, earned Mill's wrath in a magazine article he called *The Nigger Question*, in which he advocated that Britain return to the practice of slavery, on the theory that blacks were created lazy by God and could be productive only when held in slavery. So angered was Mill that he fired off to the magazine a letter, which was printed in the very next issue, assailing Carlyle's article as "a true work of the devil," that preached the cause of "human tyranny and injustice."[15] The two former friends did not meet again.

Mill's interest in left-wing causes was, as we have noted, stimulated by his wife Harriet, under whose guidance Mill published in 1852 a revised edition of his *Principles of Political Economy*, which had first appeared eight years earlier. The years that elapsed between the two editions were dramatic years, marked by a wave of socialist revolutions across Europe. It was in 1848 that Marx and his colleague, Friedrich Engels, published their *Communist Manifesto*, a document that stirred leftist intellectuals on both sides of the Atlantic. Mill's earlier *Principles*, true to his dedication to fusing together opposing points of view, sought to find common ground between laissez-faire capitalist doctrine and a program of government intervention, but now Mill was announcing himself in favor of communism "over the present state of society with all its sufferings and injustices."[16] At the time, there is no indication that Mill had been influenced by the work of Marx, now banished from France and writing *Das Kapital* from his workbench in the British Museum.

In any case, Mill was no more committed to communism, or socialism, than he was to laissez-faire capitalism. He was constitutionally unable to accept any "ism." He was in fact an elitist, in the way that Jefferson was an elitist, believing in an aristocracy of talents, but his elite was always a *creative* elite. As Max Lerner points out, Mill shrank from making this theory explicit: "He was committed to the idea that the mass of the people would somehow rise through education."[17] His sympathies always lay with the workers, but he was unwilling to accept the socialist assumption that Ricardo had suggested, that conflict between social classes was inevitable, "one of God's ordinances." To Mill, writing in 1834, relations between the classes were likely to change "in the progress of society."[18] He did not alter this position even as he grew more attracted to some of the lure of socialism. In any case, Mill believed that the radicals would rise to the top by virtue of their own efforts. Like de Tocqueville, he saw voluntary participation in local associations as providing a critical mechanism for progress. But, true to his commitment to synthesis, Mill refused to deny government an equally powerful role in the growth of a good society.[19] Individual behavior ought to be regulated only when that regulation was required to benefit society. And intervention by government was also to be limited to action working for the benefit of society. In this view, Mill was the epitome of the good liberal. In this view, which at other times would be characterized as the doctrine of social responsibility, Mill stood foremost in the pantheon of those who have contributed to the professional ideology of American journalists.

CHAPTER 28

Marx and the Other Side of Synthesis

Although it does not appear that Marx and Mill ever met, they were certainly aware of each other, and it is only natural that historians have tended from time to time to examine them together, either for purposes of comparison or contrast. We will return to that theme, but first it is important to sketch out the main lines of Marx's ideas and to place them in the perspective of the belief system of American journalists. Certainly, few among American journalists would be likely to credit their ideas to Marx, since his name is so often associated with communism and an ideology not only foreign to Americans but also hostile to American thought.

A number of Marx's ideas, especially those involving his analysis of capitalism and its institutions, have been incorporated into modern communist ideology, but even those have been adapted to a world that has changed immensely in the century or more following Marx's death in 1883. Many others among Marx's ideas relating to sociological and historical matters have, however, made their way unobtrusively into the beliefs of many Americans, journalists prominent among them.

Marx grew up in an atmosphere that bears no comparison with Mill's world in his father's "house of intellect." The only direct comparison that can be made is that both boys were recognized early as intelligent and as potential scholars. The son of a middle-class Jewish family in Trier on the Moselle River that links Germany with France, Marx went to Berlin to complete his studies and emerged as a journalist eager to change the world that he had seen around him. While each boy was hostile to the oppression of workers by large landowners and factory owners, Mill saw himself as a reformer while Marx's self-image was that of a revolutionary.

The most powerful shaping agent for Marx was his education in the philosophy of Hegel, at that time the dominant feature in German intellectual life. Marx despised Hegel's metaphysics, his argument that "the end of history" would be realized in the triumph of the Idea, which he characterized as the World-Spirit.[1] Marx thought that Hegel misunderstood human nature, "man living in a real, objective world and determined by that world."[2] But Marx accepted as revealed wisdom Hegel's concept of dialectical analysis. So, Marx found it his mission to "stand Hegel on his feet."

Using Hegel's own methodology, he converted dialectical *idealism* into dialectical *materialism*. Both Hegel and Marx believed that there was a definable end of history to be found, but while Hegel had seen operating behind the movement of history the institutions that would ultimately fulfill the World-Spirit, Marx imagined that operating force to be capitalism. The end turned out to be very different, of course. Hegel wanted mankind to reconcile itself to the workings of his Spirit. Marx wanted mankind to overthrow the tyranny of the vampire capital.[3]

By the time Marx set forth these ideas, he had written with passion about the plight of farm workers in his native Moselle Valley, published his *Communist Manifesto*, participated in the abortive French revolution of 1848, been expelled from that country, and settled in England, which was already pulsating with criticism about the plight of exploited workers.[4] It will be recalled how the English press, under the tutelage of James Mill, had served as an important agent in British reform. The year of publication of Marx's *Critique of Political Economy* was 1859, the same year in which Mill's *Essay on Liberty* appeared. *Das Kapital* followed three years later.

Where Marx parted company with Hegel most sharply was in their views about ideas. Hegel had accepted Kant's theory that a thing, in other words matter, exists for us only through our understanding, through our mind. Our consciousness of the world around us develops from our ideas, Kant and Hegel agreed. In other words, ideas are what move the world. In standing Hegel "on his feet," Marx argued the precise opposite. "Ideas," Marx wrote, in one of his most telling passages, "are not the motors of history." It is *matter* that is the moving force; hence, materialism. And of what does this matter consist? Marx had his answer: objective conditions, which he characterized as the forces of production and the class struggle. We will return shortly to Marx's economics.

Contradictions are a crucial feature of the dialectic. Hegel had maintained that every idea, every historical development, contains its own internal contradictions, and that it is as a result of the struggle between an idea, or thesis, and its contradiction, its antithesis, that there arises a new idea, a synthesis—which, of course, contains its own contradictions. Marx replaced the *idea* as the centerpiece of the struggle, with *matter*, the forces of production and the class struggle. He saw this struggle not as ideological but in fact as biological. It requires no explanation; it simply *is*. It is part of the human condition. Since there is no such thing as an idea, there is obviously then no such thing as an ideology. This conclusion would seem to pose a problem for Marx, since one of his aims was to overthrow the ideology of capitalism. He had a resolution to this dilemma also. He redefined ideology. In so doing, he developed his remarkable doctrine of the superstructure, a doctrine that, in its own strange manner, has made its way into the belief system of many journalists.

Ideology, Marx maintained, is not something that occurs naturally in the world; it is invented. Here Marx tied this concept to his analysis of capitalism. The capitalists, that is, the bourgeoisie—Marx was inclined to use the words interchangeably—had invented bourgeois ideology to enable them to retain power. "The class which has the means of material production at its disposal," he wrote, "has control at the same time over the means of mental production."[5] The bourgeois ideology thus produced is so powerful that it makes its way undetected into the consciousness of everyone who lives under the system of capitalism. All members of society, even the workers exploited under the system, simply believe in the ideology that is part of their daily lives—or, rather, they go on believing this until they are made aware of the real world. In others words, it is necessary that their consciousness be raised; it is necessary that they come to recognize that they are indeed being exploited by those of the bourgeois class who control the means of production. They have to *learn* the objective truth: that they are victims of the class struggle.

It is the forces of production, in Marx's analysis, that provide the *structure* of the real world, the structure being that of the struggle between the capitalists or bourgeoisie and the workers or proletariat. It was not a long step from Ricardo to Marx. But Marx went further, to his brilliant conception of the *superstructure*.[6] It is through its manipulation of the thoughts and behavior of the working classes, Marx held, that the bourgeoisie is able to retain power. It accomplishes this manipulation through the institutions it creates: governments, churches, schools, press. These institutions constitute the superstructure. So, in fact, does the philosophy that accompanies the institutions. Marx and Engels rejected not only ideology but also philosophy. They did this through the device of making ideology and philosophy elements of the superstructure. Their point was that when one speaks of ideology or philosophy, one actually means *bourgeois* ideology or *bourgeois* philosophy. The real world, the objective world, is free of such concepts.

The point was made sharply in *Critique*. Marx and Engels wrote that when they were younger they had cheerfully examined philosophical questions, but that was before they had understood the insidious workings of the superstructure, before they had understood how the capitalist system had alienated workers from their real, biological selves. They were now, they said, abandoning philosophy, discarding it like a worn-out old blanket, and replacing philosophy with *scientific socialism*.[7] "We are prepared," they wrote, "to settle accounts with our erstwhile philosophical conscience."[8]

Alan Ryan remarks that, try as hard as he might, Marx was never able to shed Hegel and German idealism. Rather than being a garden-variety agnostic content with down-to-earth accounts of things, Marx seems to Ryan to resemble the Satan of Milton's *Paradise Lost*. Satan saw God everywhere and revolted against him. To Marx, it was the philosophical illusions that he saw around himself against which he was compelled to rebel.[9]

Just as Hegel had discovered his World-Spirit in his analysis of history. Marx found the triumph of socialism in his analysis of history. In the Marxian interpretation, the end of history would come about when the contradictions had ended, in the form of the ultimate synthesis. It was thus that he defined communism, the state that exists at the end of history. It is the inevitable outcome, when no one any longer controls the means of production, when the class struggle has come to an end, when the institutions that have been created by the bourgeoisie have withered away into nothingness, when there is no more superstructure, when the consciousness of all people has been raised, when everyone is aware of his or her true self. This was Marx's conception of communism. He rejected "crude communism," which he said negated the personality of man.[10] The aim of the *Communist Manifesto* was to restore man to his "true identity."

Marx himself was an outspoken foe of utopian ideas; in fact, he argued with great passion that what was utopian was traditional socialism, the product of thinkers such as Rousseau, Comte, and his German colleague, Ferdinand Lassalle. His version, he argued, was scientific. Karl Korsch says that Marx's life work was to transform socialism from a theoretical, utopian fantasy into "a realistic and material science."[11] Yet, it is clear that Marx was himself a believer in ideal worlds. Erich Fromm sees him as proposing a form of socialism that "is essentially prophetic Messianism."[12] Ironically, for a man who preached the cause of science and who railed against moralizing, Marx was himself a moralizer par excellence. Behind all of Marx's words lay an appeal for what Ryan calls "an ethic of freedom."[13] In his early writings, Marx was a dedicated humanist, with views scarcely distinguishable from those of Mill. Most students of Marx believe that he put aside his youthful democratic impulses to become the "red terrorist doctor," as his enemies described him in his later years.[14] Fromm, on the other hand, insists that Marx remained a humanist all his life, "concerned with the enslavement of man (worker *and* capitalist) by things and circumstances of their own making."[15] What Marx sought was a world free of one person's exploitation of another, a world free of misery, poverty, fear, and oppression, a world of justice—even, astonishingly, a world of individual liberty, a world in which humanity at large might reestablish its control over its own social and economic organization. Marx would have dismissed this conception as romantic, but his own writings refute the claim. In this assessment, Marx and Mill were more brothers than foes.

In Marx's theory of economics, private property is another of the institutions established by the bourgeois to maintain their power. Following Adam Smith's analysis of labor and Ricardo's theory of value, Marx went on to argue that it is the unhappy laborer whose work produces the property and who plays no part in determining the fate of the property. It is the bourgeois property owner who reaps the profit. In fact, the institution of private property represents a way of alienating the worker from his true self. To Marx, alienation meant being removed from one's awareness of one's true self. The value of anything is measured in terms of the cost of raw materials and the labor expended. The capitalist himself contributes nothing; all he has to do in order to earn a profit and maintain his class position is to pay the lowest wages possible and keep the laborers in poverty.[16] Marx did not appear to be interested in morally chastizing the capitalist for this heinous behavior, which Adam Smith said would be prevented by the operations of his invisible hand. Marx simply took it for granted that the greedy capitalist exploits workers. But it is capitalism, not the individual capitalist, that is the target of Marx's curious moralizing.

Mill, the reformer, was convinced that through education, capitalism could be transformed, could be moved to abandon the repressive practices both he and Marx could observe for themselves in industrial England. Marx said no; it was another of his acts of faith. Those modifications in capitalist society that had occurred as a result of government regulation, he said, were not caused by any humanitarianism or reforming zeal but were simply acts of prudence or "frightened avarice." Capitalism was historically incapable of ending the class struggle; that would come about only when it was overthrown by the newly self-aware workers, the proletariat.[17]

The press, in Marx's view, tends to work inside the superstructure to maintain the capitalist ideology and keep the workers from becoming aware of their class and the exploitation they are suffering. In this conceptualization, the press operates simply as an instrument of the bourgeoisie, gaining special favors and status as a result of its pivotal role in maintaining the system. It is, like the schools and churches and indeed like the governmental institutions, an agency of social control. In terms of potential for revolution, however, Marx believed the press could serve as an important arm of the rising working class, acting as an instrument both of education about the real world and as agitator for change and revolution. While working toward a different economic end, the press in this construction would operate like the rebel press in colonial America as the newspapers agitated for rebellion against the British. In modified form, this portrait of the press is held by many journalists, notably those attracted to the banner of investigative reporters, who see themselves as rebels against entrenched tyranny.[18]

As a journalist, in Germany and France and as a special European correspondent for Horace Greeley's *New York Journal*, Marx made a substantial contribution to the literature of press freedom.[19] The thrust of Marx's journalism was that free inquiry is good and that censorship is not only evil but also counterproductive. The purpose of journalism was the search for truth:

> *The purposes of journalistic activity are subsumed under the one general concept of "truth." . . . Not only the result but also the*

> *route belongs to the truth. The pursuit of truth must also be true; the true inquiry is the developed truth, whose scattered parts are assembled in the result.*[20]

Marx, whose newspaper articles were repeatedly suppressed by Prussian censors when he was a young man, pleaded again and again for courage on the part of editors. He concluded, however, that unless public opinion were on the side of a free press, there was no way to avoid censorship. Once again, the remedy was to raise consciousness, of readers and publishers.[21]

Superficially, Marx the man is not difficult to pin down. Certainly, his demeanor was usually indignant, angry, impatient. Psychohistorians trace Marx's truculence to his childhood, to his splitting from his family's middle-class life-style and the religion of his forefathers. In any case, his impatience was manifest in his unwillingness to wait for social change. Above all, Marx was temperamentally unable to deal in partial solutions. He contemptuously dismissed any idea that there is such a thing as "the nature of man." Men, in his vision, are the products of social forces. Their "nature" depends on historical forces. To realize their nature, men have to become aware of their class. Marx considered Bentham absurd for imagining that there is "a normal man," the English shopkeeper. "Whatever is useful to this queer normal man, and to his world, is absolutely useful," Marx wrote caustically.[22]

Marx's perception can best be described as holistic, as all or nothing. Scientific materialism explains everything. Capitalism and society are blind forces, entire and complete. They cannot be modified in part, because the parts are not separable. Engels said so: "The real unity of the world consists in its materiality, and this is proved."[23]

In any case, although Marx preached revolution, he himself was not an activist; his natural abode was the library, and it was there that he spent most of his working life. His contributions to human thought are immense. His studies of history, philosophy, economics, and sociology have helped form the ideas of all important thinkers who lived after him. Yet, there is no general agreement on what constitutes "Marxism." Indeed, Marx himself once commented playfully that he was himself not a Marxist. Those who have puzzled over Marx's prose to try to find the essence of the "ism" associated with him are legion. One writer has characterized Marx as agitator, propagandist, philosopher of history, economist, economic historian, sociologist, political scientist, moralist, and humanist.[24]

The ends forecast by Marx and Mill are different, Marx envisaging the ultimate triumph of society over the selfish desires of individuals and Mill foreseeing the victory of the individual over the pressures of society. Yet, these two men shared a great deal more than they themselves may have imagined. Felix Oppenheim argued that Marx and Mill shared a powerful commitment to freedom, "the same ultimate goal of society in which the free development of each would be the condition of the free development of all."[25] W. A. Kaufman expressed the same idea a bit more moderately: "Mill's idea of the good life is more like Marx's conception of unalienated man than it is like Bentham's happy man."[26] Graeme Duncan saw that, despite the clash between their ideas, there was a definite affinity "between their conceptions of man—autonomy, activity, a true consciousness and sociality loom large in each."[27] And, it might be added, there was a ring of utopianism in their imagery of what lay ahead for humankind, despite the fact that each insisted on his rationality and his opposition to ideal worlds. Other writers, like Jacob Talmon, saw a vast gulf between the two men, portraying Marx's messianic ideas as totalitarian, "longing for a final resolution of all contradictions," and Mill's as liberal and open-minded.[28] J. Salwyn Schapiro was even more certain: "Anyone who passes from the pages of Mill to those of Marx becomes acutely aware of a . . . change from tolerant, democratic liberalism to intolerant, authoritarian communism."[29]

The dispute between these writers tends, ultimately, to sink into a dispute over ideology. Clearly, Marx was the more prescriptive of the two. His mindset was holistic, that is, he saw societies as thoroughly integrated, with the various parts joining to make up a clearly defined totality. The class struggle is at the center of Marx's society; it will, he said, go on and on, until the day that capitalism is dethroned and the ruling class ceases to exploit the workers. Mill's vision was pluralistic: societies are not integrated, but are made up of many different parts. When these parts are not working, they can be reformed. No, they cannot, said Marx: the parts cannot be separated from the whole. Only revolution can fix the system; reform can't do it. Both Mill and Marx saw the society around them as unfair, overbearing. Mill believed it could be remedied through gradual reforms. Marx believed that Mill's liberal prescriptions were useless.

Indeed, in one of his rare comments on Mill, Marx said as much. He thought Mill an amiable writer, but a man trying to accomplish the impossible, trying to reconcile the irreconcilable, the capitalist political economy on the one hand and the working class on the other. He was too much the confused compromiser. Yet, Marx, who was harsh in nearly all his criticisms of bourgeois writers, was curiously gentle with regard to Mill:

> *Although men like John Stuart Mill are to blame for the contradiction between their traditional economic dogmas and their modern tendencies, it would be wrong to class them with the herd of vulgar economic apologists.*[30]

When all is said and done, the affinity between Marx and Mill cannot be denied, especially with regard to the role of the press. Each of them, in his own way, perceived the press as a manipulator, as an instrument of great potential benefit to society. To Marx, the press was to be used to make the reader aware of the reality of his own life; to Mill, as to his father, the press was an instrument to point the way to changes needed to bring about a better life. Their routes were different, but in a curious way, they were each synthesizers, Marx finding the synthesis between contradictory forces; Mill finding the synthesis that brought harmony to contradictory ideas. The professional ideology of the American journalist owes much to both Mill and Marx.

PART VI

The Mass Society: Capitalism and Darwinism

Walt Whitman (1819–1892): "You shall no longer take things at second or third hand . . . nor look through the eyes of the dead . . . nor feed on spectres in books, you shall not look through my eyes either, nor take things from me, you shall listen to all sides, and filter them from yourself."

Horace Greeley (1811–1872): "He who is not conscious of having first interpreted events, suggested policies, corrected long-standing errors, or thrown forward a more searching light in the path of progress, has never tasted the luxury of journalism. It is the province of journalism to lead."

CHAPTER 29

Introduction: The Land of Unlimited Opportunity

On the American continent, the nineteenth century was a period of growth. The country expanded its borders ever westward and its economy ever upward. To the European man it was the land of unlimited opportunity. No institution promoted this image with greater determination than the press: if you staked out a claim for yourself and worked as hard as you could, you would not only improve yourself economically, perhaps earn a fortune, but you might even elevate yourself to a higher social class, a far more difficult task. Equality, as Alexis de Tocqueville observed, was the reigning deity. Of course, equality was limited. Blacks could not aspire to it, nor could Indians or women, but white men did not much trouble themselves over such trivialities. They were too busy seeking the rewards that growth promised.

Nineteenth-century growth was not an American phenomenon alone. The fruits of the Industrial Revolution were also available throughout Europe—but with a significant difference. In Europe, there were severe limitations on land. There, it was impossible for the enterprising individual to stake out a claim for himself. The lure of America was the lure of land. And with land came equality of opportunity. Across the ocean to seek their fortune came hordes of immigrants, from every country of Europe. They brought with them different cultural perspectives, they spoke different languages, and they remembered different histories. What unified them was their irrepressible optimism, their belief that in the New World there was always the chance that their dreams might come true.

In the unification of the new country, newspapers and magazines were indispensable. Where communities of interest developed among the multitude of diverse elements, it was the press as much as any other institution that was responsible. Only the schools could compare as unifying instruments.[1] In order to understand the ideology of the American press, it is important to keep in mind that the press was never an outsider to the nineteenth-century expansion of America. It was rather a necessary ingredient in the expansion process. It was in fact the trumpet of progress, the evangel of optimism.

The nineteenth century marked the rise of mass society. Technology provided the tools for mass production, mass marketing, mass advertising, and, of course, mass media. Few if any among the goals and aspirations that were broadcast in newspapers and magazines were original with the press. These were the goals and aspirations of capitalism, of an expanding free market economy. In that free market, newspapers and magazines were important vehicles of upward economic and social mobility. Editors and reporters are creatures of their environment, so it should not be surprising that the press spread the gospel of the emerging mass society. Variations on the theme were sounded, to be sure, mainly in the last third of the century, but these writers quarreled with means and not ends; they modified but did not turn aside the hopes and the optimism of the people, who, like the journalists themselves, remained faithful to what we speak of today as the American dream.

The Founding Fathers were themselves men of science, and they had foreseen a world of opportunity and progress. They had envisaged a land of milk and honey, and it was at hand. Since the ideas of journalists are for the most part derivative, the contributions to a philosophy for Americans offered by the great men of nineteenth-century journalism lay not in the originality of their thought but rather in what in twentieth-century terminology we might call public relations.

Several things need to be kept carefully in mind as one pursues the growth of a belief system among American journalists through the nineteenth and twentieth centuries, an ideology that, while it has remained for the most part unarticulated, has been perhaps even more powerfully held for its being silent. We are speaking here of attitudes, of concepts locked away in the heart, almost altogether outside the sphere of thought and conscious philosophy. One must not forget that Americans, editors among them, pictured themselves as living in a kind of laboratory where the ideas of the English and French Enlightenment were being put into practice. Ideas might always be modified by experience, but the basic ideology remained, unchanged and glorified. One must bear in mind also that chronological patterns are often useless in examining the growth of ideas. Some ideas disappear and suddenly reappear in another form. For this reason, the approach we are adopting here is one of themes and topics rather than of chronology. We are not moving from one decade to another in an orderly manner. Ideas do not rise and fall in orderly patterns.

This part, and the four that follow it, therefore, are each meant to be viewed as a package, each covering a definable element in the professional ideology, the belief system of American journalists. The unifying element of Part 6 is *optimism*, a quality that has always been central to the

American experience and which grew dramatically, among the people and in the pages of newspapers as the country expanded westward during the nineteenth century. Part 7 takes as its unifying theme *pragmatism*, the greatest American contribution to philosophy, born at the turn of the twentieth century and long since converted into a Way of Life for American reporters and editors. In Part 8, the unifying theme is *investigative journalism*, a press tradition that rose to new heights in the age of the muckrakers and has continued to the present day. Part 9 concerns itself with *power*, raising questions that have come to dominate public discussions of the mass media, questions about the relative power of the media, especially television, in an American setting in which technological advances appear to have changed the course of the country, indeed of the entire world. In Part 10, the unifying theme is *skepticism*, which as an ideal may in fact represent the expressed professional ideology of contemporary American journalists.

The interaction of ideas and experience in the nineteenth and twentieth centuries is never easy to follow. The Swiss historian Jacob Burckhardt warned against "the terrible simplifiers" who would bedazzle us by reducing complex events to pablum, leaving us with a distorted picture of the world.[2] Distortion often arises simply out of the attempt to force events into a chronological pattern. A thematic approach avoids the distortions of chronology, but poses a different problem, that is, how to avoid circularity and repetition. We are here following the advice of Burckhardt, so that when we slip, it is in being repetitive rather than in looking for simple resolutions of complex problems.

We begin in this part by examining the belief system of American journalists under four themes related to philosophical optimism, themes that are units in themselves but which like melodies in a song also act upon each other and react to each other.

The first theme grows out of the conviction that the United States was and still is a land of opportunity, no longer unlimited as it seemed in the early years, but still a place where you can, as the saying goes, pull yourself up by your bootstraps and create your own opportunities. The second theme deals with the pull of the market economy, capitalism, which to this day commands the hearts and minds of most Americans, journalists among them, and the interaction of this system of economics with the revolutionary ideas let loose in America by Darwin's theory of evolution. The third theme deals with the expansion of America to the west and the southwest, to the Rio Grande and the Pacific, an expansion that attracted millions of immigrants, and to the accompanying development of a mass society, a place where every man (and sometimes every woman) is held to be of equal value and significance, a mass society made possible by the achievements of science and technology, which in the United States are awarded places of honor comparable to that of capitalism. The fourth theme of Part 6 covers the importance of the local community in American life, not only as a place for "belonging" under the social contract promulgated by Locke and Rousseau but also as something to be envied by everyone not fortunate enough to live there. In this context, we observe the importance in the ideology of American journalism of the inwardness of this "localism," which was often accompanied by contempt for places beyond the local borders, to a peculiar American insularity.

In Part 7, we turn our attention to the impact on the ideology of journalists of the reformist impulses that motivated the reformist Populist and Progressive movements as they interacted with the expansion of America beyond the shining seas. At the same time, we turn to the primacy in American thought of pragmatism, the philosophy that is most native to the United States; here, we inspect the philosophical contributions of William James and John Dewey, and demonstrate the overwhelming impact these men have exerted on the ideas of American journalists. In this context, we consider the philosophical roots of the concept of the people's right to know, and direct attention to the intensity of patriotism that is a by-product of faith in the local community.

In Part 8, we turn to the impact of the ideas and behavior of the yellow journalists and the muckrakers, who arose towards the end of the nineteenth century, when it had become clear that hopes had been too high, that the dream had been too intense, that the image was flawed, and that unlimited progress was an illusion. With the fading of the passion of the early optimism, many newspapers and magazines became vehicles for the critics and nay-sayers. But even the muckrakers were loathe to revile the image. Instead, for the most part, they limited themselves to criticism of the practices and not the dream. They were following in the tradition of the critical press of the colonial period, but they were no less optimistic than Zenger or Alexander. It was simply a different kind of optimism. The dream was the same. Before turning to the modern playing-out of muckraking, a phenomenon known today as investigative journalism, we examine shifts in the prevailing belief system of journalists evidenced by an increasing volume of self-criticism and by criticism from outsiders, including the influential Hutchins Commission.

In Part 9, we turn to recent inputs into the belief system of journalists, influenced by the trauma of the McCarthyist period (which we also discuss) as well as the writings of social and political thinkers of the Right and the Left, including those of the journalist-philosopher Walter Lippmann and the theologian Reinhold Niebuhr. We direct attention also to a series of "new" journalisms that rival the growth of investigative journalism. The question of the "power" of journalists was raised most dramatically in speeches by former Vice President Spiro Agnew. We review the essence of Agnew's arguments and place them in the perspective of the belief system of journalists.

In Part 10, we trace the impact of modern technology and its high priests, the optimist Marshall McLuhan and the pessimist Harold Innis. We subject to close scrutiny the argument that the belief system of modern American journalists has strayed from the mainstream of American thought and has come to constitute an "adversary culture." In this context, we subject to close scrutiny recent attention given by journalists and students of the mass media alike to the ethics of journalism, and point to the idea of "professional skepticism" as representing the basic ideology of American journalists.

For the moment, though, our concern is with those who, like the journalist-poet Walt Whitman, perhaps the chief PR man of the Age of Unqualified Optimism, extolled the dream, so much so that he could hear it being sung by America.[3]

CHAPTER 30

Walt Whitman and the Gospel of America

Faith was a critical element in the belief system of nineteenth-century America. And with that faith came the curious kind of optimism that was peculiar to the United States. To the people of the older countries of Europe, nothing about the New World was of greater attractiveness than its aura of optimism. Bertrand Russell has described the nineteenth century as "the epoch of liberal optimism."[1] The United States was the visible symbol of that optimism.

Philosophical optimism is a teleological doctrine, rooted in a particular set of beliefs about the nature of humankind. Our lives must have a purpose. It is not enough for a human being to affirm life merely as a form of heroic endurance, as did the ancient Stoics, nor is it enough simply to tolerate earthly existence in order to gain admission to the hereafter, as was advocated by Roman Catholic philosophers. To philosophical optimists, life is in no way a tragic experience; it is a positive good. By behaving as free and individual human beings, each person is expressing the will of God—and at the same time reaping his rewards here on earth.

No American has captured the spirit of optimism invoked by the Enlightenment philosophers more powerfully than Walt Whitman, the most celebrated poet in the country's history.[2] Whitman may not have coined the phrases, the glory of America, the religion of America, the Idea of America, but he was the chief spokesman for the ideology that underlay the metaphors. One can see in these metaphors the heritage of Hegel's Idea brought across the Atlantic by American intellectuals studying in Europe, particularly the poet-essayist Ralph Waldo Emerson, whose influence on Whitman was vast.

The greatness of America, Whitman wrote, lay in its appeal to the common people of the entire world, in its unquenchable optimism, in its vision of the fusion of the individual into the social fabric of the country, in the endless opportunities offered by the land that stretched to the western shores. More perhaps than anyone else, Whitman embodied the passionate devotion to America that has dominated the history of the country and the pages of its newspapers. And, like so many of the evangelists of America, Whitman began his career as a journalist.

The "American Idea," Whitman wrote, lies in the social and spiritual solidarity of its people, all its people.[3] Half a century after the death of Thomas Paine, Whitman, an outspoken admirer of Paine,[4] was reasserting the fundamentals of Paine's ideology of optimism, with this significant distinction: Whitman was acting as reporter, not as essayist. He was describing the carrying out of ideas rather than discussing their philosophical content. To Whitman, *facts* were absolute.[5]

Whitman's journalistic career began in 1831 when he was a 16-year-old apprentice and continued off and on most of his life although he abandoned full-time newspapering a few years after the publication of his revolutionary poetic masterpiece, *Leaves of Grass*, in 1855.[6] He seems to have given up journalism somewhat reluctantly, convinced finally that the limitations imposed by time, space, and the wishes of editors were too constricting for him. Many others have shared this conviction. In any case, Whitman maintained that he had never had the makings of a good journalist because his opinions were hazy, "so slow to come. I am no use in any situation that calls for an instant decision."[7] Actually, Whitman might have remained a journalist to the end of his days if he had ever found a boss with whose politics he could agree.[8] Newspapering in Whitman's day was, as one historian puts it, a "notoriously unstable profession."[9] Certainly, Whitman considered newspapers a crucial factor in American life. He once explained the difference between the United States and Europe by saying that the American people were ruled by newspapers rather than monarchs.[10]

Most biographers do not treat Whitman's journalism as distinguished, but he displayed in his reportage a remarkable flair for vivid, factual documentation of the world of New York, developing the style that was to dominate his later work. As a journalist and later as a poet, he was intrigued by facts. A very sharp-sighted reporter, he brought an imaginative eye to a series of "strolls" along the streets of New York City for the *Aurora*.[11] Whitman said, in an image that later would conclude Walter Cronkite's CBS evening news show nightly, that he was providing "pictures of life as it is."[12]

Fact, Whitman said, was inevitably superior to fiction or romance. In an article in the *New York Post*, in 1851, Whitman wrote that drama interested him less than the fields, the water, the trees and the people that he encountered on his strolls.[13] Four years later, in his preface to *Leaves of Grass*, Whitman proclaimed his belief in "the superiority of genuineness over all fiction and romance."[14] Then he went on to assert: "The United States themselves are essentially the greatest poem. . . . As soon as histories are properly told there is no more need of romances."[15]

Whitman also linked together the facts of the journalist, the imagery of the poet, and the ideal of America in urging his readers: "You shall no longer take things at second or third hand. You shall listen to all sides and filter them from yourself."[16]

It was Whitman's image of democracy that captured the public imagination and that filtered, however unbidden, into the belief system of Americans, journalists not the least among them. Whitman's image of democracy was by no means unique. There was nothing new in the idealization of the pioneer; after all, America was quite simply a nation of pioneers. Whitman, however, added something new. In his images of democracy, the central figure was certainly the builder—the carpenter and the mason—but this builder constructed not only the log cabins of the frontiersman but also the structures of the city. This was the "new democratic man," in Whitman's imagery, pulled by the challenge of the frontier, whether it was embodied in the skyscraper or the ranch. And, advancing beyond the ideal of equality that de Tocqueville had detected (with some anxiety) in America, Whitman extolled the ideal of fraternity, the blood brotherhood of Americans, the "unity-within-diversity" or the "many-in-one." In this, he went beyond his contemporaries to paint a portrait of America that has endured—both as metaphor and as image of reality—down to the present day, one that swept together in perpetual embrace the sacred individual and the equally sacrosanct unified social order he or she inhabits. We will see later that a similar vision of democracy appeared in the twentieth century to the great American philosopher, John Dewey.

Democracy, in Whitman's imagery, married "perfect individualism" with "the idea of the aggregate." The "great word" was solidarity. Nations, he wrote of the Civil War, were, like individuals, in paradoxical conflict, struggling, sometimes violently, to find their own "One Identity."[17] In Whitman's metaphorical language, the "many-in-one," the total sum of Americans, joined each other in this one identity, as humanists, idealists, revolutionaries, all striving to create a just and enlightened social order:

> *The meaning of America is democracy. The meaning of Democracy is to put in practice the idea of sovereignty, license, sacredness of the individual. The idea gives identity and isolation to every man and woman—but the idea of Love fuses and combines all with irresistible power. . . . A third idea, also, is or shall be put there,—namely Religion,—the idea which swallows up and purifies all other ideas and things—and gives endless meaning and destiny to a man and condenses him in all things.*[18]

There was something apocalyptic in Whitman's vision of America, as it so often has been among the American journalists before him and those who came after him. America was great and good and when it became sullied, there was cause for a great gnashing of teeth and rending of clothes. The biblical illusion is unmistakable. In fact, Whitman frequently spoke of *Leaves of Grass* as "a New Bible."[19] Like many thoughtful

Americans of his day, Whitman was indebted to the vision of a self-reliant, democratic America publicized by the poet-essayist, Ralph Waldo Emerson (1803–1882), whom Whitman quoted in his preface to the original edition of *Leaves of Grass* as saying: "The World is young. We too must write Bibles, to unite again the heavens and the earthly worlds."[20] The mission of writing a secular gospel, of creating new Bibles, was a familiar one. In this, Emerson and his contemporaries, Henry David Thoreau (1817–1862) and Herman Melville (1819–1891), were heavily influenced by the German romantics like Johann Wolfgang von Goethe (1749–1832) and Friedrich von Schiller (1759–1805) and their English admirer, Thomas Carlyle (1795–1881).

Those were heady days, the years of Whitman's life. Not only was it an age of growth and expansion for the United States, but it was also a period in which the ideas that had dominated the thinking of Western man were subjected to questioning by an amazing group of thinkers and writers, nearly all of them incidentally at one time or another journalists. Whitman, whose life extended throughout almost the entire century, was born in 1819 and died in 1892. Among his European contemporaries were Carlyle, John Stuart Mill (1806–1873), Charles Darwin (1809–1882), and Karl Marx (1818–1883). Among the influential American writers and intellectuals who were also his contemporaries were Emerson, Thoreau, Melville, Horace Greeley (1811–1872), and even Mark Twain (1835–1910). Although each of these men made his mark on the ideology of American journalists, arguably it was Whitman who more than any other fired the passionate sense of "Americanism" that has dominated the American press ever since.

Emerson and Twain were also major intellectual influences on the thinking of American journalists, although in quite different ways. Emerson was the supreme optimist, filled with wonder about the potentialities of humankind. Twain was the bitter pessimist, dismayed over the wickedness in the human spirit. The "many-in-one" image of Whitman was broad enough to embrace Emerson and Twain, although in the end both Emerson and Twain found occasion to condemn the exuberant excesses in Whitman. We will have more to say about both Emerson and Twain later.

Whitman did not like the term *reformer*, but both as journalist and poet he was an unconquerable reformer. The tradition of journalist-as-reformer is a venerable one, and still very much with us. In a study of Washington correspondents in 1937, Leo Rosten commented: "Scratch a journalist and you'll find a reformer."[21] What did Whitman the reformer seek? He argued the cause of education for all the new democratic men, of free land for everyone, of an end to slavery, of government so just and perfect that government itself was no longer needed. It was the familiar call for limited government that had been voiced by Rousseau, Jefferson, and Paine, but in the imagery of Whitman its appeal was infectious. What John Stuart Mill demanded in prose, Whitman breathed in poetry. They were contemporaries and in their own ways fired the imagination and dreams of all Americans. American journalists have not yet ceased to heed the call of Whitman, he who despised the "putridity" of political life and the grossness of commerce and wealth, and rested his faith in "sound men, women and children," whose wisdom was on the march.[22]

It is important to note here that it was during Whitman's lifetime that the free market system of capitalism became firmly established as the economic underpinning of the United States. Printers and editors learned during these years that the press was an avenue that led to prestige and wealth. It was natural enough that most newspapers that grew and flourished during the nineteenth century would give their full endorsement to the economic system under which they themselves had flourished. Most editors accommodated themselves comfortably to the system. It was spirits like Whitman, constrained by the institutional imperative of journalism, who challenged the system. Yet, while Whitman found fault with the system, he was the greatest cheerleader of all for the country in which the system operated. The anomaly was not recognized then any more than it is today. In his later years, Whitman lost some of his optimism, but it is his earlier, passionately optimistic writings that have survived.

In Whitman's concept of America, one ought not to ignore the past, but it is the future that is of overriding consequence. He deplored the importing of European culture and proclaimed a new American culture. Daniel Czitrom says this culture came to fruition a generation after Whitman's death in the form of the motion picture.[23] In any case, Whitman's dream of a culture for Americans was clearly for the common man, based on a practical application of American experience, by no means to be limited to classrooms but to be available everywhere, to include "the west, the working man, the facts of farm and jackplane and engineers, and of the broad range of the women also of the middle and working strata."[24]

Whitman's appeal for an American culture rooted in the interests and experiences of the "common man" rather than in those of an effete intellectual elite has found fertile ground in the pages of newspapers (and among the broadcast media). Indeed, criticism of the press as pandering to the lowest tastes has been a familiar element on the American scene from the days of de Tocqueville to the present.

CHAPTER 31

The Press and Frontier Society

The song, the religion, of America that Whitman sang may have been of both cities and frontier but to the country at large in those days it was the frontier that was the centerpiece of the religion of America. Like Whitman, the American people rejoiced in their New World, which was not only free and democratic but also a place of confidence, strength, and optimism. Frontiersmen, editors as well as adventurers, saw this as contrasting with the Old World, which they perceived as closed and unchanging, given to collective rather than individual solutions of problems, decadent, barren, resigned, pessimistic.[1]

It was not until the final years of the century that what looked like scientific support for the American Idea appeared—in a widely circulated paper presented to the 1893 meeting of the American Historical Association by a University of Wisconsin professor named Frederick Jackson Turner.[2] What came to be known as Turner's "frontier thesis" portrayed the pioneer as the quintessential American, who made American democracy possible. This was a scholarly redrawing of Whitman's new democratic man. Turner's thesis was, as a leading historian observed, "a declaration of faith, a romantic invocation of a great national experience."[3]

Few historians have achieved such fame during their lifetime; Turner quickly became the most prominent among a group known as Progressive historians, the writers of "Whig history," a term used to describe an optimistic image of history that saw events as moving always forward, to ever loftier heights of achievement. Journalists had already seen this vision of America. The religion of America invoked by Whitman, the "romantic invocation of a great national experience," had long since become the daily stuff of the daily press.

The message that was delivered, not only to Americans but to the people of Europe, was one of expansion, growth, and a brimming-over spirit of optimism. It was best summed up by another journalist, Horace Greeley, in his famous admonition. “Go West, young man,” Greeley told the readers of his *New York Tribune* in 1837, “Go West and grow up with the country.” The phrase was not original with Greeley (he had come across it in reprinting an essay by John Soule in the *Terre Haute* (Ind.) *Express*[4]), but it was Greeley who repeated the message again and again, sounding the trumpet call to one and all to head into the undeveloped western lands, to build up fortunes, and, not coincidentally, to fulfil the dream of a bountiful and just America. As a boy, Greeley had gone “west” from his native Vermont (at that time, western New York was west to a New Englander) and dreamed the agrarian dream that had captivated Jefferson: of virgin land that could be developed by the sweat of one’s own brow.[5] America, in this image, would be the new Eden.

To the poetic spirit of Walt Whitman, this virgin land was like a virgin woman waiting to be taken. One cluster of new poems Whitman wrote in 1860 for the third edition of *Leaves of Grass*, now triple the length of the original, was titled, appropriately enough, “Children of Adam.” Among other things, this cluster was overtly sexual, a direct challenge to the prim model of European poetry. Even Emerson thought Whitman had gone too far.[6]

The telling and retelling of the mobility of Americans creates a very powerful myth indeed. The tale of Abraham Lincoln growing into greatness as he moved ever westward, from Kentucky to Indiana to Illinois, is an American parable, one that supplies a vivid symbol for a nation that in order to achieve its destiny had to abandon the Old World and to find new roots in its native soil. As James Oliver Robertson has pointed out, in frontier America, heaven became a “Kentucky of a place”; paradise was there for the taking if one had but “spunk enough . . . to leave behind the village where Pa and Ma do stay.”[7] In truth, the number of Americans who actually left their birthplace to heed the call of Greeley and his fellow visionaries was nowhere near so great as legend would have it, but the myth, often spread far and wide by the American press, was irresistible.[8] Certainly it drew immigrants to the American shores in numbers unparalleled in history.

No one knows exactly how many persons crossed the Atlantic and the Pacific in the nineteenth century to seek their fortune in the United States, but it is thought that some 32 million immigrants reached America between 1820 and 1930, some 14 millions during the last four decades of the nineteenth century.[9] One scholar has characterized this movement as “an epic odyssey of privation, of hopes, and of participation in building a new civilization.”[10] The impact of this migration on the development of the United States was enormous, for not only did the U.S. population increase manyfold but the nation also had to learn how to accommodate its native-born and its foreign-born in a single social order. In this pattern of accommodation, the press was inevitably a major factor. Not only were the practices of the press affected but also its ideas.

Each wave of immigrants brought fresh demands for new newspapers that could be read by those who spoke little or no English. An extensive foreign-language press appeared; some of the country's most distinguished journalists, including Joseph Pulitzer himself, began their careers in the foreign-language press. And the English-language press adapted to the needs of millions of new readers by stressing simplified language that could be read by those with limited language skills. This was Voltaire and Rousseau triumphant. And, since even illiterates had to be entertained, heavy stress was placed on headlines and on photoengraving and photography, as the new technology made this possible. Action and dramatic events now became a staple of the "news" diet, inasmuch as those to whom the language was unfamiliar could not be expected to comprehend the world of ideas.

Although a land of immigrants from the beginning, by the end of the revolutionary era the United States had satisfied itself that it was culturally English: in its language, in its institutions, in its press. The immigrants who crossed the Atlantic in the nineteenth century joined a land of "Anglo-conformity."[11] In 1818, John Quincy Adams, then secretary of state, put it this way: the new immigrants are welcome so long as they "cast off their European skin, never to resume it."[12] They had to look forward, never backwards, Adams said, uttering a refrain that has been sung through the decades to the present: if you don't like it here, you can always go back to where you came from. "The Atlantic," Adams said, "is always open to them to return to the land of their nativity and their fathers."[13]

It was at this time that the metaphor appeared of the United States as a great "melting pot" of nationalities and cultures. Perhaps it was Emerson himself, some of whose writings appeared in Greeley's *Tribune*, who was the originator of the "melting pot" image. In 1855, Emerson confided to his journal how much he detested those racists and anti-Catholics who had thronged into what had come to be called the Know-Nothing party, and added:

> *. . . as in the old burning of the Temple at Corinth, by the melting and intermixture of silver and gold and other metals a new compound more precious than any, called Corinthian brass, was formed; so in this continent—asylum of all nations,—the energy of Irish, Germans, Swedes, Poles, and Cossacks, and all the European tribes,—of the Africans, and the Polynesians,—will construct a new race, a new religion, a new state, a new literature, which will be as vigorous as the new Europe which came out of the smelting-pot of the Dark Ages. . . .*[14]

The idea of the melting pot caught on with the American press. As the trauma of the Civil War was ending, the *Chicago Tribune* cheerily envisioned the distant uplands of a growing, glorious America:

> *Europe will open her gates like a conquered city. Her people will come forth to us subdued by admiration of our glory and envy of*

> *our perfect peace. On to the Rocky Mountains and still over to the Pacific our mighty populations will spread.*[15]

A generation later the *New York Times* was greeting the immigrants just as effusively, promising that the United States would gladly transform a million Italian beggars into prosperous citizens.[16] But strikes and other threats to the social order soon flawed the image of the melting pot. Idealists like Emerson and Whitman may have glorified the arrival of the immigrants, but the press began to sing a somewhat different tune.

Even so, one cannot doubt the impact of the transcendentalist Emerson on American thought. Generations of schoolchildren were raised to celebrate his admiration for the fiercely individualistic American spirit, generous to immigrants, committed to self-reliance, contemptuous of conformity ("a foolish consistency is the hobgoblin of small minds"), comfortable in God's blessings on this piece of earth, gratified by the great men of America who "serve us as insurrections do in bad governments."[17]

Emerson's imagery of intellectual passion was a curious blending of the abstract philosophical idealism of Hegel and the romantic ferocity of the Scot Carlyle, who preached the romanticism of Goethe and Schiller to England and America. Both Emerson and Whitman were devotees of Carlyle, whose name is forever associated with the concept of hero worship.[18] They were also following in the intellectual footsteps of Jean-Jacques Rousseau, for whom passion was more powerful than thought. It is perhaps curious that the revolutionary Rousseau and the conservative Hegel could each qualify as the intellectual father of Karl Marx. But theirs were also the ideas behind Whitman and Emerson and much of the often contradictory throught of American journalists.

The power of Emerson's legacy can be seen in the acknowledged influence his writings had on the industrialist Henry Ford, in his early years the darling of hero-worshipping American journalists. Ford left behind heavily marked editions of Emerson's essays and on frequent occasions bespoke his reliance on the transcendentalist. He found congenial Emerson's concept that God resides in the soul of every human being and that man's divinity is released by escaping from the deadening limitations of reason and surrendering to the erratic, creative impulses of our own genius. A marginal check in Ford's edition called attention to this passage from Emerson: "Only in our easy, simple, spontaneous action are we strong. We love characters in proportion as they are impulsive and spontaneous."[19] The same can be said of the conventions of journalism. It is the character who is impulsive and spontaneous who makes the front pages.

As for the immigrants from Europe, the less intellectually driven Americans did not, like Emerson and the tiny American intellectual community, appear to have taken kindly to their arrival. Nativist movements epitomized by the Know-Nothing party emerged to heap scorn upon those who spoke foreign languages and who practiced Roman Catholicism, which to the nativists was a "foreign religion." That love of equality, which de Tocqueville had observed, was in fact a love of equality for native-born Americans, bearers of a cultural tradition that was white, male, Protestant, essentially Anglo-Saxon. The idea that Americans belonged in some sense to an Anglo-Saxon "race" lurked below the consciousness of the American people. But it was there nonetheless, and it affected the ideas held by the journalists as well as the content of their newspapers.[20] Optimism and faith in the future, it seems, were American (or Anglo-Saxon) qualities. And the American press, while dramatizing its content to appeal to the immigrants was, like John Quincy Adams, urging the newcomers to "Americanize" themselves.

At one time, however, historians of the American scene accepted uncritically the story of America as the melting pot. Yet recent scholarship is skeptical of this image, calling attention to the power and extent of the nativist movement, especially in the last quarter of the nineteenth century when refugees fleeing tyranny streamed across the Atlantic from poverty-ridden southern Italy, the balkanized Austro-Hungarian Empire, and pogrom-afflicted Poland and Russia.[21] They were for the most part peasants, Catholic and Jewish. They were not fair-haired and blue-eyed; they looked different, they behaved differently, and they were for the most part forced to settle in the slum areas of the great cities.[22]

The period of American expansion coincided with a spiraling fascination with racial questions everywhere in the world, and especially in the "melting pot" of the United States. The publication of Darwin's theory of natural selection, to whose influence on American ideology we will turn shortly, gave rise to profound doubts about the "fitness" of those who did not square with the Anglo-Saxon ideal. By the end of the nineteenth century, scholars and politicians alike were expressing fears about what wicked effect the wave of immigrants from southern and eastern Europe would have on the "Nordic" American ideal. Charles Davenport, a leader of the American eugenics movement, feared the new immigrant population would not only make Americans darker and smaller in stature but would also cause them to be "more given to crimes of larceny, kidnaping, assault, murder, rape, and sex-immorality."[23] More than half the states passed laws legalizing sterilization of those deficient physically and morally, identifying them in the term popular in those days as "feeble-minded."[24] Theodore Roosevelt, noting higher birth rates among the non-Nordic, scolded middle-class advocates of birth control for practicing "racial suicide."[25] Supreme Court Justice Oliver Wendell Holmes, so revered by the press for his ringing libertarian support of free speech, ruled in favor of the sterilization of a 17-year-old girl whose mother and grandmother had seemed mentally backward, asserting it was appropriate to require sacrifices of "those who already sap the strength of the State."[26]

In Emma Lazarus's 1886 poem, carved in stone on the Statue of Liberty, the new arrivals are perceived as the wretched refuse of Europe, "tempest-tost and yearning to be free." The beautiful vision of the melting pot remains in the folklore of America, but it is apparent that there were ugly blemishes on this lovely portrait, in which the hordes of non-Nordics were seen as threats to American values. When the National Socialists, in twentieth-century Germany, put into practice the ultimate in racial contempt, they were not alone in their ideology, although of course racial genocide was a peculiarly Nazi creation. In the early years of the twentieth century, a Park Avenue socialite named Madison Grant achieved considerable popularity with a book warning that intermarriage between Nordics and Mediterraneans, let alone Jews, would lead to "mongrelization" of Americans.[27] The restrictive immigration law of 1924 sought to prevent this kind of mongrelization.

Even Emerson, that devotee of the melting pot, was thankful that the earlier foreigners arriving in the United States had been blue-eyed and light-skinned.[28] If even Emerson found himself confused, one cannot wonder at the mixed messages in the press. Stereotypes were everywhere, clear expression of a mounting fear of the unknown. The dark-skinned immigrants were now a "foreign peril" to native American values. The nativist newspapers and magazines that sprang up, eager to defend these values, cast the immigrants as un-American, as "the very scum and offal of Europe," as "long-haired, wild-eyed, bad-smelling, atheistic, reckless foreign wretches, who never did an honest day's work in their lives."[29] Italian immigrants were special targets. The *Baltimore News* saw as a character trait of "this impulsive and inexorable race" a disposition to assassinate.[30]

With the eyes of the country fixed on itself, on its growth free of the entanglements and confusion of the European continent, it is not surprising that the press preoccupied itself with internal matters. The ideology of America, Whitman's song, was anchored in expansion, south of the border towards Mexico, westward towards the Pacific, and what was spoken of as the country's "manifest destiny." The world beyond the seas was forgotten in the country's preoccupation with itself. The American press remains today, in contrast to the press of other countries, an overwhelmingly inward-looking press. The power and passion of American growth and expansion has been etched on the pages of newspapers even as it has been carved in the granite sculptures on the face of Mount Rushmore. When the United States turned its eyes outward in the final decade of the century, its mission remained "manifest destiny," although that drive was no longer directed to contiguous physical territory but rather to an intangible missionary zeal to "Americanize" the world. Moral justification for expansion appeared not only in the speeches of politicians and in the essays of literary figures but also in the newspapers. We will turn to this aspect of American ideology later.

CHAPTER 32

Darwin and the Optimistic Society

America in the nineteenth century was fractured into two halves by the Civil War. In all history, few events have provided so sharp a division as the War between the States. The historian Henry Adams, returning to America in 1868 after a decade's absence in England, remarked that a Mediterranean trader absenting himself from his home for such a period 3,000 years earlier "could hardly have been stranger on the shore of a world so changed from what it had been ten years before."[1] What upset Adams most of all was the apparent decline of a tradition of small-town liberalism and the rise of a new urban "business ethic."[2] It was, however, not only the bitterly divisive war that had wrought the changes deplored by Adams. It was also the revolutionary biology announced by Charles Darwin in 1859, two years before the start of the war.

In the United States, Darwin's message was superimposed on the doctrine of capitalism, which was by now widely accepted in America; it was this peculiar juxtaposition of ideas that exerted such an enormous impact on the ideology of the New World, on journalists as well as on the business and scientific communities and the public at large.

The student of the nineteenth century is inevitably drawn to what appears to be an unbridgeable network of contradictions and paradoxes. Henry Adams's observation points to the fact that it was indeed an unsteady period of transition—from the agrarian world of the Enlightenment years to the modern world of science and technology. And yet, contradictions and paradoxes notwithstanding, certain qualities in American life continued as dominant characteristics of the entire century, shifting, changing and modifying under the impact of growth, but remaining curiously alive and markedly affecting the ideas of American journalists. No characteristic was more enduring than that of America's optimistic faith in the future.

When Darwin's theory arrived in the New World, it encountered a set of values that made it easy for those who followed to apply his study of animal life to human society. It met a "can do" society with unbounded faith in the future and an optimistic belief that there were no problems that could not be solved. Americans were children of Enlightenment liberalism and of its worship of the methods of science. The social application of Darwinism did, however, raise serious questions about something that all philosophical liberals had known in their bones: that no individual (at least no male, white, and Protestant individual) was inferior to his fellow men and that what *he* did mattered as much as what was done by all other individuals, including his "betters."

The old pre-Darwin philosophical optimism was anchored in a particular set of beliefs about humankind: that our life has a purpose, that it is not enough for a human being to affirm life merely as a form of heroic endurance. To philosophical optimists, life is not at all a tragic experience; it is a positive good. By behaving as free and individual human beings, each person is expressing the will of God—and at the same time reaping his rewards here on earth.

No one conceived this liberal vision more vividly than the Scot, Adam Smith. It is to be recalled that it was in the very year that the Declaration of Independence was being announced that Smith was publishing his classic analysis of the basic doctrine of capitalism, *The Wealth of Nations*. The "can do" spirit that Smith invoked with his insistence on action was the glue that unified the society-in-transition that was the nineteenth century, as the United States extended its borders from coast to coast, driven by men of action who made no effort to hide their desire for wealth and power. Adam Smith and the Social Darwinists who followed provided assurances that the quest for wealth and power was good in itself, beneficial for all of society.

Although some nineteenth-century journalists excoriated the commercial and industrial entrepreneurs, for most editors these men were a new breed of hero. They did not stand around and wait for God's beneficence to descend on them. In an adaptation of the Protestant work ethic that had accompanied the Puritans on the *Mayflower*, these men demonstrated that the Lord helped those who helped themselves. Such was indeed the message of the Social Darwinists who followed Smith.

There was little room in the country's newspapers for those who engaged in mere talk. From the beginning, it was men of action who were the chief figures in the pages of the American press. What they *did* was more significant to the editors than their points of view. It was the event that was the staple. This concentration on action was already apparent to de Tocqueville at the dawn of the age of a mass press. As technology changed the face of the press, as the early penny press was succeeded by the yellow press and the muckraking press, editors remained fascinated by men of action, seemingly spellbound by the allure of doers, of movers and shakers.

When nineteenth-century editors spoke out in criticism of a politician, what they were condemning was his behavior, what he had done, rarely what he thought. Judgment was utilitarian: the ethical values of editors derived from the wellspring tapped by Jeremy Bentham and John Stuart Mill and their American adherents. If an act worked for what editors saw as the greatest good of the greatest number, then that act was to be endorsed; if not, it was to be condemned.

Richard Hofstadter has shown that a thread of anti-intellectualism has run through all of American history.[3] The interests of the communities of businessmen and Protestant churchmen lay in the acquisition of wealth and power, not in the development of art, music, and literature. The intellectual impulse was not dedicated to contemplation, to the quiet study of history and philosophy, to the search for knowledge or the conduct of pure research, but rather to the invention of machines that would aid in the production process, machines that meant greater consumption of goods by the public, in other words applied research with clearly practical results.

The nineteenth-century press was permeated with this view of the nature of mankind. The most decisive questions were: Does it work? Does it increase the nation's wealth, the nation's power? If it did these things, it was "good"; if it did not, it was "bad." Social Darwinism gave scientific validity to the religion of Progress and Growth. The extrapolation of Darwin's biological insights into the social fabric, achieved by Herbert Spencer and his cohorts under the rubric of Social Darwinism, found its strongest following in the United States, where the land had already been prepared, not leastly by the editors of the popular press.

It was Spencer who introduced the unfortunate phrase, "the survival of the fittest," and applied it to human development. The idea of evolution was not itself new; it had been considered by the ancient Greeks—but it was not until Darwin that scientific evidence could establish that only those species of life that were able to adapt to changes in their environment could be certain to survive those changes. What was "natural selection" to Darwin was to Spencer "the survival of the fittest."[4]

Darwin's theory, that only those species that were *able* to adapt would survive the evolutionary process, was recast to imply that only those that were *best* able to adapt would survive—in other words, that those *not* best at adaptation were condemned to death. Darwin, a naturalist, had in mind animal biology; Spencer converted his concept to human behavior. His *Social Statics* enchanted those Americans who were emerging from the Civil War with a vast new industrial machine at their feet. Under the spell of Social Darwinism, the old law of nature that had been thought to lead to the triumph of justice and love now became the natural law of competition, a law to provide moral justification for the circulation battles that dominated the yellow press era at the close of the century. This "law" was given expression by Spencer's leading American disciple, William Graham Sumner:

> *The struggle for existence is aimed against nature. It is from her niggardly hand that we have to wrest the satisfaction for our needs, but our fellow-men are our competitors for the meager supply. Competition, therefore, is a law of nature. Nature is entirely neutral; she submits to him who most energetically and resolutely assails her. She grants her rewards to the fittest, therefore, without regard to other consideration of any kind.*[5]

Sumner went on to say that if we try to remedy the natural imbalance that results from this law of competition by taking *from* the fittest, that is, the wealthiest, and giving *to* the unfittest, that is, the poorest, we will be destroying our human freedom to work for our ends through legitimate competition. From the theories of Spencer and Sumner there emerged what industrialist Andrew Carnegie proudly proclaimed "the gospel of wealth."[6] Carnegie, following the teachings of many religious leaders of the time, saw it as the duty of the wealthy to use that wealth to benefit the poor. Others, like Sumner, despised "utopians" who tried to interfere with the freedom of individuals seeking to gain the just profits they had earned by succeeding in the marketplace of competition and thus demonstrating their fitness.

The doctrine preached by Sumner was the laissez-faire doctrine of Adam Smith's classical economics as incorporated by Spencer into his "reassuring theory of progress based upon biology and physics."[7] The pursuit of one's enlightened self-interest, selfishness, was not only economically virtuous but also a signal of one's moral virtue. So popular did Spencer become in the United States that in the last four decades of the nineteenth century, no fewer than 365,000 volumes of his writings were gobbled up by American buyers.[8] Spencer, optimist par excellence and prophet of the perfectibility of man, offered Americans a theory that seemed both scientific and comprehensive, large enough, in Hofstadter's vivid image, that it could unite "under one generalization everything in nature from protozoa to politics."[9]

The case of a New York baker named Martin Lochner illustrates the power of the ideas of Social Darwinism in the United States at the turn of the twentieth century. In 1905, the Supreme Court struck down a New York State law that had fixed maximum work hours for bakery employes as a safeguard for their health. Lochner won on the basis of his argument that the law violated his constitutional right to run his property, his bakery, according to his own work policies, relying as it were on the Spencerian law of competition. It was a direct confrontation of what later would be described as a conflict between property rights and human rights. The vote to overturn the law was close, 5 to 4, and it was not long before the minority opinion written by Justice Holmes would become law, invalidating the Lochner ruling. Holmes's opinion was remarkable in that it declared a death sentence on the doctrine of laissez-faire. Referring to the post–Civil War constitutional amendment binding states to uphold the civil liberties in the Bill of Rights, Holmes wrote, his pen dripping venom:

> *The Fourteenth Amendment does not enact Mr. Herbert Spencer's Social Statistics. . . . A constitution is not intended to embody a particular economic theory, whether of paternalism and the organic relation of the citizen to the State or of* laissez faire.[10]

CHAPTER 33

Mass Society and a Mass Press

Growth was inevitably associated with business in nineteenth-century America. Business wore two faces, each of them rooted in the advance of technology that accompanied the Industrial Revolution. One face was that of heavy industry, which emerged with the steam engine and introduced the ships and trains that made expansion possible. The other was that of consumer businesses, which created and developed the goods that were sent out on those ships and trains. In both cases, the press was deeply involved. Production of printing presses, newsprint, linotype machines, cameras, photoengraving equipment, telegraph, typewriters—innovations in these and other fields were part of the growth pattern of heavy industry that allowed the press to find a mass audience. Advertising in the pages of the newspapers and magazines promoted growth of the consumer businesses that attracted more and more readers to the columns of advertising. Small wonder that early in the nineteenth century the American press emerged as a cheerleader for the business environment that made all these developments possible. Commercial information had always been a staple in the American press but with the introduction of the penny newspaper in 1833, a new business relationship between the press and its audience was established. The penny newspaper was the brainchild of a clever New York City entrepreneur named Benjamin Day who found astonishing commercial success by reducing the price of his daily paper from the going rate of six cents to a penny.[1] Since the six-cent charge was too great for most residents of the city, only the wealthy had been subscribers to the newspapers, which for obvious reasons had been catering primarily to their interests, largely commercial. The mass audience that appeared with the penny press provided enterprising publishers with a different class of readers. The face of newspapers changed and with that change of face came revisions in content. Mass audiences had mass interests. There was no need for new ideologies. A belief system was already firmly in place. Benjamin Franklin had observed more than a century earlier that newspapers would bring in greater profits when they were written in an entertaining manner that appealed to wider audiences. In the laissez-faire doctrine of Adam Smith, American editors found a value system that served as a model for their efforts to reach broader audiences.

With Darwinism, as we have seen, there arrived even more ammunition for the values of a business economy. Darwin, Spencer, American editors—all seemed to be engaged in justifying, even glorifying, competition, expansion, and growth. The westward expansion promoted so vigorously by Greeley was seen as a part of God's design. The new glory of American cities seemed the fulfillment of Whitman's prophecy. The borders of the country spread westward. Canals were dug to connect the system of rivers so that raw materials could be transported to market and the wondrous goods that were being manufactured could be dispatched to more distant regions. Rail made it possible to distribute the goods over even wider geographical areas. On every side the message delivered by the press was glorification of growth and the beneficent face of America, whose growth seemed limitless and whose special place among God's elect was clearly illustrated by the very growth of its wealth and power. The Civil War was a dark interlude, an unfortunate but temporary interruption in the Story of Growth; to some, like Whitman, it was symbolic of the perils of unchecked growth.[2] The uninhibited expansion of the later years of the century, imbued with the spirit of Social Darwinism, propelled newspapers into the age of the yellow press. Some journalists, notably Mark Twain, rose up to challenge the excesses, but science and growth remained sacred values, quite untouchable.

As the country grew and expanded before, during, and after the Civil War, the press grew and expanded with it. The success story of Day's *New York Sun* was repeated by newspapers in New York City, along the industrially developing Atlantic Coast, and in the newer cities and towns to the west.[3] The message of the press was that in the crucible of struggle success was at hand for any American with a little bit of luck and a penchant for hard work, and who would lead an exemplary life according to the moral code of militant Christianity. The hundred or more books written by Horatio Alger served as a living symbol of this message. They achieved great popularity, relating in a variety of forms the story of struggling, ragged, and heroic young men who by hard work, the sweat of their brows, and a smiling Providence managed to achieve respectability in middle-class American society.[4] Alger's heroes did not, as the popular imagery has it, rise to the very top and become millionaires, but they were nonetheless on their way, models of upward social mobility. The fable of rags-to-riches was transformed into political propaganda for the virtues of laissez-faire capitalism in a world of boundless opportunity. In fact, Alger's tales are retellings of the lives of the men like those who became the leading journalists of the nineteenth century, Day, Greeley, James Gordon Bennett, Charles Dana, Adolph Ochs, and Joseph Pulitzer, each of whom progressed from humble beginnings to positions of wealth, prestige, and power.

Journalists, as we have pointed out, do not often originate ideas. Rather they are the great transmitters of ideas. The transmission is presented in dramatic form, and the ideas make up the raw material of what we often identify as public opinion. The abstractions that people believe come not from within themselves but from without, from their parents, their friends, their teachers, their leaders, and from what they read in their newspapers, hear on radio, and see on television. Thus, while the news media do not originate ideas, they conform to received ideas and broadcast them to the public.

The value system of business was not invented by journalists, but the most prominent among them were beneficiaries of that system, accommodated themselves to it, and helped to promote its ideology. We will see a dramatic change in this pattern with the rise of the muckrakers late in the century. It is to be remembered that the early tycoons of journalism were self-made men, themselves living illustrations of the message that Horatio Alger was to popularize. Horace Greeley, born of modest parentage in backwoods Vermont in 1811, began his working career at 15 as apprentice to an unsuccessful printer, and journeyed to the metropolis of New York City five years later to seek his fortune. He arrived, the archetype of the Alger hero, with a mere $10 to his name (that sum probably not encased, as legend would have it, inside a red bandana attached to a pole slung across his shoulder), armed only with confidence and great expectations. But luck, diligence, and drive fulfilled the dream. He secured work as a compositor and earned enough money to buy a small paper three years later. By 1841, he was able to put together $1,000 of his own money and an equal sum from borrowed sources so that he could launch a penny newspaper of his own, which he called the *New York Tribune*. Fame and fortune were now his; he rose so high in the journalistic and political firmament that he was a generation later to campaign for president of the United States in opposition to Ulysses S. Grant. By the time of his death in 1872, Greeley's wealth was estimated at $100,000.[5]

Yet his ideas about the press were by no means those of a yellow journalist. To him, a newspaper was not so much an instrument of potential profit as it was a tool to be used to educate the people, to provide for them not merely information but also instruction in the virtuous life, an instrument with which to lead the new Americans, especially the honest folk who tilled the fields in the new West, to a new and brighter future. Like Whitman and the New England humanists who were his intellectual compatriots, Greeley's image of America was drawn on a scale that was larger than life. He was, in the apt description of Constance Rourke, a "trumpet of Jubilee."[6] We will return to this aspect of Greeley's career later.

In the penny press years, an even more startling journalistic and financial success was achieved by Greeley's greatest rival, James Gordon Bennett, whose *New York Herald* was established in 1835 and quickly became the country's most widely read paper, a pioneer in what has become the hallmark of the American newspaper: dedication to "hard" news about crime, business, and politics and to softer news about personalities and entertainment. Like so many of his contemporaries, Bennett was born abroad, in Scotland in 1795. When he was 23 he emigrated to America, as he said, "to see the place where Franklin was born."[7] Bennett found work in various places as teacher, salesman, and proofreader, and ultimately scratched up the $500 with which he was able to launch the *Herald*, announcing this as his paper's motto:

> *Motto of the* Herald*—take no shinplasters—all damned rogues who issue them—live temperately—drink moderately—eschew temperance societies—take care of the sixpennies—never trust a saint—go to bed at 10—rise at six—never buy on credit—fear God almighty—love beautiful girls—vote against Van Buren—and kick all politicians and parsons to the devil.*[8]

Within a year Bennett had parlayed that motto into a circulation of 10,000. To his son, James Gordon Bennett, Jr., he bequeathed a fortune. When the latter died in 1918 even a lifetime of dissipation and squandering of the paper's assets had failed to destroy the golden egg left behind by his father, so that the *Herald* and the Bennetts' subsequent press acquisitions could be sold for $4 million.[9] The *Herald* as well as the *Sun* and many other successful newspaper empires had no reason to speak ill of laissez-faire and the religion of business that was inflaming the imagination of millions of native-born Americans and the additional millions who followed in the elder Bennett's footsteps and emigrated to the Land of Unlimited Opportunity.[10]

We can see that as far back as the middle of the nineteenth century, two different patterns had emerged in the ideological fabric of the American press, with Greeley and Bennett standing as symbols of the division. To Greeley, the primary mission of the press was to educate; to Bennett, its primary purpose was to inform. Each argued that he was operating in the public interest and was being fully responsible to the needs of society. In Greeley's view, Bennett's methods of informing his readers were so wicked and immoral that he was moved to declare "a moral war" against the *Herald* and the other penny papers that followed Bennett's example. Typical of Greeley's moral war was this passage from an 1841 *Tribune* article condemning a sensationalized penny press report of a murder case:

> *The avidity with which all the particulars attending this horrid butchery, the murderer's trial, execution and confessions, real or manufactured, said to have fallen from his lips, have been*

collected, published and read, evinces no less a depraved appetite in the community, than a most unprincipled and reckless disregard of consequences on the part of those who are willing—nay, eager, for the Sake of private gain, to poison the fountains of public intelligence, and fan into destroying flames the hellish passions which now slumber in the bosom of Society. We weigh well our words when we say that the moral guilt incurred, and the violent hurt inflicted upon the social order and individual happiness by those who have thus spread out the loathsome details of this most damning deed, are tenfold greater than those of the wretched miscreant himself. . . .[11]

In the article, Greeley called attention to the argument by penny press editors that they were offering graphic crime reports so as to fulfil "the duty of the Press to Society" to keep the public informed, a phrase that sounds like the contemporary theory of "the public's right to know." To Greeley, however, such an argument was "a wretched plea" by hypocrites to "stab the public good" while turning "a deaf ear to the higher duties which they owe to the best interests of society, to the good of their fellow-men and to the requirements of decent morality as well as of the highest justice."

Greeley regularly downplayed the idea of profit. Bennett, on the other hand, offered no pretenses. When he wrote that his paper would accept no shinplasters, he was referring to a derogatory popular term for paper money of little value that had been issued on insufficient security or had greatly depreciated. Like the Benjamin Franklin he admired, Bennett was in the newspaper business primarily to earn profits for himself. At the same time, he interpreted the very presentation of information to the public as great moral force. Bennett's ideas about the press were supremely clear in the pages of his *Herald*: by the fact that it ties indissolubly together the private acquisition of wealth and the resulting public good, the daily paper is a beneficent institution.[12] He put it this way:

I am determined to make the Herald *the greatest paper that ever appeared in the world. The highest order of mind has never yet been found operating through the daily press. Let it be tried. What is to prevent a daily newspaper from being made the greatest organ of social life? Books have had their day—the theatres have had their day—the temple of religion has had its day. A newspaper can be made to take the lead of all of these in the great movements of human thought and human civilization. A newspaper can send more souls to heaven, and save more from hell, than all of the churches or chapels in New York—besides making money at the same time. Let it be tried.*[13]

What is in fact the function of the editor in the belief system of American journalists? We have encountered Franklin's image of a "rare" man of great scholarship and writing skills.[14] To Bennett he was a man with the power to direct the course of history more forcefully than might a churchman or political leader. Greeley, on the other hand, saw the editor chiefly as a teacher. With Madison, he believed that knowledge is power, and he regularly referred to himself as a "public teacher."[15] While he portrayed his *Tribune* as an instrument of information and opinion, there can be no doubt that it was the missionary role of the editor that was most fascinating to him. Far more devoted to the literary and the abstract than was Bennett, Greeley saw his ideal editor as a moralist: "Nothing but his passion for the dissemination of sound and true views can compensate the editor for his intense and unremitting labor."[16] The proper role of the editor was to *lead* the people:

> *He who is not conscious of having first interpreted events, suggested policies, corrected long-standing errors, or thrown forward a more searching light in the path of progress, has never tasted the luxury of journalism. It is the province of journalism to lead.*[17]

Historian Henry Steele Commager has observed that Greeley was "not only the greatest and most influential editor of his day," but also the most complete reformer to be found in New York. "He had," Commager wrote, "perhaps a wider acquaintance with reformers than any other American of his day, for his interests were political and economic as well as moral and intellectual, western as well as eastern."[18]

Whitman's vision of the editor was more reportorial and literary, but still in accord with the images of Franklin, Bennett, and Greeley. To Whitman, the editor's job was to cultivate "a sharp eye, to discriminate the good from the immense mass of unreal stuff floating on all sides of him."[19] What was "good" to Whitman was not far from the good in Greeley's vision.

Whitman and Greeley did, however, envision different futures for America: Whitman saw a brilliant social order rising in the urban East, Greeley a romantic rustic Arcadia in the West. In fact, Greeley's influence on rural American society was vast, mainly through the instrument of his *Weekly Tribune*, which reached rural communities across the land and made "Papa Horace" a farmer's hero. In the 1850s, visitors arriving in New York from the west and New England made it a point to visit Greeley in the *Tribune* office, there to consult him about the condition of the world, the country, upcoming elections, and even his views about their crops. He visited them in their fields and reassured them their subscriptions hadn't run out.[20]

Progressive historians have always revered Greeley, particularly for his unremitting devotion to reform causes in an age itself dedicated to reform—in education, prisons, family life, and especially slavery. "In the history of the world," Emerson announced in 1841, the year of the founding of the *Tribune*, "the doctrine of Reform has never had such scope as at the present hour."[21] Vernon Parrington called Emerson the consummate Yankee radical, "an incorrigible idealist" who possessed the "romantic faith" of developing democracy.[22] Indeed, in what to his opponents sometimes seemed a veritable frenzy of reform, Greeley promoted at one time or another the cause of organized labor, feminism, the elimination of slavery, even a rudimentary kind of communism, all argued with passion in the pages of new newspapers.

Greeley's model was a generally obscure product of the French Enlightenment named Charles Fourier (1772–1837), an out-and-out utopian who leveled criticism not only at capitalist economics but also at such entrenched institutions as religion, marriage, and the family.[23] Fourier's "future" consisted of a network of "phalanxes"—modified in the imagery of Greeley and his American cohorts to "associations"—of thousands of small, politically independent, self-sustaining communal units. Fourier's phalanxes were copied in a series of American communes, the most noteworthy of them Brook Farm in New Hampshire, which attracted not only Greeley and Emerson but also Thoreau and another major American journalist, Charles Dana, whom Greeley took on as his chief editor.[24]

The pages of Greeley's papers contained essays, poetry, and political analysis by the giants of the era. Emerson and Whitman appeared in the *Tribune*. Charles Dickens's novel, *Barnaby Rudge*, was serialized in the paper. And when Editor Dana went on a trip to Europe, he signed Karl Marx as a political commentator. Marx's columns ran for ten years in the *Tribune*.[25]

Greeley's reform activities were never entirely consistent; he jumped enthusiastically back and forth between advocacy and caution. In so doing, he earned the wrath not only of Bennett but also of Henry J. Raymond, a former *Tribune* writer who went on to found the *New York Times* and build it into an important rival. This is not the place to repeat the oft-recounted tale of Greeley's—or America's—flirtation with communal society, but it is important to recognize the indelible impact Greeley's series of crusades exerted on the growth of the image of the journalist-as-crusader in the belief system of the American press.

Fourier maintained that the problems of the world were fundamentally social, not political, but although Greeley argued the cause of social reform, he was never far away from the world of politics. He dabbled in New York State politics for years and served a term as a Whig member of Congress, where he introduced the country's first Homestead Act, a free-land measure that was to become law under President Lincoln. In his appeal for free land, Greeley's dream was of the millennium, "the creation of a universally land-holding people such as has not been since the earlier and purer days of the Israelite commonwealth."[26]

Perhaps it was because of his rumpled, baggy appearance, as he peered near-sightedly from behind narrow spectacles, strands of silver-yellow hair littered around the edges of his frayed collar, or perhaps it was because of his squeaky, high-pitched voice, but Greeley seemed to attract political opposition and indeed ridicule and contempt. Henry Raymond of the *Times*, whom the Whigs chose over Greeley to become New York's lieutenant governor, accused Greeley not only of labor agitation but of being a communist and, what's worse, of advocating free love; Bennett blamed the Civil War on him. No one was more vicious to Greeley than the celebrated cartoonist Thomas Nast, who gained fame for his cruel caricatures of New York's William Marcy "Boss" Tweed in the pages of *Harper's Bazaar*. In Greeley's losing presidential campaign against Grant in 1872, Nast pictured him as "liar, villain and scoundrel" in running his *New York Trombone*. In Nast's image the editor was "Horrors Greedey"; his crowning blow was to portray Greeley shaking hands with John Wilkes Booth over the grave of Lincoln. A broken, bitterly disappointed man, Greeley collapsed and died less than a month after the election.[27]

CHAPTER 34

Localism and the Insular Frontier Press

A crucial element in Frederick Jackson Turner's frontier thesis was his concept of the "escape valve." Throughout the nineteenth century, the frontier was America's escape valve. One could always, in Greeley's phrase, go west. The frontier was a marvelous place to go whenever the going got tough. An American man who lost his job or his wife or his confidence could always pull up stakes and head west. Whether or not Turner's thesis correctly interprets American history, it is certainly true that from the very beginnings of the country, many Americans have been on the move. They converted the two oceans into two seas and made of their homeland a vast island, totally separated from Europe and the past.

The legend of America as the land of mobility is just as popular today as it was a century and a half ago. All legends are based on reality and certainly the nineteenth century was marked by thousands of caravans of Conestoga wagons heading west. It was marked also by the bands of footloose individuals on the move, migrants heading "somewhere else," gold rushers looking beyond the rainbow in California and Alaska, men and women always on the lookout for something better on the other side of the mountains. Their concerns were private and immediate, and insular. The outside world was a matter of almost no interest.

Wherever they settled, they founded new communities. And among the first enterprises that they established was a community newspaper. The small-town paper was at the very center of the lives of the new settlements. Land was plentiful, and farms and ranches were far removed from the towns. Only through the pages of the newspaper could farmers and ranchers keep up with what was going on. The local newspaper became and remained a bulletin board for the community. Without the local paper there was in fact no community. Novels and motion pictures of the western frontier illustrate the point clearly enough. The local editor was a prominent fixture on the frontier.

The ideas that these editors carried with them and that they circulated to their readers were familiar enough. In the new communities, it must have seemed to them, they could put into practical application that remark of Thomas Jefferson so venerated by journalists: that in a pinch newspapers were to be preferred to governments. In the early years on the frontier, there was little enough of local government. For law and order to be preserved, it was necessary that local citizens join together in cooperative peacekeeping ventures. Inevitably, the leading advocate of law and order was the local newspaper. After all, conflict disrupted the operations of the newspaper.

The newspaper became in short order the conscience of the community. Not only that. Editors quickly came to associate the future of the newspaper with the future of the community. The dream of one town after another was to erect on the prairie a new Philadelphia or a new Athens. Editors nurtured and circulated this dream. De Tocqueville called attention to this tendency in his journeys early in the century, when he observed that the vastness of America made it possible for nearly every journalist who so desired to start his own newspaper and begin exercising his personal influence. The visiting Frenchman found the number of newspapers in America to be "almost incredibly large."[1] Moreover, he observed, their pages were concentrated almost entirely on local affairs.

In this observation, de Tocqueville was identifying one of the most enduring and significant of all the ideas held by American journalists: that the true business of the newspaper is the reporting of *local* news. On this fundamental point, the ideas held by American journalists differ from the ideas held by journalists of other countries. The differences between American and French newspapers was noticed by de Tocqueville in the early years of the century: the American paper was made up of advertisements, brief political intelligence, and "trivial anecdotes" about local matters, whereas the French papers were filled with "passionate discussions" of national political issues.[2] This pattern still holds today.

Had de Tocqueville been able to return to the United States half a century later, he would have found not only that his earlier observations were still valid but that the number of papers and the number of towns had multiplied manyfold and that the press was even more devoted to community-building than were the rather ragamuffin papers he had seen.[3]

Localism in the American press is in part the heritage of the way the country grew. But its roots can also be found in the ideas that the editors carried with them into the West. The theory of the social contract so significant to Locke and Rousseau, so much a part of Jefferson's Declaration of Independence, the Rights of Man so dear to the French Revolution and to Thomas Paine—all these traveled west with the grassroots editors. The social and economic boundaries of the aristocratic world they had left, even that of the "effete" eastern seaboard, were no part of the West.

Here was individualism writ large, the individualism of the cowboy and the individualism of the editor.

The frontier community was the social contract theory put into practice: each free man cooperated freely with his fellow men in building a new society where justice reigned. What mattered was not faraway Washington or even further away Europe but what was going on *here*, at home, in the local community.

That much of this network of beliefs was myth did not alter its impact.[4] In fact, illusion is often more important than reality in our belief systems. As practiced on the frontier, the Rights of Man by no means provided rights for all men, Indians, blacks, immigrants, certainly not for women. Justice rarely prevailed on the frontier. Social and economic boundaries soon arose establishing a class system as ubiquitous as that of Europe or the East, but neither politicians nor editors spoke of these boundaries. And, who knows, perhaps they did not even recognize their existence.

The editor soon became a significant part of the local power structure. He was, as one student of the pioneer press has put it, "the unofficial greeter of visiting dignitaries, the recorder of historical highlights, the master of ceremonies on key occasions, the adviser to political and civic leaders."[5] In fact, editors often used their newspapers as springboards into politics.

Moreover, the local community newspaper was an instrument to intensify the sense of national unity or, especially in the case of the antebellum South, of sectional unity. Since mail delivery was so slow and uncertain, the local paper represented in a real sense the only window through which the settlers could see the world. The system of "exchanges" that had been operating in the East was even more important in the West. Since exchange of newspapers was permitted postage free, editors devoted large segments of their papers to reprinting material in the exchanges sent to them by other editors.[6] In deepening the passions of Americanism, the influence of frontier editors cannot be underestimated. The community of editors that emerged, united in the bonds of their brotherhood, was to a man dedicated to the ideals of American democracy, linked together in the universal portrait of a nation and its people on the move advancing into a future of unlimited bounty.

No matter how far west the frontier press traveled, its language was that of optimism. This was true in the farmlands of Iowa and Kansas, on the cattle and sheepherding ranches of Colorado and Wyoming, in the Gold Rush atmosphere of Nevada and California and even Alaska. The editors were as optimistic as the portraits they painted; America was a nation to them, as it was to Whitman, of builders. Optimism is always accompanied by belief in the future. When in Europe and in the more industrialized states of the East it became apparent that industrial growth was not an unmixed blessing and holes were detected in the shining future, frontier editors for the most part scoffed. In their belief system, pessimism was downright un-American. And why not? The future of their local communities seemed unbounded.

Not all editors of course preached this message. The excesses associated with industrial development disturbed, even disillusioned, some. The gloomy Vernon Parrington saw "the illusion of optimism [as] the great illusion of American civilization."[7] It so happens that chief among those Parrington identified as the architects of this "illusion" was William Allen White, one of the heroes of American journalism. To Parrington, White together with Booth Tarkington, a popular novelist of sentimental Hoosier romances, promoted a false doctrine of the "beautiful people" and the "folksy village."[8]

A native of Emporia, Kansas, White was from his youthful days both a hopeful novelist and a dedicated journalist. His novels were moderate successes and he also gained a measure of fame as a young muckraker in New York City at the turn of the century, but it was as the grassroots editor of the weekly *Emporia Gazette* that White made his mark. A leading journalism historian says that White "became a citizen of America and a spokesman for its small towns—of which Emporia became the symbol."[9] Despite the turbulent days through which he lived, White retained his optimism and his dedication to moral values in journalism. In fact, he was not only spokesman for the ideas of a moral and virtuous American journalism, but their symbol as well. He was the small-town editor that American reporters and editors would themselves have liked to be if only they had not been seduced by the quest for the wealth and power that Adam Smith had seen as virtuous and that Frederick Jackson Turner had honored on the frontier. To be another White, free and outspoken on the frontier, was the passionate dream of the wistful journalistic idealists who feared that wealth and power might lure reporters and editors away from simple moral values. That White was urbane and well read as well as a grassroots editor only added to the appeal. The modern, intellectualized examination of the ethics of journalism grows in substantial degree out of the cold awareness that simple moral values do not fit into a world where wealth and power are the goals.

Nowhere was White's devotion to the loftiest of journalistic principles more evident than in 1905 when he refused to print material that the Standard Oil Company had sent him as well as all Kansas editors, inviting them to publish the material and to ask "their own figure." *McClure's*, the muckraking magazine for which White sometimes wrote, said this offer meant a windfall of as much as $1,000—to papers whose annual revenue came to little more than double that figure. The article noted that whereas White refused to be tempted, other Kansas newspapers did in fact eat the tainted apple.[10]

Editors made regular pilgrimages to Emporia, where White often held court, never hesitating to speak out on behalf of the ideals of American journalism, never hesitating to condemn editors he believed were untrue to those ideals. White's columns appeared in the *Gazette* from the time he purchased the struggling weekly in 1895 until his death in 1944. From his most famous essay, "What's the Matter with Kansas?" written in 1896, through his remarkable discussion of freedom of the press in 1939, White was a man to be venerated by fellow editors, even when he was excoriating them.[11] For his message was the one that they would have liked to write, if only they could. Running a grassroots weekly, it was generally argued, gave an editor far more freedom than ever he could have had on a great metropolitan daily.

The ideas to which White gave expression were the ideas of the social contract discerned by Locke and Rousseau, the Rights of Man whose dimensions were glimpsed by Paine and Jefferson, the power of education to destroy ignorance argued by Madison, the utilitarian arguments of Bentham and Mill, as well as the social progress perceived by Marx, refined in the crucible of nineteenth-century American journalism.

White wove together these strands of the visions of the past into a model that has endured for a century. It is of course a model of optimism, with its eyes on the future and its faith in the integrity, even the nobility, of humankind, especially that branch of humankind that resides in the United States. Following the New England transcendentalists, Emerson and Whitman, Thoreau and Henry Ward Beecher, White, like Greeley and the idealistic journalists who came after, expressed confidence in democratic government and faith in the common man, paralleling the passion of Tom Paine and of the "coonskin democrats" of the frontier.

Beecher, the most renowned preacher of his age and brother of the author of *Uncle Tom's Cabin*, had preached this gospel of love and faith from his pulpit at Plymouth, Massachusetts. "The life of the common people is the best part of the world's life," he declaimed. "The life of the common people is the life of God."[12] Whitman, whose faith in the common man was powerful enough to conquer his revulsion over the killings in the Civil War and the exploitation of "robber barons," was nevertheless able to say towards the end of his life in 1888: "The older I grow . . . the more I am confirmed in my optimism, my democracy."[13]

Faith in the common man and optimism about the future was then the substance of the journalistic belief system throughout most of the nineteenth century and it continued on into the twentieth. Shaken from time to time by events, these beliefs were nevertheless strong enough to withstand the shocks of war, of industrial greed, and of evidence of man's inhumanity to man. It was the journalist-novelist Mark Twain who gave name to that era of greed and exploitation, the Gilded Age; yet through most of his life, even Twain was able to sustain belief in the virtue of ordinary people.

This pattern of faith and optimism had a profound impact on the behavior of those ordinary people. In a real and very important sense, it rendered them satisfied with their lives, or at least sufficiently oriented to the future that they were prepared to accept their present lot. It was a faith that in this respect was similar to that of the Greek Stoics and the medieval Christians: the message was to endure the present in the expectation of a better future. Even the downtrodden immigrants, as we have seen, adopted this belief system, what Whitman spoke of as the religion of America. It was also a local religion, confined to Americans inside their giant island. Newcomers might participate, but first they had to be Americanized. Foreigners belonged in another world.

In this way Americans accommodated themselves to the conditions of the present. Newspaper editors, swept away like all Americans by the emotional power of this mystical faith and reinforced in their hearts by the fact they were growing wealthy and powerful under the new religion, were in the first row of the parade of celebrants. With the climb to prominence at the end of the century of the Populist and Progressive movements, the faith came under heavy pressure. Whitman was assailed by doubts, White entered the lists against the defilers of the Dream. And Twain flailed at everyone.

PART VII

The Pragmatic Americans: Reform and Democracy

William James (1842–1910): "[Philosophy] is our more or less dumb sense of what life honestly and deeply means. It is only partly got from books; it is our individual way of just seeing and feeling the total push and pressure of the cosmos . . . Pragmatism is uncomfortable away from facts . . . The pragmatist clings to facts and concreteness, observes truth at its work in particular cases, and generalizes."

John Dewey (1859–1952): "The invention of language is probably the greatest single invention achieved by humanity. The development of . . . symbols in place of arbitrary power was another great invention . . . but symbols are significant only in connection with realities behind them . . . The method of democracy is to bring . . . conflicts out into the open where their special claims can be seen and appraised, where they can be discussed and judged."

CHAPTER 35

Introduction: Gloom Is Not Our Style

America has never been altogether free of pessimism. From the beginning European culture inevitably had its impact on the new nation, and although Paine was triumphant over Burke in the great intellectual struggle that marked the closing years of the eighteenth century, faith in mankind and its institutions was never total. The sunny capitalist future envisaged by Adam Smith and his followers escaped those who were unable to enjoy the bounty; the promise of Herbert Spencer and the Social Darwinists seemed far away to the urban masses dislocated by the Industrial Revolution and to the farmers unable to compete with the new commercial giants. Few among the millions of immigrants found it easy to taste of the American Dream. In the years of explosive industrial and commercial growth, Whitman's vision seemed beyond the reach of most Americans.

Yet, curiously, the waves of pessimistic thought that swept the continent of Europe in the late nineteenth century made only superficial incursions into the lifeblood of America. For every inroad of the pessimists there was an American counter. This pattern was as true of the press as it was of the rest of society. The elder Greeley encountered despair. So indeed did Whitman in his later years. Mark Twain, raging against the excesses of the Gilded Age, turned increasingly bitter. In the 1890s, Ambrose Bierce, another San Francisco journalist, wrote with unremitting gloom and despair. E. L. Godkin, hero of many a modern journalist, lost his earlier optimism in the face of what seemed to him a mindless generation. The Social Darwinist William Graham Sumner turned to the sternest preachings of the Stoics. All these men were heavily influenced by the naturalism and despair of European intellectuals and writers, Nietzsche and Schopenhauer, Zola and Flaubert. Stephen Crane, Jack

London and Theodore Dreiser, all journalists-turned-novelists, saw mankind as helpless in the grip of an impersonal fate. Sigmund Freud's discovery that mankind was motivated less by conscious thought than by the blind forces of emotions further weakened the framework of rationality on which an optimistic perception of the nature of man had been erected.

Yet the darkness in their souls was not strong enough to destroy the native optimism of America even among those gloomy writers. In short, unlike their European counterparts, they saw a way out. Mankind was not condemned to sit idly by and merely await the working out of its fate. People could, like Prometheus, try to defy their fate and make an effort to gain the power that would enable them to hurdle whatever blocked their paths. Carlyle offered a solution. Frank Norris, one of the gloomiest of the turn-of-the-century American novelists, put it this way: "The world wants men, great, strong, harsh, brutal men—men with purpose who let nothing, nothing, nothing stand in their way."[1]

Brooks Adams (1848–1927), great-grandson of John Adams and younger brother of Henry, stands as a symbol of the power of American optimism. Adams had as a young man written a history that was a ferocious counter to Turner's vision of democratic progress, indeed foreseeing the collapse of all Western civilization, but by the turn of the century, American optimism had changed Adams's vision: it was European civilization that was declining, not American. "I am for the new world—the new America, the new empire," he wrote. "We are the people of destiny."[2]

The final decades of the nineteenth century also marked great changes in both the content and appearance of the press in the United States. The age of yellow journalism was at hand, with its flashy stories and even flashier makeup; it was also a period of sensational growth among magazines, both phenomena directly related to changes in society. Rapid industrialization, assisted by an even speedier growth in technological capacity, accelerated the development of a mass market: audiences eager to participate in the New Society, eager to consume the latest products of commerce and industry, eager to read the news reports about the rich and the famous. The future of America looked very bright indeed; Brooks Adams was not alone in envisaging the new empire. The American people did indeed seem to be the people of destiny. Such, in any case, was the message of the press in its Darwinian struggle for success. Circulation zoomed along with the new American empire.

CHAPTER 36

William James: The Rise of Pragmatism

Unquestionably the greatest contribution made by the United States to philosophical thought is the concept known today as pragmatism. Indeed, American journalists, when asked to identify their philosophical orientation, almost invariably report themselves to be pragmatists. In this identification they are certainly accurate—if by pragmatism they mean applause for the practical and jeers for the theoretical. Yet the concept of pragmatism is a good deal more complicated than that. In fact, according to William James, the man often identified as the father of pragmatism, it is not a philosophy at all but a method. In this respect, pragmatism can be compared with the vision of the German idealist Hegel, whose greatest contribution to philosophical thought lies in his method of inquiry, dialectical analysis.

Although it is difficult to arrive at a description of pragmatism that will satisfy everyone,[1] its basic dimensions are unclouded and its relevance for the American journalist is supremely clear. The word itself is drawn from the Greek *pragma*, which means "action" and is the source of the familiar words *practice* and *practical*. Even in its etymological roots, it stands in opposition to theory and the abstract. Yet, pragmatism is by no means as simple as an endorsement of the practical and rejection of the theoretical.

Let us begin our examination of pragmatism by placing it in its historical context. In this way we will be able to see how it is related to the other major themes developed in this segment of the book, all of them associated with modern views of American democracy and the basic beliefs of American journalists: (1) the development of the political and reform movements known to historians as Populism and Progressivism, (2) the rise to prominence of faith in "the public's right to know," and (3) the acceleration over the past century of the patriotic impulses that have marked American life in general and the content of the mass media in particular.

The Civil War, it will be remembered, put an end to the movement for social reform pursued by Horace Greeley and his cohorts as well as to the philosophical inquiry of men such as Emerson and Thoreau. Those in quest of intellectual ferment, like Henry Adams, turned to Europe. There the ideas of Kant and Hegel on the one hand and Marx and Engels on the other attracted their share of American adherents. In the postwar years, as we have seen, Darwinism and the new determinism of Herbert Spencer challenged the foundation of religion and politics, of democracy itself. Whitman greeted the Gilded Age with no more enthusiasm than did Mark Twain. Within a decade of the end of the war, the winds of change were once more in the air. To some, the followers of Marx in particular, the times were revolutionary. In Paris, birthplace of the revolutionary call for the Rights of Man nearly a century earlier, enemies of the social order created a short-lived communal government in 1871, a leftist regime that inflamed the spirits of the new breed of American radicals. To others, the appeal was for reform rather than revolution. For both forces, the time was ripe for questioning the past and engaging in philosophical experimentation. Pragmatism was at hand.

The term was first used in 1878 in an article in *Popular Science Monthly* by Charles S. Peirce, a Harvard University philosopher who came to his views on pragmatism by reflecting on the ideas of his mentor, Kant. Why not, Peirce wondered, try to clear up the muddles of metaphysics by thinking of the practical consequences of ideas![2] A moralist like all the leading pragmatists, Peirce was motivated also by his hatred of Spencer and Social Darwinism. In addition to Kant, he was much indebted to Locke, especially Locke's ideas about the overriding importance of language and of the other signs with which human beings communicate. The modern studies of semiotics and semantics owe much to Peirce.[3]

Peirce's venture into pragmatism drew little attention at the time. It was not until 20 years had passed that another Harvard professor, William James, breathed life into the concept of pragmatism, in an address at the new western outpost of American culture, the University of California at Berkeley, an institution that a few years earlier James had dismissed as "a poor place."[4] Unlike the speech of the introverted Peirce, James's address stirred interest on university campuses around the country and within a decade he had made pragmatism the most widely discussed philosophical concept in the country. Arguably the most influential of all American thinkers, James was a passionate campaigner for the ideas he cherished.

The last decade of the nineteenth century was a period of intellectual innovation. We have already encountered the emergence of the frontier thesis of Frederick Jackson Turner five years before James's Berkeley address. That same decade marked the fantastic growth of American magazines, a major factor in the growth of the muckraker movement to which we turn later. In architecture the 1890s were marked by Frank Lloyd Wright's revolutionary switch from European-derived styles to indigenous "Prairie School" designs. John Philip Sousa's patriotic firebrand, "The Stars and Stripes Forever," appeared in 1896. A culture of youth, of the outdoors, of athleticism, sprouted and flourished. In Europe, the impulses of the turn of the century were similar—a rejection of the past, a glance into the future—but there was a difference. The reaction to Darwin and Freud in Europe was mainly one of looking inward and succumbing to resignation and despair, whereas in the United States, now flexing its muscles, the view was primarily outward, rejoicing optimistically in the glorious future that was unfolding.[5] Pragmatism provided the philosophical underpinning for this faith in the American future.

The slow healing of the wounds of the Civil War and the rapid expansion of ugly factory towns and teeming cities in the Reconstruction years had almost stilled the song of America that Walt Whitman had heard. The turn-of-the-century experimenters rediscovered Whitman and located in his writings a new, more philosophical content. A prominent nature writer saw America threatened by the effete and skeptical worldliness of a decaying Europe and found in Whitman an antidote for the "dry rot of culture" imported from Europe. Turner quoted from him; Wright adored him. And James, naming Whitman the chief celebrant of "the religion of healthymindedness," found in his work a poetic assertion of the principles of optimistic pragmatism, especially in his rejection of what James called "all contractile elements."[6]

It was revulsion over "contractile elements" in the philosophy of Hegel and his idealist followers, notably the Englishman T. H. Green and the American Josiah Royce, that awoke the passion in James's heart for the concept of pragmatism. James pointed out that there was nothing new about the ideas embodied in pragmatism; he loved to say that Socrates and Aristotle, Locke, Hume, and Mill had all been pragmatists without ever using the word. Certainly, editors along with many other Americans had been acting in accord with James's ideas for a long time. James notwithstanding, the thrust of pragmatism was indeed new, and it did, as he said, provide a framework for integrating the theories of knowledge of both empiricists (such as Locke and Hume and the French Enlightenment thinkers) and rationalists (such as Kant and Hegel). Moreover, it offered a code to which journalists could turn for philosophical support.

What James hated above all was what he called the idea of a "block universe," that is, the image of a world in which everything is structured and organized according to a dogma or a guiding principle or, in terms of his reference to Whitman, a dogma of "contractile elements." Pragmatism makes no effort to supply answers to cosmic questions; rather, as the word itself suggests, it provides a series of guidelines for action. A pragmatist is at home in his laboratory or his editorial offices; he does not sit in his armchair contemplating. Pragmatism draws its strength from experience, not from thought. Some critics indeed accuse it of being anti-intellectual. Others write it off as simplistic.[7] In pragmatism, what is true is what works. Its gospel is the Gospel of Science. Moreover, as it is widely interpreted, it preaches a theory of moral relativity. An action is neither good nor bad in itself; it is to be judged purely on the basis of its consequences. Relative or not, the founders of pragmatism, Peirce, James, and John Dewey, were all men of impeccable morality, utterly dedicated to the fundamental principles of freedom, democracy, and justice. James was in fact a religious mystic who found plenty of room in his theories of pragmatism for emotional understanding, for platonic thought, indeed for religious expression.[8]

The clearest expression of James's philosophy was set forth in two lectures in 1907, no doubt the most influential lectures on philosophy ever given by an American. At that time, James, brother of the renowned novelist, Henry James, was a very popular professor of philosophy at Harvard University, then the El Dorado of American thought. His early training had been as a psychologist, and on the whole he was more concerned with *how* people thought than with what they *ought* to be thinking. His approach to philosophy was inevitably psychological. Pragmatism, he said, is a belief system that satisfies both rationalists like Kant and empiricists like Locke, whom he described, respectively, in a particularly telling passage as, respectively, "tender-minded" and "tough-minded." Indeed, he saw pragmatism as "a happy harmonizer" of what at first glance seemed to be opposed ways of thinking.[9] Of the philosophy of pragmatism, he said: "It can remain religious like the rationalisms, but at the same time, like the empiricisms, it can preserve the richest intimacy with facts."[10]

Although James saw pragmatism as a way to unify empiricist and rationalist thought, there was no doubt that he was rejecting the rationalist way of thinking. Rather than the block universe that he detested, James espoused a pluralist world, a world of the Many rather than the One, in which there were no answers but a multitude of questions. He was especially hostile to Hegel, whom he had read while in Germany in 1867, finding the latter's devotion to the Idea morally reprehensible. Ideas do not exist independently in the mind, James argued; they arise only in terms of our experiences, in facts and not in thought, as Hegel maintained. James, totally committed to free will and free choices, would have no truck with Hegel's determinism. Good was meaningful, James believed, only when man had the freedom to choose it or evil.[11] James was more sympathetic to the gentle Kant than to the harsh Hegel, but he found him too intellectual; in any case, James would not accept the argument that there was any kind of unity in the world.[12]

Pragmatism, he said, rejected all abstractions and all realities based on "fixed principles, closed systems, and pretended absolutes and origins." In short, it was open-minded, dedicated to the concrete, "towards action and towards power."[13] For this reason, as well as because of his dedication to both moral principles and the dignity of the individual, James found fault with Spencer and the Social Darwinists. Spencer was on the right track by concerning himself with biological facts, James wrote, but he erred in "turning positive religious constructions out of doors."[14] James acknowledged that Darwin had demonstrated clearly the lack of a heavenly design but said he by no means eliminated the likelihood of a deity in nature "working *in* things rather than above them."[15]

No other philosopher is more clearly associated with the concept of pluralism in American society than James. In accepting pluralism as part of the basic American belief system and in dedicating themselves to facts, the vast majority of American journalists are comfortably at home with James. The contract philosophers, Hobbes and Locke, Rousseau and Montesquieu chief among them, envisaged a society that struck a balance among its plural elements, balancing out each other in the common interest. It was an intellectual statement of what in Whitman was a passionate declaration. There was no room for a view of the world that was holistic, or unitary, or "monist." James rejected the traditional "monist" Christian concept of the One in God as well as the Hegelian portrait of the One in the Prussian state or the Marxist vision of the One in the Material world. Moreover, he turned his back on the "dualist" perception of the world, in which philosophers from Plato to Kant had seen the world as a place where Mind competed with Matter, where the Spirit vied with the Animal. There was room on earth for everything, James maintained.

The pragmatic method, in James's view, was mainly a way to settle metaphysical, or ideological, disputes that otherwise might go on forever. The challenge was to check out what difference it made. In a much-quoted passage, James made this key point:

> *If no practical difference whatever can be traced, then the alternatives mean practically the same thing, and all dispute is idle. Whenever a dispute is serious, we ought to be able to show some practical difference that must follow from one side or the other's being right.*[16]

It was the consequences of action that counted. And in many instances, James pointed out, stressing the importance Peirce attached to verbal symbols, the crucial factor in disputes comes from the very way that ideas are signified, in the words that are used to express them. Language is a source of power. In the case of magic, he wrote, when the magician gives a name to his spirit or genie, he is able to control that creature's power. Pragmatism, James said, teaches similarly that words, just like theories, are means—instruments, he said—"not answers to enigmas, in which we can rest."[17]

The British philosopher, Bertrand Russell, was sharply critical of pragmatism on the ground that as it embraced action it ignored thought. James had, he said derogatorily, built an ideology "upon a foundation of skepticism."[18] When James argued that what was true was only what could be observed and that what was good was based only on the consequences of actions, Russell maintained, he seemed to be an American incarnation of the utilitarian doctrine that moral behavior was whatever brought the greatest happiness to the greatest number of people. Hence, for James, if belief in God made you happy, then you ought to believe in God. In this way, you would make yourself happy and no one would be hurt. To Russell: "This is only a form of subjective madness which is characteristic of most modern philosophy."[19] Another critic finds James's philosophy simply confused, succumbing to his own often-quoted portrait of the world of infants, "a blooming, buzzing confusion."[20]

How ironic that a belief system that so admired the objective values of empiricism could be attacked for its "subjective madness." Yet, Russell's criticism of James was in fact the very prototype of the kind of criticism to which the modern, "empirical" press has fallen prey. Journalists whose belief system is anchored in objectivity have had to defend themselves repeatedly against charges of subjective sensationalizing or slanting of the news.

James did not, however, see himself as endorsing utilitarian values. In fact, he said, pragmatism was able to embrace within its folds the values of many philosophical systems, including those utilitarianism. In any case, he dismissed altogether the idea that there was any kind of objective truth. To see an objective truth was to James the work of "the ultra-abstractionist who shudders at concreteness."[21]

Russell's dispute with James and that of many readers with many journalists is concerned with the nature of truth. To James, truth does not exist; it is to be found.[22] Pragmatism provides both a way to find truth and a theory of truth, for truth in James's view is "the name of whatever proves itself to be good."[23] In other words, something is "true" when its consequences are good. A reporter is following James when he turns to the traditional belief system of American journalism for his defense against charges of sensationalism or bias: his article, the journalist says, following reasoning that dates back to Aristotle, represents a *search* for the truth. It is not *the* truth, for that is only to be approached by collecting facts and by objectively presenting all sides of whatever is in dispute. In this way, he is helping the reader to locate the truth for himself. In language to cheer the heart of any journalist who sees himself as interpreter and not as mere transmission vessel, James treated truth as a matter of relationships. Ideas are true, he said, insofar as they help us "to get into satisfactory relation with other parts of our experience."[24]

CHAPTER 37

John Dewey and the Press as Instrument

Unlike William James, John Dewey made no effort to try to find within the doctrine of pragmatism a place for religion. His concern was with ethics, not dogma. In fact, Dewey said, in clarifying his ethical position, it is absolutely necessary to test one's actions on the basis of their good or bad consequences if one is going to discourage "dogmatism and its child, intolerance."[1] Dewey's concern was always with the *consequences* of thought and action, not their *causes*. He sought to go beyond pragmatism into what he called "experimentalism" and "instrumentalism," transforming the methods of science into a system of ethical values.

Known as the father of progressive education, Dewey is properly honored as encouraging learning-by-doing rather than through the traditional method of absorbing wisdom from teachers and professors. Since life is development, he held, the ideas and value systems that people embrace arrive through communication—from teachers and (although he paid little attention to the press as such) through the news media:

> *Schooling is a part of the work of education, but education in its full meaning includes all the influences that go to form the attitudes and dispositions (of desire as well as of belief), which constitute dominant habits of minds and character.*[2]

More the activist than James, Dewey was animated by a fierce desire to control the human environment, to subdue nature and bend it to the needs and wants of human beings. To this end, Dewey's instrumentalism maintained that thinking was the chief of mankind's instruments.[3] In this, his attitudes were not markedly different from those of Hegel or, more dramatically, Marx: Don't just sit by idly philosophizing or interpreting the world around you. Get out there and act. Use your mind to bring about change. Progressive education did not mean only to learn by doing, but to go beyond mere learning to change the world.[4] Dewey's pragmatism was a doctrine of power. In his concept of progressive education, there was no room for a rigid, fixed curriculum, as had been standard in advanced education for centuries. Introduce new studies, Dewey advised. Make use of the methods of scientific inquiry to bring about a better world. Yet, curiously enough, one of the major criticisms directed at Dewey by his followers was that for all his campaigning for social reform, for all his demand for the concrete rather than the general, he almost never actually proposed specific, concrete programs. Like Marx, he seemed to be more at home in the library than on the barricades.[5]

James died at the age of 67 in 1910, before the appearance of the modern totalitarian state and the advent of two great wars. Dewey, on the other hand, lived to a great age. Born in 1859, he lived on until 1952, and many of his ideas were affected by the realities of the twentieth century. In his later years, he abandoned the traditional optimistic worldview of those who saw the triumph of democratic ideas as inevitable. In this, his views were somewhat similar to those of the muckrakers, to whom we turn in Part 8. Dewey saw himself as neither optimist nor pessimist. Instead, he said, he was a "meliorist," one who tried to find truth in the real world experiments and through discussion. Like his fellow pragmatists, he recognized the way in which words could be manipulated by propagandists; he observed that technology had made it far easier for demagogues to manipulate the public through the words—the symbolic language—that appeared in the press:

> *. . . symbols are significant only in connection with realities behind them. No intelligent observer can deny, I think, that they are a substitute for realities instead of as a means of contact with them. Popular literacy, in connection with the telegraph, cheap postage and the printing press, has enormously multiplied the number of those influenced.*[6]

Thus Dewey moved away not only from optimism but also from the individualism of Locke and Jefferson as well as of James and other devotees of scientific inquiry. He found room in his "meliorism" for the ideas of Rousseau as well. Genuine democracy, he wrote, means the carrying out of the "public will" through cooperative rather than individual action.[7] Whereas James, following Carlyle and Emerson, took the position that the course of history was often directed by the actions of great men, Dewey concurred with Rousseau that great social movements were the chief molding force. To combat these pressures and to bend nature to the human will, individual human beings had to unite and engage in collective action. Dewey saw this new kind of activism as an extension of Jefferson's individualism. In fact, he wrote, man in a modern democratic society has the positive duty to engage in social and political action in the sphere of economics so as to insure full equality and freedom for all human beings.[8]

To Dewey democracy was "a fighting faith" that could be realized only through the instrument of the combined intelligence of the American people.[9] To be able to turn that intelligence loose required that all thoughts and ideas be disseminated among the people. Their "right" to hearing about these thoughts and ideas was implicit in Dewey's analysis. Here in modern dress was a restatement of the underlying assumption of American democracy, with its emphasis on education, through the schools and through the press.

In his image of the individual-in-association, Dewey envisioned democracy as the "ideal" that united two usually contradictory belief systems, not as a utopian dream but as an ideal still to reach full fruition.[10] People tend to view the universe in one of two ways, either as concentrated on the individual whose freedom is paramount (as in Adam Smith's laissez-faire system) or on the needs of society, of human beings taken collectively rather than individually (as in the Marxist conception). Dewey saw the true meaning of democracy as lying in the marriage of these two ideas, "liberation of individuals on the one hand and promotion of a common good on the other."[11] In other words, democracy provided for Dewey a "moral ideal" to join conservative and radical philosophy. It can be seen here how closely Dewey the philosopher was following the vision of Whitman the poet, who found the genius of democracy lying in the solidarity of a "perfect individualism" joined with "the idea of the aggregate" and merging into the many-in-one.

Dewey's instrumentalism was challenged as extensively as was James's pragmatism. Both men were accused, especially by non-Americans, of abandoning thought in favor of action, accused, in short, of anti-intellectualism. Dewey's contemporaries Bertrand Russell and George Santayana rejected his concentration on *methods* and his apparent lack of concern about the *ends* of experimentation. There was in Dewey, according to the Hegelian Santayana, a tendency to dissolve "everything substantial and actual into something relative and transitional."[12] Santayana found Dewey's pragmatism "a serpent in the garden of Eden," by making a dogma of nonthought, by introducing a "lay religion" from which God and unending moral values were excluded.[13] Santayana, a colleague of James at Harvard, was an important intellectual influence on the young Walter Lippmann, overcoming to some degree the latter's earlier attraction to James's views, and is as a result a factor of some importance in the development of the ideas of modern American journalists. How distressed Dewey, the avowed enemy of dogmatism, must have been to be identified as a dogmatist one can readily imagine.

Russell, even though a personal friend and a staunch admirer of Dewey's goals, found in his ideas a continuing source of distress. In holding that the people who live in a community can realize their desires by acting together in the spirit of democracy, Dewey was, Russell maintained, embracing a dangerous philosophy of power. He was accepting the idea that with technology and know-how, a community with "social power" could ignore the forces of nature and achieve whatever goal it was seeking. Russell saw in this the tragedy of arrogance, of pride, that accompanies "a certain kind of madness—the intoxication of power . . . to which modern men, whether philosophers or not, are prone."[14] This intoxication, Russell maintained, was "the greatest danger of our time."[15]

In responding to his critics, Dewey said that it was true that the social power of human beings working together was not of itself adequate to guarantee them a happy future but that it was preferable to try than to give up:

> *I for one do not believe that Americans living in the tradition of Jefferson and Lincoln will weaken and give up without a whole-hearted effort to make democracy a living reality.*[16]

In saying this, Dewey was giving expression to what may well be the most fundamental of the ideas held by American journalists, that the presentation of public questions in print and over the air is absolutely necessary for the future of democracy. Such a declaration may well be arrogant and prideful but even a recognition of the arrogance and pride does not disturb the belief system. Dewey may have seen himself as a meliorist and not an optimist, but nothing is more optimistic than faith, and like Whitman, Dewey and the other pragmatists all had a basic faith in a democratic political system and in the ultimate wisdom of the people. The philosophical pessimism infiltrating the ideology of European editors and reporters has remained for the most part outside the belief system of American journalists.

Even the mature Mark Twain, embittered and contemptuous of the values embraced by Americans, still managed to retain his faith in the optimistic journalistic belief system that holds the search for truth to be good not only in itself but as working for the good of society as a whole. In his mythical account of a Connecticut Yankee in the court of King Arthur written in 1889, Twain gave enduring expression to the essence of this belief system. He had his nineteenth-century Yankee transplanted in the sixth-century Arthurian court make this observation:

> *You see my kind of loyalty was to one's country, not to its institutions or its office-holders. The country is the real thing, the substantial thing, the eternal thing; it is the thing to watch over, and care for, and be loyal to; its institutions are extraneous, they are its mere clothing, and clothing can wear out, become ragged, cease to be comfortable, cease to protect the body from winter, disease, death.*
>
> *To be loyal to rags, to shout for rags, to worship rags—that is a loyalty to unreason, it is pure animal; it belongs to monarchy, was invented by monarchy; let monarchy keep it. I was from Connecticut, whose Constitution declares "that all political power is inherent in the people, and all free governments are founded on their authority and instituted for their benefit; and they have* at

all times *an undeniable and indefeasible right to* alter their form of government *in such manner as they may think expedient."*

Under that gospel, the citizen who thinks he sees that the commonwealth's political clothes are worn out, and yet holds his peace and does not agitate for a new suit, is disloyal; he is a traitor. That he may be the only one who thinks he sees this decay, does not excuse him; it is his duty to agitate anyway, and it is the duty of others to vote him down if they do not see the matter as he does.[17]

Dewey was equally dismayed by the "feudalized commercialism" of his age. Thought and discussion were to him, as they were to Twain, "instruments" with which to combat what he called "the new dogma." For the American, he wrote:

There is a genuine idealism of faith in the future, in experiment directed by intelligence, in the communication or knowledge, in the rights of the common man in the fruits of the spirit.[18]

Dewey's fascination with ethical questions has made him of special interest to the increasing number of journalists and journalism students searching for guides to moral conduct as they attempt to carry out their duties as editors and reporters. Kantians, those who believe in irrevocable value systems, tend to heap scorn on Dewey, whose ethical values were inevitably pragmatic, totally opposed to any all-encompassing system. At one point, in a critique of the metaphysics of the neo-Hegelian, T. H. Green, Dewey made the point clearly enough:

I wish . . . to point out the inadequacy of metaphysical theories, on the ground that they fail to meet the demand . . . of truly ethical theory, that it lend itself to translation into concrete terms, and thereby to the guidance, the direction of actual conduct.[19]

Put another way, Dewey was saying that moral values must be concrete: they must relate to the specific conduct under study. In other words, morality is relative, based on actual situations. This position is quite similar to Hume's view that values are inevitably drawn from custom and conventional behavior. Dewey's doctrine has come, often enough, to be criticized as "situational ethics" and hence devoid of real values. Dewey rejected this argument throughout his long career. What he was saying, Dewey insisted, was that a person could not find "concrete directions for moral action" in some social theory, for "that which is serviceable now may prove injurious at a later time."[20] Moreover, he wrote, any other system of moral values, like Hegel's "institutional idealism," must necessarily conform to an authoritative view of what is best and the individual is therefore not free to think for himself.[21] At another point, Dewey observed:

> *There are countless illustrations of the way in which a problem of personal conduct is so complicated by social conditions that a person has to decide about the latter in order to reach a conclusion in the former.*[22]

Dewey's switch from pacifism prior to World War I to support for the war and then back to pacifism again is one indication of his struggle with a system of relative moral values. Like Lippmann and other liberal thinkers, Dewey was ultimately persuaded to support that war as a step towards the achievement of a more just and more democratic world that would be driven by the machinery of benevolent science. One of Dewey's early disciples, Randolph Bourne, turned on him with a scornful reference to the "relative ease with which "the pragmatist intellectuals, with Professor Dewey at the head, had moved out their philosophy, and baggage, from education to war."[23] Years later, as war threatened Europe once again, Dewey repudiated his own support for American participation in the first war. Like many others, Dewey said, he had been misled by Allied propaganda.[24] Journalists and others struggling with moral issues would no doubt find comfort in an examination of the intellectual struggles of John Dewey, who is to many the leading philosopher produced by the United States.

CHAPTER 38

Journalists and Pragmatism

The pragmatists exerted a direct and powerful effect on Walter Lippmann, the leading philosopher among American journalists, who made James's acquaintance while a student at Harvard. James's pragmatism was by no means the only intellectual influence on Lippmann. In fact, the neo-idealist Santayana, another Harvard professor and one of James's intellectual foes, played a critical role in Lippmann's development. Still, belief in science and experimentation dominated Lippmann's thinking, which was also influenced by Dewey, whose writings were often published in the *New Republic*, the journal edited by the youthful Lippmann.

We will turn our attention to Lippmann more closely in Part 9 but it is useful to note here that it was in 1908, the year after the publication of *Pragmatism*, that James spotted an essay by the 17-year-old Lippmann in a magazine put out by Harvard undergraduates, an essay in which Lippmann spoke out in condemnation of the elitist views of another Harvard professor named Barrett Wendell.[1] James invited Lippmann to take tea with him on Thursdays and these occasions offered the cheerful, high-spirited philosopher a chance to encourage his new disciple to abandon logic—"fairly, squarely, and irrevocably"—and instead to embrace "reality, life, experience, concreteness and immediacy." Rely on science, on experimentation and an inquiring mind, James argued; seek out the facts, and you will never go wrong. The first article Lippmann published under his own name was a eulogy on the occasion of James's death in 1910. James, he wrote, was a man who "listened for truth from anybody, and from anywhere, and in any form, from Emma Goldman, the pope or a sophomore; preached from a pulpit, a throne or a soap box."[2]

Small wonder that so many journalists identify themselves as pragmatists. After all, since pragmatism is concerned primarily with the search for "facts," it seems almost made for the American journalist. Yet James and Dewey were always careful to avoid equating truth with facts and to make sure that pragmatism and the practical were not identified as the same thing. Indeed, at one point, James seemed to equate pragmatism with "humanism," a doctrine advanced by a colleague, Ferdinard Schiller, at Oxford University in England.[3] Schiller and Dewey, following the strictures of Darwin and other biologists, argued that truth emerges by the process of piling new facts on top of the old established facts by a process of induction, from the particular to the general. Truth is not a fact, but a series of facts that *works*. Truth is something that *grows*.

"Pragmatism," James said, in a passage that would produce cheers at almost any gathering of American journalists, "is uncomfortable away from facts." The rationalist, on the other hand, he said, "is comfortable only in the presence of abstractions."[4]

Facts are concrete. "The pragmatist clings to facts and concreteness," James said, "observes truth at its work in particular cases, and generalizes."[5] He might have been making the same statement about the American journalist.

As for the other side, James said that the typical "ultra-abstractionist" shudders at concreteness. He prefers the pale and spectral, "the skinny outline rather than the rich thicket of reality," the thicket of course much beloved of the fact-minded journalist. There was to James even a moral quality in the factual: "It is so much purer, clearer, nobler."[6]

Quite clearly, James's philosophy touches the intellectual and emotional needs of American journalists, as it does those of the "can do," action-oriented American people as a whole. Actually, however, this view of pragmatism as simply practical, concerned only with facts, is a simplification or even a misreading of the philosophy of James and Dewey, a philosophy that demands the utmost in rigor and open-mindedness. Dennis Chase, who regards journalists as "aphilosophical," that is, as almost unanimous in denying philosophy and in rejecting theory in favor of practice, points out how closely journalists adhere to certain aspects of pragmatism. To Chase, however, rejection of theory has tragic consequences.[7] He remarks that those leading journalists who do reflect on philosophical matters tend to identify themselves as pragmatists or empiricists.[8] Michael Schudson says that journalists have indeed been "naive empiricists,"[9] an accurate enough characterization of those who see themselves as "practical," but fail to recognize the stern demands of "pragmatism."

James made an effort to separate the concept of pragmatism from that of "radial empiricism," another idea with which he was associated, but he was not always successful in clarifying the differences. Followers of James have inevitably linked the two, and in Dewey's case, pragmatism seems to be almost identical with the scientific method, which is rooted in empirical inquiry.

Belief in the standard of objectivity arises from dedication to the scientific method. Heap fact upon fact, facts arrived at through painstaking research, and truth will emerge. Such has been the message of empirical philosophers since the days of John Locke. Yet James, in a little-noted passage, directed attention to perhaps the trickiest trap that lies beneath what appears to be the solid ground of objectivity. Often, James wrote, "the day's contents oblige a rearrangement."[10] Facts do not merely *exist*. They are deceptive. What is accepted as scientific truth today may tomorrow turn out to be false. The discovery of radium, James noted, seemed to shatter mankind's ideas about the very nature of the world. This problem did not, however, dismay the sunny-spirited James who, as we have observed earlier, rejected any idea of objective truth. New truths are found, he said, by getting themselves accepted. To do that, they have to work. In other words, it is not immoral to knowingly print a lie; it will be found to be untrue if it doesn't work. This appears to reflect the standard empirical view that research, the quest for the truth, is a process free of values. The value—or truth—emerges only after the quest has been rigorously pursued.

The contrary philosophical view holds that printing a lie in no way helps to find the truth and that, furthermore, the consequences of this value-free search for truths are insidious. The challenges to pragmatic thought by Santayana and Russell and by others whom James and Dewey identified as rationalists (Kant and Hegel significant among them) are rooted in this conviction. James dismissed their argument as the handiwork of "ultra-abstractionists," who believe that truth and morality are phenomena existing independent of whether or not they "work." Basic in the belief system of most American journalists is the Jamesian conviction that goodness lies in the search itself. This is a restatement of the ethical system of Aristotle as modified by James and Dewey. In Chase's terminology, to be "aphilosophical" means to accept whatever philosophy is culturally dominant in any given period. The "passive, osmotic acceptance" of pragmatism, he writes, "is strangling the chance for a science of journalism."

> *With nothing fixed, with everything continually evolving, the editor is free to unleash his reporters at whatever strikes his or his readership's fancy. There is never an obligation to inquire about the function of a newspaper, or to define a newspaper's chief commodity, news. This last is the most tragic terror.*[11]

Some editors, among them Greeley, William Allen White, and E. L. Godkin,[12] have of course concerned themselves with larger questions, but it is certainly correct, as Chase notes, that traditionally editors have neither asked questions about the functions of newspapers nor sought to find definitions for news. Following patterns dating back to Bennett and Greeley, they have relied on their own judgment in deciding what is to be reported and for what purpose.[13] They have relied on their experience; in this, they are indeed behaving in the spirit of pragmatism

The "can do" society, which American editors seem always to have revered, is a society of action. It is one into which nearly all the ideas of the American journalist can fit comfortably. It is optimistic; it believes without qualification in progress and growth under the banner of science and empirical inquiry; its social order is democratic and moral; education is the key to the future, and the people have a right to education in their schools and in their newspapers. In this system of beliefs, under this set of attributes, the press is without doubt an instrument of vast power with an enormous potential for good. Under this belief system, no one can question the validity of the moral crusades to which in their various forms many journalists have been dedicated.

Moral crusades have been a conspicuous element in American journalism from its outset. We have seen the crusading impulse in the work of colonial printers and antebellum activists—in James Franklin and Horace Greeley and many of their fellows. Sometimes it has seemed almost compulsory for the American journalist to stand foursquare on the side of the "common man" and the "democrat" and against the "aristocrat" and the "corrupt." In no period of American history has this tendency been more marked than during the age of the "robber barons," the industrialists of the Gilded Age.

The name that has come to designate that period, covering roughly the last third of the nineteenth century and the early years of the twentieth, was the creation of Mark Twain, who with a fellow journalist, Charles Dudley Warner, published *The Gilded Age* in 1873. In it and in so much of his other writings, Twain, perhaps the most famous writer in American history, lashed away at the hypocrisy he saw all around him. This sense of moral outrage appeared in Twain's journalism, written over a 25-year period (1847–1871), and in the fiction that followed, as he, like Whitman before him and so many creative writers afterwards, found the conventions of journalism too restrictive for his tastes.

Twain is in many ways the most fascinating figure in American literature, a self-made man who rose unexpectedly to the heights of international fame through his biting, incisive irony, a frustrated optimist, who saw his task, both as reporter and novelist, to lie in the unmasking of hypocrisy and lies. He once berated a fellow journalist for saying it was the duty of the public to search for and correct abuses. Twain thundered: "Any editor in the world will say it is YOUR duty to correct them. What are you paid for? What use are you to the community? What are you fit for as conductor of a newspaper, if you cannot do these things?"[14]

Twain was a thoroughgoing pragmatist; he inevitably preached an open mind and specifically rejected all dogmas inherited from the past. And yet, although he was frequently consumed by despair, he continued to retain an existential faith in humankind and in the promise of the American Eden.[15] He expressed contempt for Whitman's visionary democracy, but he was himself always ambivalent about it. Perhaps not surprisingly, there was an unmistakable coolness between Twain and Whitman.[16] As we shall see, in his later years Whitman was himself ambivalent about the behavior of America. Here we find a familiar enough paradox. Throughout the course of America's history, many journalists have stood with Twain, brothers in his apparently contradictory stance: critical in the pages of their papers of the weaknesses, the excesses, the hypocrisies, of what they saw about them, but still managing to retain—and indeed to repeat—the utopian credo.

Sentimentality came under attack from Twain as much as lying. Among his targets, in addition to corruption in business and the persecution of blacks, were the chivalric novels of Sir Walter Scott and the romantic treatment given to Europe in American fiction, journalism, and travel books. In 1867 he took a trip around the world as a correspondent for a San Francisco newspaper and sent back articles that appeared in both Greeley's *Tribune* and Bennett's *Herald*.[17] Those articles as well as his open assault on the decadence of the Old Country in *A Connecticut Yankee in King Arthur's Court*, helped feed the anti-European, imperialistic impulse that dominated American society in those years, a development that could not have been especially pleasing to the enemy of war and hypocrisy.

Like Whitman, Twain found the publishers of the newspapers for which he wrote less willing to face tough and bitter truths than he was. In fact, his newspapers often refused to print what he wrote. In writing *A Connecticut Yankee*, he hit back at that kind of censorship, turning to a device often used by frustrated journalists, the device of fiction. In that book Twain, whose love for newspapers was boundless, had his Yankee in Arthurian England create the Camelot *Weekly Hosannah and Literary Volcano!* and found room for some pithy observations about the press.[18]

The newspaper, Twain's Yankee commented ironically, was too flip, too irreverent, and too loud. This was of course a dig at his own editors who found his articles unseemly and concerned themselves, in Twain's view, more with refusing to offend readers and advertisers than with printing facts. Twain's Yankee commented that the *Volcano!*, with its offensiveness to authority and its amusing typographical errors, was guilty of "Arkansas journalism," a short-cut term for the kind of irreverent if sloppy journalism that Twain admired. He had this tongue-in-cheek advice for the *Volcano!* editor, a recipe perhaps for the dishonest journalist:

> *The best way to manage—in fact, the only sensible way—is to disguise repetitiousness of fact under a variety of form: skin your fact each time and lay on a new cuticle of words. It deceives the eye; you think it is a new fact; it gives you the idea that the court is carrying on like everything; this excites you, and you drain the whole column, with a good appetite, and perhaps never notice that it's a barrel of soup made out of a single bean.*[19]

Despite, and perhaps because of, his tendency to rely on exaggeration and burlesque as literary devices, Twain was committed to presenting his reader with facts and reality. His tall tales, he said, were written in an attempt to show the difference between the real and the counterfeit. In a very real sense, Twain was an adherent of what a century later would be spoken of as the "new journalism." Reality did not reside in a boring repetition of dull facts but in showing the reality behind the facts. Indeed, Twain the journalist could not resist hoaxes. In Nevada, for example, he reported deadpan the excavation of a century-old stone dummy with a wooden leg found sitting, winking, and thumbing his nose at those who dug him up. Gullible editors across the country reprinted the story without comment; so indeed did a London journal of chemistry.[20] Twain maintained that he had written the piece in order to poke fun at "the growing evil" of digging up petrifications. It was for similar reasons that Twain berated Scott for his "sham grandeurs, sham gauds and sham chivalries."[21] It was only through meticulous attention to concrete detail that the writer could demonstrate reality. The careful use of idiom and accent in *Huckleberry Finn* is testimonial enough to Twain's efforts to achieve reality. A century later, some persons were still trying to exclude words such as "nigger" from *Huckleberry Finn*, precisely what Twain in his search for truth had fought against.

As we have noted, the excesses of the Gilded Age shook the confidence of many Americans, to whom it was now evident that industrial growth, which at first had seemed an unmitigated good, had its darker side. The wealth and power that Adam Smith had seen as the goals of all people had indeed been achieved—but not by everyone, rather by only a small number—industrialists, bankers, factory operators, land speculators, railroadmen. Frequent depressions not only slowed industrial growth but threatened to ruin factory workers in the cities and farmers in the rural areas of the West and the South. The political movements known today as Populism and Progressivism gathered strength and became forces to be reckoned with. As with all such movements, their impact on the ideas of American journalists was substantial.

CHAPTER 39

Journalists and the Age of Reform

In the Civil War period, editors of both North and South drew their ideas from the same sources, Locke and Jefferson, Voltaire and Mill. Their interpretations differed sharply, of course, especially in their analyses of the virtues or evils of slavery. The pattern did not change as the century approached its close. Few persons aside from iconoclasts like Twain challenged basic doctrine. It was too powerful. The American dream of equal opportunity for all individuals was endorsed by everyone. To the Populist editors in the West, however, this dream had been shattered by greedy men, who in their view were preventing ordinary American individuals from gaining their fair share of the fruits of the dream.

The chief targets of these editors were the men who built their industrial empires during the Gilded Age, villains, according to an army of editorialists, on the ground that they had betrayed that dream, that their behavior had subverted the country's ideals. Populist editors began to turn away from the glorification of the individual. Only through collective action, they wrote, could individual freedom be protected. That meant direct intervention by government. The poet Hamlin Garland, who was in the forefront of Populist agitation, harked back to Paine and Jefferson when he argued that the fight was for "human liberty and the rights of man."[1] Paine's phrase was a rallying cry for dozens of Populist editors.[2] The "robber barons," these editors wrote, were seizing not only money and property but also the fruits of the labor of ordinary Americans. A newspaper in Columbus, Nebraska, attacked industrialists and bankers as "moral cowards and public plunderers."[3]

It was not only industrialists, however, who came under attack from Populist editors. Congress, which refused to enact the laws that were being demanded for the protection of the interests of farmers and wage-earners, was held in contempt. Populist orators, their words enshrined in the small western dailies and weeklies, assailed the politicians in Congress as cringing men who performed the will of the moneyed interests and thus betrayed the common people.

The holding up of politicians as targets had become a tradition. The doctrine of individualism invoked by Locke and advanced by American editors down to the present day has contained within it scorn for politicians. For the most part, it is true, contempt for politicians has been directed against those political figures whose views ran contrary to those of the editors involved. Even so, however, the underlying thread has been to condemn politicians in general. No editor was more explicit than James Gordon Bennett, the founder of the *New York Herald*, whose guiding principles included the fear of God, the love of beautiful women, and a campaign against Martin Van Buren. But more than that: to "kick all politicians and parsons to the devil."[4]

Bennett was of course no Populist, but his admonition, to condemn "politicians and parsons," was part of the belief system of the Populists. White's diatribe against Populist politicians was in the same spirit.[5] Earlier in the century, Dickens and de Tocqueville had called attention to the press's contempt for politicians.[6] Although the retreating frontier has by now been replaced by an urban society with its companion social graces and gentility, press contempt for politicians has not notably declined. The scorn continues to be reflected in references to public figures as "mere politicians." Among the ideas circulated by the American press, few have been more enduring than expressions of disdain for politicians. In this, American journalists, as de Tocqueville noted a century and a half ago, have differed sharply from their fellows in other parts of the world.

(These expressions of contempt for politicians may be more ritual than reality. It is in any case the opinion of the author that American journalists are far less contemptuous of politicians in the flesh than they appear to be in their writings. American history is full of accounts of enduring friendships between journalists and politicians; indeed many reporters and editors have themselves undertaken political careers. An idea need not be carried out in practice for it be held and to be given expression. Readers of newspapers and viewers of television may be excused for failing to recognize the distinction between ritual and reality.)

Bennett was critical not only of politicians but of parsons as well. In this, he was giving voice to another of the ideas often communicated by American journalists: suspicion of, or at least skepticism about, the claims and the practices of organized religion. From the earliest days to the present, churchmen have spoken up in criticism of the contents of the press. They have seen journalists sometimes merely as unbelievers, but more often as infidels or threats to religious life, sometimes even as allies of the devil.

Much of the criticism of the press by religious fundamentalists has derived from the dedication of journalists to a liberal or progressive belief system, in which science and technology are raised to a position of centrality. There have always been exceptions. In the United States, a position of prominence has always been maintained by the religious press. But as an institution, the mainstream press has adopted the philosophical views of the Founding Fathers, who were utterly convinced that the way to knowledge, to truth, to virtue, was to be found through application of the methods of science, which were essentially empirical. Faith in religion seemed to be in sharp conflict with the tenets of science, which held that a man could know only that which he could himself observe and which he could then subject to scientific tests in order to confirm the validity of those observations.

There was in the air in America in the final years of the nineteenth century a revolutionary spirit that bore some resemblance to the socialist course in Europe, but that somehow lacked the emotional power of the European movement. By the turn of the century it had lost its drive. The rowdy, rustic, almost proletarian quality of Populism was replaced first by the more genteel reformers of the Progressivist movement, later by the New Deal under the aristocratic leadership of Franklin Delano Roosevelt.

Throughout this era, the country underwent substantial social change, and the government did indeed move into private economic and social reaches that had been considered sacrosanct by the supporters of the laissez-faire theories of Adam Smith. Yet the changes were always moderate. The idea of individualism was powerful enough to turn aside demands for collective action even in the cause of the rights of man. Indeed, prevailing American ideology has from the beginning rejected collective solutions for human problems. Exceptions there have always been, but journalists, themselves successful individuals, have rarely found it difficult to condemn collective action.

In fact, collective action by organized labor has rarely won the support of the mainstream press in the United States. Journalists were among the last group of workers to form a union and when they did, in the 1930s, they were careful to call themselves a *guild* rather than a *union*, since the latter term smacked of collective, perhaps even of "foreign" elements. In any case, the wave of strikes that marked the domestic scene during the Gilded Age came under attack in the press, even among those journalists who tended to support the aims of the strikers.

Agitation for an eight-hour work day, for better wages and working conditions by railroad workers in the 1870s and 1880s led to a series of strikes, and to a massive intervention of police when a group of people, many among them immigrants, gathered for a rally in 1886 in Chicago's Haymarket Square. The rally was a peaceful affair until jittery police moved in. A bomb suddenly exploded and although the identity of the bomb-thrower was never established, six immigrants were sentenced to death. The Chicago press, followed by the majority of newspapers in the industrial East and Midwest, reacted with horror to the violence and applauded the death sentences. The *Chicago Tribune* summed up the attitude of the press: "Chicago has become the rendezvous for the worst elements of the Socialistic, atheistic, alcoholic European classes."[7]

Although the three leading Chicago newspapers disagreed about the justice of the workers' demands, they nonetheless applauded the same general set of values: an obsession with commercial order and social harmony and a commitment to public interest consumerism.[8] A. J. Liebling has documented this same set of values in examining press reports of labor disputes in the twentieth century.[9] Concentration in reports about strikes and labor unrest was inevitably on inconveniences caused to the consumer; the social and economic issues always took second place.

In reporting the Haymarket story and labor affairs generally, the Chicago press demanded that the weight of public opinion be brought to bear on those agitating for industrial change so that issues could be peacefully resolved in an atmosphere that was "calm, rational, and deliberate."[10] These papers were giving expression to an attitude that is widespread in the value system of American journalists and which Twain had deplored: that the duty of the press lies in filing the reports that will enable the public to arrive at those calm, rational, and deliberate judgments on which the future of American democracy depends, not to demand sweeping, revolutionary change. The assumption was, and is, that law and order, peace on the streets, and the absence of violence—all of these—are required for orderly growth and progress. Those who challenge this assumption are by definition not committed to the American Way. They are, in short, "foreign elements." Although America has from its very beginnings been a scene of considerable violence, violent conflict has been alien to the vision held by most newspapers of the American value system of "communication, consensus, and community." If conflict has been seen as alien, it is not surprising that aliens have been blamed for conflict.[11] The same kind of condemnation of foreign elements, Jews and Italians, Russians and Poles, as well as support for "Americanism" filled the pages of the press throughout the Gilded Age and beyond.

The collectivism endorsed by the Populists found little support among the press. Even William Allen White, who was later to be celebrated for half a century of unswerving liberalism in defense of principle and in support of the "common man," was originally a bitter foe of Populism. In fact, the editorial that made him famous was an out-and-out attack on the political leadership of the Populist movement in his native Kansas. The impetus for the essay came, as White recalled in his *Autobiography*, after he had written an article critical of William Jennings Bryan, the Populists' 1896 Presidential candidate. He was, he said, stopped on the street by a "hooting, jeering, nagging" band of Bryan supporters as he was on his way to work at his *Emporia Gazette*.[12]

While neighboring states were gaining in wealth and population, White wrote, Kansas was losing both. Still, there was "absolutely nothing wrong with Kansas," he said, that could not be resolved by ridding the state of its Populist political leaders whom he identified as "wild-eyed fanatics," attracted only by "ragged trousers . . . lazy, greasy fizzle," despisers of everyone who was successful.[13] The essay, coming from the Midwest, which was heavily Populist, won great favor among the Republican leadership, and White became a protege of the party's national chairman, Mark Hanna, and ultimately a close friend of Theodore Roosevelt, this despite the fact that Bryan and the Democrats were successful in the election in Kansas.

Historians have been unable to arrive at a clear verdict on the Populists.[14] Some have seen the movement as an an outpouring of democratic, even radical, rage over a betrayal of American ideals, as perhaps the most clear-cut expression of the Voice of the People in this country's history. Others, in the spirit of White's essay, have condemned the Populists not only as disruptive of traditional values but also as negative, anti-individual, anti-Semitic nativists. There is evidence on both sides. Historians are in no greater agreement about the Progressives than they are about the Populists, yet it is clear enough that the two "reform" movements contributed much to the glorification of the "common man" and to the companion ascendance of one of the cardinal beliefs of American journalists: the concept of the people's right to know. After all, it is only in a democratic society in which the people decide issues that the knowing makes much difference. Journalists played a critical role in both of these movements and in so doing helped to make the concept of the people's right to know a part of conventional wisdom, a part of the belief system of Americans in general and journalists in particular.

Whatever else it was, Populism had most of the ingredients of a revolutionary movement. It did indeed swell up among those at the bottom of the social order. It was only when it declined in the 1890s and was replaced by the urban and urbane intellectualism of the Progressives that reform became truly palatable to White, who wrote that Populism had "shaved its whiskers, washed it shirt, put on a derby, and moved up to the middle class."[15] The Progressives, he said, "caught the Populists in swimming and stole all their clothes except the frayed underdrawers of free silver."[16]

Many, even in later periods, accepted White's analysis and viewed the Progressives as lineal descendants of the Populists, as people who built on the antibusiness heritage of the Populists.[17] Most contemporary scholars, however, reject the idea that the Progressives were antibusiness, let alone revolutionary.[18] Reform was no longer rural and provincial, but "urban, middle-class and nationwide."[19] As such it exerted a powerful attraction over the crusading spirit of journalists, especially those who had earned for themselves a place among the nation's intellectual elite, who were themselves men of power and influence, the leaders admired by William James and other pragmatists. Theodore Roosevelt, the great hero of the Progressives and a man much admired by the reform journalists, saw himself as exactly such a leader. The youthful Lippmann observed that Progressives were convinced the people were on the lookout for a "benevolent guardian" to lead them and that the political leaders of the movement, Roosevelt and Wilson among them, saw themselves as just such guardians.[20]

Philosophically this was a reference to Plato's concept of the ideal state, where "guardians," a kind of benevolent police force, insured social justice largely through providing the people with a model of strength and courage, both physical and moral. In Plato's ideal state, it was not the guardians but the small band of intellectuals—he identified them as philosopher-kings—who established the philosophical principles on which the republic rested. Plato's ideal republic was of course an elitist state, exactly the kind dreamed of by the Progressives who, like Plato's guardians, were anything but men of the people. No doubt Roosevelt and Wilson saw themselves as healthy combinations of guardian and philosopher king. That, in any case, is the way Lippmann perceived them.

The Progressive movement arose parallel to the new theory of history circulated by Frederick Jackson Turner, who was himself celebrated as the epitome of the Progressive historian. The frontier became a symbol for the Good Life; it took its place in the national longing for days gone by, a mood fanned by the uncomfortable disruptions and distress of urban life. As we shall see shortly, it also played a role in the upsurge of patriotism and imperialism that dominated American life at the turn of the century. Moreover, the urban reforms promoted by the Progressives, with muckraking journalists in the fore, fit conveniently into the nostalgic impulse of romanticizing the past.

Typical of the upper-class Progressive reformers was the editor Joseph Medill Patterson, grandson of the founder of the *Chicago Tribune*. He and his cousin, Robert McCormick, the very archetype of the Establishment newspaper publisher, assumed control of the *Tribune* in 1914, but Patterson was of a different mold from that of his cousin. In his youth a fiery socialist orator, he wrote novels in which he argued that under capitalism neither the city of Chicago nor the nation itself could be reformed. The two managed to resolve their political differences by agreeing that the *Tribune* would remain under McCormick's control while they acquired a new paper to be run by Patterson. Thus was born the *New York Daily News*, the country's first tabloid, which publisher Patterson saw as the "people's paper," designed to meet the needs of the poor and the oppressed, primarily the immigrants, whose knowledge of English was limited.[21] For many years, Patterson's paper supported the liberal Democratic party, much to the chagrin of his cousin, Bertie McCormick, but in the end Patterson split with Franklin D. Roosevelt, mainly over foreign policy issues.[22]

Perhaps it was the difference in mindset that separated the Populists most clearly from the Progressives. Populism arose at the bottom of the unusual swing of national mood towards pessimism, impelled by the dislocations that accompanied the Gilded Age and the spectacular rise of the new moneyed class of bankers, industrialists, and entrepreneurs. The mood that accompanied the Progressive period was, however, the exact opposite. Economically, the country was on an upswing following the Panic of 1893. The national mood was expansive, serene and sunny, brimming with optimism, quite in the maintream of American history.[23] One historian writes that the grimness of Populism had been replaced by "a gusty, dawn-world confidence" that cheerfully accepted the business values of America.[24] The hero of the Progressives, as we have noted, was

Theodore Roosevelt, whose presidency was marked by fewer major reforms than his followers wished, but whose leadership role cannot be minimized. He fit precisely the image of the great leader demanded by William James and novelists like Frank Norris. He was the darling of the muckrakers, at least until he turned on them. He was also a wizard of the English language, he who spoke softly and carried a big stick, and he spoke passionately in support of such Progressive reforms as the establishment of an impartial civil service system and an end to the unrestricted might of monopolies. Again and again, Roosevelt invoked the glory of America and the muscular spirit of the common American folk who would make the nation great in the spirit of the pragmatic men of the frontier.[25]

CHAPTER 40

The Doctrine of the Right to Know

It was the Progressivist faith in a popular majority that spoke directly to the concept of the people's right to know. The intellectual leader of the Progressives was Robert La Follette, a man who served Wisconsin as both governor and U.S. senator. There can be little doubt that "Fighting Bob," as he was called by his friends, had an abiding faith in a democratic system in which decisions were made by an active, aware, and *informed* public. "The composite judgment is always safer and wiser and stronger and more unselfish than the judgment of any one individual mind," La Follette maintained, echoing the wisdom of Jean-Jacques Rousseau. "The people have never failed in any great crisis in history. . . . The very backbone of true representative government is the direct participation in the affairs of government by the people."[1]

It was a clear and precise endorsement of a public right to know. Small wonder that La Follette was so popular with the press. He was to be defeated for the presidency in 1924, when, like Theodore Roosevelt before him, he ran as the candidate of the Progressive party, but he continued to enjoy a favorable press. In this La Follette the man was like his Progressive party, or like the Progressive movement in its historiography under Turner, or its politics under Roosevelt, or its journalism under White and Lippmann—all these men stood as visible embodiment of faith in the people, of the spirit of optimism and of the people's right to know. Curiously enough, none of them was a "man of the people." Each was in his own way a member of the nation's elite, even as are the journalists who pronounce themselves the "guardians" of the people's right to know.

John Dewey's voice was added to the chorus endorsing the ideal of a public right to know. The concept was very much a part of the "fighting faith" that Dewey saw in democracy, which he equated with liberalism and with pragmatism. This stance grew stronger as Dewey aged and as he saw free speech vanishing in Hitler's Germany. "The greatest menace to freedom," Dewey wrote in 1935, "is an inert people."[2] It was, to Dewey, quite simply "a political duty" to discuss political issues in public and no one had a right to keep the people from knowing what was going on around them.

The doctrine of a public right to know is of course rooted in confidence in the common man and optimism about the future. Whether the journalist actually has such confidence in the common man is a question that cannot be answered easily. In any case, whether such confidence and optimism are genuine ingredients in the belief system of the American journalist, he or she is not likely to give expression in public to the opposite, that is, to a lack of confidence in the people or despair about the future. Certainly, whatever else one may say, today's American journalist is likely to agree with Madison that knowledge is power and to argue whole-heartedly that all free men and women are entitled to access to knowledge, to the wisdom of the ages. Such an article of faith was a hallmark of the Enlightenment.

Indeed, the concept of the right of the people to know about the practices of their government goes back to a period well before the Enlightenment. It is in fact one of the oldest ideas given expression on the American continent. In 1641, a mere generation after the arrival of the *Mayflower*, a memorandum appeared in Boston known as the Massachusetts "Body of Liberties." According to it, every male resident of the colony had "free liberty" to examine the records of any court or office, aside from those of the governing council, and to have a copy of the document made available to him.[3]

This concept was comfortably embraced by the doctrine of civil liberties enunciated in the Bill of Rights, whose guarantee of due process of the law assured the citizen that he could not be brought into federal court (and, after the Fourteenth Amendment was adopted in 1868, into any state court) without being given knowledge of the charges against him. Nor could anything he owned be taken from him or searched unless he could be shown the legal document that authorized such invasion of his property. He had the "right to know" the charges and to be shown the documents.

In emphasizing the refreshing quality of education, Madison and Jefferson enshrined knowledge in the American belief system: it provided the American citizen the raw substance he needed to carry out his constitutional role. In order that he might be able to acquire this knowledge, the citizen had a positive right to be kept informed of what his government was doing. Official stenographers recorded the proceedings of the Congress and these proceedings were accordingly published. The Government Printing Office was created in the spirit of this "right to know" on the part of the citizen. The Founders were relying also on Milton's self-righting principle, which might be (and later was) interpreted as implying a public right to know, since how else might truth enter the marketplace?

It is not at all surprising that the earliest newspapers and magazines endorsed the principle of the public's "right to know," although there is no indication that the term itself was in use in those days. Editors saw themselves as performing a public function: they were the eyes and ears of their readers. It was indeed as representatives of the public that they enjoyed the benefits of the First Amendment. These benefits were not properly theirs as individuals but only as servants of the people. In a sense, then, they were the beneficiaries of a right accorded to the press as an institution, whose function in a democratic society was to provide information to the people.

Actually, of course, what the Founders were guaranteeing was not the provision of information to the public but rather the right to express opinions in print. In either case, it is clear that the Founders were expressing a profound faith in the reasonableness and wisdom of the people. It was absolutely necessary for the editors in the villages and towns that were in the process of becoming communities to echo such faith in the people. Few persons could be expected to read the newspapers of editors who held them in contempt. To say this is not to suggest that the early editors were hypocrites who scorned their readers. It is merely to indicate how profoundly the idea was held that editors guarded some not altogether clearly articulated right of the readers they served. The most powerful article of faith held by American journalists is belief in freedom of the press. From a philosophical standpoint, it is difficult to sustain this article of faith without a companion dedication to some concept of service to the point.

The phrase, "the public's right to know," did not make its modern appearance until 1945 in an address by the general manager of the Associated Press, Kent Cooper.[4] In seeing the press as serving the right of the people "to know," Cooper was occupying the mainstream of American journalism, whether the concept was expressed openly or simply accepted as obvious. Cooper was able to justify the rights and privileges of the American press as residing in their custodial role—as instruments and indeed as servants of the people. Cooper was joined in his new crusade eight years later by Harold Cross, who justified a public right to know on the basis of a three-century-old demand for the government to open up its documents to citizens who needed to make use of them.[5] Cooper followed with a book in 1956 and the campaign was in high swing.

It needs to be pointed out that nowhere in American law can one find anything so clearly established as "a right to know." The legal protections that do exist are highly specific. The people do have a legal right to certain information; they are, for instance, entitled to know the specific charges brought in a lawsuit. But they do not have any sweeping right that requires a newspaper to keep them informed about anything. In the case of broadcasting, the Supreme Court has ruled that the viewing public has a right to be kept informed, but even here such a right is not altogether clear. "It is," Justice Byron White wrote in a landmark decision in 1969, "the right of the viewers and listeners, not the right of the broadcasters, which is paramount."[6] Neither jurists nor scholars are likely to settle the legal status of a public right to know any time soon.

The most forceful legal claim of a right to know was issued in 1960 by a Yale professor named Alexander Meiklejohn, who held that one could justify the First Amendment protections for the news media only in order that the media keep the people informed about the behavior of their government. What matters, Meiklejohn said in an oft-quoted remark, "is not that everyone shall speak, but that everything worth saying shall be said."[7] Thomas Emerson, a leading student of constitutional law, agreed that the public as sovereign "must have all information available in order to instruct its servants, the government."[8] But neither Meiklejohn nor Emerson was prepared to argue for an *absolute* right to know.

Scoffers take the position that the idea of a public right to know was something invented by journalists in the hope that they could badger the courts and the legislatures into guaranteeing the press access to confidential information.[9] The point is often made that the effort to give to the news media an institutional right frustrates the very basis of the First Amendment, which was designed to protect *individuals*, not institutions, against government abuse.[10] We have seen that the concept of the press as eyes and ears of the public gives the institution of journalism a preferred position over other institutions, which are not protected by the First Amendment. Newspaper publishers were dismayed in 1982 to read an article by Karl Luedtke, the former managing editor of the *Detroit Free Press*, calling them "insolent" for "inventing new rights and privileges for [them]selves." In that same year, Luedtke wrote that the idea of a public right to know was something that journalists had made up to serve their own interests:

> *The public knows what you choose to tell it, no more, no less. If the public did have a right to know, it would then have something to say about what it is you choose to call news.*[11]

His point was that if the public has a right to know, it must also have the authority to tell the press what to publish. Others have made it clear that a legal guarantee of a right to know would open the way for government censorship, for the government would then be in a position to enforce the right.[12] If courts were to recognize a right to know, said the chief legal representative of the *New York Times*, they would soon find themselves playing the role of editors, "since only the courts can apply the qualifications inherent in the right to know."[13] The courts have made it clear that under the Constitution, newspapers have the sole right to decide what they publish. Neither the government nor the public may tell them. Most media legal scholars agree. In fact, one leading law journal article concluded that the phrase "the right to know" is at best "sloganeering" and at worst, "a pernicious constitutional doctrine which is destructive of first amendment rights."[14]

The legal argument in the service of a public right to know is far less powerful than the philosophical, or ethical, argument. Meiklejohn, Emerson, and those of like mind inevitably turn to Milton and Madison for the assumptions on which American democracy rest and to James and Dewey for their concept of cultural pluralism, which makes a place available for all views, however hateful they may be, in what Justice Oliver Wendell Holmes called "a marketplace of ideas."[15] The complexity of the issue can be seen in the 1978 Supreme Court ruling on whether or not comedian George Carlin's "seven filthy words" were fit for radio broadcast. In its majority opinion, the Court seemed to be saying they could be aired, on the ground that it is "a central tenet of the First Amendment that the government must remain neutral in the marketplace of ideas." Somewhat surprisingly in the light of that comment, the Court proceeded to hold the language unsuitable on the ground that Carlin's satire was without redeeming social value. Closer to the "right-to-know" value system of most journalists was the dissenting opinion of Justice William Brennan, who excoriated the majority for failing "to appreciate that in our land of cultural pluralism, there are many who think, act, and talk differently from the members of this Court, and who do not share their fragile sensibilities."[16]

Whether or not a legal mechanism can be found to incorporate a public right to know in law, Emerson wrote, Americans ought to consider such a right "an integral part of the system of freedom of expression, embodied in the first amendment."[17] The press, he maintained, "is a principal source of knowledge about the inner workings, sometimes devious or corrupt, of the government apparatus."[18]

Agreeing with Emerson, educator John Merrill found a right to know present by inference in the First Amendment. And, he added, in impassioned language, such a right "is at the very foundation of American government, of public discussion, of intelligent voting, of public opinion, of the very fabric and essence of democracy."[19] This was why, Merrill said, the Founding Fathers wrote the press guarantees into the Bill of Rights:

> *If the people of the republic (the sovereign rulers of the country) do not know about public affairs and government business, they surely cannot be good sovereigns; they cannot govern themselves well. They, in the philosophical framework they find themselves in,* must *know. Their government is built upon the assumption that they will know; therefore, certainly it is their "right" to know.*[20]

The issue of a public right to know continues today to provoke impassioned discussions, but as with all philosophical questions, the issue can be resolved only in terms of one's own belief system, one's own ideology. For the most part, then, American journalists today cling firmly to their conviction that in reporting the news of the day they are serving not only the interests but also the rights of their readers. It is a belief that is central to the journalist's system of values. Still, not *everything* can be known and the great unanswered question, in any philosophical discussion that claims a public right to know, is this: the right to know *what*?

CHAPTER 41

The Jubilee: The Patriotic Press

The insularity of America is both a geographical fact and a psychological reality. The two oceans to the east and west of the United States have not only isolated the country physically from the Old World but they have also established the pattern of beliefs that has made this country one of the most inward-looking great nations the world has ever experienced. The ideas of American journalists have been profoundly affected by both the geography and the psychology of this insularity. For instance, there is the concept of "Americanization" that we have encountered before.

The press of the nineteenth century and indeed of the twentieth, as in the case of Patterson's *New York Daily News*, undertook as a mission the "Americanization" of the immigrant population so that they might assist the new arrivals to become good American citizens. There was little doubt among journalists that to be an American citizen was a great blessing, perhaps the greatest that could befall a human being. This conviction seems to have been present from the beginning, for we can see it expressed in the writings of Franklin and Paine. Then, with the arrival of millions of new citizens and the expansion of the frontier, what had been conviction took on the quality of religion. The elegies of Whitman and the nativist impulses of the Populists were of course closely allied to this "Americanization" ideal. The expansion of the United States carried with it the same kind of missionary zeal. To extend the nation from the Atlantic to the Pacific was to achieve the "manifest destiny" of the country; to carry the blessings to the disadvantaged, be they Indians or Mexicans or whatever, was a missionary calling. What was being carried to the Indians, the Mexicans, and the immigrants was the glory of the democratic Way of Life. Among the intellectual leaders of this mission was the journalist E. L. Godkin, a native of Ireland, who came to the

United States in 1856 after a brief, distinguished career as a war correspondent in the Crimea for the *London Daily News*, and who nine years later founded the *Nation*, the influential intellectual publication.

It was Godkin's declared mission to preach across the land the wonders of democracy and to broadcast the libertarian philosophy of the man he called his "prophet," John Stuart Mill. Like de Tocqueville a generation earlier, Godkin was dismayed by the rough and turbulent American frontier. But what de Tocqueville had seen as inherent in democracy was, in Godkin's view, merely a reflection of the primitive conditions in the American West. The difference between the New World and the Old, Godkin wrote in 1865, a generation earlier than Turner, lay in "the frontier life," in which he found the source of American democracy.[1] But now it was time, Godkin said, to convert the raw energy of the frontier into the cultural and literary values of the educated man. This meant, in the spirit of Godkin's hero, Mill, the glorification of the individual. A fierce individualist and enemy of the collective state, Godkin like Burke before him abhorred any attempt to try to equalize humankind by action of the state, for this would surely reduce all mankind to the lowest cultural denominator.[2]

Under Godkin, the *Nation* did not exceed 10,000 in circulation, but its influence was substantial. Leading literary and political figures of the era, William James prominent among them, were faithful readers and correspondents of the *Nation* and of the *New York Evening Post*, which Godkin edited during the last 20 years of his life (he died in 1902).[3]

The great Whig intellectual historian, Vernon Parrington, claimed Godkin was a leader without a following, "little more than a voice crying in the wilderness," but Parrington was in this case blinded by Godkin's politics.[4] Godkin despised the Whig endorsement of government intervention in business. To Godkin, "national greatness" rested not on the growth of industry but on "the stock of individual honor, of self-respect, and of public spirit, of a loyalty to ideals."[5] It was Adam Smith's laissez-faire doctrine writ large. By no means a mere voice in the wilderness, Godkin was in fact a mouthpiece for the spirit of the frontier, the spirit in which the individual was promoted to the center of the world stage. However Godkin may have hated the hurly-burly of frontier life however much he may have been the aristocratic easterner, he gave expression to that American missionary idea: that American greatness rests on the shoulders of her people, as individuals and not as collective entities. In fact, this impassioned editor "sold" the frontier to the eastern intellectual.

In the nineteenth century, as the frontier was extended to the Pacific, the American people, the farmer and rancher of the West as well as the factory worker of the East, were accommodating themselves to the developing, optimistic, sociopolitical system, one that was rooted in the liberal philosophies of John Locke, Adam Smith, Thomas Jefferson, and John Stuart Mill, one that not only accepted the centrality of the individual citizen but also very much included belief in the basic morality of the country.

The fact that so many immigrants accommodated themselves to this system, which to them was as foreign as the languages they spoke, puzzled analysts of the Marxist school, who were appearing in increasing numbers in the Old World. There were some Marxists in America as well, but their day had not yet arrived. One modern Marxist analyst has observed that the immigrants, even those who settled far from the frontier in the growing, ugly urban sprawl of the new cities, were "drawn into the new society by a process that encouraged accommodation and rendered disciplined protest difficult."[6]

The role of the press in this pattern of accommodation has not been adequately appreciated. The pages of Godkin's *Nation* helped win the approval of the intellectuals of the eastern elite. In the West, it was other newspapers, like White's *Emporia Gazette*, that preached the mystique of democracy and of individualism.

The expansionist wars reflected the same missionary impulse. As a result of the Mexican War, which American troops launched in 1846, the country was able to annex the entire Southwest, from Texas to California. The power motives and economic rationale for the war were downplayed if not totally ignored by President Polk's government and by the press, which by and large saw an American military victory as bringing democracy to Mexico and helping fulfil the divine plan under which the fertile soil of the Mexican territory would be placed in the hands of a superior people for its "beneficent utilization."[7]

An editorial in the *New York Sun* is typical of the Americanization myth that afflicted much of the press during the Mexican War. The Mexican "race," the editorial held, was used to being conquered, and if the Mexicans were smart, they would recognize that they could only profit by the experience of being conquered:

> *To* liberate *and* ennoble—*not to* enslave *and* debase—*that is our mission. . . . If they [the Mexicans] have not—in the profound darkness of their vassal existence—the intelligence and manhood to accept the ranks and rights of freeman at our hands, we must bear with their ignorance. There is no excuse for the man educated under our institutions, who talks of our "wronging the Mexicans," when we offer them a position infinitely above any they have occupied, since their history began. . . .*[8]

Whitman was an equally fierce advocate of war with Mexico. In the *Brooklyn Eagle*, he equated the people of Mexico with the Indians, against whom he lashed out in biblical wrath for their perpetration of "devilish massacres" on Americans:

> *Who has read the sickening story of those brutal wholesale murders so useless for any purpose except gratifying the cowardly appetite of a nation of braves, willing to shoot down men by the hundred in cold blood—without panting for the day when the*

prayer of that blood should be listened to—when the vengeance of a retributive God should be meted out to those who so ruthlessly and needlessly slaughter in His image?[9]

Of course, not all American newspapers expressed such fiercely retributive or imperialistic sentiments (those in the Northeast in particular spoke up in opposition), but the overriding message was the carrying out of manifest destiny. The wars that came afterwards followed a similar tack, even the Civil War, where the central issue was precisely the question of manifest destiny: would the dispute between North and South shatter the nation and its destiny? The war came about because North and South were unable to reach a compromise on either the slavery question or the relative power of the nation and its states. The biblical exhortations of the antislavery Northern orators and the rallying cries of the proslavery Southern firebrands, their words carefully recorded by the sectional press, were highly moralistic in tone, bespeaking an immoderate passion that occupied the pages of the American press from its outset. But, as historian Stanley Elkin has observed, there was no institution in American life to provide a channel for focusing these fierce moralistic outbursts so that rational compromise might be achieved.[10] Both the proslavery and antislavery movements, Elkins wrote, were "for practical purposes devoid of intellectual nourishment."[11] The fiery press, on both sides of the Mason-Dixon line, certainly did not help prevent bloodshed, any more than did the moralistic press of the Mexican War period.

As the slavery issue mounted in intensity, both Northern and Southern newspapers devoted an increasing volume of space to the issue.[12] The Northern papers were full of spicy tales of mistreatment of Negroes; the Southern papers teemed with reports of Negro insurrections, nearly all of them rumored or simply imagined.[13] No major black uprising took place after Nat Turner's revolt in 1831. De Tocqueville's warning had come to pass. In America, the Frenchman had written a generation before the Civil War, that the power of the majority was so great that it might repress all controversy.

Constance Rourke's study of Horace Greeley, to which we have referred earlier, is aptly titled *Trumpets of Jubilee*. Greeley is not the only trumpet of whom she writes. Among the others are the members of the righteous Beecher family of Massachusetts, including the preacher of temperance Lyman Beecher, and his children, Henry Ward Beecher, the antislavery Congregationalist orator, and Harriet Beecher Stowe, author of *Uncle Tom's Cabin*, the century's best-known novel about Southern blacks. Rourke drew the key word of her title from the words to the poem, "Marching Through Georgia," which, set to music, became the battle cry of Northern vengeance. "Hurrah" "Hurrah!" the poem read, "we bring the Jubilee! The flag that makes you free!"[14] It was the message of manifest destiny, of the militant Church of America on the march. The North was bringing the Jubilee, the American dream, to the enslaved blacks of the South.

It is fitting that the word *jubilee* should be biblical in origin. The ancient Jewish people used a ram's horn to proclaim the Year of Jubilee, a period of emancipation and restoration every 50 years announced by the blast of trumpets throughout the land. During the Jubilee year, fields were to be left untilled, Hebrew slaves were to be set free, and the land and houses in open country were to revert to their original owners.[15] Figuratively, the year of the Jubilee is a time of restitution, remission, release.

Of all the wars in which the United States has participated, none has been more openly imperialistic than the Spanish-American War. With the West and the South secure, manifest destiny had accomplished its mission on the American continent. In the final decade of the nineteenth century, it was clear that to expand the scope of the American dream, it was necessary to transmit it beyond the American shores. Fanned by the expansionist rhetoric of the jingoist yellow press of Hearst and Pulitzer, American troops wrested Cuba and the Philippines from Spain. Manifest destiny was now *jingoism*, a term that came to be applied to the most blatant of expansionist patriots. The term was derived from an English song that gained popularity in music halls when England and Russia came close to war in the 1870s: "We don't want to fight/ But, by Jingo, if we do,/ We've got the ships, we've got the men,/ We've got the money too."[16]

The yellow press clamoring for war with Spain drew the wrath of Godkin, true to the end of his long life to his belief in the virtue of a responsible press. As Hearst and Pulitzer, in their quest for huge circulations, grew more and more sensational, especially in clamoring for war with Spain, Godkin turned the pages of the *Nation* into a forum for attack on the yellow journals. Two months before war was declared, Godkin wrote:

> *Nothing so disgraceful as the behavior of two of these newspapers in the past week has ever been known in the history of American journalism. Gross misrepresentation of the facts, deliberate invention of tales calculated to excite the public, and wanton recklessness in the constitution of headlines which outdid even these inventions, have combined to make the issues of the most widely circulated newspapers firebrands scattered broadcast through the community. . . . It is a crying shame that men should work such mischief simply in order to sell more papers. . . .*[17]

In his final years, Godkin's was indeed a voice crying in the wilderness, as he sought to buck the public tide by condemning American imperialism. To him the conquest of the Philippines in 1899 was "a badge of national degradation."[18] The greatest villain of the period, in Godkin's eyes, was the British poet Rudyard Kipling, whose frank advocacy of imperialistic ventures had become so popular in the United States that his poem, "White Man's Burden," was cabled to America and printed as the lead item in *McClure's* magazine.[19]

Kipling's poem was composed specifically for America, which Kipling saw as partner if not actually successor to Britain in transmitting the values of the Anglo-Saxon world to the less fortunate around the world. It was the "White Man's Burden" to bring the blessings of his world to the black, brown, and yellow races. No music hall jingoist, Kipling was a moralist who had learned about India as a young reporter on the scene. Filled with a passionate hatred of corruption in any form, Kipling believed that no matter what sacrifices were called for, it was up to Americans to "send forth the best ye breed" to bring light and hope to the people of the Orient, the "new-caught, sullen peoples, half devil and half child."[20]

This was a message that could do no more than warm the heart of Kipling's ally, Theodore Roosevelt, whom Kipling brought together with Cecil Rhodes, the creator of the British imperial empire in Africa, at a dinner at the Savoy House in London in 1898, not long before Roosevelt formed his Rough Riders to gallop up San Juan Hill in Cuba and thus to emerge as the heroic, athletic patriot who would lead America into the twentieth century.[21]

Godkin was by no means alone in opposing the war against Spain, but his was a minority voice. This was, after all, the age of expansion, and Roosevelt was joined by Hearst, Pulitzer, and other editors in the quest for a sane and orderly Pax Anglo-Saxonica, for a world free of anarchy and foreign tyranny. That quest did not disappear in the twentieth century, even after Britain had surrendered her empire, for it became, as Kipling wished, the task of the United States, usually allied with Britain, to carry the White Man's Burden, that is to say Anglo-Saxon democracy, to the nations, new and old, of the Far East, the Middle East, Africa, and Latin America.

The missionary zeal was also very much present in the First World War, which was, as it was said, fought to bring about the global triumph of democracy. Even John Dewey, that enemy of violence, came to endorse a war fought for such praiseworthy ends. Only the war in Vietnam, the longest in American history, would produce serious opposition in the press, and then only after the fighting had been dragging on indecisively for nearly a decade.

As for Godkin, he slowly changed from the wide-eyed idealist of his younger days to an embittered old man. In his later years, as the western frontier reached the Pacific and the "safety valves" disappeared from the continent, as war loomed with Spain, Godkin grew pessimistic and feared for the future of democracy. The antagonisms that sprang up among farmers, workers, and capitalists especially embittered Godkin. He fell, as Parrington observes in a telling phrase, "to mouthing like any newspaper writer."[22] (Parrington's phrasing is typical of the contempt of many scholars, then and now, for the content of newspapers and especially of radio and television. Godkin was an important personality to Parrington so long as he was something "more" than a mere journalist. In truth, however, Godkin's importance is *as* a journalist.)

In periods of warfare, it is clear, the American journalist has, like nearly all mainstream Americans, rallied to the Cause, be that Cause sectional, national, or international. For the most part, the Cause, for Americans in their insular environment, has been identified as the Cause of America, a Cause inevitably seen as synonymous with democratic virtues. When Americans have been challenged (or have perceived themselves to be challenged) by outsiders, the American journalist has tended to serve as spokesman for the Cause. Sometimes the Cause has, on reflection, been seen to be a jingoistic cause (as in the wars with Mexico or Spain) and sometimes it has been seen as a response to a genuine threat to national survival, as in the Civil War or the Second World War. In each case the belief system of American journalists has been indistinguishable from that of the American people as a whole. The same cannot be said of challenges that have come from *inside* the country. It is in this connection that American journalists have often distinguished themselves as opponents of those who hold political power, as members of a Fourth Estate, as investigators. We turn now to an examination of the belief system that accompanies what today is identified as investigative journalism.

PART VIII

The Investigative Role of the American Journalist

*Lincoln Steffens (1866–1936): "When a reporter no longer saw red at a fire, when he was so used to police news that a murder was not a human tragedy but only a crime, he could not write police news for us [*New York Commercial Advertiser*]. We preferred the fresh staring eyes to the informed mind and the blunted pencil."*

A. J. Liebling (1904–1963): "The function of the press in society is to inform, but its role is to make money. The monopoly publisher's reactions, on being told that he ought to spend money on reporting distant events, is therefore exactly that of the proprietor of a large, fat cow, who is told that he ought to enter her in a horse race." (photo reprinted with permission of Ray Driver)

CHAPTER 42

Introduction: An Essential Element

Critical in the belief system, or professional ideology, of the American journalist is the conviction that he or she is a watchdog, a person who occupies a central position in American society, who provides for the citizen the surveillance that shows which persons in power are wise and honorable enough to deserve their positions of power. Not only is it essential, in this belief system, for the journalist to help educate the citizen, to supply him with information, but it is equally necessary for the journalist to serve as the citizen's eyes and ears in scrutinizing the powerful. It is in this ideological framework that the journalist functions as investigative reporter.

In contemporary times, attention to the investigative role of the journalist intensified in the period that has come to be identified as the Watergate Era. But journalists have, from the very beginning of the American experience, seen themselves as investigators: the opportunity to bring down the crooked and the corrupt has always been a magnet for attracting men and women to the nation's newsrooms. Never before the Watergate Era, however, was it possible for the journalist to claim credit for bringing down a corrupt person who had reached the highest position in the country, the presidency. In 1974, Richard M. Nixon resigned as president of the United States under attack for overstepping the law, for actions that had been described in careful detail by the press. Thereafter, fed by the applause of admirers and the rewards both in prestige and in wealth that accompanied that applause, Americans in increasing numbers poured into journalism schools in a new quest for the glamour that was suddenly accompanying the career of investigative reporter.

In Part 8, we will see the development of this emphasis on the investigative function, both in philosophical constructs and models of behavior, and also in practice. Critics of the news media often point to the investigative or watchdog role as demonstrating arrogance and elitism in the journalist. The validity of these differing points of view on the watchdog function can be examined only in terms of the philosophical roots of the journalist's professional ideology. Support for the watchdog function appears as early as John Milton's *Areopagitica*, in which the English poet-essayist demands that the journalist challenge the orthodoxy of power by printing the truth, for truth will then shatter the strength of the error that has taken control of the political arena. This philosophical construct, as we have seen, soon came to be associated with the belief that the reader has a *right to know*—to be informed, so that he can act, in order to preserve his individual rights under the social contract described by John Locke and Jean-Jacques Rousseau. Not only is this right guaranteed by the social contract but it is also in the service of Rousseau's General Will. Only through the investigative work of journalists can the right of rebellion promised by Locke be secured. Mill offers philosophical support for the journalistic precept that the reporter may not be censored by those in power even when the journalist writes stories that are anathema to the powerful. In the United States, the Democratic-Republican clubs pledged themselves to the cause of the watchdog. Mark Twain, as we have seen, went as far as journalist could go when he insisted that the reporter *lead* the attack against crooked rulers. In the twentieth century, John Dewey gave fresh philosophical support for the idea expressed earlier by Karl Marx, that the investigative journalist in a democratic society is—and ought to be—an instrument for change, a mighty force to challenge corrupt leadership.

In short, the philosophical roots for the belief system of the watchdog run deep in the soil of American journalism.

The chapters in Part 8 examine this belief system from a number of perspectives. First, we trace the ideas that fired the investigative practices of the powerful modern watchdogs operating in the ages of yellow journalism and the muckrakers. After pausing to explore criticisms of the press that come from inquiring thoughtful writers, we look at the philosophical response to those criticisms raised under the banner of social responsibility—a banner lofted proudly by the members of a commission chaired by Robert Hutchins and advanced by the authors of a prominent study that introduced the idea of four theories of the press. Finally, we trace the important role investigative reporting has assumed in the contemporary world of American journalism.

In all these cases, it will be seen, a powerful moral base is found for the idea of a watchdog role for the American press.

CHAPTER 43

The Yellow Journalists

The fact that "yellow journalism" has always had a bad press has tended to obscure its significance and even its meaning in American life. For, while yellow journalism is thought of by journalists and the public alike as a practice to be avoided like a pestilence of horrors in the interests of truth and objectivity, its chief ingredients nevertheless conform to many of the universally accepted values of the American media system.

The goals, the values, of yellow journalism were given repeated expression by the two men most frequently associated with the practice, the publishers Joseph Pulitzer and William Randolph Hearst: to serve the people, to inform, to teach, to entertain, and to expose graft and corruption, wherever in American life it is to be found, especially when it can be uncovered in the very citadels of power.

In his first editorial in his *St. Louis Post-Dispatch* in 1878, Pulitzer declared that his paper would "serve no party but the people," that it would be "the organ of truth," that it would "advocate principles and ideas rather than prejudice and partisanship." He went even further in 1893 in his first editorial in his *New York World* by asserting:

> *There is room in this great and knowing city for a journal that is not only cheap, but bright, not only bright, but large, not only large, but truly Democratic—dedicated to the cause of the people rather than that of the purse-potentates—devoted more to the news of the New than the Old World—that will expose all fraud and sham, fight all public evils and abuses—that will serve and battle for the people with earnest sincerity.*[1]

Although less given to lofty phrases than Pulitzer, Hearst proclaimed a similar belief system. He embraced the cause of the people, spoke up for the underdog, and spent vast sums of money in order to provide information and entertainment to the reading public. Like Pulitzer, he considered himself a teacher. Even those biographers who condemn Hearst's splashy sensationalism acknowledge the importance of this controversial editor in the firmament of investigative journalism. W. S. Swanberg, for instance, notes that in his first three years as editor of the *San Francisco Examiner*, Hearst launched a dozen or so crusades, several of them of major importance, especially his long campaign against the unscrupulous might of the Southern Pacific Railroad.[2]

Hearst made no pretense to impartiality. His papers were, he said, not only expressing but actually guiding a "great national movement, a new spirit in the American people." A perceptive interviewer of Hearst in 1906 quoted him as saying, "I mean to restore democracy in the United States," but argued that the intensely egoistic Hearst was thinking more of the "I" than the "democracy," that Hearst "simply has a movement of his own. This isn't democratic, this is plutocratic, aristocratic."[3]

In his later years, Hearst offered an explanation for why he had for so long printed what later came to be identified as "bad news," stories about the transgressions of the mighty and about the seamy underside of American life. It was a statement that fit elegantly into the belief system of the American journalist:

> *People are interested in the fundamentals, love, romance, adventure, tragedy, mystery. The world is not all sweetness and light—not all sunshine. There are storms and darkness. There is suffering and death. Whoever paints the world must paint the deep shadows as well as the bright lights.*[4]

The relationship between yellow journalism and the watchdog syndrome is apparent. No voices were raised during the heyday of Pulitzer and Hearst, as they were later, to accuse the press of supporting an "adversary culture," but political leaders and businessmen might have done so—had they turned to thoughts of that kind or if the yellows had been less securely situated in the mainstream of the American spirit. Instead, politicians and businessmen joined their voices with those of intellectuals railing at the lurid excesses of the yellow press, at what came to be known as sensationalism. Hearst himself rejected that word. He described his product instead as "striking."[5] Indeed, the yellow press—so named because of the prominence of Pulitzer's cartoon figure, the Yellow Kid, a child clad, at the dawn of the age of rotary presses able to reproduce color, in a yellow dress—was anything but adversarial. It stood, as Pulitzer and Hearst demonstrated, for the traditional American values of patriotism, loyalty, honesty, thrift, and sentimentality. Arthur McEwen, editor of Hearst's *New York Journal*, said that what he wanted from the authors of his articles was the "gee-whiz" emotion. "We run our paper," he declared in what would become a classic definition of the yellow press, "so that when the reader opens it, he says: 'gee-whiz!' "[6] The first paragraph of each story was, McEwen said, to express romance, sympathy, hate, gain. The emphasis was on what he called the basic passion, "love for the woman, power for the man."

This period and the first years of the twentieth century marked, as we have seen, the rise of the values of the Progressive moment in the United States. The sociologist Herbert J. Gans has pictured those as the values journalists hold, now as well as then.[7] He called them "enduring values," identical with the values of the "altruistic democracy" model of the Progressive movement. In an uncanny way, Gans said, journalists shared with the great majority of Americans belief

> *in the common advocacy of honest, meritocratic, and anti-bureaucratic government, and in the shared antipathy to political machines and demagogues, particularly of populist bent.*[8]

This was in fact the ideology expressed by the yellow press, even as it rose to new heights in readership and circulation, even as it staged its sensationalist stunts, even as it drew the wrath of moderate critics such as Will Irwin, and those who followed.

Splitting with the Greeley past, Hearst and Pulitzer and the other yellow editors simply gave a new definition to news. They offered the reading public what it, the public, wanted—a skillful blend of not only the "gee-whiz," the sensational, the open appeal to the heart rather than the intellect, not only the innovative and dazzling, but also the appeal of the challenge to the high and the mighty. The yellows claimed to serve as the arm of the "voiceless masses" in protecting them from the ugly might of the powerful. Readership and circulation soared. Between 1880 and 1890, when the yellow press was in its first bloom, circulation increased 135 percent. In the period between 1880 and 1920 the total circulation of newspapers in the United States rose from 3,566,395 to 33,741,742.[9]

Some of the political leaders who felt the wrath of the yellows scoffed at the alleged leadership role of the press. William Jennings Bryan, three-time Democratic candidate for president, found the press utterly devoid of courage. "Newspapers," he said, "watch the way people are going and run around the corner to get in front of them."[10]

Never far from the surface, in those dying days of the nineteenth century, was the concept of the press as investigator, as sentinel on the ramparts where those in power were being monitored on behalf of what Pulitzer and Hearst depicted as the common man. The announced goal of the sentinels was to lead these common men, these underdogs, in defense of their economic and political interests. They declared themselves foes of power, supporters of liberal causes—in short, watchdogs. They portrayed themselves as a "living creature" with a heart and conscience, that loved and hated, pitied and protected, but were always motivated by their mission of educating and informing the common man.[11]

The yellows joined Mark Twain and E. L. Godkin as enemies of the Gilded Age. Despite this, neither Twain nor Godkin was a friend of the yellow press. It is to be recalled how bitterly Godkin assailed Hearst and Pulitzer for their "disgraceful ... misrepresentation of the facts" in promoting war with Spain in the 1890s.[12]

Even though Pulitzer and Hearst concerned themselves less with their editorial pages than their news columns, they nonetheless dwelt philosophically in the tradition of the editors of the penny press, the Greeleys and Bennetts, adherents all of the strictures of the English and French libertarians, those who like Locke endorsed the right of rebellion, or who like Rousseau envisioned the General Will, those who portrayed the press as serving in the vanguard of investigative activism.

It was not only the yellows who were the crusaders. There was also the gentler Charles Dana who, after leaving Greeley, embarked on a long career as editor of the *New York Sun*, and who coined the battlecry of the crusading journalist, "turn the rascals out."[13] Dana's *Sun* exposed the corruption of the Grant administration, just as the *New York Times* had earlier reported the graft of the Boss Tweed government in New York City.[14] The time was clearly ripe for the investigating surge of the yellow press and its successor, the muckrakers.

But what a display of journalistic excess! No more vivid description of the excesses of the sensationalist yellow press has appeared than that of Will Irwin, a journalist who lived through the period and reported it in a thorough, 15-part account in *Collier's* magazine in 1911, the year of Pulitzer's death. This is what Irwin wrote:

> *There followed the climax of the yellow craze, an episode in social history which we may yet come to regard with as much amazement as the tulip craze in Holland or the Mississippi Bubble. Now did the* World *and the* Journal *go insane with violent scareheads, worded to get the last drop of sensation from the "story," and throw it to the fore; now did they make fact out of hint, history out of rumor; now did they create, for their believing readers, a picture of a world all flash and sensation; now did they change their bill day and night like a vaudeville house, striving always for some new and startling method of attracting a crowd. Now they hunted down the criminal with blaring horns, so playing on the mob weakness for the thief chase; now, with the criminal caught and condemned and sentenced, they howled for his reprieve, glorified him in hysterics, so availing themselves of the old mob sympathy for the victim of the law, mob hatred for the executioner. Now they dressed out the most silly and frivolous discussion of the day with symposiums of solemn opinion from prominent citizens; now they went a step further in audacity and headed an interview from Bishop Potter or Chauncey M. Depew "By Bishop Potter" or "By Chauncey M. Depew," as though these eminent citizens were real contributors. Now they discovered the snob in all humanity and turned reporters, artists, and—after the half-tones became possible—photographers loose on "Society."*

> *The Four Hundred of New York, largely a newspaper myth, was the target for this army. Their doings, with the follies emphasized, bedecked column after column, daily and Sunday, of hysterical slush. Life, as it percolated through the* World *and* Journal, *became melodrama, the song of the spheres a screech.*[15]

A remarkable shift in the policies and behavior of Pulitzer's *World* took place after the turn of the twentieth century, a change often ascribed to the fact that Pulitzer was going blind and to his selection of the distinguished journalist, Frank I. Cobb, as his chief editor. By the time of Pulitzer's death, the *World* had parted company with the yellows and blatant sensationalism. It had placed on its payroll the most outstanding journalists in the country and was to become known, before it itself died in 1931, as "the newspaperman's newspaper." The young Walter Lippmann had became director of its editorial page and the paper included on its staff such prominent writers as the playwright Maxwell Anderson, humorist Frank Sullivan, and columnist Heywood Broun.[16] Pulitzer insisted to the end that his paper was "a moral agency and a sounding board for the public interest." His defense of the practice of investigative journalism was eloquent, as he argued one of the most powerful cases ever made for an inquiring, inquisitive press:

> *This complaint of the "low moral tone of the press" is common but very unjust. A newspaper relates the events of the day. It does not manufacture its record of corruptions and crimes, but tells of them as they occur. If it failed to do so it would be an unfaithful chronicler. . . . The daily journal is like the mirror—it reflects what which is before it. . . . Let those who are startled by it blame the people who are before the mirror, and not the mirror, which only reflects their features and actions.*[17]

It would be an error to characterize the entire American press of the yellow age as sensationalist, as portraying life on these shores as melodramatic. Dana's *Sun*, Adolph Ochs's *Times*, Steffens's *Commercial Advertiser*—these and many others turned their backs on the "gee-whiz" syndrome and, while still seeking profits, sought to pursue the literary and moral values espoused by Walt Whitman: to calmly enlighten readers about the true face of the world around them. In abandoning the sensationalism of the yellows and still seeking to make money, these men were emulating the model set for them by Benjamin Franklin, who wrote in 1731 that in his quest for truth he was rejecting the higher profits he could have earned if he had stooped to the lowest common denominator.[18]

Steffens, whom we will encounter later in examining the investigating muckrakers, was a direct descendant of Whitman, urging his young reporters to look for and "express the beauty in the mean streets of a hard, beautiful city."[19] Still, Steffens was not so dedicated a socialist that he failed to see the increased circulation and higher profitability that investigative reporting could bring.[20] Meanwhile, he condemned what he saw as the cynicism of the Pulitzers and Hearsts and envisioned a "new journalism" half a century before the term was popularized in the United States. Speaking at the time in the traditional spirit of American optimism, Steffens found journalistic cynicism to be a mere pose; he turned his back on all veteran reporters who had grown jaded and world-weary from the practice of journalism. His newspaper, he said, did not want reporters whose vision of a fire was simply of redness or who saw murder as merely a crime and not a human tragedy: "We preferred the fresh staring eyes to the informed mind and the blunted pencil."[21] Steffens, as we will see, did not retain that spirit of optimism through his entire life.

Dana, like Steffens, condemned stilted, stuffy writing. He pictured the press as the "little sister of literature,"[22] and demanded clarity, simplicity, and detail in his columns, a recipe that was to be repeated by Pulitzer in his later years, after he had turned away from sensationalism and trivialities.

It is important to note that it was not only the "gee-whiz" formula and the investigative reporting of the yellows that made possible the remarkable rise in circulation of the yellow press and the companion expansion of investigatory practices by the entire American press. Those practices were combined in the final years of the nineteenth century and the early years of the twentieth with the rapid urbanization of the country and startling advances in technology.

In any case, the age of the yellow press completed the passage of the American journalist from editorialist or commentator to reporter or transmitter of news, a process that began with the inexpensive newspapers of the penny press era. Irwin was among those who deplored the passing during the age of the yellows of "the editorial press," when, he wrote, truth gave way to news, and the editorial, or opinion, function of the newspaper yielded to an emphasis on "hard news," with special emphasis on the dramatic and heartrending.[23] The professional ideology remained, however, and the newspaper still portrayed itself as the tribune of the people. In other words, journalists depicted themselves as watchdogs, or investigators—or, as they were called by Theodore Roosevelt, muckrakers.

CHAPTER 44

The Muckrakers as Watchdogs

In the mythology of the American journalist, and among Americans as a whole, the muckraker stands as the symbol of the investigating spirit of the press. To some, muckraker is a dirty word, the embodiment of all the excesses of the yellow press; to others, it epitomizes the virtues of a democratic press, of the journalist as indeed the tribune of the people. A number of the central elements in the ideology of American journalists is reflected in the spirit of muckraking. It is in fact at this very point that we can see the coming together of philosophical strains which on the surface may seem contradictory but which in the special environment of the United States found points of commonality. Here we see manifestations of the ideas of philosophers as different as Locke and Rousseau, Voltaire and Marx, Mill and Hegel!

At the heyday of Social Darwinism, the United States seemed to embrace Andrew Carnegie's Gospel of Wealth,[1] although the forces of Populism and Progressivism were already rising to challenge the pseudo-biological premises of that Gospel. Carnegie considered the concentration of economic power in the hands of the few as being "not only beneficial but essential to the future progress of the race." Many political leaders and indeed newspaper editors endorsed the Carnegie hypothesis.[2] Spurred by the appeal of Social Darwinism, railroads, oil companies, steel companies, banks, and holding companies grew into incredible instruments of personal and corporate power. Politicians often seemed merely puppets dangling by the economic strings of the industrialists. These—the railroadmen, the oilmen, and their brethren—were the chief targets of the muckrakers, surfacing as an antidote to the excesses of Twain's Gilded Age. Of course there were other reformers in addition to the muckrakers, many of them on university campuses, but the driving force for social change came with the new political movements that we have already encountered.

In the final years of the nineteenth century and the early years of the twentieth, the economy of the United States expanded rapidly, spurred by the impact of an amazing urbanization.[3] The switch was on from the farm to the cities. In 1870, only about 20 percent of the people lived in towns of 8,000 or more. By 1903, in one generation, this figure had grown to 33 percent. The old rural society was on the way out. The teeming megalopolis arrived to dominate the American landscape—and with it came the fantastic waves of immigrants. In Chicago and New York, more than 50 percent of the population increase was immigrant, creating the legend of the melting pot, with its shifting political structures. Urban working conditions were ghastly: the normal work day was ten hours, and most workers were on the job six days a week. The rate of accidents was heavy. Child labor was exploited ruthlessly. The immigrant quarters of cities bulged with ugly tenements. Disease was rampant in these unsightly slums. At the other end of the scale were the nouveau riche, who came under attack from the muckrakers. The task of this breed of watchdogs was eased mightily by a revolution in communications. Railroads spread across the continent. The telegraph and the telephone made communication over distances possible for the first time. Communications from end to end of the country was suddenly possible through the medium of the national magazines. These were the successors to the yellow press of the daily newspaper. Indeed, Hearst expanded his horizons and his influence through his muckraking magazine, *Cosmopolitan*. Pulitzer, Hearst, and other publishers of daily newspapers sought national circulation in their newly established Sunday editions, the very bellwether of the yellow press.

The year 1893 was as important for magazines as 1833 had been for the dailies when Ben Day made newspapers a commodity for the masses through the introduction of the penny edition. A depression that damaged the national economy made it possible for magazine editors to reduce their prices sufficiently to attract for the first time a mass magazine audience. Lower prices for subscribers were made possible both by the new technology, which sharply reduced the costs of publishers, and by the advertising industry, which now could seek to attract customers to the new and burgeoning array of consumer products. The pacesetter among the national magazines was *McClure's*, which could announce two and a half years after its first issue of 1893 that: "We had, month by month, more pages of paid advertising than any other magazine at any time in the history of the world."[4]

Until the arrival of the muckrakers, national magazines had tended to be sedate affairs, devoted chiefly to literary articles and to columns on moral and political subjects. Godkin's *Nation* was an early and prominent member of the traditional magazine press.

The new editors were not literary men. S. S. (Sam) McClure, an enterprising young editor, launched his magazine, the most widely acclaimed of the muckraker journals, in June 1893 and then dramatically slashed the per-issue rate from a quarter to 15 cents. Jumping swiftly onto the bandwagon, as was his wont, Hearst cut the price of his *Cosmopolitan* to 12½ cents and *Munsey's*, another magazine that joined the ranks of the muckrakers, reduced its rate to a dime. The lower middle class was at last able to enter the market of magazine consumers.

The catchword of these journals was nothing short of investigative reporting, with a no-holds-barred assault on corporate power and political evil. Friendly critics have tended to manufacture the stuff of legends in their adulation for the muckrakers. Vernon Parrington, for instance, described their "dramatic discovery [wherein] the corruption of American politics was laid on the threshhold of business like a bastard on the doorsteps of the father."[5] As a result the muckraking journals soon had a combined circulation of 3 million copies a month, or one copy for every seven families.[6]

The muckrakers were not given to pulling punches. Consider the opening paragraphs of Thomas W. Lawson's renowned article titled "Frenzied Finance" that appeared in *Everybody's* magazine in 1904.

> *Amalgamated Copper was begotten in 1898, born in 1899, and in the first five years of its existence, plundered the public to the extent of over one hundred millions of dollars. It was a creature of that incubator of trust and corporation frauds, the state of New Jersey, and was organized ostensibly to mine, manufacture, buy, sell and deal in copper, one of the staples, the necessities of civilization. From its inception it was known as a "Standard Oil" creature, because its birthplace was the National Bank of New York (the "Standard Oil" bank) and its parents the leading "Standard Oil" lights, Henry H. Rogers, William Rockefeller and James Stillman.*[7]

Lawson, a Boston stock market gambler and promoter, is not accorded a place of honor in the firmament of the muckrakers. His "Frenzied Finance" series brought spectacular circulation increases for *Everybody's*, but Lawson's motive was exposed as that of seeking his own private gain rather than the interests of the public. The American belief system cannot tolerate accolades for such motivation. In a letter to E. J. Ridgway, the editor of *Everybody's* in 1907, Lawson is said to have disclaimed any debt to the people. "What do I owe to the gelatine-spined shrimps? What have the saffron-blooded apes done for me?" he asked, adding: "Forgive me, my dear Ridgway, but the people, particularly the American people, are a joke."[8]

Perhaps the most influential of all the articles written at the height of the muckraking era was a series by Lincoln Steffens, the onetime cheery editor of the *Commercial Appeal*, titled baldly "The Shame of the Cities." Political theorist Max Lerner considers Steffens a national hero "to be celebrated in every school and college" for his "usefulness in creating a richer and healthier American culture."[9] The first of Steffens's series on cities appeared in the January 1903 issue of *McClure's*, along with an attack on the inhumanity of coal mine operators by Ray Stannard Baker and an outspoken blast by Ida Tarbell at John D. Rockefeller and the Standard Oil Company. It was Tarbell who coined the phrase that has often been used to characterize the mind-set of the investigating journalists of the muckraking era, "righteous indignation."[10]

Calling attention in his own editorial to the remarkable series of articles, McClure proudly proclaimed his magazine the representative of "all of us" in defending law, justice, and indeed the liberty of the people against the "capitalists, workingmen, politicians, citizens—all breaking the law, or letting it be broken."[11] This was not Lawson the profit-maker, of course; it was the muckraker, the investigating journalist, in his finest hour. Such indeed is the legend of that era. It is central in the professional ideology of the American journalist.

The term *muckraker* became part of the language thanks to a comment by President Theodore Roosevelt, who was in the early days of the era the darling of the investigative journalists but who later came to heap scorn on them for concentrating only on the bad news—or the muck—that they could rake up and paying no attention to the good news, that is to say, the accomplishments of people like Roosevelt. In this, TR was staking out ground that would become familiar in later years when news-media critics would charge reporters with operating outside the mainstream of American life. Roosevelt invoked the image from John Bunyan's seventeenth-century *Pilgrim's Progress* of the "Man With the Muckrake" who can "look no way but downward." Roosevelt said that the journalist "who never thinks or speaks or writes save of his feats with the muckrake, speedily becomes not a help to society, not an incitement to good, but one of the most potent sources of evil."[12] Muckraker Baker on the other hand maintained that he and his colleagues launched their investigations "not because we hated our world but because we loved it."[13] Pulitzer, it is to be recalled, made the same point.

The most intriguing and one of the most influential of the muckrakers was a California socialist named Upton Sinclair. Sinclair's book, *The Jungle*, which he published privately in 1906, was an all-out assault on the meatpacking industry, a book that moved President Roosevelt to conduct an investigation that a year later produced the Pure Food and Drug Act.[14] As the fierce rhetoric of the muckrakers seemed to dissipate with the achievements of the Roosevelt reforms and the imminence of world war, as the steam of the Progressive movement seemed to vanish into thin air, Sinclair refused to silence himself. In the end, he turned his investigative pen on the industry that had spawned him and his muckraking colleagues, the press itself.

The Brass Check appeared in 1919, a year after the end of the First World War, at a time when the revolutionary ideas let loose by the Russian Revolution two years earlier were sweeping the world and producing socialist demonstrations even in the United States. Sinclair wrote that muckraking had died because the press itself had turned against investigative reporting, against all reformist movements. "A capitalist system," he wrote, "lives by the capitalist system, it fights for that system, and in the nature of the case cannot do otherwise."[15]

Sinclair was the very incarnation of the investigative journalist. Nothing was sacred to him. His mission, he wrote over and over again, was to work for social justice, no matter what forces lined up against him. "I'm the only one of the muckrakers who kept on muckraking," he declared proudly on the occasion of his eightieth birthday in 1958.[16] He had lived to see his dream of the unionization of journalists come true with the formation of the American Newspaper Guild in 1933—although the union was never as leftist and socialist as Sinclair had wished.

Sinclair told journalists in *The Brass Check*—named for the "john" given to a client by a prostitute—that he was declaiming against "the knavish press [which] saps your strength . . . eats out your soul . . . smothers your thinking under mountain-loads of lies. You fall, and the chariot of Big Business rolls over you." He went on:

> *I cry to you for the integrity of your calling, for the honor and dignity of Journalism. I cry to you that Journalism shall no longer be the thing described by Charles A. Dana, master-cynic of the "New York Sun," "buying white paper at two cents a pound and selling it at ten cents a pound." I cry to you that Journalism shall be a public ministry, and that you who labor in it shall be, not wage-slaves and henchmen of privilege, but servants of the general welfare, helping your fellow-men to understand life, and to conquer the evils in nature outside them, and in their own hearts.*[17]

The romantic nature of Sinclair's imagery is apparent. It is less noticeable in the writings of the other muckrakers, Steffens, Tarbell, Baker, Lawson. But it was there. Without question, these journalists were the philosophical offspring of Rousseau and Paine; they envisaged themselves as radical forces devoted at whatever cost to the good of the General Will. They were, however, also followers of the more conservative concepts of Milton and Locke, defenders of the idea that truth must be given a free hand to challenge error, of the idea that the social contract endows them with the authority to incite to rebellion against power when that power is used for arbitrary and hurtful ends.

Sinclair was alien to the moderate Progressivism that attracted the muckrakers. Were the others friendly to the capitalist system, or were they moles serving as a kind of vanguard for socialist—or collective—concepts challenging the mystique of individualism in the United States?

In any case, it was Steffens who was the quintessential muckraker. He was, as his biographer, Justin Kaplan wrote, "morally impassioned," a champion of the "desperate cause," a man driven by a compulsion to "make people think."[18] Steffens, like Sinclair, seemed to be possessed of what some critics called a "Jesus complex." In fact, the muckrakers often claimed Jesus as the greatest of their remote antecedents.[19]

Ronald Steel, the biographer of Walter Lippmann, who once worked as a legman for Steffens, portrayed the muckrakers as "the watchdogs" of the Progressive reform movement:

> *Exposing corruption of political machines, detailing the stranglehold of the giant corporations, crying shame on the cities where immigrants and blacks were exploited, these journalists roused the middle-class conscience and made reform a mass movement.*[20]

Kaplan was often critical of the romantic streak in Steffens, but he nonetheless credited him and his colleagues with the ultimate in investigatory reporting, the "letting in of light and air," which they accomplished in the face of widespread government corruption and resistance to press attacks. It would not be until the resurgence of the modern investigators "in the era of Ralph Nader, My Lai and Watergate" that journalists would find themselves faced with "quite so much to expose or so strong a resistance to exposure."[21]

CHAPTER 45

The Journalism Critics

The American press has never been free of criticism, especially by the disaffected among its own practitioners. In fact, as David Rubin has pointed out, "the media have long been poking around in each other's backyards."[1] Over the years, dating back at least to the appearance of Lambert Wilmer's *Our Press Gang* in 1859, American journalists have attacked what Wilmer described as "the corruptions and crimes" of American newspapers.[2] Wilmer had some very harsh words for the press of his day. "I charge the newspaper press of America," he wrote just before the outbreak of the Civil War, "with checking the diffusion of useful knowledge among the people, by withdrawing the attention of the reading public from useful, salutary, and legitimate objects of study."[3]

Additional and often very sharp criticism came, as we have seen, from European visitors, including Dickens, de Tocqueville, and English moralist Harriet Martineau.[4] Dickens was so offended by the American press that he was able to rake up some vintage invective about the New York newspapers in his novel, *Martin Chuzzlewit*. His image of the New York journalist was bitter, overstated, witty. He had his hero, Martin, arriving at the wharf to be greeted by the "shrill yells" of newsboys peddling papers named the New York *Sewer, Stabber, Peeper, Spy, Plunderer:*

> *Here's the* Sewer's *exposure of the Washington gang, and the* Sewer's *exclusive account of a flagrant act of dishonesty committed by the Secretary of State when he was eight years old; now communicated, at a great expense, by his own nurse. Here's the* Sewer![5]

Dickens, whose novels appeared serially in magazines, found little to applaud in America, especially the sensational penny press. His judgment about the press was, like that of de Tocqueville and other critics, unsystematic. Many critiques were directed against the excesses of the penny press, and had little to do with any sense of philosophical mission on the part of the newspapers. The criticism tended to appear in books such as Wilmer's or in articles in political and literary magazines of small circulation like Godkin's *Nation* or in weekly newspapers such as White's *Emporia Gazette*.

The criticism was often on moral and political grounds. Editors came under attack for their conservative stance. For the most part, these critiques came from the political left. As one of the most persistent of the later press critics, George Seldes, said frankly, he could not conceive of a great newspaper without a liberal policy.[6] Oswald Villard, editor of the *Nation* from 1918 to 1932, lamented "the deterioration of the editorial pages," which he said resulted from "the stupidity, the ignorance and the lack of responsibility to the public" of many owners of journals.[7]

In general, what Seldes, Villard, and their fellow liberal critics wanted was a press that had a more investigative outlook, that embarked on political crusades to ferret out evildoers, that worked for the benefit of the downtrodden. Their heroes were the muckrakers, whom they saw as the heirs of the revolutionary press of colonial days. Adolph Ochs's *New York Times*, which openly concerned itself more with profit than with muckraking, was a favorite target. Among those who condemned the *Times* was Silas Bent, a journeyman reporter and publicist, who was also a professor of journalism at the University of Missouri. Of Ochs, Bent had this to say:

> *His property has none of the fine frenzy of the crusading press. It has no mission to save the people from themselves or from their overlords. It shares the same mystical faith which William Allen White attributes to Mr. [President Calvin] Coolidge, that prosperity is godliness, or at least godly. It never "makes" news, unless the Hundred Neediest Cases can be called that. It never campaigns to expose corruption or industrial ills. Its editorial premise is America-as-it-is.*[8]

Few among the critics spoke favorably of the drive for profit of newspaper owners. It was Upton Sinclair, of course, who launched the most virulent attack, directed against what both Seldes and Harold Ickes, Franklin Roosevelt's secretary of the interior, labeled the "lords of the press."[9] Sinclair's *The Brass Check* stands as the classic portrait of venal press owners. In Sinclair's symbolism, it is to be recalled, the check was presented to a prostitute as proof that payment had been made for services to be performed at brothels.[10] Sinclair did not invent the metaphor. In 1859, Wilmer described the receipts of newspapers as "the wages of prostitution."[11] Half a century later, another critic likened to "editorial prostitution" the sale of a journal's opinions to the highest bidder.[12] An anonymous article in *Forum* magazine charged that "prostitutes and reporters are damned by their very calling."[13] Sinclair at one time meant to pursue the metaphor further by subtitling his book, "A Study of the Whore of Journalism."[14]

Obviously, criticism of the press has always been accompanied by a great deal of passion. For example, Villard, a fervent supporter of racial equality and grandson of the abolitionist William Lloyd Garrison, let fly at the *New York Times* in 1923 with all his verbal artillery. He called the newspaper "unsurpassed [as] a teacher of race hatred [that left] no stone unturned to make clear its belief that there are two kinds of American citizens—the privileged and the disadvantaged—the blacks and the whites."[15]

In his thorough study of media self-criticism, Rubin isolated six principal areas in which the press has come under attack from journalistic critics:[16]

1. *"Feeding the mob."* This is Rubin's term for the practice of sensationalizing the news in order to cater to the basest tastes of readers or, as is often said, to "the lowest common denominator." Bent, in his collection of press articles that he called *Ballyhoo*, condemned the "deranged standards" of news judgment that led to "orgiastic" coverage of Babe Ruth, Gertrude Eberle, Charles Lindbergh, Jr., and the Spanish-American War. He called the press a "Sancho Panza" following the appetites of the mob.[17]
2. *Monopoly ownership of the press.* Widespread condemnation of mergers and of the elimination of competing media enterprises found expression in a 1946 report that censured "communication empires," chains, and the cost of entry into the marketplace.[18] We will return to that report in the next chapter.
3. *Invasion of personal privacy by the press.* Allegations that the press disregards individual feelings in its quest for the dramatic and sensational is an old one, argued by critics as dissimilar as Alexis de Tocqueville, Charles Dickens, and William Allen White, the celebrated editor of the *Emporia Gazette*. Allen wrote in a 1911 column that newspapers playing up details of crimes and scandals and pawing among the ashes of ruined marriages were "bad for the public morals" and ought to be "suppressed under the police power of the state."[19]
4. *Advertiser control of news content.* White, who was also a long-time foe of commercialism in the press, declared sadly: "We have ceased to be a profession and are now an industry."[20]
5. *Antagonism by the press to organized labor.* Liberal press critics censured publishers for their opposition to the labor movement even before Sinclair launched his all-out attack. E. A. Ross wrote in 1910 that newspapers usually distort facts against labor, serving as "mouthpieces of the financial powers."[21] A. J. Liebling,

perhaps the best known of the press's self-critics, wrote tellingly about the press and organized labor.[22]

6. *The "sins" of news agencies*. News agencies, especially the Associated Press, have long been targets of press critics, almost from its earliest days in the nineteenth century. The *Atlantic Monthly* said in 1914 that the AP was a news trust.[23] Sinclair accused it of being the "great concrete wall" that suppressed information unfavorable to business interests.[24]

In none of these areas, aside perhaps from the "feeding the mob" category, Rubin noted, did the criticism deal with fundamental questions of press philosophy. Rather, it concerned itself with specific press practices, and was for the most part, directed at the *content* of the news columns and not at the philosophy behind the selection of that content. Nor was there any examination of the *form* in which news is identified, selected, and reported. Charges continue today that the media sensationalize the news, invade privacy, are run by the advertisers, "talk down" to the public, lower popular taste, and represent the interests of powerful business interests against those of the public. These accusations have turned increasingly to television programming, but here too they have remained almost always specific in nature, directed at particular programs on television. The deeper philosophical issues, discussed at exhaustive length by academics, have throughout the history of the American press been of little more than passing interest to journalists themselves.

Perhaps the most searching and analytical critique of the press by a journalist came in Will Irwin's 15-part series in *Collier's* in 1911. We encountered that series earlier in our examination of the yellows. Irwin was himself a prominent muckraker, at one time managing editor of *McClure's* magazine. He went on to become chief of the foreign department for the George Creel propaganda committee in World War I. Irwin was especially critical of what he perceived to be control by advertising interests of the content of newspapers. He saw publishers in cahoots with advertisers in a kind of conspiracy designed to misinform the public.[25] The earlier criticism of the press for being in the hands of Big Business has been reversed in modern times, when investigative reporters are often accused of being antibusiness.

Still, one of the most persistent criticisms of the American press has been that they are dominated by business, and that the profit seekers dominate American society. Muckraker Steffens argued that all American institutions, including journalism, are businesses, and that they are all under the control of the business of politics. He summed by this view succinctly in an attack on the coal and steel tycoon Mark Hanna, who had worked behind the scenes to choose Warren Harding as the Republic candidate for president in 1920. What Hanna and other party bosses wanted, Steffens wrote, was "the management of the American people in the interest of the American businessman for the profit of American business and politics."[26]

The community of businessmen embraced publishers, who were themselves businessmen but who assailed Steffens and the community of journalists generally as fundamentally hostile to business, a stance that has persisted to this day. For example, James L. Ferguson, the chairman of General Foods, has recently been quoted as accusing the news media of an "underlying hostility toward the business community and all its works."[27] Despite these accusations, journalists, as citizens of the capitalist society of the United States, tend to be overwhelmingly supportive of its system of economics. Even Steffens ultimately abandoned socialism. But journalists are always hungry for news stories that stir the emotions and that depict people in conflict.[28]

The first major academic examination of the attitudes of journalists to the business world, as well as of their perceptions about their work, was undertaken by Leo Rosten in his doctoral dissertation at the University of Chicago. His work, published in 1937, dealt with "the function, the techniques, and the composition of the press corps, and the relationship of the Washington correspondents to the news, to their news sources, to their employers, and to their society."[29]

Other researchers have pursued Rosten's pioneering work, but have made little headway in attracting the interest of journalists.[30] It was Liebling who of all the press critics won the most respect among reporters and editors themselves.

> *The function of the press in society is to inform, but its role is to make money. The monopoly publisher's reactions, on being told that he ought to spend money on reporting distant events, is therefore exactly that of the proprietor of a large, fat cow, who is told that he ought to enter her in a horse race.*[31]

Liebling was a journalist whose column, "The Wayward Press," appeared in the *New Yorker* from 1944 to 1963.[32] For 20 years, his columns drew a sizeable readership among journalists as well as among the intellectuals to whom the magazine was directed. Like most of the journalist critics who came before and after, Liebling had printer's ink in his veins. In the introduction to his book of collected columns, *The Wayward Pressman*, Liebling described his love affair with newspapers: "I would spread them on the floor and lie down on my belly on them, or take them to bed with me, or into the bathroom."[33] Although he was often passionately critical of the way the press dealt with this or that news event and especially of what he saw as a violently antilabor bias, Liebling refrained from relying on the metaphor of "the press as prostitute" which was popular among many other critics.[34]

Liebling condemned what he saw as "formula thinking" on the part of journalists, especially on labor issues and foreign affairs:

> *The formulas most newspapers have fallen back on for foreign news are few. One is "Man go to church, good man, no lie. Man*

> *not go to church, bad, lie." Ergo "Franco, Salazar, Adenauer, Christian Democrats, good, truthful. Communists, bad, whatever they say lie." In handling any story outside the United States, then, it is necessarily true, and you have solved your problem without trouble or expense.*[35]

Liebling was on the staff of Pulitzer's *World* when it was abandoned and sold by Pulitzer's heirs in 1931, a sale that produced one of his more memorable columns. Deploring the loss of some 3,000 jobs on what had often been described as the best newspaper in the country, Liebling wrote bitterly: "The end of the *World* marked the beginning of realism in the relation of American newspaper employees to their employers. The employers had been realistic for a long time. It took the abandonment of an 'institution' like the *World* to drive the message home."[36]

Liebling no doubt thought he was recording the death of the romantic strain that had echoed through the belief system of American journalists for many years. He was recognizing for the first time, he thought, that the news media industry was like all other industries, subject to the push and pull of the marketplace. Liebling was wrong. That romantic strain has by no means vanished from the professional ideology of the American journalist. It has found a secure home in the sphere of investigative journalists, the successors to the reporters of the yellow and muckraker periods. The death of the *World* and of the many other great newspapers that followed did not kill the romantic investigators, for they have gained even greater fame and prestige in the contemporary world.

There is, in any case, little evidence that the criticism of Liebling and his colleagues had much influence on the behavior of owners, editors, or reporters. Rubin's conclusion was that the mass media in the United States "do not change at all in response to commission reports, resolutions, or importuning of the critics."[37] That conclusion is, of course, always subject to revision. The romantic strain has, in any case, persisted in the face of Liebling's "realism."

CHAPTER 46

The Doctrine of Social Responsibility

Criticism of the techniques and practices of the press achieved its high mark in the formal report of the Hutchins Commission. This body, named after its chairman, Chancellor Robert M. Hutchins of the University of Chicago, was created just after the Second World War to inquire into questions of whether news reports were unfair, slanted, and sensational rather than factual, whether the press was indeed putting out the kind of "junk Journalism" that Tom Stoppard examined in his play *Night and Day*.[1] The Hutchins Commission concerned itself especially with the kind of articles offered by the yellow journalists and the muckrakers. In its report, published in 1947, the commission, while standing firmly behind press freedom and the First Amendment, condemned the journalism of the day for its "meaninglessness, flatness, distortion, and the perpetuation of misunderstanding."[2]

The centerpiece of the commission's report was insistence that the press provide five basic services: (1) an accurate, comprehensive account of the day's news; (2) a forum for exchange of comment; (3) a means of projecting group opinions and attitudes to one another; (4) a method of presenting and clarifying the goals and values of the society, and (5) a way of reaching every member of the society.[3] As it turned out, however, the most enduring of the commission's demands was that the press not only present facts in a meaningful context, but that it must also disclose *the truth about the facts*, thus sealing into the professional ideology of journalism the essence of investigative reporting. Under the banner of the Hutchins Commission, the press was now burdened with the moral obligation to go beyond the "objective" facts, to read between the lines of information given by sources, to look at what lay under, over, and behind events, and to seek out and present the truth of what the reporters had uncovered. The commission rejected sensationalism but provided a moral foundation for investigative reporting.

Here was a restatement three centuries later of John Milton's message. Do not, Milton and the Hutchins Commission declared, accept what you are told as truth. If it is falsehood, then it is your duty to print the truth, putting truth and error to the test in "the marketplace of ideas." Here too was confirmation of the belief that the public has a right to know—a right to know not only the facts but also the truth about the facts. Voltaire urged the journalist to be skeptical about the facts he was given by his sources, to go instead for the truth behind those facts. The wisdom of the English and French Enlightenment was now affirmed in the professional ideology of the American journalist. The journalist, the Hutchins Commission argued, was required not only to present the facts, not only the truth behind the facts, but to be accountable to society if he or she failed to do so.

The accountability side of the issue was cemented into the framework of American journalism in a series of essays published a decade after the report of the Hutchins Commission. These essays comprised what their authors, Fred S. Siebert, Theodore Peterson, and Wilbur Schramm, labeled the *four theories of the press*, of which one was a value system specifically directed at American journalists. They called this the *social responsibility doctrine*, and used it to charge the American press community, as had the Hutchins Commission, with telling the truth behind the facts and thereby becoming responsible and accountable to the American public.

In his essay on social responsibility, Peterson reviewed criticism of the press by Will Irwin, George Seldes, Harold Ickes, and Upton Sinclair, criticism that already had influenced the Hutchins Commission. Peterson proclaimed himself in complete accord with the major conclusions of the Hutchins Commission. All of these earlier critics had sworn allegiance to the most basic chapter in the book of the American journalists' ideology: the belief in free expression. It was of course this belief that was asserted again and again by the Founding Fathers. Madison, it is to be recalled, was prepared to forgive the press even the most grievous of its abuses on the ground that without the knowledge afforded by education and the press, the social order would be doomed to ignorance. In announcing the doctrine of social responsibility, however, Peterson goes well beyond a simple faith in free expression:

> *Under social responsibility theory, freedom of expression is grounded on the duty of the individual to his thought, to his conscience. It is a moral right. . . . Freedom of expression is not something which one claims for selfish ends. It is so closely bound up with his mental existence that he ought to claim it. It has value both for the individual and for society.*[4]

Freedom then is not something simply to enjoy. Whoever is free is obliged to use that freedom responsibly. According to the authors of *Four*

Theories, the social responsibility doctrine replaced belief in utterly untrammeled press freedom. Still, however modified, the doctrine continued to uphold freedom as essential to human development. Peterson wrote that he and the Hutchins Commission had a more modern view of the nature of man than existed under pure libertarianism. Social responsibility doctrine, he said, did not deny the libertarian view that man is a rational creature. But, in the spirit of pragmatism, it was, he said, a more skeptical doctrine. "Man is viewed not so much as irrational as lethargic," he said. "He is capable of using his reason, but he is loath to do so. Consequently, he is easy prey for demagogues, advertising pitchmen, and others who would manipulate him for their selfish ends."[5] The investigative work of the press, however, might steer rational, lethargic Americans to recognition of what their leaders were actually doing. This view was very much in keeping with libertarian doctrine, as it had been outlined in Siebert's essay. There, Siebert saw libertarian theory as the intellectual underpinning of the concept of the press as watchdog, wherein it was "the right and duty of the press to serve as an extralegal check on government."[6]

We have called attention earlier to the fact that the exact intentions of the Founding Fathers are unclear as to whether the right to free expression was to be absolute or limited. It may well be that the idea of the press as being responsible to society at large was present from the very beginnings of the United States. This idea was of course an essential element in Rousseau's doctrine of the General Will and of the press philosophy enunciated by Tunis Wortman and his fellows in the Democratic-Republican societies at the close of the eighteenth century. Marx, in envisaging the press as part of the vanguard leading the workers away from exploitation by the capitalists, was giving expression to a different form of social responsibility. Even Mill, holding up the ideal of the completely free individual, pictured the press as serving society—the sum of all the individuals in the land.

In short, while social responsibility as terminology is a modern expression, it is an ancient doctrine, one that had already been alluded to in the writings of Plato and Aristotle, one that has been reaffirmed in every generation since Milton.

Yet, the question must remain as to whether the doctrine of social responsibility is a valid philosophical concept. An ideology may be true or false, or perhaps somewhere in the middle. Philosophical discourse is bound up in complexities and contradictions. In fact, the author of this work has elsewhere taken the position that "the term social responsibility is a term devoid of meaning . . . a term whose content is so vague that almost any meaning can be placed upon it."[7] Neither Mill nor Rousseau would have been pleased to hear that an uncertain entity called "society" had the duty—or the power—to decide whether the press was being responsible to it or accountable to it. If "society" does not have this duty or power, who does? Only those who already wield political and economic power have that kind of power. Thus, the social responsibility doctrine might ultimately squeeze the press into an instrument for maintaining the powerful in power, frustrating its very intentions under the prescription of the Hutchins Commission and the authors of the "four theories."

For a journalist to be responsible requires active thought. You can not be responsible simply by rote or by chance. There must always be a choice. You must have an option to be either responsible or irresponsible. And of course you must be free to make the choice. If your choice is not free, if you are forced to act under threat, you are not responsible for your behavior. The one doing the threatening is responsible. It is not as simple as it may sound, however, for a journalist to act on the basis of thought. In all jobs, there is a good deal of routine. Most decisions are in fact made without thought, simply by force of habit or custom or by the conventional way certain kinds of work are performed. David Hume held that goodness could be defined only in terms of the standards existing in particular times and places, by customs, habits, and conventions. Journalism is a practice where convention is king. Late-twentieth-century sociologists have found much to study in the practice of journalism, especially its conventions.

The point here is that conventional behavior often gets in the way of the kind of social responsibility advocated by Hutchins and the "four theories." William James's doctrine of pragmatism awards virtue in accordance with whether or not behavior works. James's most prominent journalist student, Walter Lippmann, called attention to the importance of conventions in the selection of what constitutes news. Every newspaper, he wrote, "is the result of a whole series of selections as to what items shall be printed, in what position they shall be printed, how much space each shall occupy, what emphasis each shall have."[8] Leon Sigal has identified what he calls "the journalist's creed," based chiefly on the elements that go into his definition of news.[9] The key elements in a journalist's definition of what is newsworthy are well known: timeliness (what happens today is more newsworthy than what happened yesterday), proximity (what takes place close to home is more newsworthy than what takes place further away), authoritativeness (the higher the authority, the more newsworthy), relevance to the lives of readers, dramatic qualities, degree of conflict, and so forth.

All of these conventional definitions of news render it difficult for the reporter or editor to follow the prescription of the Hutchins Commission and the "four theories": to tell the truth about the facts, even if it were possible for the journalist to know the truth about them. Max Ways, who has campaigned for a new definition of news, has suggested there is an "artistic bias" in the conventional behavior of American journalists. This bias turns up not in the content of newspapers and broadcasting stations but rather in the *form* in which news is presented.[10] Ways parted from the traditional view that journalism is a craft or a profession; to him, journalism is an art—"crude and unbeautiful, but nevertheless an art." All artists are influenced by traditions and canons, and journalism is especially under the influence of the tradition of journalism forms:

> *Preference for "the story" that journalism* knows *can be communicated leads it to neglect the changes that need to be told but do not fit the standards of familiarity, simplicity, drama. This artistic bias has nothing to do with the ideology or partisanship of the journalist himself. He may take sides concerning the substance of a news story, but such substantive bias will often be overridden by his formal bias. A journalist who sees a story that is attractive—artistically speaking—will tell it even if it runs contrary to his political prejudices, hurts the interests of his friends, and brings sorrow to his mother's heart. This laudable independence exacts, however, a heavy price: if the artistic standards by which the story is selected and shaped are themselves out of phase with reality the consequent distortion may be greater than that produced by a journalist's substantive bias toward one "side" of an issue.*[11]

It is not difficult to fit the issue of whether journalists are hostile to business into Ways's analysis of journalism forms. It is the *story* that is important, not right and wrong. In any case, if the bias of journalism lies more in its forms than in its substance, the philosophical underpinning of the doctrine of social responsibility and indeed of investigative reporting is seriously undermined. Whether this be true or not, *belief* in the virtue of investigative reporting continues to be firmly held, the gloom of A. J. Liebling notwithstanding.

The forms of journalism have altered, of course, with the rise of television as a source of news. While broadcasters maintain that public understanding of the truth behind the facts has increased sharply in the age of television, critics such as Neil Postman argue that the emphasis on entertainment in television "has made entertainment itself the natural format for the representation of all experience. . . . The problem is not that television presents us with entertaining subject matter but that all subject matter is presented as entertaining."[12]

However Postman may rail against television, however Ways may insist on the existence of an artistic bias in journalism, the doctrine of social responsibility, embodying its vision of the journalist as watchdog, retains its central position in the belief system of American journalists. We turn our attention now to investigative reporting in contemporary America.

CHAPTER 47

Investigative Journalism: The Conscience of Society

At one level, of course, "investigative" journalism is a redundant concept, since *all* journalism requires some kind of investigation on the part of the reporter. At another level, the investigative journalist is expected somehow to dig more deeply behind the "facts" than the ordinary reporter. The term is difficult to define—and some newspersons scoff at the very idea of an investigating journalist. Even so, courses in investigative reporting have become commonplace in schools of journalism, and many students make it clear their goal in the field is to become an investigator. However the term is defined, philosophically the investigative reporter sees himself or herself as the Conscience of Society, pursuing corruption in high places without fear or favor, the incarnation of the New Muckraker. The investigator is seeking to carry out the doctrine of social responsibility.

One prominent journalism text, noting that the American journalist has always been dedicated to the public interest, asserts that today there is an even "stronger emphasis on *public service* journalism and on the work of the investigative reporter" than in the past.[1] All texts on reporting stress the importance of journalism. Max Ways notwithstanding, another author says reporting is not only art, not only craft, but "a principal means of building and maintaining the kind of society a democratic people wants."[2] Yet another text identifies the journalist as "a vital cog in the democratic system."[3] Investigative reporters, one teacher says, are considered in the field "as the imagined defender of the public trust, the politician-slayer à la Steffens and Sinclair, the St. George of dragon-killing fame."[4] To him, the investigative reporter uses two talents not found to the same extent in other reporting, the ability to use public records and the ability to see and understand. Still, it is difficult to distinguish these talents from those valued by reporters in general.

A number of guidebooks for journalists provide tips for the investigative reporter. The dean of authors on journalism techniques, Curtis MacDougall, writes that the investigator is careful not to trespass, eavesdrop, wiretap, intercept mail, or perform other illegal acts "if for no other reason than fear of being fired or arrested," but adds that it may be handy for the investigative reporter to use "some of the techniques of a professional detective."[5] A recent text advises the investigator that if he (or she) is going undercover and must invent a phony background for himself he ought to stay as close to the truth as possible, using his own first name so that he will remember to respond when someone calls him. This text argues that it is impossible to overdo stories on topics such as child abuse, government corruption, medical fraud, or prison reforms, the mainstays of investigative reporting, because such problems are always at hand.[6]

Avoid the traditional stance of just laying out the facts for the reader and allowing him to draw his own conclusions, says yet another guidebook. Rather, lay out the facts and make sure to tell the reader what they mean, for journalists, "like scientists, are not advocates. They are seekers of truth."[7] Here is the vision of the Hutchins Commission at work in the newsroom. This text also offers advice on whom to use as sources for investigative reports: enemies, losers, and people in trouble, for these persons are most likely to find out what is bad about those under investigation.

To the investigator, style is not especially relevant. The task of the investigator is not only to dig below the surface for information but also to publicize it as widely as possible, to lift the dark facts into the brightest glare of day. He studiously avoids taking sides in issues, except insofar as he stands opposed to wrongdoing of any kind; hence, he does not see himself as partisan or as editorial writer. All he is after, in his view, is the truth. He shuns nothing, including whatever official documents he needs to prepare his case.

To speak of preparing a case is in fact to identify the modus operandi of the investigative journalist. Although he was by no means the first investigative reporter, Don Bolles of the *Arizona Republic* became a symbol for this kind of reporter after he was killed when his car was blown up in typical gangland fashion in 1976 in downtown Phoenix. He was at the time in the midst of a journalistic investigation of crookedness in Arizona land development projects. A year before he was murdered, Bolles and a group of like-minded journalists had formed an organization they called IRE, for Investigative Reporters and Editors, Inc.[8] After Bolles's death, some three dozen journalists joined forces to investigate the bombing, and succeeded in helping locate three persons who were then convicted of the bombing.[9] Bolles himself had identified the investigative journalist with the frontier marshal. "Newspapers," he said, "are the one force between us and total chaos. Every major advance or cleaning up of corruption in this state has been made by the newspapers of Arizona."[10]

Like the muckrakers whom they emulate, the investigators have taken as their targets the great and the powerful. Moreover, they often link their investigative work with the concept of the people's right to know. A posthumous citation given to Bolles in Arizona was named the John Peter Zenger Award for Freedom of the Press and the People's Right to Know.[11] There can be little doubt that investigators see themselves as the Fourth Estate, with power comparable to that of the president, the Congress and the Supreme Court. They have achieved considerable prominence. The names of *Washington Post* investigators Bob Woodward and Carl Bernstein became household words as a result of their probing of the Watergate story.[12] The investigators who conduct the interviews on the television series *60 Minutes* are as familiar to the viewing audience as the president or the pope. The program is one of the most highly rated on the air, proof that investigative reporting has not only an altruistic side but that it pays off in cold cash as well.[13]

Nonetheless, there is an unmistakable ring of selfless service in the sound of the term investigative journalist. Few Americans would discard the idea that the people have a right to know. Some critics have, however, criticized investigative journalists for falling prey to the deadly sin of pride and for arrogating to themselves a position that properly belongs to elected agents of justice.[14] Television journalist Robert MacNeil has called the investigators "the macho arm of American journalism" and said they have contributed to "a public perception of unfairness" among the news media.[15] While MacNeil was critical of the investigators, he held in contempt other "new" journalism groups, which we will address in Part 9.[16]

It has appeared to some commentators that the primary goal of investigative journalists is personal prestige and power, as if they were after more and more victims so that they might tally up and take pride in the notches in their belts. Daniel Yankelovich, pollster and president of the Public Agenda Foundation, has blamed the media's "love affair" with investigative reporting for failure to distinguish fact and fiction, and for bringing on public disaffection with the press. Yankelovich commented that it seemed to him investigative journalists are saying to themselves: "Well, as long as our heart is in the right place and we know that those bastards are really guilty, so what if we have to fudge the facts a little bit?"[17] Yankelovich was referring specifically to the most celebrated case of journalistic fraud in recent times, the case of Janet Cooke, a reporter for the *Washington Post*, who was awarded a Pulitzer Prize for a 1980 story that, it was later revealed, she had manufactured. The Cooke case will be discussed in more detail in Chapter 58.[18]

Second only to the Watergate exposure among the most celebrated triumphs of investigative reporters was the 1970 report by Seymour Hersh, a freelance journalist for the Dispatch News Service of the massacre by American soldiers of Vietnam civilians at the village of My Lai, for which he won the Pulitzer Prize. A two-part *Rolling Stone* report was so laudatory that Hersh emerged as a kind of saviour of American democracy.[19] Hersh later recalled the difficulty he had in convincing American newspapers to publish the story for fear that they would be accused of libeling the named individuals even though Hersh had taken photographs of the scene and shown the pictures to editors. His organization, the Dispatch News Service, hired a prominent Washington law firm, which took the stand that "the public's right to know far outweighed any disadvantages to some involved individuals." Hersh speculated about why papers responded as they did to his reports:

> *What made some responsible and careful newspapers publish my stories and others, equally as responsible and careful, not publish them? I think part of the answer is instinct, the instinct many reporters and editors feel for a story or a source.*[20]

Investigative reporting experienced its great surge in the 1970s and 1980s, after the decline of the heady revolutionary period of the 1960s. The *Weltgeist*—the Spirit of the Times—of the later decades was markedly different from that of the romantic 1960s. By asking Americans in 1961 to dedicate themselves to the service of the country rather than to pursue their own interests, President Kennedy had touched the temper of the 1960s. But after he and his brother Robert as well as Martin Luther King had been assassinated, after the continuing strife and turbulence in the streets, after the battles between police and dissident groups, the country longed for "peace and quiet," and sought a return to placidity. The optimism that had marked the 1960s disintegrated, and a mood of pessimism, close in spirit to the strain of cultural pessimism that had long marked European society, settled over the country. The investigative journalists were among the chief disseminators of cultural pessimism.

The strain has, for the most part, been absent from the American scene. The question to be considered here is: can the American press consecrate itself to challenging the high and the mighty with such intense zeal without adopting, or at the very least appearing to adopt, a belief system shot through with cultural pessimism? In selecting the skeptical stance of the yellows, the muckrakers, and the investigators, does the journalist reject the optimism of Locke, Jefferson, and John Stuart Mill and embrace the pessimism of such European philosophers as Rousseau and Kant? Is it their perception that the American press is permeated with pessimism that leads critics to question its place in today's society? Insistence that the press plays up bad news and ignores the good in society is a salient part of the criticism not only of investigative journalism but of the news media altogether.

To MacNeil, public perception of unfairness in the mass media is associated with what he calls the "aggressive negativism, sometimes of a rather theatrical posturing kind, that has pervaded so much reporting, especially from Washington, since Vietnam and Watergate."[21] The public, he said, wants "fairness—even-handedness, balance, objectivity— . . . and the greatest complaint I hear is lack of it."[22]

Journalists, as we have been careful to point out, do not on the whole involve themselves consciously in questions of philosophical complexity. Yet beneath the conscious awareness of the investigative reporter and indeed of most practitioners of journalism, the old and the new, an uneasy sense of doubt has appeared. Are these practices *right*? Are they *moral*? What are the ethical implications? Journalists, like those pursuing most activities, have in a sense "discovered" ethics. This discovery places greater weight than ever before on the ideology of journalists, on how that belief system came into being and how it operates. We will return to the subject of the ethics of journalism in Part 10. Now, we turn our attention to another issue related both to the rise in importance of the investigative function of the journalist and to the ethical questions that grow out of this function. The issue is one of power, the power of American journalists.

PART IX

An Ideology Without an Ideology

Walter Lippmann (1889–1974): "The press is . . . very much more frail than the democratic theory has as yet admitted. It is too frail to carry the whole burden of popular sovereignty, to supply spontaneously the truth which democrats hoped was inborn. And when we expect it to supply such a body of truth we employ a misleading standard of judgment. We misunderstand the limited nature of news, the illimitable complexity of society; we overestimate our own endurance, public spirit, and all-round competence."

Reinhold Niebuhr (1892–1971): "Some over-all philosophy of mass communication is required ... It is difficult to enforce responsible behavior upon the producer, though the theory [of social responsibility] is right in holding the producer morally responsible for the product of news and entertainment in the mass media. It is difficult to compel responsible behavior." (photo used with permission of Union Theological Seminary)

CHAPTER 48

Introduction: Media and Power

Part 9 is about power, a crucial issue that dominates the media field today, both in theory and practice. The number of books, tracts, monographs, essays, and chapters that have been flooding the market testify to the vast public interest in the question of how much power the media possess and—if it is as great as many people seem to think—how that power could be used in different (presumably better or wiser) ways. The greater share of that outpouring is produced by the people most directly involved—journalists and the powerful about whom they write. But a good deal of the literature is being written also by scholars, often political or social philosophers. Fascination with the news media has been intensified in modern society as television has gained an increasingly dominant role in the daily lives of Americans.

Certainly no journalist has failed to be affected by the plethora of articles and commentary about the power of the news media. It is clear that the ubiquity of news programs on television has resulted in the creation of a new firmament of journalism stars. They have become so prominent, so much a part of the everyday lives of Americans, that they seem to be very powerful individuals indeed, with a capacity to shape the thoughts and beliefs of viewers and thus to be a dominant factor in American public life. Francis Bacon's epigram much beloved of Madison, that knowledge is power has been replaced by the assertion that *information* is power. Whoever controls the news media, the primary source of information about public affairs, it is said, has the power to control societies and nations. Now that the age of television has arrived, we no longer encounter any philosophical examination of power that does not in some way focus on the news media.

Although the pattern has changed somewhat recently, over the years the press has rarely been reluctant to proclaim vast powers for itself.

Pulitzer for instance went so far as to argue that the *World* "should be more powerful than the President. He is fettered by partisanship and politics and has only a four years' term."[1]

Like all abstractions, the concept of power is subject to a good many interpretations. The economist, John Kenneth Galbraith, defines power as a universal means to gain personal, organizational, or political goals, but he holds also that it may be sought simply for itself. The mere possession of power, in Galbraith's view, may bring emotional rewards quite apart from whatever ends are being sought.[2] Galbraith sees the mass media as exercising "conditioned power" through its capacity for manipulation and persuasion. This exercise of power is particularly worrisome, he says, since the influenced individual has no idea that he or she is being controlled; he is simply conditioned to submit to the power of the media: "The belief that was once accorded the priest—and perhaps in lesser measure the schoolmaster—is now accorded the spokesmen and -women of television and the press."[3]

In making somewhat the same point, Neil Postman argues that the information the viewer receives from television is inevitably out of context, patterned into small, neat segments between commercials. The absence of context, the absence of relationships, discourages thinking, so that the viewer does not realize he is being controlled or conditioned.[4] Put another way, the power of the mass media, particularly television, rests in part on the premise that the target audience is used but does not know it is being used. Ideology is transmitted, but painlessly, without being noticed. Todd Gitlin holds that the mass media, like other forms of popular culture, never manufacture or create beliefs.[5] Rather, he says, the beliefs of social elites and social movements are relayed, reproduced, processed, and *packaged* by the mass media. In this way, then, the conditioning power of the mass media is used not in order to overwhelm opposition anywhere in society but rather to domesticate opposition, absorbing it, co-opting it,[6] as we will see in our examination of the phenomenon known as the underground press.

However defined, the word *power* usually has a pejorative connotation. "The lust for power, for dominating others," the Roman historian Tacitus wrote in a sentiment that has not yet been repealed, "inflames the heart more than any other passion."[7] "Power tends to corrupt," Lord Acton proclaimed a century ago, "and absolute power corrupts absolutely."[8] Most of us probably believe this aphorism, however much we may in our own secret heart yearn to gain and exercise power.

In the five chapters that follow, the power question is approached from a number of different perspectives. First, the general growth of philosophy during the years after the Second World War is explored. That war marked a watershed in human history. By 1945, the years of dominance of the European colonial empires had come to an end and the United States had emerged as the unchallenged bearer of the glories of the European past, figuratively at least now, the porter of Kipling's "white man's burden." The foe was seen for the first time as an *ideological* challenger, the Soviet Union, with its message of collectivism and unequivocal state control.

These political changes were accompanied by the appearance of nuclear power and the threat to human survival posed by the new mechanisms of destruction. This threat spread itself over all philosophy, and both theory and practice were now required to take into consideration the death of the planet. New challenges were raised to the dominant concept of pragmatism, from both the political Right and the political Left. In this context of media power, special attention is devoted to the writings of Reinhold Niebuhr and Walter Lippmann, whose impact on American thought, particularly that of journalists, was extensive.

Next, we consider the responses of American journalism to the many challenges of the postwar world. Investigative journalism, the most widely discussed of the responses, has already been examined, but there were others. These are taken up one by one, and their ideological implications are explored. Critical elements in the belief system of journalists are involved, including the concepts of professionalism, objectivity, social responsibility, the public's right to know, and press freedom itself.

In the postwar years, "professionalism" appeared as a norm in the mass media, as it did in fact in many other occupations. While the notion may have suited the journalist better than it did the bridge builder or insurance salesman, nonetheless professionalism as a standard spread through the entire society. The idea of being professional meant, of course, adhering to certain widely observed, if not indeed mandatory, standards. For journalists, chief among these standards was the universally accepted norm of objectivity. Following the Hutchins Commission report, social responsibility also became a yardstick for measuring journalism excellence. In the postwar years, as the power of the mass media appeared to be expanding enormously, all these values came under challenge, and journalism found itself under increasing attack from the holders of political power and from the public at large.

The argument advanced by Vice President Agnew in 1969 was the most celebrated of the challenges raised to the power of the mass media, since it brought into question the relative power of the press and the government. Our third major theme in this chapter covers both the attacks and the responses, as we examine the ideological implications of this question of relative power.

We all like to group things by decades, the Roaring '20s, for example, or the Depression '30s. Decades are really guideposts, short cuts to understanding that help provide some kind of order in a disorderly world. We need to be careful about the use of decades; the Depression began in 1929 and was by no means ended in 1940. Purists find fault with the use of decades as guideposts, but they are useful nevertheless, so long as we remember that they represent rough approximations rather than descriptions of reality. For a relatively clear portrait of the United States (and indeed of all Western society) in the contemporary world, we need not fear to divide the years into decades, all with general descriptions—the conservative '50s, the revolutionary '60s, the complacent '70s, the transitional '80s. As central figures in their society during these decades, journalists in general have been equally conservative, revolutionary, complacent, and transitional.

The public mood in the years immediately following the Second World War reflected a wish to return to an orderly social environment; experiments of any kind were discouraged. On the surface there was a remarkable national consensus. In fact, historians and other scholars were saying that it was on the basis of this national consensus that the United States had grown, flourished, and won the war.[9] Literary critic Lionel Trilling wrote in 1949 that Americans were unanimous in their belief in liberalism, not only as "the dominant but even the sole intellectual tradition."[10] How hollow those words sounded by the close of the '80s when *liberal* had become a pejorative word, used by President Reagan and his followers to attack the adherents of Lionel Trilling. But in the postwar world, to some it appeared that nirvana had arrived, as if the intellectual community of the West, journalists among them, had reached agreement on the virtues of the welfare state and a mixed, fundamentally capitalist, economy. In 1960, sociologist Daniel Bell proclaimed the victory of pragmatism and political pluralism and the end of ideology.[11]

Dewey's prediction that pragmatism would become the basic belief system of the United States seemed to have been confirmed. Yet, at this very time, on university campuses and in intellectual journals there was taking place a serious reexamination of the basic postulates on which the country rested.

By the 1960s, consensus had evaporated. A curious pattern of polarization, unusual in America's intellectual history, had developed. The key word in the challenge was *new*. James Oliver Robertson points out the overriding importance that newness has had in American history beginning with the idea of this as the New World, as "a fresh place, a new beginning, an opportunity."[12] On the American scene there appeared the New Left. And the New Conservatism, the New History, the New Politics, the New Sociology. And of course there was the New Journalism. None of these movements was in itself new, but each portrayed itself as new and different, and each first invaded, and then adapted itself to, the increasingly homogenized and technologized social order.

CHAPTER 49

The New Conservatives and the New Radicals

Among the leaders in the ranks of the New Conservatives was Peter Viereck, whose lodestar was balance. He extolled proportion, self-restraint, freedom, and aimed his bitter pen directly at Rousseau, who, he said, argued for revolt and against tradition, seeing only natural virtue in mankind and ignoring evil out of "satanic pride in (his) own unchecked ego."[1] To Viereck, freedom was foremost among the principles of the New Conservatism, a freedom that to him derived from the teachings of Plato, Burke, Hegel, and the German historians. Viereck despised "conviction" and "passionate intensity" and argued not only against Rousseau but also against "liberal" press commentators, insisting on "gradualism" under rational codes of law and ethics.[2] To him, the preachings of Rousseau were filled with the defiance of adolescence instead of mature reasoning. Viereck wrote his major contribution to the conservative cause in 1949. A little more than a decade later, the underground press movement was rejecting his declaration of principles and arguing for precisely the kind of "adolescent defiance" that he despised.

Russell Kirk, another spokesman for the New Conservatism, also turned to Burke for his model, rejecting both Locke and Jefferson, finding stability not in innovation but in the family, private property, religion, and above all in the American tradition of a constitutional balance of powers.[3] Like Viereck, Kirk announced his rejection of "ideology"—in favor of adherence to accepted traditions. Historian Clinton Rossiter, himself a member of the New Conservatives, observed sagely that while Kirk, like his mentor Burke, professed to despise ideology, he was nevertheless "forced by the loneliness of his intellectual and temperamental position to be an unvarnished ideologue."[4]

It is worth a reminder here that we are all ideologues if by an ideology we mean, as this book argues, a system of beliefs. This point is one to keep in mind. Journalists, like the bulk of "pragmatic" Americans, denigrate ideology. The news as it appears on radio and television and in the columns of newspapers and magazines is likely to condemn, either directly or by intimation, "mere ideologues." It is not often recognized that anyone who proclaims the virtues of "the American tradition"—or indeed of its opposite—is an ideologue, quite as unvarnished as Viereck. Rights that are "self-evident," as those of life, liberty, and the pursuit of happiness, are in particular the fruit of an ideology, for these are based on what we *believe*, not on what we *know*. It is well to pause every now and then and ask oneself how it is possible to adhere at the same time to that often-recited national belief in both liberty and the pursuit of happiness. For is not one's own liberty inevitably limited by the pursuit by someone else of his or her happiness? Might not restrictions on one's own liberty add to the other's happiness? And the other way around. In other words, there is no escaping ideology!

The most revolutionary of the New Conservatives was the historian Willmoore Kendall, whose ideas in the decades to come were to appeal to many American intellectuals. Kendall's targets were the very pillars of American liberalism: he attacked the majoritarian ideas of Locke, the egalitarian principles of Mill, and the pragmatism of James and Dewey. In the writings of these philosophers Kendall found an absence of moral standards and support for an "open society," which he frankly abhorred.

Kendall's ideas, as well as those of the entire fraternity of New Conservatives, were rooted in the view that democracy cannot function properly if control is placed in the hands of ordinary human beings, busy in their own daily pursuits, morally corruptible, inevitably ill trained intellectually. It is *community*, not individuals, that must be the pivot of a viable human society.

In this, Kendall's stance was akin to that of the great English conservative, Matthew Arnold, who had argued that the genius of the English nation is greater than that of any individual. And it resonated with that of the influential American philosopher of economics, Joseph Schumpeter, who held that democracy could survive only if its leaders were qualified and its public played only a limited role in decision making.[5]

In short, according to this view, people need to be led. They are incapable of carrying out the decision-making role assigned to them by traditional liberalism. Community is the answer. Locating a link to Rousseau that the Frenchman would not have liked, Kendall turned to the General Will to support the banning of books and the proscribing of communists, if to do so were "the deliberate sense of the community."[6] In an argument that provided intellectual rationale for condemning a licentious but free press, Kendall maintained that the country must not allow an unrestricted right for citizens, media included, to say what they wish to say.[7]

The seeds of conservative revolt lay germinating throughout the late 1940s and the 1950s, giving rise along the way to support for the anticommunist "crusade" of Senator Joseph McCarthy and his colleagues in Congress and exploding into the mainstream with the triumph of Ronald Reagan and the political right in the 1980s. This is not to say that the philosophers of the New Conservatism were admirers of McCarthy, but it is true that they saw communism and other "alien" ideologies as threats to the conservation of American values. Some American journalists, including several of the most prominent among them, embraced many of the ideas of the New Conservatism, a shift from the past in which journalists had tended to be associated with liberal and pragmatic values.

Rejection of what Lionel Trilling and Daniel Bell saw as a liberal American consensus came not only from conservatives but from the New Left as well. In a modern updating of Marx, the sociologist C. Wright Mills found "the power elite" every bit as exploitative of the masses as Marx's bourgeoisie. Mills's immensely influential book, appearing in 1956, portrayed America as anything but consensual; instead, he wrote, it is controlled and manipulated by business, military, and political elites.[8] Rather than being a watchdog, in Mills's analysis the press is but a feeble entity cheerfully locked away in the hip pockets of the ruling aristocracy. This was far removed from the analysis of the press that President Nixon and Vice President Agnew would soon present.

The New Left, drawing on Mills, argued that power had to be withdrawn from "the Establishment." Instead, the New Left's ideal was "power and uniqueness rooted in love, reflectiveness, reason, and creativity." In the 1962 Port Huron manifesto of Students for a Democratic Society (SDS), violence was specifically rejected as a means to achieve these ends but as the mood of revolution gained strength in the 1960s, some New Left radicals began to express belief in the "creativity of violence."[9] As the 1960s wore on, the consensus doctrine vanished, replaced by an ideological struggle between the political Right and Left.

Among the weapons discovered by the New Left and their allies was the "media event." Groups that were convinced they could not gain through ordinary means the space in the press they needed to be recognized as legitimate forces on the social scene turned to street marches and protest demonstrations, convinced that newspapers and particularly television journalists would give them extended coverage. In this their reasoning proved correct, and in short order every group that believed itself discriminated against began to plan "media events" in order to attract coverage. The New Left saw this mechanism as a means to counter the dominance of the press by antagonistic political forces.

While the New Conservatives turned to Viereck, Kirk, and Kendall, the New Left found its intellectual underpinning in the works of Mills and, even more, in those of Herbert Marcuse and the Frankfurt school of social scientists in Germany. To Marcuse, in contradistinction to Burke and Viereck, a man can be free only when he is "free from constraint, external and internal, physical and moral—when he is constrained neither by law nor by need."[10] Thus, "the Establishment" is to be opposed wherever and whenever it is found. Inasmuch as the mass media are devices of the Establishment, Marcuse wrote, it is proper that they be censored.[11]

The Frankfurt school was Marxist in its methods of analysis but was by no means communist. Juergen Habermas, perhaps the most influential of its members in the United States, in fact endorsed traditional capitalist political philosophy. Others such as Max Horkheimer, Theodor Adorno, Claus Mueller, Oskar Negt, and Alexander Kluge, were more "radical"; that is, they proposed solutions to social and political problems outside the mainstream of American social thought. Negt and Kluge, for example, demanded a "counter-public" that would do battle on behalf of the working class against the news media, which, they claimed, are mere puppets in the hands of an industrial-military complex.[12] The members of the Frankfurt school were profoundly concerned with the cultural aspects of communication. They saw the entertainment function of the mass media as a device used by "the Establishment" to maintain control over society.[13] Journalists, in this view, are simply tools in the hands of Mills's power elite. The thrust of the Frankfurt school, whose hallmark was "critical theory," was never practical; in fact, Mueller saw the *intellectual* as the "only hope" for survival of a democratic society, since only intellectuals have the resources to criticize the social order.[14]

To Habermas, criticism of society and its standards could come only from "psychoanalysts," a role those journalists who followed Habermas cheerfully adopted as their own, since in their commentary they would not only interpret events but provide psychological explanations for the behavior of "newsmakers."[15] He saw "public opinion" in the modern world as a mere fiction. It simply does not exist, he said, because power has moved into the hands of "bureaucrats, organizations and parties." These groups have taken unto themselves the carrying out of journalistic activities through their public relations agents, who carefully conceal their own goals not only from the people but also from their governments and indeed from most members of their own groups.[16] Habermas's analysis of a "fictional public" (Negt and Kluge called it "a pseudo-public") challenged the very heart of American communications studies, which have been devoted increasingly to the study of what they identify as "public opinion."[17]

New Left scholars and a small band of like-minded journalists found especially appealing Habermas's adaptation of Mills's power elite to the field of communications. Habermas's solution, the establishment of psychoanalysts and an effort by informed citizens to create their own communications network outside the control of the Establishment, suggested a function for journalists far removed from the generally accepted role of objective observer and disinterested reporter.[18]

CHAPTER 50

Niebuhr and Lippmann

Like the great majority of the American public, conditioned as they have been to the virtues of pragmatic, empirical thought, journalists have seemed for the most part to continue to express their traditional optimism in the face of the challenges posed by the New Conservatives and the New Radicals. Professionalism appeared to represent a satisfactory strategy for ignoring the prophets of Right and Left. Even today, despite two generations of pressure from the extremes, the old "can do" virtues—of optimism, moderation, even insularity—continue to dominate American thought. Ronald Reagan, who seemed to embody all those virtues, may have been the most popular chief executive in office that the country has produced.

Lurking below the surface, however, have been concepts that are quite contrary to the prevailing belief system. They have, as we shall see, exerted a strong impact on the ideas of some journalists. Among the most influential of the spokesmen for this contrary philosophy have been the journalist Walter Lippmann and the theologian Reinhold Niebuhr. There is more of Madison than Jefferson in both Lippmann and Niebuhr. Like Burke and Rousseau, they have been less than certain that the nature of mankind is good. Neither Lippmann nor Niebuhr was ready to sing Whitman's song of America. Both found sympathetic ears in the circles of journalistic intellectuals.

Niebuhr (1892–1971) and Lippmann (1889–1974) both abandoned the socialism they espoused when they were young men. And despite the fact that both men considered themselves liberal, they have been criticized by the intellectual Left as secret conservatives. This viewpoint has some merit, although it goes too far. In any case, as we have seen, Lippmann did shift from whole-hearted admiration for William James to the antipragmatic stance of Santayana.

Over the course of their long lives, which spanned the Great Depression and two world wars, they of course modified their views considerably, and the careful critic can find many examples of self-contradiction. In essence, though, the messages of the mature Lippmann and the mature Niebuhr were considerably more gloomy about the nature of humankind than the traditional American belief system would have it. In the end, both men concluded that it is a fatal error to rely on "the people" in a democratic society. One cannot blame faulty institutions if things go wrong, Niebuhr asserted. Echoing Shakespeare's message that the fault lies not in the stars but in ourselves, Niebuhr asserted that evil is to be found in human beings who are themselves blind to the fact that their actions are motivated by self-interest. It was the question of power, our central theme in Part 9, that fascinated both Lippmann and Niebuhr.

What Niebuhr found especially troublesome was the virtue claimed for innocence. It is, he asserted, not enough for a person to justify his behavior by claiming that he is pure of heart and that he operates out of the best of motives. Popular image to the contrary, Niebuhr said, America is not in a state of innocence. An accurate portrait of America would, he said, show that its actual posture was one of power—power over the political, social, and economic environment, power over the quality and extent of information, indeed power over life and death. To claim good motives was not enough, for the irony of life is that there is a vast difference between what we think we believe and what we actually believe and do.

> *Our moral perils are not those of conscious malice or the explicit lust for power. Rather, they are the perils which can be understood only if we realize the ironic tendency of virtues to turn into vices when too complacently relied upon; and of power to become vexatious if the wisdom which directs it is trusted too confidently.*[1]

For a metaphor of contemporary life, the theologian Niebuhr turned to a passage from Luke: "The children of this world are in their generation wiser than the children of light."[2] To Niebuhr, the children of this world are in fact children of darkness, who although filled with evil and malice are nevertheless wise, for it is they who "understand the power of self-interest."[3] Since the innocent, good-hearted children of light are blind to reality, they are just as much to be condemned as the children of darkness, perhaps even more so because they are afflicted with arrogance and pride, believing, no matter what the evidence might show, that they are moral and good. Niebuhr argued that moral cynicism has an advantage over moral sentimentality:

> *Its advantage lay not merely in its own lack of moral scruple but also in its shrewd assessment of the power of self-interest,*

> *individual and national, among the children of light, despite their moral protestations.*[4]

However much he may have been tempted to do so, Niebuhr never rejected democracy. But his image of democracy was a great deal narrower than that of the traditional American belief system, which he insisted needed to be radically rethought. In any case, although he saw himself as a pragmatist, his approach was more moral than pragmatic. Democracy requires that each man be tolerant of the ideas of his fellow men. But, like Mill, he insisted that this is not the only way. At best, he wrote in a much-quoted passage, "democracy is a way of finding proximate solutions to insoluble problems."[5] In other words, all answers are partial, and only fools believe in absolute solutions to complex problems. In an epigram that is equally well known, Niebuhr asserted, with his usual sense of irony: "Man's capacity for justice makes democracy possible; but man's inclination to injustice makes democracy necessary."[6] Thus, if democratic institutions are to be preserved, Americans will need "the wisdom of the serpent and the harmlessness of the dove."

> *The children of light must be armed with the wisdom of the children of darkness but remain free from their malice. They must know the power of self-interest in human society without giving it moral justification. They must have this wisdom in order that they may beguile, harness and restrain self-interest, individual and collective, for the sake of the community.*[7]

Despite this somewhat cynical comment on human nature, Niebuhr was not one to resign himself to disaster. Instead, he turned for comfort to his own rather ascetic code of Christianity; his reverence for self-transcendence marked a return to the ideas of Emerson. Merely to affirm ideals is wasted effort, he said; far better to try to gain enough power to be able to combat the wicked uses of power by others. He was fascinated by ambiguities and paradoxes and argued that despair was unacceptable. What was crucially important for Niebuhr was the capacity to *recognize* the irony of life and to turn away from a bipolar view of good and evil, to avoid the blind optimism that, once exposed, brings about the "danger that sentimentality will give way to despair and that a too consistent optimism will alternate with a too consistent pessimism."[8]

In an observation that recalls the views of Edmund Burke, Niebuhr maintained that men would always abuse freedom. For to be free means that one is free to do evil as well as good. Thus, freedom is as much a burden as it is a gift. Psychiatrist Erich Fromm, thinking along the same lines, argued that mankind does not really desire freedom anyway. In a contest between freedom and security, Fromm said, humankind would always choose security.[9]

Niebuhr's sense of the irony of life caused him to reject the faith in rationality and social planning that had sustained Dewey. In a marked shift away from the very foundation of the Enlightenment, Niebuhr turned his back on any idea of relying on the scientific method in the study of mankind, that is to say in any of the social sciences. To do so was to introduce "an ideological taint," Niebuhr wrote, because the so-called scientific inquirer could never exclude himself from his own experiments.[10] Mankind can never be understood empirically, Niebuhr held, because scientific inquiry can never take into account the spiritual dimension of human existence and "the illogical and contradictory patterns of the human drama."[11]

As one of the members of the Hutchins Commission, Niebuhr campaigned actively for the doctrine of "social responsibility," arguing that it was correct "in holding the producer morally responsible for the product of news and entertainment in the mass media." True to his doubts about the wisdom of humankind, however, he acknowledged that it was enormously difficult to induce the consuming public to exert pressure "to police the media."[12]

It can be seen how subversive Niebuhr's ideas were of the traditional concepts that had become central elements in the belief system of American journalists. He rejected, one after another, the chief elements in that belief system. He disavowed the basic innocence and goodness of Americans. He challenged an optimistic image of the future. He cast in doubt the principles of empirical, scientific inquiry. He questioned the idea that America had created something better when it "turned its back on Europe and made a new beginning."[13] He turned *his* back on insularity and nationalism, which he equated with collective pride, and to him pride was the very essence of Original Sin. Most important of all, he repudiated the very idea that freedom was a virtue.

Lippmann was rarely as harsh in his judgments as Niebuhr, but his direct influence on journalists was greater. After all, he was himself a journalist and so widely respected in his field that on the occasion of his seventieth birthday, the celebrated *New York Times* columnist James Reston could assert that Lippmann had given his generation of journalists "a wider vision of our duty." Of Lippmann, Reston wrote:

> *The point is not that he was never wrong or that he did not change his ideas and even on occasion contradict his theories, but that he provoked thought, encouraged debate, forced definition, and often revision of policies, and nourished the national dialogue on great subjects for over half a century.*[14]

On all points, Reston was entirely correct. It can surprise no one that Lippmann changed his mind or that his output was often contradictory. After all, he wrote 18 books, some as a quite young man; he also wrote hundreds of essays and magazine articles and for nearly 40 years a newspaper column, "Today and Tomorrow," which appeared three times a week. The powerful of the world were among his readers; presidents consulted him before making decisions. And Lippmann often directly influenced those decisions. He also exercised considerable sway over journalists who read him or came into contact with him. For two generations, Lippmann was the Pontiff of the Press.[15] In short it can be said that Lippmann was the most powerful journalist the United States has ever produced. Professional journalists regularly pored over his column for "news" as much as for his commentary, since it was recognized how close Lippmann was to the seat of power. It was often proposed to him that he run for public office, but he thought he could exercise greater influence as a journalist than as an officeholder.[16]

Many, but not all, of Lippmann's views paralleled those of Niebuhr. Lippmann also believed that evil was to be found in mankind, not in its institutions. He also questioned the wisdom of the common man and doubted the efficacy of democratic institutions. At certain points in his career, he too turned his back on the scientific method. But ultimately Lippmann split with Niebuhr and found his guiding star in science and in scientific detachment and disinterest. As a journalist, he devoted much of his thinking to questions that were of direct interest to reporters and editors. Public opinion fascinated him all his life.

Lippmann's journalistic career, it is to be recalled, began as legman for the muckraker, Lincoln Steffens. But, even though he always considered Steffens a kind and sweet man, he parted company with him after a year with *Everybody's*, because Steffens was "too whimsical" in his belief that the path to good government came through emulating Jesus. Lippmann was too much the intellectual to buy Steffens's romanticism.[17] Still, some of Steffens's skepticism about the inherent goodness of the average man rubbed off on Lippmann, as did Steffens's belief that corruption was an inherent part of the American system. The solution lay, Lippmann believed, in mastery, not drift. The title of his 1914 book, three years after leaving Steffens, emphasized his very point.

On the whole, Lippmann's message was not a cheery one. He had almost no faith in the common man and, in his masterpiece, appropriately titled *Public Opinion*, he challenged one of the most cherished beliefs in the American journalist's professional ideology: the "democratic assumption" that what newspersons write in the press provides the raw stuff for democratic decision making. Since, Lippmann wrote, we all think in stereotypes, we interpret what we read according to our stereotypic view of the world rather than on the basis of the "objective facts" that appear in print.[18] We are, he said, like the people in Plato's cave, impressed not by reality but by the shadows on the wall that we see before us. Rejecting muckraker Upton Sinclair's condemnation of the press as the whore of big business, Lippmann concluded:

> *If the press is not so universally wicked, nor so deeply conspiring, as Mr. Sinclair would have us believe, it is very much more frail than the democratic theory has as yet admitted. It is too frail to carry the whole burden of popular sovereignty, to supply spontaneously the truth which democrats hoped was inborn. And when*

we expect it to supply such a body of truth we employ a misleading standard of judgment. We misunderstand the limited nature of news, the illimitable complexity of society; we overestimate our own endurance, public spirit, and all-round competence.[19]

The press, that frail reed, can never provide a reliable picture of the world, Lippmann wrote. It is because they must act without any reliable picture of the world that governments, schools, churches, and even newspapers "make such small headway against the more obvious failings of democracy," which Lippmann identified as violent prejudice, apathy, and preference for the trivial over the significant. This failure, he concluded, "is the primary defect of popular government, a defect inherent in its traditions."[20] We cannot find resolution of the problems of democracy, Lippmann said, in any of its institutions, but only in what he called "social organization."[21] Here, Lippmann was promoting the instrumentalism of Dewey, but without Dewey's enthusiasm. Dewey himself was dismayed by *Public Opinion*. He called Lippmann's book "perhaps the most effective indictment of democracy as currently conceived ever penned."[22]

Dewey's comments appeared in a 1922 issue of the *New Republic*, which Lippmann edited. Two years later Lippmann became director of the editorial page of the *New York World*, the Pulitzer paper by now free of its yellow past, so much so that Lippmann's biographer, Ronald Steel, could call it "the voice of America's liberal conscience."[23] Lippmann saw himself as a political and philosophical realist. Although his outlook on the world sometimes seemed bleak, still he did not surrender to bitterness and cynicism, perhaps because he never entirely overcame the romantic idealism of his youth. In some ways he was a throwback to the ancient Stoics, whose message was simply to endure. But Lippmann's Stoicism was modified by the views of his boyhood mentor, Santayana.

Measure, restraint, and detachment—these made up the stance that Santayana proposed for the moral man. Lippmann embraced them all. The moral journalist, he wrote, stands aloof from the struggle, possibly (but probably not) unaware of the intensity of his own involvement. However much he supped at the table of the powerful of the earth, Lippmann always viewed himself as the outsider, the detached observer. He might have been writing of himself when as a young man he wrote of "the tragic barrier" that separated Santayana from ordinary men:

It's as if he saw all forests and no trees. He filled active souls with a sense of the unbridgeable chasm between any ideal of perfection and the squeaky, rickety progress of human affairs. There is something of the pathetic loneliness of the spectator about him. You wish he would jump on the stage and take part in the show.

> *Then you realize that he wouldn't be the author of* The Life of Reason *if he did. For it is a fact that a man can't see the play and be in it too.*[24]

It was for lack of detachment that Lippmann condemned his onetime friend and Harvard classmate, John Reed, who went to Russia as a journalist and remained to join Lenin's revolution. Since Reed could not be detached about what he reported, Lippmann concluded, "he is not a professional writer or reporter."[25] Except in his earlier writings, Lippmann joined Santayana's search for absolute moral values; like Santayana, he was concerned lest excessive democracy produce the tyranny of the majority that de Tocqueville feared a century earlier. In *The Public Philosophy*, which appeared in 1955 when he was nearly 65, Lippmann complained that the people had acquired too much power and that only a return to a stronger executive could rescue the country from a "morbid derangement of the true functions of power." Even Niebuhr wrote that Lippmann had gone too far.[26]

Still, this book was in keeping with Lippmann's fundamental belief that there is a "higher law" to which humankind must answer. Lippmann's higher law is, however, quite different from Niebuhr's, for it is altogether free of religious content. It is "the denial that men may be arbitrary in human transactions."[27] In other words, all behavior must be rational, based on a detached calculation of the pluses and minuses. No decision is a wise one unless it has been thought through. There is simply no room for a decision based on mere emotion. The public philosophy—or "civility" as Lippmann called it—is founded on "the laws of a rational order of human society."[28] To this higher law all members of a democratic society must yield. It was, in Lippmann's view, the culmination of Enlightenment thought.

In sum, Lippmann can best be seen as a skeptical Enlightenment rationalist, and although his views sometimes read as extreme, he rarely was out of step with the popular mood of the country.[29] His greatest asset was his capacity to take the most complex of issues and write about them with such clarity that they could be understood by any intelligent reader.

Niebuhr and Lippmann are stunningly contemporary in their fascination with power. At various times in his long career, Lippmann addressed himself to the power of governments, of the president, of the wealthy, of the ordinary citizen alone and in the mass, and of the press itself. Despite his frequent assertions of disinterest, Lippmann was very much interested in the extent of his own power. And it was considerable. His biography abounds with tales of presidents counseling with him and occasionally offering him official positions in the government. Lippmann always rejected these, reflecting accurately enough that his own influence was greater *outside* government. Lippmann was prepared at various times to turn over almost unlimited power to the two Roosevelts, but at other times he called for restraints on power.

In his often-quoted Farewell Address, delivered to an admiring group of journalists in Washington after he had written his final "Today and Tomorrow" column in 1967, Lippmann said that his long career in journalism had convinced him "many Presidents ago that there should be a large air space between a journalist and a head of state."[30] Although he may have been convinced of the need for such air space, he did not heed his own advice. To him, it was absolutely essential that he remain very close indeed to power, for only then might he be able to recognize and illuminate the great issues of the day. The belief system of American journalists encourages that air space, but the practice seems to deny the conviction.

In the end, Lippmann agreed with Niebuhr that the only way to control seemingly unrestrained power is through the exercise of counter-power. Among those counters, the press inevitably stood front and center. Sometimes Lippmann was prepared to offer similar power to the men of science, to dispassionate experts, sometimes to professional scholars, but always to the journalistic observers.

Morality was inevitably a matter for the higher law of balance, moderation, detachment, and disinterested reason, but never the church. He did not put his faith in America's Holy Writ, that is to say its compacts, covenants, and constitutions.[31] Nor, of course, in the common man, whose destiny, in Lippmann's view, was never to lead, always to be led.

Foreign affairs always was dominant among Lippmann's political interests. It was there that his influence was greatest and, in one sense at least, subversive. He was thoroughly opposed to the insularity that dominated much of American life, arguing in his books, monographs, and columns for an end to the traditional American stance of isolation and neutrality, especially inside the "Atlantic community," a phrase Lippmann created.[32] If he would not involve himself, he would work unceasingly to induce his fellow citizens, presidents prominent among them, to involve themselves. This globalism may have been Lippmann's chief contribution to the philosophy of journalism, for those who followed, James Reston chief among them, embraced Lippmann's global view so thoroughly that at least in the urban centers along the East Coast the old insularity of the press slowly gave way to a greater concern for world affairs.

No journalist has appeared to take Lippmann's place. As one analyst has observed, readers no longer look to journalists for wisdom.[33] But perhaps most readers never did. In any case, it is the television anchorman who is today's journalistic celebrity, but primarily for his appearance and style, rarely for his wisdom. It is to be doubted that, even in his heyday, few among the masses that Lippmann held in such contempt went out of their way to look for his column, just as average citizens were unconscious in their day of Locke and Voltaire, Marx and Mill. But the powerful often paid close attention to these men, and during Lippmann's lifetime they read and pondered everything he wrote and said. Similarly, it was the wielder of power who fascinated Lippmann, not the average reader. Still, he liked to see himself, as do most contemporary journalists, as reporter, not as philosopher.

CHAPTER 51

The Shock of McCarthyism

We must now backtrack a little bit in time to events that were central in the lives of both Niebuhr and Lippmann as well as the other new apostles of Right and Left who challenged the central belief system of Americans, journalists prominent among them. Never may we allow ourselves to forget that American journalists are more than mere newspersons. They are also citizens of their own country and indeed of their own socioeconomic milieu. The value system of the people they come in contact with—their teachers, the novelists, essayists, and poets whose works they read, their parents and friends, above all their fellow journalists and their news sources—is their value system as well.

As had been the case in the past, the American journalists of the first half of the twentieth century paid little attention to scholarly examination of the beliefs of the society of which they were part. Nor did they interest themselves for the most part in communicating those interpretations of values to their audience. In their practical orientation, they went about their daily routines, optimistic as usual, dedicated to the ideals of press freedom enunciated by Jefferson and Mill. They were far too busy with the practical matter of reporting the "news" to pay close attention to the polarization that was going on around them, not really aware that hostility to "freedom of the press" was growing among the public at large as well as in academic circles. Depending on where in the political spectrum the hostility arose, it was aimed either at a docile, manipulated press in the service of entrenched power or at a licentious press challenging the moral and political values of society.

In the modern, fiercely competitive world of the mainstream journalist, practitioners have seemed even less concerned with ideas than were their colleagues of the past. Crusading has by no means disappeared, but the modern investigative journalist has been devoted more to tracking down wrongdoers than to promoting causes. Journalists have often appeared to go about their work by rote, adhering without reflection to the conventions that traditionally have defined news: dealing in facts and not opinions; reporting today's news today; discovering the unusual and bizarre; reporting what is closer to home rather than what is far away; writing about the affairs of political leaders and celebrities; searching out the conflictual and dramatic—in short, in serving their communities as professionals. It is no doubt less fun for a journalist to operate as a cool professional than it is to slash his sword to right and to left, contemptuous of the conventions as he follows his own star, moved by a Rousseauean commitment to his own feelings. His job is more secure, however, when he pursues the "higher law" of Walter Lippmann.

To operate professionally is indeed to operate under the conventional journalistic definitions of news, and in the contemporary world no standard of excellence in journalism is more acceptable than that of professionalism. When objectivity or social responsibility are invoked, it is almost always done in order to meet professional standards, rarely to challenge popular wisdom. Individual political leaders and individual actions may be and often are challenged, but not systems, institutions, or even ideas. To do so is unprofessional.

While editors in their newsrooms have continued to demand professionalism and empirical inquiry, hostility, as we have seen, has been developing among intellectuals on both the political Right and Left to pragmatism and empiricism. From both Right and Left, critics have mounted arguments against blind adherence to empirical method, arguing that its concern is only with means, with technology, and not with ends, not with human values. Sharp criticism was voiced by Niebuhr and Lippmann to the mere accumulation of "facts," details, and minutiae. Demands came for redirecting attention to the "whole man," for an end to "social engineering" and value-free research.

The Right called for a return to platonic standards and for insistence on absolute morality. Kendall inveighed against the "moral relativism" of the ethic of pragmatism and insisted on acceptance of the fundamentals of Christianity.[1] Leo Strauss, a student of classical political philosophy, rejected the study of behavior, which dominated the disciplines of sociology, economics, and political science, and demanded a "deeper understanding of political things" than could be learned just by examining the way people acted. He saw behaviorism as not only value-free but as a synonym for "dogmatic atheism."[2] The appeal of religious fundamentalism and the "born again" movement was at hand.

From the Left came an insistence on rising above politics into the reaches of poetry. Norman Brown, a classic scholar, saw the scientific method as an attempt to substitute method for insight or, as he said, "mediocrity for genius."[3] Theodore Roszak argued that when man is studied "objectively," he can be equated only with the stupid unfeeling things of the world. Instead, Roszak advised, people must be seen subjectively, as individual, "whole and integrated," human beings.[4]

From both Left and Right, reliance on "facts" and other objective data that can be used as computer inputs was viewed as morally wrong. Both sides, following Rousseau, were seeking to replace reason with passion, to replace science with love. These movements had their counterparts in the world of journalism, as we shall see.

Philosophical movements notwithstanding, it was more than anything else the rise to prominence of Senator Joseph R. McCarthy of Wisconsin that smashed the comfortable philosophical floor that had long served as the foundation of the belief system of the American press. Two other factors were important: the astonishing explosion of new technologies that provided opportunities and imposed restraints on the traditions of journalism, and the impact of two world wars.

Periods of reaction come after all great wars. World War I was followed by a decade of unrivaled growth when the watchwords of America were peace and prosperity. Since revolution was feared and the agreed-upon enemy was communism, dissident movements were repressed. The Great Depression of the 1930s shattered the calm and generated a decade of revolutionary activity that was marked by a reaction against the entrenched power of wealth and tradition. Following the path that was prepared by the muckrakers, the journalists of the 1930s flirted with revolution, formed labor unions, and condemned wealth and tradition. The years following World War II were a mirror of the era that came after the first war: first, there was a period of growth, when the watchwords once again were peace and prosperity, when the enemy once again was revolution and communism. It was in this era that the "cold war" began. The comfortable code of objectivity was supreme.

It was in 1950, only five years after the end of World War II, that McCarthy launched his "crusade" against communism. The McCarthy experience caused journalists to question their traditional value system, for it became clear how easy it was for the code of objectivity to be used by unscrupulous politicians to present utter falsehood to the public. Some writers suggest that shifts had taken place in the definition of news even before the rise of McCarthy. These writers maintain that the traditional separation whereby news went on the news pages and editorials on the editorial pages was already vanishing.[5] Certainly, the Hutchins Commission as early as 1947 had urged an increase in explanatory articles, in telling the truth about the facts, but most newspapers continued to cling to the traditional value system of objectivity.

By the time the Wisconsin senator appeared on the scene and the word *McCarthyism* had been coined, a remarkable degree of uniformity had developed in the self-image of the American reporter and editor. Journalistic virtue was held to reside in the concept of objectivity, in locating the facts and presenting those facts to the public. The journalist himself or herself was not part of the story reported. It was enough to publish the statements and declarations made by newsworthy subjects.

The truth of those statements and declarations was a matter of less than overriding interest to the reporter so long as "both sides" of controversial questions were presented and given equal treatment. The reader was supposed to judge the truth for himself or herself. This self-image has in fact never been replaced. An historical account of the relationship between McCarthy and the press concludes that the discovery that McCarthy had used the press for his own dishonest and deceptive purposes led to "lasting changes in the media," but that nevertheless:

> *The primary function of a newspaper is to tell people what is happening. It is not the duty of a newspaper to decide what is good for the people to know nor to be concerned about the effect of the news it publishes. Its duty is to furnish the information. In the case of McCarthy, the press did not properly fulfill this function.*[6]

That idea, that journalists ought not to be advocates of any causes other than the Cause of America or the Cause of Democracy, remains deeply embedded in the belief system of America's reporters, despite the popularity of investigative journalism. So powerfully is this idea held that it is expressed even by a historian relating the story of Joseph McCarthy himself. To Edwin Bayley, the press erred not in practicing objectivity but rather in failing to provide enough *information* so that McCarthy's lies might be exposed.

McCarthy emerged as a national figure during the fiercely anti-Communist postwar atmosphere. His claims, later shown to be untrue, that the highest levels of government were infested by Communists and Communist sympathizers, resulted in the condemnation of many persons. Under attack from McCarthy and his fellow investigators, some lost their jobs, many more their reputations. The Washington press, operating under the code of objectivity, reported McCarthy's charges as well as the denials of the accused. Denials, often in later editions, never overtake accusations and McCarthy was, as Bayley wrote, a master of making use of deadlines and the reporter's thirst for drama to get his allegations before the public. Editorials often condemned McCarthy but readership of editorials is limited; only one in ten read the editorial page.[7]

It was after the exposure of McCarthy that a powerful demand arose for "interpretive reporting." The idea of social responsibility promoted by the Hutchins Commission joined forces with the idealism of the postwar generation of journalists and scholars, led by Curtis MacDougall of Northwestern University, in a campaign to end the practice of blind objectivity and turn instead to more explanatory writing.[8] The path was now clear for fresh ideas in journalism, similar in spirit to those that were bubbling up in the community of social and political philosophers. Recognition of how effectively they had been manipulated brought on in the post-McCarthy period a widely expressed reaction among journalists against the code of objectivity and led indirectly to a long list of "new" conceptualizations about the role and function of the American journalist.

It was in this environment that investigative journalism was reincarnated, although it has tended to concern itself more with tracking down wrongdoers than with promoting causes. None of the "new" conceptualizations is in fact entirely new.

So familiar to its practitioner is the language of his field that it is next to impossible to explain the precise meaning of his jargon to anyone else. All institutions develop their own languages and their own ways of doing things. To the nonjournalist, the jargon of the mass media is as obscure as plant terminology is to one who is not a biologist. For the journalist, however, the term "inverted pyramid" instantly brings to mind a specific image of a style of writing. For the editor to "shirttail" the pyramid is simply to be doing his job. Everyone in television knows what a "standupper" is, although to the layman the term may seem a description of a certain posture.

The phrase "news judgment" is another such term. The journalist under attack inevitably defends himself by turning to his news judgment. "New" modes of journalism represent a fundamental challenge to the standards of news judgment that accompanied the rise of technological society. The term "new journalism" had appeared before. It was used as a concept nearly a century earlier by Matthew Arnold, the English poet and literary critic, when in 1887 he attacked plans for self-rule in Ireland and the journalists who supported those plans. What was needed, Arnold wrote, was a "new journalism" that was more responsive to the real needs of the people. In fact, Arnold endorsed a "new culture" to be based on understanding of the best that had been thought and said in human experience.[9] As had Bennett during the age of the penny press, Pulitzer turned to the term once again in the yellow period, in connection with the crusading spirit of his *New York World*.[10]

The modern campaign for a new journalism and for greater "social responsibility" was as much a response to the social upheaval brought on by technological innovations and by two world wars as it was a reaction against the use of the code of objectivity by Senator McCarthy.[11] In fact, "new" ideas surged onto the journalistic scene after each of the wars. The major new thrust in journalism in the 1930s was economic. Among the direct results of the social changes introduced by Roosevelt's New Deal were increased pay and increased social status for the journalist, thereby introducing a generation of well-educated, socially advancing news personnel. Under President Kennedy's call for moral greatness, hordes of young men and women, journalists among them, arrived in Washington to join the team identified by journalist David Halberstam as "the best and the brightest."[12] By the thousands young Americans signed up for the Peace Corps and streamed into journalism offices, convinced that in print and broadcasting there was a marvelous weapon to use in their search for the truth and indeed to serve the Cause of America and of democracy.

Each of the new movements in journalism was a reaction against the commonplace press standard of the journalist as mirror, as one who was himself (there were few herselves then) a nonparticipant in the "news," but rather a figure *through* whom news was presented. Among the differences between these movements and those of the past was the great advance that had been made in the technology of public relations. These changes made it far easier than ever before to communicate with fellow believers and to convert what once would have been slow-simmering local activity into national and even international movements.

Among the new movements we can identify at least nine strains, one, of course, being that of investigative journalism. Let us first describe each of the remaining eight movements briefly and then, in Chapter 52, examine them in some detail. Discussion of the various kinds of "new" journalism has been quite confused, since the terms have frequently been used interchangeably despite the fact that among them there are many differences in kind as well as in degree. Here then is a brief characterization of these movements.

Enterprise journalism: The concept appeared chiefly among the news agencies, which came under sharp attack for their "objective" and noncritical treatment of McCarthy's charges. Under enterprise journalism, the reporter refuses to rely on handouts provided by news sources or press conferences arranged by the sources and instead "digs" behind the scenes to uncover the "real" news rather than the news selected by sources who have their own axes to grind. He or she searches for the truth about the facts but remains an objective reporter by concealing his or her own opinions.

Interpretive journalism: The journalist in this model, sometimes identified as "news analyst," educates himself or herself in the subject matter of the stories covered by reading the available literature, interviewing a multitude of sources, or perhaps by attending classes or seminars, so that he or she becomes an expert in the subject matter and is able to write stories that are in fact enlightened analyses of complex and controversial questions. The analyst explores "both sides" of issues and thus retains objectivity inasmuch as he or she is capable of keeping his own opinions out of the story.

New journalism: The journalist rejects altogether the goal of objectivity and searches instead for the hidden truths that lie in human consciousness and memory. The journalist becomes a living and breathing part of the story, using as his or her model the practices and techniques of the novelist.

Underground journalism: This is the designation that was given to the newspapers published in the 1960s by young men and women of what they proudly identified as "the counterculture," often on university campuses, who rejected the traditional patterns and practices of mainstream journalism in favor of articles and journalistic forms hostile to the traditional politics and life-styles of those in power. Objectivity and "facts" were rejected in favor of what was seen as truthful reporting.

Advocacy journalism: The journalist is here a frank spokesperson for a cause. He or she picks and chooses among the available source material in search of weapons to help the cause. Objectivity in this situation is considered offensive and wicked. The advocacy journalist is in fact an editorialist operating on the "news" pages.

Adversary journalism: The journalist is here playing the part of an unabashed watchdog, placing himself or herself in the position of foe of authority, whether the person in power is liberal or conservative, Democrat or Republican, club owner or player. The journalist remains objective and dispassionate, but eternally in the opposition.

Precision journalism: The journalist consciously adopts the methods of science and turns to public and official documents as his primary source material, conducting his own research, usually through questionnaires and surveys, or hiring professional researchers to do the work and then analyzing the data himself with the aid of computers and other technological instruments. In seeking information from the public, he relies on scientific sampling techniques rather than haphazard interviews. His values are scientific detachment and he adopts the yardstick of objectivity.

Celebrity journalism: While not representing a philosophy, this development expresses a noteworthy trend, resulting from the vastly enhanced status and popularity of television news personnel, particularly those close to the seat of national power in Washington. It is a commonplace that the anchorman of a network news program has been considered the most trustworthy person in America. The celebrity journalist is not an objective observer but rather teacher or guide. He interprets, but he also expresses his own opinions; he stands aloof, perhaps even above those of whom he writes or speaks.[13]

CHAPTER 52

A Potpourri of "New Journalisms"

None of the movements described in Chapter 51 was revolutionary. Each was very much a product of America's philosophical and intellectual heritage. Nearly all the ideas were "democratic." After all, Locke and Hobbes, Jefferson and Madison had all argued that it was the duty of the individual to perform his role in the community, to refuse to accept the pronouncements of authority blindly, and in fact to "enterprise" by digging behind the pronouncements for the truth. The "investigative" thread runs throughout the history of American journalism. Zenger was an early enterprise journalist. The contempt of Voltaire and Milton for censorship and Jefferson's hostility to tyranny over the mind were "interpretive." Rousseau and his collectivist followers taught both "adversary" and "advocacy" themes. An "underground" press inspired Rousseau and the colonists, whose editors expressed the General Will as they saw it, even as did the editors of the twentieth-century underground press. The moral crusades that are imagined by "advocacy" as well as "underground" and "investigative" journalists have been an integral element in American journalism from its earliest days. The "great" editors and reporters of the American past were in their own way all "celebrity journalists." James and Dewey endorsed the principles of "new" journalism, a journalistic practice reminiscent of the writings of Benjamin Franklin and his English fellows, Addison and Steele, as indeed of Walt Whitman and Mark Twain.

The phrase "new journalism" had by the early 1960s become a magnet for the writers and reporters seeking a new literary art form. The "new" journalism rejected altogether the standard of objectivity and sought frankly to make use of the conventions of fiction to produce accounts of news events. Truman Capote, the novelist, an early proponent of the new journalism, labeled his book, *In Cold Blood*, "a non-fiction novel."[1] Tom Wolfe, the movement's chief theorist, endorsed a disciplined "psychology of realism" wherein reporters sought to touch emotions rather than the minds of their readers. "The most gifted writers," Wolfe wrote, "are those who manipulate the memory sets of the reader in such a rich fashion that they resonate with the reader's own real emotions. The events are merely taking place on the page, in print, but the emotions are real."[2]

One analyst saw Wolfe as rejecting "the instinctual view of journalism" in which reporting was static, "to be learned and relearned by succeeding generations of untrained persons."[3] Wolfe was taking a slap at both the all-knowing city editor who trained his staff in his own image and the professors of journalism who taught how-to courses in high school and college. To Everette Dennis, the old code of objectivity with its dedication to the empirical accumulation of raw facts was "primitivism," both in style and in reportorial methods. Dennis argued that the writing style of "primitive" investigative reporters like Jack Anderson and Seymour Hersh was neither memorable nor graceful. He added:

> *The primitives' lack of imagination in written expression is matched only by their conservative adherence to a case-by-case method of gathering information. In an age of computers it is truly amazing that journalists rigidly cling to the same methods of news-gathering that James Gordon Bennett used in the 1830s.*[4]

Wolfe, Capote, and other leaders in the new journalism movement—Gay Talese, Jimmy Breslin, Norman Mailer—specifically rejected primitivism in *style*. As Dennis points out, they also addressed themselves to *content*, exploring the emotion-laden social questions of drugs, the youth culture, and the peace movement. Wolfe made popular the idea of "radical chic" among "high-cult" figures like conductor Leonard Bernstein, and explored such arcane journalistic topics as the excesses in contemporary architecture.[5] Yet, within a decade of its arrival, the steam had gone out of new journalism. The mainstream press community could not stomach the whole-hearted denigration of the cult of objectivity and wrote off Wolfe and his colleagues as authors of fiction, hence not journalists at all. Misreading the point that the main concern of the new journalism was with style and not with content, critics tended to equate it with "adversary" journalism. By 1974, Wolfe himself had abandoned the banner of new journalism.[6]

The "underground" movement bore a superficial similarity to new journalism, although its quest was never for elegance in literary style. It served frankly as the voice of the counterculture. Indeed, *voice* was the name chosen by one of the most successful underground newspapers, the *Village Voice*, which began publication in New York's Greenwich Village in 1955. To the underground journalists, the mainstream press's standard of objectivity was anathema. Ray Mungo, who helped establish the Liberation News Service, an underground news agency, wrote: "Cold facts are nearly always boring, and may even distort the truth, but Truth is the highest achievement of human expression."[7] Shock value was the stock-in-trade of the underground press as it sought to outrage the "straight community." It embraced youth and denigrated maturity.[8] The young journalists wrote with unreserved enthusiasm about rock music, drugs, uninhibited sex, four-letter words, and fashions in hair and clothing that offended their elders. No underground newspaper attracted more readers than *Rolling Stone*, which began as the bible of rock music and which, long after most of the underground press had perished in the 1970s, found its own niche by adapting to the basic values of the overground press.

The values of the counterculture were not only contrary to those taught in the schools but also outside the professional value system of American journalism. The social revolutionaries of the 1960s were by no means ready to conform to the ideas of Locke and Jefferson in journalism or in public affairs. Underground journalists had little room in their belief system for objectivity or a public right to know or even for social responsibility. More significant to these revolutionary journalists than any traditional press values was the right of the individual journalist to serve his own conscience.

The targets of counterculture journalists were tradition and complacency in the mainstream press. They wanted no part of "the buttoned-down excellence" of the *New York Times*. Still, these youthful protesters were no more charting new philosophical ground than were Tom Wolfe and Norman Mailer. In historical context the output of underground journalists was no more outrageous than the output of the newspapers that de Tocqueville and Dickens had condemned more than a century earlier. Like the revolutionary colonial press and the "libellistes" of Rousseau's day, the underground journalists despised tradition and made no pretense of keeping their contempt to themselves. But their movement died when the rebellious 1960s came to an end.

As had the new journalists, the underground editors and reporters left an important legacy in style. Adapting computer technology to their own ends, the counterculture explored new possibilities in graphics and in nonverbal approaches to communication. Offset printing techniques challenged and ultimately dispelled the old black-and-white newspaper format with its rows of eight solid columns. White space became important. Columns often ceased to be vertical or even horizontal. Messages, colors, artwork, poetry, prophecy, astrology—the content of these newspapers ran sometimes upside down, sometimes sideways, sometimes in wrap-around fashion. Psychedelic color schemes emerged. The overground press has always borrowed technological innovations whenever and wherever they appeared and in this situation they soon came to adopt many of the typographical departures of the underground press.

Just as "adversary" and "investigative" journalism are sometimes confused with one another, the "underground" press is often mistaken for the "advocacy" press. But there are important distinctions. Certainly a number of underground editors were advocates of particular causes, chiefly an end to the Vietnam War, but these editors were so far removed from the modern American tradition of "balanced" journalism that they might just as well appear as mere footnotes in any scheme of journalistic classification. By the 1970s, in any case, many among these editors had chosen either to abandon journalism or to join the ranks of the mainstream.

To the most dedicated of the underground activists the press was an instrument to be used for purposes of counterpropaganda; they thought of the overground press as an instrument of propaganda in the hands of "the Establishment" and perceived of themselves as providing the antidote. The black press in the United States had long seen itself in the same light.[9] There sprang up in the ranks of the underground press a battery of newspapers dedicated to improving the social and economic status of blacks as well as papers demanding greater rights for women, Latin Americans, homosexuals, and other groups that felt themselves to be exploited. The black separatist movement developed its own underground press. All of these latter groups were practitioners of advocacy journalism. Far removed as they were from the attention of the overwhelming majority of American citizens, they drew on the popular belief in rebellion when rebellion was demanded. Although their ideas were taken from Locke and Jefferson, their perception of the social scene differed substantially from that of the community of overground journalists. In the end, the mainstream press took over, in softened form, their passion for social reform and provided in its own pages greater attention to issues involving blacks, women, Chicanos, homosexuals, and other minorities.

The values held by "adversary" journalists go back to the very beginnings of the American press. It was in the colonies on the Atlantic seaboard that the tradition arose of American editors monitoring the behavior of sovereigns, governors, and other lords of power, and calling attention to tyranny and abuses. These were the first American press watchdogs, drawing their inspiration from English commentators as far back as Milton. Of course, to the pure adversary journalist, it is unthinkable to support power lords in any way and therefore the Milton who served as censor for Oliver Cromwell would have to be seen as a turncoat no longer worthy of endorsement. That American journalists have ever been pure in their adversarial stance, however, is unlikely. Most journalists have copied Milton, standing vigilant in the role of watchdog when those they were watching angered them but growing blind when the watched ones were acceptable to them.

"Precision" journalism is concerned entirely with method and technique.[10] In many ways it is similar in spirit to the pragmatic enterprise journalism. One might think "scientific" could be substituted for "precision" since the goal is to apply the methods of scientific inquiry to the practice of journalism, but there is something that does not quite ring true about the idea of "scientific" journalism, which sounds deterministic. Hitler's Germany and Stalin's Soviet Union both proclaimed that they were in the vanguard of "scientific" history. Moreover, James refused to accept any kind of fixed principles and argued for open-mindedness. In theory, precision journalism proclaims no fixed principles and conducts its inquiries free of prejudgments or indeed of values. It is to be remembered that Russell argued that the pragmatists in their "scientific investigations" ignored thought. If this is what James was in fact doing, then he would resemble the journalists Dennis condemned as primitives.

In any case, the practice of precision journalism, as urged by its backers, involves the study of empirically assembled data in order to clarify the complex subject matter with which today's journalist is faced. The leading examples of precision journalism involve reliance on census tracts and other official documents for the raw material on which analytical, or interpretive, news stories are based. Since the collection of such data is expensive and time-consuming, the practice of precision journalism seems limited to the largest and most profitable news enterprises. Whether precision journalism ought to qualify as a separate category rather than as a subdivision of interpretive journalism is debatable. The standards of journalism in general call on reporters and editors to be as precise as they possibly can be in everything they write.

Celebrity journalism is quite different; it is anything but precise. Celebrity journalists are not new, but they have always been associated with political power. Nineteenth-century editors were all celebrities of a sort. So have been the newspaper columnists of more contemporary times, men in the image of Walter Lippmann. But it was not until television invaded the American home that reporters and anchorpersons achieved celebrity status and their opinions began to matter to the public. The impact of these celebrities on the belief system of journalists can be illustrated by the case of George Will, who is at once newspaper columnist, television commentator, talk show participant, book author, and lecturer. James Fallows notes that Will's manner differs markedly from the "interpretive" stance of earlier journalistic celebrities such as Lippmann, or the "investigative" demeanor of Watergate's Woodward and Bernstein. The new model of journalistic success achieved by Will and his cohorts has, Fallows writes, begun to spread a new journalistic philosophy that has "helped make political debate more catty and dismissive."

> *The put-down is essentially because there is such a large gap between the sweeping philosophical statements now printed in opinion journalism and the inconvenient, irregular world of fact.*[11]

It has never been easy to distinguish these "new" forms of journalism from one another. Each movement is itself an abstraction and the way it has been defined has depended in part on who did the defining.

There remains in contemporary journalism another critical question of definition, one whose impact is powerful politically, financially, and morally, affecting at once the courts, the schools of journalism, and the news media themselves. It is this: what constitutes the press and the news media? How in fact is journalism to be defined? Well over half the space in both the print and broadcast media is taken up by material that can by no stretch of the imagination be characterized as "news." Journalists are said to deal in news; they are not supposed to be in the business of advertising or of public relations. Their work is, however, financed primarily by commercial interests. What then is the proper relationship between journalist and commercial interest? For generations editors have endorsed Pulitzer's dictum that news is a matter for journalists and advertising a matter for the commercial side of the newspaper.

Much of the thrust of the "new" movements we have been discussing has been to lend support to the idea of a fearless, independent journalism, willing to challenge even those financial interests that pay their salaries. Taken literally, this seems to exclude the commercial elements of the news media from the field of journalism. In this context, it becomes a legitimate question to ask whether courses in advertising and public relations properly belong in the curriculum of schools of journalism.

At one level, the question would seem to have become more pressing with the marked rise in journalism school enrollment of students interested in advertising and public relations. Yet, on the whole, most institutions avoid facing the question. It is often said that the techniques of advertising and public relations—the writing and photographing of publishable material and the layout and design of that material on newsprint or videotape—are essentially similar to the work of newspersons. This explanation deals with form only, not with content. The concept of news is excluded from the definition. Neither advertising nor public relations can realistically be considered to be elements of journalism if by journalism is meant the publication of news, however news may be defined. There is no pretense in either advertising or public relations that what they seek is a fair presentation of all arguments and points of view about their products and personnel.

By their very nature, they are partial and exclusive. They do not desire to present the truth about the facts. Their interest is in publicizing only those truths that aid in the marketing of their products. For this reason journalists face a difficult if not insurmountable obstacle in convincing the public that their unalterable goal is the presentation of the truth about the facts when considerably more than half the product of their organization is devoted, at best, to presenting a slanted and partial version of the truth. All disputes over the power of the media must be viewed against this background.

CHAPTER 53

The "Power" of Journalism

The "Agnew Doctrine" was given expression by the then vice president on November 13, 1969, before a group of Republican party loyalists in Des Moines, Iowa, shortly after a speech by President Nixon that the White House had billed as an important pronouncement on his Vietnam War policies.[1] Nixon's address, carried live by all three TV networks, had been followed immediately by sharp criticism from television newsmen, especially on CBS and NBC. The networks were employing a practice known among broadcasters as "instant analysis," that is, providing immediate comment at the end of a televised speech. In this case, the reporters had been handed a text of Nixon's speech to study some hours earlier. In their instant analysis, they summarized the highlights of the speech and then concluded that, despite the fact it had been publicized as a new peace initiative, it contained no departures from previous policy.

When Agnew's speech was announced, all three TV networks, aware that they were to be targets of attack, chose to give it live coverage. In the speech Agnew focused attention on what he called "this little group of men who not only enjoy a right of instant rebuttal to every Presidential address, but more importantly wield a free hand in selecting, presenting and interpreting the great issues of our nation." He went on to ask:

> *How is this network news determined? A small group of men, numbering perhaps no more than a dozen "anchormen," commentators and executive producers, settle upon the 20 minutes or so of film and commentary that is to reach the public. . . . Their* powers of choice *[italics added] are broad. They decide what 40 to 50 million Americans will learn of the day's events in the nation and in the world.*[2]

The vice president was careful to point out that it was only when licensed by an arm of the government, the Federal Communications Commission, that a television station might commence broadcasting. In no way, Agnew said, was he proposing censorship, but he contended that the public

> *would rightly not tolerate this kind of concentration of power in government. Is it not fair and relevant to question its concentration in the hands of a tiny and closed fraternity of privileged men elected by no one, and enjoying a monopoly sanctioned and licensed by government?*[3]

Many newspapers and Nixon's political opposition joined the TV networks in responding with unconcealed anger and resentment. But Agnew, clearly operating under a go-ahead signal from Nixon, refused to retreat. In fact, he advanced. In a second address, this one to the Chamber of Commerce of Montgomery, Alabama, on November 20, Agnew called attention to the numerous allegations that the administration was seeking to stifle dissent, and dismissed them as "nonsense." He belittled critics who, he said, had condemned his first speech as "sinister," and "disgraceful, ignorant and base," and as having led the nation "into an ugly era of the most fearsome suppression and intimidation." He continued:

> *The president of one network said it was an "unprecedented attempt to intimidate a news medium which depends for its existence upon government licenses." The president of another charged me with "an appeal to prejudice" and said it was evident that I would prefer the kind of television that would be subservient to whatever political group happened to be in authority at the time. And they say* I *have a thin skin. Here are classic examples of overreaction.*[4]

In this second address, Agnew broadened the base of his attack by including two prominent liberal newspapers, the *New York Times* and the *Washington Post*, as targets. One sentence stands out: "The day when the network commentators and even gentlemen of the *New York Times* enjoyed a form of diplomatic immunity from comment and criticism of what they said—that day is past."

> *Just as a politician's words—wise and foolish—are dutifully recorded by the press and television to be thrown up to him at the appropriate time, so their words should likewise be recorded and likewise recalled. When they go beyond fair comment and criticism they will be called upon to defend their statements and their positions just as we must be called upon to defend ours.*[5]

The flow of rhetoric—from Agnew and from his opponents—swirled across the country and set in motion a public debate that has not yet come to an end.[6] The representatives of the press, especially those at the networks and in the offices of the *Times* and the *Post*, seemed surprised to learn that Agnew had struck a responsive chord in the American breast. Far from reacting with hostility to Agnew, the public turned out to agree with him. Telephone response to the speech showed the public favoring his remarks by at least two to one. At one station in Oklahoma City, the switchboard operator received 350 calls and all but two praised the speech. One caller was reported to have said: "Oh Lord, you are wonderful. He said just what I've been thinking for years."[7] The remark was typical. Subsequent polls testing public opinion indicated that two-thirds or more of the American people were alarmed at the growing power of the news media.[8] In voluminous number, letters from the public poured into newspaper offices; the switchboards of broadcasting stations were filled with hostile telephone calls. There could be little doubt that the credibility of the news media was under challenge.

Julian Goodman, president of NBC, accused Agnew of appealing to "prejudice" in an effort to "deny to television freedom of the press."[9] Frank Stanton, president of CBS, called the address "an unprecedented attempt by [Agnew] to intimidate" the television industry. Whatever the deficiencies of CBS reporters, Stanton said, "they are minor compared to those of a press which would be subservient to the executive power of government."[10] Fred Friendly, former president of CBS News and at the time consultant for Public Broadcasting to the Ford Foundation, acknowledged that there had been some overreaction on the part of the broadcasters, but added that the Agnew comments—taken together with remarks and suggestions from officials of the Nixon administration, including Clay Whitehead, director of Telecommunications Policy, and Herbert Klein, then director of Communications—had a "chilling" effect on the industry.[11]

No word, incidentally, has been more widely used than "chilling" to describe the power of authority to curb free expression in the press. The "chilling" concept is old, dating back at least to the middle of the nineteenth century. "Nothing chills the heart like . . . distrust," a British churchman declared in a famous sermon.[12] Government pressure to force radio stations to censor their own views in order to provide reply time to individuals attacked on the air exerted a "chilling effect" on free expression, asserted David Bazelon, a libertarian federal judge, in a 1972 dissent.[13]

Richard Harwood and Laurence Stern, correspondents for the *Washington Post*, said they were convinced that "wrapping oneself in the First Amendment" would not evaporate Agnew's charges: "The media are as blemished as any other institution in American society."[14] Another *Post* reporter, Lou Cannon, said he could understand "how overly sensitive—timid, if you want—the broadcasters were," but said he could not see any reason for the *Post* or the *Times* to feel outraged.[15] Alexander Bickel, law professor at Yale University and attorney for the *Times* in the celebrated Pentagon Papers case, said he considered the press to be overly sensitive to the Agnew speech, and took the position that the vice president had no real power. "Why in the world," he asked, "should there be such a terrific brouhaha that the Vice President of the United States has criticized the media? It was intimidation only because it was taken that way."[16]

Press critic Ben Bagdikian, who offered a thorough analysis of the Agnew matter and who was himself a very sharp critic of the vice president, took the position some years later that the public antagonism against the press demonstrated by the widespread support for Agnew's charges served as a reminder to the press of its proper stance, which he said was not one of adversary to government. "The ideal relationship," Bagdikian said, "is one of independence of the media from government, and no assumption of governmental obligations by the media."[17]

It is useful to analyze Agnew's observation dispassionately, outside the realm of the purely political. Agnew was without question serving the interests of President Nixon. When he took office as president in 1969, Nixon was determined to weaken the influence of the liberal press, especially the television networks, the *Times*, and the *Post*. Opposition to his Vietnam War policies was especially anathema to him: to succeed in his Vietnam program, he needed widespread national support. And he was not getting that support from the news media. In fact, the response by Eric Sevareid, David Brinkley, and others to his November 3 speech must have been especially painful to him. Hence the highly unusual course of a direct attack on the news media; it is to be remembered that few administrations had taken on the press frontally. Even Roosevelt and Truman had been careful to criticize only "the fat cat publishers"; they had continued to applaud the individual newsmen.

Stripped of its political overtones, what can we say constitutes the Agnew Doctrine? For, in fact, careful analysis shows that Agnew or his speechwriter had constructed something approaching a full-blown theory. It is, simply, this: the news media exert a tremendous (and perhaps dangerous) influence over public affairs in this country. The theory can be demonstrated in four propositions:

1. The media, especially television, are run by a very small group of people.
2. This small group of people decides what the public is told about public affairs.
3. The decisions of the public in the voting booth are controlled in large measure by the picture of the world supplied by the news media. The people decide for whom they will vote on the basis of that picture.
4. Finally, then: a small group of journalists determine the public policy of the United States.

If one dissects the Agnew Doctrine, one finds oneself faced at last with an extraordinary doctrine. It suggests astronomical power for the news media.

It should be pointed out that the Agnew Doctrine concerns itself exclusively with the "national" news media and with information about national and international news events. How far one should extend the Agnew Doctrine to cover the local press and local news events is difficult to say. Agnew himself was careful to dissociate the national media from the small-town press; in fact, his speeches sought to separate the small-town press from the great institutions he was attacking. Unquestionably, he found support for his position among some representatives of the small-town press. Still, it is possible to extend the doctrine to the local press; some American readers and viewers have inveighed against what they perceived to be the vast power of the local press over local public affairs.

It is important to stress that the Agnew Doctrine exists as a theoretical construct even in the absence of partisan political motivations. Indeed, the perception of press power that Agnew presented is shared not only by conservative opponents of the liberal press, but also by many liberals and radicals and, even more surprising, by members of the news media themselves! The growing mass of literature about the power of the press seems boundless, whether it come from scholars, from politicians, from authors of letters to the editor or from journalists themselves.[18] A Harvard University study more than a decade after Nixon and Agnew were forced from power discovered that Washington policy makers viewed news media power as on the increase. This increase in power, the study reported, was marked also by a sharp rise in the number of journalists in Washington; the mid-1980s total of 10,000 represented a tripling of the Washington press corps in a single generation. One professor went so far as to say the country had become a "media democracy," with the press replacing political parties as an influence on national decisions.[19]

The power question is at the center of all discussions about the place occupied by the mass media in contemporary life. There is nothing especially new about linking the press with questions of power. It has always been recognized that anyone who could control the flow of information was in a position to exercise power over the receivers of "news." With the rise of television, however, greater attention than ever before has been given to the source of public information. It was in the context of television that the Agnew Doctrine was announced. Nearly all those who rejected Agnew's argument took the position that the news media were nowhere near so powerful as he claimed, that in any contest with political authority, the president for example, the media were certain to be the losers. The ousting of Nixon from office following persistent challenges by the news media did nothing, certainly, to weaken the arguments of those who claimed vast power for the media.

Whatever the reality of the power relationship (and it does seem unlikely that one could show the press exercising greater power than the government), it is quite clear that in today's world the news media have as never before become fascinated with the question of power relationships. The widespread publicity given to reporters Bob Woodward and

Carl Bernstein of the *Washington Post* for their role in the fall of President Nixon turned the attention not only of the American public but of the entire world to the question of the power of the press and increased interest in investigative journalism.

Whenever power enters a picture so does earnestness. How can anyone be light-hearted when reflecting on questions of power? When faced with questions of power, humor simply abandons belly laughs; it turns to satire rather than farce. The journalist who ruminates about the level of his or her power is serious; the questions he considers are grave ones. Little opportunity remains for frivolity. To stress power is to take the fun out of being a journalist. Perhaps this emphasis on power plays a part in the demand made by management consultants for frivolous badinage on news programs shown on local television stations. The consultants are convinced that the viewing public, unwilling to live in a world of earnestness, is more likely to choose TV channels in which the news is not treated with deadly seriousness.[20]

Still, it is difficult to challenge the claim that the Woodward-Bernstein story and a number of less dramatic but similar cases have increased the tendency among many journalists to use their position as platforms for swatting the powerful, for acting out the role of watchdog that has long been associated with the journalist. Ironically, the fascination with power relationships has produced an interest not only in the relationship of the journalist to those who wield political power but also in the question of power relationships inside the field of journalism itself.

An interesting sidelight of the controversy over Agnew's speech appeared in the raising of questions about the weak position of minorities within the field of journalism. The civil rights movement of the 1960s represented a watershed in the development of awareness of the weakness of minorities within the press establishment. Blacks, it was clear, held no power at all in the mainstream American press, and women held practically none. The report of the special commission appointed by President Johnson to examine racial violence in the country devoted a significant chapter to the impotence of blacks in the white press establishment.[21] In the underground press movement of that same revolutionary decade, blacks, women, and representatives of minority political causes joined force to, among other things, demand positions of prominence for themselves in the world of American journalism. It became all too apparent that the institution of the press resembled all other institutions in American society in assigning the greatest degree of power within its own domain to its own elite. Agnew may have been wrong in speaking of journalism as being dominated by a band of "effete eastern snobs" but he was not far from the target in suggesting a closely knit media power structure. In that structure, minority groups were as weakly represented as they were in all other social institutions in the country. The self-image of American journalists was that of watchdog of power but their own institutional practices were similar to those of other power bureaucracies. As we have seen throughout this book, reality did not equal self-image.

It is uncertainty about power relationships that has, to a large degree, led modern American journalists to embrace pragmatism and to follow the ghost of the muckrakers. Inevitably, this uncertainty has moved reporters and editors to define themselves as skeptics—about the practice of journalism, about the integrity of news sources, about the seriousness of the reading and viewing public, indeed about the social order they see around themselves. There are those who take the position that the journalist has departed from the mainstream of American life. We turn now to an examination of this serious question and of its impact on the morality of the American journalist.

PART X

The "Skeptical" Adversaries

Daniel Patrick Moynihan (1927-): "Journalism has become, if not an elite profession, a profession attractive to elites . . . The political consequence of the rising social status of journalism is that the press grows more influenced by attitudes generally hostile to American society and American government . . . The issue is not one of serious inquiry, but of an almost feckless hostility to power."

Marshall McLuhan (1911–1980): "The medium is the message. This is merely to say that the personal and social consequences of any medium—that is, of any extension of ourselves—result from the new scale that is introduced into our affairs by each extension of ourselves, or by any new technology . . . [It] is the medium that shapes and controls the scale and form of human association and action. The content or uses of such media are as diverse as they are ineffectual in shaping the form of human association. Indeed, it is only too typical that the 'content' of any medium blinds us to the character of the medium." (photo used with permission of University of Toronto.)

CHAPTER 54

Introduction: Skepticism and Modernism

The unifying theme of this concluding part is *skepticism*. For most American journalists, the self-image that must rise to mind is that of the cool observer, the wary student of humankind who holds suspect the statements and comments, yes, even the physical appearance of everyone he or she encounters. This is the disciple of Hobbes and Hume, who insisted that nothing can be taken for granted, that all information must be subject to scientific scrutiny. This is the disciple of Voltaire, whose advice to the eighteenth-century journalist was to treat with dispassionate skepticism everything that he could see or hear. This is the disciple of James and Dewey, who demanded that all evidence be dealt with by the rigorous investigation required by pragmatism. This is the disciple of Lincoln Steffens and Walter Lippmann, who dismissed prepared statements and sought answers only in the responses to questions they themselves raised.

The chief task of the skeptic is inevitably defined in terms of asking questions. Only by posing questions can one approach the truth about the facts. The image of the investigative journalist is that of the skeptical watchdog par excellence. He or she trusts no one who cannot document his case with verifiable evidence. Truth can be arrived at only by empirical—that is to say, verifiable—proof. Facts are sacred, but first they must be verified.

This emphasis on watchdoggery may have led the journalist, in the twentieth century, to what Daniel Patrick Moynihan, whom we encountered in Part 1, calls "the adversary culture." The term was not new with Moynihan. In fact, it grew out of the American literary tradition. But it was he who applied the term to newspeople, thereby raising vital questions about the professional ideology of the American journalist. If the prevailing belief system of Americans remains one of optimism, adhering to the virtues of individualism, the so-called myth of Adam, is the pragmatic skepticism of the journalist not outside the mainstream? Is it not part of an "adversary culture" that embraces the dogma of the European cultural pessimists? Do the recent meanderings of American journalists make them, as Spiro Agnew charged, hostile to the American belief system? We will explore these questions in Part 10.

First, however, we turn our attention to a related matter: the changes in the power equation brought about by the growth of the broadcasting industry and what has come to be called "new technology," the cybernated, computerized world in which we now have arrived. This equation has produced both encouraging and discouraging scenarios, ranging from the concept of a peaceful global village to that of an armed world in which the values of America—democracy and equality—vanish in a totalitarian fog. In this context, we examine the thoughts and influence of two Canadian thinkers, Marshall McLuhan and Harold Innis, who relate the promises and the perils of technology to the skeptical premises of today's journalist. We conclude with an examination of the relevance of the themes of individualism, optimism, pragmatism, power, and skepticism to the ethics of journalism.

CHAPTER 55

Modern Technology: McLuhan and the Global Village

No one can say with any degree of confidence what has brought about the soul-searching character of the last quarter of the twentieth century. Certainly the incredible technological accomplishments of the postwar world are central to any understanding of America's contemporary belief system. At the same time, we have witnessed the increasing urbanization of society, with its frightening assault on quiet and privacy in the impersonal megalopolis. We have experienced also the rise of nuclear power and the threat it poses to the future existence of humankind. Accompanying these developments has been a marked decline in orthodox religious practices and a companion increase in leisure time. In any case, the field of journalism has not been immune from this process of soul-searching. The multiplication of college and university courses on the role and function of journalism in society is testament to the significance of this process in the field of journalism. So indeed have been the posing of serious questions about the relationship of the mass media to matters of politics, law, science, and ethics.

Profound moral questions have arisen. How powerful are the media? it is asked. What role do the media play in what we learn, in what we know? How can the power of the media, however great or small it may be, be employed for the benefit of humankind? Ought brakes to be placed on the media so that they do not abuse their power? How can the media themselves be made more responsible, more accountable, to the public they claim to serve, both externally in the outside world and internally in their own studios, newsrooms, and front offices?

At the same time, American journalism has extended itself further into the world of pure entertainment, spurred on by the increasing popularity and profitability of television. The entertainment industry has mushroomed, expanding the number of jobs in the allied pursuits of advertising and public relations. Codes of ethics have been adopted in every branch of the mass media, all in the end accepting as gospel a trio of moral values: professionalism, objectivity, and social responsibility, all of which we have encountered earlier. The "new" modes of journalism have been adopted in one way or another by the mainstream media.

As conglomerates and holding companies have entered the field, control of the information business has been concentrated into fewer and fewer hands. These vast enterprises dedicated to profit and expansion have inevitably concerned themselves less than did editors of the past with "hard" news and more with marketable commodities: "soft" features, human interest, gossip about celebrities, and heavily dramatized stories of conflict and confrontations. "Packaging" of the news into short punchy paragraphs has become a common practice. Schools of journalism have concentrated on instructing students in the practical application of the accepted norms of American journalism, although in many cases, especially at the graduate level, courses have multiplied in the ethics and philosophy of journalism.

In modern America, the scientific method has been consecrated among journalists as well as among the citizenry at large. The practical has been extolled, but too often it has been mistakenly equated with the pragmatic. Reason, science, and pragmatism have, as we have seen, become entrenched in the belief system of Americans, ritualized on the nation's television screens. The Corporate State has been justified rationally by empirical inquiry. There has in fact flourished in all walks of life a consensus on the general standards of professionalism, objectivity, and social responsibility.

The increasingly visible role of new media forms brought on by technological developments—first radio, later television, and then the advanced fruit of electronic experimentation, computers, and the other "new media"—has deepened the interest of social and political philosophers in questions about the power of the media. Technological progress has inflamed the optimistic utopian vision that has been present in the American spirit from its very outset. But it has had the contrary impact as well. It has also raised to its highest level the strain of cultural pessimism imported from its European roots.

American growth has always been associated with the fruits of scientific inquiry. The nation's earliest heroes were not only patriots but scientists as well. Benjamin Franklin's fame rests more on his kite-flying experiments with electricity than on his role in politics and journalism. Thomas Paine was a builder of bridges. Thomas Jefferson was an architect and designer. From the wilderness these "can do" Renaissance men created, with their hands as well as their brains, an America that was meant to be a model for the world. The rolling back of the frontier was the next step in what has sometimes been identified as the myth of Eden.[1] The heroes of the Old West have passed on. So have the captains of industry. But another frontier remains. It is not to be symbolized by the pony express or the steel mill, but it is no less part of America's optimistic heritage. Its symbols are the television set, the cable, and the computer. The Garden of Eden was now to be found through modern communication and new media. The chief prophet of this new Eden was an unlikely person, a feisty Canadian student of English literature named Marshall McLuhan. Its watchword was the global village.

Time has not dealt kindly with McLuhan the man. Even during his heyday in the 1960s he was the target of attacks by literary critics and academics, partly as the result of his tendency to poke fun at conventional wisdom, partly because of fatal weaknesses in his methodology.[2] Nonetheless, McLuhan gained widespread publicity among the public and many supporters among television people. The heart of his creed, belief in the centrality of the electronic media in public affairs and the power of the media to bring about a better world, has become a salient unit in the belief system of optimistic Americans, in and out of the television industry.

McLuhan was part of the tradition that honored Franklin and Jefferson and the technological innovators who followed them. Samuel Morse, father of the telegraph, was no less forceful than McLuhan when he forecast not only faster communications through the telegraph but a better world as well. More than a century before the appearance of McLuhan's work, Morse was telling Congress that through electromagnetic telegraphy humankind would be able to create an artificial nerve system to "diffuse, with the speed of thought, a knowledge of all that is occurring throughout the land; making, in fact, one neighborhood of the whole country."[3] One day after Morse demonstrated his telegraph publicly for the first time, the *Baltimore Patriot* repeated his feat and informed its readers that it had succeeded in "the annihilation of space."[4] That was in 1838. In 1964, McLuhan published his *Understanding Media*, which he appropriately subtitled "The Extensions of Man." The nerve system was no longer merely a figurative by-product of telegraphy but an actual expansion of the biological human being. In fact, McLuhan said in the phrase most widely associated with his thought, "the media is the message."

> *This is merely to say that the personal and social consequences of any medium—that is, of any extension of ourselves—result from the new scale that is introduced into our affairs by each extension of ourselves, or by any new technology—[It] is the medium that shapes and controls the scale and form of human association and action. The content or uses of such media are as diverse as they are ineffectual in shaping the form of human association. Indeed, it is only too typical that the "content" of any medium blinds us to the character of the medium.*[5]

Form in this imagery had overtaken content. One could no longer be separated from the other. Coming from a background in literature,

McLuhan was particularly interested in the form, the language, the structure, of the media. In this he was part of a new wave in scholarly studies that concerned itself particularly with the importance of the *way* information was communicated. This new wave has appeared in many guises, among them linguistics, structuralism, semiotics, structural anthropology, and ethnomethodology.[6] We have already encountered these fields in tracing the history of ideas in the United States. Locke's reflections on language were influential in the thought of Charles Peirce and thus in the growth of pragmatism. The critical philosophers in Germany and the United States, Habermas, Adorno, and Marcuse prominent among them, were fascinated by the impact of the language of television on popular culture. Hegel's metaphysics dominated the growth of the various studies of popular culture and language, within which the work of McLuhan must be classified. Madison long ago spoke of knowledge as power and, as Hegel said, knowledge cannot be disseminated except through language.[7]

McLuhan's statement that the media is the message has to be seen in its Hegelian context. Hegel was no empiricist; in fact, he was the polar opposite. Ideas, he said, come from thought, not from the accumulation of data through experimentation and observation. One gains ideas through reading and conversation, and ideas are expressed in language which is "the child and the instrument of intelligence."[8] Only through language, he said, are human beings able to exist for one another. The American journalist is not likely to have immersed himself in the murky metaphysics of Hegel, but he is familiar with the concept of human kinship through the media, as promoted by McLuhan and by Morse, Whitman, and Emerson before him. Emerson, who like Hegel saw the world as indivisible and the hand of God transcendent in all human behavior, wrote that "machinery" agreed with transcendentalism. "Our civilization and these [technological] ideas are reducing earth to a brain," he wrote. "See how by the telegram and steam the earth is anthropologized," that is, made human.[9]

The American journalist is not likely to have read the work of the influential French symbolist, Stéphane Mallarmé, but for Mallarmé, thought was both "a message and a message about the message."[10] In a phrase foreshadowing Max Ways, Mallarmé wrote that meaning lay in the form as well as the content. The literary scholar McLuhan adapted the ideas of Hegel and Mallarmé, whose world of communications was that of print, to the age of electronics. McLuhan endorsed Mallarmé's idea that the popular press of the technological age is no longer fragmentary, reflecting single points of view but that it embraces a global perspective, and is, in McLuhan's words, "a mosaic of the postures of the collective consciousness."[11]

The French literary scholar, Georges Poulet, influential in the English-speaking world through a career at Johns Hopkins University, has pointed out that language as embodied in print or even in speech is too slow to convey thought. People simply think faster than they can speak or write.[12] McLuhan solved that problem by proclaiming the end of the linear age and the arrival of a new world, which offered total experience through the electronic media.[13] The linear transmission of thought, as reflected by the lines on a page or even the one-to-one communication of speech, has in McLuhan's imagery been replaced in the electronic age by the total environment of the TV screen, which merges into a single image what we see and what we hear.

Here there was no failure of language, as perceived by Poulet, but the exact opposite—the triumph of language, the new language of the new media. McLuhan had a new version of the myth of Christianity.[14] Paradise was lost in Eden; the Fall was completed in Babel when a multiplicity of tongues destroyed human communication. But with the arrival of the new media, Paradise is regained. Here, McLuhan is in a sense following the logic of Milton, but where Milton saw Paradise regained by the triumph of reason over passion, with Christ besting Satan in debate, McLuhan's image of Paradise regained was through modern electronics.[15] In McLuhan's vision, Babel is conquered by cybernetics; the communal world of the ancient villages is reconstructed through the global village that has been established by the new media. The computer, said McLuhan, "promises by technology a Pentecostal condition of universal understanding and unity."[16]

McLuhan was not always so optimistic about technology. In his early career, he wrote disparagingly about the media, following in the spirit of his mentor, Harold A. Innis (to whose work we turn shortly), in condemning the media as being trivial instruments and mere mouthpieces for commercial and political propaganda. But beginning with his first serious study of media content, *The Mechanical Bride*, in 1951, McLuhan grew more and more extremist in his adoration of the potential of technology. By the time *The Gutenberg Galaxy* appeared in 1962, McLuhan had envisioned the modern age as the fruition of the Renaissance that had begun with Gutenberg's discovery of movable type.[17]

Modern technology, McLuhan wrote, has "liberated" humankind from the linear world that emerged with the "Guternberg galaxy." From now on, he said, "the vision will be tribal and collective," no longer fragmented and "crude," as he called the individualistic ideas of the eighteenth century.[18]

That McLuhan's image was mythic in no way detracts from the impact of his concept of electronic technology opening the gates to Paradise. Our belief system is made up of myths of all kind. Myth is, as the French literary scholar René Girard has written, "a fleeting revelation of truth."[19] The influential colonial farmer, Crèvecouer, declared that America was producing "a new race of men."[20] Whitman, in similar religious imagery, perceived a Yankee genesis in America and offered his own account of the creation of the world. To Whitman, "The United States are essentially the greatest poem."[21] Although Whitman's "American dream" is a piece of folklore, that has not detracted from the power of his image any more than the myth of the Garden of Eden has prevented it from making its way into the belief system of Americans, either as truth by creationists or as metaphor by Darwinists. Paradox is everywhere in the development of the myths and folklore of America in, as elsewhere, the religious imagery of men as diverse as Whitman and McLuhan. It is, after all, to be recalled that Whitman's Adam was cavorting about in unabashed sexuality in his Garden of Eden. Neither Milton nor McLuhan examined that aspect of Paradise.

In any case, no less a figure than Franklin Delano Roosevelt, first or second in historians' rankings of greatness among U.S. presidents, was an uncritical adherent of a belief system encompassing the acceptance of the United States as a reincarnation of Paradise on Earth. In fact, as biographer Ted Morgan has written, Roosevelt was in his self-perception the very embodiment of this optimistic myth:

> *FDR had struck his bargain with God. He had made the moral compact. He was an expression of the collective American will, and America had God on its side, and he had incorporated America, was the embodiment of America, and therefore God was with him.*[22]

In McLuhan's vision the myth was positive and promising. In the conceptualization of his mentor, Innis, it was negative and terrifying. Both men were technological determinists, that is, people who see human behavior as dominated by the instruments of technology, which exert an immense power in the affairs of humankind.[23]

Technology is never neutral. Neil Postman makes the point vividly in his examination of the impact of technology on one's belief system. Changes in the technology of communication, he says, inevitably force changes in one's values: "Introduce the alphabet to a culture, and you change its cognitive habits, its social relations, its notions of community, history and religion."[24] By introducing speed-of-light transmissions, "you make a cultural revolution," he argued. "Here is ideology, pure if not serene."[25] Americans make a serious mistake, he said, by assuming that the fruits of technology are automatically positive. They may indeed have the reverse effect.

While agreeing with Innis that the rise of the television society has damaged American culture, Postman is in complete accord with McLuhan's vision that the metaphors of the media ("the medium is the message") explain and organize the world for us. And, he concludes, by converting nearly all information into entertainment, television is amusing America to its cultural death.[26] In fact, Postman sees the world, led by the United States, in "the third great crisis" in Western education. The first took place in Athens in the fifth century before Christ, when an oral culture was replace by an alphabet-writing culture, giving rise to the writings of Plato. The second came with the invention of the printing press, giving rise to the writings and influence of John Locke. The third, he held, "is happening now, in America, as a result of the electronic revolution, particularly the invention of television. To understand what this means, we must read Marshall McLuhan."[27]

Postman comes from a humanist tradition. Social scientists, who dominate the field of communication studies, tend to downplay the importance of both Innis and McLuhan, largely because their media studies do not fall within the prevailing system of empirical analysis.[28] Still, the ideas of both men are mighty ingredients in the belief system of many Americans, including journalists. For those of an optimistic bent, it is McLuhan whose thought predominates. For those of pessimistic inclination, like Postman, the greater influence is that of Innis.

CHAPTER 56

Harold Innis: The Dark Side

Like McLuhan, Innis was a Canadian, and much of his thought was swayed by Canadian disaffection with the power and influence of the United States that was encroaching on Canada across its long southern border. As Daniel Czitrom put it, the key referent in the works of both men was "the brute and seemingly irreversible fact of American power, particularly American technological power."[1] To Innis (and the early McLuhan), American society and American media were powerful threats to Canadian culture. The later McLuhan rejected Innis's views and came to exalt that power, bubbling over with optimism about the glorious future that he saw looming before the United States and the world through the unifying force of new media.

Innis was always pessimistic about the media and must be seen in the context of those less optimistic commentators, past and present, who would in no way credit the machine with the power to create a better life. The historian Henry Adams, who held the individual in mystic veneration and insisted that "power is poison," wrote in the early years of the twentieth century that it was the mechanization of modern life that was destroying harmony and beauty.[2] Mark Twain, long a skeptic about power, turned his bitter pen against mechanization in his *Connecticut Yankee*. The downfall of Twain's Yankee arrived when he himself was trapped by the very electric fence he had created as a protective device against the primitive early Britons with whom he was contending. The work of contemporary analysts, such as Lewis Mumford, Alvin Toffler, and Jacques Ellul, is part of this tradition.[3] No one has examined the media and communications with greater insight than Innis, whose influence on media analysts, especially Marxists and other leftists, has been considerable. Ironically, however, Innis was no Marxist and can be more accurately characterized, like Henry Adams, as a man determined to conserve the intellectual grace and elegance of the past.

It is extraordinarily difficult to portray Innis's thought in a few paragraphs. Innis was unable during his lifetime, cut short in 1952 at the age of 57, to put together in clear, coherent form his analysis of communications, although he devoted the last third of his life to attempting to fashion a theory of human history as tied together by communication. As Hegel focused his philosophy of history on nation-states and Marx on the means of production, Innis turned to communication as the unifying force in human existence.[4]

As economist and historian, Innis arrived at his theory of communication through his studies of the lumber industry. His fundamental assumption was that true power lies in the ability to control space and time. This can be accomplished only through control of the technology of communication, for only then can one direct the political process—within one's own territory and within one's own time frame. At its most fundamental, the power to control is economic, since technology is so expensive. This power can belong, then, only to those who control the technology of communication. From his study of the lumber industry, he drew the conclusion that newspapers in the United States had gained true power through their exploitation of the forests of his beloved Canada in search of a cheap supply of paper.[5]

Innis traced the history of humankind through past "cultures." For him a culture comprised the interdependent political and economic systems of the social order under study. He explained, as no one had done before, how those cultures used both the *material means* of communication—roads, rivers, canals, railways, and the vehicles that rode them—and the *language* of communication. Whoever managed the language of communication, he said controlled the culture and thus exercised true power. To advance the culture, his argument went, those who controlled the language turned to technology. Since they were in command economically and politically, they were able to direct the path of technology and thus to establish, on purpose or unwittingly (it didn't matter which to Innis), the biases and stereotypes of the system both in terms of how communication was applied and, of greater importance, what was the *content* of the communication.

In his examination of U.S. history, Innis maintained that by creating their own media of communications, the holders of political and economic power were able to manipulate the voters so that they might be retained in power. He cited Jefferson, Jackson, Lincoln, and the two Roosevelts as illustrations. The media of communication circulated the myths, the slogans, and the stereotypes on which control of the culture and hence the country's belief system rested.

Motivated by a passionate distrust of U.S. power, Innis said that the entrenched power position of newspapers led them to create vast communication monopolies, which then worked systematically and ruthlessly to destroy everything valuable in the past. Change itself became the only permanent virtue. Writing during the McCarthy era, Innis commented that the old protections given the individual in the U.S. Constitution had declined under the weight of "the jackals of communication," whose work was dedicated to maintaining the power of the already powerful in the United States. The distinguished English scholar, Eric Havelock, a onetime colleague of Innis at Toronto and on the whole an admirer, has written that Innis's postwar output constituted "an increasingly vehement polemic against the United States and its institutions."[6]

Clearly a fierce vein of pessimism ran through the writings of Harold Innis. Like most pessimists, he was a moralist. He was horrified by what he saw as the immense power of the media in the United States and at what he believed to be the destruction of the cultural heritage of Western civilization. His work stopped with the appearance of radio, and he left to McLuhan a study of the influence of television. But what Innis saw was a social order preoccupied with instantaneous experience—space, in his imagery—and entirely unconcerned about the past of mankind—time, and the wonders of history:

> *The overwhelming pressure of mechanization evident in the newspaper and the magazine has led to the creation of vast monopolies of communication. Their entrenched positions involve a continuous systematic ruthless destruction of elements of permanence essential to cultural activity. The emphasis on change is the only permanent characteristic.*[7]

In much the same way, Postman argued that Americans' sense of history and continuity was being destroyed by the immediate "disconnected" images presented by television. The typographic mind, with its "sophisticated ability to think conceptually, deductively and sequentially," Postman held, was being replaced by "the Age of Show Business."[8]

What was coming, in Innis's increasingly pessimistic perspective, was anything but a brave new world. He echoed Santayana's aphorism in his argument that a historyless society was condemned to repeat the errors of the past, with even more terrible reults than Santayana had foreseen—because of the advances made in technology. It would be an error to dismiss Innis as an effete radical, for his pessimism over man and his technology represents a recurring theme in the passage of ideas in the American experience.

Whereas McLuhan's views were those of innocents incarnate, the mystics who proselytize the vision of Walt Whitman and the myth of a new Eden in America, Innis, like many before and after him, rejected innocence and turned to despair. Habermas, Adorno, and others of the Critical school have, like Postman, been equally dismayed over the assault on cultural tradition by the entertainment industry, notably motion pictures and television, and by the mythology disseminated by advertisers and public relations specialists. Innis showed that new technologies have shaped all societies from Babylon to the present through their production and distribution of information. To him the effect of new technologies has been unsettling. Jacques Ellul has gone further. He says that "social propaganda," the handiwork of the entertainment industry and public relations agencies, has greater impact on Americans than the political propaganda of Hitler's National Socialists or the Communist agitators of the Stalin era had on Germans and Russians. Ellul maintains that all technological progress exacts a price, since it itself has no moral values and pursues its own ends "blind to the future," whether these ends operate for the good of human beings or not:

> *A principal characteristic of technique . . . is its refusal to tolerate moral judgments. It is absolutely independent of them and eliminates them from its domain. Technique never observes the distinction between moral and immoral use. It tends, on the contrary, to create a completely independent technical morality.*[9]

Let us remember that at the center of the Agnew Doctrine lies the conviction that newspaper and especially television journalists are exponents of a pessimistic culture that is threatening American values. Innis thought not: his perception of the media was of cheerleader and propagandist for the myths and the optimistic stereotypes of those who hold political and economic power. In this connection, it is interesting also to recall Niebuhr's fear that innocence opened the doorway to tyranny and his advice to his countrymen to beware their tendency to "a too consistent optimism."[10]

It has in the twentieth century become commonplace to speak harshly of the excesses to which innocence has led and to call attention to the threads of pessimism that have always been present in one form or another in the belief system of Americans, the ideas for instance of John Adams, Edmund Burke, and Jean-Jacques Rousseau. Curiously, however, this reexamination of the past had led not to a turning away from optimism but to a new, even more powerful formulation of this mystique. Herbert Croly, editor of the *New Republic*, for which Lippmann toiled, was one who argued that Americans in the past had been too optimistic and who interpreted the Progressivist movement as an attempt to counter the tendencies to blind optimism. Progressives, he wrote, were abandoning innocence and unreality and replacing them with a "sense of serious national purpose."[11] The manifest destiny that had been a rallying cry on the frontier was now converted into a sense of national purpose, a dedication in short to a new cause. McLuhan's global village is drawn from this same imagery.

Croly was a good deal more optimistic than he himself seemed to see. His villain was not faith in the future but rather the "blind optimism" that he detected in Whitman and the other singers of the Song of America in the past. The modern incarnation of optimism appeared in more measured terms than Whitman's hyperbole, but it has been there all the same, manifested in such optimistic declarations as President John F.

Kennedy's inaugural speech when he invited Americans to join with him in asking not what they could get from their government but what they could do for their fellow men.

That not especially attractive element in the American belief system that we have encountered in the nativist movement and in impulses towards insularity became allied in the twentieth century with philippics against pessimists. These attacks were often accompanied by expressions of dedication to a "pure" kind of Americanism, manifested in the campaigns against the "hyphenated Americans" during World War I, that is, against "impure" strains such as those to be found in Polish-Americans or Italian-Americans.[12] In our more enlightened age, we no longer hear the term "hyphenated" applied to Americans but the concept lingers in terms like Afro-Americans and Asian Americans. The anticommunist "crusade" of Joseph McCarthy was a cousin to the hyphenation campaigns. In fact, loyalty to the government and its symbols, such as the flag and the pledge of allegiance, continue to be critical ingredients in the popular American belief system. Questions about the overt expression of these symbols of loyalty figured prominently in the presidential election campaign of 1988.

The communications media were always crucial in the dissemination of the symbols of America, its myths, and its folklore. The power of the media to spread a belief system, for good or ill, is incalculable. Whatever other power may be possessed by the print and broadcast media, there can be no question that they represent the chief mechanism through which ideas, myths, stereotypes, opinions, and attitudes are dispersed to the people of America.

It is small wonder then that the question of media power has become such an important subject of discussion in the contemporary world. Innis, like Lord Acton before him, insisted that power corrupts those who hold it. Honesty, decency, truth, justice—all these may be eliminated or censored from public dialogue by those who control the media. John Milton and untold millions of journalists after him have insisted that those who control the media must endow the media with the authority to report "all the news that's fit to print." Others, including even Thomas Jefferson, have proposed restraints on a licentious press. Since the discussion is not only political and economic but also moral, attention has increasingly been directed to the position of ethics in any philosophy of journalism, to which we will turn shortly.

CHAPTER 57

The Adversary Culture: Optimism and Pessimism

In 1971 Daniel Patrick Moynihan raised eyebrows in the journalistic community by describing the investigative press as belonging to an adversary culture. His examination of the news media was, like that of Spiro Agnew, made in terms of the relationship between the press and the president. His widely discussed essay in *Commentary* followed Agnew's critique by two years.[1] In fact, neither before nor after the presidency of Richard Nixon (1969–1974) has there been such open and extended public discussion of the role played by the news media in the public life of the country.

Was the press, as Moynihan suggested, usurping presidential power to the detriment of the country? It is of course possible, as critics of Moynihan have suggested, that this was a frivolous question, raised by a man of wit and charm. Moynihan, a U.S. senator from New York, is a Democrat and a former Harvard University professor who might himself have been placed among another of Agnew's target groups, an "effete corps of impudent snobs who characterize themselves as intellectuals."[2] Moynihan was quite capable of concealing his philosophical questions behind a bit of whimsy; it was certainly obvious to him that whatever power the press might have been thought to hold, that power was in a real sense of trivial significance compared with that of the chief executive.

In whichever case, behind Moynihan's question of relative power lay an inquiry of deeper philosophical import: what in fact is the belief system of American journalists?

The tradition of muckraking is certainly enshrined in that belief system, Moynihan pointed out, noting that ever since the turn of the century, the American press has taken "as a primary mission" the search for corruption in government. More recently and potentially of "far more serious consequence," he said, was the rise, among journalists reporting for the leading national newspapers and newsmagazines, of what he called an "adversary culture."

He might of course have included television network journalists, since their social and economic origins are similar to those of reporters for the national print publications. Once upon a time, Moynihan wrote, when journalists took pride in rejecting higher education in favor of learning in the School of Hard Knocks, their attitudes were "surprisingly close" to those of working people. But journalism has now become, if not altogether an elite profession, then at least "a profession attractive to elites,"[3] so that the ideas of journalists working for the national news media have become "Ivy League." It is in the fabled universities of the East, Harvard, Yale and Princeton, said Harvard's Moynihan, that there is being ground out this adversary culture, which he identified as an elitist culture of "disparagement":

> *The political consequence of the rising social status of journalism is that the press grows more influenced by attitudes generally hostile to American society and American government. . . . The issue is not one of serious inquiry, but of an almost feckless hostility to power.*[4]

This is a remarkable statement, of the same order as Agnew's remark about the power of the press. It suggests a revolutionary shift in the ideas of American journalists, at least among those based in Washington who report on events of major national significance. For the news media—even if only those based in Washington—to reject the fundamental values of American society, the optimistic individualism of Locke and Jefferson, Madison and Mill, would place the media somehow outside the mainstream of American life. Journalists would have become the effete eastern snobs of whom Agnew spoke, out of touch with what Agnew and Nixon spoke of as middle America.

The concept of an adversary culture was not original with Moynihan. It appears to have been mentioned first in 1965 by the literary essayist, Lionel Trilling. And his definition of an adversary culture was set forth in the strongest of terms. He spoke of the "subversive intention . . . that characterizes modern writing," an effort to separate the reader from his habits of thought and feeling and to give him "a ground and a vantage point from which to judge and condemn, and perhaps revise, the culture that produced him."[5] This was a revolutionary idea, the idea that writers were trying to drive their readers into condemning the thoughts and the feelings among the families and the very society that had bred and educated them. It split an intellectual elite from the belief system of ordinary Americans. The fallout from this conception has continued to fire the polemics of Left and Right to this day. Trilling went so far as to identify "a class" that had formed around the adversary culture, one that had developed its own habits of responding to its environment, a class that "is not without power" and that, like all power groups, was seeking "to aggrandize and perpetualize itself" *and its ideology*.[6]

In other words, Trilling was saying, those in the adversary culture make up a kind of fifth column in the body politic, a class of subversives who are endeavoring to foist their own belief system on the public. Americans are uncomfortable with the idea of classes. As James Oliver Robertson has pointed out, in American mythology, America is simply a classless society. Classlessness, he has written, is one of the most important elements in American definitions of democracy: "It is the ultimate guarantee of equality and freedom."[7] In the class-ridden society of nineteenth-century England, the press was already being seen as the very reverse of a class. In a journal article in 1855, Henry Reeve, a distinguished correspondent for the *Times* of London, argued that the press was indeed "the 'Fourth Estate' of the Realm" and served as an antidote to the rigid class structure of British society.[8] That image—of the press as an independent observer and critic standing somewhere outside of society—has never departed from the belief system of journalists. The idea of the media as a class not only does violence to this perception but also runs strongly counter to the ideology of American democracy.

Trilling did not refer to journalists specifically in his analysis of an adversary culture. His reference point was to poets, novelists, and playwrights. But, as Moynihan pointed out, journalists, especially the prominent Washington reporters and columnists, have become members of the kind of cultural elite that embraces the community of creative writers.

It remained for the sociologist Daniel Bell to give journalists a specific assignment inside an adversary culture. Newspapers along with publishing houses, museums, cultural weeklies, the theater, the cinema, and the universities, Bell wrote in 1976, are substantially influenced if not dominated by the adversary culture. Although the specific themes and life-styles of the adversary culture have varied from decade to decade, there is nevertheless a pattern wherein "the cultural intelligentsia brooded on themes of despair, anomie, and alienation."[9] Thus, in Bell's view, there was born a "bad news syndrome" against which much of "middle America," in the spirit of Agnew, have protested.

Morris Dickstein, an English professor who lived through the dramatic revolutionary '60s at Columbia University, drew sharp distinctions among the decades of the '50s, '60s, and '70s, but still concluded that one product of this entire era was a deviation by journalists from their traditional path. Amid the turbulence stirred by the utopian visionaries of the '60, many journalists discarded the traditions of value-free objectivity and learned not only to accept it as safe to "participate in the events they described but that their presence and private feelings belonged to the final account."[10] Thus, the stage was set for the use of an adversary press, participating in the news events it reported.

In the 1970s, Dickstein wrote, President Nixon had the press "on the run," but that even the failure of his Vietnam policies and the exposure of his abuse of presidential power did not dissipate the adversary culture. "A shattering blow," he said, was administered to "the 'idea' of America, the cherished myth of America."[11]

Since the concept of an adversary culture is inevitably linked to what Dickstein identifies as "high culture," an obvious target for Agnew and others was the Eastern seaboard literary set, into which he and many successors dumped the journalists for the *New York Times*, the *Washington Post*, the television networks, and the leading newsmagazines. Indeed, one essayist has taken the position that blue-collar Americans do not like the news media on the ground that it is an upper-class instrument whose interests are adversarial to those of blue-collar workers.[12] Many commentators have taken the position that in modern society, journalists and those in power have become so closely intertwined socially and culturally that the idea of their being adversaries is ludicrous. Tom Bethell maintains that the power of journalists is indistinguishable from the power of government. "Government and media figures are increasingly interchangeable anyway," he has written, "just as their roles are symbiotic. Even their pay is comparable."[13]

One ought not in any case to confuse the idea of an adversarial culture with the concept of an adversarial relationship between media and government. The idea of an adversary culture goes far deeper into the social and philosophical fabric of the society than power struggles between the media and government. The image of humankind in the adversary culture, assuming such a thing actually does exist, is certainly not sunny. Society is seen as basically unfair. Man, at least when he is in power, is seen as egocentric, selfishly materialistic. Justice is available only for those in dominant positions; it is not available for the poor or for minority races or for those whose social views are held to be deviant, such as atheists or homosexuals.

Sociologist Gaye Tuchman has held that journalists are so busy meeting their daily deadlines that they have no time or inclination to engage in philosophical speculations.[14] Certainly, on the whole, reporters and editors spend very little time asking themselves whether or not they dwell in an adversary culture. We can pretty well assume that they picture themselves as squarely in the middle of the American mainstream. The conventions under which the journalist exercises his or her news judgment may very well serve as a substitute for a conscious value system. Just as Trilling and Bell speak of an adversary culture as being inhabited by a "class," Moynihan holds that American journalists share a "culture"—even though they do not have any conscious awareness of embracing an ideology. As have others, Tuchman among them, Moynihan has pictured journalism as a field of action and not of thought. *Philosophy and ideology are there surely enough, but they are not recognized as being a belief system.*

It is a pity that the lengthy comments in response to Moynihan's essay that appeared in *Commentary* four months after his essay failed to deal with the philosophical questions that had been raised, except peripherally.[15] The lengthiest comment, an essay in itself, was written by

Max Frankel of the *New York Times*, later the newspaper's chief editor, who rejected as an "absurd standard of pedigree" Moynihan's view that the Washington press is a "social elite" infected by an adversary culture that incorporates attitudes hostile to American society and government. Frankel observed that a journalistic career requires no specific set of credentials, but is open to "any bright lad [*sic*] of proletarian or another origin."[16] Moreover, he took the position that, even though the field is made up of a better-educated cadre of journalists than there have been in the past, their value system remains similar to that of their audiences. "We are," he wrote, "mutually influenced by the attitudes and values of our communities."[17]

In fact, Frankel said, the readers of newspapers shape *it* as much as it shapes *them*. The community to whom the newspaper is addressed is itself often divided—some on one side of an issue and some on the other—but on the whole, he said, readers are pleased with the stance of the serious modern journalist. This, he described as one of "informed skepticism."[18]

Although rarely defined clearly, this stance is consonant with the conception of pragmatism held by James and Dewey. A pragmatist, James declared in 1907, "turns his back resolutely once and for all upon . . . abstractions and insufficiency. . . . He turns towards fact, towards action and towards power."[19] In other words, "informed skepticism." Three quarters of a century later, Frankel defined the stance of the *Times*: "We practice this skepticism not in the spirit of persecution or prosecution, but from a sense of wishing to serve our readers with reports of what is really going on."[20]

He did not discuss the Rashomon effect.[21] Indeed, Frankel's letter concerned itself with the *practice* of skepticism, not the philosophy behind it; in his lengthy response there was no mention of the epistemological question raised by Moynihan. It is to be recalled that at the center of Moynihan's criticism of the investigative press was his assertion that journalism is not really a profession since it lacks a shared epistemology under which all members of the "profession" recognize a mistake when it is made. Of paramount importance is the fact that Frankel was giving expression to one of the most basic of the ideas held by American journalists, however troublesome it may be for reporters or editors to place the idea in a theoretical framework. Yet, what precisely is "informed skepticism"? Lack of faith? Lack of trust? Cynicism about human nature? An adversary culture?

Frankel's response to Moynihan's concern about the lack of a tradition of self-correction in journalism was also a practical one. Remarking that newspapers appear daily, he noted that "in one sense . . . we correct ourselves every morning, a requirement and an opportunity that most other institutions, including the Presidency, lack."[22] These sentiments echoed those of Franklin and Jefferson, Greeley and Bennett, Pulitzer and Godkin. The fundamental ideas held by journalists about the nature of the press had changed little from the early years of American history.

Frankel also noted another long-standing practice in journalism, the making available of letters-to-the-editor columns to those who wish to raise challenges to articles in the newspaper. In any case, neither letters-to-the-editor columns nor other proposed corrective suggestions, such as press councils and ombudsmen, deal with the substance of what Moynihan considered the most important of his observations, that the lack of a professional tradition of self-correction illustrates the lack of an epistemology shared by all respected journalists.

The ideas of American journalists, even of leaders in the field, are fundamentally practical rather than theoretical. Press critics seem to follow a similar pattern. Among the nine other letters responding to Moynihan's article, only one dealt with the question of self-correction. This was written by Elie Abel, a former journalist for the *Times* who was at the time dean of the Graduate School of Journalism at Columbia University. Abel wrote that if the press wanted to be taken seriously as a profession, it must "learn to acknowledge its mistakes. . . . The effect would be to increase, rather than diminish, respect for the press."[23] Still, Abel also bypassed discussion of the question of epistemology. It seems clear that the "philosophy" of journalism held by American reporters and editors is inarticulate, firmly held but vague in content, practical rather than conceptual, based on conventions rather than analytical thought. In observing that it is a "culture" that journalists share rather than a "philosophy," Moynihan was on solid ground.

Abel denied the adversarial argument. There is, he wrote, no reason why better-educated and better-paid Washington correspondents should become infected by an adversary culture. It is not logical, Abel said, to hold that an Ivy League education accompanied by upward social mobility "necessarily conditions a young journalist to adopt attitudes hostile to American society."[24] Another letter writer, Joann C. Cazden, also challenged Moynihan's assertion that the attitudes of journalists are hostile:

> *There are some segments of American society that welcome informed skepticism and an enlightened outlook in the press. If it were not for enterprising journalists, new breed or old, such pretty occurrences as My Lai would not have come to light.*[25]

This debate was taking place in an era when, as Dickstein wrote, after the assassinations of the 1960s, after the continuing strife and turbulence in the streets, after the battles between police and dissident groups, the country sought a return to the placid life. The optimism of the 1960s evaporated and a mood of pessimism, close in spirit to the cultural pessimism that had long marked European society, settled over the United States. It was not to last; in the Reagan years the old spirit of optimism returned, although in somewhat different form. The investigative journalists, exposing every pustule in the body politic, remained perhaps the chief disseminators of cultural pessimism in the United

States. Small wonder that questions were raised about the proper role and function of the press and indeed about the relationship between the new muckrakers and an adversary culture.

Frankel did not postulate a clear relationship between informed (or enlightened) skepticism and cultural pessimism, nor does the nexus seem to be widely recognized by the community of journalists. That community may—and does—reject out of hand the very idea that newspaper and broadcasting reports paint a pessimistic portrait of the social order, but their dedication to "informed skepticism" is so complete that it can today be considered a primary journalistic value, part of the contemporary newsperson's professional ideology.

Few reporters or editors would want to be identified as gullible, as persons who accept what they are told at face value and who do not look for contrary claims or for corroboration, just as do other professionals, the historian, the attorney, the biologist. In this, as we have pointed out, journalists are empiricists, pragmatists, following the methods of science. Whether journalists are as skeptical as their value system would have it is another matter. It is the private opinion of this writer, both from long experience as a journalist and as academic researcher, that journalists often become quite gullible in the hands of expert managers of the news.

In practice, informed skepticism seems clear enough as a *method*. Yet, what does it mean in terms of one's system of beliefs, one's ideology, to be an informed skeptic? The scientist may challenge the techniques and conclusions of fellow scientists in their research without raising questions about their truthfulness and honesty. The historian may offer similar challenges. The lawyer or the journalist, on the other hand, cannot question a statement, political or otherwise, without raising doubts about the integrity of his source. Skepticism on the part of a journalist is inevitably not far removed from cynicism, yet to be cynical is in no way considered desirable for a journalist.

To most of us, skepticism no doubt automatically implies lack of trust. Not so, apparently, in the belief system of journalists. The dictionary defines a skeptic as one who "instinctively or habitually doubts, questions, or disagrees with assertions or generally accepted conclusions."[27] At a deeper level, however, the concept has a somewhat different connotation. The philosophical doctrine of skepticism holds that since absolute knowledge is impossible, inquiry must involve continual testing: *all propositions are to be doubted, even if one is to arrive at relative knowledge*.

Perhaps it was to the philosophical doctrine that Frankel was referring, even though he avoided the philosophical by equating skepticism with the quest for "what is really going on." The philosophical skeptic accepts the Rashomon effect, satisfied that he can *never* learn what is really going on but at best only an approximation of it, relative reality rather than what is absolutely certain.

To most journalists, discussions of this character are mere quibbling; they properly belong to the arcane dialogues of learned societies. The belief system of the reporter or editor follows James's pragmatic model.

The good is to be located in the practical; the abstract is to be avoided. Still, whether concrete or abstract, whether practical or theoretical, the posture of skepticism is inescapably adversarial.

The word *skepticism* clearly means different things to different people, however expressed. Yet, skepticism is not really part of the tradition of optimism that has for so long marked so much of American society and indeed the practice of journalism. Americans have long been able to adhere at the same time to the contradictory belief systems of philosophical optimism and pragmatic skepticism. The strain of cultural pessimism has, for the most part, been absent from the American scene.[28] The question to be considered here is this: how can the American journalist practice skepticism without adopting or, at the very least, appearing to adopt, a belief system shot through with cultural pessimism? The tendency of Americans, especially those less classically educated, towards a positive outlook, has been widely documented.[29] In selecting the stance of skepticism, does the journalist reject the optimism of Locke, Jefferson, and John Stuart Mill? Is it viewing the American press as permeated with pessimism that leads critics to challenge its credibility and to question its place in today's society? Insistence that the press plays up bad news and ignores the good in society is a salient part of the criticism not only of investigative journalism but of the news media altogether.

For a better understanding of what is behind much of the criticism of American journalism, one might turn to a variant definition that can be given of philosophical skepticism: denial of "the sincerity, rectitude, or existence of motives of human conduct other than selfish" and the "moroseness, surliness, or pessimism growing out of [such] cynicism."[30] It seems clear enough that anyone who is continually on the lookout for examples of man's wickedness is subject to becoming cynical, defeatist about the possibility of human salvation even in the United States, where the underlying belief system has generally tended to be (and in the Reagan years remained) the exact opposite.

It is interesting to note that the philosophical school of the Cynics was composed of the most highly motivated followers of Socrates, austere men who preached the renunciation of wealth, fame, and honor in favor of a life of contemplation and painful honesty. These intellectuals condemned the pursuit of pleasure; their earthly reward lay in ridding the world of corruption.[31] The classical Cynic was Diogenes, he who roamed the streets of Athens in the fourth century before Christ with a lighted lantern in search of an honest man. Diogenes and his fellow Cynics were accused, even as are today's journalists, of being know-it-alls who held mankind in arrogant contempt.[32] The term *cynic*, once one of honor, has now fallen into disrepute. The Agnew Doctrine and the companion criticism of the journalist as preaching an adversary culture is a curious twentieth-century reincarnation of the condemnation of the Cynics made 2,500 years ago.

CHAPTER 58

Ethics: The New Wave in Journalism

Philosophy has traditionally been divided into five subdivisions: (1) *metaphysics*, the study of the nature of reality; (2) *logic*, the study of the processes and laws of thinking; (3) *epistemology*, the study of knowledge and of the theory of knowledge; (4) *aesthetics*, the study of the meaning and experience of beauty, and (5) *ethics*, the study of the formation of moral values and of principles of right and wrong. While ethics has become a prominent topic and subject for study in all fields today, there has never been universal agreement among philosophers on its precise scope. Still it must inevitably involve the development of moral values. Some believe that ethics ought to provide us with a set of principles to guide our behavior; others think that ethics should be a tool for use in analysis of moral statements.[1]

As a subject for study, ethics went into a severe decline in the early years of the twentieth century. That decline seemed to parallel the rise of pragmatism. Emphasis on what worked made it appear to many that there might no longer be any urgent need to deal with moral questions. Furthermore, the triumph of behavioral theories in the study of psychology caused many to see the actions of human beings as largely instinctual, and thus amoral. There was also general misunderstanding of Einstein's theory of relativity, a different kind of factor in the decline of ethics. If behavior were a relative matter to be judged in terms of the practical and the instinctual, why worry about questions of morality? This is not to say that Americans stopped being interested in issues of right and wrong, or good and evil, but rather that these matters were on the whole judged to be questions of faith to be left to religion and churches. The business of scholars and universities, it seemed, was to deal with matters of mind, not faith, not morality.

In this environment, occupational values were often described as professional, implying a close linkage with morality but in actual fact far removed from questions of right and wrong. It is not entirely clear what it was that brought ethics back into good standing in the American community; perhaps it was the creation of the atomic bomb, since that device raised a threat to continued human existence and renewed interest in the question of why we are here on earth in the first place. Or perhaps it was the rediscovery, often by journalists, of unethical behavior in public life.

The definition of the Greek philosopher Epicurus, written around 300 B.C., covers the ground well: "Ethics deal with things to be sought and things to be avoided, with ways of life and with the *telos*."[2] *Telos* refers to the chief good, the aim, the end of life, the *summum bonum*. In philosophy, teleology is the theory of purposes, ends, goals, final causes, values, the Good.

Few thinking human beings have failed at some time in their lives to ask themselves: what is the end of life? why we are here on earth? It is a dreadful oversimplification to narrow hypotheses about the *summum bonum* down to a mere three, but we are not far off if we settle on three *basic* concepts, those associated with Aristotle, Kant, and Hume. Kant, the most iron-willed of philosophers, saw the Good in absolute terms. Never do anything, Kant held, that you would not want to be a universal rule for everybody at all times. Never, for instance, tell a lie, however pure you believe your motive to be. To Aristotle, the Good lay in the *search* for the Good. It was always virtuous to try to find the Good and live up to it. To Hume, there were no absolutes. All moral codes, all habits, all virtues, were relative; they depended on the time and place in which they arose. They were rooted not in any ultimate teleology, but in customs. Hume distinguished carefully between what *is*, that is to say, reality, and what someone tells us we *ought* to do. Hume was very adventurous for a man of the eighteenth century, but he still saw moral rules as natural and not man-made. On the other hand, modern commentators who shared Hume's general views, saw no such things as fixed rules. "Moral concepts change as social life changes," wrote Alasdair MacIntyre.[3] He pointed out how, during the centuries of philosophical discussions about "justice," its meaning has changed and changed again from the conception of justice held by Socrates two and a half millennia ago.

The psychiatrist, Erik Erikson, has drawn a useful distinction between ethics and "moralism," in which he offers a quiet critique of both Kant's absolutism and of Hume's relativism. Writing about the nonviolent stance adopted by India's Mohandas Gandhi, Erikson judged "moralism" to be "blind obedience" to whatever moral values are handed down to one by any kind of authority figure, be it the Deity or a parent or political leader. Ethics, Erikson said, "is marked by an insightful assent to human values," implying that it is conscious and thought out. Moreover, he said, "ethics is transmitted with informed persuasion, rather than enforced with absolute interdicts."[4] Informed persuasion, to Erikson, was accomplished by the force of one's reason and logic. There can, Erikson wrote, be no distinction between personal, professional, and political ethics. To Erikson, there is no moral distinction between what you do as a journalist and what you do as a human being.

Whatever the reason for the newfound interest in ethics and morality, by the latter third of the twentieth century, just about every occupation in the country had produced codes of ethics and was running seminar after seminar in the practice of morality. Here, the emphasis was inevitably on professional standards of morality. Journalism, of course, participated in this movement. It was no accident that it was at the end of the war in which nuclear weapons were first employed that the Hutchins Commission raised questions about the very foundations of journalism. Why, the commission asked, ought there to be a press system anyway, and by what right ought it to be free and independent? In short, what was the ethical raison d'être of journalism? Taking a position that was at least as old as the writings of John Milton, the Hutchins Commission decided that the proper end of journalism—its justification—lay in its being responsible to human society. To be an ethical journalist, the practitioner had to be working in the service of mankind, not merely seeking his or her own ends. It was imperative that he or she be socially responsible, socially accountable.[5] This was a value system identical to that of Diogenes and the Cynics.

Such an expression of morality is, of course, utopian. It rejects self-interest and may even represent a denial of human biological nature. Yet "social responsibility" and "service to the public" remain the fundamental ethical standards not only of journalism but of most occupations in the country. The paradox is one that has by now attracted the attention of people in every human activity, ranging from churchmen and governments to philosophers and commercial businessmen: how can we, limited as we are by our biological nature, behave ethically? Where once there appeared codes of professional standards, there are now codes of ethics.[6] Neither codes of professional standards nor codes of ethics resolve the paradox, but in the world of journalism they illustrate the passionate concern with matters of morality that today grips both practitioners and scholars.[7]

It is part of the belief system of virtually all American journalists that the rationale for newspapers and broadcasting outlets—all the mass media for that matter—is public service. Put another way, the professional ideology holds that if the media do not serve the public, there is no justification for their existence other than selfish or commercial ones. And selfish, commercial media would not likely deserve the special status provided for the press in the First Amendment to the Constitution. Nor could they easily wrap themselves in the rainment of disinterested service. The heritage of Aristotle and Plato, Milton and Locke, Voltaire and Rousseau, Jefferson and Madison, Mill and James, places emphasis on the value, the irreplaceable value, of an institution that helps expand human knowledge and virtue. For such an institution to be but another instrument of selfish grasping or of mere commercialism is utterly unacceptable in the belief system of journalists.

The commercial nature of the mass media creates a mighty paradox. As individuals have struggled to cope with this paradox, the issue of morality in the mass media has become ever more dominant in the institution of journalism. This is so even though there is a nagging recognition of the fact that whenever we human beings face tough moral questions, we frequently do our best to dodge the ethical implications and to attempt, often passionately, to find some other basis for making decisions. To do this seems to be part of the human condition. Thus, whether the gathering be of publishers, editors, reporters, professors, or students, there is a tendency to deal with moral dilemmas on the basis not of morality but on the basis of written codes of ethics or of legal or professional standards.

The current fascination with ethical questions in the media has been increased by a series of troublesome developments in the years following the Second World War: the "payola" scandals that afflicted the disc jockey business, the discovered dishonesty of television quiz shows, the revelations about the manipulation of sports reporters, political writers, and fashion correspondents through "freebies," the providing of free tickets and other gifts, the questionable tactics of investigative journalists, the revelation of outright fraud by some reporters.

In 1972, the Associated Press Managing Editors (APME) Association created for the first time a Professional Standards Committee, a body that was charged with looking into questions of "professional ethics." As part of its work, the committee gathered information on the gifts and other gratuities given to the press by clothing manufacturers and other commercial interests. A report by Carol Sutton, managing editor of the *Louisville Courier-Journal*, told not only of plane fares and meals being paid for by manufacturers but also of door prizes that included round-trip air fares to Europe, crystal ware, and a great variety of dresses, boots, watches, jewelry, and other items. Moreover, dress manufacturers provided discounts to journalists of around 50 percent.[8] That report, and others, led to severe crackdowns by many newspapers and broadcasting outlets not only on the freebies offered by clothing manufacturers but on free tickets by theatres, motion picture houses, sporting promoters, and political organizations.

The great adulation that came to Bob Woodward and Carl Bernstein of the *Washington Post* for their investigative work in covering the Watergate story was replaced some years after the event by troubling moral questions about their tactics in getting the story. Sissela Bok, for example, noted that they had given false information to persons they interviewed, that they had impersonated other people in telephone calls, and had lied to their chief source, "Deep Throat," in an attempt to gain corroboration for a fact they otherwise would not have received.[9] Another student of journalism ethics observed that Woodward and Bernstein "employed these immoral means toward immoral ends, namely, the self-interest of protecting themselves and the *Post*." The tough moral question involved was: on what ethical basis, if any, may a journalist claim justification in the use of immoral means? In the language of the ethics of journalism, are there occasions when the end justifies the means?

The most celebrated case of journalistic fraud in modern times is the case of Janet Cooke, a reporter for the same *Washington Post* who was awarded a Pulitzer Prize for an article about an eight-year-old "Jimmy," who, according to the article, dosed up on heroin. It turned out that Cooke had not only manufactured the entire story but had also lied to the newspaper about her education and previous employment. The embarrassed *Post* editors fired Cooke and forced her to return the prize. An internal investigation by the newspaper's ombudsman, Bill Green, blamed "the failure of a system" for not checking up thoroughly on Cooke's story. The failure to check was in part, Green said, the result of the fact that Cooke was black and that white editors did not want to be seen as racist. Green tagged Cooke "a young and talented reporter, flaming with ambition," who was afflicted by "the front page syndrome," that is to say, a kind of infection of misdirected zeal—to get articles on Page One and thus to win prizes, enhanced prestige, salary and power.[10] It was ironic that Ben Bradlee, the editor of the *Post*, who was idolized in the film version of *All the President's Men*, had, some five months before the fraud was discovered, challenged those who were condemning the press for being too aggressive in pursuing stories. "We are," Bradlee said at that time, "writing what Phil Graham [the former publisher of the *Post*] once called 'the first rough draft of history'—not the unquestionable truth."[11]

It is that troublesome topic of truth, and of the means used in seeking it, that have become the primary thrust of studies of ethics, not only those of journalists but of people in all occupations. We have seen how basic truth is in the belief system of American journalists. Is the search for truth the *summum bonum* of journalism ethics? Aristotle might have said so. In any case, the traditional self-image of reporters and editors has, from the beginning, as we have seen through all the pages of this book, been as seeker and printer of the truth. Or, as Frankel put it, of the informed skeptic telling it as it is.

In writing about the Janet Cooke case, the *Columbia Journalism Review* observed that there was nothing particularly new about journalistic hoaxes but commented that a new ingredient had entered the craft as a result of the rise of the various forms taken by new journalism—enterprise, interpretive, precision, investigative. "Journalists," the magazine wrote, "have become anthropologists, and works of anthropology are held up as models for students at journalism schools."[12] The implication was that rigorous examination of ethical questions is urgently demanded under these circumstances.

If journalists have become anthropologists, then they have become bad anthropologists—at least inasmuch as the structure of Cooke's story was typical. Her story began, as has become the standard style of contemporary journalism, with an anecdote:

> *Jimmy is 8 years old and a third-generation heroin addict, a precocious little boy with sandy hair, velvety brown eyes and*

needle marks freckling the baby-smooth skin of his thin brown arms.

He nestles in a large, beige reclining chair in the living room of his comfortably furnished home in downtown Washington. There is an almost cherubic expression on his small, round face as he talks about life. . . .[13]

Cooke's article drew this observation from one student of the case: "The tradition in journalism of using an anecdotal lead to describe a larger problem cannot justify the shorthand of describing a particular problem and letting the reader imagine the generalized situation. . . ."[14]

One of the issues confronting the student of journalism ethics is contextual. Is it possible to establish rules that apply from case to case or must each situation confronted be dealt with differently? Are there in fact rules in the world of journalism? With the rise of ethical questions, students of journalism have now, perhaps for the first time, addressed themselves to the great moral challenges raised by Aristotle, Hume, and particularly Kant. For it was Kant who insisted that morality cannot be divided, that means are as important as ends.

John Merrill, who has written extensively on the subject, has rejected situational ethics, or what he calls "whim" ethics, and has agreed with Kant:

If every case is different, if every situation demands a different standard, if there are no absolutes in ethics, then we should scrap the whole subject of moral philosophy and simply be satisfied with each person running his life by his whims or "considerations" which may change from situation to situation.[15]

Others hold that in real life, questionable means are permissible when the end is good. Let us take as an example the case of a hypothetical investigative reporter who gains admission as a patient at a mental hospital in order to be able to get at the truth about what is taking place behind the locked doors of the hospital. In this situation, the journalist is clearly being dishonest; he gives a false name and lies about his identity. However, under professional standards of sound journalistic behavior, his dishonesty is not usually taken as unethical, since there are no alternatives available for learning the truth. Sometimes, under these standards, dubious means must be employed in the service of a "higher" end, namely the service of the public—in order to be responsible to society. The public, these standards hold, has a right to know the truth about the hospital. In this situation, it is easy for the reporter to lose sight of the fact that the story he writes may win him a promotion, a subsequent salary raise, perhaps even a Pulitzer Prize. He may dodge the ethical question altogether by calling on the newspaper's attorneys so that he might gain the secure knowledge that he is not breaking the law. He is also secure in the awareness that he is following the professional standards of his craft: he is giving the public what it has a right to know; he is objective in the article he writes; he makes sure that he gets the side of the hospital officials into his story as well as that of aggrieved patients. On all counts, he has sidestepped the tough ethical question. He has relied on professional standards rather than on morality. In fact, he is practicing what Erikson spoke of as blind obedience—to a code that demands facts, that demands indeed the truth about the facts. In short, he has justified his deception on the ground that if the end is good, then means of questionable morality may be used, for the public has a right to know the truth about the facts.

Sissela Bok has called it "rhetorical nonsense" to rely on a public right to know as moral justification for dubious behavior.[16] This, she adds, is not to say that there is no legitimate public interest in being given access to news about the day's events. But to justify one's acts on the basis of that phrase is to beg the ethical question involved, which deals with systematic inquiry into when and how it becomes legitimate for the journalist (or for anyone else, for that matter) to engage in practices, such as deception, that otherwise might be considered unethical. Bok makes it clear how very easy it is to justify such practices on some other basis, such as a public right to know, or the professional standards of journalism.

No moral transgression is more seductive than one done for some "higher good," she has written, as when a parent deceives a child or a doctor deceives the sick, yet such lies "form the most dangerous deceit of all," for the moral transgressor rarely has a problem in duping himself.[17] The *Columbia Journalism Review*, in commenting on the Janet Cooke case, made this observation:

> *The birth and death of Jimmy may serve to arm us against the seductions of that "higher truth" consisting of what reporters and editors believe—and desire—to be true but which they lack the evidence to prove.*[18]

After Cooke's story was printed and before its falsity was disclosed, the publisher of the *Post*, Don Graham, wrote her a note saying: "If there's any long-term justification for what we do, it's that people will act a bit differently and think a bit differently if we help them understand the world even slightly better."[19] It is indeed part of the belief system of the great majority of American journalists that not only is the public good served by what he or she writes or broadcasts, but that the articles may well help the reader or viewer to understand the world a little better. The new wave of interest in the ethics of journalism has asked for a reexamination of that belief system.

There is a dualism here, as in so many of the philosophical questions in the field of journalism. There is the conflict between one's own personal moral values and the professional standards in the field. Does a public right to know, for instance, permit one to lie and deceive? Which ranks higher, the *collective* good—that is, the interests of the public—or the integrity of the *individual*? Rousseau, among others, perceived the *summum bonum* in the General Will, the collective needs and desires of us all. Mill, among others, saw the Good in terms of our own individual needs and desires. Is it best, do we serve best, if we conceive the human animal as good, if we are optimistic about the nature of humankind? Or is it best, do we serve best, if we are pessimistic about the nature of humankind, if we ask whether it makes sense to place our reliance in the press? Lippmann said it didn't make sense; he dismissed the press as a frail reed incapable of carrying out the educating function that Paine perceived it as having—and, still, he continued to practice journalism for half a century. Even though intellectually he rejected the idea of this educating function, he spent his entire life trying to educate his readers. It is a mighty paradox indeed.

Is, then, the belief system of the American journalist realistic in its dedication to Madison's claim that to the press—above all other institutions—the world owes "all the triumphs which have been gained by reason and humanity, over error and oppression." Or is it more rational to accept as inevitable Liebling's loss of illusions about the press when he and 3,000 colleagues lost their jobs with the death of the *New York World*? Is the true face of American journalism the "informed skepticism" espoused by Max Frankel? Were the reporters for the *New York Sewer* who greeted Dickens's Martin Chuzzlewit figments of his tortured imagination or did they embody the investigative zeal that produced a Janet Cooke? Are American journalists believers in the collective or the individual? In optimism or pessimism? A review of the dispute between Tom Paine and Edmund Burke provides the extremes. For the most part, American journalists have inclined to the Paine side of the dispute. If they are part of an adversary culture, then, in this view, the public is best served by the adversary culture, under the professional banner of Frankel's informed skepticism. Most journalists at the close of the twentieth century would cheerfully endorse Max Frankel's recipe for virtuous journalism.

But the pendulum has always swung back and forth. It will no doubt go on swinging back and forth as long as there are journalists in America.

Notes

Introduction: Journalism as Fire and Light

1. Tom Stoppard, *Night and Day,* New York: Grove Press, 1979, p. 32.
2. Voltaire, *Conseils à un journaliste,* May 10, 1737, in *Oeuvres complètes de Voltaire,* Louis Moland, ed., Paris: Garnier Frères, 1879, 22:243–246.
3. Max Weber, cited in Hanno Hardt, *Social Theories of the Press: Early German and American Perspectives,* Beverly Hills, Calif.: Sage Publications, 1979, p. 179. This remark is taken from Weber's prophetic speech to the German Sociological Association on the need for systematic research on the press in modern societies.
4. William James, *Pragmatism: A New Name for Some Old Ways of Thinking,* New York: Longmans, Green, 1907, p. 4.
5. G. K. Chesterton, *Heretics,* New York: John Lane Co., 1905, in James, op. cit., p. 3.
6. C. Wright Mills, *The Sociological Imagination,* Harmondsworth, England: Penguin Books, 1970, p. 11.
7. Thomas Jefferson, letter to James Madison, September 6, 1789, reprinted in John Somerville, and Ronald E. Santoni, eds., *Social and Political Philosophy: Readings from Plato to Gandhi,* Garden City, N.Y.: Doubleday Anchor Books, 1963, p. 264.
8. Robert N. Bellah, Richard Madsen, William M. Sullivan, Ann Swidler, and Steven M. Tipton. *Habits of the Heart: Individualism and Commitment in American Life,* Berkeley: University of California Press, 1985, p. 306.
9. Stoppard, op. cit., p. 108.

PART I: JOURNALISM AND THE STUDY OF PHILOSOPHY

1 Introduction: To Keep "Us Always Alive with Excitement"

1. Oliver Wendell Holmes, "Bread and the Newspaper," *Atlantic,* September 1861, reprinted in Edward Weeks and Emily Flint, eds., *Jubilee: One Hundred Years of the Atlantic,* Boston: Little, Brown, 1957, p. 132. Holmes, though not as well known today as his jurist son, was a fascinating character in his own right. He was one of the founders of the *Atlantic,* served as a regular contributor, and may have been the person who named the publication. For an up-to-date biography of the younger Holmes, see Sheldon M. Novick, *The Honorable Justice: The Life of Oliver Wendell Holmes,* Boston: Little, Brown, 1985.
2. Holmes, op. cit., p. 125.
3. Ibid., p. 133.
4. Henry David Thoreau, *Walden,* reprinted in Brooks Atkinson, ed., *Walden and Other Writings of Henry David Thoreau,* New York: Modern Library, 1937, pp. 46–47.
5. Ibid., pp. 84–85.
6. Steven Thomas Seitz, "Political Ideologies and the Essence of Politics," in L. Earl Shaw, ed., *Modern Competing Ideologies,* Lexington, Mass.: Heath, 1973, p. 3; Alvin W. Gouldner, *The Debate of Ideology and Technology: The Origins, Grammar, and Future of Ideology,* New York: Seabury, 1976, p. 11; Roger Scruton, *A Dictionary of Political Thought,* New York: Hill and Wang, 1982, pp. 213.
7. Seitz, op. cit., pp. 3–4.
8. Gouldner, op. cit., p. 13. See Karl Marx, and Friedrich Engels, *The German Ideology,* New York: International Press, n.d.
9. Daniel Bell, *The End of Ideology,* New York: Free Press, 1962, pp. 393–407.
10. W. Lance Bennett, *News: The Politics of Illusion,* New York: Longman, 1988, p. 148.
11. Mark Fishman, *Manufacturing the News,* Austin: University of Texas Press, 1980, pp. 134–140.
12. Robert E. Lane, *Political Ideology: Why the Common Man Believes What He Does,* New York: Free Press, 1962.
13. William James, *Pragmatism: A New Name for Some Old Ways of Thinking,* Longmans, Green, 1907, p. 4.

2 Ideology and the Missing Theory of News

1. Walter Lippmann, "Some Notes on the Press," in Clinton Rossiter and James Lare, eds., *The Essential Lippmann,* New York: Random House, 1963, pp. 398–399. The essay is an excerpt from Lippmann's book, *The Stakes of Diplomacy,* published in 1915.
2. Ibid., p. 399.
3. Edward Jay Epstein, *Between Fact and Fiction: The Problem of Journalism,* New York: Vintage Books, 1975, p. 3.

4. Ibid., p. 18.
5. John C. Merrill, *The Imperative of Freedom: A Philosophy of Journalistic Autonomy,* New York: Hastings House, 1974, pp. 17–18.
6. Dennis Chase, "The Aphilosophy of Journalism," *Quill,* September 1971, pp. 15–17.
7. Daniel Patrick Moynihan, "The Presidency and the Press," *Commentary,* March 1971, p. 47. Moynihan's essay (pp. 41–52) was reprinted in abridged form in the *National Observer,* March 29, 1971.
8. Ibid., p. 47.
9. See, for instance, Leon V. Sigal, *Reporters and Officials: The Organization and Politics of Newsmaking,* Lexington, Mass.: Heath, 1973. See also Mark Fishman, *Manufacturing the News,* Austin: University of Texas Press, 1980.
10. See, for instance, J. Herbert Altschull, "What Is News?," in *Mass Comm. Review,* November 1974, pp. 17–23.
11. Judge Murray L. Gurfein, U.S. District Court, New York, denied a preliminary injunction against the *New York Times* in the Pentagon Papers case, 1971, later adjudicated by the U.S. Supreme Court. For the text of Gurfein's opinion, see Martin Shapiro, ed., *The Pentagon Papers and the Courts: A Study in Foreign Policy-Making and Freedom of the Press,* San Francisco: Chandler, 1972, pp. 90–98.
12. James Carey, "But Who Will Criticize the Critics?", in Everette M. Dennis, Arnold H. Ismach, and Donald M. Gilmore, eds., *Enduring Issues in Mass Communication,* St. Paul, Minn.: West, 1978, pp. 362–368, reprinted from "Journalism and Criticism: The Case of an Undeveloped Profession," *Review of Politics,* 36, no. 2 (April 1974): 227–249.
13. Ibid., p. 366.
14. Ibid., pp. 365–366.
15. Gaye Tuchman, "Objectivity as Strategic Ritual: An Examination of Newsmen's Notions of Objectivity," *American Journal of Sociology,* 77 no. 4 (January 1972): 662.
16. David Hackett Fischer, *Historians' Fallacies: Toward a Logic of Historical Thought,* New York: Harper Torchbooks, 1970, pp. 87–90.
17. Quoted ibid., p. 88. See Woolf's *Collected Essays,* New York: Harcourt, Brace and World, 1967, 4:234.
18. Cited in Edward Jay Epstein, *News from Nowhere: Television and the News,* New York: Random House, 1973, p. 57. See also Herbert J. Gans, *Deciding What's News: A Study of CBS Evening News, NBC Nightly News, Newsweek and Time,* New York: Vintage Books, 1980. Gans calls attention (p. 188) to the adoption by NBC journalists of what their news director, Reuven Frank, called "artificial innocence . . . the refusal of journalists to alter the story for the purpose of controlling its effects [and] . . . the newsman's necessary deliberate detachment from aiming his work or letting someone else aim it to changing society—even for the noblest motive."
19. Fischer, op. cit., p. 268.

3 Philosophy and Some Fundamental Questions

1. Cited in Dennis Chase, "The Aphilosophy of Journalism," *Quill,* September 1971, p. 15.

2. Warren Breed, "Social Control in the Newsroom: A Functional Analysis," in *Social Forces,* May 1955, pp. 187–188.
3. J. Herbert Altschull, "The Amoral Morality of Editors: Uniformity and the Nose of the Camel," in Anne van der Meiden, *The Ethics of Journalism,* Utrecht: State University Press, 1982, p. 107.
4. The careful distinction was made by Louis W. Hodges, director of the program, "Society and the Professions: Studies in Applied Ethics," at Washington and Lee University.
5. Joseph A. Leighton, *The Individual and the Social Order,* New York: Appleton, 1926, p. 7.
6. Robert N. Bellah, Richard Madsen, William M. Sullivan, Ann Swidler, and Steven M. Tipton, *Habits of the Heart: Individualism and Commitment in American Life,* Berkeley: University of California Press, 1985, p. 76.
7. M. Caplan, "Who Ever Told You Ethics Would Be Easy?" in Frank McCulloch, ed., *Drawing the Line: How 31 Editors Solved Their Toughest Ethical Dilemmas,* Washington: American Society of Newspaper Editors Foundation, 1984, pp. 96–97.
8. Leighton, op. cit., p. vii.
9. Cited in Chase, op. cit., pp. 15–17.
10. Walter Lippman, *A Preface to Morals,* London: George Allen & Unwin, 1929, p. 157.

PART II: THE ENGLISH LIBERTARIANS AND THE THEORY OF LIBERTY

4 Introduction: The Dawn of the Modern Age

1. Quoted in A.J. Beitzinger, *A History of American Political Thought,* New York: Dodd, Mead, 1972, p. 3.
2. Quoted in William Haller, *Tracts on Liberty in the Puritan Revolution,* 1934, 1:28. in Fredrick Seaton Siebert, *Freedom of the Press in England 1476–1776: The Rise and Decline of Government Control,* Urbana: University of Illinois Press, 1965.
3. James Harrington, *Oceana,* quoted in George H. Sabine, *A History of Political Theory,* 3rd ed., New York: Holt, Rinehart and Winston, p. 502. Harrington's *Oceana* was published in 1656, in the long-standing tradition of political utopias. (Note: *Leviathan* appeared in 1651.)
4. Siebert, op. cit., p. 85.

5 John Milton and the Self-Righting Principle

1. See Frederick Seaton Siebert, *Freedom of the Press in England 1476–1776: The Rise and Decline of Government Control,* Urbana: University of Illinois Press, 1965, p. 195; Don M. Wolfe, *Milton in the Puritan Revolution,* New York: Thomas Nelson and Sons, 1941, pp. 120–138; and James H. Hanford, *John Milton, Englishman,* New York: Crown, 1949, pp. 113–120. For the most thorough study of Milton, see the massive six-volume work of David Masson, *The Life of Milton,* Gloucester, Mass.: Peter Smith, 1965. See also

Joseph A. Witterich, Jr., *The Life of John Milton by William Hayley,* Gainesville, Fla.: Scholars' Facsimiles and Reprints, 1970. For an excellent modern biography, see William Reilly Parker, *John Milton: A Biography,* 2 vols., New York: Oxford University Press, 1968. See also Christopher Hill, *Milton and the English Revolution*, New York: Penguin Books, 1979.

2. John Milton, *The Doctrine of Divorce,* quoted in Hanford, op. cit., p. 115.
3. Ibid.
4. Wolfe, op. cit., p. 57.
5. Hanford, op. cit., pp. 125–126. One of the four children died in infancy. Milton was married twice more, but had no children other than the three daughters who survived from his marriage to Mary Powell.
6. Bertrand Russell, *A History of Western Philosophy,* New York: Simon and Schuster Touchstone, 1972, p. 783. Russell saw a similar "fire and passion" sweeping Europe in 1848 and resulting in the *Communist Manifesto* of Karl Marx and Friedrich Engels.
7. Ibid., pp. 42–44. One who suffered painfully was Dr. Henry Burton, rector of St. Matthew's Church, London, who had his ears shaved so closely that the temporal artery was cut and blood "gushed forth in torrents upon the scaffold." See Benjamin Brook, *The Lives of the Puritans*, London: printed for J. Black, 1813, 3: 50.
8. Russell, op. cit., pp. 172–173. Near the Red Lion Inn, where Milton hid out for a while, he lived, as Hanford wrote, "in perpetual danger of being assassinated."
9. Wolfe, op. cit., p. 13, 37.
10. Ibid., p. 1.
11. George H. Sabine, *A History of Political Theory,* 3rd ed., New York: Holt, Rinehart and Winston, 1965, p. 496.
12. The distinguished English poets John Dryden and William Blake were among the first to identify Milton's Satan as the "true hero" of his epic poem.
13. John Milton, *Paradise Lost,* bk. 2: lines 258–263. Reprinted in *Great Books of the Western World,* Chicago: Encyclopedia Britannica, 1955 32:93–333. The cited passage appears on p. 99 of this edition.
14. Ibid., bk. 1, lines 254–255. See also Russell, op. cit., pp. 135, 224.
15. Wolfe, op. cit., p. 246.
16. *The Shorter Oxford English Dictionary,* 1973, S.V. "areopagitic."
17. John Milton, *Areopagitica,* reprinted in Great Books, 32:379–412. The cited passage appears on p. 390.
18. Ibid., p. 391.
19. Ibid., p. 406.
20. Ibid., p. 402.
21. Ibid., p. 409.
22. Ibid.
23. Ibid.
24. Wolfe, op. cit., p. 351.
25. Sabine, op. cit., p. 509.
26. Isaiah Berlin, *Four Essays on Liberty,* New York: Oxford University Press, 1969, pp. 187–188. The cited material is from Berlin's essay, "John Stuart Mill and the Ends of Life," delivered in London, December 2, 1959.
27. A.J. Beitzinger, *A History of American Political Thought,* New York: Dodd, Mead, 1972, p. 18.

28. John Milton, *Observations upon the Articles of Peace with the Irish Rebels.* This pamphlet appeared May 15, 1649, four months after the execution of Charles. The pamphlet represented, among other things, justification for the massacre of Irish troops at Drogheda and Wexford by Cromwell's men. See Wolfe, op. cit., pp. 85–87.
29. John Milton, *The Tenure of Kings and Magistrates.* See Hanford, op cit., pp. 133–135. The *Tenure* appeared February 13, 1649, two weeks after the execution of Charles, which took place January 30.
30. Milton, *Areopagitica,* p. 394.
31. Ibid., p. 396.
32. Parker, op. cit., 1:666.

6 Thomas Hobbes and Society by Contract

1. Richard Peters, *Hobbes,* Westport, Conn.: Greenwood Press, 1956, p. 13. The story was told originally by John Aubrey, in his *Brief Lives,* ed. Oliver L. Dick, Ann Arbor: U. of Michigan Press, 1957, p. 147. Aubrey's colorful account is the usual source for details of Hobbes's life. See the brief biographical account in Michael Oakeshott, ed., *Leviathan: Or the Matter, Forme and Power of a Commonwealth Ecclesiastical and Civil,* Oxford: Basil Blackwell, 1946, pp. vii–viii. This is the edition of Hobbes's masterpiece hereafter as *Leviathan.*
2. Peters, op. cit., p. 44.
3. Bertrand Russell, *A History of Western Philosophy,* New York: Simon and Schuster Touchstone, 1972, p. 548.
4. David D. Raphael, *Hobbes: Morals and Politics,* London: George Allen & Unwin, 1977, p. 18.
5. Ibid., p. 19. See also James H. Hanford, *John Milton, Englishman,* New York: Crown, 1949, p. 81.
6. Peters, op. cit., p. 260.
7. Raphael, op. cit., pp. 24–25; Russell, op. cit., p. 548; George H. Sabine, *A History of Political Theory,* 3rd ed., New York: Holt, Rinehart and Winston, 1965, pp. 548–549.
8. *Leviathan,* pp. 21, 24. See also Russell, op. cit., p. 549.
9. *Leviathan,* pp. 17–25. See also Peters, op. cit., p. 136. Hobbes's interest in names and signs contributed to the modern study of semiotics. We will return to this theme in our examination of pragmatism in Part 7.
10. Vernon L. Parrington, *Main Currents in American Thought,* vol. 1, *The Colonial Mind 1620–1800,* New York: Harcourt Brace Harvest Books, 1954, p. 284.
11. *Leviathan,* p. 82. For a reprint of some of the most significant passages from the *Leviathan,* see John Somerville and Ronald E. Santoni, eds., *Social and Political Philosophy: Readings from Plato to Gandhi,* Garden City, NY: Doubleday, Anchor Books, 1963, pp. 139–168.
12. See Job, chaps. 40 and 41.
13. Ibid., chap. 17.
14. The illustration is reprinted in *Leviathan,* p. 1. See also Raphael, op. cit., p. 14.
15. Job 41:33.

16. *Leviathan,* pp. 113–120. Hobbes's theory of obligation has intrigued many scholars. See Oakeshott's excellent, brief summary, ibid., pp. lviii–lxi. See also Howard Warrender, *The Political Philosophy of Hobbes: His Theory of Obligation,* Oxford: Clarendon Press, 1957.
17. Russell, op. cit., pp. 553–554.
18. *Leviathan,* p. 112.
19. Ibid., pp. 115–117. See also Raphael, op. cit., p. 37.
20. Ernst Cassirer, *The Philosophy of the Enlightenment,* Princeton, N.J.: Princeton University Press, 1979, p. 256.
21. For an interesting examination of this characteristic, see Russell, op. cit., pp. 550–551.
22. *Leviathan,* pp. 93–105, 109–110.
23. John Locke, *Second Treatise of Civil Government,* ed. Thomas I. Cook, New York: Hafner, 1947, p. 132.

7 John Locke and the Paradox of Democracy

1. Bertrand Russell, *A History of Western Philosophy,* New York: Simon and Schuster Touchstone, 1972, p. 642. Russell calls attention to Shelley's noteworthy dictum, clearly derived from Locke: "When a proposition is offered to the mind, it perceives the agreement or disagreement of the ideas of which it is composed."
2. John W. Yolton, *The Locke Reader,* Cambridge: Cambridge University Press, 1977, pp. 4–5.
3. John Locke, *An Essay Concerning Human Understanding,* ed. Peter H. Niddich, Oxford: Clarendon Press, 1975, bk. 3, chap. 6. See also the citation in Yolton, op. cit., pp. 148–149: "Words are general . . . when used for signs of general ideas, and so are applicable indifferently to many particular things." See also Ruth W. Grant, *John Locke's Liberalism,* Chicago: University of Chicago Press, 1987, pp. 37–39.
4. John Locke, *Two Treatises of Government,* ed. Thomas I. Cook, New York: Hafner, 1947, hereafter identified simply as *Treatise.* The citations report the chapter and paragraph number in Locke's *Second Treatise.*
5. There is considerable biographical material on Locke. See, for instance, Maurice Cranston, *John Locke: A Biography,* London: Longman, Greens, 1957; and Richard I. Aaron, *John Locke,* 3rd ed., Oxford: Oxford University Press, 1971. Most collections also contain brief biographical notes. See, for instance, Yolton, op. cit., pp. 1–9; and Cook's introduction to *Treatise,* pp. vii–xxxix.
6. For an interesting assessment of Descartes's influence, see Russell, op. cit., pp. 564–565.
7. Grant, op. cit., pp. 119–120. For the original, see Sir Robert Filmer, *"Patriarcha; or The Natural Powers of the Kings of England Asserted" and Other Political Works of Sir Robert Filmer,* ed. Peter Laslett, Oxford: Basil Blackwell, 1949.
8. *Treatise,* 8:95, p. 168.

9. Ibid., 8:119, p. 182. For further on the subject of tacit vs. express consent, see Grant, op. cit., pp. 123–128, and Yolton, op. cit., p. 296.
10. For more on Locke's two contracts, see Cook's introduction to *Treatise,* pp. xx–xxi. See also George H. Sabine, *A History of Political Theory,* 3rd ed., New York: Holt, Rinehart and Winston, 1965, pp. 531–534.
11. Russell, op. cit., p. 624.
12. *Treatise,* 8:97, p. 169.
13. Cook, introduction to *Treatise,* p. xxi.
14. *Treatise,* 10:133, p. 187.

8 A Blueprint for Revolutionary Thought

1. John Locke, *Two Treatises of Government,* ed. Thomas I. Cook, New York, Hafner, 1947, 10:123, p. 184. The citations report chapter and paragraph number in the *Second Treatise.*
2. Ibid., 10:124, p. 184.
3. Ibid., 5:27, p. 134.
4. Ibid., 19:222, p. 233.
5. Ibid., 19:242, p. 246.
6. Ibid., 13:155, pp. 201–202.
7. Ibid., 19:222, p. 233.
8. Ibid., 19:225, pp. 235–236.
9. Ruth W. Grant, *John Locke's Liberalism,* Chicago: University of Chicago Press, 1987, p. 189. See also Richard Hofstadter, *The Idea of a Party System: The Rise of Legitimate Opposition in the United States, 1780–1840,* Berkeley: University of California Press, 1969.
10. Lord Peter King, *The Life and Letters of John Locke,* London: Bell and Daidy, 1858, pp. 202–209. See also Leonard W. Levy, ed., *Freedom of the Press from Zenger to Jefferson,* Indianapolis: Bobbs-Merrill, 1966, pp. xxi–xxii.
11. John Locke, *A Letter Concerning Toleration,* 2nd ed., Indianapolis: Bobbs-Merrill, 1955, pp. 44–46. See also John W. Yolton, *The Locke Reader,* Cambridge: Cambridge University Press, 1977, pp. 4–5. p. 273.
12. Levy, op. cit., p. xxi.

9 David Hume: The Roots of a Skeptical Press

1. The British stupidities of the colonial era are outlined brilliantly in Barbara Tuchman, *In Praise of Folly: From Troy to Vietnam,* New York: Alfred A. Knopf, 1983.
2. A. J. Ayer, *Hume,* New York: Hill and Wang, 1980, p. 1. Not all commentators on Hume are so effusive in their praise. In fact, one of the most influential of modern reviewers of Hume is sharply critical of his errors in analysis and exposition. See Norman Kemp Smith, *The Philosophy of David Hume: A Critical Study of its Origins and Central Doctrines,* London: Oxford University Press, 1941.
3. Ayer, *op. cit.,* p. 18. In his *Prolegomena,* Kant credited Hume with giving his "investigations in the field of speculative philosophy quite a new direction."
4. George H. Sabine, *A History of Political Theory,* 3rd ed., New York: Holt, Rinehart and Winston, 1965, p. 605.

5. Quoted ibid., p. 14. See also Charles W. Hendel, *The Philosophy of David Hume,* Indianapolis, Bobbs-Merrill, 1963, p. 5. Smith's comments appeared in a tribute to Hume published in 1846.
6. A. J. Beitzinger, *A History of American Political Thought,* New York: Dodd, Mead, 1972, p. 11. For an interesting discussion of the role played by Hume in British philosophy, see Hendel, op. cit., pp. xxi–li.
7. Ayer, op. cit., p. 11. Ayer quotes Lytton Strachey: "He was flattered by princes, worshipped by fine ladies, and treated as an oracle by the *philosophes.*" It was in Paris that he made the acquaintance of the French philosopher, Jean-Jacques Rousseau, with whom he was to engage in a bitter dispute. See Ayer, pp. 12–13.
8. Hume said in a contemporaneous letter that in writing his *Treatise,* he had the works of Cicero "in my eye in all my reasonings." See Hendel, op. cit., pp. 90–91.
9. L. A. Selby-Bigge, *Hume's Treatise of Human Nature,* Oxford: Clarendon Press, 3rd ed., 1978, 3:2:2, p. 493. This is the edition of Hume's major philosophical work hereafter referred to as *Treatise.* The first edition appeared in 1888. The work is divided into books, chapters, and sections, designated here as 3:2:2. Selby-Bigge produced a splendid, detailed index, pp. 641–709, to which interested readers are referred for additional notes on Hume's ideas.
10. *Treatise,* 1:1:1, pp. 1–7. For examinations of Hume's examination of perceptions, see, among others, Hendel, op. cit., passim.; Ayer, op. cit., pp. 25–26; Beitzinger, op. cit., pp. 11–13; and Bertrand Russell, *A History of Western Philosophy,* New York: Simon and Schuster Touchstone, 1972, pp. 660–663.
11. *Treatise,* 1:3:8, p. 98. See also Ayer, op. cit., p. 25.
12. *Treatise,* 1:3:8, p. 98.
13. Ibid., 1:1:1, p. 2.
14. Ibid., 1:4:6, p. 252.
15. Hume's theory of abstractions can be found in *Treatise,* 1:1:7, pp. 17–25.
16. Ibid., 1:3:8, p. 103. See also Russell, op. cit., p. 670.
17. *Treatise,* 1:4:7, p. 270. See also Russell, op. cit., p. 672.
18. Hendel, op. cit., p. 376, maintains that Hume "is as much a 'philosophical dogmatist' as a 'philosophical skeptic.' "
19. *Treatise,* 1:3:9, pp. 106–117.
20. Ibid., 1:4:1, p. 183.
21. Sabine, op. cit., p. 600–601, points out that a large part of Hume's philosophy is devoted to showing the presence of conventions in the natural social sciences.
22. David Hume, *Inquiries Concerning Human Understanding, and Concerning the Principles of Morals,* 3rd ed., L. A. Selby-Bigge, ed. Oxford: Oxford University Press, 1978, p. 75. See also Ayer, op. cit., p. 66.
23. *Treatise,* 3:2:2, p. 497.
24. Ibid., 1:3:8, p. 103.
25. A. H. Basson, *David Hume,* London: Pelican Books, 1958, p. 104.
26. *Treatise,* pp. 577–579. See Hendel, op. cit., pp. 226–235, for an excellent analysis of Hume's concept of sympathy.
27. *Treatise,* 3:9:1, pp. 550–551.
28. Ibid., 3:9:10, pp. 553–554.
29. Ibid., 3:2:2, pp. 486–487.
30. Russell, op. cit., p. 660.

31. David Hume, "Of the Liberty of the Press," pp. 3–7, and "Of Civil Liberty," pp. 101–108, in Charles W. Hendel, ed., *David Hume's Political Essays,* New York: Liberal Arts Press, 1953.
32. Hume, "Liberty of the Press," p. 6.
33. Hume, "Civil Liberty," p. 104.
34. See Rousseau's *Confessions,* and Ayer, op. cit., pp. 12–13.

PART III: THE FRENCH, SOCIETY, AND THE POWER OF FEELINGS

10 Introduction: Les Philosophes

1. Isaiah Berlin, "Two Concepts of Liberty," in *Four Essays on Liberty,* London: Oxford University Press, 1984, pp. 118–172. This is a revised edition of Berlin's Inaugural Lecture at the University of Oxford, October 31, 1958.
2. For brief, clear accounts of the ideas of Zeno and the Stoics and Cicero, see, e.g., George H. Sabine, *A History of Political Theory,* 3rd ed., New York: Holt, Rinehart and Winston, 1961, pp. 141–173; and Bertrand Russell, *A History of Western Philosophy,* New York: Simon and Schuster Touchstone, 1972, pp. 252–270.
3. See, e.g., Norman L. Torrey, ed., *Les Philosophes: The French Philosophers of the Enlightenment and Modern Democracy,* New York: Capricorn Books, 1960, pp. 15–20. See also Sabine, op. cit., pp. 542–551; and Ernst Cassirer, *The Philosophy of the Enlightenment,* Princeton, N.J.: Princeton University Press, 1979, pp. 197–233.
4. For an account of Benjamin Franklin and Helvétius's widow, see Carl Van Doren, *Benjamin Franklin,* New York: Viking, 1938, pp. 648–650. See also Torrey, op. cit., p. 185; and S. G. Tallentyre, *The Friends of Voltaire,* London: Smith, Elder & Co., 1906, p. 204.
5. See Richard E. Amecher, *Franklin's Wit and Folly,* 1983, for a fascinating account of Franklin's life in Passy, examining his relationship not only with Madame Helvétius but with prerevolutionary Parisian society of 1779. For Madame Helvëtius and others, Franklin composed his *Bagatelles,* most of which were not published until after his death in 1790. Amecher's book includes the complete *Bagatelles.* Franklin's role in the development of the ideas of American journalists will be examined more closely in Chapter 16.
6. Ibid., p. 54.
7. Montesquieu is cited extensively in James Madison's *Notes of Debates in the Federal Convention of 1787.* See the edition edited by and including an introduction by Adrienne Koch, New York: Norton, 1966. Montesquieu also is relied upon in the *Federalist Papers,* essays by Madison, Alexander Hamilton and John Jay, published in 1787, and often reprinted. See the edition edited by and including introduction by Jacob E. Cooke, Cleveland: World Press Meridian Books, 1961, pp. 52–54, 56, 292, 295, 324–327, 523. The references are to *Federalist* nos. 43 and 47 by Madison and to nos. 9 and 78 by Hamilton.

8. Lytton Strachey, "The Rousseau Affair," in *Books and Characters: French and English,* London: Chatto and Windus, 1922, pp. 193–205. Strachey saw Rousseau as different from the other *philosophes* who, he wrote, continued to belong to the past.

11 Montesquieu: The Spirit of Laws

1. Paul Spurlin, *Montesquieu in America 1760–1800,* Baton Rouge: Louisiana State University Press, 1940, pp. 6–7. See also A. J. Beitzinger, *A History of American Political Thought,* New York: Dodd, Mead, & Co., 1972, pp. 18–19, and some of those quoted by him. Spurlin rejects successfully certain earlier interpretations of American history wherein the French influence was discounted. For example, James B. Perkins, *France in the American Revolution,* Boston: Houghton Mifflin, 1911, pp. 418–419 said the ancestors of colonials were essentially English, "unaffected by French thought."
2. Spurlin, op. cit., p. 259. Howard Mumford Jones, "The Importation of French Literature in New York City 1750–1800," *Studies in Philosophy,* 28:4. (October 31), pp. 235–251, cites 8 advertisements for Montesquieu's works in New York newspapers (there were 30 for Voltaire, 11 for Rousseau) and 17 in Philadelphia papers (45 for Voltaire, 35 for Rousseau).
3. George H. Sabine, *A History of Political Theory,* 3rd ed., New York: Holt, Rinehart and Winston, 1961, p. 558.
4. Beccaria, *Of Crimes and Punishment,* reprinted in Alessandro Manzoni, *The Column of Infamy,* trans. Kenneth Foster and Jane Grigson, London: Oxford University Press, 1964, p. 13. A. P. d'Entrèves, in the introduction to this book, cites Beccaria's powerful "feeling with victims of injustice, with the defenceless and the oppressed" (p. 13).
5. Ibid., p. 67.
6. See, for instance, Montesquieu's early work, *Lettres persanes,* published in 1721, 27 years before his renowned *Les Esprits des lois.* In the *Persian Letters,* chap. 83, Montesquieu wrote: "Justice is a harmonious relationship which really exists between two things. The relationship never varies, whether it is viewed from the perspective of God, an angel, or of man. . . . Even if God did not exist, we ought always to love justice. . . . Justice is eternal and nowise dependent on human conventions." The citations from Montesquieu are taken from the Thomas Nugent translation of *The Spirit of Laws*, New York: Hafner Press, 1949, hereafter cited as *Spirit.* The Nugent translation, as revised by J. V. Prichard, is published in *Great Books of the Western World,* vol. 38, Chicago: Encyclopedia Brittanica, 1952. (This volume also includes Rousseau's *A Discourse on the Origin of Equality, A Discourse on Political Economy,* and *The Social Contract* but not *Persian Letters.*)
7. Voltaire, *A Commentary on the Book, Of Crimes and Punishment (by Beccaria,* 1777, cited by Peter Gay, *Voltaire's Politics,* Princeton, NJ: Princeton University Press, 1959, pp. 287–288.
8. *The Federalist Papers,* edited by and with introduction by Jacob E. Cooke, Cleveland: World Meridian, 1961. Madison's *Federalist* No. 10 appears on pp. 56–65. This essay has been reprinted frequently.

9. *Spirit,* 5:3. See *Great Books* 38:1–331.
10. Spurlin, op. cit., pp. 261–262. Madison made this memorable comment during debates on the Constitution at the Virginia Convention.
11. *Spirit,* 4:5. See *Great Books,* 38:15–16. For a slightly different translation, see Norman L. Torrey, ed., *Les Philosophes: The French Philosophers of the Enlightenment and Modern Democracy,* New York: Capricorn Books, 1960, p. 96.
12. *Spirit,* 11:4. "If power is not to be abused, things must be so disposed that power checks power." See *Great Books* 38:69.
13. *Spirit,* 23:29, cited by Norman Hampson, *Will and Circumstances: Montesquieu, Rousseau and the French Revolution,* London: Gerald Duckworth & Co., 1983, p. 22.
14. *Spirit,* 12:12/13. See *Great Books,* 38:89–90; Torrey, op. cit., pp. 114–115.

12 Voltaire: "I Will Defend to the Death"

1. Peter Gay, *Voltaire's Politics: The Poet as Realist,* Princeton, N.J.: Princeton University Press, 1959, pp. 31–32.
2. The bibliographical essay in Gay's *Voltaire's Politics,* pp. 355–395, is must reading for an overview of Voltaire scholarship. Among readable biographies, see Georg Brandes, *Voltaire,* London: Tudor, 1930; A. Owen Aldridge, *Voltaire and the Century of Light,* Princeton, N.J.: Princeton University Press, 1975; and A. J. Ayer, *Voltaire,* London: Weidenfeld, 1986. For an outstanding study of the entire period, see Ernst Cassirer, *The Political Philosophy of the Enlightenment,* paperback ed., Princeton, N.J.: Princeton University Press, 1979.
3. See Jacquelin Marchand, ed., *Essai sur les moeurs et l'esprit des nations et sur les principaux faits de l'histoire, depuis Charlemagne jusqu'à Louis XIII* [An Essay on the Customs and Spirits of Nations, and on the Major Historical Facts from Charlemagne to Louis XIII], Paris: Editions Sociales, 1975. This work, whose preface contains Voltaire's theory of history, appeared between 1753 and 1756 but was not known under its celebrated title until 1769. See Haskell M. Block, ed., *Voltaire: Candide and Other Writings,* New York: Modern Library, 1956, p. 572. An English translation of the introduction to the *Essai* appears in Block, pp. 313–320.
4. See Voltaire's *Conseils à un journaliste sur la philosophie, l'histoire, le théâtre, les pièces de poésie, les mélanges de littérature, les anecdotes littéraires, les langues et la style,* May 10, 1737, reprinted in Louis Moland, ed., *Oeuvres complètes de Voltaire,* vol. 22, *Mélanges,* Paris: Garnier Frères, 1879, pp. 241–266. See also Voltaire, *Philosophical Dictionary,* trans. Peter Gay, 2 vols., New York: Basic Books, 1962; and Theodor Besterman, ed., *Voltaire's Correspondence,* Geneva: Institut et Musée Voltaire, les Délices, 1956.
5. George H. Sabine, *A History of Political Theory,* 3rd ed., New York: Holt, Rinehart and Winston, 1961, p. 561.
6. From Voltaire's *Correspondence,* February 3, 1769, cited by Kathleen O'Flaherty, *Voltaire: Myth and Reality,* 2nd ed., Cork: Cork University Press, 1945, pp. 77–79. O'Flaherty's debunking book was written as an antidote to the laudatory work by the English poet Alfred Noyes, *Voltaire,* New York: Sheed and Ward, 1936. Gay, op. cit., p. 389, speaks of Noyes's book as "a witty plea" for his flawed (and astonishing) argument that Voltaire was really a good Catholic.

7. For a discussion of Voltaire's shift in attitudes during the repression in Geneva, see Gay, op. cit., pp. 259–265. It was during this period that Voltaire, critical of the Geneva religious authorities, delivered his famous aphorism, "If God did not exist, one would have to invent him" (p. 265).
8. See especially Voltaire's *Republican Ideas,* which was published anonymously as a precautionary measure, either in 1762 or 1765. For a discussion of the date, see Gay, op. cit., pp. 346–351.
9. Voltaire's "Essay on Locke" is translated and reprinted in Block, op. cit., pp. 340–346, and in Torrey, op. cit., pp. 73–78. This was Letter No. 13 in Voltaire's *Philosophical Letters,* written between 1726 and 1734 and published in 1734. The *Letters* were condemned by the French Parlement and publicly burned by the hangman. See Block, p. 572.
10. Thomas Jefferson, letter to Dr. Benjamin Rush, September 23, 1800, cited in Paul L. Ford, ed., *Writings of Thomas Jefferson,* New York: Putnam's Sons, 1892–1899, 7:460.
11. Letter to Jacob Vernet, June 1, 1744, reprinted as Letter No. 2778 in Besterman, op. cit., 14:203–204. The reference is to the accession by Agiluf to the throne of the dukedom of Turin, although the date of 615 may be in error. I am indebted to Diana Johnstone for the translation of this letter.
12. Voltaire, *Conseils à un journaliste,* p. 243.
13. Ibid., pp. 264–265. See George Orwell, "Politics and the English Language," This frequently reprinted essay is included in Orwell's *Inside the Whale and Other Essays,* Harmondsworth: Penguin Books, 1971, pp. 143–157.
14. Voltaire, *Conseils à un journaliste,* p. 244.
15. Voltaire, "Essays on Locke," in Block, op. cit., p. 342.
16. Ibid., p. 345.
17. Voltaire's *Philosophical Dictionary* was begun in 1752 and published 12 years later, containing, according to Gay, op. cit., p. 208, what "Deists, skeptics and humanitarians had been preaching . . . for a century." Especially readable are his sections on Liberty (including liberty of the press), 2:111–114. This dictionary was Voltaire's second bomb. His first, the *Philosophical Letters,* appeared in 1734. Many historians, beginning with Gustave Lanson in 1909 have likened the two works to "a declaration of war" against the Old Order. See Lanson's edition of the *Letters,* p. 52.
18. Peter Gay, ed., *Philosophical Dictionary,* 2:114.
19. Voltaire, *Philosophical Letters,* 2:205–6, quoted by Gay, op. cit., p. 22.
20. Letter to Vernes, April 25, 1767, quoted by Gay, op. cit., p. 3.
21. For an account of the La Barre affair, see Aldridge, op. cit., pp. 336–342. See also Voltaire's treatise on Beccaria *(A Commentary on the Book, Of Crimes and Punishments).* Excerpts from that treatise appear in most collections of Voltaire.
22. Gay, op. cit., p. 293.
23. C. A. Helvétius, *De l'esprit; or Essays on the Mind and Its Several Faculties,* ed. and trans. William Mudford, London: M. Jones, 1807.
24. S. G. Tallentyre, *The Friends of Voltaire.* London: Smith, Elder & Co., 1906, pp. 198–199. See also Norman L. Torrey, eds., *Les Philosophes,* New York: Capricorn Books, 1960, p. 185.
25. Gay, op. cit., p. 74.
26. This idea appears in Bentham and also in earlier utilitarians dating back to the ancients, Cicero, Seneca, Epictetus, and Marcus Aurelius, and to some

degree also in Hobbes and Hume. Bentham, who was generous in giving credit to Helvétius for many of his ideas, also honored Hume. When he first encountered Hume's *Treatise of Human Nature,* Bentham wrote, he felt as if the scales fell from his eyes. See A. Seth Pringle-Patterson, *The Philosophical Radicals and Other Essays,* Edinburgh: William Blackwood and Sons, 1907, p. 7.

27. Helvétius, op. cit., 2:24.
28. Tallentyre, op. cit., p. 198.

13 Rousseau: The General Will and Social Responsibility

1. See Isaiah Berlin, *The Hedgehog and the Fox,* New York: New American Library Mentor Books, 1957, p. 74.
2. Norman Hampson, *Will and Circumstances: Montesquieu, Rousseau, and the French Revolution,* London: Gerald Duckworth & Co., 1983, p. 27.
3. Ibid.
4. George H. Sabine, *A History of Political Theory,* 3rd ed., New York: Holt, Rinehart and Winston, 1961, pp. 577–596.
5. Cf. Dennis Chase, "The Aphilosophy of Journalism," *Quill,* February, 1970, pp. 15–17.
6. Robert Darnton, "The Social Life of Rousseau," in *Harper's,* July 1985, p. 69. See the story of Janet Cooke in Chapter 58.
7. Robert Darnton, *The Literary Underground of the Old Regime,* Cambridge Mass: Harvard University Press, 1982, p. 68.
8. For a good, readable account of Rousseau's life, see Will and Ariel Durant, *Rousseau and Revolution: A History of Civilization in France, England and Germany from 1756 and in the Remainder of Europe from 1715 to 1789,* New York: Simon and Schuster, 1967.
9. Lytton Strachey, "The Rousseau Affair," in *Books and Characters: French and English,* London: Chattop and Windus, 1922, p. 205, says the abyss between Diderot and Rousseau was not the abyss between heaven and hell but rather the divide between the Old World and the New.
10. Rousseau, *The Confessions,* trans. and with an introduction by J. M. Cohen, Harmondsworth: Penguin Classics, 1984, p. 190. See also Durant, op. cit., p. 13.
11. Darnton, "The Social Life of Rousseau," p. 73.
12. For a current reprint of *The Social Contract,* see John Somerville and Ronald E. Santoni, eds., *Social and Political Philosophy: Readings from Plato to Gandhi,* Garden City, NY: Doubleday Anchor Books, 1963, pp. 205–238, which gives the sentence as "Man is born free and yet we see him everywhere in chains." The citations list book and chapter numbers. See also *Great Books of the Western World,* Chicago: Encyclopedia Britannica, 1952, vol. 38, pp. 387–439.
13. Ibid, 1:9. The translation is Cole's, G. D. H. Cole's translation in *Great Books,* 38:394.
14. Ibid., I:9.
15. Jean Lacroix, "Rousseau: Conscience and Confession," in *Le Monde,* retrospective commemorating the 200th anniversary of the death of Rousseau, reprinted in *The Guardian Weekly,* September 10, 1978.

16. Rousseau, always the paradox, has indeed succeeded in climbing out of the demimonde into cafe society, but he himself turned his back on that society. See *Confessions,* passim. Hampson, op. cit., pp. 37–41, argues that Rousseau himself was in no way a revolutionary, although his ideas anticipated those of Marx and Lenin as well as the French revolutionaries.
17. Rousseau, *Social Contract,* 2:3.
18. Ibid., 2:6.
19. Ibid., 2:7.
20. Ibid.
21. Reynolds Packer, *The Kansas City Milkman,* New York: Dutton, 1950.
22. Rousseau, Emile: *A Treatise on Education,* 1762. This translation from Book 2 is in Norman L. Torrey, *Les Philosophes: The French Philosophers of the Enlightenment and Modern Democracy,* New York: Capricorn Books, 1960, pp. 164–165.
23. Ibid., p. 165.
24. Hampson, op. cit., pp. 43–45.
25. Darnton, "Social Life of Rousseau," p. 73.
26. Lewis Carroll, "Through the Looking-Glass and What Alice Found There," in *The Annotated Alice,* rev. ed., ed. Martin Gardner, Harmondsworth: Penguin Classics, 1970, p. 269. Here Humpty was expressing the nominalist position advanced during the medieval age by William of Ockham, that universal terms do not refer to objective existence but are mere verbal utterances. This position is held today by most logical empiricists. See also Michel Tournier, "Jean-Jacques' Ideal Child," in *Le Monde* commemorative (see n. 15).
27. Darnton, *Literary Underground,* p. 29.
28. Ibid., p. 35.
29. Ibid., p. 25.
30. Ibid., pp. 203–204.
31. Isaiah Berlin, "Two Concepts of Liberty," in *Four Essays on Liberty,* London: Oxford University Press, 1984, pp. 118–172. See also Robert G. Picard, *The Press and the Decline of Democracy: The Democratic Socialist Response in Public Policy,* Westport, Conn.: Greenwood Press, 1985, pp. 41–42; and Robert Nisbet, *The Social Philosophers,* New York: Thomas Crowell, 1973, p. 152.
32. Larry Siedentop, "Two Liberal Traditions," in Alan Hale, ed., *The Idea of Freedom: Essays in Honour of Isaiah Berlin,* London: Oxford University Press, 1979, p. 169.
33. Cited in Durant, op. cit., p. 890.
34. Ernst Cassirer, *Rousseau, Kant and Goethe,* Harper & Row, 1963, p. 25, quoted in Durant, op. cit., p. 543. See also *Kritik der reinen Vernunft Critique of Pure Reason,* 1st ed., Riga, Latvia: J.F. Hartknoch, 1781, p. 819.

14 Revolution: The Rights of Majorities and Minorities

1. "Declaration of the Rights of Man and of the Citizen," reprinted in Norman L. Torrey, *Les Philosophes: The French Philosopher of the Enlightenment and Modern Democracy,* New York: Capricorn Books, 1960, pp. 284–287. For an examination of public opinion in revolutionary France, see William Doyle,

Origins of the French Revolution, London: Oxford University Press, 1980, pp. 78–95. See also Jack R. Censer, *Prelude to Power: The Parisian Radical Press 1789–1794,* Baltimore: Johns Hopkins University Press, 1976, especially pp. 37–48; A. Martin, and G. Walter, *Catalogue de l'histoire de la révolution française,* Paris; 1943; and André Cabanis, *La presse sous le consulat et l'empire,* Paris: Société des études robespierristes, 1975, p. 9. Cf. J. Herbert Atlschull, *Agents of Power: The Role of the News Media in Human Affairs,* New York: Longman, 1984, pp. 14–15.

2. Torrey, op. cit., p. 286.
3. Quoted in Cabanis, op. cit.
4. Metternich, *Fuerst Metternich ueber Napoleon Bonaparte,* Vienna: Wilhelm Braunmueller, 1875, p. 14. See also Metternich's *Denkschrift Metternichs ueber den Charakter und die Eigenheiten Napoleons,* 1814; and Martin and Walter, op. cit.
5. The role of Paine will be discussed further in Chapter 20.
6. E.g., in Lafayette's letter to James Madison, October 27, 1827. The original is in the possession of the Historical Society of Pennsylvania. See Madison's reply, February 20, 1828, in *The Writings of James Madison,* ed. Gaillard Hunt, New York: Putnam, 1910, 9:307.
7. For an account of French press history, especially of the early years, see among others Claude Bellanger, et al., *Histoire générale de la presse française,* Grenoble: Presses; Universitaire de Grenoble, 1976; Jean Sgard, *Dictionaire des journalistes,* Paris: Presses Universitaire de France, 1969–1976; Henri Avenel, *Histoire de la presse française,* Paris: Flammarion, 1900; and Charles Ledré, *La presse à l'assaut de la monarchie 1815–1848,* Paris: Armand Colin, 1960.
8. Altschull, op. cit., pp. 30–34. See also French history works cited above and Frederick B. Artz, *France Under the Bourbon Restoration 1814–1830,* New York: Russell and Russell, 1931.
9. Daniel L. Rader, *The Journalist in the July Revolution in France: The Role of the Political Press in the Overthrow of the Bourbon Restoration, 1827–1830,* The Hague: Nijhoff, 1973; and David H. Pinkney, "The News Media and the Monarchy of France, 1827–1830," *Reviews in European History* (March 1985): 519–523. See also Irene Collins, *The Government and the Newspaper Press in France 1814–1881,* London: Oxford University Press, 1959.
10. Alexis de Tocqueville, *Democracy in America.* All citations are from *The Henry Reeve Text as Revised By Francis Brown Now Further collected And Edited With a Historical Essay, Editorial Notes, and Bibliography By Phillips Bradley,* 2 vols., New York: Vintage Books, 1945. The young Frenchman arrived in the United States in May 1831 and returned to France nine months later. His two-volume report on his trip appeared in France in 1835; a four-volume English translation was completed in 1840. The two-volume 1945 English text was a complete revision.
11. Ibid., bk. 2, *Influence of Democracy in the Feelings of Americans,* chap. 1, "Why Democratic Nations Show a More Ardent and Enduring Love of Equality Than of Liberty," 2:102.
12. Ibid., 2: pp. 101–102.
13. Ibid., 2:106.
14. Ibid., vol. 1, chap. 11, "Liberty of the Press in the United States," 1:195.

15. Ben Hecht and Charles MacArthur, *The Front Page,* New York: Covizi-Friede, 1928.
16. *New York Times,* November 14, 1959.
17. Tocqueville, op. cit., 1:193–194.
18. Ibid., p. 192.
19. Ibid.
20. Ibid., p. 194.
21. Ibid., p. 195.
22. Larry Siedentop, "Two Liberal Traditions," in Alan Hale, ed., *The Idea of Freedom: Essays in Honor of Isaiah Berlin,* London: Oxford University Press, 1979, pp. 167–174.

PART IV: THE AMERICAN BELIEF SYSTEM ARISES

15 Introduction: Call for Rebellion

1. Cited in Edward Bean Underhill, ed., *Tracts on Liberty of Conscience and Persecution, 1614–1661,* London: J. Haddon, 1846, p. 32.
2. Thomas Jefferson, "An Act For Establishing Religious Freedom," reprinted in John Somerville and Ronald E. Santoni, eds., *Social and Political Philosophy: Readings from Plato to Gandhi,* Garden City, N.Y.: Doubleday Anchor Books, 1963, p. 248. See also Paul L. Ford, ed., *The Writings of Thomas Jefferson,* New York: Putnam, 1892–1899, 2:237–239. See also *The Papers of Thomas Jefferson,* compiled by Elizabeth J. Sherwood and Ida T. Hopper, Princeton, N.J.: Princeton University Press, 1954–1958.
3. Barbara W. Tuchman, *In Praise of Folly: From Troy to Vietnam,* New York: Alfred A. Knopf, 1983, p. 197. The reference is to the dismissal of Benjamin Franklin as deputy postmaster of the American colonies. Franklin recalls that he was wearing the same suit of Manchester velvet that he had worn when he was dismissed by Lord Wedderburn. Tuchman's reference is drawn from *Memoirs* of William Temple Franklin, cited in *Papers of Benjamin Franklin,* ed. William Willcox, New Haven, Conn.: Yale University Press, 1978, 21:41 n. 9.
4. Tuchman, op. cit., p. 192.
5. David Ramsey, quoted in Arthur M. Schlesinger, *Prelude to Independence: The Newspaper War on Britain 1764–1776,* Boston: Northeastern University Press, 1980, p. xiii. Schlesinger's book, the classic discussion of the rise of the American press, was originally published in 1957. Ramsay's *The History of the American Revolution,* was published in Philadelphia in 1789.

16 Benjamin Franklin and the "Price of Truth"

1. James Franklin, *New-England Courant,* November 27, 1721.
2. Edwin Emery and Michael Emery, *The Press and America: An Interpretative History of the Mass Media,* 4th ed., Englewood Cliffs, N.J.: Prentice-Hall, 1978, pp. 35–36. More extravagant praise for Franklin can be found in the earlier editions of this standard history text.

3. J. Edward Gerald, "Truth and Error—Journalism's Tournament of Reason," *Quill,* July 1969, reprinted in John C. Merrill and Ralph D. Barney, eds., *Ethics and the Press: Readings in Mass Media Morality,* New York: Hastings House, 1975, pp. 136–142.
4. Leonard W. Levy, *Legacy of Suppression: Freedom of Speech and Press in Early American History,* Cambridge, Mass.: Harvard University Press, 1960, p. 3. In his *Emergence of a Free Press,* New York: Oxford University Press, 1985, Levy sharply revised his earlier thinking in *Legacy.* In the later work, he perceives Franklin as superficial (p. 121) and as no friend of press freedom (p. 57). For a contrary view of Franklin, see Adrienne Koch, *Power, Morals, and the Founding Fathers: Essays in the Interpretation of the American Enlightenment,* Ithaca, N.Y.: Cornell University Press, 1961, p. 22.
5. Clinton Rossiter, *Seedtime of the Republic,* New York: Harcourt, Brace, 1953, p. 300.
6. See Chapter 12.
7. Benjamin Franklin, reprinted in Albert Henry Smythe, ed., *The Writings of Benjamin Franklin,* 10 vols., New York: Macmillan, 1905–1907, 2: "Preface to the Pennsylvania Gazette," October 2, 1729.
8. Benjamin Franklin, "An Apology for Printers," *Pennsylvania Gazette,* June 10, 1731, reprinted in Smythe, op. cit., p. 174. For additional on Franklin as entrepreneur, see Stephen Botein, " 'Meer Mechanics' and an Open Press: The Business and Political Strategies of Colonial American Printers," in Donald Fleming and Bernard Bailyn, eds., *Perspectives in American History,* vol. 9, 1975, pp. 179–183.
9. For reference to central tension, see J. Herbert Altschull, *Agents of Power: The Role of the News Media in Human Affairs.* New York: Longman, 1984, pp. 21–26.
10. Franklin, op. cit., p. 178.
11. Ibid.
12. Leonard W. Larabee, ed., *The Papers of Benjamin Franklin,* New Haven, Yale University Press, 1959–1965, 8:28–40, 87–88, cited in Levy, *Emergence,* p. 57. Levy comments with ironic bite: "Thus spoke America's foremost printer and reputed champion of freedom of the press." Levy does not appear to entertain much if any tolerance for views contrary to his own. He does acknowledge, however, in *Emergence* that he had gone too far in his earlier *Legacy,* remarking that that work had been written in part out of spite. See his preface, p. vii. His *Emergence,* he said, was meant to correct the earlier work but not to revise his main theme, that the Founding Fathers did not mean to overthrow the seditious libel doctrine of Blackstone. See Chapter 19 for additional on Blackstone. The minister condemned by Franklin, the Reverend William Smith, founder of the *Philadelphia Zeitung,* editor of *The American Magazine* and provost of the University of Pennsylvania, appears to be one of Levy's personal heroes.
13. Levy, op. cit., p. 173.
14. Benjamin Franklin, "On Freedom of Speech and the Press," in *Autobiography, Memoirs of Benjamin Franklin,* Philadelphia: McCarty and Davis, 1834, 2:431–439, reprinted from *Gazette,* Philadelphia, November 1737, n.d.
15. Ibid., p. 431. The metaphor of a tree pruned of fruitful growth appears to have been a popular one in the colonies. It appears not only in Franklin but in the writings of James Madison and Tunis Wortman, among others.

16. Ibid., p. 434.
17. "An Account of the Supremest Judicature in Pennsylvania, Viz, The Court of the Press," published as a newspaper essay, 1789, and reprinted in Smythe, op. cit., 10:38, 40.
18. Ibid.
19. Levy, *Emergence,* p. 192; James M. Smith, *Freedom's Fetters: The Alien and Sedition Laws and American Civil Liberties,* Ithaca, N.Y.: Cornell University Press, 1956, p. 137.

17 James Madison and Free Expression

1. Andrew Bradford, in *The American Weekly Mercury,* Philadelphia, April 25, 1734, reprinted in Leonard W. Levy, ed., *Freedom of the Press from Zenger to Jefferson,* Indianapolis, Bobbs-Merrill, 1966, pp. 38–43.
2. Ibid., p. 39.
3. For the classic account of the Zenger case, see James Alexander's report reprinted in Livingston Rutherford, *John Peter Zenger: His Press, His Trial, and a Bibliography of Zenger Imprints,* New York: Dodd, Mead, 1904, pp. 198–241. Zenger was printer of the *New-York Weekly Journal,* and worked for Alexander and his partners.
4. Anna Janney DeArmond, *Andrew Bradford: Colonial Journalist,* Newark, Del.: University of Delaware Press, 1949, chap. 4, "The Bradford-Hamilton Controversy." See also Leonard W. Levy, *Emergence of a Free Press,* New York: Oxford University Press, 1985. p. 50.
5. Quoted in Josiah Quincy, ed., *Reports of Cases Around and Adjudged in the Superior Court of the Province of Massachusetts Bay, Between 1761 and 1772,* Boston: Little, Brown, 1865, pp. 236–237.
6. Quoted in Rutherford, op. cit., p. 239.
7. James Alexander, "Free Speech as a Pillar of Free Government," four essays published in the *Pennsylvania Gazette,* November 17–December 8, 1737, excerpts reprinted in Levy, *Freedom,* pp. 62–74.
8. Levy, *Emergence,* p. 125.
9. Alexander, op. cit., pp. 62–63.
10. See J. Herbert Altschull, *Agents of Power: The Role of the News Media in Human Affairs,* New York: Longman, 1984, pp. 12–14, for a brief discussion of Cato. See also Levy, *Freedom,* pp. 10–11.
11. Adrienne Koch, ed., *Notes of Debates in the Federal Convention of 1787, Reported by James Madison,* New York: Norton, 1966, p. 630.
12. For a brief summary of the legislative history of the Bill of Rights, see Levy, *Emergence,* pp. 257–266.
13. Alexander Hamilton, *Federalist* No. 84, in *The Federalist Papers,* edited and with introduction by Jacob E. Cooke, Cleveland: World Meridian, 1961, pp. 575–587. For Madison's views, see his *Federalist* No. 41, p. 277.
14. James Madison, *Federalist* No. 10, ibid., pp. 55–65.
15. Ibid. See also Madison's *Federalist* No. 47, pp. 324–327, in which he cites "the oracle," Montesquieu, to support his position that the citizen can be secure only when governmental powers are separate.
16. Letter to Thomas Jefferson, October 17, 1788, in Robert A. Rutland, ed., *The Papers of James Madison,* Charlottesville: University of Virginia Press, 11:297–298.

17. Edmund S. Morgan, *Inventing the People: The Rise of Popular Sovereignty in England and America,* New York: Norton, 1989. See the excellent review article by Pauline Maier in the *New York Times Book Review,* July 3, 1988, p. 10.
18. See, for instance, Jefferson's letter to Madison of March 15, 1789, in Julian T. Boyd, ed., *Papers of Jefferson,* Princeton, N.J.: Princeton University Press, 1950, 14:659–661.
19. Letter to William T. Barry, August 4, 1822, in Gaillard Hunt, ed., *The Writings of James Madison,* New York: Putnam, 1910, 9:103–109. See also Marvin Meyers, ed., *Sources of the Political Thought of James Madison,* Indianapolis: Bobbs-Merrill, 1973, pp. 435–436. Barry was lieutenant governor of Kentucky and also a professor who had sought Madison's endorsement for publicly supported higher education. For the classic biography, see Irving Brant, *James Madison,* 4 vols., Indianapolis, IN: Bobbs-Merrill, 1941–1961.

18 The "Best Friend" of the Press: Thomas Jefferson

1. Thomas Jefferson, letter to Edward Carrington, January 16, 1787, in Paul L. Ford, ed., *The Writings of Thomas Jefferson,* New York: Putnam, 1892–1899, 6:357–361. For a one-volume summation of Jefferson's life and writings, see *The Portable Jefferson,* New York: Viking Press, 1965. For an extended biography, see Dumas Malone's six-volume life published by the University of Virginia Press, Charlottesville, Va.
2. Thomas, Jefferson, letter to Thomas Kean, February 19, 1803, ibid., 8:218–219.
3. See John Somerville and Ronald E. Santoni, eds., *Social and Political Philosophy: Readings from Plato to Gandhi.* Garden City, N.Y.: Doubleday Anchor Books, 1963, pp. 240–245, for a reprint of the Declaration of Independence, including the phrases of Jefferson's original which he subsequently edited out.
4. Ibid., p. 277. The letter was addressed to John B. Colvin, editor of the *Republican Advocate,* Frederickstown, Md., September 20, 1810. Cited in Ford, op. cit., 9:279–281.
5. See, among others, Leonard W. Levy, *Jefferson and Civil Liberties: The Darker Side,* Cambridge, Mass.: Belknap Press of Harvard University Press, 1963; and Fawn W. Brodie, *Jefferson: An Intimate History,* New York: Norton, 1974.
6. Thomas Jefferson, [document quoted or collected in Peden], in William Peden, ed., *Thomas Jefferson: Notes on the State of Virginia,* Chapel Hill: University of North Carolina Press, 1955, Query 16, p. 155, cited by Leonard W. Levy, *Emergence of a Free Press,* New York: Oxford University Press, 1985, pp. 178–179.
7. Thomas Jefferson, letter to James Madison, July 31, 1788, in *The Papers of Thomas Jefferson,* compiled by Elizabeth J. Sherwood and Ida T. Hopper, Princeton, N.J.: Princeton University Press, 1954–1958, 6:304, cited in Levy, *Emergence*, pp. 250–251.
8. *An Act for Establishing Religious Freedom, Passed in the Assembly of Virginia in the Beginning of the Year 1786.* The Preamble, from which the

famous citation is drawn, is reprinted in Somerville and Santoni, op. cit., pp. 247–248. See Sherwood and Hopper, op. cit. for original.

9. Levy, *Emergence,* p. 195.
10. Thomas Jefferson, Second Inaugural address, March 4, 1805, in Ford, op. cit. 8:341–347. See also Leonard W. Levy, *Freedom of the Press from Zenger to Jefferson,* Indianapolis: Bobbs-Merrill, 1966, pp. 367–368; J. Herbert Altschull, *Agents of Power: The Role of the News Media in Human Affairs,* New York: Longman, 1984, p. 29, and Jefferson's letter to John Norvell, June 11, 1807, abridged in Levy, *Freedom,* pp. 372–373.
11. Spiro Agnew, speech at Des Moines, Iowa, reprinted in the *New York Times,* November 14, 1969.
12. David Hackett Fischer, in *Historians' Fallacies: Toward A Logic of Historical Thought,* New York: Harper Torchbooks, 1970, pp. 297–298, writes, amusingly: "... it is a rare political proposal which is not, in some fashion, legitimized by an out-of-context quotation from the Founding Fathers. Consider, for instance, the rhetorical raids that have been made upon the writings of Thomas Jefferson...." Fischer than proceeds to cite historical errors by some of the more distinguished modern historians.
13. For a discussion of the significance of promises among American journalists, see Sissela Bok, *Secrets: On the Ethics of Concealment and Revelation,* New York: Pantheon, 1982, pp. 116–135, 249–264.
14. Thomas Jefferson, letter to John Adams, October 28, 1813, in Somerville and Santoni, op. cit., pp. 266–270; and in Ford, op. cit., 9:424–430.
15. Ibid.
16. Leslie J. Cappon, *The Adams-Jefferson Letters,* Vol. 2, Chapel Hill: University of North Carolina Press, 1959 (Adams to Jefferson Aug. 16, 1813, pp. 365–367; Sept. 2, 1813, pp. 370–372; Jefferson to Adams, Oct. 28, 1813, pp. 387–392) See also Adrienne Koch, ed., *Adams and Jefferson: "Posterity Must Judge,"* in Charles Sellers, ed., *The Berkeley Series in American History,* passim, Chicago: Rand McNally, 1963.
17. William James, *Pragmatism: A New Name for Some Old Ways of Thinking,* New York: Longmans, Green, 1907. The work of James will be examined in Chapter 36.
18. Thomas Jefferson, letter to N. G. Dufief, April 19, 1814, excerpted in Levy, *Freedom,* pp. 374–375.
19. Jefferson, *An Act,* pp. 247–248.

19 That "Great Bulwark of Liberty"

1. Zechariah Chafee, review of Alexander Meiklejohn, *Free Speech and its Relation to Self-Government, Harvard Law Review,* (1949) 62:898. See also Chafee's *Free Speech in the United States.* New York: Atheneum, 1969 (originally published in 1941), pp. 3–35, for an earlier examination of the origin and significance of the First Amendment.
2. Alexander Meiklejohn, *Free Speech and Its Relation to Self-Government,* New York: Harper, 1948, p. 17.
3. See Alexander Hamilton, Federalist No. 84, in Jacob E. Cooke, ed., *The Federalist Papers,* Cleveland: World Publishing Co., 1965, pp. 575–587. See

also Benjamin Franklin, "The Court of the Press," 1789, in Albert Henry Smythe, ed., *The Writings of Benjamin Franklin,* 10 vols., New York: Macmillan, 1905–1907, 10:37, cited in Leonard W. Levy, *Emergence of a Free Press,* New York: Oxford University Press, 1985, p. 204.

4. For a thorough history of the development of the ten amendments in the Bill of Rights, see Bernard Schwartz, ed., *The Bill of Rights: A Documentary History,* 2 vols., New York: Chelsea House, 1971. The text of the first two proposed amendments that were not ratified by the states can be found in vol. 2, p. 1164. Discussion of Madison's proposals is reported throughout the volumes.
5. Levy, op. cit., pp. 173–184. See also Claude H. Van Tyne, *The Loyalists in the American Revolution,* reprint, Gloucester, Mass.: P. Smith, 1959, pp. 327–329, and Philip Davidson, *Propaganda and the American Revolution,* Chapel Hill: University of North Carolina Press, 1941.
6. With ratification by Virginia on December 15, 1791, the ten amendments of the Bill of Rights were added to the Constitution. See Levy, op. cit., pp. 264–266.
7. For an outstanding summary of the origin and application of the First Amendment, see Marvin L. Summers, *Free Speech and Political Thought,* Lexington, Mass.: Heath, 1969. See also J. Herbert Altschull, *Agents of Power: The Role of the News Media in Human Affairs,* New York: Longman, 1984, pp. 17–34.
8. Sir William Blackstone, *Commentaries on the Laws of England,* 4 vols., Oxford: Clarendon Press, 1765–1769. See especially bk 4, chapter 11, pp. 151–154, on prior restraint.
9. Ibid., p. 152.
10. Schenk v. U.S., 249, United States Reports, 47: "The question in every case is whether the words used are used in such circumstances and are of such a nature as to create a clear and present danger that they will bring about the substantive evils that Congress has a right to prevent."
11. See Patterson v. Colorado, 205 U.S. 454, 462 (1907) and Abrams v. U.S., 250 U.S. 616, 630 (1919). See also the intersting discussion of the views of Holmes in Levy, p. 281.
12. Potter Stewart, "Or of the Press," mimeo, address at Yale University convocation, Nov. 2, 1974.
13. Douglass Cater, *The Fourth Branch of Government,* Boston: Houghton Mifflin, 1963.
14. Levy, op. cit., p. 273.
15. On the Alien and Sedition Laws, see John C. Miller, *Crisis in Freedom,* Boston: Little, Brown, 1951. See also James M. Smith, *Freedom's Fetters.* For opposing viewpoints, see Levy, op. cit., p. 330, and Walter Berns, "Freedom of the Press and the Alien and Sedition Laws: A Reappraisal," in Philip B. Kurland, *The Supreme Court Review,* Chicago: University of Chicago Press, 1970, p. 141. Berns' views are given thorough expression in his *In Defense of Liberal Democracy,* Chicago: Regnery Gateway, 1984.
16. James Madison, *The Virginia Report of 1799–1800, Touching on the Alien and Sedition Laws; Together with the Virginia Resolutions of December 21, 1798, the Debate and Proceedings Thereon in the House of Delegates of Virginia, and Several Other Documents,* Richmond Va: J. W. Randolph, 1850, pp. 210–229.

See also "Report on the Virginia Resolutions of 1798," in *Letters and Other Writings of James Madison, Fourth President of the United States, in four volumes, published by Order of Congress,* New York: R. Worthington, 1884, 4:218–227. See also *Virginia Resolutions of 1798,* ibid., pp. 506–507.

17. James Madison, *The Virginia Report,* p. 222.
18. Altschull, op. cit., p. 90. Marx's article appeared in the *Anekdota,* February 1843.
19. Madison, *The Virginia Report,* p. 222. Note that Madison repeats the pruning metaphor cited earlier.
20. Letter to William T. Barry, August 4, 1822, Madison, *Letters and Other Writings*. 9:103.
21. For a contrary view, see Edmund Burke on community, in *Reflections on the Revolution in France.*
22. Hamilton, op. cit., p. 580. For Marx and the need for public support of the press, see Altschull, op. cit., p. 92.
23. For a reference to the competition between Freneau and Fenno, see e.g., Edwin Emery and Michael Emery, *The Press and America: An Interpretative History of the Mass Media,* 4th ed., Englewood Cliffs, N.J.: Prentice-Hall, 1978, pp. 82–83. The authors label the competition "vituperative partisanship."
24. Julius Goebel, ed., *The Law Practice of Alexander Hamilton: Documents and Commentary,* vol. 1, New York: Columbia University Press, 1964, pp. 808–835.
25. Ibid., p. 831.
26. James Kent, *Croswell ads (sic) the People,* pp. 41–64, cited in Goebel, op. cit., p. 833.
27. Ibid.

20 Paine, Burke, and the "Rights of Man"

1. Thomas W. Copeland, "Burke, Paine and Jefferson," in *Our Eminent Friend Edmund Burke: Six Essays,* New Haven, Yale University Press, 1949, p. 148.
2. For biographical material on Paine, see, among others, David Hawke, *Paine,* New York: Harper & Row, 1974; Audrey Williamson, *Thomas Paine: His Life, Work, and Times,* New York: St. Martin's Press, 1973, and Samuel Edwards, *Rebel!,* New York: Praeger, 1974. For a review of these works, see Fawn Brodie, "Tom Paine: Relevant Founding Father," *New Republic,* May 4, 1974.
3. Michael Foot, "Shatterproof Paine," *Sunday Times* (London), January 1982, reprinted in *Guardian Weekly,* Jan. 24, 1982. Foot was reviewing a British television documentary on the life of Paine. See also, Brodie, op. cit.: "Paine was an 18-century hippie . . ."
4. Thomas Paine, "The American Crisis," reprinted in Moncure D. Conway, *The Writings of Thomas Paine,* 4 vols., New York: AMS Press, 1967, 1:170. See also Paine's "Common Sense," 1:69–120. It was in "Common Sense," a pamphlet published January 10, 1776, that Paine called for independence from "British barbarity" (p. 96). Moreover, he demanded a key role for the

colonial press in rebellion, warning against British-backed "printers who will be busy in spreading specious falsehoods" (p. 117).

5. Copeland, op. cit., pp. 166–167.
6. An account of the facts of Jefferson's "endorsement" of Paine's *Rights of Man* can be found in Dumas Malone, *Jefferson and the Rights of Man,* vol. 2 of Malone's six-part biography. Boston: Little, Brown, 1951, pp. 351–358.
7. Edmund Burke, *Reflections on the Revolution in France,* Garden City NY: Doubleday Anchor, 1973, p. 62. This edition includes also Paine's *The Rights of Man,* but eliminates most of the notes and contains no editor's comments. For a more useful reprint, see Burke's *Reflections,* edited by and including an introduction by Thomas Mahoney, New York: Liberal Arts Press, 1955. For examination of Burke's life and thought, see, i.a., F.P. Lock, *Burke's Reflections on the Revolution in France,* London: Allen & Unwin, 1985; Frank O'Gorman, *Edmund Burke: His Political Philosophy,* Bloomington: Indiana University Press, 1973, and David R. Cameron, *The Social Thought of Rousseau and Burke,* Toronto: University of Toronto Press, 1973.
8. Thomas Paine, *The Rights of Man,* Garden City, NY: Doubleday Anchor, 1973, p. 281.
9. Paine, op. cit., p. 406. Interestingly, Paine and Burke each argued that his reasoning was a close following of that of Montesquieu.
10. Ibid., p. 415.
11. Quoted in Foot, op. cit. See also Alan Ryan, *The Listener,* March 24, 1988, in review article on the publication of A.J. Ayer, *Tom Paine,* London: Secker, 1988: "When he went back to America in 1802, he found himself refused transport by a New Jersey coach driver who said that his coach and horses had once been struck by lightning; and he had no wish to risk it happening again." For additional on Paine's tribulations with the law, see *The Prosecution of Thomas Paine: Seven Tracts, 1783–1798,* New York: Garland, 1974.
12. Paine, op. cit., p. 357. See also pp. 393–397, 416–445.
13. Burke, op. cit., p. 71.
14. Copeland, op. cit., p. 166, n31.
15. Foot, op. cit.
16. Quoted in Levy, *Emergence of a Free Press,* New York: Oxford University Press, 1985, pp. 285–289. See Rex v. Paine, Massachusetts State Trials, 1791, 22:357.
17. Paine, op. cit., p. 419.
18. Thomas Paine, article in *The American Citizen,* New York, October 20, 1806, reprinted in William M. Van der Weyde, *The Life and Times of Thomas Paine,* New Rochelle, N.Y.: Rimington and Hoopes, 1928, vol. 10, pp. 287–290.
19. Alexander M. Bickel, "Reconsideration: Edmund Burke," *New Republic,* March 17, 1973, p. 34. For an opposing viewpoint, see Ryan, op. cit., who writes that it is likely Burke "simply got carried away by his own rhetoric: Paine was a victim of the violence and folly predicted by Burke, a self-deceived and self-destructive rationlist." The furious collision between Burke and Paine enthusiasts continues.
20. Bickel, op. cit., p. 34.
21. Burke, op. cit., p. 73.
22. Ibid.

23. Robert Rea, *The English Press in Politics, 1760–1774,* Lincoln: University of Nebraska Press, 1063, p. 192.

21 Revolution: A Mystique for Journalists

1. Harry H. Clark, "Thomas Paine's Relation to Voltaire and Rousseau," *Revue Anglo-Americaine,* (April–June, 1932).
2. Eugene Perry Link, *Democratic-Republican Societies 1790–1800,* New York: Columbia University Press, 1942. This was a doctoral dissertation at Columbia University. See also A. J. Beitzinger, *A History of American Political Thought,* New York: Dodd, Mead, 1972, p. 304.
3. William Duane, *A Letter to George Washington,* written under the pseudonym of Jasper Wright. See Link, op. cit., p. 115.
4. Thomas Jefferson, undated memo of 1801 in Paul L. Ford, ed., *The Writings of Thomas Jefferson,* New York: Putnam, 1892–1899, 8:56. See also Leonard W. Levy, *Emergence of a Free Press,* New York: Oxford University Press, 1985, p. 307.
5. Joel Barlow, *A Letter to the National Convention of France, on the Defects in the Constitution of 1791, and the Extent of the Amendments Which Ought to Be Applied,* New York: Thomas Greenleaf, 1793, p. 32. A copy of this book was owned and initialed by Thomas Jefferson and it was among those donated to the Library of Congress. See William K. Bottorff, and Arthur L. Ford, eds., *The Works of Joel Barlow,* 2 vols., Gainesville, Fla.: Scholars' Facsimilies and Reprints, 1970, 1:52.
6. Link, op. cit., p. 124.
7. Tunis Wortman, *A Treatise Concerning Political Enquiry and the Liberty of the Press,* New York: George Forman, 1800, pp. 261–262.
8. Ibid., p. 245.
9. George Hay, ("Hortensius"), *An Essay on the Liberty of the Press, Respectfully Inscribed to the Republican Printers Throughout the United States,* Richmond, Va.: Samuel Pleasants, Jr., 1803, pp. 21–30.
10. Ibid., p. 23. See also Levy, *Emergence of a Free Press,* New York: Oxford University Press, 1985, p. 195. Walter Berns offers an interpretation of the ideological struggle over the Alien and Sedition Acts that differs substantially with that of this book and of Levy. See, e.g., Berns, *The First Amendment and the Future of American Democracy,* New York: 1976; and "Freedom of the Press and the Alien and Sedition Laws: A Reappraisal," in Philip B. Kurland, ed., *The Supreme Court Review,* Chicago: University of Chicago Press, 1971, pp. 265–322.
11. Hay, op. cit., p. 29. Hay wrote a second essay on press freedom in 1803. The two were published in a single volume by Pleasants (see note 9 above). Hay was not only a member of the Virginia House of Delegates and a U.S. attorney under Jefferson but also a son-in-law of James Monroe. For more on Hay, see Stephen H. Hochman, "On the Liberty of the Press in Virginia: From Essay to Bludgeon, 1798–1803," *Virginia Magazine of History and Biography,* 84 (1976):431–435.

12. Hay, op. cit., pp. 26–28.
13. Link, op. cit., p. 161.

22 Kant, Hegel, and the Counterrevolution

1. The literature on Hegel is enormous. Studies particularly relevant to the present work include Bruce Mazlish, "Hegel," in his *The Riddle of History: The Great Speculators from Vico to Freud,* New York: Harper & Row, 1966; Jean Hyppolite, *Studies on Marx and Hegel,* New York: Basic Books, 1969; Daniel J. Cook, *Language in the Philosophy of Hegel,* The Hague: Mouton, 1973; George D. O'Brien, *Hegel on Reason and History,* Chicago: University of Chicago Press, 1975; and Charles Taylor, *Hegel,* Cambridge: Cambridge University Press, 1975. For a critical analysis of Hegel's work, see Karl Popper, *The Open Society and Its Enemies,* 4th ed., Princeton, N.J.: Princeton University Press, 1963. See also Bertrand Russell, *A History of Western Philosophy,* New York: Simon and Schuster, 1972, pp. 730–746.
2. Mazlish, op. cit., p. 135.
3. See Isaiah Berlin, "Two Concepts of Liberty," in *Four Essays on Liberty,* London: Oxford University Press, 1984, p. 148. See also Russell, op. cit., pp. 730–746; George H. Sabine, pp. 628–668; and Geoffrey Hawthorn, *Enlightenment and Despair: A History of Sociology, A History of Political Theory,* 3rd ed., New York: Holt, Rinehart and Winston, 1961, Cambridge: Cambridge University Press, 1976.
4. Mazlish, op. cit., p. 141.
5. This group of traveler-scholars included Ralph Waldo Emerson, Horace Greeley, Henry Adams, and many others. For an analysis of the impact of the Teutonic model on American learning see Gerald Graff, *Professional Literature: An Institutional History,* Chicago: University of Chicago Press, 1987.
6. In the literature of journalism ethics, see, e.g., references to Kant in Clifford G. Christians, Kim B. Rotzoll, and Mark Frackler, *Media Ethics, Cases and Moral Reasoning,* 2nd ed., New York: Longman, 1987; and in Edmund B. Lambeth, *Committed Journalism: An Ethic for the Profession,* Bloomington: Indiana University Press, 1986. See also Sissela Bok, *Lying: Moral Choice in Public and Private Life,* New York: Vintage Books, 1979, passim.
7. The portrait of Kant by poet Heinrich Heine, pointing up the importance of Kant's daily walks in Koenigsberg is part of the cultural tradition and imagery of Prussia. Among the voluminous literature on Kant, see, e.g., Carl J. Friedrich, *The Philosophy of Kant,* New York: Modern Library, 1969; Ernst Cassirer, *Kant's Life and Thought,* New Haven, Conn.: Yale University Press, 1981; and John Stuckenberg, *The Life of Immanuel Kant with a New Preface by Rolf George,* Lanham, Md: University Press of America, 1986. See also Mazlish, op. cit., pp. 101–125, and Russel, op. cit., pp. 701–718. For Kant's own work, see especially his *A Critique of Pure Reason,* New York: St. Martin's Press, 1965; and *Perpetual Peace and Other Essays on Politics, History and Morals,* Indianapolis, Hackett, 1983.
8. Quoted in Dagobert D. Runes, ed., *Dictionary of Philosophy,* Towota, N.J.: Littlefield, Adams and Co., 1982, p. 158.
9. See Sabine, op. cit., pp. 745–753; and Russell, op. cit., pp. 717–718. See also Raymond Williams, *Culture and Society 1780–1950,* New York: Harper & Row, 1966.

10. Quoted in Runes, op. cit., p. 159.
11. Hawthorn, op. cit., pp. 41–42.
12. The literature on Kant's categorical imperative is also extensive. See, e.g., Christians et al., op. cit.; and Bok, op. cit., passim. See Kant's extended discussion of the topic in his *A Critique of Pure Reason.*
13. Hegel specifically rejected the compact idea. See Mazlish, op. cit., p. 171.
14. Quoted in Berlin, op. cit., p. 148.
15. Mazlish and some others deny that Hegel was a romantic. See Mazlish, op. cit., pp. 132–134.
16. Quoted in Hawthorn, op. cit., p. 42.
17. Ibid.
18. Friedrich, op. cit., 1954, pp. 9–14.
19. Mazlish, op. cit., p. 167, describes the German people as Hegel's Chosen People but adds that he was not speaking about the citizens of any particular German country, rather the Germanic people who inhabited Europe after the fall of Rome.
20. Ibid., pp. 156–158.
21. Ibid., p. 97. Hegel traced the course of history from origins in the Orient to the present day wherein the Germanic peoples had shown "the capacity to be the bearers of this higher principle of Spirit."
22. Ibid., p. 128.
23. Russell, op. cit., pp. 743–745. For a discussion of holistic fallacy, see also David Hackett Fischer, *Historians' Fallacies: Toward a Logic of Historical Thought,* New York: Harper Torchbooks, 1970, pp. 65–66.

PART V WEIGHING THE INDIVIDUAL AGAINST SOCIETY: THE PARADOX OF DEMOCRACY

23 Introduction: Jeremy Bentham and the Pleasure-Pain Principle

1. Emery Neff, *Carlyle and Mill: Mystic and Utilitarian,* New York: Columbia University Press, 1924, pp. 87–88.
2. See, for instance, *The World Almanac and Book of Facts,* 1989, p. 373.
3. See A. Seth Pringle-Patterson, *The Philosophical Radicals and Other Essays,* Edinburgh: William Blackwood and Sons, 1907, and Elie Halevy, *The Growth of Philosophic Radicalism,* London: Allen & Unwin, 1928.
4. Jeremy Bentham, *An Introduction to the Principles of Morals and Education,* London: 1787, reprinted in Mary Peter Mack, ed., *A Bentham Reader,* New York: Pegasus, 1969, pp. 85–86. The italics are Bentham's.
5. For a good, concise review of Bentham on utilitarianism, see Alan Ryan, ed., *John Stuart Mill and Jeremy Bentham: Utilitarianism and Other Essays,* New York: Viking Penguins, 1987, pp. 43–60.
6. Jeremy Bentham, *A Fragment on Government,* 1776, reprinted in Mack, op. cit., p. 62–63.
7. For commentary on Bentham's work, see, among others, Eric Halévy, *The Growth of Philosophical Federalism,* London: Faber, 1972; John Plamenatz, *The English Utilitarians,* 2nd ed., Oxford: Basil Blackwell, 1958; Leslie

Stephen, *The English Utilitarians,* London: Duckworth & Co., 1900; Bhikhu Parekh, ed., *Bentham's Political Thought,* London: Croom Helm, 1973; David Baumgardt, *Bentham and the Ethics of Today,* Princeton, N.J.: Princeton University Press. See also Neff. op. cit., pp. 61–147. An intriguing view of Bentham can be found also in the study by his disciple, John Stuart Mill, *Mill on Bentham and Coleridge,* with an introduction by F. R. Leavis, London: Chatto and Windus, 1950. See also Ryan, op. cit.

8. Pringle-Patterson, op. cit., p. 6.
9. Plamenatz, op. cit., pp. 83–88.
10. See, for instance, John Rawls, *A Theory of Justice,* Oxford: Oxford University Press, 1972.
11. Quotes from Mack, op. cit., p. viii.
12. Mill, op. cit., p. 93.
13. For discussion of these points, see especially Neff, op. cit., pp. 72–78; and Mack, pp. xii–xix.
14. Mack, op. cit., p. x.
15. Ibid., p. xxv.
16. Ibid.
17. Bentham, *Fragment,* in Mack, op. cit., p. 44.
18. Bentham, *Introduction,* chap. 10, "Of Motives," in Mack, op. cit., 107–113.
19. Ryan, op. cit., pp. 8–9.
20. Bentham, *Introduction,* chap. 12, "Of the Consequences of a Mischievous Act," in Mack, op. cit., pp. 117–120.

24 Radical Economies and the Rise of Capitalism

1. A. J. Beitzinger, *A History of American Political Thought,* New York: Dodd Mead, 1972, pp. 189–193.
2. Adam Smith, *A Theory of Moral Sentiments,* pp. 303–305, reprinted in Benjamin A. Rogge, ed., *The Wisdom of Adam Smith,* selected and edited by John Haggarty, Indianapolis: Liberty Press, 1976, p. 125.
3. Adam Smith, *Wealth of Nations,* p. 423, excerpted in Rogge, op. cit., pp. 123–124. An excellent, relatively brief, segment from the book can be found reprinted in L. Earl Shaw, ed., *Modern Competing Ideologies,* Lexington, Mass.: Heath, 1973, pp. 236–248.
4. Graeme C. Duncan, *Marx and Mill: Two Views of Social Conflict and Social Harmony,* Cambridge: Cambridge University Press, 1973, p. 253.
5. Ayn Rand, with Nathaniel Branden, *The Virtue of Selfishness: A New Concept of Egotism,* New York: Signet Books, 1964.
6. Rogge, op. cit., p. 50.
7. Ibid., p. 51.
8. Thomas R. Malthus, *Essay upon Population,* London: J. Johnson, 1798. For an excellent review of Malthus's works, see Leslie Stephen, *The English Utilitarians,* vol. 2, London: Duckworth & Co., 1900, pp. 137–185.
9. Stephen, op. cit., p. 148.
10. Ibid., p. 162.
11. Ibid., p. 147.
12. Malthus wrote: "Improvement in the condition of the great mass of the labouring classes should be considered as the main interest of society. To improve their condition, it is essential to impress them with the conviction that they can do much more for themselves than others can do for them, and

that the *only* source of permanent improvement is the improvement of their moral and religious habits." Cited in Stephen, pp. 174–180.

13. Ibid., p. 187.
14. David Ricardo, *Principles of Political Economy and Taxation,* London: G. Bell and Sons, 1891, p. 1.
15. Stephen, op. cit., p. 223.
16. Quoted in Emery Neff, *Carlyle and Mill: Mystic and Utilitarian,* New York: Columbia University Press, 1924, p. 87.
17. Quoted in George H. Sabine, *A History of Political Theory,* 3rd ed. New York: Holt, Rinehart and Winston, 1961, p. 690.
18. James Mill, "Liberty of the Press," article in a special supplement to the *Encyclopedia Britannica,* 1825, reprinted by J. Innes, London, n.d. See also Joseph Hamburger, *James Mill and the Art of Revolution,* New Haven, Conn.: Yale University Press, 1963, p. 28.
19. Neff, op. cit., p. 89.
20. Bertrand Russell, *A History of Western Philosophy,* New York: Simon and Schuster Touchstone, 1972, p. 776.
21. Neff, op. cit., p. 88.
22. Russell, op. cit., p. 777.
23. See Stephen, op. cit., passim; and A. Seth Pringle-Patterson, *The Philosophical Radicals and Other Essays,* Edinburgh: William Blackwood and Sons, 1907, pp. 7–8.
24. Neff, op. cit., pp. 143–144.

25 James Mill: The Press as Agitators

1. James Mills, "Liberty of the Press," in *Essays on Government, Jurisprudence, Liberty of the Press, and Law of Nations,* London: ca. 1825, pp. 14–15, excerpted in Joseph Hamburger, *James Mill and the Art of Revolution,* New Haven, Conn.: Yale University Press, 1963. p. 29.
2. Mill, op. cit., quoted in Hamburger, op. cit., p. 28.
3. Quoted in Hamburger, op. cit., p. 51n.
4. James Mill, letter to Albany Fonblanque, October 25, 1831, *Mill-Taylor Collection 49A,* British Library of Political and Economic Science, cited in Hamburger, op. cit., p. 61. Fonblanque was so enthusiastic for Benthamism that he named a son Jeremy after his mentor.
5. *Examiner,* September 25, 1831, quoted in Hamburger, op. cit., p. 62.
6. *Morning Chronicle,* September 19, 1831, quoted in Hamburger, op. cit., p. 63.
7. *Times* (London), October 3, 1831, quoted in Hamburger, op. cit., p. 64.
8. Joseph Parkes, letter to G. Grote (an early Bentham disciple), July 21, 1835, quoted in Hamburger, op. cit., p. 274. For an interesting, early examination of press power and public opinion, see G. C. Lewis, *An Essay on the Influence of Authority in Matters of Opinion,* London: 1849.
9. Alexis de Tocqueville, *Journeys to England and Ireland,* reprint, London: Faber and Faber, 1918, September 7, 1833, pp. 66–68, quoted in Hamburger, op. cit., pp. 263–264.
10. See, for instance, Edward Jay Epstein, *News from Nowhere,* New York: Random House, 1973.
11. Quoted in Hamburger, op. cit., p. 273.
12. Ibid., p. 281.

13. Joseph Parkes, letter to Edward Ellice, December 16, 1841, quoted in Hamburger, op. cit., pp. 281–282.
14. For a sketch of Cobbett, see Justin Wintle, ed., *Makers of Nineteenth Century Culture 1800–1914,* London: Routledge and Kegan Paul, 1982, pp. 123–124. See also Samuel Bradford, *The Imposter Detected, or, A Review of Some of the Writings of "Peter Porcupine" by Timothy Tickletoby: to which is Annexed A Refreshment for the Memory of William Cobbett,* Philadelphia: privately printed, 1796; and George Spater, *William Cobbett, the Poor Man's Friend,* London: Routledge and Kegan Paul, 1982.
15. Thomas Jefferson, letter to Samuel Smith, August 22, 1798, reprinted in Leonard W. Levy, ed., *Freedom of the Press from Zenger to Jefferson,* Indianapolis: Bobbs-Merrill, 1966, pp. 353–354. See also Edwin Emery and Michael Emery, *The Press and America: An Interpretive History of the Mass Media,* 4th ed., Englewood Cliffs, N.J.: Prentice-Hall, 1978, pp. 79–80.
16. Quoted in A. Seth Pringle-Patterson, *The Philosophical Radicals and Other Essays,* Edinburgh: William Blackwood and Sons, 1907, p. 21.

26 John Stuart Mill: Utilitarianism Revisited

1. Max Lerner, ed., *Essential Works of John Stuart Mill,* New York: Bantam Books, 1961, p. vii.
2. Isaiah Berlin, "John Stuart Mill and the Ends of Life," in *Four Essays on Liberty,* Oxford: Oxford University Press, 1984, p. 179. The essay was originally delivered as the Robert Whaley Cohen Memorial Lecture in London, December 2, 1959, on the 100th anniversary of Mill's birth.
3. Mill's *On Liberty* has been reprinted frequently, sometimes in separate volumes, sometimes in collections. It can be found in unabridged form in Lerner, op. cit., pp. 249–360.
4. George H. Sabine, *A History of Political Theory,* 3rd ed., New York: Holt, Rinehart and Winston, 1961, p. 709.
5. John Stuart Mill, *A System of Logic, Ratiocination and Inductive,* London: John W. Parker, p. 5. See also Graeme C. Duncan, *Marx and Mill: Two Views of Conflict and Social Harmony,* Cambridge: Cambridge University Press, 1973, p. 209.
6. Quoted in A. J. Mill, "The Education of John—Some Further Evidence," *Mill Newsletter,* no. 11 (Winter 1976), pp. 10–12. See also Peter Glassman, *J. S. Mill: The Evolution of a Genius,* Gainesville, Fla.: University of Florida Press, 1985, pp. 7–8.
7. John Stuart Mill, *The Autobiography of John Stuart Mill,* reprint, ed. Jack Stillinger, London: Oxford University Press, 1971. For the work of psychohistorians, see, among others, Glassman, op. cit.; Bruce Mazlish, *James and John Stuart Mill,* New York: Basic Books, 1975, and A. W. Levi, "The 'Mental Crisis' of John Stuart Mill," *Psychoanalytic Review,* 32 (January 1945):86–101. For a somewhat more charitable view, see Emery Neff, *Carlyle and Mill: Mystic and Utilitarian,* New York: Columbia University Press, 1924, pp. 181–182.
8. Berlin, op. cit., p. 175.
9. Glassman, op. cit., p. 10.

10. Levi, op. cit., is convinced that John Stuart grew up hating his father but without being able to recognize this feeling. Glassman op. cit., pp. 21–39, agrees and takes the position that Mill was the victim of a classical Oedipus syndrome.
11. Lerner, op. cit., p. xi. Lerner credits the phrase to Jacques Barzun.
12. Mill, *Autobiography,* p. 89. The most powerful of all influences in stirring Mill's dormant feeling were the *Mémoires d'un père* of Jean François Marmontel, whose moving passage about the death of his father brought Mill to tears as he thought for the first time of the potential death of his own father. Levi says Mill's crisis resulted from a repressed death wish toward his father that he could now release, and he thus was enabled to express his feelings as well as his tears. Glassman agrees. See Levi, op. cit., p. 94; and Glassman, op. cit., p. 89.
13. On the dedication page of *On Liberty,* Mill wrote: "Were I but capable of interpreting to the world one half of the great thoughts and noble feelings which are buried in her grave, I should be the medium of a greater benefit to it than is ever likely to arise from anything that I can write, unprompted and unassisted by her all but unrivaled wisdom." Quoted in Lerner, op. cit., p. xv.
14. Neff, op. cit., p. 184.
15. John Stuart Mill, *Essay on Bentham, London and Westminster* Review, 1838, reprinted in Alan Ryan, ed., *John Stuart Mill and Jeremy Bentham: Utilitarianism and Other Essays,* New York: Viking Penguin, 1987, p. 172. See also F. R. Leavis, ed., *Mill on Bentham and Coleridge,* London: Chatto and Windus, 1950.
16. Ryan, op. cit., pp. 17–18.
17. Mill, *On Bentham,* in Ryan, op. cit., p. 172.
18. Ibid., pp. 173–174.
19. John Stuart Mill, *Utilitarianism,* London: 1863, reprinted in Ryan, op. cit., pp. 303–304. The italics are Mill's.
20. Mill. *On Bentham,* in Ryan, op. cit., pp. 149–150.
21. Bertrand Russell, *A History of Western Philosophy,* New York: Simon and Schuster Touchstone, 1972, p. 778.
22. Mill, *On Bentham,* in Ryan, op. cit., p. 151.
23. John Stuart Mill's *Essay on Coleridge,* reprinted in Ryan, op. cit., p. 189.
24. Ibid., p. 178.
25. Ibid., pp. 183–184.

27 The Gospel of Liberty

1. John Stuart Mill, *Essay on Liberty,* London: 1859, reprinted in Max Lerner, ed., *Essential Works of John Stuart Mill,* New York: Bantam Books, 1961, p. 266. Lerner describes Mill's "religion" in these words: "[He] wants to extract the 'essence' of religion from its supernatural trappings. The essence turns out to be . . . the religion of humanity—or, as it now tends to be called, humanist religion." (p. xxvii).
2. Ibid., p. 263.
3. Ibid., p. 269.
4. Ibid.

5. Ibid., p. 315.
6. Ibid., p. 321.
7. Isaiah Berlin, "John Stuart Mill and the Ends of Life," in *Four Essays on Liberty,* Oxford: Oxford University Press, 1984, p. 193.
8. It was for this reason that Mill described himself as a man of "no system." *Autobiography of John Stuart Mill,* ed. Jack Stillinger, London: Oxford University Press, 1971, p. 136. See also Graeme C. Duncan, *Marx and Mill: Two Views of Conflict and Social Harmony,* Cambridge: Cambridge University Press, 1973, p. 211.
9. John Stuart Mill, *Utilitarianism,* London: 1863, reprinted in Alan Ryan, ed., *John Stuart Mill and Jeremy Bentham: Utilitarianism and Other Essays,* New York: Viking Penguin, 1987, pp. 234–238.
10. Ryan, op. cit., p. 43.
11. Berlin, op. cit., pp. 187–189.
12. Mill, *On Liberty,* p. 280.
13. Berlin, op. cit., p. 205.
14. John Stuart Mill, "Law of Libel and Liberty of the Press," reprinted in G. L. Williams, ed., *John Stuart Mill on Politics and Society,* Hassock, England: Harvester Press, 1975, p. 169. The essay appeared originally in *Westminster Review,* 3 (1825).
15. Emery Neff, *Carlyle and Mill: Mystic and Utilitarian,* New York: Columbia University Press, 1924, pp. 33–37. The articles in question appeared in *Fraser's* magazine, Mill's under the title, *The Negro Question.* Neff's book is an intriguing study of these two powerful figures in the intellectual life of nineteenth-century Britain.
16. John Stuart Mill., *Principles of Political Economy,* quoted in op. cit., p. xxiii.
17. Lerner, op. cit., p. 252.
18. John Stuart Mill, "On Miss Martineau's Summary of Political Economy," *Monthly Repository,* (May 1834):320.
19. John Stuart Mill, "Centralization," *Edinburgh Review,* 115 (April 1862): p. 342. See also Duncan, op. cit., pp. 248–250.

28 Marx and the Other Side of Synthesis

1. See Chapter 22 for an examination of Hegel's ideas.
2. Karl Marx and Friedrich Engels, *The Holy Family,* trans. R. Dixon, Moscow: 1956 [originally published in 1845], p. 24, quoted in Graeme C. Duncan, *Marx and Mill: Two Views of Conflict and Social Harmony,* Cambridge, Cambridge University Press, 1973, p. 59.
3. For an excellent analysis of this distinction, see Alan Ryan, "Marx and the Philosophers: More Like Milton's Satan Than an Agnostic," *Listener,* May 8, 1986, pp. 13–14.
4. See J. Herbert Altschull, *Agents of Power: The Role of News Media in Human Affairs,* New York: Longman, 1984, pp. 85–98, for an account of Marx's life, with special emphasis on his press ideology. See the bibliographic notes, pp. 316–318.
5. Karl Marx and Friedrich Engels, *The German Ideology,* 1846, quoted in Philip Corrigan, Harvie Ramsay, and Derek Sayer, *Socialist Construction and Marxist Theory: Bolshevism and its Critics,* New York: Monthly Review Press, 1978, pp. 22–23.

6. See Altschull, op. cit., pp. 95–97, for a discussion of the problem of translating Marx's writings from German to English.
7. See Karl Korsch, *Marxism and Philosophy,* New York: Monthly Review Press, 1970, p. 48. Korsch's study appeared originally in the form of four essays published between 1922 and 1930.
8. Karl Marx and Friedrich Engels, preface to *Critique of Political Economy,* 1859, cited in Erich Fromm, *Marx's Concept of Man,* New York: Frederick Ungar, p. 74. Fromm considers this commentary superficial on the ground that, in later works, Marx continued the patterns of philosophical thought that he had demonstrated in earlier works such as his *Philosophical and Economic Manuscripts,* published in 1844. Ryan, op. cit., p. 14 tends to agree, although offering a different analysis: "When Marx rejected the philosophy he had grown up on, it was a rejection of moralising; indeed, in his eyes, it was a rejection of 'morality.' "
9. Ryan, op. cit., p. 13.
10. Fromm, op. cit., p. 39.
11. Korsch, op. cit., p. 152.
12. Fromm, op. cit., p. 5.
13. Ryan, op. cit., p. 14.
14. Of the many biographies of Marx, the one that best blends together a study of his life and his philosophy is Isaiah Berlin, *Karl Marx: His Life and Environment,* London: Oxford University Press, 1963. See also Korsch, op. cit. For a compendium of Marx's writings, see John Lachs, *Marxist Philosophy, a Bibliography,* London: Oxford University Press, 1968.
15. Fromm, op. cit., pp. 48–49.
16. Marx's economic theories have been discussed in many places, not always with the same interpretation. For a clear, concise description, see Duncan, op. cit., pp. 97–138.
17. Ibid., pp. 154–155.
18. For discussions of the press in Marxist ideology, see, among others, Altschull, op. cit., pp. 93–97; and Patrick Daley, and John Solosky, "Marxism and Communication," paper presented at the annual convention of the Association for Education in Journalism, Seattle, 1978.
19. See Henry M. Christian, *The American Journalism of Marx and Engels: A Selection,* New York: New American Library, 1966.
20. Quoted in Altschull, op. cit., p. 91.
21. Ibid., p. 92. See also Lloyd D. Easton, and Kurt H. Guddat, eds., *Writings of the Young Marx on Philosophy and Society,* Vol. 1, Garden City, N.Y.: Doubleday, 1967, p. 146.
22. Karl Marx, *Das Kapital,* London: Swañ Soññeñscheiñ, Lowrey, 1887, 1:609.
23. Friedrich Engels, *Anti-Duehring,* Moscow: 1959, cited in Andrew Collier and Timothy O'Hargan, *Social and Political Philosophy,* Atlantic Highlands, N.J.: Humanities Press, p. 58. Robert Kilroy-Silk, *Socialism Since Marx,* Harmondsworth: Penguin Books, 1972, p. 4, considers Engels's *Anti-Duehring* the best general summary of Marxism.
24. Kilroy-Silk, op. cit., p. 5.
25. Felix Oppenheim, *Moral Principles in Political Philosophy,* New York: Random House, 1968, p. 54.
26. W. A. Kaufman, "Wants, Needs, and Liberalism," *Inquiry,* 14, no. 3 (Autumn 1971): 202.

27. Duncan, op. cit., p. 293.
28. Jacob Talmon, *The Rise of Totalitarian Democracy,* Boston: Beacon Press, 1952, p. 254.
29. J. Salwyn Schapiro, "Comment on Lewis Feuer's Discussion of John Stuart Mill and Marxian Socialism,'" *Journal of the History of Ideas* 4 (1943):304.
30. Marx, *Das Kapital,* pp. 610–611. See Duncan, op. cit., pp. 293–294.

PART VI THE MASS SOCIETY: CAPITALISM AND DARWINISM

29 Introduction: The Land of Unlimited Opportunity

1. For an account of the importance of schools and associations in the development of the American social order, see Peter Dobkin Hall, *The Organization of American Culture, 1700–1900: Private Institutions, Elites, and the Origins of American Nationality,* New York: New York University Press, 1984. See also Carl Kaestle, *Pillars of the Republic: Common Schools and American Society 1780–1860,* New York: Hill and Wang, 1983.
2. Jakob Burckhardt, *Kultur und Macht,* ed. Michael Freund, Potsdam: Alfred Protte, 1934, quoted in Peter Viereck, *Conservativism Revisited: The Revolt Against Revolt,* New York: Scribner's, 1949, pp 34–36, 143. "My picture of the terrible simplifiers who will overrun Europe," Burckhardt wrote before World War I, "is no pleasant one . . . Naked force in command, and the silencing of opposition . . . This power can derive only from evil . . . Long voluntary subjection under individual Fuehrers is in prospect." For additional on Burckhardt's views, see his *Force and Freedom,* New York: Pantheon Books, 1943.

30 Walt Whitman and the Gospel of America

1. Bertrand Russell, *A History of Western Philosophy,* New York: Simon and Schuster Touchstone, 1945, p. 746.
2. Vernon L. Parrington, in his *Main Currents in American Thought,* 3 vols, New York: Harcourt Brace, 1958, 2:86, calls him "the greatest [figure] assuredly in our literature." The first two volumes of Parrington's monumental work were published in 1927, the third posthumously in 1930. Volume 2 is subtitled *The Beginnings of Critical Realism in America, 1860–1920.* The first edition of Whitman's classic contribution to American poetry, *Leaves of Grass,* hereafter cited as LOG, was published in 1855. Whitman revised it continually and the final edition appeared in 1892, the year of his death. The literature on Whitman is extensive. We have relied heavily on the excellent biography by Justin Kaplan, *Walt Whitman: A Life,* New York: Simon and Schuster Touchstone, 1986. For a brief sketch, see Parrington, op. cit., 3:69–86.
3. Cited in Horace Traubel, *With Walt Whitman in Camden,* 5 vols., Philadelphia: University of Pennsylvania Press (1906–1964), 1:13.
4. Whitman judged Paine a great man who was "double-damnably lied about." See Moncure D. Conway, *The Writings of Thomas Paine,* New York: AMS

Press, 1967, 2:422–423. Conway cites a poetic tribute to Paine from Whitman. See also Kaplan, op. cit., p. 57, 116–117.

5. For an excellent examination of the influence of Whitman's journalism on his artistry as a poet, see Shelley Fisher Fishkin, *From Fact to Fiction: Journalism and Imaginative Writing in America,* Baltimore, Johns Hopkins University Press, 1985, pp. 13–51. See also Kaplan, op. cit., passim. Another Whitman biographer, Paul Zweig, *Walt Whitman: The Making of a Poet,* New York: Basic Books, 1984, pp. 3–4, expresses utter contempt for Whitman's journalism, which he describes as "drab." Zweig surprisingly questions whether Whitman in fact wrote some of the articles attributed to him.
6. Unless otherwise identified, citations from Whitman's *Leaves of Grass* are from the first edition published in 1855 and reprinted in Malcolm Cowley, ed., *Leaves of Grass,* New York: Penguin Books, 1975.
7. Kaplan, op. cit., p. 248; Traubel, op. cit., 1:249.
8. Kaplan, op. cit., passim.
9. Ibid., p. 104.
10. Ibid., p. 128. The citation is drawn from an article in the *Brooklyn Eagle*.
11. As, for example, in this excerpt from Whitman's report about approaching a fire scene ("Scenes of Last Night," *New York Aurora,* April 1, 1842): "Puddles of water and frequent lengths of hosepipe endangered the pedestrian's safety: and the hubbub, the trumpets of the engine foreman, the crackling of the flames, the lamentations of those who were made homeless by the conflagration all sounded louder and louder as we approached, and at least grew to one continued and deafening din. . . . The most pitiful thing in the whole affair was the sight of shivering women, their eyes red with tears, and many of them dashing wildly through the crowd, in search, no doubt, of some member of their family, who, for what they knew, might be buried 'neath the smoking ruins nearby." Reprinted in Fishkin, op. cit., pp. 20–21.
12. "Life in a New York Market," *New York Aurora,* March 16, 1842, reprinted in Fishkin, op. cit., p. 15.
13. *New York Evening Post,* July 27, 1851, cited in Emory Holloway, ed., *The Uncollected Poetry and Prose of Walt Whitman,* Garden City, N.Y.: Doubleday, Page, 1921, p. 248.
14. Whitman, LOG, p. 5.
15. Ibid. LOG, p. 5.
16. Ibid., p. 26. On the second page, Whitman wrote the following, which although not so intended is clearly good advice for the journalist:

Stop this day and night with me and you shall possess the origin of all poems. . . .
You shall no longer take things at second or third hand . . . nor look through the eyes of the dead . . . nor feed on spectres in books,
You shall not look through my eyes either, nor take things from me,
You shall listen to all sides, and filter them from yourself.

17. Kaplan, op. cit., p. 300.
18. Whitman, introduction to LOG, in C. J. Furness, ed., *Walt Whitman's Workshop,* Cambridge, Mass.: Harvard University Press, 1928, p. 171.
19. Kaplan, op. cit., p. 228. See also Richard Maurice Bucke, *Notes and Fragments,* London: A. Talbot & Co., 1899, p. 57.
20. Whitman, LOG, 3rd ed., Quoted in Kaplan, op. cit., p. 228.

21. Leo C. Rosten, *The Washington Correspondents,* New York: Arno Press, 1984, p. 6.
22. Furness, op. cit., pp. 56–62.
23. Daniel J. Czitrom, *Media and the American Mind: From Morse to McLuhan,* Chapel Hill: University of North Carolina Press, 1982, p. 37.
24. Walt Whitman, *Democratic Vistas,* New York: J.S. Redfield, 1871, p. 43.

31 The Press and Frontier Society

1. I am indebted for this classification of perceptions of the differences between the New and Old World to Gene Wise, *American Historical Explanations: A Strategy for Grounded Inquiry,* Homewood, Ill.: Dorsey Press, 1973, p. 191.
2. The title of Turner's paper was "The Significance of the Frontier in American History." It was published in the 1983 AHA *Annual Report,* Washington, D.C.: 1984, pp. 199–227. For an examination of Turner's writings and comments both favorable and unfavorable, see Ray Allen Billington, *The Frontier Thesis: Valid Interpretation of American History?* New York: Holt, Rinehart, 1966, which reprints the original essay on pp. 9–20. The introduction by Billington provides a good summary of the extensive literature on the Turner thesis.
3. John Higham, "The Divided Legacy of Federick Jackson Turner," in his *Writing American History: Essays on Modern Scholarship,* Bloomington: Indiana University Press, 1970, pp. 118–129. The citation here is to be found on p. 121. Higham's analysis is brief and perceptive.
4. Robert W. Jones, *Journalism in the United States,* New York: Dutton, 1947, p. 227. See also Maria Cooper, *Horace Greeley als publizistische Persoenlichkeit,* Duesseldorf: Rheinisch-Bergische Druckerei, 1966, p. 104. Henry Luther Stoddard, *Horace Greeley: Printer, Editor, Crusader,* New York: Putnam's, 1946, p. 40, notes that the New York editor was known to many as "Go-West Greeley" after he launched his campaign in 1837.
5. For more on Greeley, see, among others, Glyndon G. Van Deusen, *Horace Greeley: Nineteenth Century Crusader,* Philadelphia: University of Pennsylvania Press, 1953; Luther D. Ingersoll, *The Life of Horace Greeley,* New York: Beekman, 1974 (a reprint of the 1873 edition); Constance Rourke, *Trumpets of Jubilee, Henry Ward Beecher, Harriet Beecher Stowe, Lyman Beecher, Horace Greeley, P. T. Barnum,* New York: Harcourt, Brace and World Harbinger Books, 1927 and 1963, pp. 180–275; and Vernon L. Parrington, *Main Currents in American Thought,* vol. 2, New York: Harcourt Brace, 1927, pp. 238–249. I am especially in debt to Constance Rourke's excellent study.
6. Justin Kaplan, *Walt Whitman: A Life,* New York: Simon and Schuster Touchstone, 1986, p. 248. Many other critics pilloried Whitman, especially for his frank sexual references. In that Victorian Era, the mere mention of nakedness or the limbs of the body was taboo. Women's sexuality, Kaplan notes, "was an unholy secret" (see pp. 248–250). Emerson's complaint was not with the content of "Children of Adam" but with the problems in marketability Whitman was imposing on himself.
7. James Oliver Robertson, *American Myth, American Reality,* New York: Hill and Wang, 1980, pp. 147–148.
8. Ibid., p. 151: " 'Mobility'—physical, social, economic, tied together by belief and practice—for Americans is both symbol and reality of the free, indepen-

dent individual. The lives Americans actually lead are often immobile and frustrating. Physical and economic mobility are not, and have not actually been, very great. But the reality is not so important to Americans as the symbols and logic with which they perceive the reality. They *believe* they are mobile so strongly that mobility has been a constant in descriptions of Americans life by Americans and by foreigners. And the belief has, for two hundred years or more, been reinforced by stories, histories, and statistics of Americans on the move."

9. *Columbia-Viking Desk Encyclopedia,* 3rd ed., New York: Viking Press, 1968, 1:503. See also Charles Sellers, and Henry May, *A Synopsis of American History,* 2nd ed., Chicago: Rand McNally, 1969, p. 255.
10. Abraham S. Eisenstadt, *American History: Recent Interpretations,* 2nd ed., New York: Crowell, 1970, 2:169.
11. The phrase was originated by Stewart G. Cole and Mildred Wiese Cole in their *Minorities and the American Promise,* New York: Harper, 1954, chap. 6.
12. Adams's letter, in answer to a query posed by one Baron von Fuerstenwaerther, was published in *Niles' Weekly Register,* 18 (April 29, 1820): 157–158.
13. Ibid.
14. Quoted by Stuart P. Sherman in his introduction to *Essays and Poems of Emerson,* New York: Harcourt Brace, 1921, p. xxxi. See also Milton M. Gordon, "Assimilation in America: Theory and Reality," *Daedalus,* 90 (Spring 1961): 263–285. Reprinted in Lawrence W. Levine, and Robert Middlekauff, *The National Temper: Readings in American History,* New York: Harcourt, Brace, 1968, pp. 265–284; the Emerson quotation is cited on p. 274.
15. "Our Country's Future," *Chicago Tribune,* September 28, 1864, cited in John Higham, *Strangers in the Land: Patterns of American Nativism 1858–1925,* 2nd ed., New York: Atheneum, 1969, p. 14. Higham's *Strangers* is the well-deserved classic in the field.
16. *New York Times,* June 2, 1874, cited in Higham, *Strangers,* p. 47.
17. For a summary of Emerson's thoughts, see the charming little pamphlet, *Emerson on Man and God,* Mount Vernon, N.Y.: Peter Pauper Press, 1961. See also Emerson's *Essays,* New York: Oxford University Press, 1936.
18. Carlyle's most influential works in America were his spiritual autobiography, *Sartor Resartus,* published in *Fraser's History Magazine,* 1833–1834, and *On Heroes, Hero-Worship, and the Heroic in History,* London: Chapman and Hall, 1841. For trenchant analyses of Carlyle's ideas, see Sir Leslie Stephen, *History of English Thought in the Eighteenth Century,* 2 vols., 2nd ed., New York: Putnam's 1881; and Emery Neff, *Carlyle and Mill: An Introduction to Victorian Thought,* 2nd ed., New York: Columbia University Press, 1926. Isaiah Berlin classifies Carlyle and Marx as "great Victorian preachers." See his "John Stuart Mill and the Ends of Life," in *Four Essays on Liberty,* Oxford: Oxford University Press, 1984, p. 173.
19. Robert Lacey, *Ford: The Men and the Machine,* London: Heinemann, pp. 113–114, quoting from Emerson's *Essays,* op. cit., p. 93. Emerson taught Ford to learn from his weaknesses. He marked a page in Emerson's *Essays:* "It is more his interest than it is theirs (his enemies) to find his weak point." Lacey, p. 206.
20. Higham, *Strangers,* p. 9.
21. The bibliographic notes in Higham's *Strangers,* pp. 401–405, provide good hunting ground for those who wish to conduct research on the way the press

handled immigration issues. See also Milton M. Gordon, "Assimilation in America: Theory and Reality," *Daedalus,* 90 (Spring 1961): 163–185.

22. Stephan Thernstrom, "Urbanization, Migration, and Social Mobility in Late Nineteenth-Century America," in Barton J. Bernstein, ed., *Towards a New Past: Dissenting Essays in American History,* New York: Random House Pantheon Books, 1968, pp. 158–175. The citation here can be found on p. 160. See also Higham, *Strangers,* pp. 3–11, 91–96.
23. Charles B. Davenport, *Heredity in Relation to Eugenics,* New York: Holt, 1911, pp. 216–222. For an excellent study of the role of the eugenics movement in American life, see Daniel J. Kelves, *In the Name of Eugenics: Genetics and the Uses of Human Heredity,* New York: Alfred A. Knopf, 1985. Kelves provides a thorough portrait of Davenport and his influence: see especially pp. 44–56.
24. Kelves, op. cit., p. 111.
25. Ibid., p. 74.
26. Buck v. Bell, 247 U.S. 280 (1927). The case of Carrie Buck seems to have been largely overlooked by journalism scholars combing the Supreme Court files in civil liberties cases. Holmes, who had for years expressed fears about the potential impact of overpopulation on society, was 86 when he wrote (in an 8–1 decision): "We have seen more than once that the public welfare may call upon the best citizens for their lives. It would be strange if it could not call upon those who already sap the strength of the State for these lesser (!) sacrifices . . . in order to prevent our being swamped with incompetence . . . The principle that sustains compulsory vaccination is broad enough to cover cutting the Fallopian tubes. . . . Three generations of imbeciles are enough." See Henry J. Abraham, *The Judiciary: The Supreme Court in the Governmental Process,* 4th ed., Boston: Allyn & Bacon, 1977, pp. 65–66.
27. Madison Grant, *The Passing of the Great Race,* Scribner's, 1916, cited by Kelves, op. cit., p. 329. See also Higham, *Strangers,* pp. 143–144, 271–272. F. Scott Fitzgerald, in *The Great Gatsby,* New York: Scribner's, 1925, has his hero, Tom Buchanan, refer to what may have been Grant's book: "The idea is if we don't look out the white race will be—will be utterly submerged. It's all scientific stuff; it's been proved. . . . It's up to us, who are the dominant race, to watch out or these other races will have control of things." (p. 13).
28. Higham, *Strangers,* p. 65.
29. Ibid., pp. 52–54.
30. Ibid., p. 90.

32 Darwin and the Optimistic Society

1. Henry Adams, *The Education of Henry Adams,* New York: Random House Modern Library, 1931, pp. 237–238.
2. Van Wyck Brooks, *New England: Indian Summer,* New York: Dutton, 1946, p. 97.
3. Richard Hofstadter, *Anti-intellectualism in American Life,* New York: Macmillan, 1976.
4. Herbert Spencer, *The Principles of Biology,* published as vols. 2 and 3 of Spencer's *A System of Synthetic Philosophy,* New York: Appleton, 1896, 3:12.

See also Spencer's *Social Statics,* New York: Appleton, 1892–1897. Note that Darwin apparently endorsed this view. Bergen Evans, *Dictionary of Quotations,* New York: Delacorte Press, 1968, observes (p. 238): "Fittest was a word unfortunately adaptable to almost any value that anyone desired to repose in it. It was a long time before the chilling fact emerged that, in this context, it could mean 'fittest to survive.' "

5. Cited by A. J. Beitzinger, *A History of American Political Thought,* New York: Dodd, Mead, 1972, p. 405, from William Graham Sumner, "Earth Hunger or the Philosophy of Land Grabbing," in Albert G. Keller, and Maurice R. Davie, eds., *Essays of William Graham Sumner,* New Haven, Yale University Press, 1934, 1:174. For biography, see Harris E. Starr, *William Graham Sumner,* New York, H. Holt, 1925. On Social Darwinism generally, see Richard Hofstadter, *Social Darwinism in American Thought,* rev. ed., New York: Braziller, 1959.
6. Andrew Carnegie, "Wealth," *North American Review* 148, (June 1889): pp. 653–664. Reprinted in Gail Kennedy, ed., *Democracy and the Gospel of Wealth,* Lexington, Mass.: Heath, 1968, pp. 1–8. See also Beitzinger, op. cit., pp. 410–411, wherein he notes that the attempt to justify acquisition on theological or religious grounds were of two types, dignified and vulgar. For example, Russell H. Conwell (1843–1925) said in his popular lecture, "Acres of Diamonds," that it was a Christian duty to "get rich" and that "to make money honestly is to preach the gospel."
7. Hofstadter, *Social Darwinism,* pp. 31–32. For his evaluation of Spencer, see pp. 35–44.
8. Sidney Fine, *Laissez-Faire and the General-Welfare State: A Study of Conflict in American Thought, 1865–1901,* Ann Arbor, University of Michigan Press, 1956, p. 41. For his evaluation of Spencer, see pp. 32–46.
9. Hofstadter, *Social Darwinism,* pp. 31–32. Spencer became, Hofstadter wrote, "the metaphysician of the homemade intellectual, and the prophet of the cracker-barrel agnostic." To Spencer, God was irrelevant, the "Unknowable." It is curious that so many Protestant religious leaders were so positive about the preachings of Social Darwinism.
10. Lochner v. New York, 198 U.S. 45 (1905). Three years later, in Muller v. Oregon, 208 U.S. 412 (1908), the Supreme Court upheld an Oregon statute fixing a ten-hour work day as a minimum for women laundry workers. For an interesting account of the two cases, see John A. Garraty, ed., *Quarrels That Have Shaped the Constitution,* New York: Harper Colophon Books, 1966, pp. 176–190. See also Alfred H. Kelly, and Winfred A. Harbison, *The American Constitution: Its Origin and Development,* 3rd ed., New York: Norton, 1963, pp. 523–528.

33 Mass Society and a Mass Press

1. The first edition of Day's *Sun* appeared on September 3, 1833. See Edwin Emery and Michael Emery, *The Press and America: An Interpretive History of the Mass Media*, 4th ed., Englewood Cliffs, N.J.: Prentice-Hall, 1978, pp. 120–121.

2. For the wretchedness caused Whitman by the Civil War, see especially his *Democratic Vistas,* an 84-page pamphlet published in 1871. See also Justin Kaplan, *Walt Whitman: A Life,* New York: Simon and Schuster Touchstone, 1986, pp. 334–339.
3. For a brief history of the penny press, see Emery and Emery, op. cit., pp. 119–135, especially their bibliography, pp. 133–135.
4. For a balanced account of Alger (1834–1899) and his place in literary and political history, see Gary Scharnhorst, with Jack Bales, *The Lost Life of Horatio Alger,* Bloomington: Indiana University Press, 1985. For additional material on Alger, see Ralph D. Gardner, *Horatio Alger; or, The American Folk Era, including Road to Success: The Bibliography of the Works of Horatio Alger,* rev. ed., New York: Arco, 1978.
5. Emery and Emery, op. cit., pp. 128–130. See Greeley's *The Autobiography; or Recollections of a Busy Life,* new ed., Port Washington, N.Y.: Kennikat Press, 1971. The *Autobiography* first appeared in 1872.
6. See Constance Rourke *Trumpets of Jubilee,* New York: Harcourt, Brace and World Harbinger Books, 1927 and 1963.
7. Cited in Isaac C. Pray, *Memoirs of James Gordon Bennett and His Times,* New York: Stringer & Townsend, 1855, p. 37.
8. *New York Herald,* September 25, 1835.
9. Emery and Emery, op. cit., p. 432. See also Richard O'Connor, *The Scandalous Mr. Bennett,* New York: Doubleday, 1962, pp. 308–319.
10. Between 1821 and 1850, an estimated 2.5 million persons emigrated to the United States. See *The New York Times Encyclopedic Almanac* 1971, p. 192.
11. *New York Tribune,* April 19, 1841, quoted in Robert W. Jones, *Journalism in the United States,* New York: Dutton, 1947, p. 277; and Maria Cooper, *Horace Greeley als publizistische Persoenlichkeit,* Duesseldorf: Rheinisch-Bergische Druckerei, 1966, p. 150.
12. On Bennett's moral stance, see Emery and Emery, op. cit., p. 125. For lengthier treatments, see Pray, op. cit., pp. 264–282; Willard G. Bleyer, *Main Currents in the History of American Journalism,* Boston: Houghton Mifflin, 1927, pp. 293–296; and Frank Luther Mott, *American Journalism,* 3d ed., New York: Macmillan, pp. 236–237.
13. *New York Herald,* August 11, 1836.
14. For Franklin's views, see Chapter 16.
15. Greeley, *Autobiography,* p. 456.
16. *New York Tribune,* February 24, 1868, quoted in Bleyer, op. cit., p. 233.
17. Ibid.
18. Henry Steele Commager, *The Era of Reform 1830–60,* Princeton, N.J.: Van Nostrand, 1960, p. 29.
19. Quoted in Emery Holloway, *Whitman: An Interpretation in Narrative,* New York: Knopf, 1926, p. 7. See also Shelley Fisher Fishkin, *From Fact to Fiction: Journalism and Imaginative Writing in America,* Baltimore: Johns Hopkins University Press, 1985, p. 23.
20. Rourke, op. cit., pp. 199–200.
21. Quoted ibid., p. 200. Rourke goes on to say: "here was the poor lad risen to eminence, one of themselves; the American legend was crystallizing, and Greeley, with his rustic ostentation was composing it."

22. Vernon L. Parrington, *Main Currents in American Thought,* 3 vols., New York: Harcourt, Brace, 1954–1958, 3: passim.
23. Jonathan Beecher, *Charles Fourier: The Visionary and the World,* Berkeley: University of California, Press, 1987. For information on Fourier and his influence on Greeley and his friend Arthur Brisbane, see Rourke, op. cit., p. 194, 201–204, 208, 214, 219–222; Parrington, op. cit., 2:243; A. J. Beitzinger, *A History of American Political Thought,* New York: Dodd, Mead, 1972, pp. 346–347, and Leon P. Baradat, *Political Ideologies: Their Origins and Impact,* Englewood Cliffs, N. J.: Prentice-Hall, 1979, pp. 180–182.
24. For a brief account of the role of Brook Farm in the lives of Yankee individualists, see Parrington, op. cit., 2:338–342. Emerson, as Parrington points out, had little sympathy for Fourier, and called his system "the imagination of a banker." See also Katherine Burton, *Paradise Planters*, New York: AMS Press, 1973.
25. The accounts in the following works about Greeley's career as a journalist are all interesting, although with different emphases: Rourke, op. cit.; Maria Cooper, *Horace Greeley als publizistische Persoenlichkeit,* Duesseldorf: Rheinisch-Bergische Druckerei, 1966; Henry Luther Stoddard, *Horace Greeley: Printer, Editor, Crusader,* New York: Putnam's, 1946; and Glyndon G. Van Deusen, *Horace Greeley: Nineteenth Century Crusader,* Philadelphia: U. of Pennsylvania Press, 1953. See also standard journalism histories.
26. Rourke, op. cit., p. 211.
27. Ibid., pp. 246–247.

34 Localism and the Insular Frontier Press

1. Alexis de Tocqueville, *Democracy in America,* ed. Phillips Bradley, 2 vols., New York: Vintage Books, 1945, 1:193–194.
2. Ibid.
3. In 1840, the number of dailies published in the United States totaled 138 in a population of 17 million. By 1900, the totals had increased to 2,226 newspapers and a population of 76 million. See Alfred Lee McClung. *The Daily Newspaper in America,* New York: Macmillan, 1937, p. 718.
4. John Higham calls this America's "most cherished myth." See his "The Divided Legacy of Frederick Jackson Turner," in *Writing American History: Essays on Modern Scholarship,* Bloomington: Indiana University Press, 1970, p. 127. See also James Oliver Robertson, *American Myth, American Reality,* New York: Hill and Wang, 1980, passim.
5. William H. Taft, "Local Newspapers and Local History," in Ronald T. Farrar, and John Stevens, eds., *Mass Media and the National Experience,* New York: Harper and Row, 1971, p. 174.
6. Culver Smith, *The Press, Patronage and Politics,* Athens: University of Georgia Press, 1977, especially pp. 68–71.
7. Vernon L. Parrington, *Main Currents in American Thought,* vol. 3, New York: Harcourt, Brace, 1958, p. 376.
8. Ibid. Among Tarkington's best-known works are *The Magnificent Ambersons* (1899) and *Penrod* (1914).

9. Edwin Emery and Michael Emery, *The Press and America: An Interpretive History of the Mass Media,* 4th ed., Englewood Cliffs, N.J.: Prentice-Hall, 1978. See also Sally Foreman Griffith, New York: Oxford University Press, 1988.
10. J. Herbert Altschull, *Agents of Power: The Role of the News Media in Human Affairs,* New York: Longman, 1984, p. 68. See also William Allen White, *Autobiography,* New York: Macmillan, 1946.
11. The Kansas editorial appeared in the *Gazette* on August 16, 1896, the press freedom editorial on July 2, 1939.
12. Quoted in Constance Rourke, *Trumpets of Jubilee,* New York: Harcourt, Brace and World Harbinger Books, 1927 and 1963, p. 171.
13. Quoted in Horace Traubel, *With Walt Whitman in Camden,* 5 vols., Philadelphia: University of Pennsylvania Press, 1906–1964, 1:195. See also Justin Kaplan, *Walt Whitman: A Life,* New York, Simon and Schuster Touchstone, 1986, pp. 338–339; and Rourke, op. cit., p. 211.

PART VII: THE PRAGMATIC AMERICANS: REFORM AND DEMOCRACY

35 Introduction: Gloom Is Not Our Style

1. Quoted in John Higham, *American History: Essays on Modern Scholarship,* Bloomington: Indiana University Press, 1962, p. 93. Higham provides an excellent analysis of the final years of the nineteenth century, pp. 73–102. See also Donald Pizer, "Romantic Individualism in Garland, Norris and Crane," *American Quarterly,* 10 (Winter 1958): 463–475; and Kenneth S. Lynn, *The Dream of Success: A Study of the Modern American Imagination,* Boston: Little, Brown, 1955.
2. Higham, op. cit., pp. 91–94. See also Brook Adams, *The Law of Civilization and Decay: An Essay on History,* London: S. Sonnenschein, 1895; and Arthur Beringause, *Brooks Adams, A Biography,* New York: Knopf, 1955.

36 William James: The Rise of Pragmatism

1. See Arthur O. Lovejoy, "The Thirteen Pragmatisms," *Journal of Philosophy,* 5 (1908): 29–39. The article by Professor Lovejoy appeared one year after James published his classic work on pragmatism.
2. Charles Hartshorne and Paul Weiss, eds., *Collected Papers of Charles Sanders Peirce,* vol. 5, Cambridge, Mass.: Harvard University Press, 1931, p. 18: "In order to ascertain the meaning of an intellectual conception one should consider what practical consequences might conceivably result by necessity from the truth of that conception; and the sum of these consequences will constitute the entire meaning of the conception."
3. Thomas A. Seboek, "A Signifying Man," *New York Times Book Review,* March 30, 1986, pp. 14–15. Seboek was reviewing *The Semiotic of John Poinsot,* edited and translated by John N. Deely, with Ralph Austin Powell, Berkeley: University of California Press, 1986.

4. James's Berkeley lecture, "Philosophical Concepts and Practical Results," was delivered in 1898. For background material on the lecture, see Justin Kaplan, *Lincoln Steffens: A Biography,* New York: Simon and Schuster, 1974, pp. 29–30. For an exhaustive and dispassionate examination of James's philosophical thought, see Gerald E. Myers, *William James: His Life and Thought,* New Haven, Conn.: Yale University Press, 1986.
5. I am again indebted to John Higham's "American Culture in the 1890s," in *American History: Essays on Modern Scholarship,* Bloomington: Indiana University Press, 1962, for this analysis of the mood of the decade.
6. Ibid., pp. 98–99. See also John Burroughs, *Whitman: A Study*, New York: Haskell House, 1896, p. 223; William James, *The Varieties of Religious Experience: A Study in Human Nature*, New York: Longmans, Green, 1902, p. 84. See also Charles B. Willard, *Whitman's American Fame,* Providence, R.I.: Brown University Press, 1950.
7. Stuart Sutherland, review of *William James: His Life and Thought,* by Gerald E. Myers, *Listener,* January 15, 1987, pp. 21–22.
8. Ibid. Sutherland says James's work was flawed by a belief that man's thought should serve his moral instincts, "a belief that is scarcely the best road to scientific or even philosophical truth."
9. James's classic statement of his views is contained in his *Pragmatism,* a collection of the Harvard essays published in 1907 by Longmans, Green, New York. A reprint of important sections of that book, together with commentary and articles containing various pros and cons about pragmatism can be found in Gail Kennedy, ed., *Pragmatism and American Culture,* Lexington, Mass., D. C. Heath, 1950, in Heath's series on Problems in American Civilization. The reference to "a happy harmonizer" is to be found in *Pragmatism,* p. 66 (Kennedy, p. 20). For additional material on James see among others Myers, op. cit.; and Ralph Barton Perry, *The Thought and Character of William James,* Boston: Little, Brown, 1936. A good summary of the views of James and Dewey can be found in A. J. Beitzinger, *A History of American Political Thought,* New York: Dodd, Mead, 1972, pp. 461–481.
10. James, *Pragmatism,* p. 33, reprinted in Kennedy, op. cit., p. 9.
11. For James's views on Hegel, see his *The Will to Believe,* New York: Longmans, Green, 1897, pp. 294–295. See also Burleigh T. Wilkins, "James, Dewey, and Hegelian Idealism," *Journal of the History of Ideas,* 3 (1956): 336–338.
12. William James, *A Pluralistic Universe,* New York: Longmans, Green, 1909, pp. 238–241.
13. James, *Pragmatism,* p. 51, reprinted in Kennedy, op. cit., p. 14.
14. Ibid., p. 40 (Kennedy, p. 12).
15. Ibid., p. 70 (Kennedy, p. 20).
16. Ibid., p. 45 (Kennedy, p. 13). See also Ernst Cassirer, *Language and Myth,* New York: Dover, 1946; and John C. Condon, *Semantics and Communication,* 2nd ed., New York: Macmillan, 1975.
17. James, *Pragmatism,* p. 53, reprinted in Kennedy, op. cit., p. 15.
18. Bertrand Russell, *A History of American Philosophy,* New York: Simon and Schuster Touchstone, 1972, p. 818.
19. Ibid.
20. Sutherland, op. cit.
21. James, *Pragmatism,* p. 68, reprinted in Kennedy, op. cit., p. 19.
22. Ibid., p. 64 (Kennedy, p. 18).

23. Ibid., p. 76 (Kennedy, p. 22).
24. Ibid., p. 58 (Kennedy, p. 16).

37 John Dewey and the Press as Instrument

1. John Dewey, "Pragmatic America," *New Republic,* April 12, 1922, pp. 185–187, reprinted in Gail Kennedy, ed. *Pragmatism and American Culture,* Lexington, Mass.: D. C. Heath, 1950, p. 58. The writings of Dewey are vast, including some 30 books and hundreds of articles and monographs published during his lifetime. For a partial listing of Dewey's writings and commentary on him, see A. J. Beitzinger, *A History of American Political Thought,* New York: Dodd, Mead, 1972, p. 480 n. 18. An excellent portrait may be found in Sidney Hook, *John Dewey: An Intellectual Portrait,* Westport, Conn.: Greenwood Press, 1971 [originally published in 1939]. See also John J. McDermott, ed., *The Philosophy of John Dewey,* New York: Putnam's, 1973. To be read with profit is the section from the 1908 revised edition of Dewey's *Ethics,* chaps. 16 and 17, reprinted in John Somerville, and Ronald E. Santoni, eds., *Social and Political Philosophy,* Garden City, N.Y.: Doubleday Anchor, 1963, pp. 478–499.
2. John Dewey, *Liberalism and Social Action,* New York: Putnam's, 1935, p. 58. Critical excerpts are contained in the like-titled section reprinted in Kennedy, op. cit., pp. 94–111. This passage appears on p. 95.
3. John Dewey, *Reconstruction in Philosophy,* New York: Holt, 1920, pp. 86–121; *Essays in Experimental Logic,* New York: Dover, 1953, p. 30. See also Beitzinger, op. cit., p. 472; and Somerville and Santoni, op. cit., pp 488–490.
4. Dewey, *Reconstruction,* pp. 31–33; and Beitzinger, op. cit., p. 470. Dewey often quoted with approval Sir Francis Bacon's aphorism, "knowledge is power." Cf. Karl Marx, "Feuerbach's Thesis," reprinted in Erich Fromm, *Marx's Concept of Man,* New York: Praeger, 1961, p. 74. See Chapter 28.
5. Sidney, Kaplan, "Effects of World War I on Some Liberals," *Journal of the History of Ideas,* 17, no. 3 (1956): 348: "The fatal flaw of his own thought has been precisely the absence of usable policies." See also M. G. White, *Social Thought in America: The Revolt Against Formalism,* New York: Viking Press, 1949, p. 161.
6. Dewey, *Liberalism and Social Action,* p. 72, reprinted in Kennedy, op. cit., p. 101.
7. Ibid., p. 87, reprinted in Kennedy, op. cit., p. 108.
8. John Dewey, *Freedom and Culture,* New York: Putnam's, 1939, pp. 156–160.
9. Dewey: Liberalism and Social Action, op. cit., pp. 91–92, reprinted in Kennedy, op. cit., p. 110.
10. Dewey, reprinted in Somerville and Santoni, op. cit., *Ethics,* pp. 497–499. There is of course some similarity between Dewey's vision of democracy and the Marxist-Leninist image of a still-to-be-realized communistic future.
11. Ibid.
12. Bertrand Russell, *A History of Western Philosophy,* New York: Simon and Schuster Touchstone, 1972, p. 827.
13. George Santayana, (1863–1952), "Dewey's Naturalistic Metaphysics," reprinted in Richard C. Lyon, ed., *Santayana on America: Essays, Notes, and*

Letters on American Life, Literature, and Philosophy, New York: Harcourt, Brace and World, 1968, pp. 109–126. See also Paul A. Schilpp, *The Philosophy of George Santayana,* Evanston: Northwestern University Press, 1940, p. 522.

14. Russell, op. cit., p. 828.
15. Ibid.
16. Dewey, *Liberalism and Social Action,* p. 92, reprinted in Kennedy, op. cit., p. 110.
17. Mark Twain, *A Connecticut Yankee in King Arthur's Court,* rev. ed., with introduction by Justin Kaplan, Harmondworth, England: Penguin Books, 1986 [originally published in 1889], pp. 128–129.
18. Dewey, "Pragmatic America," reprinted in Kennedy, op. cit., p. 60.
19. John Dewey, "Green's Theory of the Moral Values," cited in Burleigh T. Wilkins, "James, Dewey, and Hegelian Idealism," *Journal of the History of Ideas* 3 (1956): 346. See also Dewey's "The Philosophy of T. H. Green," *Andover Review,* 11 (1889): 344–345.
20. Dewey, *Ethics,* chap. 5, "Historic Individualism," reprinted in Somerville and Santoni, op. cit., p. 479.
21. John Dewey, *Democracy and Education: An Introduction to the Philosophy of Education,* New York: Macmillan, 1916, p. 351, cited in Wilkins, op. cit., p. 341.
22. Dewey, *Ethics,* chap. 16, "Morals and Social Problems," reprinted in Somerville and Santoni, op. cit., p. 479.
23. Randolph Bourne *Education and Living,* New York: Century, 1917, p. 66, cited in Kaplan, op. cit., p. 360.
24. John Dewey, "No Matter What Happens—Stay Out," *Common Sense,* 8 (March 1939): 11, cited in Kaplan, op. cit., p. 362.

38 Journalists and Pragmatism

1. Ronald Steel, *Walter Lippmann and the American Century,* New York: Vintage Books, 1981, pp. 17–23.
2. Walter, Lippmann, "An Open Mind: William James," *Everybody's Magazine,* December 1910.
3. William James, *Pragmatism,* New York: Longmans, Green, 1907, p. 65, reprinted in Gail Kennedy, ed., *Pragmatism and American Culture,* Lexington, Mass.: D. C. Heath, 1950, p. 18.
4. Ibid., p. 67 (Kennedy, p. 19).
5. Ibid., p. 68 (Kennedy, p. 19).
6. Ibid.
7. Dennis Chase, "The Aphilosophy of Journalism," *Quill,* September 1971, p. 15.
8. Ibid.
9. Michael Schudson, *Discovering the News,* New York: Basic Books, 1978, pp. 6, 122. Schudson's book is an excellent review of the rise of the goal of objectivity among fact-oriented journalists.
10. James, *Pragmatism,* p. 62, reprinted in Kennedy, op. cit., p. 18.
11. Chase, op. cit., p. 15.
12. James was a great admirer of Godkin, at whose life and thoughts we take a closer look in Chapter 41. James wrote: "Godkin's was certainly the towering

influence in all thought concerning public affairs," quoted in Justin Kaplan, *Lincoln Steffens: A Biography,* New York: Simon and Schuster, 1974, p. 55.

13. J. Herbert Altschull, "What Is News?" *Mass Comm. Review,* Winter 1978, pp. 17–23. For a more detailed discussion, see Altschull, *Agents of Power: The Role of the News Media in Human Affairs,* New York: Longman, 1984, pp. 45, 224–238.
14. Quoted in Henry Nash Smith, *Mark Twain of the Enterprise: Newspaper Articles and Other Documents 1862–1884,* Berkeley: University of California Press, 1969, p. 160. This remark appeared in an article in *The Territorial Enterprise,* (Virginia City, Nev.) February 13, 1864.
15. Justin Kaplan, introduction to Mark Twain, *A Connecticut Yankee in King Arthur's Court,* rev. ed., Harmondsworth, England: Penguin Books, 1986, p. 22.
16. Justin Kaplan, *Walt Whitman: A Life,* New York: Simon and Schuster Touchstone, 1986, p. 27. Whitman's characterization of Twain: "He might have been something. He comes near something, but he never arrives." When 20 years after Whitman's death, Twain was asked to give a Senate committee a list of American authors whose work he considered of value, he simply left Whitman's name off the list. He also omitted the names of Melville, Thoreau, Hawthorne, and Henry James.
17. Shelley Fischer Fishkin, From Fact to Fiction: Journalism and Imaginative Writing in America: Baltimore, Johns Hopkins University Press, 1985, p. 66.
18. Ibid., p. 65.
19. Twain, *Yankee,* p. 249.
20. Fishkin, op. cit., pp. 60–61. Twain's story first appeared in the *Territorial Enterprise,* October 4, 1862.
21. Mark Twain, *Life on the Mississippi,* Boston: J. R. Osgood, 1883, pp. 375–376. See Fishkin, op. cit., p. 75.

39 Journalists and the Age of Reform

1. Quoted in Norman Pollack, "Populism: Realistic Radicalism," in Allen F. Davis, and Harold D. Woodman, eds., *Conflict or Consensus in American History,* Boston: Heath, 1966, p. 244.
2. Ibid., p. 245. See also Pollack's *The Populist Response to Industrial America,* Cambridge, Mass.: Harvard University Press, 1962.
3. Quoted in Pollack, "Populism," p. 248.
4. *New York Herald,* September 22, 1835.
5. William Allen White, "What's the Matter with Kansas," *Emporia Gazette,* August 16, 1896. In that essay, White wrote that the Populist party candidate for governor was nothing more than "an old mossback Jacksonian who snorts and howls because there is a bathtub in the State House."
6. See the notes to Chapter 14 for references on de Tocqueville. See Dickens' *American Notes for General Circulation,* Middlesex: Penguin Books, 1972, especially pp. 282–287.
7. Quoted in David Nord, "The Business Values of American Newspapers: The 19th Century Watershed in Chicago," *Journalism Quarterly,* 61, no. 2 (Summer 1984): 265–277. The cited passage from the *Chicago Tribune,* May 6, 1886, can be found on p. 270. For a more elaborate treatment of the theme,

see a similarly titled paper by Nord, delivered to the Qualitative Studies Division, Association for Education in Journalism, July 1982, mimeo. See also John Higham, *Strangers in the Land: Patterns of American Nativism 1858–1925,* 2nd ed., New York: Atheneum, 1969, pp. 52–96. For additional material on the Haymarket affair, see Henry David, *The History of the Haymarket Affair,* New York: Farrar & Rinehart, 1936.

8. Nord, op. cit., p. 272.
9. Several articles in the collection of Liebling articles titled *The Press,* New York: Ballantine Books, 1964, deal with the theme of press coverage of labor union activities. See, for instance, "The Great Gouamba," pp. 90–98, written December 7, 1946; and "The Impossible Headline," pp. 98–107, written October 18, 1947.
10. Nord, op. cit., p. 272.
11. Ibid. See also Michael Wallace, "The Uses of Violence in American History," *American Scholar,* vol. 40/41, 1971, pp. 81–102. See also Shalom Endelman, ed., *Violence in the Streets*, Chicago: Quadrangle, 1968, pp. 19–23.
12. William Allen White, *Autobiography,* New York: Macmillan, 1946. See the brief commentary by Richard Hofstadter, ed., in his *Great Issues in American History: A Documentary Record,* vol. 2, *1864–1957,* New York: Random House Vintage Press, 1958, pp. 173–174.
13. White, "What's the Matter with Kansas?" pp. 174–177.
14. The literature on Populism is substantial. It includes analyses by those, like Norman Pollack, who generally endorse Populist ideas, and those, like Richard Hofstadter, who see the Populist movement as retrograde rather than progressive. See, among others, the classic pro-Populism historical document, John D. Hicks, *The Populist Revolt,* Minneapolis: University of Minnesota Press, 1931; and the classic anti-Populist work, Hofstadter's *The Age of Reform,* New York: Knopf, 1956. Davis and Woodman, op. cit., include brief excerpts from Hofstadter's book as well as an excerpt from Thomas Cochran, and William Miller, *The Age of Enterprise,* New York: Macmillan, 1942. For a brief roundup of pro and con material, see Irwin Unger, ed., *Populism: Nostalgic or Progressive?* Chicago: Rand McNally, 1964. Little original material is available on the extensive examination of political and philosophical issues by the contemporary press.
15. Quoted in George Mowry, *The Era of Theodore Roosevelt 1900–1912,* New York: Harper & Row, 1958, excerpted in Davis and Woodman, op. cit., p. 302.
16. Ibid. The reference to free silver is to the centerpiece of the program of William Jennings Bryan, the Populist leader who three times lost out as the Democratic candidate for the presidency. Progressives, while endorsing reform, were hostile to Bryan. Their hero among Democrats was Woodrow Wilson.
17. The chief spokesman for this view among historians is Russell Nye. See his *Midwestern Progressive Politics,* East Lansing: Michigan State University Press, 1951, excerpted in Davis and Woodman, op. cit., pp. 304–314.
18. A leading spokesman for this view among historians is Mowry, op. cit. See also Robert Wiebe, *Business and Reform: A Study of the Progressive Movement,* Cambridge, Mass.: Harvard University Press, 1962; Richard Hofstadter, *Social Darwinism in American Thought,* New York: Braziller, 1959.
19. Hofstadter, *Age of Reform,* excerpted in Davis and Woodman, op. cit., p. 302.

20. See Walter Lippmann, *Drift and Mastery,* p. 189. See also Theodore Roosevelt, "Who Is A Progressive?" New Outlook, vol. 102 (1912), cited in Davis and Woodman, op. cit., p. 318.
21. Edwin Emery and Michael Emery, *The Press and America: An Interpretive History of the Mass Media,* 4th ed., Englewood Cliffs, N.J.: Prentice-Hall, 1978, pp. 364–368. See also Mowry, op. cit., excerpted in Davis and Woodman, op. cit., p. 314; Joseph Medill Patterson, *Little Brother of the Rich,* Chicago: Reilly and Britton, 1908, and his articles in the *Independent,* 61 (1906): 493–495, and the *Public,* April 8, 1905. For additional related material, see Simon M. Bessie, *Jazz Journalism,* New York: Dutton, 1938; and John Chapman, *Tell It to Sweeney: The Informal History of the New York Daily News,* New York: Doubleday, 1961.
22. Emery and Emery, op. cit., pp. 367–368.
23. Mowry, op. cit., excerpted in Davis and Woodman, op. cit., p. 325.
24. Eric Goldman, *Rendezvous with Destiny: A History of Modern American Reform,* New York: Knopf, 1932; see Davis and Woodman, p. 328. The contemporary leftist historian, John Chamberlain, in *Farewell to Reform,* New York: John Day, 1932, saw a darker side to Progressivism and regarded it as a forerunner to the fascism he saw arising.
25. Nye, op. cit., excerpted in Davis and Woodman, op. cit., pp. 311–314.

40 The Doctrine of the Right to Know

1. Quoted in Russell Nye, *Midwestern Progressive Politics,* East Lansing: Michigan State University Press, 1951, excerpted in Allen F. Davis and Harold D. Woodman, eds., *Conflict or Consensus in American History,* Boston: Heath, 1966, pp. 309–310.
2. John Dewey, *Liberalism and Social Action,* New York: Putnam's, 1935, p. 66, excerpted in Gail Kennedy, ed., *Pragmatism and American Culture,* Lexington, Mass.: D. C. Heath, 1950, p. 99. Dewey was, among other things, deploring a recent decision by the U.S. Supreme Court that seemed to him to go against freedom of expression. He especially applauded the dissenting opinion of Justice Louis D. Brandeis.
3. *The Public Interest and the Right to Know: Access to Government Information and the Role of the Press, A Selective Bibliographic Guide,* Boston Public Library, 1971, p. ii. This invaluable little monograph was meant to provide the layman with background reading in this field in preparation for the third annual New England Book Festival, which was dedicated to the theme, "Freedom to Write, Freedom to Print, Freedom to Publish."
4. Cooper's speech was given at a meeting of B'nai B'rith, on February 18, 1945. See the *New York Times,* February 19, 1945. See also Kent Cooper, *The Right to Know,* New York: Farrar, Strauss and Cudahy, 1956.
5. Harold L. Cross, *The People's Right to Know—Legal Access to Public Records and Proceedings,* New York: Columbia University Press, 1953.
6. Red Lion Broadcasting Co. v. Federal Communications Commission, 394 U.S. (1969).
7. Alexander Meiklejohn, *Free Speech and its Relation to Self-Government,* New York: Harper, 1948, reprinted in his *Political Freedom,* New York: Harper,

1960. p. 26. For a more recent, sturdy defense of the right-to-know doctrine, see Franklyn S. Haiman, *Speech and Law in a Free Society,* Chicago: University of Chicago Press, 1981.

8. Thomas I. Emerson, "Legal Foundations of the Right to Know." *Washington University Law Quarterly,* Vol. 1976, no. 1, p. 14.
9. Everette E. Dennis, and John C. Merrill, *Basic Issues in Mass Communication,* New York: Macmillan, 1984, p. 32.
10. Ibid.
11. Kurt Luedtke, article in *Bulletin of the American Society of Newspaper Editors,* May–June 1982, p. 16, and in "The Twin Perils: Arrogance and Irrelevance," speech at convention of American Newspaper Publishers Association, San Francisco, 1982.
12. On this subject, the writings of John C. Merrill are interesting. In *"The People's 'Right to Know' Myth," New York State Bar Journal* 45 (November 1973): 461–466, Merrill argued there was no such thing. In an essay published in 1984, he took the opposing position. See his "There Is a Right to Know," in Dennis and Merrill, op. cit., pp. 38–41. Dennis and Merrill provide an intriguing examination of a number of the questions considered in the present book. On each question, they offer opposing viewpoints. For other viewpoints in opposition to the right-to-know ideology, see Gerald J. Baldasty, and Roger A. Simpson, "The Deceptive 'Right to Know": How Pessimism Rewrote the First Amendment," *Washington Law Review,* 56: (1981): 365–395; Walter Gellhorn, "The Right to Know: First Amendment Overbreadth?" *Washington University Law Quarterly,* vol. 1976, no. 1: 25–28, and James C. Goodale, "Legal Pitfalls in the Right to Know," pp. 29–36.
13. Goodale, op. cit., p. 32.
14. Baldasty and Simpson, op. cit., pp. 393–394.
15. Holmes's assertion of the marketplace of ideas concept came in his dissenting opinion in Abrams v. United States, 250 U.S. 616 (1919). See discussion in J. Herbert Altschull, *Agents of Power: The Role of the News Media in Human Affairs,* New York: Longman, 1984, p. 21.
16. Federal Communications Commission v. Pacifica Foundation, 438 U.S. 726 (1978).
17. Emerson, op. cit., p. 2.
18. Ibid., p. 18.
19. Merrill, "There *Is* a Right to Know," p. 39.
20. Ibid., p. 38.

41 The Jubilee: The Patriotic Press

1. E. L. Godkin, "Aristocratic Opinions of Democracy," *North American Review,* January 1865.
2. See Chapter 20 on Burke.
3. Among these were President Charles W. Eliot of Harvard University, President Daniel Coit Gilman of Johns Hopkins, James Russell Lowell, James Bryce, and Charles Eliot Norton. See Edwin Emery and Michael Emery, *The Press and America: An Interpretive History of the Mass Media,* 4th ed., Englewood Cliffs, N.J.: Prentice-Hall, 1978, p. 189.

4. Vernon L. Parrington, *Main Currents in American Thought,* vol. 3, New York: Harcourt, Brace, 1958, p. 162.
5. *Nation,* January 30, 1873.
6. Stephan Thernstrom, "Urbanization, Migration, and Social Mobility in Late Nineteenth Century America," in Barton J. Bernstein, ed., *Towards a New Past: Dissenting Essays in American History,* New York, Random House Pantheon Books, 1968, p. 173.
7. Cited in Armin Rappaport, ed., *The War With Mexico: Why Did It Happen?* Berkeley: University of California Press, 1964, p. 1.
8. *New York Sun,* October 22, 1847, quoted in Rappoport, op. cit., p. 45. See also p. 47, where Rappoport quotes from the *Baltimore Sun,* October 15, 1847: "Would it not be an act of benevolence, clothed too with an inexpressible moral sublimity, to revolutionize such a state of things, and restore the powers of government to the sovereignty of the people?".
9. "The Mexican War Justified," *Brooklyn Daily Eagle,* May 11, 1846, quoted in Shelley Fisher Fishkin, *From Fact to Fiction: Journalism and Imaginative Writing in America,* Baltimore: Johns Hopkins University Press, 1985, p. 47. Nine years later, Whitman used some of the same war-justifying phraseology in *Leaves of Grass*. In the poem, the image generated, however, is one of horror, not of a causus belli. See Fishkin, op. cit., p. 48.
10. Stanley Elkins, *Slavery, A Problem in American Institutional and Intellectual Life,* Chicago: University of Chicago Press, 1959, pp. 193–222, especially p. 202.
11. Elkins, op. cit., pp. 205–206.
12. Donald L. Shaw, "News About Slavery from 1820–1860 in Newspapers of South, North and West," *Journalism Quarterly* 61, no. 3 (Autumn 1984): 483–492. Shaw's study of a random selection of newspapers shows that news items about slavery did not rise to above 10 percent of the Southern papers studied until 1845. From then until the outbreak of the war, the figure stood at more than 20 percent. No doubt Twain's *Huckleberry Finn,* published in 1884, was in part motivated by his dismay about the dehumanized way most newspapers reported the slavery matters.
13. Elkins, op. cit., p. 221.
14. Henry Clay Work, "Marching Through Georgia," Chicago: Root and Cody, 1865.
15. *The Shorter Oxford English Dictionary,* Vol. 1, s.v. "Jubilee."
16. The words appeared in W. G. Hunt's, poem, "We Don't Want to Fight," in 1878. "By Jingo," as a euphemism for "By God" or "By Jesus," was borrowed from the jargon of conjurers. Rabelais substituted "by jingo" for "par Dieu" in 1694. See *The Shorter Oxford English Dictionary,* s.v. "jingo."
17. *Nation,* February 24, 1898. The reference to two papers is to Hearst's *New York Journal* and to Pulitzer's *New York World.* Yellow journalism and the roles of Hearst and Pulitzer will be examined in Part 8.
18. The phrase is by Parrington, op. cit., p. 166.
19. The poem was written in 1898 and appeared on pp. 2–3 of the February, 1899, issue of *McClure's* magazine. It appeared in Kipling's collection, *The Five Nations,* in 1903. Among Kipling's output are such standbys as "Mandalay," "Gunga Din," and the "Recessional" for Queen Victoria's Diamond Jubilee in 1897. The most outspoken literary devotee of British imperialism, Kipling

was his nation's first Nobel Prize winner in literature (1907). For additional comment on Kipling, see Rutherford and the *Listener* review.

20. Kipling's poem was subtitled, "The United States and the Philippine Islands." According to Angus Wilson, *The Strange Ride of Rudyard Kipling: His Life and Works,* London: Secker and Warburg, 1977, p. 196, that poem and the "Recessional," written a year earlier, "turned a popular, very well-known writer into a controversial figure of world fame." This is a reference to the bitterness directed at Kipling by anti-imperialists. For the complete text, see *Rudyard Kipling's Verse, Definitive Edition,* New York: Doubleday, Doran & Co., 1940, pp. 321–323. R. Thurston Hopkins, *Rudyard Kipling: A Literary Appreciation,* New York: Frederick A. Stokes, 1915, p. 221, comments that within a decade the phrase, "the white man's burden," had become a stock reference for writers and speakers.
21. Roosevelt received an advance copy of "The White Man's Burden," in January 1899, and sent it to Senator Henry Cabot Lodge of Massachusetts, later a bitter opponent of President Woodrow Wilson's peace policy and of the League of Nations. Roosevelt commented in the letter that Kipling's work was "rather poor poetry, but good sense from the expansionist standpoint." See J. I. M. Stewart, *Rudyard Kipling,* New York: Dodd, Mead, 1955, p. 180.
22. Parrington, op. cit., p. 163.

PART VIII THE INVESTIGATIVE ROLE OF THE AMERICAN JOURNALIST

43 Introduction: An Essential Element

1. *New York World,* May 11, 1883. George Juergens, *Joseph Pulitzer and the New York World,* Princeton, N.J.: Princeton University Press, 1966, pp. 14–15.
2. W. S. Swanberg, *Citizen Hearst,* New York: Charles Scribner's, 1961, pp. 48–50. "By the time he had been editor for a year, the pink-cheeked young playboy, heir to a mining fortune, was recognized as the spokesman for "the people," the voiceless masses with whom he had not the slightest apparent kinship" (p. 50).
3. Lincoln Steffens, "Hearst, Man of Mystery," *American Magazine* 57 (November 1906): 14. See Justin Kaplan, *Lincoln Steffens: A Biography,* New York: Simon and Schuster, 1974, pp. 156–158, for a fine analysis of Hearst and the Steffens interview.
4. Quoted in Swanberg, op. cit., p. 195, from an undated letter in the year 1933 from Hearst to Mrs. W. J. Chalmers, presently in the archives of the Chicago Historical Society.
5. Steffens, op. cit., p. 11.
6. Swanberg, op. cit., p. 68.
7. Herbert J. Gans, *Deciding What's News: A Study of CBS Evening News, NBC Nightly News, Newsweek and Time,* New York: Vintage, 1980, pp. 39–69.
8. Herbert J. Gans, "The Messages Behind the News," in Michael C. Emery, and Ted Curtis Smythe, eds., *Readings in Mass Communication: Concepts and Issues in the Mass Media,* Dubuque, Iowa: William C. Brown, 1988, 6: 167–168.

9. Robert E. Park, "The Yellow Press," *Sociology and Social Research,* 12 (September–October 1927): 11.
10. W. J. Bryan and M. B. Bryan, *The Memoirs of William Jennings Bryan,* Philadelphia: John Winston, 1925, p. 299.
11. Lydia K. Commander, "The Significance of Yellow Journalism," *Arena,* 34 (August 1905): 151.
12. See Chapter 41.
13. Willard, G. Bleyer, *Main Currents in the History of American Journalism,* Boston: Houghton Mifflin, 1927, p. 303. For biographical material on Dana, see Frank M. O'Brien, *The Story of the Sun,* rev. ed., New York: Appleton-Century-Crofts, 1928; and Candace Stone, *Dana and the Sun,* New York: Dodd, Mead, 1938. For a critical view of Dana, see Vernon L. Parrington, *Main Currents in American Thought,* vol. 3, New York: Harcourt, Brace, 1958, pp. 43–47.
14. For a brief summary of the *Times'* role in the exposure of the Tweed government, see J. Herbert Altschull, *Agents of Power: The Role of the News Media in Human Affairs,* New York: Longman, 1984, pp. 76–77.
15. Will Irwin, part 3 of his series originally published in *Collier's* in October 1911, reprinted in Irwin's *The American Newspaper,* ed. Clifford F. Weigle, and David Clark, Ames, Iowa: University of Iowa Press, 1969, p. 17, col. 2.
16. Ronald Steel, *Walter Lippmann and the American Century,* New York: Random House Vintage, 1980, passim. Lippmann spent nine years at the *World* (1922–1931) and was the author of some 1,200 *World* editorials.
17. Quoted in Juergens, op. cit., pp. 70–71.
18. See Chapter 16, notes 10–14.
19. Lincoln Steffens, *The Autobiography of Lincoln Steffens,* New York: Harcourt, Brace, 1931, p. 587.
20. Ibid., p. 316.
21. Ibid., pp. 314–315.
22. Bleyer, op. cit., pp. 297–298. For Dana's views on what a journalist ought to be, see Charles A. Dana, *The Art of Newspaper Making,* New York: Appleton, 1895, pp. 29–65. He saw newspapers as a "great civilizing engine" and placed great emphasis on original literary style.
23. Irwin, op. cit., p. 15.

44 The Muckrakers as Watchdogs

1. See Chapter 32 for a discussion of Carnegie's Gospel of Wealth.
2. Bernard M. Weisenberger, *Reaching for Empire: The Life History of the United States,* vol. 8, New York: Time, Inc., 1964, p. 10.
3. For a dated but thorough report on the rapid changes in the face of the United States in the last half of the century, see Arthur M. Schlesinger, *Political and Social Growth of the American People,* New York: Macmillan, 1941.
4. Harold Wilson, *McClure's Magazine and the Muckrakers,* Princeton, N.J.: Princeton University Press, 1979. See also Robert Stinson, "S. S. McClure and His Magazine: A Study in Editing of *McClure's* 1893–1913," dissertation, Indiana University, Bloomington, 1972. See Theodore S. Greene, *American Heroes: The Changing Models of Success in American Magazines,* New York: Oxford University Press, 1970, p. 91, for McClure commentary on attacking the success syndrome.

5. Vernon L. Parrington, *Main Currents in American Thought,* vol. 3, New York: Harcourt, Brace and World, 1958, p. 406.
6. Louis G. Geiger, "Muckrakers—Then and Now," *Journalism Quarterly,* 43 (Autumn 1966): 469.
7. Lawson's article later was expanded into a successful book. See Thomas W. Lawson, *Frenzied Finance,* New York: Ridgway-Thayer, 1905.
8. Quoted in C. C. Regier, *The Era of the Muckrakers,* Chapel Hill: University of North Carolina Press, p. 130.
9. Quoted in Arthur Weinberg and Lila Weinberg, eds., *The Muckrakers: The Journalists Who Opened the Public's Eyes to Corruption Everywhere, and Shocked America into an Era of Reform,* New York: Capricorn Books, 1964, p. 121. The Weinbergs' book provides an outstanding collection of muckraker articles with clear, accompanying text.
10. For a brief summary of the essence of the muckraking movement, see J. Herbert Altschull, *Agents of Power: The Role of the News Media in Human Affairs,* New York: Longman, 1984, pp. 77–82. See the bibliographies in Altschull, pp. 314–315, and in Weinberg and Weinberg, op. cit., pp. 441–449.
11. Quoted in Weinberg and Weinberg, op. cit., pp. 4–5.
12. Quoted in Altschull, op. cit., p. 81.
13. Ray Stannard Baker, *American Chronicle: The Autobiography of Ray Stannard Baker,* New York: Scribner's, 1945, pp. 122–123. See also Altschull, op. cit., pp. 81, 314–315.
14. Weinberg and Weinberg, op. cit., pp. 205–206.
15. Upton Sinclair, *The Brass Check,* Muscatine, Iowa: Norman Baker, 1928, pp. 224. The original edition was published by Sinclair in Long Beach, Calif., in 1919.
16. Weinberg and Weinberg, op. cit., p. 433.
17. Ibid., pp. 427–428.
18. Justin Kaplan, *Lincoln Steffens: A Biography.* New York: Simon and Schuster, 1974, pp. 192–193.
19. Ibid., pp. 117–118.
20. Ronald Steel, *Walter Lippman and the American Century,* New York: Random House Vintage, 1980, p. 36.
21. Kaplan, op. cit., pp. 331–332: "Lincoln Steffens' bold thrust and Theodore Roosevelt's seemingly operatic parry prefigured a conflict of as yet unsettled dimension and outcome."

45 The Journalism Critics

1. David M. Rubin, "Liebling and Friends: Trends in American Press Criticism, 1859–1963," paper presented at session of Mass Communications and Society division, Association for Education in Journalism, Ottawa, August 16–19, 1975, p. 3. See also Michael J. Robinson, "Fifty Years in the Doghouse: Blaming the Press is Nothing New," *Washington Journalism Review,* March 1986, pp. 44–45; Les Brown, *The Reluctant Reformation: On Criticizing the Press in America,* New York: David McKay, 1974; and Tom Goldstein, ed., *Killing the Messenger: 100 Years of Media Criticism,* New York: Columbia University Press, 1989.

2. Lambert A. Wilmer, *Our Press Gang; or, A Complete Exposition of the Corruptions and Crimes of American Newspapers,* Philadelphia: J. T. Lloyd, 1859, p. 53.
3. Ibid.
4. Harriet Martineau, *The Martyr Age of the United States,* Boston: Weeks, Jordan & Co., 1839; and *The "Manifest Destiny" of the United States,* New York: Amsterdam Anti-Slavery Society, 1857.
5. Charles Dickens, *The Life and Adventures of Martin Chuzzlewit,* London: Thomas Nelson and Sons, n.d., p. 278. The book was originally published in 1844.
6. George Seldes, *Lords of the Press,* New York: Julius Messner, 1938, p. 183.
7. Oswald Garrison Villard, *How Stands Our Press?* no. 19 in the Human Events Pamphlet Series, Chicago: Human Events Associates, 1947, p. 10.
8. Silas Bent, *Ballyhoo,* New York: Boni and Liveright, 1927, p. 168. See also Rubin, op. cit., p. 13. For other press critics, see among others the celebrated critique of *New York Times* coverage of the Bolshevik Revolution by Walter Lippmann, Charles Merz, "A Test of the News; Some Criticisms," *New Republic,* September 8, 1920; Oswald Garrison Villard, *Some Newspapers and Newspapermen,* New York: Knopf, 1923 and 1926; and the 15-part series by the muckraking journalist Will Irwin that appeared in Collier's, in October 1911, later collected in Irwin's *The American Newspaper* ed. Clifford F. Weigle and David Clark, Ames, Iowa: Iowa State University Press, 1969.
9. Seldes, op. cit. Harold L. Ickes, *America's House of Lords,* New York: Harcourt, Brace, 1939, p. 11. Like many other presidential aides throughout history, Ickes was particularly critical of press coverage.
10. Upton Sinclair, *The Brass Check,* Muscatine, Iowa: Norman Baker, 1928 [originally published in 1919]. It was Sinclair's original intention to subtitle his book, "A Study of the Whore of Journalism." See Rubin, op. cit., p. 32.
11. Wilmer, op. cit., p. 150.
12. Hamilton Holt, *Commercialism and Journalism,* Boston: Houghton Mifflin, 1908, p. 75.
13. "What Is the Matter with the Press" *Forum,* April 1914, pp. 565–571.
14. Sinclair, op. cit., p. 437.
15. Villard, *Some Newspapers and Newspapermen,* pp. 11–12.
16. Rubin, op. cit., pp. 16–29.
17. Bent, op. cit., pp. 34–35.
18. Commission on Freedom of the Press, *A Free and Responsible Press,* Chicago: University of Chicago Press, 1947, pp. 43–44.
19. Rubin, op. cit., pp. 16–29.
20. Quoted on Ickes, op. cit., p. 11.
21. Cited in Rubin, op. cit., p. 26.
22. See A. J. Liebling, *The Wayward Pressman,* Garden City, N.Y.: Doubleday, 1947; and *The Press,* New York: Ballantine Books, 1961. Both are compendiums of Liebling's essays in the *New Yorker,* together with additional commentary. For a biography, see Raymond Sokolov, *Wayward Reporter: The Life of A. J. Liebling,* New York: Harper and Row, 1980.
23. "The Problem of the Associated Press," *Atlantic Monthly,* July 1914, pp. 132–137.
24. Sinclair, op. cit., pp. 87–88.

25. Irwin, op. cit., p. 15.
26. Quoted in Justin Kaplan, *Lincoln Steffens: A Biography,* New York: Simon and Schuster, 1974, pp. 97–98.
27. Howard Simons, and Joseph A. Califano, Jr., *The Media and Business,* New York: Vintage Books, 1979. This book reports the proceedings of an October 1977 weekend seminar of leaders from media and business, sponsored by the Ford Foundation. See also J. Herbert Altschull, "Journalist Aren't Anti-Business—They're Just Pro-Drama," *Business Horizons,* September–October 1972, p. 5.
28. Altschull, "Journalists Aren't Anti-Business," p. 5: "I mean to suggest that those voices being heard in the business community about a bias in the press against business are off the mark. The bias is against anything that is neither conflictual nor heart-warming."
29. Leo C. Rosten, *The Washington Correspondents,* New York: Harcourt, Brace, 1937, p. 6.
30. Among the distinguished studies of opinions and attitudes of journalists, see Jeremy Tunstall, *Journalists at Work: Specialist Correspondents, the News Organizations, News Sources and Competitors-Colleagues,* London: Constable, 1971. See also Leon V. Sigal, *Reporters and Officials: The Organization and Politics of Newsmaking,* Lexington, Mass.: Heath, 1973. See also John W. C. Johnstone, Edward J. Slawski and William Bowman, *The News People: A Sociological Portrait of American Journalists and Their Work,* Urbana: University of Illinois Press, 1976. Also David H. Weaver and G. Cleveland Wilhoit, *The American Journalist: A Portrait of U. S. News People and Their Work,* Bloomington: Indiana University Press, 1986.
31. Liebling, *The Press,* p. 7.
32. Rubin, op. cit. The title, "The Wayward Press," was used originally in a similar column in the *New Yorker* by Robert Benchley, writing under the name of Guy Fawkes from 1927 to 1939.
33. Liebling, *Wayward Pressman,* p. 16.
34. Rubin, op. cit., pp. 31–32.
35. Liebling, "The Pretzels," in *The Press,* p. 193.
36. Liebling, *The Press,* pp. 40–41. The article was a reprint of the original, which had appeared in *Wayward Pressman.* Liebling refers approvingly to Jim Barrett, *The World, the Flesh and Messrs. Pulitzer,* New York: Vanguard, 1931, and speaks of Barrett's claim that Pulitzer's heirs made more than $25 million in profit after the founder's death: "They had plowed back nothing into the property—the same story as the New England textile men, except that newspaper publishers like to advertise themselves as more idealistic than bag-spinners."
37. Rubin, op. cit., p. 33.

46 The Doctrine of Social Responsibility

1. See Introduction.
2. *A Free and Responsible Press: A General Report on Mass Communication: Newspapers, Radio, Motion Pictures, Magazines, and Books,* 2 vols., Chicago: University of Chicago, 1947. For a summary of the Hutchins Commission

report, see J. Herbert Altschull, *Agents of Power: The Role of the News Media in Human Affairs,* New York: Longman, 1984, pp. 179–187.
3. Altschull, op. cit., p. 181.
4. Theodore Peterson, "The Social Responsibility of the Press," in Fred S. Siebert, Theodore Peterson, and Wilbur Schramm, *Four Theories of the Press: The Authoritarian, Libertarian, Social Responsibility and Soviet Communist Concepts of What the Press Should Be and Do,* Urbana: University of Illinois Press, 1956, pp. 96–97.
5. Ibid., p. 100.
6. Fred S. Siebert, "The Libertarian Theory of the Press," in Siebert, Peterson, and Schramm, op. cit., p. 56.
7. Altschull, op. cit., p. 302.
8. Walter Lippmann, *Public Opinion,* New York: Macmillan, 1922, p. 223.
9. Leon V. Sigal, *Reporters and Officials: The Organization and Politics of Newsmaking,* Lexington, Mass.: D. C. Heath, 1973, pp. 65–100. Sigal's study is a first-rate examination of the conventions, catchphrases, and self-image of American journalists.
10. Max Ways, "What's Wrong With News?" *Fortune,* October 1969, reprinted in William Hammel, *The Popular Arts in America: A Reader,* 2nd ed., New York: Harcourt Brace Jovanovich, 1977, pp. 409–425. See especially pp. 415–418.
11. Ibid., pp. 417–418.
12. Neil Postman, *Amusing Ourselves to Death: Public Discourse in the Age of Show Business,* New York: Viking Penguin, 1975, p. 87.

47 Investigative Journalism: The Conscience of Society

1. John C. Hohenberg, *The Professional Journalist: A Guide to the Practices and Principles of the News Media,* 4th ed., New York: Holt, Rinehart and Winston, 1978, p. iii.
2. Mitchell V. Charnley and Blair Charnley, *Reporting,* 4th ed., New York: Holt, Rinehart and Winston, 1979, p. x.
3. Julian Harriss, et al., *The Complete Reporter: Fundamentals of News Gathering, Writing and Editing,* New York: Macmillan, p. 3.
4. Stephen Hartgen, "There's More Here than Meets a Dragon's Eye," *Quill,* April 1975, pp. 12–15.
5. Curtis MacDougall, *Interpretive Reporting,* 8th ed., New York: Macmillan, 1982, p. 10.
6. Ibid.
7. Brian S. Brooks, ed., *News Reporting and Writing,* New York: St. Martin's Press, p. 2. 1980, For a similar work, see M. Harry, *The Muckraker's Manual: How to Do Your Own Investigating Reporting,* Port Townsend, Wash: Loompanics Unlimited, 1980. See also Louis Rose, *How to Investigate Your Friends and Enemies,* St. Louis: Albion Press, 1981; and James Phelan, *Scandals, Scamps and Scoundrels,* New York: Random House, 1982.
8. Edwin Emery and Michael Emery, *The Press and America: An Interpretive History of the Mass Media,* 4th ed., Englewood Cliffs, N.J.: Prentice-Hall, 1978, p. 372. See also John M. Harrison, and Harry H. Stein, *Muckraking—Past, Present and Future,* University Park, Pa.: Pennsylvania State University Press, 1973; and Michael F. Wendland, *The Arizona Project,* Kansas City: Sheed, Andrews and McNeel, 1977, for details on what happened after the murder of Bolles.

9. Emery and Emery, op. cit., p. 372.
10. Bolles is quoted in the preface to J. Edward Murray, *The Investigative Reporter and the Democratic Process,* Tucson: University of Arizona Press, 1977. The slim book is a transcript of Murray's speech at an awards ceremony.
11. Ibid.
12. The experiences of Carl Bernstein and Bob Woodward is documented in their book, *All the President's Men,* New York: Simon and Schuster, 1974. The book became a best-seller and the movie returned a handsome profit. The literature on the "Woodstein" phenomenon is vast.
13. *60 Minutes* has consistently ranked in the top ten in the Nielsen ratings. It stood sixth in 1987 with a 23.1 share. *World Almanac* and *Book of Facts*, 1989, p. 357.
14. Some comdemned the lengthy report by IRE journalists on the Bolles case, maintaining it drew faulty conclusions because of a lack of documentary evidence. The IRE firmly defended its report. See Wendland, op. cit.; and Melvin L. DeFleur and Everette E. Dennis, *Understanding Mass Communication,* Boston: Houghton Mifflin, 1981, p. 436. For articles critical of the practice of investigative reporting, see, e.g., John Lancaster, "Woodstein in Des Moines," *Columbia Journalism Review,* January–February 1983, pp. 51–52; and Timothy Ingram, "Investigative Reporting: Is It Getting Too Sexy?" in Michael Emery and Ted C. Smythe, eds., *Readings in Mass Communication,* 4th ed., Dubuque, Iowa: Wm. C. Brown, 1980, pp. 243–255.
15. Robert MacNeil, "The Mass Media and Public Trust," New York: Gannett Center, 1985, p. 6. remarks at dedication of the Gannett Center for Media Studies, Columbia University, March 13, 1985.
16. Ibid., p. 5: "the new journalism . . . died because it excused mediocre practitioners from the drudgery of gathering facts. . . . advocacy journalism . . . regards fairness as effete and unmanly, and thinks telling both sides of a story and letting the public decide the merits is wimpy and even irresponsible. . . ."
17. Daniel Yankelovich, comment to staff of National News Council; see *Washington Post,* April 30, 1981.
18. Janet Cooke's article "Jimmy's World," appeared in the *Washington Post* on September 28, 1980.
19. Eszterhas, "Rolling Stone Interview with Seymour Hersh," *Rolling Stone,* April 10 and 24, 1975.
20. Seymour M. Hersh, "The Story Everyone Ignored," *Columbia Journalism Review,* Winter 1969–1970, reprinted in Emery and Smythe, op. cit., 1st ed., 1972, pp. 434–439. Quoted material can be found on p. 439.
21. MacNeil, op. cit., p. 5.
22. Ibid., p. 4.

PART IX AN IDEOLOGY WITHOUT AN IDEOLOGY

48 Introduction: Media and Power

1. Quoted in Harold A. Innis, *The Press: A Neglected Factor in the Economic History of the Twentieth Century,* London: Oxford University Press, 1949, p. 24.

2. John Kenneth Galbraith, *The Anatomy of Power,* Boston: Houghton Mifflin, 1983, pp. 10–11.
3. Ibid., p. 177. Galbraith identifies three types of power: *condign,* power, which grows out of the capacity to inflict punishment in cases of noncompliance; *compensatory,* which promises rewards, and *conditioned.* See also p. 6, pp. 29–30, 176–180, for Galbraith's interesting discussion of the power of the news media.
4. Neil Postman, *Amusing Ourselves to Death: Public Discourse in the Age of Show Business,* New York: Viking Penguin, 1975, p. 70, 75, 90.
5. Todd Gitlin, "Prime Time Ideology: The Hegemonic Process in Television Entertainment," in *Social Problems,* 26:3 (February 1979), p. 254.
6. Ibid., p. 274. See also Raymond Williams, *Marxism and Literature,* New York: Oxford University Press, 1977.
7. Tacitus, *Annals,* Chicago: *Great Books of the Western World,* Encyclopedia Britannica, XV, p. iii.
8. Quoted in Bergen Evans, *A Dictionary of Quotations,* New York: Delacorte Press, 1968, p. 547. The famous aphorism of Lord Acton (John Emerich Dalberg), appeared in a letter to Bishop Mandell Creighton in 1887.
9. For landmark works by some leading spokesmen for the "consensus" or "accommodation" school, see, e.g., Clinton D. Rossiter, *The First American Revolution,* New York: Harcourt, Brace, 1956: Hammond Bray, *Banks and Politics in America from the Revolution to the Civil War,* Princeton, N.J.: Princeton University Press, 1957; and David N. Potter, *People of Plenty,* Chicago: University of Chicago Press, 1954. For a review of the "consensus" theory and of the opposed "conflict" theory, see Allen J. Davis, and Harold D. Woodman, eds., *Conflict or Consensus in American History,* Boston: Heath, 1966.
10. Lionel Trilling, *The Liberal Imagination,* Garden City, N.Y.: Doubleday, 1950, p. 5.
11. Daniel Bell, *The End of Ideology; on the Exhaustion of Political Ideas in the Fifties,* Glencoe, N.Y.: The Free Press, 1960, p. 397. The literature on pluralism is voluminous. See, for instance, Robert A. Dahl, *Pluralist Democracy in the United States: Conflict and Consent,* Chicago: Rand McNally, 1967; and his *A Preface to Democratic Theory,* Chicago: University of Chicago Press, 1956. See also Gabriel Almond and Sidney Verba, *The Civic Culture: Political Attitudes and Democracy in Five Nations,* Princeton, N.J.: Princeton University Press, 1963; and David Truman, *The Governmental Process: Political Interests and Public Opinion,* 2nd ed., New York: Knopf, 1971.
12. James Oliver Robertson, *American Myth, American Reality,* New York: Hill and Wang, 1980, p. 29.

49 The New Conservatives and the New Radicals

1. Peter Viereck, *Conservatism Revisited: The Revolt Against Revolt 1815–1949,* New York: Scribner's, 1949, p. 35.
2. Ibid., pp. 132–133. The writings of Burke, Viereck wrote, were especially applicable in the years that followed the second world war: "Today, any number of so-called political commentators claim to interpret the news.

Americans will find none timelier than Burke though his *Reflections on the Revolution in France* are dated 1790. He teaches us to answer world revolution not by outbidding it with a leftism of our own nor by reactionary rightist tyranny but by conserving the free institutions of the west." (p. 83–84).

3. Russell, Kirk, *The Conservative Mind, from Burke to Santayana,* Chicago: Regnery, 1953, p. 32.
4. Clinton Rossiter, *Conservatism in America: The Thankless Persuasion,* 2nd ed., New York: Knopf, 1962, p. 16.
5. Joseph Alois Schumpeter, *Capitalism, Socialism and Democracy,* 3rd ed., New York: Harper & Row, 1962.
6. Willmoore Kendall, *The Conservative Affirmation,* Chicago: Regnery, 1963 cited in Allen Guttmann, *The Conservative Tradition in America,* New York: Oxford University Press, 1967, pp. 158–160. See also Jeffrey Hart, *The American Dissent: A Decade of Modern Conservatism*, Garden City, N.J.: Doubleday, 1966.
7. Kendall, Ibid. A. J. Beitzinger, *A History of American Political Thought,* New York: Dodd, Mead, 1972, (p. 580) notes that Kendall also believed, in an apparent contradiction, that society ought to keep its doors open. See also Kendall's *John Locke and the Doctrine of Majority-Rule,* Urbana, Ill.: University of Illinois Press, 1941.
8. C. Wright Mills, *The Power Elite,* New York: Oxford University Press, 1956. For an attempt to explain the later decline and ideas of Mills and other radical writers of the era, see Norman Birnbaum, *The Radical Renewal: The Politics of Ideas in Modern America,* New York: Pantheon, 1988.
9. The Port Huron manifesto, drafted by Tom Hayden, is reprinted in Paul Jacobs and Saul Landow, eds., *The New Radicals: A Report with Documents,* New York: Random House, 1966, pp. 150–162. The manifesto declared (p. 156); "It is imperative that the means of violence be abolished and the institutions—local, national, international—that encourage nonviolence as a condition of conflict be developed." For more on this topic, see Arthur M. Schlesinger, Jr., *The Crisis of Confidence: ideas, power, and violence in America,* Boston: Houghton Mifflin, 1969, especially pp. 30–31. Schlesinger writes: "What distinguishes the New Left is not only its unwillingness to define what it aims for after the revolution but its belief that such mystification is a virtue." See also Beitzinger, op. cit., p. 585, and George Kennan, *Democracy and the Student Left,* Boston: Little, Brown, 1968.
10. Herbert Marcuse's thought can be found in English translation in his *Eros and Civilization: A Philosophical Inquiry into Freud,* Boston: Beacon Press, 1955; *Reason and Revolution: Hegel and the Rise of Social Theory,* Boston: Beacon Press, 1960; *One Dimensional Man: Studies in the Ideology of Advanced Industrial Society,* Boston: Beacon Press, 1964, and "Repressive Tolerance" in *A Critique of Pure Tolerance,* Boston: Beacon Press, 1965.
11. Marcuse, "Repressive Tolerance," p. 111.
12. Oskar Negt and Alexander Kluge, *Oeffentlichkeit und Erfahrung,* Frankfurt-am-Main, Germany: Suhrkamp, 1972, p. 33.
13. Much of the work of the Frankfurt school has not been translated into English. Among the important translated works are Theodor W. Adorno, *Philosophy of Modern Music,* New York: Continuum, 1973. Also Adorno and

Max Horkheimer, *Dialectic of Enlightenment,* New York: Herder and Herder, 1972, and Juergen Habermas, *Knowledge and Human Interests,* London: Heineman, 1978. For reviews of German critical theory, see Hanno Hardt, *Social Theories of the Press: Early German and American Perspectives,* Beverly Hills, Calif: Sage, 1979, and Nicholas Petryszak, "The Frankfurt School's Theory of Manipulation," in *Journal of Communication,* 27, no. 3 (Summer 1977), pp. 32–40. For those who read German, see Antje Stein, "Das 'Gespenst' der Oeffentlichkeit in der Kommunikationswissenschaft," unpublished thesis, University of Munich, 1986. Frauelein Stein, a student of mine at Munich, produced an excellent study of what she called the "apparition" of public opinion.

14. Claus Mueller, *The Politics of Communication: A Study in the Political Sociology of Language, Socialization and Legitimation,* New York: Oxford University Press, 1973.
15. Juergen Habermas, *Strukturwandel der Oeffentlichkeit,* Neuwied, Germany: 1974, p. 235. See Stein, op. cit., passim.
16. Habermas, op. cit., pp. 248–249, 278. See also Thomas A. McCarthy, *The Critical Theory of Juergen Habermas,* Cambridge, Mass.: MIT Press, 1978.
17. Negt and Kluge, op. cit., p. 70. These commentators use the word *Scheinoeffentlichkeit,* which can be translated by "pseudo-public" or perhaps "sham" or "phony" public.
18. Habermas, op. cit., pp. 230–250. Habermas wrote that "as far as the normative demands of public order (rules) are concerned, the liberal model of the public has no value other than merely historical. We simply cannot use that term any more to describe the factual relationships within an industrially developed mass democracy."

50 Niebuhr and Lippmann

1. Reinhold Niebuhr, *The Irony of Human History,* New York: Scribner's, 1962, p. 133. The book is drawn from lectures at Westminster College, Fulton, Mo., in 1949 and 1951. For examinations of Niebuhr's thought, see Gene Wise, *American Explanations: A Strategy for Grounded Inquiry,* Homewood, Ill.: Dorsey, 1973, especially pp. 271–315; Robert M. Brown, *The Essential Reinhold Niebuhr: Selected Essays and Addresses,* New Haven, Conn.: Yale University Press, 1986; and A. J. Beitzinger, *A History of American Political Thought,* New York: Dodd, Mead, 1972, especially pp. 551–562.
2. The Gospel According to Luke, 16:8.
3. Reinhold Niebuhr, *The Children of Light and the Children of Darkness: A Vindication of Democracy and a Critique of Its Traditional Defense,* New York: Scribner's, 1944, pp. 9–10. The book is drawn from lectures given at Stanford University, Palo Alto, Calif., 1944.
4. Ibid., pp. 11–12.
5. Ibid., p. 118.
6. Ibid., p. xiii.
7. Ibid., pp. 40–41.
8. Ibid., p. xiv.
9. Erich Fromm, *The Sane Society,* New York: Rinehart, 1955, pp. vii–viii, 95–97.

10. Cited by Beitzinger, op. cit., p. 556. This is a reference to what has come to be identified as the Hawthorn effect. See *Encyclopedia Britannica* (1988) 29:942–943.
11. Niebuhr, *Irony,* pp. 83–88.
12. Niebuhr, "Introduction," in Wilbur Schramm, *Responsibility in Mass Communication,* New York: Harper & Brothers, 1957, p. xv.
13. Niebuhr, *Irony,* p. 28. Niebuhr said he might have been more inclined to accept the portrait of American virtue as exceeding that of other countries if it were not for this country's "spiritual pride" in overstating "the innocency of American social life."
14. Quoted in Ronald Steel, *Walter Lippmann and the American Century,* New York: Vintage Books, 1980, pp. 512–515.
15. The author met Lippmann personally twice, and spoke with him on the telephone on two or three other occasions. Even though these occasions were all professional, there was about them the aura of an audience with the pope.
16. Steel, op. cit., passim., especially pp. 208, 423, 496.
17. Ibid., pp. 37–38; Justin Kaplan, *Lincoln Steffans: A Biography,* New York: Simon and Schuster, 1974, pp. 176–178.
18. Walter Lippmann, *Public Opinion,* New York: Macmillan, 1922, pp. 29–38, holds that human beings interpret the world on the basis of stereotypes.
19. Ibid., pp. 361–362.
20. Ibid., p. 365.
21. Ibid., p. 364.
22. John Dewey, "Public Opinion," *New Republic,* May 3, 1922. See Steel, op. cit., p. 183.
23. Steel, op. cit., pp. 274–275.
24. Quoted in Steel, op. cit., pp. 21–22. The article "Santayana—A Sketch," appeared in *International,* vol. 8 (1911).
25. Ibid., p. 82. The article appeared in the *New Republic,* December 12, 1914. The motion picture, *Reds,* produced by Warren Beatty, was a fictionalized biography of Reed.
26. Beitzinger, op. cit., p. 494.
27. Walter Lippmann, *The Good Society,* Boston: Little, Brown, 1937, p. 346.
28. Walter Lippmann, *Essays in the Public Philosophy,* Boston: Little, Brown, 1955. chap. 1.
29. John Leonard, in review of Steel, op. cit., in the *New York Times,* August 22, 1980. Leonard sums up Lippmann: "Although often perceived as lonely and brave, he was usually close to the public opinion he so dismissed—a populist progressive, a Wilsonian, a New Dealer, a semi-isolationist, an interventionist, an internationalist, as the times seemed to demand."
30. Quoted in Steel, op. cit., p. 582.
31. See James Oliver Robertson, *American Myth, American Reality,* New York: Hill and Wang, 1980, pp. 65–69, for a discussion of America's Holy Writ.
32. Elie Abel, in a review of Steel's op. cit., in the *Washington Post,* August 24, 1980, in noting Lippmann's coining of the phrase in 1917, points out the narrowness of Lippmann's internationalism, dedicated as it so clearly was to an internationalism that embraced almost entirely the nations of Western Europe in whose tradition the United States evolved.
33. Ibid. Abel, himself an experienced reporter, wrote that there were in 1970 "plenty of Washington columnists still at work. But we do not look to them—as we once looked to Lippmann—for wisdom, bottled in bond. The

contemporary crowd are reporters, not philosophers." See also John Morton Blum, ed., *Public Philosopher: Selected Letters of Walter Lippmann,* New York: Ticknow & Fields, 1986. In reviewing this volume of Lippmann's letters, Robert Manning wrote in the *Washington Journalism Review,* February 1986, p. 58; "One cannot finish this volume . . . without suspecting that Walter Lippmann, far from wanting distance between himself and princes, would have liked to be one of them and probably believed he should have been. He certainly had the brains for high public office, but he was saved for journalism by his disdain for the sweaty arena and his distrust of the popular majorities by which men are chosen for power in America."

51 The Shock of "McCarthyism"

1. See A. J. Beitzinger, *A History of American Political Thought,* New York: Dodd, Mead, 1972, p. 580. See also Allan Guttmann, *The Conservative Tradition in America,* New York: Oxford University Press, 1967, and Frank Meyer, *In Defense of Freedom,* Chicago: Regnery, 1962 p. 41, who maintained that Freedom does not mean merely to do that which is right but also "the choice between virtue and vice." Beitzinger repeats Kendall's question: "Can a society long exist if a complete moral relativism obtains among its members?"
2. Leo Strauss, epilogue in Herbert J. Storing, ed., *History of Political Philosophy,* 2nd ed., Chicago: University of Chicago Press, 1981, pp. 313–327.
3. Norman O. Brown, *Life Against Death: The Psychoanalytical Meaning of History,* 2nd ed., Middletown, Conn.: Wesleyan University Press, 1985, pp. 314–315. See also Leo Hamalian, and Frederick R. Karl, eds., *The Radical Vision: Essays for the Seventies,* New York: Crowell, 1970, pp. 107–112, especially pp. 109–111.
4. Theodore Roszak, *The Making of a Counter-Culture: Reflections on the Technocratic Society and the Youthful Opposition,* Garden City, N.Y.: Doubleday, 1969, pp. 236–242.
5. Edwin B. Bayley, *Joseph McCarthy and the Press,* New York: Pantheon Books, 1981, p. 219.
6. Ibid., Bayley's book is indispensable. For those interested in exploring the career of McCarthy, especially as it bore on the news media see, among others, Jack Anderson, and Ronald W. May, *McCarthy: The Man, the Senator, the "Ism,"* Boston: Beacon Press, 1952; Fred J. Cook, *The Nightmare Decade: The Life and Times of Senator Joe McCarthy,* New York: Random House, 1971; Fred W. Friendly, *Due to Circumstances Beyond our Control,* New York: Random House, 1967; and Richard H. Rovere, *Senator Joe McCarthy,* New York: Harcourt, Brace, 1959.
7. See Bayley, op. cit., pp. 113–124, for an examination of press reaction to McCarthy. See also J. Herbert Altschull, *Agents of Power: The Role of the News Media in Human Affairs,* New York: Longman, 1984, p. 128.
8. Curtis MacDougall, *Interpretative Reporting,* New York: Macmillan. Before MacDougall's death, his book went through eight editions, the last appearing in 1982.
9. Matthew Arnold, "Up to Easter," *Nineteenth Century,* May 1887, pp. 638–639. See also John Hollowell, *Fact and Fiction: The New Journalism and the*

Nonfiction Novel, Chapel Hill: University of North Carolina Press, 1977. Arnold's work can be profitably skimmed in Matthew Arnold, *Essays, Letters, and Reviews*, Cambridge, Mass.: Harvard University Press, 1960. See also Edwin Emery and Michael Emery, *The Press and America: An Interpretive History of the Mass Media,* 4th ed., Englewood Cliffs, N.J.: Prentice-Hall, 1978.

10. Emery and Emery, op. cit., pp. 220–221.
11. For a discussion of the origin of the term "social responsibility," see Altschull, op. cit., pp. 301–305.
12. David Halberstam, *The Best and the Brightest,* New York: Random House, 1972.
13. James Fallows, "The New Celebrities of Washington," *New York Review of Books,* June 12, 1985, pp. 41–49.

52 A Potpourri of "New Journalism"

1. Truman Capote, *In Cold Blood,* New York: Random House, 1966. John Hollowell, *Fact and Fiction: The New Journalism and the Nonfictional Novel,* Chapel Hill: University of North Carolina Press, 1977, especially p. 40, which provides a classification of the "main themes" of the new journalism.
2. Tom Wolfe, and E. W. Johnson, eds., *The New Journalism,* New York: Harper & Row, 1973, p. 48.
3. Everette E. Dennis, "Journalistic Primitivism," *Journal of Popular Culture,* 9 (Summer 1975): 122–135, reprinted in Everette E. Dennis, Arnold H. Ismach, and Donald M. Gillmor, eds., *Enduring Issues in Mass Communication,* St. Paul, Minn.: West, 1978, pp. 205–215. The quoted comment appears on p. 206. See also the endnotes, p. 215. Dennis's views on objectivity altered a bit over the years. For a more recent viewpoint, see his essay, "Journalistic Objectivity is Possible," in Everette E. Dennis, and John C. Merrill, *Basic Issues in Mass Communication,* New York: Macmillan, 1984, pp. 111–118. For Merrill's opposing view, see pp. 103–110. See also the writings of Irving Kristol and Paul Weaver, among others.
4. Dennis, "Journalistic Primitivism," reprinted in Dennis, Ismach and Gillmor, op. cit., p. 209.
5. See the Bantam Books editions of some of Wolfe's well-known works of "new journalism," such as *Radical Chic* (1978), *The Electric Kool-Aid Acid Test* (1968), and *The Right Stuff* (1979). For further leading works of the genre, see Norman Mailer, *The Armies of the Night: History as a Novel, the Novel as History,* New York: Signet, 1967; Jimmy Breslin, *How the Good Guys Finally Won: Notes from an Impeachment Summons,* New York: Viking, 1975; and Gay Talese, *Honor Thy Father,* New York: World, 1971.
6. Dennis, "Journalistic Primitivism," reprinted in Dennis, Ismach, and Gillmor, op. cit., p. 206. The reference is to a letter Dennis received from Wolfe in March 1974.
7. Raymond Mungo, *Famous Long Ago: My Life and Hard Times with Liberation News Service,* Boston: Beacon Press, 1970, pp. 75–76.
8. The literature on the underground press is rich. Perhaps the most comprehensive study is Robert J. Glessing, *The Underground Press in America,* Bloomington: Indiana University Press, 1970. Other important studies include Howard Good, *Outcasts,* Metuchen, N.J.: Scarecrow Press, 1989;

Lauren Kessler, *The Dissident Press,* Beverly Hills, Calif.: Sage, 1984; Laurence Leamer, *The Paper Revolutionaries,* New York: Simon and Schuster, 1972; and Roger Lewis, *Outlaws of America,* London: Heinrich Hanau, 1972. For a study of the underground press in a single city, see Gaye S. Smith, *The Underground Press in Los Angeles,* privately published, Los Angeles, 1968.

9. For a thorough examination of the black press, see Roland Wolseley, *The Black Press U.S.A.,* Ames, Iowa: Iowa State University Press, 1989. This is an updated version of Wolseley's earlier work of 1971. For additional material see Armistead S. Pride, *The Black Press: A Bibliography,* prepared for the Association for Education in Journalism, Ad Hoc Committee on Minority Education, 1968. An interesting and gloomy report on the role of the black press is contained in *Report of the National Advisory* [Kerner] *Commission on Civil Disorders,* Washington, D.C.: U.S. Government Printing Office, 1968, pp. 362–380. See also James D. Williams, *The Black Press and the First Amendment,* New York: National Urban League, 1976; and J. Herbert Altschull, *Agents of Power: The Role of the News Media in Human Affairs,* New York: Longman, 1984, pp. 199–201, 330.
10. Philip Meyer, *Precision Journalism,* Bloomington: Indiana University Press, 1979.
11. James Fallows, "The New Celebrities of Washington," *New York Review of Books,* June 12, 1985, p. 47.

53 The "Power" of Journalism

1. See the *New York Times,* November 14, 1969, p. 24, for the text of Agnew's November 13 speech in Des Moines, Iowa.
2. Ibid. The italics are added to emphasize the significance of the association of press power with choice.
3. Ibid.
4. See the *New York Times,* November 21, 1969, p. 22, for the text of Agnew's November 20 speech in Montgomery, Ala.
5. Ibid.
6. Books and monographs on the Agnew phenomenon flooded the market for a while, but fell off sharply with the passage of time. Among the most interesting: Robert Marsh, *Agnew: The Unexamined Man,* Philadelphia: Lippincott, 1971; John R. Coyne, *The Impudent Snobs,* New Rochelle, N.Y.: Arlington House, 1972; Theo Lippman, *Spiro Agnew's America,* New York: Norton, 1972; Robert W. Peterson, *Agnew: The Coining of a Household Word,* New York: Facts on File, 1972; and Richard M. Cohen, *A Heartbeat Away,* New York: Viking Press, 1974. See especially Ben Bagdikian, "The Fruits of Agnewism," *Columbia Journalism Review,* January–February 1983, pp. 9–21. See also Spiro T. Agnew, *Frankly Speaking,* Washington, D.C.: Public Affairs Press, 1970.
7. *New York Times,* "Most Callers Back Agnew," November 15, 1969, p. 20.
8. A poll commissioned by the Republican National Committee found that 64 percent of the respondents supported Agnew's stance and only 24 percent opposed. Surveys by CBS and ABC turned up similar responses. See Lippman, op. cit., p. 194.

9. Peterson, op. cit., p. 61.
10. *New York Times,* "Rebuttal by Network," November 14, 1969, p. 24.
11. *New York Times,* "Burch's Letter Appears to Rebuff Critics of TV," November 22, 1969, p. 16.
12. Sermon by the Rev. Frederick William Robertson (1816–1853), author of five volumes of sermons, cited in the *Oxford English Dictionary* (1933), S.V. "chill."
13. Brandywine–Main Line Radio, Inc. v. Federal Communications Commission, 473 F 2d 16 (1972), cert. denied, 93 S. Ct. 2731.
14. Coyne, op. cit., p. 49.
15. Ibid.
16. *New York Times,* November 24, 1969.
17. Ben H. Bagdikian, *Bagdikian on Political Reporting, Newspaper Economics, Law and Ethics,* Fort Worth: Texas Christian University Press, 1976, pp. 27–28. See also Bagdikian, "The Fruits of Agnewism," on the Agnew case.
18. See, for instance, Thomas R. Dye, and L. Harmon Ziegler, *American Politics in the Media Age,* Monterey, Calif.: Brooks Cole, 1983; and David L. Paletz, and Robert M. Entman, *Media Power Politics: A Timely, Provocative Look at How the Media Affect Public Opinion and Political Power in the United States,* New York: Macmillan, 1981. See also J. Herbert Altschull, *Agents of Power: The Role of the News Media in Human Affairs,* New York: Longman, 1984, especially chap. 6.
19. Martin Linsky, *Impact: How the Press Affects Federal Policy-Making,* New York: Norton, 1986. The quotation is from the preface, a "conceptual essay," written by Gary R. Orren.
20. See, e.g., Richard Townley, "The News Merchants," excerpted from *TV Guide,* March 9 and 16, 1974, in Barry Cole, ed. *Television Today: A Close-Up View, Readings from TV Guide,* New York: Oxford University Press, 1981, pp. 158–165.
21. *Report of the National Advisory* [Kerner] *Commission on Civil Disorders,* Washington, D.C.: U.S. Government Printing Office, 1968. See also Louis L. Knowles, and Kenneth Prewitt, eds., *Institutional Racism in America,* Englewood Cliffs, N.J.: Prentice-Hall, 1969, and Carolyn Martindale, *The White Press and Black America,* New York: Greenwood Press, 1986.

PART X The "Skeptical" Adversaries

55 Modern Technology, McLuhan and the Global Village

1. We have encountered the myth of Eden earlier, in Part 6. For a thorough analysis of this phenomenon, see R. W. B. Leavis, *The American Adam: Innocence, Tragedy, and Tradition in the Nineteenth Century,* Chicago: University of Chicago Press, 1955. To illustrate the longevity of this myth, Leavis, interestingly, cites the twentieth-century English writers D. H. Lawrence and T. S. Eliot on "the true myth of America."
2. For a brief and interesting discussion of the work of McLuhan and the reaction to his theories of communication, see Daniel J. Czitrom, *Media and the American Mind: From Morse to McLuhan,* Chapel Hill: University of

North Carolina Press, 1982, pp. 165–182. See also Raymond B. Rosenthal, *McLuhan: Pro & Con,* New York: Funk and Wagnalls, 1968.

3. Quoted in Czitrom, op. cit., p. 227. Morse's remark was made before a meeting of the House Commerce Committee in 1838. Morse's telegraph underwent a successful test in 1844.
4. Alvin F. Harlow, *Old Wires and New Waves: The History of the Telegraph and Wireless,* New York: Appleton-Century, 1936, p. 11. See also Neil Postman, *Amusing Ourselves to Death: Public Discourse in the Age of Show Business,* New York: Viking Penguin, 1985, p. 66.
5. Marshall McLuhan, *Understanding Media: The Extensions of Man,* New York: McGraw-Hill, 1964, p. 7, 9.
6. For an interesting account of thought in these fields, see Richard Macksey and Eugenio Donato, eds., *The Structuralist Controversy: The Languages of Criticism and the Sciences of Man,* Baltimore: Johns Hopkins University Press, 1972. See also Czitrom, op. cit., p. 182; and Varda L. Leymore, *Hidden Myth: Structure and Symbolism in Advertising,* London: Heinemann, 1975.
7. Jean Hippolyte, "Hegel's Philosophic Language," in Macksey and Donato, op. cit., p. 162. See the references to Hegel in his views in Chapter 22.
8. Ibid., p. 161. Hippolyte is relying in part on Emile Benveniste, *Problèmes de linguistique générale,* Paris: Gallimard, 1966, pp. 63–74.
9. Quoted in the classic by Leo Marx, *The Machine in the Garden,* New York: Oxford University Press, 1966, pp. 232–234. See also Gene Wise, *American Explanations: A Strategy for Grounded Inquiry,* Homewood, Ill.: Dorsey, 1973, and Wilson P. Dizard, Jr., *The Coming Information Age: An Overview of Technology, Economics, and Politics,* New York: Longman, 1982, pp. 22–43.
10. See the discussion between Jean Hippolyte and Reinhardt Kuhn in Macksey and Donato, op. cit., pp. 183–184. For biographical material, see Stephen Mallarmé, *Mallarmé,* Harmondsworth, England, 1977, and Jean-Paul Sartre, *Mallarmé,* Paris: Gallimard, 1986.
11. Marshall McLuhan, *The Gutenberg Galaxy: The Making of Typographic Man,* Toronto: University of Toronto Press, 1962, p. 272.
12. Georges Poulet, cited in Macksey and Donato, op. cit., p. 177.
13. Czitrom, op. cit., pp. 173–174.
14. Ibid., pp. 174–175.
15. See John Milton, *Paradise Regained,* bk. 1. For an excellent analysis of this work, see James H. Hanford, *John Milton, Englishman,* New York: Crown, 1949, pp. 200–205.
16. Cited in James W. Carey and John J. Quirk, "The Mythos of the Electronic Revolution," in *American Scholar,* Summer 1970, p. 402.
17. Marshall McLuhan, *The Mechanical Bride: Folklore of Industrial Man,* New York: Vanguard Press, 1951; *The Gutenberg Galaxy,* op. cit. See Czitrom, op. cit., pp. 171–181.
18. McLuhan, *Gutenberg Galaxy,* pp. 272–273.
19. René Girard, in Macksey and Donato, op. cit., p. 181. Cf. Claude Levi-Strauss's remark in his *Structural Anthropology* that "Myth grows until the intellectual impulse which has produced it is exhausted," quoted in James Oliver Robertson, *American Myth, American Reality,* New York: Hill and Wang, p. 294. For additional (and fascinating) material on myths, see Robertson, passim. The literature on myths is extensive. Among others who

deal extensively with myths in the field of journalism is of course Walter Lippmann in *Public Opinion,* New York: Macmillan, 1922.

20. St. John de Crèvecouer, *Letters From An American Farmer,* Gloucester, Mass.: P. Smith, 1968. The original appeared in 1782.
21. See Justin Kaplan, *Walt Whitman: A Life,* New York: Simon and Schuster Touchstone, 1986, pp. 100–101, 196–197. See also the references to Emerson's views in Chapter 30.
22. Ted Morgan, *FDR: A Biography,* London: Grafton Books, 1986, p. 552.
23. Theories of technological determinism have been produced throughout most of Western civilization. For reviews, see the previously cited works of Leo Marx and Gene Wise.
24. Postman, op. cit., p. 157.
25. Ibid.
26. The title of Postman's book, *Amusing Ourselves to Death,* illustrates his point with lugubrious irony. He helps support his position by citing (p. 10) a passage from the German social thinker, Ernst Cassirer: "Physical reality seems to recede in proportion as man's symbolic activity advances. Instead of dealing with the things themselves [cf. Kant] man is in a sense constantly conversing with himself. He has so enveloped himself in linguistic forms, in artistic images, in mythical symbols or religious rites that he cannot see or know anything except by the interposition of [an] artificial medium." Cassirer, *An Essay on Man,* Garden City, NY: Doubleday Anchor, 1956, p. 43.
27. Postman, op. cit., pp. 144–145.
28. See Melvin L. DeFleur and Sandra Ball-Rokeach, *Theories of Mass Communication,* 4th ed., New York: Longman, 1982, pp. 184–185.

56 Harold Innis: The Dark Side

1. Daniel J. Czitrom, *Media and the American Mind: From Morse to McLuhan,* Chapel Hill: University of North Carolina Press, 1982, p. 147. See also Robin Neill, *A New Theory of Value: The Canadian Economics of H. A. Innis,* Toronto: University of Toronto Press, 1972.
2. Henry Adams, *Mont-Saint-Michel and Chartres: A Study of Thirteenth Century Unity,* Washington, 1904. See also James Oliver Robertson, *American Myth, American Reality,* New York: Hill and Wang, 1980, pp. 172–174.
3. Lewis Mumford, *The Myth of the Machine,* 2 vols., New York: Harcourt, Brace and World, 1967; Alvin Toffler, *Future Shock,* New York: Random House, 1970; and Jacques Ellul, *The Technological Society,* New York: Vintage Books, 1964.
4. Innis's clearest expression of his views on communications appears in his *Empire and Communication,* Oxford: Clarendon Press, 1950; in *The Bias of Communication,* Toronto: University of Toronto Press, 1971; and in his celebrated lecture, *The Press: A Neglected Factor in the Economic History of the Twentieth Century,* London, Oxford University Press, 1949. See also Czitrom, op. cit., p. 161, and his bibliographic notes, pp. 221–224.
5. Eric A. Havelock, "Harold Innis: The Philosophical Historian," *Et Cetera* 38 (Fall 1981): 262–263. Havelock, who taught at both Harvard and Yale and was a one-time colleague of Innis at Victoria College in Canada, is perhaps

the best source of information about both Innis and his complex theories. Havelock was himself a distinguished communications scholar. The entire Fall 1981 issue of Neil Postman's *Et Cetera* was dedicated to Harold Innis, "A Man of his Times." For additional material on Innis, see the biography by another colleague at Victoria College, Donald Creighton, *Harold Adams Innis: Portrait of a Scholar,* Toronto: University of Toronto Press, 1972.

6. Havelock, op. cit., p. 250: "He discerned with accuracy, from the vantage point of a Canadian observer, the increasing militarization of the politics and economy of the U.S., at a time when few if any American liberals showed any awareness of it."
7. Quoted in Havelock, op. cit., p. 259.
8. Neil Postman, *Amusing Ourselves to Death: Public Discourse in the Age of Show Business,* New York: Viking Penguin, 1975, p. 63.
9. Ellul, op. cit., pp. 96–97. See also Wilson P. Dizard, Jr., *The Coming Information Age: An Overview of Technology, Economics, and Politics,* New York: Longman, pp. 1–21.
10. See Reinhold Niebuhr, *The Children of Light and the Children of Darkness: A Vindication of Democracy and a Critique of Its Traditional Defense,* New York: Scribner's 1944, p. xiii. See also Gene Wise, *American Explanations: A Strategy for Grounded Inquiry,* Homewood, Ill.: Dorsey, 1973, p. 282.
11. Quoted in Robertson, op. cit., pp. 297–299.
12. For a discussion of hyphenated Americans, see ibid., pp. 327–328.

57 The Adversary Culture: Optimism and Pessimism

1. Daniel Patrick Moynihan, "The Presidency and The Press," *Commentary,* March 1971, pp. 41–52, reprinted in abridged form in the *National Observer,* March 19, 1971.
2. Quoted in Theo Lippman, Jr., *Spiro Agnew's America,* New York: Norton, 1972, p. 188. The speech in which this passage appeared was delivered in New Orleans on October 19, 1969. See also Robert W. Peterson, ed., *Agnew,* New York: Facts on File, 1972.
3. Moynihan, op. cit., p. 43.
4. Ibid.
5. Lionel Trilling, *Beyond Culture: Essays on Literature and Learning,* New York: Viking, 1965, pp. xii–xiii.
6. Ibid., pp. xv–xvi.
7. James Oliver Robertson, *American Myth, American Reality,* New York: Hill and Wang, 1980, pp. 258–259.
8. George Boyce, *Newspaper History from the Seventeenth Century to the Present Day,* Beverly Hills, Calif.: Sage, 1978, pp. 23–24. The excerpt is from chap. 1. "The Fourth Estate: The Reappraisal of a Concept."
9. Daniel Bell, *The Cultural Contradictions of Capitalism,* New York: Basic Books, 1976, pp. 40–41.
10. Morris Dickstein, *Gates of Eden: American Culture in the Sixties,* New York: Basic Books, 1977, p. 249. The epilogue of Dickstein's book, pp. 248–277, provides an excellent, personalized account of the ideas at work during three decades of American life. Dickstein, a disciple of Trilling, also gives an interesting account of Trilling's influence.

11. Ibid.
12. Michael Novak, "Why the Workingman Hates the Media," in John C. Merrill, and Ralph D. Barney, eds., *Ethics and the Press: Readings in Mass Media Morality,* New York: Hastings House, 1975, pp. 108–117. "What people resent is the new economic power of the media, the myth-making which erects great new realities. They also resent the arrogance that tells people every day: "We're smarter, better-informed, more critical, more skeptical than you."
13. Tom Bethell, "The Myth of an Adversary Press: Journalist as Bureaucrat," *Harper's,* January 1977, p. 40. For a discussion of the symbiotic relationship of government and press, see J. Herbert Altschull, *Agents of Power: The Role of the News Media in Human Affairs,* New York: Longman, 1984, pp. 193–201.
14. Gaye Tuchman, "Objectivity as Strategic Ritual: An Examination of Newsmen's Notions of Objectivity," *American Journal of Sociology,* 77, no. 4 (January 1972): 662.
15. The July 1971 issue of *Commentary* contained a lengthy collection of "Letters from Readers" responding to the Moynihan article. These letters are quite revealing as illustrations of the ideology of American journalists. Cited hereafter as Letters.
16. Letters, pp. 12–16.
17. Ibid., p. 18.
18. Ibid., p. 16.
19. William James, *Pragmatism,* New York: Longman, Greens, 1907, p. 52.
20. Letters, p. 18.
21. See discussion of Rashomon effect in Chapter 2.
22. Letters, p. 20.
23. Ibid., p. 22.
24. Ibid.
25. Ibid., p. 24.
26. Seymour Hersh's Pulitzer Prize–winning account of the My Lai incident as discussed in Chapter 47.
27. *American Heritage Dictionary of the English Language,* 1969. s.v. "skeptic."
28. See, for instance, Gabriel A. Almond, and Sidney Verba, *The Civic Culture:* Princeton, N.J.: Princeton University Press, 1963.
29. David O. Sears, and Richard E. Whitney, "Political Persuasion," in Ithiel de Sola Pool, and Wilbur Schramm, eds., *Handbook of Communication,* Chicago: Rand McNally, 1973, pp. 271–276. For a somewhat contrary view, see Robertson, op. cit., pp. 347–353.
30. Dagobert D. Runes, *Dictionary of Philosophy,* Totowa, N.J.: Littlefield, Adams & Co., 1962, p. 278.
31. William S. Sahakian, *Ethics: An Introduction to Theories and Problems,* New York: Barnes and Noble, 1974, pp. 12–13.
32. Ibid.

58 Ethics: The New Wave in Journalism

1. William S. Sahakian, *Ethics: An Introduction to Theories and Problems,* New York: Barnes and Noble, 1974, p. 1.
2. Quoted in Sissela Bok, *Lying: Moral Choice in Public and Private Life,* New York: Vintage Books, 1979, p. xix.

3. Alasdair MacIntyre, *A Short History of Ethics,* New York: Macmillan, 1966, p. 1.
4. Erik H. Erikson, *Gandhi's Truth,* New York: Norton, 1969, p. 251.
5. The Hutchins Commission report is discussed in Chapter 46. See J. Herbert Altschull, *Agents of Power: The Role of the News Media in Human Affairs,* New York: Longman, 1984, pp. 301–305, for an examination of the origin of the term *social responsibility*.
6. The Society of Professional Journalists, a professional association then known as Sigma Delta Chi and at that time consisting only of newspaper people, adopted a code of ethics as early as 1926. It was revised in 1973. All other groups associated with journalism, including broadcast journalists, publishers, managing editors, photographers, and public relations people, have since adopted similar codes. For a detailed discussion of these codes, see Clifford G. Christians, and Catherine L. Covert, *Teaching Ethics in Journalism Education,* New York: Hastings Center, 1980. Bok, op. cit., p. 260, holds that such codes of ethics, in journalism and other fields, "function all too often as shields: their abstractions allow many to adhere to them while continuing their ordinary practices."
7. The literature on journalism ethics has grown voluminous in recent years. See, among others, Clifford G. Christians, Kim B. Rotzoll, and Mark Fackler, *Media Ethics: Cases and Moral Reasoning,* 2nd ed., New York: Longman, 1987; Edmund B. Lambeth, *Committed Journalism: An Ethic for the Profession,* Bloomington: Indiana University Press, 1986; H. Eugene Goodwin, *Groping for Ethics in Journalism,* Ames, Iowa: Iowa State University Press, 1983; John C. Merrill, and S. Jack Odell, *Philosophy and Journalism,* New York: Longman, 1983, and Thomas W. Cooper et al., *Communications Ethics and Global Change,* New York: Longman, 1989.
8. *Louisville* (Ky.) *Courier-Journal,* November 16, 1972.
9. Bok, op. cit., pp. 127–128.
10. Janet Cooke's article appeared in the *Washington Post* September 28, 1980. The edition featuring Bill Green's report appeared April 19, 1981.
11. *Bloomington* (Ind.) *Herald-Telephone,* April 6, 1981. Bradlee was the keynote speaker at a seminar on journalism practices in nearby Nashville, Ind.
12. *Columbia Journalism Review,* July–August 1971, p. 28.
13. *Washington Post,* September 28, 1980.
14. Anne Singletary, unpublished paper, in my seminar on "Media and Society," Indiana University, Spring 1984.
15. Excerpted from John C. Merrill, *The Imperative of Freedom,* New York: Hastings House, 1974, reprinted from John C. Merrill and Ralph D. Barney, eds., *Ethics and the Press: Readings in Mass Media Morality,* New York: Hastings House, 1975, p. 16.
16. Sissela Bok, *Secrets: On the Ethics of Concealment and Revelation,* New York: Pantheon, 1982, p. 254.
17. Bok, *Lying,* p. 175.
18. *Columbia Journalism Review,* July–August 1971, p. 28.
19. Don Graham, unpublished note to Janet Cooke 1981.

Recommended Readings

Among my many goals in writing this book was to put together an unusually extensive set of notes and bibliographic material that would provide research guides for students of journalism, be they university undergraduates or graduates, be they political scientists, historians, sociologists, journalism scholars or simply interested citizens. One may browse through the dozens of pages of notes (pp. 365–434) at one's leisure. At the same time, the notes may serve as guideposts for further research.

Each of the chapters contains notes covering material from the writings of the philosophers examined in this book as well as biographic material and secondary sources. The output of the selected philosophers is so voluminous that no list of recommended readings could cover all the available material. This means, of course, that the list of selections is quite subjective, containing writings that I have found useful and significant. Another author would no doubt choose a different list.

Each historian of ideas begins his work from his own social and political perspective. Some commentators are of the Left, some of the Right; some are open to new thoughts; some are closed to them. The careful reader must sift through the work of these historians and choose the interpretations that most satisfy him or her. Here is a listing of the leading general historians of ideas on whom I have relied most heavily.

Although I do not agree with all the constructions offered by the following general historians of ideas, I recommend them all heartily, both for cogent thought and writing style. They are listed in alphabetical order.

Beitzinger, A.J., *A History of American Political Thought,* New York: Dodd, Mead & Co., 1972.

Gouldner, Alvin W., *The Debate on Ideology and Technology: The Origins, Grammar, and Future of Ideology,* New York: Seabury, 1976.

Mazlish, Bruce, *The Riddle of History: The Great Speculators from Vico to Freud,* New York: Harper & Row, 1966.

Parrington, Vernon L., *Main Currents in American Thought,* 3 volumes: 1, *The Colonial Mind 1620–1800,* New York: Harcourt Brace Harvest Books, 1954.

Russell, Bertrand, *A History of Western Philosophy,* New York: Simon and Schuster Touchstone, 1972.

Sabine, George H., *A History of Political Thought,* 3rd ed., New York: Holt, Rinehart and Winston, 1965.

Wise, Gene, *American Historical Explanations: A Strategy for Grounded Inquiry,* Homewood, IL: Dorsey Press, 1973.

Among histories of ideas that deal extensively with journalism and free expression, the following books and/or selections are recommended:

Altschull, J. Herbert, *Agents of Power: The Role of the News Media in Human Affairs,* New York: Longman, 1984.

Berlin, Isaiah, *Four Essays on Liberty,* New York: Oxford University Press, 1969. See especially his essay, "John Stuart Mill and the Ends of Life."

Cassirer, Ernst. *The Philosophy of the Enlightenment,* Princeton NJ: Princeton University Press, 1979.

Czitrom, Daniel J., *Media and the American Mind: From Morse to McLuhan,* Chapel Hill NC: University of North Carolina Press, 1982.

Hardt, Hanno, *Social Theories of the Press: Early German & American Perspectives,* Beverly Hills CA: Sage Publications, 1979.

Levy, Leonard W., *Emergence of a Free Press,* New York: Oxford University Press, 1985.

Merrill, John C., *The Imperative of Freedom: A Philosophy of Journalistic Autonomy,* New York: Hastings House, 1974.

Merrill, John C., and Odell, S. Jack, *Philosophy and Journalism,* New York: Longman, 1983. See the excellent bibliographical material on logic (p. 29), semantics (pp. 47–48), epistemology (p. 75), ethics (pp. 105–106), values (p. 127), and press freedom (pp. 182–83).

Siebert, Fred S.; Peterson, Theodore, and Schramm, Wilbur, *Four Theories of the Press: The Authoritarian, Libertarian, Social Responsibility and Soviet Communist Concepts of What the Press Should Be and Do,* Urbana IL: University of Illinois Press, 1956.

Williams, Raymond, *Culture and Society, 1780–1950,* New York: Harper and Row, 1966.

Among the best collections of readings of the work of political and social philosophers, see especially:

Somerville, John, and Santoni, Ronald E., *Social and Political Philosophy: Readings from Plato Gandhi,* Garden City, NY: Doubleday Anchor Books, 1963.

For readable sketches on philosophy and ideology, see:

Bell, Daniel, *The End of Ideology; on the Exhaustion of Political Ideas in the Fifties,* Glencoe, NY: Free Press, 1960.
Runes, Dagobert D., ed., *Dictionary of Philosophy,* Totowa, NJ: Littlefield, Adams and Co., 1982.
Shaw, L. Earl, ed., *Modern Competing Ideologies,* Lexington, MA: Heath, 1973.

For a useful compilation of American court decisions on free expression, see:

Hachten, William A., *The Supreme Court on Freedom of the Press: Decisions and Dissents,* Ames, IA: Iowa State University Press, 1970.

For analyses of language in ideas, see

Cassirer, Ernst, *Language and Myth,* New York: Dover, 1946.
Condon, John Jr., *Semantics and Communication,* 2nd ed., New York: Macmillan, 1975.

For fascinating examinations of the methodological errors and myth-making of historians of ideas, see:

Fischer, David Hackett, *Historians' Fallacies: Toward a Logic of Historical Thought,* New York: Harper Torchbooks, 1970.
Robertson, James Oliver, *American Myth, American Reality,* New York: Hill and Wang, 1980.

The number of studies of journalistic ethics is growing geometrically. Some of the best follow:

Bok, Sissela, *Lying: Moral Choice in Public and Private Life,* New York: Vintage Books, 1979.
Bok, Sissela, *Secrets: On the Ethics of Concealment and Revelation,* New York: Pantheon, 1982.
Christians, Clifford G.; Rotzoll, Kim B., and Fackler, Mark, *Media Ethics: Cases and Moral Reasoning,* 2nd ed., New York: Longman, 1907.
Cooper, Thomas W., et al., *Communications Ethics and Global Change,* New York: Longman, 1989.
Lambeth, Edmund B., *Committed Journalism: An Ethic for the Profession,* Bloomington, IN: Indiana University Press, 1986.
Rawls, John, *A Theory of Justice,* Oxford: Oxford University Press, 1972.

The following list offers suggested readings in connection with the writings of *specific* philosophers, essayists, editors, and political figures who have come under scrutiny in this book. In most cases the works of these persons and the secondary material about them are enormous. What is listed here are particularly relevant works written by these individuals and significant books written about them. The listing is presented in alphabetical order and includes, for the reader's guidance, dates of birth and death and brief notes about the writers. The cited names and volumes refer to works identified in the Notes. The numbers in parentheses refer the reader to the relevant chapters. Primary works are identified by italics.

Agnew, Spiro (1918–): former Vice President of the United States; media critic—Bagdikian, Coyne, Lippmann (57).

Bennett, James Gordon (1795–1872): journalist, editor, press innovator—O'Connor, Pray (33).

Bentham, Jeremy (1748–1832): English utilitarian, leader of Philosophical Radicals—Mack, *Ryan,* Stephen (23).

Burckhardt, Jakob (1818–1897): Swiss cultural historian—*Force and Freedom,* Viereck (29).

Burke, Edmond (1729–1797): British statesman, conservative political philosopher—Bickel, Camerson, Copeland, Lock, *Reader* (20).

Carlyle, Thomas (1795–1881): British essayist, historian, cultural philosopher—Neff, Stephen, *Sartor* (31).

Carnegie, Andrew (1835–1919): Scottish industrialist, philanthropist, moralist—*Kennedy,* "Wealth" (32).

Darwin, Charles (1809–1882): English biologist, whose theory of organic evolution revolutionized science, philosophy and theology—Hofstadter, *Origin of Species,* Spencer, Sumner (32).

Dewey, John (1859–1952): American philosopher, educator, social critic, ethicist, pragmatist, utilitarian—Hook, *Kennedy,* McDermott, *Liberalism* (37).

Emerson, Ralph Waldo (1803–1882): essayist, leader of New England transcendentalist movement—Sherman, *Pauper Press* (31).

Franklin, Benjamin (1706–1790): American statesman, scientist, journalist, moralist—*Autobiography, William Temple Franklin, Larabee,* Van Doren, (10, 15, 16).

Godkin, Earl Lawrence (1831–1902): journalist, editor, political theorist—Bleyer, Hofstadter, Kaplan, Nye (38, 39).

Greeley, Horace (1811–1872): journalist, editor, statesman, political theorist—*Autobiography,* Rourke, Stoddard (31, 33).

Habermas, Juergen (1929–): German critical social theorist—Habermas, Hardt, McCarthy (49).

Hegel, Friedrich Georg Wilhelm (1770–1831): German idealist philosopher—Cook, *Friedrich,* Mazlish, Popper (22, 54).

Helvétius, Claude-Adrien (1715–1771): French Enlightenment sensualist, early utilitarian—*Esprit* (11).

Hobbes, Thomas (1588–1679): "father" of modern analytical philosophy, political theorist, authority on logic, psychology—*Oakeshott,* Raphael, Peters, Warrender (6).

Hume, David (1711–1776): Scottish philosopher, historian, skeptic, analyst of ideas and ideology—Ayer, Hendel, Kemp Smith, *Selby-Bigge* (9).

Innis, Harold Adams (1894–1952): Czitrom, *Empire and Communication,* Havelock, *The Press,*—(48, 56).

James, William (1842–1910): American philosopher and psychologist, driving force behind pragmatism—*Kennedy,* Perry, *Pragmatism* (Intro, 36, 37).

Jefferson, Thomas (1743–1826): President, political and social theorist—*Ford,* Levy, Malone (15, 17, 18).

Kant, Immanuel (1724–1804): Developer of "critical philosophy," ethicist, authority on science and epistemology—Cassirer, *Friedrich, Kant,* Mazlish (12, 22).

Liebling, A.J. (1904–1963): journalist, critical columnist—*The Press,* Rubin, Sokolov, *Wayward Press* (39, 45).

Lippmann, Walter (1889–1974): journalist, editor, political philosopher—*Essays in the Political Philosophy, The Essential Lippmann, Public Opinion,* Steel (38, 45).

Locke, John (1632–1704): English empiricist, moral and political philosopher whose influence on U.S. development was critical—Cook, Grant, *Treatise,* Yolton (6, 7).

McLuhan, Marshall (1911–1980): Canadian literary and media scholar—Czitrom, *Mechanical Bride,* Rosenthal, *Understanding Media* (54).

Madison, James (1751–1836): President, political philosopher—Brant, *Federalist, Hunt,* Levy, Meyers, *Virginia Report* (10, 14, 17, 19).

Malthus, Thomas Robert (1766–1834): English economist and moral philosopher —*Malthus,* Stephen (24).

Marcuse, Herbert (1898–1979): American leftist political and social philosopher—*Eros and Civilization,* Peytrszak, "Repressive Tolerance"—(49).

Marx, Karl (1818–1883): German revolutionary, influential social and economic theorist, sociologist—Berlin, Collier and O'Hargan, Duncan, *Das Kapital,* Fromm, *The German Ideology,* Korsch (13, 26, 28).

Mill, James (1773–1836): Scottish philosopher, historian and economist—*Britannica, Essays,* Hamburger (24, 25).

Mill, John Stuart (1806–1873): English liberal philosopher and economist, often regarded as England's most influential philosopher—*Autobiography,* Berlin, Duncan, *Great Books,* Neff, Plamenatz, Lerner (23, 24, 26, 27).

Milton, John (1608–1674): English poet, moral and political essayist—*Areopagitica,* Masson, Parker, *Portable Milton* (5).

Montesquieu, Charles Secondat, Baron de (1689–1755): French philosopher and political theorist—*Spirit,* Spurlin, *Torrey* (10).

Moynihan, Daniel Patrick (1927–): U.S. politician, diplomat, political theorist—Dickstein, *The Presidency and the Press* (57).

Niebuhr, Reinhold (1892–1971): American theologian, social theorist—*Children, The Essential Niebuhr, Irony* (50).

Paine, Thomas (1739–1809): Journalist, author, revolutionary theorist and leader, deist—Ayer, Conway, Foot, Hawke, *The Rights of Man* (20, 21).

Peirce, Charles Sanders (1839–1914): American philosopher, physicist, mathematician, founder of pragmatism—*Papers,* Seboek (36).

Ricardo, David (1772–1823): English economist, theorist—*Ricardo,* Stephen (24).

Rousseau, Jean-Jacques (1712–1778): French philosopher, essayist, novelist, revolutionary social theorist—Berlin, Cassirer, Darnton, Durant, *Confessions, Social Contract,* Strachey (12, 13).

Santayana, George (1863–1952): philosopher, man of letters, authority on aesthetics—Kirk, *Santayana,* Schlipp (37, 40, 49).

Sinclair, Upton (1878–1968): journalist, novelist, socialist theorist—*Brass Check,* Kaplan (44, 45).

Smith, Adam (1723–1790): Scottish political economist and moral philosopher—*Rogge, Wealth of Nations* (24).

Steffens, Lincoln (1866–1936): journalist, political and economic theorist—*Autobiography,* Greene, Kaplan (43, 44).

Thoreau, Henry David (1817–1862): mystic, transcendentalist, natural philosopher—*Walden* (1).

Tocqueville, Alexis de (1805–1859): French essayist, social and political theorist—*Democracy in America,* Siedentop (14).

Twain, Mark (Samuel Langhorne Clemens) (1835–1910): Novelist, journalist, humorist, social critic—*Connecticut Yankee,* Fishkin (37, 38).

Voltaire, François Marie Arouet de (1694–1778): Philosophical skeptic, humanist, journalist, historian, reformer—*Block, Correspondence,* Gay, *Philosophical Letters* (10, 12).

White, William Allen (1868–1944): Journalist, editor, social critic—*Autobiography,* Hofstadter, "Kansas," (34, 39).

Whitman, Walt (1819–1892): American poet, social and political critic—Fishkin, Kaplan, *Leaves of Grass,* (30, 33).

Wortman, Tunis (176?–1822): Journalist, social theorist—*From Zenger to Jefferson,* Hay, Levy (21, 22).

Zenger, John Peter (1697–1746): German printer, famed for being tried and acquitted on libel charges—Rutherford (17).

Index